T0181517

Lecture Notes in Computer Science 13259

More information about this series at https://link.springer.com/bookseries/558

José Manuel Ferrández Vicente ·
José Ramón Álvarez-Sánchez ·
Félix de la Paz López · Hojjat Adeli (Eds.)

Bio-inspired Systems and Applications

from Robotics to Ambient Intelligence

9th International Work-Conference on the Interplay
Between Natural and Artificial Computation, IWINAC 2022
Puerto de la Cruz, Tenerife, Spain, May 31 – June 3, 2022
Proceedings, Part II

Springer

Editors
José Manuel Ferrández Vicente ⓘ
Universidad Politécnica de Cartagena
Cartagena, Spain

Félix de la Paz López ⓘ
Universidad Nacional de Educación
a Distancia
Madrid, Spain

José Ramón Álvarez-Sánchez ⓘ
Universidad Nacional de Educación
a Distancia
Madrid, Spain

Hojjat Adeli ⓘ
Ohio State University
Columbus, OH, USA

ISSN 0302-9743   ISSN 1611-3349 (electronic)
Lecture Notes in Computer Science
ISBN 978-3-031-06526-2   ISBN 978-3-031-06527-9 (eBook)
https://doi.org/10.1007/978-3-031-06527-9

This Springer imprint is published by the registered company Springer Nature Switzerland AG
The registered company address is: Gewerbestrasse 11, 6330 Cham, Switzerland

Preface

The main topic of these IWINAC 2022 books is the study of intelligent systems inspired by the natural world, in particular biology. Several algorithms and methods and their applications are discussed, including evolutionary algorithms. Bio-inspired intelligent systems have thousands of useful applications in fields as diverse as machine learning, biomedicine, control theory, telecommunications, and, why not, music and art. These books covers both the theory and practice of bio-inspired artificial intelligence, along with providing a bit of the basis and inspiration for the different approaches. This is a discipline that strives to develop new computing techniques through observing how naturally occurring phenomena behave to solve complex problems in various environmental situations. Brain-inspired computation is one of these techniques that covers multiple applications in very different fields. Through the International Work-Conference on the Interplay between Natural and Artificial Computation (IWINAC) we provide a forum in which research in different fields can converge to create new computational paradigms that are on the frontier between neural and biomedical sciences and information technologies.

As a multidisciplinary forum, IWINAC is open to any established institutions and research laboratories actively working in the field of natural or neural technologies. But beyond achieving cooperation between different research realms, we wish to actively encourage cooperation with the private sector, particularly SMEs, as a way of bridging the gap between frontier science and societal impact.

In this edition, four main themes outline the conference topics: neuroscience, affective computing, robotics, and deep learning.

1) Machine learning holds great promise in the development of new models and theories in the field of neuroscience, in conjunction with traditional statistical hypothesis testing. Machine learning algorithms have the potential to reveal interactions, hidden patterns of abnormal activity, brain structure and connectivity, and physiological mechanisms of the brain and behavior. In addition, several approaches for testing the significance of the machine learning outcomes have been successfully proposed to avoid "the dangers of spurious findings or explanations void of mechanism" by means of proper replication, validation, and hypothesis-driven confirmation. Therefore, machine learning can effectively provide relevant information to take great strides toward understanding how the brain works. The main goal of this field is to build a bridge between two scientific communities, the machine learning community, including lead scientists in deep learning and related areas within pattern recognition and artificial intelligence, and the neuroscience community. Artificial intelligence has become the ultimate scale to test the limits of technological advances in dealing with life science challenges and needs. In this sense, the interplay between natural and artificial computation is expected to play a most relevant role in the diagnosis, monitoring, and treatment of neurodegenerative diseases, using the advanced computational solutions provided by machine learning and data science. This requires

interchanging new ideas, launching projects and contests, and, eventually, creating an inclusive knowledge-oriented network with the aim of empowering researchers, practitioners and users of technological solutions for daily life experience in the domains of neuromotor and linguistic competence functional evaluation, clinical explainability, and rehabilitation by interaction with humans, robots, and gaming avatars, not being strictly limited to only these but also open to other related fields. The use of machine learning-based precision medicine in monitoring daily life activity and providing well-being conditions to especially sensitive social sectors is one of the most relevant objectives. Case study descriptions involving neurodegenerative diseases (Alzheimer's disease, fronto-temporal dementia, cerebrovascular damage and stroke, autism, Parkinson's disease, amyotrophic lateral sclerosis, multiple sclerosis, Huntington's chorea, etc.) are included in the proceedings. Mild cognitive impairment (MCI) is considered the stage between the mental changes that are seen between normal ageing and early-stages of dementia. Indeed, MCI is one of the main indicators of incipient Alzheimer's disease (AD) among other neuropsychological diseases. The growth of these diseases is generating a great interest in the development of new effective methods for the early detection of MCI because, although no treatments are known to cure MCI, this early diagnosis would allow early intervention to delay the effects of the disease and accelerate progress towards effective treatment in its early stages. Although there have been many years of research, the early identification of cognitive impairment, as well as the differential diagnosis (to distinguish significant causes or typologies for its treatment), are problems that have been addressed from different angles but are still far from being solved. Diverse types of tests have already been developed, such as biological markers, magnetic resonance imaging, and neuropsychological tests. While effective, biological markers and magnetic resonance imaging are economically expensive, invasive, and require time to get a result, making them unsuitable as a population screening method. On the other hand, neuropsychological tests have a reliability comparable to biomarker tests, and are cheaper and quicker to interpret.

2) Emotions are essential in human-human communication, cognition, learning, and rational decision-making processes. However, human-machine interfaces (HMIs) are still not able to understand human sentiments and react accordingly. With the aim of endowing HMIs with the emotional intelligence they lack, the science of affective computing focuses on the development of artificial intelligence by means of the analysis of affects and emotions, such that systems and devices could be able to recognize, interpret, process, and simulate human sentiments.

Nowadays, the evaluation of electrophysiological signals plays a key role in the advancement towards that purpose since they are an objective representation of the emotional state of an individual. Hence, the interest in physiological variables like electroencephalograms, electrocardiograms, or electrodermal activity, among many others, has notably grown in the field of affective states detection. Furthermore, emotions have also been widely identified by means of the assessment of speech characteristics and facial gestures of people under different sentimental conditions. It is also worth noting that the development of algorithms for the classification of affective states in social media has experienced a notable increase in recent years. In this sense, the language of posts included in social networks, such as Facebook or Twitter, is evaluated with the aim of detecting the sentiments of the users of those media tools. For this edition, the theme of affective computing and sentiment analysis was intended to be a meeting point for researchers who are interested in any of the areas of expertise related to sentiment analysis, including those seeking to initiate their studies and those currently working on these topics. Hence, papers introducing new proposals based on the analysis of physiological measures, facial recognition, speech recognition, or natural language processing in social media are included as examples of affective computing and sentiment analysis.

3) Over the last decade there has been an increasing interest in using machine learning, and in the last few years deep learning methods, combined with other vision techniques to create autonomous systems that solve vision problems in different fields. Therefore, a special session was organized to serve researchers and developers publishing original, innovative, and state-of-the art algorithms and architectures for real-time applications in the areas of computer vision, image processing, biometrics, virtual and augmented reality, neural networks, intelligent interfaces, and biomimetic object-vision recognition.

The aim was to provide a platform for academics, developers, and industry-related researchers belonging to the vast communities of the neural network, computational intelligence, machine Learning, deep learning, biometrics, vision systems, and robotics fields to, discuss, share, experience, and explore traditional and new areas of computer vision, machine learning, and deep learning which can be combined to solve a range of problems. The objective of the session was to integrate the growing international community of researchers working on the application of machine learning and deep learning methods in vision and robotics to facilitate a fruitful discussion on the evolution of these technologies and the benefits to society.

4) Finally, deep learning has meant a breakthrough in the artificial intelligence community. The best performances attained so far in many fields, such as computer vision or natural language processing, have been overtaken by these novel paradigms to a point that only ten years ago was just science fiction. In addition, this technology has been open sourced by the main IA companies; hence, making it quite straightforward to design, train, and integrate deep-learning based systems. Morcover, the amount of data available every day is not only enormous but also growing at an exponential rate. In recent years there has been an increasing interest in using machine learning methods to analyse and visualize massive data generated from very different sources and with many different features: social networks, surveillance systems, smart cities, medical diagnosis, business, cyberphysical systems, or media digital data. This topic was selected to serve researchers and developers publishing original, innovative, and state-of-the art machine learning algorithms and architectures to analyse and visualize large amounts of data.

The wider view of the computational paradigm gives us more elbow room to accommodate the results of the interplay between nature and computation. The IWINAC forum thus becomes a methodological approximation (a set of intentions, questions, experiments, models, algorithms, mechanisms, explanation procedures, and engineering and computational methods) to the natural and artificial perspectives of the mind embodiment problem, both in humans and in artifacts. This is the philosophy that continues in

IWINAC meetings, the interplay between the natural and the artificial, and we face this same problem every two years, although last year we had to postpone the conference due to the COVID-19 pandemic. This synergistic approach will permit us not only to build new computational systems based on the natural measurable phenomena but also to understand many of the observable behaviors inherent to natural systems.

The difficulty of building bridges between natural and artificial computation is one of the main motivations for the organization of IWINAC events. The IWINAC 2022 proceedings contain the works selected by the Scientific Committee from more than 200 submissions, after the refereeing process. The first volume, entitled Artificial Intelligence in Neuroscience: Affective Analysis and Health Applications, includes all the contributions mainly related to new tools for analyzing neural data, or detecting emotional states, or interfacing with physical systems. The second volume, entitled Bioinspired Systems and Applications: from Robotics to Ambient Intelligence, contains the papers related to bioinspired programming strategies and all the contributions oriented to the computational solutions to engineering problems in different application domains, such as biomedical systems or big data solutions.

An event of the nature of IWINAC 2022 cannot be organized without the collaboration of a group of institutions and people who we would like to thank now, starting with UNED and the Universidad Politécnica de Cartagena. The collaboration of the Universidad de La Laguna (ULL) was crucial, as was the efficient work of the Local Organizing Committee, chaired by Josefa Dorta Luis and Pedro Gómez Vilda with the close collaboration of Carmen Victoria Marrero Aguilar, (UNED), Carolina Jorge Trujillo (ULL), and Chaxiraxi Díaz Cabrera (ULL). In addition to our universities, we received financial support from the Universidad de La Laguna, Ayuntamiento Puerto de la Cruz, Programa de Grupos de Excelencia de la Fundación Séneca, and Apliquem Microones 21 s.l.

We want to express our gratitude to our invited speakers Hojjat Adeli, from Ohio State University (USA), Rafael Rebolo, from the Instituto de Astrofísica de Canarias (Spain), Manuel de Vega, from the Universidad de La Laguna (Spain), Athanasios Tsanas, from the University of Edinburgh (UK), and Luis M. Sarro, from the Universidad Nacional de Educacion a Distancia (Spain) for accepting our invitation and for their magnificent plenary talks. We would also like to thank the authors for their interest in our call and the effort in preparing the papers, conditio sine qua non for these proceedings. We thank the Scientific and Organizing Committees, in particular the members of these committees who acted as effective and efficient referees and as promoters and managers of preorganized sessions on autonomous and relevant topics under the IWINAC global scope. Our sincere gratitude goes also to Springer, for the continuous receptivity, help, and collaboration in all our joint editorial ventures on the interplay between neuroscience and computation.

Finally, we want to express our special thanks to BCD Travel (formerly Viajes Hispania), our technical secretariat, and to Chari García, Ana María García, and Juani Blasco, for making this meeting possible, and for arranging all the details that comprise the organization of this kind of event.

We would like to dedicate these two volumes of the IWINAC proceedings in memory of Professor Mira.

June 2022

José Manuel Ferrández Vicente
José Ramón Álvarez-Sánchez
Félix de la Paz López
Hojjat Adeli

Organization

General Chair

José Manuel Ferrández Vicente   Universidad Politécnica de Cartagena, Spain

Organizing Committee

José Ramón Álvarez-Sánchez   Universidad Nacional de Educación a Distancia, Spain

Félix de la Paz López   Universidad Nacional de Educación a Distancia, Spain

Honorary Chairs

Hojjat Adeli   Ohio State University, USA
Rodolfo Llinás   New York University, USA
Zhou Changjiu   Singapore Polytechnic, Singapore

Local Organizing Committee

Josefa Dorta Luis   Universidad de La Laguna, Spain
Pedro Gómez-Vilda   Universidad Politécnica de Madrid, Spain
Victoria Marrero Aguiar   Universidad Nacional de Educación a Distancia, Spain
Carolina Jorge Trujillo   Universidad de La Laguna, Spain
Chaxiraxi Díaz Cabrera   Universidad de La Laguna, Spain

Invited Speakers

Hojjat Adeli   Ohio State University, USA
Rafael Rebolo   Instituto de Astrofísica de Canarias, Spain
Athanasios Tsanas   University of Edinburgh, UK
Manuel de Vega   Universidad de La Laguna, Spain
Luis M. Sarro   Universidad Nacional de Educación a Distancia, Spain

Field Editors

Jesús Bernardino Alonso	Universidad de Las Palmas de Gran Canaria, Spain
Emilia Barakova	Eindhoven University of Technology, The Netherlands
Diego Castillo-Barnes	Universidad de Granada, Spain
Enrique Dominguez	Universidad de Málaga, Spain
Francisco Domínguez-Mateos	Universidad Rey Juan Carlos, Spain
Josefa Dorta Luis	Universidad de La Laguna, Spain
Jose García-Rodríguez	Universitat d'Alacant, Spain
Andrés Gómez-Rodellar	University of Edinburgh, UK
Pedro Gómez-Vilda	Universidad Politécnica de Madrid, Spain
Juan Manuel Górriz	Universidad de Granada, Spain
Victoria Marrero Aguiar	Universidad Nacional de Educación a Distancia, Spain
Carmen Jiménez Mesa	Universidad de Granada, Spain
Vicente Julián-Inglada	Universitat Politècnica de València, Spain
Carolina Jorge	Universidad de La Laguna, Spain
Krzysztof Kutt	Jagiellonian University, Poland
Fco. Jesús Martínez Murcia	Universidad de Málaga, Spain
Rafael Martínez Tomás	Universidad Nacional de Educación a Distancia, Spain
Jiri Mekyska	Brno University of Technology, Czech Republic
Ramón Moreno	Grupo Antolin, Spain
Grzegorz J. Nalepa	Jagiellonian University, Poland
Andrés Ortiz	Universidad de Málaga, Spain
Daniel Palacios-Alonso	Universidad Rey Juan Carlos, Spain
José T. Palma	Universidad de Murcia, Spain
Javier Ramírez	Universidad de Granada, Spain
Mariano Rincón Zamorano	Universidad Nacional de Educación a Distancia, Spain
Victoria Rodellar	Universidad Politécnica de Madrid, Spain
Jose Santos Reyes	Universidade da Coruña, Spain
Fermín Segovia	Universidad de Granada, Spain
Athanasios Tsanas	University of Edinburgh, UK
Ramiro Varela	Universidad de Oviedo, Spain
Yu-Dong Zhang	University of Leicester, UK

International Scientific Committee

Amparo Alonso Betanzos, Spain
Jose Ramon Álvarez-Sánchez, Spain

Contents – Part II

Machine Learning in Computer Vision and Robotics

Deep Learning

Artificial Intelligence Applications

Contents – Part I

Neuromotor and Cognitive Disorders

Affective Analysis

Affective Computing in Ambient Intelligence

Eye Tracking Measurement of Train Drivers' Attention Based on Quasi-static Areas of Interest

Paweł Węgrzyn[1]([✉])[ID], Michal Kepski[2,3][ID], and Iwona Grabska-Gradzińska[1][ID]

[1] Institute of Applied Computer Science and Jagiellonian Human-Centered Artificial Intelligence Laboratory (JAHCAI), Kraków, Poland
{pawel.wegrzyn,iwona.grabska}@uj.edu.pl
[2] Interdisciplinary Centre for Computational Modelling, Faculty of Mathematics and Natural Sciences, University of Rzeszow, Rzeszów, Poland
mkepski@ur.edu.pl
[3] Simteract SA, Kraków, Poland

Abstract. The article concerns eye tracking research conducted in order to improve simulators for train drivers' training, as well as simulator games for railway enthusiasts. The image viewed in the simulator window changes dynamically, but it can be divided into certain sectors that change in a slow and predictable way. We propose a method of analyzing the focus of the driver's or player's attention based on these quasi-static sectors. With quasi-static sectors it is possible to identify certain strategies for observing the route. These strategies are similarly used by train drivers or game players both in the case of simulators and in the case of observing the actual train passage. Such an approach can be used to analyze the attention and performance of a driver or player, as well as to assess the realism of a virtual route against a real route. In particular, an important assessment of the relevant graphic elements of the designed virtual route may be made for the developer of the simulator.

Keywords: Eye tracking measurement · Train driver's attention · Train driver's performance · Train simulators

1 Introduction

Eye tracking technology can help rail industry professionals design better driving simulators and training programs. By collecting and analyzing driver attention data, both driving simulator manufacturers and trainers can provide higher quality products and create tools to support generation of proper content for simulator applications. It also offers insights into post-evaluation and assessment based on visual attention, situational awareness, and habitual driver behavior or

Supported by the Polish National Centre for Research & Development (NCBR) within the Smart Growth Operational Programme grant No. POIR.01.01.01-00-0382/20 as a part of the European Regional Development Fund (ERDF).

J. M. Ferrández Vicente et al. (Eds.): IWINAC 2022, LNCS 13259, pp. 3–12, 2022.
https://doi.org/10.1007/978-3-031-06527-9_1

behavior in unforeseen circumstances. Some studies have tracked observational patterns in train drivers. Certain eye-gaze patterns have been observed which distinguish between less and more experienced drivers [3,8]. The article [6] analyses the monitoring of the driver's attention during some train operations, like driving at the section (without stopping) or driving through the train station (with stopping). The visual strategies that train drivers employ when monitoring and searching the visual scene were discussed in [5,9]. Eye tracking has proved useful for examining the cognitive functioning of train drivers [4,7], analyzing the degree of train driver's fatigue [12] and studying the dynamic visual field of train drivers [1,2].

In the context of creating virtual routes for simulator training, in addition to the consistency of the route, which can be controlled by training scenario creators, the perceived authenticity of the experience is important as well. It was reported that other factors, such as interactivity, play a greater role than the quality of the generated graphics [11]. Simulation realism is defined as the level to which the virtual environment and the interactions available within it are indistinguishable from the player's interaction with the real environment. Simulation realism can depend on a number of features of the virtual 3D world: representation of objects perceived as landmarks along a given route, maintenance of appropriate object scale, etc. The application of eye tracking technology in virtual route generation research can solve the questions: (1) which objects draw the special attention of simulator users and which objects are overlooked by them, and (2) whether the observation strategies of the virtual route are similar to those observed during a real ride. From a practical perspective, an answer for (1) may give a clue to how the display of different types of objects in the visual field can be optimized, and whether all of these elements must have the same quality for the entire virtual environment to evoke authenticity in players. Comparative analysis of observational patterns in participants may lead to an answer whether the virtual route corresponds in authenticity level to its real counterpart. Quantitative analysis of eye tracking recordings from route rides to capture elements (e.g., buildings, vegetation, infrastructure, etc., defined as Areas Of Interest) that attract the attention of participants (and those that do not) was performed. Moreover, the analysis of observational patterns using quasi-static areas of interest was proposed in this study.

2   Eye Tracking with Camera-on-Rail Systems

In eye tracking research, we deal usually with either a still image (photograph, painting, landscape) or a smoothly changing image (3d motion capture from video). In the former case, eye tracking methods can refer to fixed static image fragments as potential areas of interest (AoI). In the latter case, this is not possible. The image from the camera on the rails is something intermediate between a still image and a smoothly changing image. The image is changing, but it can be divided into certain sectors in which one can find certain types of objects (e.g. rails, view of the rails, views from the sides of the rails). These sectors are generally not static, but their boundaries are well defined and change slowly and in the ways that can be calculated from the camera movement. We will call these sectors quasi-static areas of interest. Therefore, as in the case of static image analysis, we can divide the observed image in eye tracking methods into well-defined sectors. These sectors can be analyzed as potential areas of interest. The extended field of the analysis consists of the individual objects faced near the axis of the movement. From the observer point of view they appear transiently for a short period of time according to the velocity difference between the object and the camera and their geometry changes dynamically while getting closer.

This is the main idea of this article. Using the approach described above, we will show that one can get various, interesting results. In particular, we have noticed that some drivers and players use similar ways of observing an image. In addition, there are differences in the average length of fixation between the defined graphic elements of routes from different sectors and there are differences in the assessment of the relevance of individual graphic elements of sectors for the authenticity of routes.

3 Pilot Study: Materials and Methods

The experiment was conducted by the researchers from Jagiellonian University and University of Rzeszów. It was conducted 26–28 February 2021 and involved 32 participants. The examined group consisted of the train drivers and track machine operators (37,50%), game players especially interested in train simulators (50%, partially intersected with the first group) and the group both not professionally engaged in railway industry and not experienced in video simulators games (34,38%). On a base of the initial survey further subgroups were defined including railway enthusiast and railway workers, but not train drivers, as well as game players, but not the simulator players.

Two 16-min films were shown to all participants: first one was the recording of the authentic train ride with the camera in the front window (real route) and the other one was the similar route but recorded as the animation generated in 3D environment of Unreal Engine (virtual route). The Tobii Pro Nano eye tracker and the Tobii Pro Lab was used to collect data. Both the Tobii Pro Lab analytical tools and the software scripts prepared by the researchers were used for analysis.

3.1 Experiment Procedure

Every participant has taken part in the same procedure:

1. A participant fulfills the initial survey: information about professional background, gaming experience and statistical information.
2. Introduction to the experiment, setting the participant position and the eye tracker calibration.

3. First part of the experiment: the participant watched the first film. Half of the participants were shown the real route recording as the first one to watch, others were shown the virtual one as the first one.
4. The short break for recalibration
5. Second part of the experiment: the other recording, respectively.
6. Participant fulfills the perceptiveness survey.

Each entry took an average of 53 min. The main goal of the experiment was to analyze the differences in perception in the main four sectors of the image on the monitor, that we have called quasi-static areas of interest. Their shape changes slightly, and taking the radius of the track curvature and other suitable data into consideration - one can calculate the borders of the sectors for any moment of time. These sectors are crucial for the perception of change during a railway ride. The eye tracking metrics were taken during the entire ride for each sector separately. The image changes continuously, but each sector contains its constant characteristic elements: bottom and front elements connected with the railway infrastructure and left and right with the traffic events and non-railway environment. Beside that, there were defined individual objects of short-time incidental appearance, which were taken into consideration in defined time period and sector. Some of these elements gave the observer crucial knowledge about environment and changes of the circumstances and participants were expected to notice them (road signs, traffic lights, opposite vehicles etc.) and others acted as distractors (people, commercials, etc.). Some of these elements were moving. For incidental objects we used the pattern on the right shown in Fig. 1. Each incidental object moves within one of the sectors of the diagram. It moves from the middle of the screen to the edge along the axis of the sector. The object becomes recognizable while getting closer to the camera, so in the middle part of the image the objects are not considered as observed deliberately. Figure 1 compares these two different schemes for dividing the image into sectors. The left pattern was used for objects that are visible to the observer for much longer.

   All informative and distracting elements appeared for a period of time depending on the distance from the track axis, velocity difference between them and the camera. The shape of the object evolved accordingly to the schema based on the camera-on-rail movement: first they appeared near the middle of the screen and then expanded to cover the part of the triangle defined by crossing point of the motion axis and the horizon line as an apex and the height of the object while passing the camera on the image edge. The period of exposition could be easily calculated according to the velocity difference.

4   Evaluation of Experimental Results

Eye movement is recorded in the form of raw quantitative data that can be statistically analyzed and various types of measures can be applied to it. This allows for an interpretation of the way how the elements of the screen image are perceived [10]. The main purpose of the eye tracking is to record and analyze two main components of eye movement: saccades and fixation. Saccades are fast,

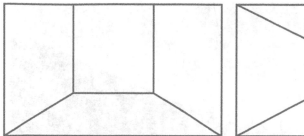
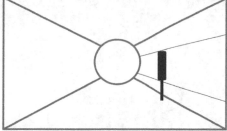

Fig. 1. Defined sectors (quasi-static areas of interest) indicated in the image (red lines) and the incidental object appearance area (black ones). (Color figure online)

Fig. 2. Real world view

intensive eye movements, and fixations are periods of steady vision. Fixations are very short and frequent, lasting on average 200–300 ms, but exactly during these fixation, the cognitive process takes place, i.e., visual information reaches the brain and is consciously processed. In this study, the distribution of average fixation time on each of the four focal areas was analyzed across groups of participants in order to compare the distributions of fixations occurring during observations of each route. The mean fixation distributions in four main areas for the 32 subjects were also clustered to analyze the similarities between the real route and its virtual counterpart. In other words, an attempt was made to find a certain pattern in the study group and to verify whether it overlaps with the observation strategies of the real and virtual route elements (Figs. 2 and 3).

Fig. 3. Virtual view

4.1 Example of Research Based on Quasi-static AoI: Common Strategies of Observation

The distribution of the average fixation time for individual subjects in each of the four sectors was analyzed. The percentage distribution of the average fixation time for train drivers for virtual and actual journeys is shown in Table 1. The research sample of train drivers is not very large, but some interesting things can be observed. First, the differences in the average length of fixation for defined sectors are no more than 3% at a statistically significant level ($p < 0.04$). This means that we can define for a single sector, a certain expected average fixation time, which will be the most likely for each driver, and we can expect a normal distribution of relatively low dispersion around this value. Secondly, the ways of observing the real route and the virtual route are almost identical for individual drivers. The train drivers have different observation strategies, but they use them in a repetitive way. For the developer, this result is also a strong argument for the realism of the virtual route.

Table 2 presents an analogous distribution of the average fixation time over four basic sectors for railway enthusiasts, railway workers, but not train drivers. In this case, the differences in the average length of fixation for the defined main areas at a statistically significant level ($p = 0.07$) are also not greater than 3%. Again, the strategies for observing the real and virtual routes are similar. The next Table 3 shows the results for a group of twenty video game and simulator players. The differences between players in fixation on individual sectors are already greater than the average of 3%. However, the way of observing the real and virtual route is still similar for each player separately. Finally, the set of 64 observations, i.e. ones related to 32 subjects on two routes - virtual and real, were clus-

Table 1. Comparison of the percentage distribution of the average fixation time on virtual and real routes for individual study participants from the group of train drivers.

	Mean fixation distribution						
	Virtual route				Real route		
ID	left	right	ahead	track	left	right	ahead	track
---	---	---	---	---	---	---	---	---
1	24%	21%	28%	27%	24%	20%	27%	29%
2	24%	26%	24%	26%	23%	25%	27%	25%
7	29%	18%	28%	25%	29%	20%	28%	23%
8	30%	23%	27%	20%	26%	24%	29%	21%
9	22%	23%	34%	21%	21%	23%	32%	24%
19	23%	26%	30%	21%	24%	24%	28%	24%
20	23%	27%	27%	23%	25%	26%	27%	22%
21	25%	22%	28%	25%	24%	25%	28%	23%

tered using the k-NN centroid algorithm for segmentation. It is an exploratory analysis of data using unsupervised learning, which is not a very sophisticated, but the most popular technique for cluster analysis. The division into four clusters (k = 4) was made. Since the data is continuous (i.e., not binary or discrete) and arranged on hyperplanes (i.e., data adds up to one for each series), the proper distance measure between items is the Euclidean metric. The optimization problem of cluster division is nonlinear, therefore the technique of nonlinear optimization using the generalized reduced gradient (GRG) method was chosen. The silhouette coefficient (SC) has been calculated, which value is always between −1 and +1. SC equal to one means that clusters are well apart and clearly distinguished. SC equal to zero means that the clusters are non-distinguishable or we can say that the distance between the clusters is not significant. SC equal to minus one means that clusters are being assigned incorrectly. For the above division, SC is 0.3709,

Table 2. Comparison of the percentage distribution of the average fixation time on virtual and real routes for individual study participants from the group of railway enthusiasts and railway employees (non-drivers).

	Mean fixation distribution						
	Virtual route				Real route		
ID	left	right	ahead	track	left	right	ahead	track
---	---	---	---	---	---	---	---	---
3	27%	23%	26%	24%	22%	23%	28%	27%
4	24%	25%	26%	25%	24%	24%	26%	26%
11	22%	26%	29%	23%	22%	25%	28%	25%
23	24%	21%	31%	24%	23%	22%	28%	27%

Table 3. Comparison of the percentage distribution of the average fixation time on virtual and real routes for individual participants of the study from a group of video game players.

	Mean fixation distribution							
	Virtual route				Real route			
ID	left	right	ahead	track	left	right	ahead	track
5	26%	24%	25%	25%	24%	27%	26%	23%
6	23%	27%	26%	24%	25%	25%	25%	25%
10	26%	24%	26%	24%	25%	26%	24%	25%
12	26%	22%	28%	24%	28%	20%	27%	25%
13	22%	21%	33%	24%	22%	24%	27%	27%
14	26%	25%	25%	24%	24%	26%	26%	24%
15	24%	26%	26%	24%	26%	25%	25%	24%
16	23%	21%	30%	26%	24%	20%	28%	28%
17	23%	22%	29%	26%	22%	20%	30%	28%
18	19%	22%	32%	27%	21%	23%	26%	30%
22	25%	24%	41%	10%	22%	24%	34%	20%
24	23%	26%	26%	25%	21%	22%	27%	30%
25	22%	24%	30%	24%	22%	23%	29%	26%
26	25%	25%	26%	24%	25%	24%	28%	23%
27	24%	25%	28%	23%	22%	22%	31%	25%
28	22%	25%	30%	23%	23%	23%	29%	25%
29	24%	25%	29%	22%	22%	23%	30%	25%
30	22%	23%	30%	25%	23%	22%	30%	25%
31	23%	23%	33%	21%	20%	20%	35%	25%
32	21%	23%	30%	26%	21%	21%	29%	29%

which is a pretty good result. This means that there are some common strategies for observing the route. The ways of observing the real and virtual route are very similar. The average distance between these methods is 0.0417 and the maximum is 0.1261. After clustering, for 22 out of 32 participants, the ways of observing the real and virtual routes are assigned to the same cluster (Table 4).

Table 4. Results of clustering of data on the route observation strategies.

cluster	left sector	right sector	ahead sector	track sector
1	23.1%	25.2%	30.7%	21.0%
2	22.4%	22.1%	29.4%	26.1%
3	24.2%	25.4%	26.2%	24.2%
4	26.8%	21.6%	27.8%	23.8%

4.2 Example of Research Based on Quasi-static AoI: The Importance of Incidental Objects and Landmarks

The proper representation of landmarks will enable drivers to recognize real routes in their virtual counterparts. To indicate the elements which draw the visual attention of users, the statistical analysis of the fixations inside AoI's of incidental objects and landmarks were performed. Two groups of corresponding AoI's were selected: one for the video route and the second for the 3D route. Mean fixation lengths (across all observers) for each AoI were calculated. The data were normalized, so the sum of all test samples is 1, the expected average for such a test sample is $1/N$ (where N is the number of defined graphic elements). Statistical analysis has shown that for both routes, certain classes of objects have mean fixation differences larger than 10% (Chi-squared test, $p < 0.02$).

5 Conclusions and Future Works

We have tested the method of eye tracking research conducted on people watching on a monitor either the actual ride of a train or the operation of a train simulator. It is convenient to divide the screen image into certain quasi-static sectors in which different objects may appear. A measure of the realism of a virtual route can be introduced as a similarity with the way of observing this route by train drivers and players in comparison to the observation of the real route. The above method was also used by the simulator developer to assess which elements of the route are important for realism and immersion. A detailed discussion of this topic will be the subject of a further work.

Acknowledgements. The presented work was part of the R&D project "Generation of the train routes realistic visualization for the professional railway simulators" (grant No. POIR.01.01.01-00-0382/20). The authors wish to express their appreciation to the CEO and CTO of Simteract SA, Mr. Marcin Jaśkiewicz and Mr. Grzegorz Ociepka for empowering this research to happen. Also the authors would like to thank the company technical team, especially Artur Szymański, Adam Rzepka, Marcin Gomoła, Miłosz Szczygielski for their help in preparing routes for planned experiments. Special thanks to Dominika Gołuńska for preparing and discussing eyetracking data.

References

1. Brook-Carter, N., Parkes, A., Mills, A.: Piloting a method to investigate the thought processes behind train driver visual strategies. In: McCabe, P.T. (ed.) Contemporary Ergonomics 2004, pp. 271–275. Ergon Soc., CRC Press Taylor & Francis Group (2004)
2. Guo, B., Mao, Y., Hedge, A., Fang, W.: Effects of apparent image velocity and complexity on the dynamic visual field using a high-speed train driving simulator. Int. J. Ind. Ergon. **48**, 99–109 (2015). https://doi.org/10.1016/j.ergon.2015.04.005
3. Horiguchi, Y., Sawaragi, T., Nakanishi, H., Nakamura, T., Takimoto, T., Nishimoto, H.: Comparison of train drivers' eye-gaze movement patterns using sequence alignment. SICE J. Control Meas. Syst. Integr. **8**(2), 114–121 (2015). https://doi.org/10.9746/jcmsi.8.114

4. Kata, G., Poleszak, W.: Cognitive functioning and safety determinants in the work of a train drivers. Acta Neuropsychologica **19**(2), 279–291 (2021). https://doi.org/10.5604/01.3001.0014.9958

5. Luke, T., Brook-Carter, N., Parkes, A.M., Grimes, E., Mills, A.: An investigation of train driver visual strategies. Cogn. Technol. Work **8**(1), 15–29 (2006). https://doi.org/10.1007/s10111-005-0015-7

6. Madlenak, R., Masek, J., Madlenakova, L.: An experimental analysis of the driver's attention during train driving. Open Eng. **10**(1), 64–73 (2020). https://doi.org/10.1515/eng-2020-0011

7. Rjabovs, A., Palacin, R.: Investigation into effects of system design on metro drivers' safety-related performance: an eye-tracking study. Urban Rail Transit **5**(4), 267–277 (2019). https://doi.org/10.1007/s40864-019-00115-1

8. Sun, C., Zhang, G., Zhai, X.: Research on specific eye movement mode of qualified railway driver. In: 2018 International Symposium on Power Electronics and Control Engineering (ISPECE 2018), vol. 1187 (2019). https://doi.org/10.1088/1742-6596/1187/5/052083. Journal of Physics Conference Series

9. Suzuki, D., Yamauchi, K., Matsuura, S.: Effective visual behavior of railway drivers for recognition of extraordinary events. Q. Rep. RTRI **60**, 286–291 (2019). https://doi.org/10.2219/rtriqr.60.4_286

10. Tobii Pro AB: Tobii Pro Lab User's Manual. Danderyd, Stockholm (2020). http://www.tobiipro.com/

11. Welch, R.B., Blackmon, T.T., Liu, A., Mellers, B.A., Stark, L.W.: The effects of pictorial realism, delay of visual feedback, and observer interactivity on the subjective sense of presence. Presence **5**(3), 263–273 (1996)

12. Yan, R., Wu, C., Wang, Y.: A preliminary study for exploring high-speed train driver fatigue using eye-gaze cue. In: Sehiemy, R.E., Reaz, M.B.I. (ed.) Proceedings of the 2016 2nd International Conference on Artificial Intelligence and Industrial Engineering (AIIE 2016). Advances in Intelligent Systems Research, vol. 133, pp. 187–190 (2016)

A Physical Cognitive Assistant
for Monitoring Hand Gestures Exercises

J. A. Rincon[✉], V. Julian, and C. Carrascosa

Universitat Politècnica de València, Institut Valencià d'Investigació en Intel.ligència
Artificial (VRAIN), Valencia, Spain
{jrincon,carrasco}@dsic.upv.es, vjulian@upv.es

Abstract. The use of cognitive assistants has grown significantly in
recent years. The recent appearance of advanced devices for the detection and monitoring of a wide range of physical tasks has allowed a great
advancement in the development of environments that facilitate the well-
being of people, particularly the elderly. In this sense, this paper proposes
the development of a physical cognitive assistant that allows the monitoring of hand gestures exercises for elderly people or people with some kind
of hand-related disease. In addition, the cognitive assistant incorporates
the detection of the patient's emotional state during the exercise.

Keywords: Cognitive assistant · Emotion detection · Elderly · Edge
AI

1 Introduction

Life expectancy is currently increasing, which is a significant demographic
change. Aging impacts society as a whole and the condition of individuals. As a
consequence, health problems (physical and mental), as well as possible mobility issues, arise. These problems have a direct impact on the autonomy of the
elderly. This dependence has led to the emergence of initiatives to improve the
quality of life of this group of people.

Within the field of support for the elderly, there are many initiatives for
their follow-up and monitoring. The most basic assistance system consists of a
series of sensors operated remotely to monitor a person's vital signs.[1] A robot is
responsible for monitoring vital signs and sending images of the patient to the
physician remotely. In turn, the physician has the possibility to perform actions
to safeguard the patient's health. There are other systems aimed at providing
personalized assistance and issuing reminders to the user [1]. If we focus on
the quality of life of the elderly and on preventing their cognitive decline, we
see that in the literature, there are proposals that suggest that physical activity
helps to improve their mood and cognitive state, resulting in less dependence and
depression. Proposals such as the PAMAP system [2], or the TAIZO robot [3]
make it possible to monitor the elderly and motivate them to perform a specific

---

[1] https://www.intouchhealth.com.

© Springer Nature Switzerland AG 2022
J. M. Ferrández Vicente et al. (Eds.): IWINAC 2022, LNCS 13259, pp. 13–23, 2022.
https://doi.org/10.1007/978-3-031-06527-9_2

physical activity. This physical stimulation is proposed based on the capabilities analyzed by the systems and according to personal needs.

Another example is the PHAROS system [4], which is a Cognitive Assistant (CA) [5] that allows to analyze the behavior of the supervised people by means of artificial vision, being able to measure the correct development of the exercise. The physical part of this assistant is a pepper[2] robot that facilitates interaction with patients.

A CA is a relatively new concept focused only on direct assistance to people with cognitive disabilities, expanding the area of Ambient Assisted Living (AAL) [6] to include complex platforms that include sensors, actuators, monitoring abilities and decision processes. Essentially, CAs are focused on people and their disabilities, providing tools that best fit them using personalization methods. CAs can range from a medication reminder to a messaging system that connects its users with their relatives. New developments like the Internet Of Things and Edge Computing have allowed the development of well-being-enhancing environments that were until now unavailable through embedded systems.

In the specific case of Edge Computing, it covers a type of computing, where computing devices are located in the same physical location as the user. This allows users to get faster and more reliable services, and enterprises can take advantage of the flexibility of hybrid cloud computing. With Edge Computing, users can employ and distribute a common set of resources across a large number of locations. This brings a number of advantages for those using it, as faster and more stable services can be obtained at lower cost. This is reflected in the users as they get a faster and more uniform experience. At the same time, this closeness of the computer systems translates into low latency and high availability applications with permanent monitoring.

Many of the applications of robotics based on Edge Computing technology are directly related to industry. Since, mainly, industrial robots need to perform different tasks under time constraints and cannot afford latency when receiving the next command to execute a welding task, manipulate an object or classify objects by means of artificial vision, etc., Edge Computing technology is being used more and more in different fields. Perhaps one of the most interesting is related to physical cognitive assistants. These assistants, mainly with a robot shape, incorporate powerful computer units, capable of executing tasks like those of industrial robots. However, decision-making takes on real importance due to the extreme and continuous contact with humans, as the aim of these robots is to have direct and continuous interaction with people.

Currently, these physical cognitive assistants have evolved thanks to Edge AI based platforms. Edge AI is a combination of Edge Computing and Artificial Intelligence. Edge AI proposes that AI algorithms are processed locally on the device itself or on a server in close proximity to the device. In this way, AI algorithms use the data obtained by the devices themselves at a low level and can make decisions quickly without having to transmit large amounts of information to the Internet or the cloud. Some examples of these physical cognitive assistants

---

[2] https://www.softbankrobotics.com/emea/en/pepper.

are: ElliQ[3] and Senter,[4] that aim to provide support for a healthier and happier aging population.

One of the disadvantages of these assistants is their price, which makes them not very accessible to people. However, with the advent of new, smaller, cheaper and more powerful devices, it has been possible to adapt a new type of low-cost physical cognitive assistants. According to this, this paper presents a physical, cognitive assistant in the form of a desktop robot that monitors certain exercises for the elderly or people with specific disabilities. Specifically, the assistant tries to determine specific gestural exercises with the hands, proposing to the patient the performance of exercises proposed by his caregivers. All activities are monitored and stored for possible follow-up by the caregiver. In addition, the assistant can detect emotional states during the performance of the exercises to determine aspects such as the patient's interest, mood, or apathy during the course of the activities.

2   Desktop Robot Description

This section describes the operation of the desktop assistant robot, detailing the different software and hardware tools used to create the system. The proposed system is shown in Fig. 1 and Fig. 2 shows the 3d model of the robot.

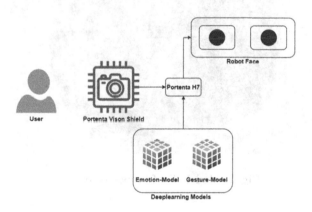

Fig. 1. Architecture of the proposed system.

The main components are the vision module, the decision making module that incorporates the classification models and the execution support framework consisting of an Arduino Pro Portenta. The following sections describe in more detail the hardware components and the developed classification models. At a general level, the desktop robot proposes exercises to the patient through

---

[3] https://elliq.com/.
[4] http://senter.io.

its displays indicating the exercise's number and the. number of repetitions. Through the camera and the classification models, the system determines if the exercise has been done correctly and also associates an emotional state to it. By means of simple messages, the robot communicates to the patient if the exercise has been performed correctly.

Fig. 2. Model 3D of proposed robot.

2.1 Hardware Description

The proposed robot was built using an Arduino Pro Portenta H7 processing system (Fig. 3a). The Portenta H7 system has a dual-core STM32H747 main processor that includes a Cortex® M7 running at 480 MHz and a Cortex® M4 running at 240 MHz. These two processors communicate via a remote procedure call mechanism that allows functions of the other processor to be called seamlessly. The carrier system allows Arduino software to run on the Arm® Mbed™ operating system, native Mbed™ applications, MicroPython and use the TensorFlow™ Lite model. The Portenta system includes connection to WiFi and Bluetooth Low Energy (BLE) networks. It is possible to connect a shield to the H7 port, which integrates a camera, two microphones and a LoRa communication system. This shield, called a vision shield (Fig. 3b), allows the robot to perceive the environment through images and sounds.

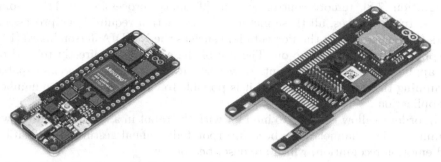

(a) Arduino Pro Portenta H7.   (b) Arduino Portenta H7 Vision Shield.

Fig. 3. Main hardware components employed in the design of the desktop robot

Two 128×64 pixel Oled screens have been integrated (see Fig. 4). These screens have a decorative function and are only used to display the animated robot's eyes.

Fig. 4. LCD Oled 128×64.

2.2   Software Description

In this section, we will describe the different software tools used for training learning models. Perhaps one of the most important aspects of robots is how they interact with humans. There are different ways to achieve this interaction: voice recognition [7,8], remote control systems [9], image processing [10,11], among others. In some cases, all these methods of interaction require large processing units (if compared with the Portenta H7) such as the NVIDIA Jetson board [12], Raspberry Pi 4 [13], and so on. The use of these devices is directly related to the application to be carried out. However, with these new processors capable of running the classification model it is possible to carry out an infinite number of applications.

In order to allow the user to interact with the robot in a non-verbal way, two communication channels have been incorporated: manual gesture identification and emotion recognition, which are described below.

2.3   Hand Gesture Detection for Basics Therapy

Hand exercises are important and necessary to help stretch and strengthen the muscles of the hands and fingers, and to reduce pain and stiffness. It is for this reason that gesture recognition is an important tool in the robot, as this process allows it to be used as a tracking system for each of the rehabilitation exercises. In this case, a dataset has been created with 100 images for each of the 9 classes, 8 of which are exercises and a ninth class that indicates that it is not recognising anything (Fig. 5a and Fig. 5b[5]) (Exercises 6, 7, 8, and 9 correspond to the contact between the thumb and each of the other 4 fingers).

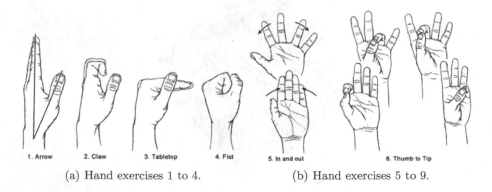

1. Arrow	2. Claw	3. Tabletop	4. Fist	5. In and out	6. Thumb to Tip

(a) Hand exercises 1 to 4.   (b) Hand exercises 5 to 9.

Fig. 5. Portenta technology

A MobileNetV1 network [14] was used for training, the images were pre-processed and resized to 224×224 to be compatible with the network architecture. Of the 600 images obtained, 80% of them were used for the training

---

[5] https://deansmithmd.com/Hand--and-Wrist-Rehabilitation.

process, 10% for testing and the remaining 10% for validation of the model. The hyper-parameters of the trained network are shown in Table 1.

Table 1. Hyper-parameters used in the training of the NN for hand gesture recognition.

Net-Type	Alpha	Dropout Rate	Depth Multiplier	Pooling	weights	Dropout Rate
Mobilenet V1	0.5	0.01	1.0	AVG	Imagenet	0.001

The number of epochs was 60, since it was observed that if more than this value was used, the network suffered from overtraining.

Table 2 shows the classification scores obtained for the detection of hand gestures, an accuracy of 97% was obtained.

Table 2. Scores of the Hand Gesture detection by the trained NN.

	Precision	Recall	F1-Score	Support
Arrow.class	0.96	1.00	1.00	161
Claw.class	0.97	1.00	1.00	160
Tabletop.class	0.98	1.00	1.00	160
Fist	0.97	0.82	0.90	155
In.class	0.955	1.00	0.92	155
Out.class	0.92	1.00	1.00	155
Thumb-1.class	0.97	1.00	1.00	95
Thumb-2.class	0.97	1.00	1.00	98
Thumb-3.class	0.96	1.00	1.00	92
Thumb 4.class	0.97	1.00	1.00	95
Accuracy	0.98	1025		
Macro Avg	0.98	0.97	0.97	1025
Weighted Avg	0.98	0.97	0.97	1025

Figure 6 shows the confusion matrix obtained with the trained model, as can be seen the diagonal of the matrix is around **97%** this means that our model can classify the different manual exercises.

2.4   Emotion Classification

Emotions are psychophysiological reactions that represent ways of adaptation to certain stimuli of the individual when perceiving an object, a person, a place, an event or an important memory. They are what we feel when we perceive something or someone. They are universal and common to all cultures.

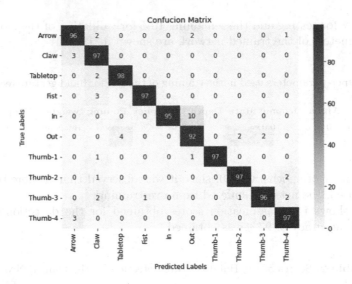

Fig. 6. Normalised confusion matrix of hand gesture detection.

The classification of emotions has become an important aspect to investigate and even more important is to be able to classify them correctly. To do this, there are different techniques and tools that help in this classification. It is possible to use bio-signals to perform this classification, signals such as skin resistance (GSR), Electro cardiography (ECG) and electro-encephalography (EEG) are perhaps the most common and most reliable signals. However, one of the problems is their high-level of intrusiveness to the user. For this reason, other techniques such as the use of an image is somewhat more common. But this technique is unreliable because the person may be sad, but show a happy face.

Due to the fact that classifying emotions using image processing is easy, this desktop robot integrates a model that classifies eight emotional states: afraid, angry, disgusted, happy, neutral, sad, surprised and bored. To train the emotion classification model we use the Karolinska Directed Emotional Faces (KDEF) database [15]. This database is a set of 4900 images of human facial expressions. The set of images is divided into 70 individuals showing 7 different emotional expressions. Each expression is viewed from 5 different angles. The subjects used for the construction of this dataset were 70 amateur actors, 35 women and 35 men, aged between 20 and 30, without beard, moustache, earrings or glasses, and preferably without visible make-up during the photo shoot.

To train the network using the KDEF dataset, a MobileNetV1 [14] network was used. The images were pre-processed and dimensionally modified to be compatible with the network architecture. In the end the images had a size of 224 × 224.

Emotion classification is a crucial tool in the robot, as it allows us to know the robot's emotions during the exercises. This will help the caregivers to determine which exercises are accepted and which are not and thus modify the therapy

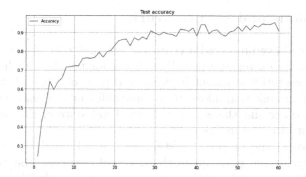

Fig. 7. Accuracy Emotion Classification.

	Precision	Recall	F1-Score	Support
Afraid	0.86	1.00	0.92	101
Angry	1.00	0.62	0.77	92
Bored	0.44	0.47	0.45	30
Disgusted	0.70	1.00	0.83	88
Happy	1.00	0.76	0.86	91
Neutral	0.99	0.96	0.97	92
Sad	0.82	1.00	0.90	105
Surprised	1.00	0.67	0.80	57
Accuracy	0.85		656	
Macro Avg	0.85	0.81	0.81	656
Weighted Avg	0.88	0.85	0.85	656

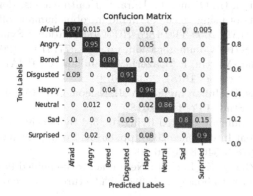

Fig. 8. Normalised confusion matrix of emotion classification.

sessions, either by decreasing the number of repetitions per exercise or the length of the exercise session (Figs. 7 and 8).

3   Conclusions and Future Work

In this paper, we have presented a cognitive assistant that allows the monitoring of hand gesture exercises especially suitable for people with hand mobility problems. The cognitive assistant integrates a series of physical devices and a decision-making module that allows to propose different exercises and to monitor them taking into account the associated emotional state of the patient during the development of the exercises.

As future work, the proposed system will be validated by caregivers and patients of a daycare centre in the northern area of Portugal. The validation will be performed through simple exercises with the patients under the supervision of caregivers. Moreover, another interesting aspect to be introduced will be a direct connection with caregivers to share information about the progress of patients in the performance of their exercises.

Acknowledgement. This work was partially supported by MINECO/FEDER RTI2018-095390-B-C31 project of the Spanish government, and the O_HAI&#10115 project of the Croatian Science Foundation.

References

1. Costa, A., Heras, S., Palanca, J., Novais, P., Julián, V.: A persuasive cognitive assistant system. In: Ambient Intelligence- Software and Applications – 7th International Symposium on Ambient Intelligence (ISAmI 2016). AISC, vol. 476, pp. 151–160. Springer, Cham (2016). https://doi.org/10.1007/978-3-319-40114-0_17
2. Bleser, G., et al.: A personalized exercise trainer for the elderly. J. Ambient Intell. Smart Environ. 5(6), 547–562 (2013)
3. Matsusaka, Y., Fujii, H., Okano, T., Hara, I.: Health exercise demonstration robot TAIZO and effects of using voice command in robot-human collaborative demonstration. In: RO-MAN 2009-The 18th IEEE International Symposium on Robot and Human Interactive Communication, pp. 472–477. IEEE (2009)
4. Costa, A., Martinez-Martin, E., Cazorla, M., Julian, V.: PHAROS-physical assistant robot system. Sensors 18(8), 2633 (2018)
5. Araujo, A., Novais, P., Julian Inglada, V.J., Nalepa, G.J.: Cognitive assistants. Int. J. Hum.-Comput. Stud. 117, 1–3 (2018)
6. Costa, R., et al.: Ambient assisted living. In: 3rd Symposium of Ubiquitous Computing and Ambient Intelligence 2008, pp. 86–94. Springer, Cham (2009). https://doi.org/10.1007/978-3-540-85867-6_10
7. Su, Y., Ma, K., Zhang, X., Liu, M.: Neural network-enabled flexible pressure and temperature sensor with honeycomb-like architecture for voice recognition. Sensors 22(3), 759 (2022)
8. Bakouri, M., et al.: Steering a robotic wheelchair based on voice recognition system using convolutional neural networks. Electronics 11(1), 168 (2022)
9. Torielli, D., Muratore, L., Laurenzi, A., Tsagarakis, N.: TelePhysicalOperation: remote robot control based on a virtual "marionette" type interaction interface. IEEE Robot. Autom. Lett. 7(2), 2479–2486 (2022)

10. Megalingam, R.K., et al.: Inverse kinematics of robot manipulator integrated with image processing algorithms. In: Bianchini, M., Piuri, V., Das, S., Shaw, R.N. (eds.) Advanced Computing and Intelligent Technologies. LNNS, vol. 218, pp. 493–504. Springer, Singapore (2022). https://doi.org/10.1007/978-981-16-2164-2_38
11. Juang, L.-H.: Humanoid robots play chess using visual control. Multimedia Tools Appl. **81**(2), 1545–1566 (2021). https://doi.org/10.1007/s11042-021-11636-y
12. Pullela, B.E.A., et al.: 3d-objekterkennung mit jetson nano und integration mit kuka kr6-roboter für autonomes pick-and-place (2022)
13. Rakhmatulin, I., Volkl, S.: Brain-computer-interface controlled robot via Raspberry-Pi and PiEEG. arXiv preprint arXiv:2202.01936 (2022)
14. Howard, A.G., et al.: MobileNets: efficient convolutional neural networks for mobile vision applications. arXiv preprint arXiv:1704.04861 (2017)
15. Lundqvist, D., Flykt, A., Öhman, A.: Karolinska directed emotional faces. Cogn. Emot. **22**, 1094–1118 (1998)

Automation of Social Media Interactions
A Framework for Online Social "Sowing"

Francisco S. Marcondes[(⊠)], José João Almeida, and Paulo Novais

ALGORITMI Centre, Universidade do Minho, Braga, Portugal
francisco.marcondes@algoritmi.uminho.pt
https://algoritmi.uminho.pt/

Abstract. A fundamental behavior in social agents is to start, keep and grow its target network, this is called "sowing" and depends on affective computing principles, methods and tools. This paper evaluates the feasibility of sowing being fully or partially automated. The discussion is grounded on a framework elaboration that addresses key-issues of such a behavior. The framework construction strengthens the case for its feasibility pointing out that its handlers are the most sensitive part.

Keywords: Social Agent · Online Social Network · Automation

1 Introduction

The chatbot technology was first proposed by Alan Turing in for presenting what he would think to be "Artificial Intelligence". That idea remains until today, yet following the "springs" and "winters" of the field [1]. It is possible to follow the development of a technology through hype cycles *cf.* [10]. According to Garter's hype cycle for artificial intelligence the Chatbot *peak of inflated expectations* was in 2019 and in 2021 reached the *trough of disillusionment* [8].

On another hand, among others, [19] claims that the chatbot marketplace is growing, especially for customer service, healthcare, and financial services. Also, that they are being used both by customers and by employees. Customers benefit from round-the-clock question and answer interactions whereas employees by digital assistance interactions.

Considering the projected market growth and the hype cycle stage of the technology, it is possible to suggest that the chatbot technology may find its way through the *slope of enlightenment*, avoiding another winter by becoming *obsolete before plateau*.

The current chatbot *innovation trigger* followed the deep-learning spring where generative models were sought. On its way through *trough of disillusionment* and due to examples such as of TAY [22], it became clear that hybrid solutions suit better for commercial enterprises [11]. The current state of the art is then a pragmatic use of both symbolic and connectionist approaches, whatever suits better for each situation.

Chatbots are not being used only for customer or employee support, but also for advertising and propaganda [15]. This sort of chatbot is often called a Social

J. M. Ferrández Vicente et al. (Eds.): IWINAC 2022, LNCS 13259, pp. 24–33, 2022.
https://doi.org/10.1007/978-3-031-06527-9_3

Agent. A Social Agent is a more restricted type of chatbot as it does not need to handle entangled dialogues acting more as a broadcast service. They work on social environments such as online social networks and retail websites that allow people to comment on products [7]. The focus of this paper is for Social Agents operating in online social networks.

As any technology, Social Agents range from virtuous to malicious. A known practice of malicious Social Agents is to interact as a normal user for a while before starting the malicious behavior [18]. This is called "sowing" and aims to gather a critical mass of target followers [20] and bubbles [24] for echoing the malicious messages. In this sense, especially during the sowing period, affective computing is a cornerstone.

This paper **hypothesis** is that it is possible to partially or totally automate the sowing procedure of a Social Agent. The **objective** for exploring that hypothesis is twofold: 1) understand the technology that may have being applied, as for propaganda and fake-news spreading; and 2) evaluate if the same sort of technology may be ethically applied, as for counter-propaganda and fighting against fake-news. As a **result**, it is presented a framework addressing key-issues of the sowing procedure. For **scope reduction** this paper considers only Twitter as its target social media.

Methodology. The first objective of this paper is to understand what sort of technology may have being applied by Social Agents during the sowing process. In this sense, the model conceptualization is kept as straightforward as possible yet seeks for most possible autonomous behavior. In addition, being a speculative model, there is no need of going further than the TRL-2. In other words, it is expected a sufficiently detailed model description, internally consistent, that people skilled in the field are able to understand and evaluate [21]. The computational model was created by the development process described in [16] and colored following [3]. The diagrams conforms with UML and OCL notations.

Paper Organization. This paper is organized according to the TRL-2. Section 2 presents theoretical elements that are necessary to laying the foundation for the sowing procedure in Twitter. That section is followed by Sect. 3 presenting an UML model built upon the presented theoretical aspects and elaborated with specific computing concerns. Finally, Sect. 4 performs the TRL-2 assessment and discusses the research issues raised in the introduction.

Ethics Statement. It is currently established that interactions on social media may have psychological consequences. Therefore, no experimentation was undertaken in social media. All ideas discussed in this paper are of theoretical nature or assessed in the laboratory environment.

2   Theoretical Modeling

From a formal perspective an open dialogue can be expressed as an entangled structure of dialogue acts. A dialogue act is a function $f : p \to p'$ with $p, p' \in P$ where P is a set of phrases, p is an input phrase (or silence) and p' a reply (could be **none**) [13]. A structured dialogue is a closer type of dialogue used specially in social media. A structured dialogue can be expressed as a recursive tree structure of chained dialogue acts like:

$$[p' = p]_0 \quad \cdots \quad [p'' = p]_n$$

The tree depth can be limited or not. The chaining is given by equating p and p', e.g. $p \to [p', p] \to [p'', p] \to \ldots$.

From a human perspective a dialogue is a social interaction. A social interaction refers to reciprocal actions between actors when sharing information [5]. Information here is not restricted to knowledge but also includes social and non-verbal cues. A symbolic social interaction is a closer type of social interaction used specially in social media that must rely just on symbols. A smooth interaction happens when parties meet, most of the time, to each other's beliefs, desires and values. In other words, it happens when they positively reinforce each other [4]. Consider the attribute expression to be applied upon dialogue acts:

$$p._{\gamma} \overset{?}{=} p'._{\gamma}$$

where γ can be a sentiment, a personality trait, a social norm, *etc.*. When it holds the interaction is considered to be *smooth* otherwise *rough*.

Based on the argumentation theory. In short, *cf.* [6], an argumentation frame is a pair $\langle ar, at \rangle$ where $ar \in Ar$ is an argument and $at \in At$ with $At \subseteq Ar \times Ar$ is an attack; existing an attack implies a conflicting situation, otherwise a conflict free one. Let $P = Ar$ then if at (renamed to reply r) exists the social interaction may proceed, otherwise does not. Then, given the reply set $R = \{(p_i, p_j)|i = n^{th}\text{input}, j = n^{th}\text{reply}\}$, it is possible to choose a reply that positively reinforces the input based on the γ value.

Suppose the following phrase with annotations from the Emolex [17] for the γ value of each word:

$$I_{null} \; love_{joy} \; my_{null} \; abacus_{trust}$$

Each word in the Emolex is annotated for eight emotions and two valences, either being classified for *true* and *false*. The annotations in this example refers to words with one of these values classified with *true*. The positive reinforcement is given by following the γ values, therefore:

$$I_{null} \; find_{null} \; it_{null} \; a_{null} \; genuine_{trust} \; gem_{joy}$$

Highlight that this works for virtually every word if it receives help from a human. Consider, for instance the words *journalist*$_{trust}$ and *jump*$_{joy}$. A phrase such as *a journalist is jumping* will not suit but tailoring it into *the journalist in me is jumping* would, and could be chained after either phrase.

Notice that replying is just part of the interaction in social media, posting is also essential. This leads to the problem about what to post. Let the graph:

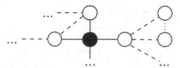

the black node is the social agent, the straight line denotes a first level connection, the dashed a second level connection and the dotted a third level connection. The presented graph is an oversimplified representation of an actual network but suffices for extract some key insights. Once again the strategy is of reinforcement based on the γ value. As a possibility may be to reinforce the first level network by calculating, for avoiding unnecessary complexity, the average $\overline{\gamma}$ for a feature (such as emotion, personality, subject, *etc.*):

$$\overline{n}_\gamma = \frac{\sum^n \overline{p}_\gamma = \dfrac{\sum^p p_\gamma}{l_p}}{l_n}$$

where n is the nodes of the graph, and p the posts made by a related profile.

Suppose then that the $\overline{n}_\gamma$ is a subject such as "flat earth". By posting material related to "flat earth" in such a network would produce a smooth interaction with most of the connections. A consequence of that average oriented posting strategy is to reinforce the bubble's segmentation by creating an "echo chamber" [2]. According to the need that affective function can be fine tuned, between other possibilities, to get $\overline{n}_\gamma$ within a given period for creating the illusion of being tuned on; build complex $\overline{\gamma}$ by including, for instance, subject and sentiment; to weight the graph edges by a criterion such as the bubble's central nodes *cf.* [24] or a target group; *etc.*

It is also possible to learn what the connections expect from the social agent by computing the received feedback. By reinforcing a given post p that got engagement it is possible to understand if it was an accident or a pattern to follow. This means that eventually it is possible to learn which γ values works better for a given group or perhaps for each individual. According to the need it is also possible to consider the $\overline{n}_\gamma$ for second and third level connections.

It is also worth highlighting that a composition of a tweet is more than composing a text. It may usually include [12] : mentions, snippets, emojis, links, hashtags and rich media. Therefore, a smooth communication in Twitter includes all these elements, properly chosen for positive reinforcement of a γ.

In addition, it is also possible to consider the group or person vocabulary e word use frequency for additional personalization. Finally, the social agent cannot engage on an abusive behavior.

3   Computational Model

Based on the theoretical model, the computational model can be elaborated. For a context, Fig. 1 presents the Use Case diagram with blue scenarios together with a high-level component diagram.

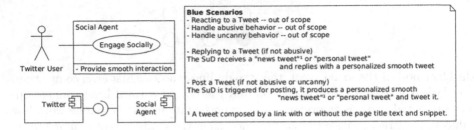

Fig. 1. Computational Model Context

There are three scenarios highlighted as out of scope for this paper. The first one is related with reacting to a tweet as far it may also be considered a reply. Reacting to a tweet involves liking, retweeting, *etc.*. It is kept out of scope since the underlying constraints of reaction are mostly disjoint of those handled in this paper. The second one relates to avoiding abusive behavior and the third involves uncanny behavior. They were kept out of scope as it was not possible to gather enough data to support a viable model. In addition to the obvious ethical issues, it may result in deboosting that would hinder the sowing [14]. The absence of these modules are not an issue as far as the research is kept within the laboratory environment.

The communication diagram elaborating the replying scenario is presented in Fig. 2 and the one elaborating the posting scenario is depicted in Fig. 3. From these two models it was derived the class diagram[1] in Fig. 4.

For a brief description of Fig. 2, when the :Social Agent object receives a tweet (to be called as *source tweet*) calls the :Profile Builder for profiling the *source tweet*'s author. It then fetches Twitter for the author's feed and evaluates the γ value. Therefore, on replying, the *source tweet*'s author is the *target profile*. After filtering for avoiding abuse the :Tweet Builder object is called and, based on the *source tweet*, calculates the *networking set* (snippet, mentions and hashtags) and the *replying set* (text, emoji, link and rich-media) for it. Finally, from these sets, together with the *target profile*, it fits the smoothest elements for building a *fitted tweet*. It is not scope for this paper to discuss the internal behavior of each handler, therefore, they can be taken as abstract to be realized in several forms.

Situations to be handled that worth to highlight are when social agent is mentioned and the *source tweet*'s author is a follower. By using the proper construction it may leverage the author's dopamine [9] strengthening the friendship bond. A mention may also be a reply from a tweet sent by the social agent. This may or may not receive treatment according to the program's purpose.

---

[1] From the reusability perspective it would be better to present it into two diagrams forming two encapsulated analysis patterns, however, due to page number limitations, it is presented merged.

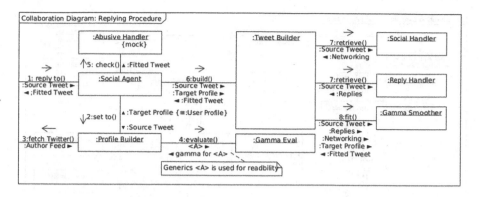

Fig. 2. Object Communication Diagram for the Replying Scenario

For an instance consider that the social agent had received the tweet:

for an emotion γ assessed using the text2emotion module, results in: *Angry: 0.5, Fear: 0.5, Happy: 0.0, Sad: 0.0, Surprise: 0.0*. By scraping this author's last 20 tweet using the twint module, results on the average *Fear: 0.352, Sad: 0.255, Surprise: 0.100, Angry: 0.048, Happy: 0.095* values. Therefore, from the emotion perspective, a smooth reply would be composed by fear, sadness and angry. Polled from the Emolex [17] the word *abandon* settles fear and sadness, for the angry it may be included and angry emoji. After including a random snippet such as '...' [12], a smooth reply would be then:

An abandon... 😡😡

For a brief description of Fig. 3, when the :Social Agent object is triggered, it receives a target audience that can be usually the the social agent's followers, a subset of them of the follower's followers. The application calls then the :Profile Builder object for retrieve the audience's feeds and calculating the γ value for the network, identify topic intersections, *etc.*. It also calls the :Topic Keeper object that retrieves from a data source suitable for the targeted audience, *e.g.* the Google News website, the trending topics for that day and evaluates their γ value. After filtering for avoiding abuse and uncanny behavior, the tweet building follows a similar path of the replying procedure.

Notice that the data source can be either an authentic news portal or a fake-news website, the social agent may also shift between these two. In addition, it

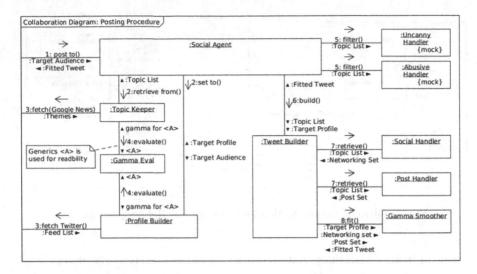

Fig. 3. Object Communication Diagram for the Posting Scenario

can be a public or private data source. This suggests that an adaptation of the presented procedure may also be considered for posting after the sowing stage.

The instance for the posting procedure would be analogous to the replying procedure provided that their differences are considered, then, omitted.

Then, from the model depicted in Fig. 2 results in the one in Fig. 4. Notice that this is a high-level diagram aiming to identify domain elements, therefore technology elements that would increase efficiency are not included. This implies that the different elements can be realized in several ways, for those using AI, it can be symbolic, connectionist or hybrid.

Highlight that a tweet can be, at least, of two types *news tweet* and *personal tweet*. It is important to differentiate them as far as they yield a whole different building in the low-level [12]. A *news tweet* is a tweet composed by a link together with the title of the link's page and may also include a text snippet. From an affective computing perspective, it does not provide information about the sender's feelings, traits or vocabulary. What can be inferred from it is its author's topics of interest and the type of media consumed by that user.

In addition there are two roles omitted in the diagram. The first is a Twitter Listener that start the replying procedure and the second is a Scheduler that is responsible for keeping track of the time, for instances, the social agent must wait a while before reply and may create a tweet schedule for scattering a group of topics throughout the day (including repackaged repetitions). Highlight that the Abusive Handler interface would not fit into a malicious social agent, however it is included in the case of that be used as a reference model. On another hand, the Uncanny Handler on a malicious bot aims to avoid being recognized as bot by the users, the online social network and applications like botometer[2].

---

[2] https://botometer.osome.iu.edu/.

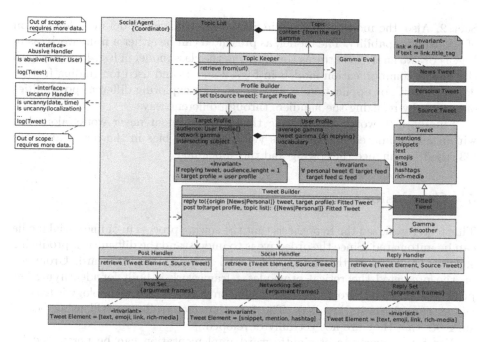

Fig. 4. Social Agent Framework for Smooth Interaction

4 Results and Discussion

It can be claimed that this paper showed that the **hypothesis** of sowing process automation is feasible.

For the first **objective**, the presented models point out key elements that may being used for sowing and therefore how the underlying technology may be. Also, it becomes clear that the handlers are the cornerstone of such systems and if properly suited the social agent is capable of almost full automation. The difficulty of building such handlers can be envisioned by the current need of humans to act as the puppet master of three to five bots [18]. Nevertheless it appears to be a matter of time until that technology is mastered, this would be revealed first by the increase in the number of bots pupped by each person and eventually by people being removed from the loop.

A question that naturally emerges is if the sowing practice is ethical, even if used for a virtuous purpose. That is not the sort of question that can be answered by technologists, then it will be left an open question. Said that, for the second **objective**, it can be said that beyond possible it is necessary as the need for critical mass of both quantity and quality for starting a campaign in online social media. Nevertheless, the applicable ethical constraints must be raised and applied in the model (realizing the `Abusive Handler` interface) before leaving the laboratory environment.

For the **result**, the presented model suits with TRL-2 as it presents a conceptual construction from straightforward mathematical principles presented in

Sect. 2. Also, the model presented in Sect. 3 is a sufficiently detailed description of a feasible capability. The model, as presented can be either a framework (as in Fig. 4) or two analysis patterns (by splitting the class model in Fig. 4 according to the object communication models in Figs. 2 and 3) and used for guiding further development. For application, it may be used for exploring different possibilities of sowing by realizing the handlers through different ways.

Finally, it is worth highlighting that a social agent never works alone but within a coordinated bot-net. This yields cognitive bias in the target audience [23] used to enhance the sowing and the spreading.

5   Conclusion

This paper explored the hypothesis that the sowing process in online social media can be automated. Since the objective is to understand the difficulty of producing such an application, the theoretical model is kept straightforward. Grounded on the presented theoretical principles a framework is built for identifying key principles on such a program. The conclusion drawn is that technology is feasible yet as capable as its handlers. The fact that fact trolls are still using people suggests that they are not yet fully developed.

For future works, a straightforward implementation can be performed for assessment in the laboratory in order to understand the extension that a simple model may reach. There could also be further research on modeling the reply procedure for messaging systems (WhatsApp and Telegram) and the cooperation model of a bot-net. In addition, perform further assessment considering the impact of the mediation algorithm of online social media.

Acknowledgments. This work has been supported by FCT - Fundação para a Ciência e Tecnologia within the R&D Units Project Scope: UIDB/00319/2020

References

1. Agapiev, B.: What caused the "AI winter" and what were the early warning signs? (2018). https://bit.ly/34PptI4
2. Choi, D., Chun, S., Oh, H., Han, J., Kwon, T., et al.: Rumor propagation is amplified by echo chambers in social media. Sci. Rep. **10**(1), 1–10 (2020)
3. Coad, P., de Luca, J., Lefebvre, E.: Java Modeling color with UML: Enterprise Components and Process with Cdrom. Prentice Hall PTR, Upper Saddle River (1999)
4. Combs, T.D., Brown, R.A.: Digital Behavioral Design. Boundless Mind (2018)
5. Degenne, A.: Type d'interactions, formes de confiance et relation. Redes, vol. 16 (2009)
6. Dung, P.M.: On the acceptability of arguments and its fundamental role in non-monotonic reasoning, logic programming and n-person games. Artif. Intell. **77**(2), 321–357 (1995)
7. Ferrara, E., Varol, O., Davis, C., Menczer, F., Flammini, A.: The rise of social bots. Commun. ACM **59**(7), 96–104 (2016)

8. Gartner Group: Smarter with Gartner: Insights that drive stronger performance. https://www.gartner.com/smarterwithgartner

9. Lanier, J.: Ten Arguments for Deleting Your Social Media Accounts Right Now. Random House, New York (2018)

10. Linden, A., Fenn, J.: Understanding Gartner's hype cycles. Strategic Analysis Report No. R-20-1971, p. 88. Gartner, Inc (2003)

11. Luo, B., Lau, R.Y., Li, C., Si, Y.W.: A critical review of state-of-the-art chatbot designs and applications. Wiley Interdisc. Rev. Data Mining Knowl. Discov. 12(1), e1434 (2022)

12. Marcondes, F.S., Almeida, J.J., Durães, D., Novais, P.: Fact-check spreading behavior in Twitter: a qualitative profile for false-claim news. In: Rocha, Á., Adeli, H., Reis, L.P., Costanzo, S., Orovic, I., Moreira, F. (eds.) WorldCIST 2020. AISC, vol. 1160, pp. 170–180. Springer, Cham (2020). https://doi.org/10.1007/978-3-030-45691-7_16

13. Marcondes, F.S., Almeida, J.J., Novais, P.: Chatbot theory. In: Yin, H., Camacho, D., Novais, P., Tallón-Ballesteros, A.J. (eds.) IDEAL 2018. LNCS, vol. 11314, pp. 374–384. Springer, Cham (2018). https://doi.org/10.1007/978-3-030-03493-1_40

14. Marcondes, F.S., et al.: A profile on Twitter Shadowban: an AI ethics position paper on free-speech. In: Yin, H., et al. (eds.) IDEAL 2021. LNCS, vol. 13113, pp. 397–405. Springer, Cham (2021). https://doi.org/10.1007/978-3-030-91608-4_39

15. Marcondes, F.S., Almeida, J.J., Novais, P.: A short survey on Chatbot technology: failure in raising the state of the art. In: Herrera, F., Matsui, K., Rodríguez-González, S. (eds.) DCAI 2019. AISC, vol. 1003, pp. 28–36. Springer, Cham (2020). https://doi.org/10.1007/978-3-030-23887-2_4

16. Martin, R.C.: UML for Java Programmers. Prentice Hall PTR, Upper Saddle River (2003)

17. Mohammad, S.M., Turney, P.D.: NRC emotion lexicon, vol. 2. National Research Council, Canada (2013)

18. Pomerantsev, P.: This is Not Propaganda: Adventures in the War Against Reality. PublicAffairs (2019)

19. Ramadass, B.: The Truth About Chatbots. Forbes (2022)

20. Shao, C., Ciampaglia, G.L., Varol, O., Yang, K.C., Flammini, A., Menczer, F.: The spread of low-credibility content by social bots. Nat. Commun. 9(1), 1–9 (2018)

21. TEC-SHS: Technology readiness levels handbook for space applications. Tec-shs/5551/mg/ap iss1 rev6, European Space Agency (2008)

22. Wolf, M.J., Miller, K., Grodzinsky, F.S.: Why we should have seen that coming: comments on microsoft's tay "experiment," and wider implications. SIGCAS Comput. Soc. 47(3), 54–64 (2017)

23. Woolley, S.C., Howard, P.N.: Computational Propaganda: Political Parties, Politicians, and Political Manipulation on Social Media. Oxford University Press, Oxford (2018)

24. Zhang, Q., Li, X., Fan, Y., Du, Y.: An SEI3R information propagation control algorithm with structural hole and high influential infected nodes in social networks. Eng. Appl. Artif. Intell. 108, 104573 (2022)

Visualization Methods for Exploratory Subgroup Discovery on Time Series Data

Dan Hudson[1]($\boxtimes$) (ID), Travis J. Wiltshire[2] (ID), and Martin Atzmueller[1,3] (ID)

[1] Semantic Information Systems Group, Osnabrück University, Osnabrück, Germany
{daniel.dominic.hudson,martin.atzmueller}@uni-osnabrueck.de
[2] Department of Cognitive Science and AI, Tilburg University,
Tilburg, The Netherlands
t.j.wiltshire@tilburguniversity.edu
[3] German Research Center for Artificial Intelligence (DFKI), Osnabrück, Germany

Abstract. This paper presents visualization methods for exploratory subgroup discovery, focusing on numeric time series data. We provide four novel visualizations for the inspection and understanding of subgroups. These visualizations facilitate interpretation in order to get insights into the data and the respective subgroups, while also supporting statistical interpretation and assessment of the subgroups and their respective parameters. Furthermore, we illustrate the approach in the context of complex time series data – specifically on team interactions in the affective computing context.

Keywords: Visualization · Subgroup Discovery · Time Series Data

1 Introduction

Subgroup discovery [1] is a versatile approach for descriptive modeling, providing powerful options for exploratory and explanatory data analysis. It focuses on the detection of subgroups according to a given quality function, which can be flexibly defined, e. g., for detecting deviating subgroups with respect to a nominal or numeric target variable [15], or more complex target relations like encompassing a set of target variables [1]. Recently, the analysis of numeric data, in particular time series data, has been receiving increased interest, especially in relation to capturing and making sense of complex relationships amongst variables. To do so requires not only advanced algorithmic methods for subgroup discovery, but also methods for inspection and visualization [4, 11, 14] of the results. Exploring, for example, the key properties of subgroups is crucial in order to enable a human-centered data analysis approach, and ultimately computational sensemaking [2].

This paper therefore focuses on visualization methods for exploratory subgroup discovery, specifically in the context of time series data. We present several visualization approaches that also include statistical assessment in order to demonstrate, explain, and provide justification for the obtained subgroups. In contrast to existing approaches for (visual) subgroup discovery, e. g., [4, 11, 14],

© Springer Nature Switzerland AG 2022
J. M. Ferrández Vicente et al. (Eds.): IWINAC 2022, LNCS 13259, pp. 34–44, 2022.
https://doi.org/10.1007/978-3-031-06527-9_4

we focus on visualization methods for exploratory subgroup discovery on time series data, emphasizing the importance of visualization as an analysis step for interpreting and making sense of subgroups. These visualizations can both present an overview of the subgroups, and also provide a statistical characterization of the distributions of important variables.

Furthermore, we provide a case study illustrating our proposed approaches in the context of multi-modal team interaction data. In teamwork, groups of individuals collaborate to achieve shared goals. Recent literature [13] has emphasized the potential of data-centric methods to reveal previously obscure insights into the time-varying processes that constitute working together. Here, a variety of sociometric sensor and unobtrusive recordings have the benefits of providing: continuous recordings which allow for the ability to examine dynamics and processes over time, affordable data collection and analysis, as well as the possibility of fast feedback. In our case, we focus on time series of body movement and speech audio, extracted from video and microphone recordings of interacting teams. In this context, we can build upon our previous work [9] centered around subgroup discovery, in which we search for subgroups of the data, defined according to features of the body movement, that are predictive of high dynamic complexity [17] in speech (suggesting that a change in the dynamics of speech interaction is imminent). Ours is therefore a multi-modal approach, that can be used to generate hypotheses about how postural behavior at certain points in time anticipates changes in speech interaction. Underlying this approach is a novel combination of four visualizations that aid inspection and interpretation of the discovered subgroups, guiding the analyst and also making the results more appropriate for presenting back to non-experts such as team members for their self-reflection. Overall, this work therefore supports faster and easier 'computational sensemaking' of time series, especially for sociometric recordings in the context of affective computing [8].

In summary, the key contributions of this paper are:

1. We provide four novel visualizations for the inspection and understanding of subgroups. These visualizations facilitate exploratory and explanatory subgroup discovery, while also providing for the statistical assessment of the subgroups and their respective parameters. We discuss this in the context of SD4Py, a python package for subgroup discovery.[1]
2. Furthermore, we illustrate these approaches via a case study that shows how to better understand time series data using subgroup discovery; here, we focus on team interactions in the affective computing context.

The rest of the paper is summarized as follows: Sect. 2 describes our proposed approach. After that, Sect. 3 illustrates this in a case study in the domain of affective computing, specifically teamwork analysis. Finally, Sect. 4 provides a discussion and concludes the paper with a summary and outlines interesting directions for future work.

---

[1] SD4Py is available here: https://github.com/cslab-hub/sd4py.

2   Method

Our approach is based on *subgroup discovery* for time series data, which aims to identify explainable subgroups within the data that possess some particular property of interest [1]. Based on prior work [9,10,18], for example, we can identify subgroups with a high *dynamic complexity* [17] on average, which is associated with an imminent phase transition (i. e., a qualitative change in the dynamics of some variable). In our case study, we focus on speech due to its importance in group interactions as well as conveying affective content [5]. Please see [9] for a detailed description of dynamic complexity in team interaction applications.

SD4PY – *An Overview.* Subgroup discovery is a process we implement using the python package SD4PY, which we present for the first time here, leading to subgroup descriptions that consist of a pattern of rules (typically in the form of feature-value pairs) for deciding which data points are members of the subgroup. Each subgroup can be used to identify a subset of points within the data. The process aims to find subgroups that maximize a given quality function, e. g., a function that trades off the size of the subgroup membership with how extreme the target variable is on average. The SD4PY package makes this a simple procedure in python. The user simply prepares the data in tabular form in a pandas dataframe, and then calls a single function to discover subgroups, passing in the target variable, and other optional parameters such as the quality function to use. This package leverages the existing VIKAMINE software in Java [3,4], providing a simple python interface, requiring no interaction with Java, to the functionality for subgroup discovery that VIKAMINE provides. This also means that it gives access to a wide range of functionality that exists in VIKAMINE, including multiple parameters for how to perform the subgroup search, and various methods to post-filter the discovered subgroups and remove those that are redundant or uninteresting. This provides a simple workflow for python users to perform subgroup discovery in a highly-configurable manner.

Visualizations for Analyzing Time Series Data. In prior work [9], we showed that subgroup discovery can be performed on time series data after applying the TSFresh python package [7] to extract relevant features (e. g., descriptive statistics, autocorrelation measures, various forms of entropy) that describe windows taken from the time series. It is then possible to search for subgroups, either looking for features that co-occur with a high value of the target variable, or by applying a lag such that the subgroups predict a high target value at a later time. For example, in this paper, we investigate how different features of the postural movement of team members within a 1-min window are associated with high dynamic complexity of speech in the same window.

This paper presents multiple ways to visualize subgroups. Since subgroup discovery identifies many possible subgroups, we provide two visualizations to help the user to compare and then select the most interesting subgroups for further inspection. We also provide two visualizations for then inspecting a specific subgroup, improving interpretation and understanding.

Subgroup discovery uses a quality function to evaluate potential subgroups; however, this gives little information about how well the 'quality' of the subgroup will generalize to new data. We introduce a visualization to indicate the variability of the target variable (dynamic complexity in our case) when the subgroup is applied to different samples of the data (overlapping, sampled with replacement). In other words, bootstrapping is used to estimate the distribution of the average value of the target variable. Since some subgroups are larger than others, identifying more points in the data, we also visualize the size of the subgroups as a fraction of the data they are applied to. This information appears together as a box plot to show the distribution of the target variable over multiple samples, with the mean size of subgroups being shown by the thickness of the boxes (see Fig. 1 for an example visualization).

Two subgroups can overlap to a greater or lesser degree in which data points they identify. To show this, we include a network diagram where edges are weighted by the Jaccard similarity between the subsets of data they identify. As can be seen in the example in Fig. 2, this can help to identify where subgroups are particularly similar, and may guide selection of a 'diverse' set of subgroups with lower redundancy for further inspection, and/or choosing subgroups that are particularly representative of a cluster, based on their position within the network diagram. An edge between two subgroups is drawn if the Jaccard similarity is greater than a threshold τ (in our case we chose $\tau = 0.2$) and thicker edges represent higher similarity.

In addition to comparative visualizations, we provide visualizations to support the interpretation and understanding of an individual subgroup. These give an indication of what is particularly special about the subgroup. The first visualization of this type (example in Fig. 3) consists of multiple panels, and provides an overview of the average values for various important variables. Each panel compares the subgroup to its complement (i.e., data from all non-subgroup members). From top to bottom, the panels show: the distribution of values for the target variable; the distribution of values for the selector variables defining the subgroup; and, the distributions of additional numeric and nominal variables, selected based on an estimate of effect size (corrected Hedge's G for numeric variables and the lesser confidence interval of the odds ratio for nominal variables).

When focusing on time series analysis, it is also possible to show where subgroup members occur in time. This appears in the final visualization (example in Fig. 4), which shows the progression of multiple numeric variables over time and uses red rectangles to identify time windows which are members of the subgroup being inspected. This helps the user to relate the subgroup members, target variable, raw time series values, and derived TSFresh features to one another. TSFresh features are computed using a sliding window to show their progression over time. Note that all of the visualizations described in this section are calculated from a specific dataset; it could be the same data used to perform subgroup discovery or it could be another set of data such as a validation set that has been held out.

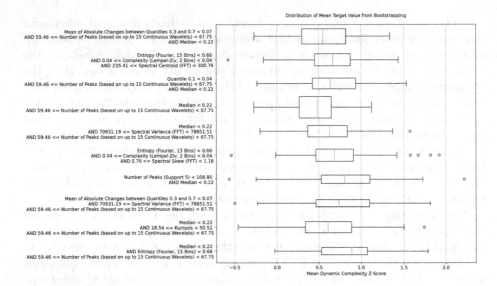

Fig. 1. The distribution of mean target values from bootstrapping simulations for multiple subgroups. The thickness of the boxes show the average size of the subgroup relative to the other subgroups.

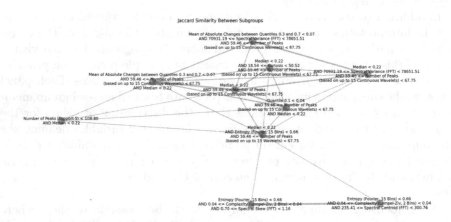

Fig. 2. Network diagram depicting the overlap between subgroups (Jaccard similarity of members) as the thickness of edge weights. Nodes connected by a thicker line are more similar, and nodes appearing more centrally in the diagram tend to have more overlap with a higher number of other subgroups.

3   Case Study: Application to Team Interaction Data

Data from the ELEA corpus of team meetings [16] was used to showcase our analysis approach and new visualizations. The ELEA corpus contains video and audio recordings of teams of three or four individuals collaborating to rank the importance of a list of items for surviving a fictional disaster scenario. Movement data was extracted from the video using Open-Pose [6] and applying the Euclidean distance to quantify the change in location (i.c., movement) of keypoints representing the posture of team members. See [10] for more details on this analysis. This led to a time series of the global magnitude of postural movement for each team member. We also quantified the dynamics of speech through the audio recordings. First, the energy within each second of audio was computed, and then the dynamic complexity of this time series was calculated using a sliding window of length 12. Further details of the dynamic complexity calculation are provided in [17].

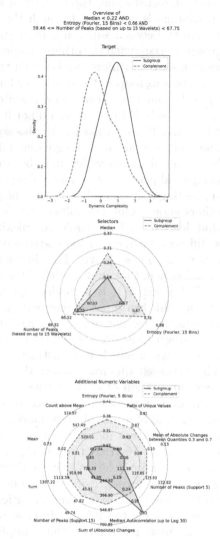

Fig. 3. Summary of a single subgroup.

Movement features were extracted for 1-min windows using TSFresh. The mean was used to aggregate each feature across team members. We then applied subgroup discovery using SD4PY on the 1-min windows, with the average dynamic complexity across the window being the target variable. Note that these dynamic complexity values were converted to z-scores per team. Subgroups of windows in which the dynamic complexity is typically high on average are those in which a phase transition in speech dynamics is especially likely to occur [17]. Subgroup discovery was performed using the binomial quality function (cf. [1,15] for an in-depth discussion) and the top 100 subgroups were retained for the following steps.

After discovering 100 subgroups, bootstrapping was used to find confidence intervals on the estimated effect size (corrected Hedge's G, comparing the mean target value of subgroup members to that of non-members) and the proportion of data points selected by the subgroup. Subgroups were filtered to only include those that have a lower bound of selecting at least 1% of data points, and then the top 10 were selected with the best lower bound on the estimated effect size. These subgroups are visualized in Fig. 1, where the distribution of target values is depicted along the horizontal axis and the relative size of the subgroup on average is portrayed through the vertical height of each box. The Jaccard similarity between subgroups is shown in Fig. 2, indicating how much each subgroup overlaps with the others. These two figures make it possible to understand more about the differences between the subgroups. For example, Fig. 1 suggests that the subgroup in the ninth row has more variability in the target value than the subgroup in the third row, despite them having a similar mean target value and size, something that would not have been obvious otherwise. A practitioner might use this information to choose one subgroup over another, for example due to it seeming to have greater reliability. Figure 2 uncovers (dis)similarities between subgroups which may be overlooked typically, with, for example, the peripheral position of 'Number Peaks (Support 5) < 108.00 AND Median <0.22' suggesting that this subgroup selects quite a different group of data points to the others shown. One possibility here is that there are different sets of conditions that lead to high dynamic complexity; this particular subgroup could reflect a different mechanism associated with increased dynamic complexity than the other subgroups shown. This is an additional hypothesis, resulting from the visualization, that may guide subsequent analysis and interpretation.

Using Fig. 3, it is possible to gain more understanding of a particular subgroup. This figure shows one particular subgroup, defined by low median body movement, low entropy, but a moderate number of peaks in body movement. The subgroup is already defined by these three variables, however there may be other ways in which it is distinctive, according to various additional features. The lower-left quadrant shows that members of this subgroup tend to have a lower proportion of values above the mean and fewer changes around the mean, compared to non-members. This is consistent with a situation where there is a background of minimal body movement, but with a moderate number of peaks in movement that increase the average value, and where changes in value around the mean are restricted to moments when increasing up to or decreasing after a peak. Autocorrelation may be increased on average for members of this subgroup by the presence of extended periods of minimal activity, which would stay highly consistent over time. Additionally, the distribution of target values is depicted in the top-left quadrant as an estimated probability distribution. This can be more informative than simply considering the mean target value, and here it shows that there is relatively less overlap between subgroup members and non-members for small values, and relatively more overlap for higher values, potentially suggesting that the subgroup does well at excluding moments of low dynamic complexity but does not capture all moments when the dynamic complexity is high. This visualization shows more of the related aspects of the subgroup than would be possible from inspecting the subgroup definition alone.

Since this analysis is based on time series, it can be helpful to visualize the different variables over time. TSFresh features computed in a sliding window were visualized alongside the audio energy per second, target variable, and movement energy per second for one particular team meeting, in Fig. 4. This clarifies some relationships between features, such as the high similarity between the median value and the change around the mean (between the 0.3 and 0.7 quantiles). It also gives a limited indication as to which variables are relatively consistent across subgroup members. For example, while the entropy and median appear to hold to a relatively consistent range of values across the subgroup members (indicated by red background rectangles), the ratio of unique values by contrast is noticeably lower in the first subgroup window than in the second. Of course, the visualization types exemplified in Figs. 3 and 4 could be used to perform a detailed inspection of any of the other subgroups to better understand how certain patterns of body movement are associated with high speech complexity are reflected.

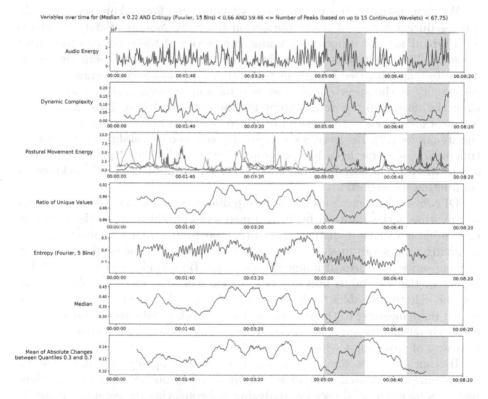

Fig. 4. The original time series, derived target variable, and other TSFresh-derived numeric variables over time. One subgroup is also visualized, such that red rectangles in the background are used to indicate windows of time that were included in the subgroup when originally performing subgroup discovery. (Color figure online)

4   Discussion and Conclusions

In this work, we advance SD4PY, a python package that includes visualizations for conducting and making sense of subgroup discovery analyses. The collective benefits of using these visualizations for subgroup discovery entail: 1) understanding the variability of the target variable for subgroups, 2) identifying similarities and dissimilarities in subgroups for the purpose of selecting subgroups for further inspection, 3) contrasting the differences between a given subgroup compared to non-subgroup data in terms of target and selector variables, and lastly 4) building intuition about the subgroups through highlighting windows of the original time series and TSFresh selector variables. Not only do we build on the capabilities of VIKAMINE for subgroup discovery, but SD4PY also makes them more accessible to python users and other data scientists.

We demonstrated the use of these visualizations for making sense of subgroups during a case of team interaction involving movement data extracted with OpenPose and using the dynamic complexity of the speech as the target variable. This allowed us to show how an example subgroup compares to the non-subgroup data (see Fig. 3). In particular, there was lower average dynamic complexity in the speech, and most selector and numeric variables were lower than the non-subgroup data, except for the autocorrelation. Most analyses of teamwork and social interactions are aimed at estimating aggregate measures of the dynamics [12]. However, we can greatly enhance our ability to understand time-series using methods like subgroup discovery that highlight distinct periods of the team or social interactions. SD4PY provides a tool and workflow for conducting such efforts.

Of course, these methods for subgroup discovery and visualization can apply to any time series data, to begin to make sense of which properties of a specific subgroup make it distinct from other subgroups. Many application areas involving time series analysis, e. g., affective computing, focusing on a variety of time-series measures of human social interaction, could benefit here. A key aspect of this will be to build on the current work to not only tailor the target and selector variables to the particular domain of interest, but evaluate and assign more meaning to these features. Future work should also investigate how these visualizations are used in the sensemaking process by scientists and also as a way of providing feedback to team members.

In conclusion, we have showcased a set of new, openly available tools for performing and making sense of subgroup discovery on time-series data. These methods have potential uses for analyzing and conveying the complex dynamics of teamwork and social interactions, more broadly. Our aim is that their use and continued development will assist in providing insights to researchers and the individuals (e.g., team members) themselves.

Acknowledgements. This work was partially supported by Interreg NWE, project Di-Plast - Digital Circular Economy for the Plastics Industry (NWE729) and by the Dutch Research Council (NWO) as part of the NWO-KIEM Creative Industries & Digital Humanities program, project number KI.18.047.

References

1. Atzmueller, M.: Subgroup discovery. WIREs DMKD **5**(1), 35–49 (2015)
2. Atzmueller, M.: Declarative aspects in explicative data mining for computational Sensemaking. In: Seipel, D., Hanus, M., Abreu, S. (eds.) WFLP/WLP/INAP - 2017. LNCS (LNAI), vol. 10997, pp. 97–114. Springer, Cham (2018). https://doi.org/10.1007/978-3-030-00801-7_7
3. Atzmueller, M., Lemmerich, F.: VIKAMINE – open-source subgroup discovery, pattern mining, and analytics. In: Flach, P.A., De Bie, T., Cristianini, N. (eds.) ECML PKDD 2012. LNCS (LNAI), vol. 7524, pp. 842–845. Springer, Heidelberg (2012). https://doi.org/10.1007/978-3-642-33486-3_60
4. Atzmueller, M., Puppe, F.: Semi-automatic visual subgroup mining using VIKAMINE. J. Univ. Comput. Sci. **11**(11), 1752–1765 (2005)
5. Baucom, B.R., et al.: The language of interpersonal interaction: an interdisciplinary approach to assessing and processing vocal and speech data. Eur. J. Psychother. Couns. **7**(1), 69–85 (2018)
6. Cao, Z., Hidalgo Martinez, G., Simon, T., Wei, S., Sheikh, Y.A.: OpenPose: realtime multi-person 2D pose estimation using part affinity fields. IEEE Trans. Pattern Anal. Mach. Intell. (2019)
7. Christ, M., Braun, N., Neuffer, J., Kempa-Liehr, A.W.: Time series feature extraction on basis of scalable hypothesis tests (tsfresh-a Python package). Neurocomputing **307**, 72–77 (2018)
8. Doan, N.N.T., et al.: Towards multimodal characterization of dialogic moments on social group face-to-face interaction. In: Proceedings Workshop on Affective Computing and Context Awareness in Ambient Intelligence. UPCT, Cartagena (2019)
9. Hudson, D., Wiltshire, T.J., Atzmueller, M.: Local exceptionality detection in time series using subgroup discovery: an approach exemplified on team interaction data. In: Soares, C., Torgo, L. (eds.) DS 2021. LNCS (LNAI), vol. 12986, pp. 435–445. Springer, Cham (2021). https://doi.org/10.1007/978-3-030-88942-5_34
10. Hudson, D., Wiltshire, T.J., Atzmueller, M.: multiSyncPy: a python package for assessing multivariate coordination dynamics. Behav. Res. (2022). https://doi.org/10.3758/s13428-022-01855-y
11. Jorge, A.M., Pereira, F., Azevedo, P.J.: Visual interactive subgroup discovery with numerical properties of interest. In: Todorovski, L., Lavrač, N., Jantke, K.P. (eds.) DS 2006. LNCS (LNAI), vol. 4265, pp. 301–305. Springer, Heidelberg (2006). https://doi.org/10.1007/11893318_31
12. Kazi, S., et al.: Team physiological dynamics: a critical review. Hum. Factors **63**(1), 32–65 (2021)
13. Kozlowski, S.W., Chao, G.T.: Unpacking team process dynamics and emergent phenomena: challenges, conceptual advances, and innovative methods. Am. Psychol. **73**(4), 576 (2018)
14. Kralj, P., Lavrac, N., Zupan, B.: Subgroup visualization. In: 8th International Multiconference Information Society (IS-05), pp. 228–231. Citeseer (2005)
15. Lemmerich, F., Atzmueller, M., Puppe, F.: Fast exhaustive subgroup discovery with numerical target concepts. Data Min. Knowl. Discov. **30**, 711–762 (2016)
16. Sanchez-Cortes, D., Aran, O., Mast, M.S., Gatica-Perez, D.: A nonverbal behavior approach to identify emergent leaders in small groups. IEEE Trans. Multimedia **14**(3), 816–832 (2011)

17. Schiepek, G., Strunk, G.: The identification of critical fluctuations and phase transitions in short term and coarse-grained time series—a method for the real-time monitoring of human change processes. Biol. Cybern. **102**(3), 197–207 (2010)
18. Wiltshire, T.J., Hudson, D., Belitsky, M., Lijdsman, P., Wever, S., Atzmueller, M.: Examining team interaction using dynamic complexity and network visualizations. In: Proceedings IEEE International Conference on Human-Machine Systems, pp. 1–6 (2021)

Real-Life Validation of Emotion Detection System with Wearables

Dominika Kunc[✉][iD], Joanna Komoszyńska[iD], Bartosz Perz[iD],
Przemysław Kazienko[iD], and Stanisław Saganowski[iD]

Department of Artificial Intelligence, Faculty of Information
and Communication Technology, Wrocław University of Science and Technology,
Wrocław, Poland
dominika.kunc@pwr.edu.pl

Abstract. Emotion recognition in real life is challenging since training
machine learning models requires many annotated samples with experienced emotions. Although collecting such data is a difficult task, we
may improve the process by utilizing a pre-trained model detecting emotional events. We conducted a study to test whether employing machine
learning models that detect intense emotions to trigger self-assessments
collects more data than triggering self-reports randomly. We have examined the performance of three models on 13 participants for three months.
Results show that our models enhance the data collection and provide
on average 21% more emotionally annotated data in the general setup.
The personalized model improves the collection even more – by up to
38%.

Keywords: Emotion Recognition · Machine Learning · Wearables ·
Real-life Validation · Emognition System

1 Introduction

The development and validation of machine learning (ML) models detecting
emotions are not trivial. The major issue is emotion-related data collection since
catching an emotional event in real life is hard. While experiencing emotions,
people do not focus on side tasks such as remembering about reporting them with
self-assessments. To mitigate this problem we created the Emognition system,
which enables more efficient and user-friendly data collection in everyday life by
using machine learning models to detect intense emotions.

Traditional validation of ML models (by using the train-test sets, cross-
validation, leave-one-subject-out, etc.) often may not be sufficient and may not

This work was partially supported by the National Science Centre, Poland, project
no. 2020/37/B/ST6/03806; by the statutory funds of the Department of Artificial
Intelligence, Wroclaw University of Science and Technology; by the Polish Ministry of
Education and Science – the CLARIN-PL Project.

The original version of this chapter was revised: an error in reference no.
12 of the paper was corrected. The correction to this chapter is available at
https://doi.org/10.1007/978-3-031-06527-9_59

J. M. Ferrández Vicente et al. (Eds.): IWINAC 2022, LNCS 13259, pp. 45–54, 2022.
https://doi.org/10.1007/978-3-031-06527-9_5

show all the predictive abilities of a model, because of the characteristics of the labeled data. The reported emotions are only a part of all experiences, and a classifier could detect emotion that would not be labeled manually. We believe that testing such models, in case of their accuracy and generalizability, should be performed in real life. Once the model detects an intense emotion, the participant can immediately report whether the prediction was true or not.

We conducted a three-month-long study in everyday life with 13 participants. It aimed to validate the ML models' performance in real life. The participants used the Emognition system to respond to emotion-related questionnaires. To provide a baseline, our study's participants responded to emotion-related assessments triggered not only by the models but also by a quasi-random trigger. Moreover, the participants could also manually trigger the assessments. ML models detected on average 21% more intense emotions than the randomly triggered assessments for not personalized models. Moreover, we tested the personalized approach, which increased the difference in detected intense emotions' rates up to 38% for personalized models.

2   Related Work

Emotion recognition from physiological signals has been present in the literature for a while. Datasets collected in the laboratory are available [8,10,12] and researchers performed various experiments using them [6,15,19]. Recent progress in technology made physiology-sensing devices pervasive (e.g., sensors in smartphones, smartwatches), and scientists begin to research emotions and affective states in real life [2,14,16,20]. Reliable emotion recognition systems could be employed in healthcare, human-computer interaction, or education to improve them [2,9]. However, conducting field studies comes with many challenges, such as sparsity of collected data, dependency of emotions on the context, or differences in people's lifestyles and experienced emotions [9,17]. Therefore, approaches employed in laboratory studies may not be appropriate for real life.

Studies in the wild frequently utilize self-assessment questionnaires for gathering data, as it is impossible to collect objective emotional annotations during everyday life [5,16,17]. Simple approaches include: (1) prompting participants at random moments in hope to catch emotional events [16,18]; (2) scheduled assessments on fixed times or events during the day [5]; (3) using self-triggered assessments while relying on participants' will and sense of duty [3,5]. Although these approaches can be employed together, such questionnaires can miss emotional events, and annotations collected through them are sparse [16]. A promising idea that aims to overcome these problems is to create a pre-trained machine learning model for emotion detection and employ it to trigger self-assessment questionnaires. Such a model may provide more emotionally-annotated data than traditional approaches.

When creating an ML model, it is important to validate it adequately. However, no standard validation procedure for affect recognition systems can be found in the literature. Some researchers used well-established validation methods when creating ML models, such as dividing the data into separate training and test sets [15], into more sets (folds) and performing cross-validation over them [11], or using a combination of both [19]. Hernandez et al. [7] utilized leave-one-day-out cross-validation (LODO) to build personalized models for stress recognition. Using LODO allowed them to create personal models while taking into account models' ability to generalize over time. Although these approaches can provide a good evaluation of a model's performance in some scenarios, they are not suitable for measuring its ability to generalize to new people. To assess a model's performance for new participants, researchers should ensure that training and testing are done on different pools of participants. Therefore, in experiments which focus on generalizability researchers tend to utilize leave-one-subject-out (or leave-k-subjects-out) cross-validation (LOSO/LkSO) [6,7,16,19].

None of these validation methods provides a way to verify how a model works in real-life. Although some of them imitate inference on unseen data, it is impossible to generate new emotional labels for already collected examples. If new models recognize emotions in unlabeled data fragments, there is no way to check if their predictions are correct. Therefore, when creating and testing models for emotion recognition in real-life, one should also consider validating them in the same manner, i.e., in everyday life.

3   Experimental Setup

3.1   Emognition System

The Emognition system enhances the collection of emotionally annotated data in real-life scenarios. It consists of mobile and smartwatch applications. We used Android smartphones connected with Samsung Galaxy Watch 3 smartwatches. The physiological signals provided by the smartwatch include: raw BVP sampled 25 Hz, heart rate (HR) sampled at 12.5 Hz, PP-interval (PPI) sampled at 12.5 Hz, and 3-axis accelerometer data (ACC) sampled 50 Hz.

Our framework uses three possible triggers for reporting emotions: **self-reports** – participants can fill in the assessment whenever they want to; **quasi-random assessments** – providing participants a limited number of questionnaires in random moments during the day; **ML model** – a real-time prediction of an intense emotion based on the physiological data from wearables. The assessments triggered randomly and by the model look the same – the participants are not able to distinguish them nor guess what was the trigger. We have limited the number of triggered assessments to six per day as our previous work [13] showed that users are comfortable with that many questionnaires. After reaching the limit, participants did not receive more triggered assessments and could only fill in the self-triggered ones. The self-assessment form consists of questions whether the participant experienced an intense emotion (possible answers: "Yes," "No," "Don't know"), the valence and arousal of the event (0–100 scale), and a free-text section for details on context. More information about the Emognition system can be found in [13,14]. The demo of the system is available at [4].

Table 1. Information about datasets used in our experiments.

ID	Participants	Size	Intense emotions/ Neutral states [%]
Dataset A	Emognition Team members	243	29.2/70.8
Dataset B	Emognition Team members	589	31.0/69.0
Dataset C	Recruited participants	1223	39.0/61.0
Dataset D	Five selected recruited participants (first four weeks of the study)	375	50.9/49.1

3.2 Datasets

In order to train an ML model to use it as a questionnaire trigger in the Emognition system, we had to collect emotion-related datasets in real life. Table 1 presents the collected datasets' properties.

Dataset A was collected from November 2020 to February 2021 by the Emognition team members (four females, seven males). It consists of 71 intense emotions and 172 neutral states labeled. All of the collected samples were manually reported (no triggers used).

Dataset B includes all samples from *Dataset A* and new samples collected by the same participants from February 2021 to May 2021. The labels' distribution in this set is close to the previous one - a total of 183 intense emotions and 406 neutral states, which results in proportions of circa 30/70.

Dataset C comes from the new study, with recruited participants (six females, seven males). Unfortunately, two participants (one female, one male) decided to leave the study before its end. One participant exited at the beginning and the second one after almost two months of the study. The study lasted from September 2021 to December 2021 and resulted in 1223 clearly labeled emotion-related samples: 477 intense emotions and 746 neutral states. This set was not used as the training set for any model but was used for the latter statistics.

Dataset D is a subset of the *Dataset C* - samples from the first four weeks of the study gathered by five participants with a sufficient number of reported intense emotions in the study's first two weeks. This choice was made to enable validating a machine learning model trained on study participants' data in real life. The total number of intense emotions was 191, and 184 samples of neutral states. One person who dropped out of the study is included in the chosen participants subsets, as we did not know that this participant was going to leave the study. The distribution of per-participant assessments answers is presented in Fig. 1. It is visible that each of the participants had different trends in their responses. This shows that it may not be trivial to create a general model working well for all participants, and the possible solution may be the personalized approach. More details on the study and the *Dataset D* can be found in [14].

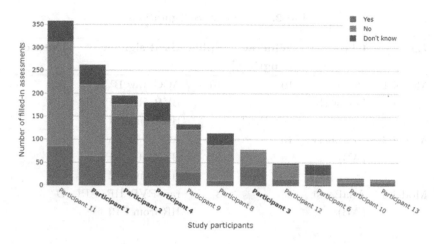

Fig. 1. Distribution of answers from filled-in assessments in the *Dataset C*. Bolded participants are the ones with a sufficient number of reported intense emotions in the study's first two weeks. Only these participants are included in the *Dataset D*.

The distributions of labels in the *Datasets C* and *Datasets D* are different than in the *Datasets A* and *Dataset B* (from 30% to 40–50% of intense emotions). This may be caused by the changes in the data collection process. The earlier datasets were collected only with self-triggers, as no ML or random-based triggers were used. The latest data was collected with the Emognition system [13, 14].

All participants gave us written informed consent and participated in the study for no compensation. The research was approved by and performed in accordance with guidelines and regulations of the Bioethical Committee at Wroclaw Medical University, Poland; approval no. 149/2020.

3.3 Procedure

In our previous work [14] we mentioned the cold start problem of emotion-related studies and suggested personalizing models with incoming data. We tested there four scenarios of models' training data. We checked whether the presence of the new participants' samples in the training set is beneficial for employed machine learning models. Our experiments showed that models perform better when previously gathered participants' samples are included in their training sets. Models in the experiment mentioned above were validated in an across-time manner - previously collected data was split into two-week parts, and the latter was used as the test set. This setting may be sufficient for the general overview of the models' performance. However, we believe that the actual predictive abilities of the model can be measured by embedding it in the Emognition system and enabling real-time predictions with an immediate response from the participant in the form of a filled-in self-assessment. The main disadvantage of testing models on previously collected data is that some emotional events may not be included because of random or not precise assessments' triggers.

Table 2. ML models configurations.

ID	Classifier	Window Length [s]	Splits	Used signals	Dataset
Model 1	Random Forest (RF)	10	10	ACC, raw BVP, BVP, HR, PPI, HR from PPI	A
Model 2	AdaBoost (AB)	10	10	ACC, raw BVP, BVP, HR, PPI, HR from PPI	B
Model 3	AdaBoost (AB)	60	3	raw BVP, HR, PPI, HR from PPI	D

The configurations of machine learning models validated in real life are presented in Table 2. The first model embedded in our application was a feature-based Random Forest classifier trained on the *Dataset A*. The input data were trimmed to 10-s windows and split into 10 parts of equal length. We used raw signals provided by the Samsung Galaxy Watch 3 and those processed by us. The used signals included: ACC (acceleration), ACC vector, raw BVP (blood volume pulse), BVP - filtered with Median and Butterworth filters, HR (heart rate) and PPI (PP intervals [ms]) derived by Samsung Galaxy Watch 3, and HR from PPI - heart rate calculated from the PP intervals. The second model was the AdaBoost classifier. The setup of the window's length, splits, and used signals remained the same as for the first model. The main difference, besides the classifier, was the training set. The last tested model was chosen based on the results of the previously mentioned experiments [14] - which was the best resulting feature-based classifier. The windows were 60 s long and were split into three equally long non-overlapping parts. Moreover, the ACC signal and its derivatives were not used in this configuration. For the training, we used the *Dataset C*.

All participants used the models in approximately the same periods of time, with only a few days of difference between them. This is due to different times of installations and updates of the application, calibration of individual thresholds for participants, and technical problems. These included problems with our software, as well as with participants' smartphones. For all participants we excluded their initial data from the further analysis, not only because they installed the application at different dates, but also to account for the time needed to get familiar with the Emognition system.

The number of filled-in assessments in each week of the study is presented in Fig. 2. During the update weeks (fourth and eighth), some participants experienced technical problems and did not use the application. This issue reflects in the decrease in the number of filled-in assessments in the fourth and eighth weeks of the study. Moreover, the study's first three weeks yielded the highest number of emotion-related samples, which may be connected with participants' moti-

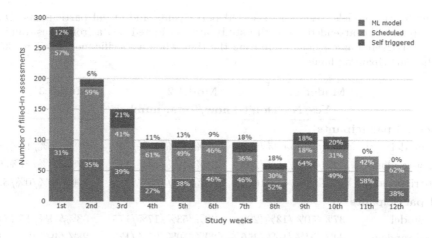

Fig. 2. Number of filled-in assessments through weeks of the study in the *Dataset C*. Percents in third and fourth weeks do not sum to 100% because of rounding.

vation at the beginning of the study. Unfortunately, their motivation decreased with time, and the latter weeks were not receiving that many reports.

After a few days during which participants were installing the application and getting to know the Emognition system, the Model 1 (RF) was used for around three weeks. Installation of the second model was disturbed because of an application problem, so we extended the time for the Model 2 (AB) to about four weeks. With the last model (AB), participants spent almost four weeks.

3.4   Results

We wanted to validate the models and check whether the assessments triggered by models report more intense emotions than randomly triggered ones. Our goal is to derive a solution that enables detecting more emotion-related samples.

The quasi-random trigger is the baseline for each model, as it is a trivial solution for reminding participants about labeling their current emotional state. It is worth noting that the assessments triggered randomly and by the model are indistinguishable for the user. The self-triggered assessments' statistics were included in the results to show how the other triggers mechanisms enabled collecting a higher number of samples. Table 3 shows the performance of each trigger used in our study divided into three stages, depending on which machine learning model was embedded in the application.

The first important analysis of the results is the percentage of "Yes" answers gathered by the triggers on each stage of the study. The first stage got the highest number of filled-in assessments, which may be caused by the participants' high motivation at the beginning of the study.

The questionnaires triggered by the first model (RF) got a 7 percentage points (pp) greater number of detected intense emotions than the quasi-random trigger for the selected participants and a 3 pp higher for all of the participants.

Table 3. ML models' results on selected participants and on all participants. Only participants who attended the entire study are considered. Data from quasi-random and self-triggered assessments were from the time when a specific model was working on the participant's phone.

	Model 1	Model 2	Model 3
	Yes/No/Don't know/Total number		
Selected participants			
ML model	49%/40%/11%/145	41%/44%/15%/73	51%/36%/13%/86
Quasi-random	42%/43%/15%/209	33%/49%/18%/112	37%/42%/21%/60
Self-triggered	100%/0%/0%/16	88%/0%/12%/8	100%/0%/0%/3
All participants			
ML model	37%/50%/13%/229	30%/53%/17%/175	33%/51%/15%/189
Quasi-random	34%/51%/15%/356	29%/50%/21%/173	28%/49%/23%/121
Self-triggered	48%/50%/2%/62	44%/49%/7%/57	28%/61%/11%/36

The second model (AB) got an 8 pp higher rate of affirmative answers than the random method for the participants' subset and 1 pp for the whole group. The last model (AB) turned out to be much better than the trivial trigger in detecting emotional events - the advantage of 14 pp for the selected participants and 5 pp for all. The rates of the "No" and "Don't know" answers were also lower for all the machine learning models for selected participants. In the case of all participants, the negative responses rates for different triggers were close to 50%.

Suppose that all models' assessments were randomly triggered (with corresponding quasi-random answers distributions). Comparing the number of detected intense emotions of such a setting with the original numbers for ML models, the number of "Yes" responses for selected participants is higher than for random trigger by 16%, 25%, and 38% for Model 1 (RF), Model 2 (AB), and Model 3 (AB), respectively. In the case of all participants, ML models provide 9%, 4%, and 17% more reports with intense emotions.

Another aspect is the models' personalization. The real-life validation results for the selected participants showed that the personalized model has the most significant advantage compared to the quasi-random trigger and has the highest true positive rate from all models. So the model trained on samples from participants is better-resulting in intense emotions detection. In our previous study, the personalized model also performed better [14].

4 Discussion and Conclusions

In the Computer Science discipline, we are used to a traditional way of validating the models based on either LOSO (leave-one-subject-out) or 10-fold cross-validation. However, the best setup to test a model is its application in a given domain/environment, which in our case is real life. This raises two crucial questions. How to translate the performance of the model measured with the F1 metric into the performance in real life? How do such metrics affect the number of detected intense emotions during everyday life? The real-life validation can clearly show us how useful the model is, i.e., how many intense emotion samples we can collect with the ML model. The results of our experiments reveal the ML models were better than quasi-random triggers: even 9% more intense emotions detected with the general model and up to 38% with a personalized solution.

However, real-life emotion detection can be affected by many factors. It depends on the participants' personality, mood, context [1], and motivation for labeling data. The inter-participant differences in distributions of assessments' responses show diversity, and it may be impossible to create one general model that will suit every person. The obvious solution would be per-participant model personalization. Unfortunately, collecting a sufficient number of samples from one subject to train a reasoning model is a very time-consuming process. Although the Emognition system enhances data collection, the average number of samples for each participant still remains relatively low. To overcome this problem, we employed a model personalized for the group of selected participants. The results showed that this approach improves the efficiency of the Emognition system in detecting intense emotions for such a selected group.

The study participants' motivation may also affect the results. To ensure that the number of incoming samples does not significantly decrease throughout the whole study, we can impose clear restrictions on the participants, e.g., they have to report at least six important events per day [18]. However, such rules may only boost the self-reporting, not the number of real emotions. We did not force our participants with any obligatory number of filled-in assessments, as we wanted the reports to be honest and unbiased.

The results of models' validation in everyday life performed during our study showed that employing a machine learning model as a trigger for self-assessments is a promising idea. ML models were better than the quasi-random trigger in catching the intense emotions that participants experienced in all considered cases. We also created a post-study survey for participants, and nine out of eleven of them answered it. Participants' responses showed that answering self-assessments was convenient for them. Interestingly, in the question about the perception of their emotions, four participants told us that they could better understand their emotions after the study. All of the above leads to the conclusion that combining machine learning models with personalization may be a game-changer for the research in emotion recognition in real life, especially in data collection. Having bigger and more varied train datasets is crucial for developing better-performing models.

References

1. Barrett, L.F.: How Emotions Are Made: The Secret Life of the Brain. Pan Macmillan (2017)
2. Dao, M.S., Dang-Nguyen, D.T., Kasem, A., Tran-The, H.: Healthyclassroom - a proof-of-concept study for discovering students' daily moods and classroom

emotions to enhance a learning-teaching process using heterogeneous sensors. In: ICPRAM (2018)

3. Dzieżyc, M., et al.: How to catch them all? Enhanced data collection for emotion recognition in the field. In: PerCom 2021, pp. 348–351. IEEE (2021)

4. Emognition system demo (2022). https://youtu.be/zgJw4krZ5tU. Accessed 25 Feb 2022

5. Exler, A., Schankin, A., Klebsattel, C., Beigl, M.: A wearable system for mood assessment considering smartphone features and data from mobile ECGs. In: UbiComp 2016, pp. 1153–1161. ACM (2016)

6. Harper, R., Southern, J.: A Bayesian deep learning framework for end-to-end prediction of emotion from heartbeat. IEEE Trans. Affec. Comput. (2020)

7. Hernandez, J., Morris, R.R., Picard, R.W.: Call center stress recognition with person-specific models. In: D'Mello, S., Graesser, A., Schuller, B., Martin, J.-C. (eds.) ACII 2011. LNCS, vol. 6974, pp. 125–134. Springer, Heidelberg (2011). https://doi.org/10.1007/978-3-642-24600-5_16

8. Koelstra, S., et al.: DEAP: a database for emotion analysis; using physiological signals. IEEE Trans. Affec. Comput. 3(1), 18–31 (2011)

9. Larradet, F., Niewiadomski, R., Barresi, G., Caldwell, D.G., Mattos, L.S.: Toward emotion recognition from physiological signals in the wild: approaching the methodological issues in real-life data collection. Front. Psychol., 1111 (2020)

10. Miranda-Correa, J.A., Abadi, M.K., Sebe, N., Patras, I.: AMIGOS: a dataset for affect, personality and mood research on individuals and groups. IEEE Trans. Affec. Comput. 12(2), 479–493 (2018)

11. Romeo, L., Cavallo, A., Pepa, L., Berthouze, N., Pontil, M.: Multiple instance learning for emotion recognition using physiological signals. IEEE Trans. Affec. Comput. (2019)

12. Saganowski, S., et al.: Emognition dataset: emotion recognition with self-reports, facial expressions, and physiology using wearables. Sci. Data 9 (2022). Article No. 158

13. Saganowski, S., Behnke, M., Komoszyńska, J., Kunc, D., Perz, B., Kazienko, P.: A system for collecting emotionally annotated physiological signals in daily life using wearables. In: ACIIW 2021, pp. 1–3. IEEE (2021)

14. Saganowski, S., Kunc, D., Perz, B., Komoszyńska, J., Behnke, M., Kazienko, P.: The cold start problem and per-group personalization in real-life emotion recognition with wearables. In: WristSense at PerCom 2022. IEEE (2022, in press)

15. Santamaria-Granados, L., Munoz-Organero, M., Ramirez-Gonzalez, G., Abdulhay, E., Arunkumar, N.: Using deep convolutional neural network for emotion detection on a physiological signals dataset (AMIGOS). IEEE Access 7, 57–67 (2018)

16. Schmidt, P., Dürichen, R., Reiss, A., Van Laerhoven, K., Plötz, T.: Multi-target affect detection in the wild: an exploratory study. In: ISWC 2019, pp. 211–219 (2019)

17. Schmidt, P., Reiss, A., Dürichen, R., Van Laerhoven, K.: UbiComp 2018 (2018)

18. Shui, X., Zhang, M., Li, Z., Hu, X., Wang, F., Zhang, D.: A dataset of daily ambulatory psychological and physiological recording for emotion research. Sci. Data 8(1), 1–12 (2021)

19. Siddharth, S., Jung, T.P., Sejnowski, T.J.: Utilizing deep learning towards multimodal bio-sensing and vision-based affective computing. IEEE Ttans. Affec. Comput. (2019)

20. Taylor, S., Jaques, N., Nosakhare, E., Sano, A., Picard, R.: Personalized multitask learning for predicting tomorrow's mood, stress, and health. IEEE Trans. Affec. Comput. 11(2), 200–213 (2020)

Sentiment Analysis Based on Smart Human Mobility: A Comparative Study of ML Models

Luís Rosa[1]([⊠]), Hugo Faria[1], Reza Tabrizi[1], Simão Gonçalves[1], Fábio Silva[2], and Cesar Analide[1]

[1] Department of Informatics, ALGORITMI Center,
University of Minho, Braga, Portugal
{pg44415,pg33877,pg42850,id8123}@alunos.uminho.pt, analide@di.uminho.pt
[2] CIICESI, ESTG, Politécnico do Porto, Felgueiras, Portugal
fas@estg.ipp.pt

Abstract. The great social development of the last few decades has led more and more to free time becoming an essential aspect of daily life. As such, there is the need to maximize free time trying to enjoy it as much as possible and spending it in places with positive atmospheres that result in positive sentiments. In that vein, using Machine Learning models, this project aims to create a time series prediction model capable of predicting which sentiment a given place cause on the people attending it over the next few hours. The predictions take into account the weather, whether or not an event is happening in that place, and the history of sentiment in that place over the course of the previous year. The extensive results on dataset illustrate that Long Short-Term Memory model achieves the state-of-the-art results over all models. For example, in multivariate model, the accuracy performance is 80.51% when it is applied on the LinkNYC Kiosk dataset.

Keywords: Machine Learning · Smart Cities · Sentiment Analysis · Human Mobility

1 Introduction

Currently, the number of Smarty Cities (SCs) is increasing and these cities have as main objective to improve the lives of citizens using Internet of Things (IoT) devices [5]. Examples of which are the implementation of existing lighting control systems in cities or the management of the flow of electricity or traffic [4]. A very common problem in cities is to control the density people in urban areas, that is, human mobility in cities that are not always the same throughout the day and that can affect people's daily lives due to existence of a high population density [6,10].

This density of people in the same geographic area, as well as the data they can generate from the interaction with digital services available in cities, allows us to make predictions at the most different levels. One of these levels is the

© Springer Nature Switzerland AG 2022
J. M. Ferrández Vicente et al. (Eds.): IWINAC 2022, LNCS 13259, pp. 55–64, 2022.
https://doi.org/10.1007/978-3-031-06527-9_6

emotion associated with a certain location at a given future time. If proven effective, it may allow for further investigation, with the goal of helping people better choose how to spend their time.

The polarity of a sentiment is a subjective topic, but there are still aspects known to affect it [12]. One the most important ones being the weather. The relevancy of weather in people's sentiment is something that can used to predict how the environment at a given place feels. One other important aspect to be considered for the sentiment a place is the possibility of there being an event occurring at said place. Additionally, all the information present in a date can help predict sentiments In other words, the day of the week, the month or even the hour of the day are all aspects that can influence sentiments.

The rest of the paper is organized as follows. Section 2 contextualizes key concepts as SCs, Artificial Intelligence (AI) and surveys about Sentiments analyzes. In Sect. 3, we detail the case study experiment used, and it explains all the processes carried out during the exploration and pre-treatment of data, address the various models developed to predict the human sentiments on New York City center. In the end of this stage (Sect. 4), we discuss the results of the case study. Finally, we summarize the work done and note on future work that be implemented to improve our work.

2   State of the Art

In this first stage of the article, we contextualize the two key concepts, the concept of Smart Cities (SCs) and Internet of Things (IoT). We intend that with the realization of the contextualization of these two concepts it is possible to have better understand the purpose of our study and the various reasons that led us to carry it out. Then, some surveys related with area of human sentiment are presented.

2.1   Smart Cities and Internet of Things

One of the most important concepts to understand is the concept of smart cities. SCs use IoT devices such as smart sensors, cameras or traffic lights. All this to improve the quality of life of citizens, stimulate the local economy and raise development indicators. Thus, the main objective of these cities is to develop innovative responses to improve infrastructure, public services and much more [3].

Through Table 1, we can see some use cases of SCs and we can easily observe cases that are constantly present in our daily lives, such as smart parking or smart street lighting. That said, building a true Smart City (SC) can be incredibly complex, not only because of the numerous tasks and functions that a city can have, but also because of the huge financial hurdle. Furthermore, to be a true SC, cities need to have an integrated approach, where various projects are interconnected, and, above all, data and IoT platforms are brought together to get all the benefits that SCs make possible.

Table 1. Examples of Use Cases and Applications of Smart Cities

Areas	Examples
Public Services	Citizen Services, Tourist Services, ...
Transportation	Smart Roads, Smart Parking, ...
Sustainability	Environment Monitoring, Smart Energy, ...
Public Safety	Smart Lighting, Emergency Response, ...
Infrastructure	Smart Buildings, Structure Health, ...

2.2   Developed Studies

This exact field of Artificial Intelligence (AI) models predicting human sentiment associated with time and place is rather scarce in terms of past research work. However, there are a few works in area of human sentiment.

E. Asani et al. [2] proposed a context-aware recommender system to extracts the food preferences of individuals from their comments and suggests restaurants in accordance with these preferences. For this purpose, the semantic approach is used to cluster the name of foods extracted from users' comments and analyze their sentiments about them. Finally, nearby open restaurants are recommended based on their similarity to user preferences.

In its turn, B. AlBadani 1 et al. [1] presents a new method of sentiment analysis using deep learning architectures by combining the Universal Language Model Fine-Tuning (ULMFiT) with Support Vector Machine (SVM) to increase the detection efficiency and accuracy. The method introduces a new deep learning approach for Twitter sentiment analysis to detect the attitudes of people toward certain products based on their comments.

Gihan Weeraprameshwara and Vihanga Jayawickramas [13] establishes benchmarks with the goal of identifying the best model for Sinhala sentiment analysis. They test on Facebook posts a set configuration, other deep learning models catered for sentiment analysis. In this study they report that the 3 layer Bidirectional LSTM model achieves an F1 score of 84.58% for Sinhala sentiment analysis, surpassing the current state-of-the-art model; Capsule B, which only manages to get an F1 score of 82.04%. Further, since all the deep learning models show F1 scores above 75% they conclude that it is safe to claim that Facebook reactions are suitable to predict the sentiment of a text.

M. Mao et al. developed an group event recommendation engine [7], based on the social relations a group of users has, that recommends them inexperienced events. At it's core, its an recommendation algorithm with the purpose of making recommendations to persistent groups, according to their criteria, past events. Since events take place at predefined location and time it is important to identify the popularity much before the occurrence of the event.

That said, it was possible to observe with the aforementioned studies that the concepts of Smart Cities (SCs) are increasingly present in society, AI has applicability in several areas, and we saw how they contribute to forecasting people's sentiments.

3   Experimental Study Case

As we have seen before, our case study is about predicting sentiments through Machine Learning (ML) techniques. Thus, in this section we start by approaching the dataset that we chose to use for our forecast and the main reasons that led us to choose it. After that, we see the main conclusions that we obtained from the exploratory analysis to better understand the data we are using. Thus, we proceed with the main steps taken in the data preprocessing to leave our dataset "clean" to later apply our ML models. The project was implemented in Python via Google Colab framework.

3.1   Exploratory Data Analysis

To build our dataset we use a public service that provided relevant information for the development of this study. Firstly, we decided to choose a service provided by NYC OpenData API, more specifically the LinkNYC Kiosk Status. The Department of Information Technology and Telecommunications (DoITT) manages the technical operations with Socrata Open Data API, ensuring that technological capabilities are always evolving to better meet user needs. This API provides data about the LinkNYC kiosks in which various data such as location, and the status of the Link's WiFi, tablet, and phone of the person connected to the network are described. This dataset consists of 2161 rows and 29 columns.

311 Open API via NYC Open Data is another resource we used on our work [9]. Although, this dataset contains several attributes, we highlight the most useful for the context of this work: Created Date, Descriptor, Latitude and Longitude. Then, a simple Python code apply Valence Aware Dictionary and Sentiment Reasoner (VADER) Analysis. VADER is a lexicon and rule-based sentiment analysis tool that is specifically attuned to sentiments expressed in social media [11]. It also uses a combination of a sentiment lexicon is a list of lexical features (e.g., words) which are generally labeled according to their semantic orientation as either positive, neutral or negative. This math formula gives Descriptor attribute their weight in the calculation of the sentiment label for every entry in the data set.

The previous distinguishable sentiments were then given a label number in a way that created somewhat of a scale of excitement in order to facilitate handling the data as well as making it better for the model. The scale chosen was the following: -1 - Negative; 0 - Neutral; 1 - Positive. After calculating sentiment weight for Descriptor attribute, the column with these weights was joined on LinkNYC Kiosk Status dataset, giving the final sentiment value each corresponding entry (based on date index).

After we apply Correlation Matrix (CM) technique, attributes such as Sentiment, Generated On, Borough, Latitude and Longitude show an import correlation coefficients. The first attribute is an attribute that contains the date and time when a user entered the kiosk. The second attribute is where the kiosks are located. The last two, as the name implies, give us the exact location in terms of latitude and longitude. We can view more detailed information about all dataset attributes in [8].

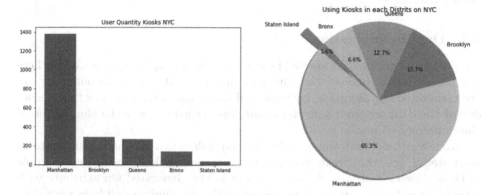

Fig. 1. Exploratory Analysis - User Quantity Kiosks NYC and Using Kiosks in each Districts on NYC.

When analyzing the Generated On attribute in detail, the most important interpretation we obtained was that this attribute had several old dates, and some of these dates even corresponded to dates from the last century. About the Borough attribute, it is important to mention that one of the conclusions we reached was that it had only 5 values, namely Manhattan, Brooklyn, Queens, Bronx and Staten Island. Thus, we can see through Fig. 1 some interesting data that we obtained in which it can be concluded that most users are from Manhattan (Manhattan has 65.3% of kiosk users).

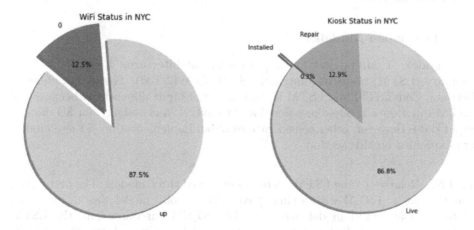

Fig. 2. Exploratory Analysis - Wifi Status in NYC and Kiosk Status in NYC.

To conclude our exploratory analysis, we also consider it interesting to observe the performance of the kiosks and WiFi. Having said that, we can observe in Fig. 2 the various states of both and we can easily conclude that both present good performances.

3.2   Data Preprocessing

As already mentioned, we started by carrying out an exploratory analysis where it was possible to conclude that the most important attributes for our study are the Generated On, Borough, Latitude and Longitude attributes. For this reason, one of the data preprocessing steps that was carried out was the elimination of the remaining columns.

Another thing that was possible to conclude when looking at the data in more detail, was that there were several null and "useless" data. One example of these "useless" data is the data present in the Generated On attribute with several dates that are too old. So, we proceeded to eliminate all lines with data below the beginning of the year 2017 and later we also proceed to the ordering of these dates. Regarding the data type of each attribute of the dataset, we also proceed to perform the conversion of the column data Generated On to the type of data that we consider most appropriate for our purpose.

To finish our data processing, in the Borough attribute that contained five distinct values, we used the fit_transform method of the scikit-learn library to improve the performance of our models. This method is used so that we can scale the training data and also learn the scaling parameters of these data and thus allow the built models to learn the mean and variance of the characteristics of the training set. These learned parameters are then used later to scale our test data. At the end of the Data Preprocessing, our dataset has 2123 rows and 4 columns and in the next step we address the various models that we implemented to achieve our goal.

3.3   Developed Models

The models of our project are based on two architectures: Long Short-Term Memory (LSTM) and Convolutional LSTM (ConvLSTM). The main difference between ConvLSTM and LSTM is the number of input dimensions, because the LSTM input data is one-dimensional and ConvLSTM is designed for 3D data as input data. However, other considerations about implementation of these models are explained on this section.

LSTM. Relative to the LSTM, were implemented three models. The first model was the classic LSTM with a single layer. The second model was an extension of the classic LSTM model, which is the LSTM Bidirectional. In the LSTM Bidirectional, instead of training just one model, are introduced two models. The first model learns the sequence from the input and the second model learns the inverse of that sequence. For this, it is necessary to have a mechanism that can combine both models, and this step is called the merge step, which can be done with addition, multiplication, average or concatenation functions. The third and last model implemented was another extension of the classic LSTM model, which is the Stacked LSTM. The classic LSTM consists of a single hidden LSTM layer followed by a feed-forward output layer, whereas Stacked LSTM has multiple hidden LSTM layers, where each layer contains multiple memory cells Figs. 3, 4 and 5.

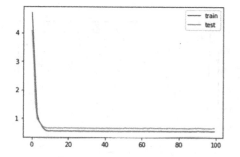

Fig. 3. Results from LSTM.

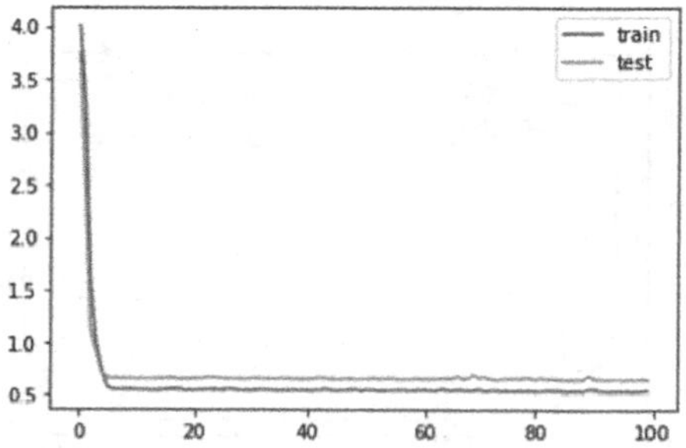

Fig. 4. Results from Stacked LSTM.

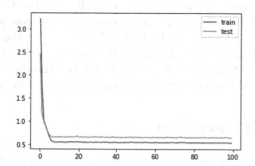

Fig. 5. Results from LSTM Bi-direction.

In these three graphs are exposed the behaviours of the models by loss function Mean Squared Error (MSE) and to optimize the models we use Adam optimizer. As we can see in the three models of LSTM, first we have a quickly reduce of the loss and then they stabilize. In a fast observation we can see that Stacked LSTM is slightly better than LSTM Bidirectional and LSTM single layer. Still, the computational cost of training of the models is higher comparing with LSTM single layer.

ConvLSTM. Relative to the ConvLSTM, were implemented two models. The first model was the CNN-LSTM, which is an integration of a Convolutional Neuronal Network (CNN) with an LSTM. In the first phase of this model, the CNN part of the model processes the data and int the second phase the one-dimensional result of the first phase is fed into an Long Short-Term Memory (LSTM) model. The second model was ConvLSTM2D, which is similar to LSTM but the input transformations and the recurring transformations are convolutional Figs. 6 and 7.

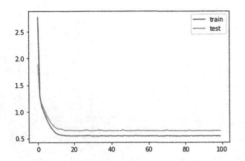 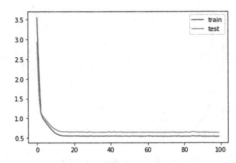

Fig. 6. Results from CNN-LSTM.   **Fig. 7.** Results from ConvLSTM2D.

In these two graphs we compare the behaviors of the CNN-LSTM model versus ConvLSTM2D. Such as the three others models that we saw of LSTM, first we have a quickly reduce of the loss and then they stabilize. We also used the loss function Mean Squared Error (MSE) and the Adam optimizer as well. The training result of these models is better than the training result of the three models of LSTM, but the computational cost to training the models is higher.

4   Results and Discussion

In this analysis we can see that we don't have big differences between the models, but of course we can see a little difference in the Convolutional LSTM (ConvLSTM) model that have a better performance.

If we have a huge and flexibility feature set to don't look at the computational cost of the training we will choose the ConvLSTM2D with a 0.632 value of loss. On the other hand, if we don't have this feature set and we need the best model with the lower computational cost we will choose Long Short-Term Memory (LSTM) single layer with a 0.650 value of loss, because in the set of the models with the lower computational cost, this is the model with the lower computational cost and just have a little bit higher value of loss. However, if we want a balance between the computational cost and the value of loss we will choose the CNN-LSTM with a 0.639 value of loss, because have a lower computational cost than ConvLSTM2D and still have one of the bests values of loss.

In the end, we made a comparison of the Multivariate models. We compare Multivariate LSTM model with the Multivariate CNN-LSTM model and how can we see in the Fig. 8 the loss function in LSTM model is much better than CNN-LSTM model. In addition, the computational cost of LSTM is extremely less than Convolutional Neural Network (CNN) models.

Models	Val_Loss
LSTM	0.650
CONVLSTM2D	0.632
STACKED LSTM	0.648
LSTM BIDIRECTIONAL	0.649
CNN-LSTM	0.639

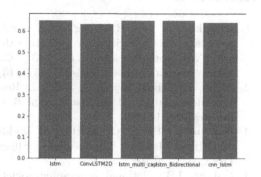

Fig. 8. Comparison of the results obtained.

5   Conclusion

This article approaches the modelling and prediction of sentiment associated with time an place. Starting with finding and processing data relevant to the problem in question, this step proved incredibly important, since finding the appropriate data for this particularly subjective topic was as difficult if not more than the making of the prediction model. The second phase of the work consisted of the model implementation that through training and some optimization ended the practical work with the conclusion of the final Long Short-Term Memory (LSTM) prediction model.

However, a critical point about data size should be mentioned. Unfortunately, our dataset is extremely small and did not have enough information to train our model. For example, we did not have the internet connection time of each cell phone and time to terminate the network connection in each kiosk. Due to these inconveniences we try to solve this problem with the cross validation method with shuffel = true, and we try to compare the models in their behavior of error loss and loss function.

In future work, we intend to predict the future sentiment values into a classification problem. In this classification problem a possible type of model to use would be decision trees. The short tests made in the data processing phase showed that a simple, unoptimized decision tree was able to reach around 75% accuracy, achieving better results than the ones obtained through the LSTM model.

Acknowledgements. This work has been supported by FCT - Fundacao para a Ciencia e Tecnologia within the R&D Units Project Scope: UIDB/00319/2020. It has also been supported by national funds through FCT - Fundação para a Ciência e Tecnologia through project UIDB/04728/2020.

References

1. AlBadani, B., Shi, R., Dong, J.: A novel machine learning approach for sentiment analysis on Twitter incorporating the universal language model fine-tuning and SVM. Appl. Syst. Innov. **5**(1), 13 (2022). https://doi.org/10.3390/asi5010013, https://www.mdpi.com/2571-5577/5/1/13/htm
2. Asani, E., Vahdat-Nejad, H., Sadri, J.: Restaurant recommender system based on sentiment analysis. Mach. Learn. Appl. **6**, 100114 (2021). https://doi.org/10.1016/j.mlwa.2021.100114
3. Balboni, C., Bryan, G., Morten, M., Siddiqi, B.: Transportation, Gentrification, and Urban Mobility: The Inequality Effects of Place-Based Policies. Preliminary Draft, p. 3 (2020)
4. Garver, J.B.: National geographic society. Am. Cartographer **14**(3), 237–238 (1987). https://doi.org/10.1559/152304087783875921
5. Hultin, J.: Smart cities: acceleration, technology, cases and evolutions in the smart city. https://www.i-scoop.eu/internet-of-things-iot/smart-cities-smart-city/
6. Joshi, S., Saxena, S., Godbole, T., Shreya: Developing smart cities: an integrated framework. Procedia Comput. Sci. **93**, 902–909 (2016). https://doi.org/10.1016/j.procs.2016.07.258
7. Liao, G., Huang, X., Mao, M., Wan, C., Liu, X., Liu, D.: Group event recommendation in event-based social networks considering unexperienced events. IEEE Access **7**, 96650–96671 (2019). https://doi.org/10.1109/ACCESS.2019.2929247
8. NYC Open Data: LinkNYC Kiosk Status (2019). https://data.cityofnewyork.us/City-Government/LinkNYC-Kiosk-Status/n6c5-95xh
9. NYC Open Data: 311 Service Requests from 2010 to Present (2021). https://data.cityofnewyork.us/Social-Services/311-Service-Requests-from-2010-to-Present/erm2-nwe9
10. Rosa, L., Silva, F., Analide, C.: WalkingStreet: understanding human mobility phenomena through a mobile application. In: Yin, H., et al. (eds.) IDEAL 2021. LNCS, vol. 13113, pp. 599–610. Springer, Cham (2021). https://doi.org/10.1007/978-3-030-91608-4_58
11. Dawra, S., Gumber, S.: Sentiment Analysis using VADER (2021). https://www.geeksforgeeks.org/python-sentiment-analysis-using-vader/
12. Taj, S., Shaikh, B.B., Fatemah Meghji, A.: Sentiment analysis of news articles: a lexicon based approach. In: 2019 2nd International Conference on Computing, Mathematics and Engineering Technologies, iCoMET 2019 (2019). https://doi.org/10.1109/ICOMET.2019.8673428
13. Weeraprameshwara, G., Jayawickrama, V., de Silva, N., Wijeratne, Y.: Sentiment analysis with deep learning models: a comparative study on a decade of Sinhala language Facebook data. arXiv preprint arXiv:2201.03941, January 2022. https://doi.org/10.48550/arxiv.2201.03941

Evaluation of Selected APIs for Emotion Recognition from Facial Expressions

Krzysztof Kutt[(✉)] ⓘ, Piotr Sobczyk, and Grzegorz J. Nalepa ⓘ

Jagiellonian Human-Centered Artificial Intelligence Laboratory (JAHCAI) and
Institute of Applied Computer Science, Jagiellonian University, Kraków, Poland
krzysztof.kutt@uj.edu.pl, gjn@gjn.re

Abstract. Facial expressions convey the vast majority of the emotional
information contained in social utterances. From the point of view of
affective intelligent systems, it is therefore important to develop appropriate emotion recognition models based on facial images. As a result of
the high interest of the research and industrial community in this problem, many ready-to-use tools are being developed, which can be used
via suitable web APIs. In this paper, two of the most popular APIs
were tested: Microsoft Face API and Kairos Emotion Analysis API. The
evaluation was performed on images representing 8 emotions—anger,
contempt, disgust, fear, joy, sadness, surprise and neutral—distributed
in 4 benchmark datasets: Cohn-Kanade (CK), Extended Cohn-Kanade
(CK+), Amsterdam Dynamic Facial Expression Set (ADFES) and Radboud Faces Database (RaFD). The results indicated a significant advantage of the Microsoft API in the accuracy of emotion recognition both
in photos taken en face and at a 45° angle. Microsoft's API also has an
advantage in the larger number of recognised emotions: contempt and
neutral are also included.

Keywords: Affective computing · Facial expression · Emotions ·
Benchmark datasets

1 Introduction and Motivation

American psychologist Albert Mehrabian published in 1968 a rule known as "7-
38-55" [16]. According to it, the content of an utterance alone conveys 7% of the
emotional state, the tone of voice accounts for 38%, while non-verbal communication (facial expressions, gestures) accounts for as much as 55%. This indicates
that the ability to recognise emotions from the face is highly important [4]. On
the other hand, it should be pointed out that emotional expressions are fairly
universal, i.e., they are recognised by members of different cultures – even those
that have had no contact with each other [5]. Both of these factors point to the
need to include emotion processing from facial expressions in information systems that deal with emotional information processing, i.e., affective computing
(AfC) systems [18].

© Springer Nature Switzerland AG 2022
J. M. Ferrández Vicente et al. (Eds.): IWINAC 2022, LNCS 13259, pp. 65–74, 2022.
https://doi.org/10.1007/978-3-031-06527-9_7

Deciphering emotions from facial expressions is a complex issue. Extensive time has been devoted to it by Paul Ekman, whose efforts were summarised in the Facial Action Coding System (FACS), developed in 1978 [3] and later updated in 2002 [6]. In the FACS system, facial expressions are encoded by more than 40 action units (AUs), which are the visually smallest muscle movements that cause changes in face expression. According to Ekman, each basic emotion is characterised by a unique expressive pattern, which may vary slightly for variants of the same emotion. As an example, there are over 60 facial expressions for anger, although all of them have two features in common: lowered eyebrows and tightened lips [3]. FACS has some limitations, among others, it is pointed out that action units are local patterns, whereas facial expressions are the result of the interaction of structures. FACS also does not take into account the temporal perspective of facial changes [18].

An alternative approach in recognizing emotions from facial expressions was proposed in [7]. This system is based on recognising emotions from the flow of movement of the whole face, rather than synthesising them from the movement of individual muscles. For this purpose, a geometric model of the facial shape was used, which was then superimposed on the face and the detected emotions were assigned based on the movement patterns of the grid. In addition to the two systems mentioned above, there are a number of other solutions (see, e.g., [2,9]). Among them, the most interesting from the point of view of creating practical systems seem to be commercial solutions, in which access to an appropriate API is provided, to which one sends photos/videos containing emotional expressions and in response receives feedback on emotions detected by the system. Thanks to this, implementation of a solution based on facial emotion recognition does not require large resources to run the model, e.g., on mobile phones or in wearable systems – only constant access to the Internet is needed.

Our research is aimed at preparing a toolkit for developing personalised intelligent affective systems [11]. The core assumption is to use affordable wearables as the basis for the whole mechanism. This requires a lightweight framework, which will not have high hardware requirements and will be adequately robust for the assumed applications [17]. This straight leads to the choice of using one of the available APIs for emotion recognition. The aim of the work described in this paper was to verify two such solutions – the key to their selection was the availability of a free version that allows testing. The results obtained will be the basis for further work, in which the usability of the selected API will be evaluated on data collected in BIRAFFE (*Bio-Reactions and Faces for Emotion-based Personalization for AI Systems*) series of experiments [12,13].

The rest of paper is organized as follows. General approach for emotion recognition from facial expressions is discussed in Sect. 2. Then, in Sect. 3, the datasets selected for experiments are outlined. Evaluation results are presented in Sect. 4. The paper is concluded in Sect. 5.

2 Emotion Recognition from Facial Expressions

The general automatic emotion recognition systems based on facial expressions consists of detecting a face in an image, extracting its features, and finally classifying them [1]. Various challenges arise in this process, for example, the face may not be captured centrally but from a semi-profile; individual differences in face shape and appearance make generalisation difficult; the classifier may be overfitting or underlearning due to insufficient teaching examples [1]. Assuming that a facial expression is a manifestation of a perceived emotion, the problem of emotion recognition can be reduced to the problem of pattern recognition. Supervised learning methods are usually used for this purpose [10].

The first step is to detect the location of the face in the image. In the case of facing the camera, this can be done using the Viola-Jones detector [21]. Its algorithm is based on extracting Haar features for each part of the image, i.e., small areas containing a vertical, horizontal or diagonal line. This is necessary to calculate whether a photo contains a face, but it is very inefficient due to the need to check a large number of features. To solve this problem, so-called cascades of classifiers were introduced: first checking which features have the biggest influence on the final classification and then grouping them into subsequent steps of the matching algorithm. In this way, if a potential face is not found in a window in the first step, the rest of the features no longer need to be checked in that window. [21] suggested that this face search algorithm has very good performance. To avoid the effect of face rotation on emotion recognition, the detected face needs to be normalised, i.e., transformed to a standard size and orientation.

Once the face is found, the next step is feature extraction based on determining the position of landmarks such as the contours of the eyes and eyebrows, the corners of the mouth, and the tip of the nose. A geometric grid is superimposed on the face, constructed from the landmarks of the universal neutral face model. Differences between the models are recalculated by the classifier to determine a specific emotion. Information about the position and orientation of key features provides input to the classifier algorithms, which return action units or final recognised emotional states as output. Most approaches to learning a classification model boil down to supervised learning, where emotions are labelled in a learning set [1,10].

There are many solutions on the market that analyse emotions based on facial expressions, working along the above described scheme. The industry is constantly growing, offering commercial applications to study the perception of advertisements, the user's sense of satisfaction, and even to check the level of anger in public places such as stadiums or airports to prevent possible dangerous events. Since creating software that recognises emotions requires having a large amount of data for machine learning, companies offering such solutions primarily aim to hide the business logic of the application. This is most often done through the use of microservice architecture: the software that recognises emotions based on a face photo runs as a service on the company's server, accessible by the API, which makes it possible to integrate this solution into your own application while having no knowledge of the specific operation of the system. It is important to note that API-based systems are usually characterised by limited availability (daily or monthly transaction limit). In addition to application access, systems may also differ in the number of emotions detected, moreover, each system has its own capabilities and limitations. For the purpose of this research, two comprehensive systems for emotion recognition based on facial expressions were selected, differing in their specifications and the emotion model used: Microsoft Face API and Kairos Emotion Analysis API. Only free variants of the above-mentioned tools were used in the experiments.

2.1   Microsoft Face API

Microsoft Cognitive Services[1] is a collection of various services including image recognition, photo identification, voice verification or intelligent recommendation systems. Among these services is the Microsoft Face API[2] for emotion detection based on facial expressions. The API takes as input an image in which it seeks a face. Then, for each face it finds—based on its expression—it returns the confidence level for each emotion in the recognised set and the coordinates of the rectangle bounding the face field in JSON format. The detected emotions are: anger, contempt, disgust, fear, joy, sadness and surprise and—additionally— neutral. During interpretation of the returned results, the emotion with the highest score should be understood as the detected emotion. All emotion scores are summed to one. Microsoft agrees not to publish the submitted data or give access to it to other users, although it reserves the right to use the images to improve its services.

2.2   Kairos Emotion Analysis API

Kairos is a company offering services related to demographic data analysis— including emotion recognition—through the use of vision systems and machine learning. The Kairos Emotion Analysis API[3] runs as a web service available in a REST architecture. The service allows recognition of emotions not only from a photo, but also from videos. A photo containing a face is uploaded to the Kairos Emotion Analysis API. The found facial features and expressions are processed by algorithms, returning in response values corresponding to the recognised emotions and the locations of facial feature points in the image. The service recognises six basic emotions: anger, disgust, fear, joy, sadness, surprise. The confidence level of the detected emotions ranges from 0 to 100 and, as with the Microsoft API, the one with the highest score should be interpreted as the recognised emotion.

---

[1]   See: https://azure.microsoft.com/en-us/services/cognitive-services/.
[2]   See: https://azure.microsoft.com/en-us/services/cognitive-services/face/.
[3]   See: https://www.kairos.com/docs/api/.

3 Datasets

Standardised sets of face images labelled by experts were used for the experiments. It was decided to select the 4 most popular datasets:

- *Cohn-Kanade (CK)* [8]. It is a dataset created at Carnegie Mellon University in 2000 consisting of a series of posed photographs, taken at short intervals, starting with a neutral facial expression and ending with a face corresponding to a certain emotion. The last photo in the series is also coded using the updated FACS system [6] and labelled with the name of the emotion. The label itself refers to the facial expression the subjects were asked to express, not to the one actually presented. The collection contains a total of 585 image series, representing the 6 basic emotions. Ninety-seven students aged between 18 and 30 were selected to create it, 65% of whom were female. In terms of ethnicity, 15% were African-American, 3% Asian or Hispanic, and the rest Euro-American. The images were taken straight on with uniform lighting and are available in greyscale at 640×490 pixel resolution.
- *Extended Cohn-Kanade (CK+)* [15]. This is the second version of the CK dataset released in 2010. In addition to posed photographs, a certain group of spontaneous expressions was included. Compared to CK, the group of subjects and the number of photo series taken has been increased. The photos are also coded in FACS and labelled with emotions, but the labels have been verified by experts. The facial expressions captured represent 8 states: 6 basic emotions, contempt and neutrality. A 593 image series covering the photographs of 123 people was recorded. The images are provided in 640×490 pixel resolution. Most of them are in grayscale, but there are also some in colour.
- *Amsterdam Dynamic Facial Expression Set (ADFES)* [20]. This dataset, created at the University of Amsterdam, consists of 648 MPEG-2 videos lasting approximately 6 s. The videos were recorded simultaneously from two angles: straight ahead and from a $45°$ angle. In addition, the database includes frames extracted from videos recorded frontally, demonstrating people expressing emotion at their peak. These are colour JPEG images with a resolution of 720×576 pixels. The people recorded are of different ethnicities, being Europeans, Africans and Turks between the ages of 18 and 25. The subject group consisted of 10 women and 12 men. They were trained so that their facial expressions corresponded to a prototype of a certain emotion according to the FACS system [6]. A major advantage of the ADFES database is the number of emotions presented – in addition to the 6 basic ones, each of the subjects presented a neutral face, contempt, as well as pride and shame.
- *Radboud Faces Database (RaFD)* [14]. The RaFD collection, created in 2010 at Radboud Universiteit in Nijmegen, consists of photos of 67 models (Europeans and Africans), of which 38 are men, 19 – women, 4 – boys and 6 – girls. Each person was trained by an expert to be able to make facial expressions corresponding to eight emotional states according to FACS [6]: 6 basic, contempt and neutral. The photograph of each emotional expression was simultaneously taken from different perspectives: en face, in profile and from a 45°

angle. The entire collection consists of 8040 colour images with a resolution of 681 × 1024 pixels.

4   APIs' Evaluation

A series of experiments were conducted using the free version of both APIs. Images were sent one at a time, response sent by the API was received, and then the detected emotion was compared with the emotion with which the image was labelled. For each of the tests—one test is an evaluation of one API on a single emotion tested on images from one set—accuracy score was calculated by dividing the number of correctly assigned labels to all images used in the test. The Kairos API does not recognise a neutral emotion, so for the purposes of testing it was assumed that the "no emotion" response returned by this API would be treated as a neutral emotion.

Due to the large number of images in the learning sets and the limitations of the free versions of the API, for the purpose of the tests, from each of the available datasets a subset was selected on which the evaluation was performed:

- for each of the series of images (one subject expressing one emotion), a single image was selected in which the emotion reached its peak of expression,
- in CK+ dataset, only images annotated by FACS experts were considered.

Finally, the evaluation was carried out on the following number of pictures:

- CK dataset: sadness – 128, joy – 103, surprise – 103, fear – 66, anger – 45, and disgust – 42;
- CK+ dataset: surprise – 83, joy – 69, disgust – 59, anger – 45, sadness – 28, fear – 25, and contempt – 18;
- ADFES dataset: 21 photos for surprise and 22 images for each of the other conditions: anger, contempt, disgust, fear, joy, sadness and neutral;
- RaFD dataset: 67 en face images for each condition: surprise, anger, contempt, disgust, fear, joy, sadness and neutral. A second set of the same size was also selected, in which the subjects were photographed at 45°.

Based on the obtained accuracy results shown in Figs. 1 and 2, and on the analysis of the confusion matrix (not included in the article, due to limited space), the following observations can be drawn:

1. Microsoft Face API dominates for most emotions and most datasets. The Kairos Emotion Analysis API achieves higher performance only for anger.
2. Only the Microsoft Face API handled photos that were not taken en face.
3. In the CK and CK+ datasets, the Kairos Emotion Analysis API most often had problems detecting faces: for these datasets, either no face or no emotion message appeared most often.
4. Both systems perform well in identifying joy and surprise, while anger, fear and sadness receive generally low accuracy scores.
5. Fear is often mistaken for surprise and sadness for no emotion.

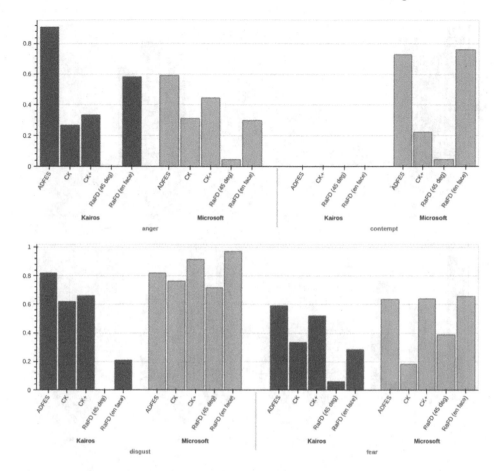

Fig. 1. Accuracy scores for each tested scenario: 8 emotions, 2 frameworks, 5 datasets (cont. on Fig. 2).

6. The model used in the Kairos system does not include contempt, so this API is unable to recognise this emotion (hence the 0 values for all tests).
7. ADFES dataset includes also faces tagged as pride and shame. Both systems are unable to recognise these emotions so this is not included in the figures, however we have considered these images in the evaluation. The confusion matrix analysis indicates that pride is often recognised as joy and shame as neutrality. This pattern is confirmed by Russell's two-dimensional emotion model [19] – pride and joy are adjacent in this space, whereas shame can be confused with neutrality because it lacks a specific facial muscle representation [20].

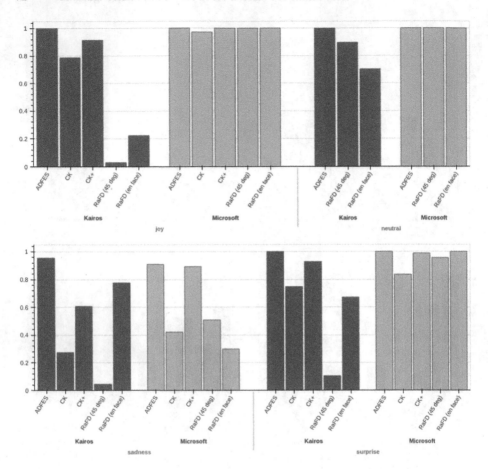

Fig. 2. Accuracy scores for each tested scenario: 8 emotions, 2 frameworks, 5 datasets (cont. from Fig. 1).

5   Summary and Future Work

This paper presents a detailed comparison of two popular web APIs for emotion recognition from facial expressions: Microsoft Face API and Kairos Emotion Analysis API. The evaluation was performed on images taken from 4 benchmark datasets: Cohn-Kanade (CK), Extended Cohn-Kanade (CK+), Amsterdam Dynamic Facial Expression Set (ADFES) and Radboud Faces Database (RaFD). The results indicated a significant advantage of the Microsoft API in the accuracy of emotion recognition both in photos taken en face and at a 45° angle. Microsoft's API also has an advantage in the larger number of recognised emotions: contempt and neutral are also included.

In the benchmark datasets used in this study, subjects were explicitly asked to produce a specific emotional expression, making the facial changes highly expressive. As part of future work, we plan to evaluate both APIs on the data obtained in the BIRAFFE1 and BIRAFFE2 experiments [12,13]. In contrast to the benchmark datasets used in the present work, in the BIRAFFE datasets emotional expressions appeared as a *by-product* of the execution of the experimental protocol related to the evaluation of emotional stimuli and to the playing of affective games. This will make these expressions more similar to natural ones and present in everyday life, so that it will be possible to obtain information about the effectiveness of APIs in more ecological conditions, which is important for the design of affective user interfaces.

References

1. Cohn, J.F., De La Torre, F.: Automated face analysis for affective computing. In: Calvo, R.A., D'Mello, S., Gratch, J., Kappas, A. (eds.) The Oxford Handbook of Affective Computing, pp. 131–150. Oxford University Press (2015). https://doi.org/10.1093/oxfordhb/9780199942237.013.020
2. Deshmukh, R.S., Jagtap, V.: A survey: software API and database for emotion recognition. In: 2017 International Conference on Intelligent Computing and Control Systems (ICICCS), pp. 284–289 (2017). https://doi.org/10.1109/ICCONS.2017.8250727
3. Ekman, P., Friesen, W.V.: Facial Action Coding System: A Technique for the Measurement of Facial Movement. Consulting Psychologists Press, Palo Alto (1978)
4. Ekman, P., Rosenberg, E.L.: What the Face Reveals: Basic and Applied Studies of Spontaneous Expression Using the Facial Action Coding System (FACS). Oxford University Press, Oxford (2005)
5. Ekman, P., Friesen, W.V.: Constants across cultures in the face and emotion. J. Pers. Soc. Psychol. **17**(2), 124–129 (1971)
6. Ekman, P., Friesen, W.V., Hager, J.C.: Facial Action Coding System (FACS): Manual. A Human Face, Salt Lake City (2002)
7. Essa, I.A., Pentland, A.P.: Coding, analysis, interpretation, and recognition of facial expressions. IEEE Trans. Pattern Anal. Mach. Intell. **19**(7), 757–763 (1997)
8. Kanade, T., Cohn, J.F., Tian, Y.: Comprehensive database for facial expression analysis. In: Proceedings of the Fourth IEEE International Conference on Automatic Face and Gesture Recognition (FG 2000), Grenoble, France, pp. 46–53 (2000)
9. Khanal, S.R., Barroso, J., Lopes, N., Sampaio, J., Filipe, V.: Performance analysis of Microsoft's and Google's emotion recognition API using pose-invariant faces. In: Proceedings of the 8th International Conference on Software Development and Technologies for Enhancing Accessibility and Fighting Info-exclusion, DSAI 2019, Thessaloniki, Greece, 20–22 June 2018, pp. 172–178. ACM (2018). https://doi.org/10.1145/3218585.3224223
10. Konar, A., Chakraborty, A. (eds.): Emotion Recognition: A Pattern Analysis Approach. Wiley, New Jersey (2015)
11. Kutt, K., Drążyk, D., Bobek, S., Nalepa, G.J.: Personality-based affective adaptation methods for intelligent systems. Sensors **21**(1), 163 (2021). https://doi.org/10.3390/s21010163
12. Kutt, K., et al.: BIRAFFE: bio-reactions and faces for emotion-based personalization. In: AFCAI 2019: Workshop on Affective Computing and Context Awareness in Ambient Intelligence. CEUR Workshop Proceedings, vol. 2609. CEUR-WS.org (2020)

13. Kutt, K., Drążyk, D., Szelążek, M., Bobek, S., Nalepa, G.J.: The BIRAFFE2 experiment. Study in bio-reactions and faces for emotion-based personalization for AI systems. CoRR abs/2007.15048 (2020). https://arxiv.org/abs/2007.15048

14. Langner, O., Dotsch, R., Bijlstra, G., Wigboldus, D., Hawk, S., van Knippenberg, A.: Presentation and validation of the radboud face database. Cogn. Emotion **24**(8), 1377–1388 (2010)

15. Lucey, P., Cohn, J.F., Kanade, T., Saragih, J., Ambadar, Z., Matthews, I.: The extended Cohn-Kanade dataset (CK+): a complete dataset for action unit and emotion-specified expression. In: Proceedings of the Third International Workshop on CVPR for Human Communicative Behavior Analysis (CVPR4HB 2010), San Francisco, USA, pp. 94–101, (2010)

16. Mehrabian, A.: Communication without words. Psychol. Today **2**(4), 53–56 (1968)

17. Nalepa, G.J., Kutt, K., Bobek, S.: Mobile platform for affective context-aware systems. Future Generar. Comput. Syst. **92**, 490–503 (2019). https://doi.org/10.1016/j.future.2018.02.033

18. Picard, R.W.: Affective Computing. MIT Press, Cambridge (1997)

19. Russell, J.A.: A circumplex model of affect. J. Pers. Soc. Psychol. **39**, 1161–1178 (1980)

20. van der Schalk, J., Hawk, S., Fischer, A., Doosje, B.: Moving faces, looking places: validation of the Amsterdam dynamic facial expression set (ADFES). Emotion **11**(4), 907–920 (2011)

21. Viola, P., Jones, M.J.: Robust real-time face detection. Int. J. Comput. Vis. **57**(2), 137–154 (2004). https://doi.org/10.1023/B:VISI.0000013087.49260.fb

Bioinspired Computing Approaches

Robust Makespan Optimization via Genetic Algorithms on the Scientific Workflow Scheduling Problem

Pablo Barredo and Jorge Puente[✉][iD]

Department of Computing, University of Oviedo, Campus of Gijón,
33204 Gijón, Spain
{uo237136,puente}@uniovi.es
http://www.di.uniovi.es/iscop

Abstract. Distributed scientific applications are commonly executed as a workflow of data interdependent tasks on a cluster of different machines. Over the last years, the infrastructure used for solving these problems has evolved from clusters of physical machines to virtual resources in a Cloud based on Quality of Service requirements and pay-per-use basis. In these settings, the total execution time of the workflow, i.e., the makespan, is one of the main objectives. The subsequent optimization problem of distributing the tasks on the available resources, called workflow scheduling problem, is often solved by means of metaheuristics. In this paper we propose an improved workflow model that considers disk times in communications costs. To solve the scheduling problem, we devise a genetic algorithm that produces robust schedules. The experimental study showed that the proposed model is able to predict the execution time of the workflow with more precision than the existing ones in a Cloud Infrastructure as a Services system.

Keywords: Scientific Workflow · Genetic Algorithm · Robust Makespan

1 Introduction

Cloud computing is a distributed computing paradigm that provides virtual, scalable and dynamic resources on a pay-as-you-use basis. Infrastructure as a Service (IaaS) is one of the main facilities that cloud computing offers. Some of the advantages of these services are efficiency, speed, accessibility and virtualization capabilities, among others. These features have made cloud computing a relevant choice for scientists when they are executing compute-intensive experiments by using scientific workflows.

Researchers need the computation results as soon as possible while trying to minimize the use time of rented processing infrastructure. Consequently, the finish time of the last workflow task (the makespan) is one of the most relevant Quality of Service (QoS) measures. The processing of scientific workflows may last from a few minutes to several days depending on the size of the workflow

© Springer Nature Switzerland AG 2022
J. M. Ferrández Vicente et al. (Eds.): IWINAC 2022, LNCS 13259, pp. 77–87, 2022.
https://doi.org/10.1007/978-3-031-06527-9_8

(from dozens to thousands of tasks, interchanging from KBs to TBs of data) and the performance of the computation infrastructure (cloud platforms have hosts with different properties and processing capacities).

A Workflow Management System (WMS) is needed to orchestrate and schedule the execution of the workflow. One of the functions of the WMS is to optimise the allocation of tasks to the heterogeneous virtual machines (VMs) in the cloud infrastructure. The difficulty of this scheduling problem (NP-complete [6]) justifies the application of approximate methods for its resolution, including evolutionary algorithms.

In this paper we propose a genetic algorithm to obtain robust schedules with low makespan. For this purpose, we present a reformulation of the makespan estimation model considering not only computation and network communications, but also disk operation times. The model is inspired by the task to VMs deployment model of a well-known WMS, as it is Pegasus, in data-intensive workflows.

The remaining of the paper is organized as follows. The workflow model is defined in the next section. In Sect. 3 we introduce the proposed genetic algorithm. The experimental study is reported in Sect. 4. Finally, the paper concludes in Sect. 5.

2 The Scientific Workflow Scheduling Model

The computational applications in distributed systems are workflows modelled as a set of tasks interconnected by precedence constraints. The execution of a task can be initiated as soon as the necessary data are available, i.e., after its predecessor tasks execution. After execution every task generates an output dataset. This dataset is required by its successor tasks in the workflow before their execution. Most workflow applications can be represented in the form of a direct acyclic graph where the nodes are the tasks, and the arcs are the precedence constraints. This is the case for multiple scientific applications in very different research fields such as bioinformatics (1000genome, soyKB), agroecosystem (cycles) or astronomy (montage) [5].

2.1 Schedule Evaluation Models

In the context of metaheuristic optimization, thousands of schedules are generated and subsequently evaluated. The evaluation models tend to simplify the workflow processing problem for the sake of speeding-up calculations. The most common evaluation model for workflow schedules [2,4,9] only considers CPU processing times and data sets network communications between different hosts. This Network-Computation model (NC) ignores all disk accesses from/to tasks in their data sets acquisition/generation. Other common simplification in NC model only considers the latest network communication time from predecessor tasks to establish the starting time estimation of a successor task. For computation-intensive workflows, NC model may generate quite accurate makespan approximations.

However, in a cloud computing environment (usually a pay-per-use infrastructure environment) not only are relevant computing times or networking communications, but also disk data input/output transference times. This extra time should be relevant in data-intensive workflows where data transfer operations are not negligible w.r.t. computing times. In this work we propose an extended evaluation definition called Disk-Network-Computation model (DNC), which considers network communications and all disk operations. In DNC model, the estimated starting time depends on whether the predecessor tasks ran on the same host or not. In the first case, local disk reading times are used; in the second case, remote disk reading times and network communications should be used. Finally, after task execution we should consider total local disk writing times for saving all generated output data sets.

Workflow Definition. Scientific workflows are represented as a direct acyclic graph $G = (T, A)$, where $T = \{t_1, t_2, ..., t_n\}$ is the set of nodes representing the n tasks of the problem, and $A = \{(t_i, t_j) | 1 \leq i \leq n, 1 \leq j \leq n, i \neq j\}$ represents the set of arcs or dependency constraints among the tasks. Nodes are labeled with their corresponding task sizes in $MFLOPs$ (Million Floating Point Operations), and the arcs are labeled $data(i, j)$, i.e., the dataset size in MB to transfer from t_i to t_j. Moreover, t_{entry} and t_{end} are fictitious tasks with null computation and communication, that represent entry and exit points of the workflow respectively.

Cloud Resource Definition. The resource model consists in a cloud service provider that offers an IaaS platform as a set of heterogeneous hosts or VMs to its clients. Let $M=\{vm_1, vm_2, ...,vm_m\}$ be the set of VMs, each one modeled as a tuple $< pc, nb, ds >$, where pc, nb and ds are the processing capacity in $GFLOPS$, network bandwidth in MB/sec and disk reading/writing speed in MB/sec respectively.

2.2 Definition of the Workflow Scheduling Problem

Given a workflow $G = (T, A)$ and an IaaS infrastructure as a set of VMs M, the goal of the Workflow Scheduling Problem - defined by the tuple (G, M) - is twofold. Firstly, we need to find a feasible solution $S = (Hosts, Order)$ where $Hosts$ is a mapping from tasks to VMs and $Order$ is a topological order of G. And then, we want this schedule be optimal in the sense that its *makespan* is minimal.

Specifically, the goal is:

$$minimize\ EFT(t_{exit}) \tag{1}$$

where $EFT(t_{exit})$ is the estimated finish time of the task t_{exit}.

The schedule of the tasks and the corresponding estimated value of *makespan* are defined in accordance with the applied evaluation model: the standard NC model or the new DNC model. In the next subsections both models are formally introduced.

Network-Computing Processing Model. In the NC model, the processing time for a workflow is modelled combining computation and communication times, in the latter considering network communications only and so ignoring all disk accesses. The *makespan* estimation is calculated applying the following definitions:

Definition 1. *The computation time of task t_i on a machine vm_k, denoted ct_i^k, is defined as:*

$$ct_i^k = size(t_i)/pc_k \tag{2}$$

where $size(t_i)$ is the size of the task t_i measured in GFLOPs and pc_k is the processing capacity of the virtual machine vm_k in GFLOPS.

Definition 2. *The data transfer time between tasks t_i and t_j mapped on vm_k and vm_l respectively is defined as:*

$$dt_{i,j}^{k,l} = \begin{cases} 0 & : k = l \\ \frac{data(i,j)}{min(ds_k, nb_k, nb_l)} & : k \neq l \end{cases} \tag{3}$$

where $data(i,j)$ is the output-data size from t_i to t_j, and vm_k and vm_l are the VMs where tasks are scheduled respectively; ds_k is the disk speed of vm_k, and nb_k and nb_l are the network bandwidths of vm_k and vm_l respectively. Note that all local disk accesses are ignored when both tasks are executed in the same VM.

Definition 3. *The estimated finish time of task t_i on vm_k is defined as:*

$$EFT(t_i, vm_k) = EST(t_i, vm_k) + ct_i^{vm_k} \tag{4}$$

where only the computation time is considered, while local saving of all output data is ignored.

Note that definition of the NC model uses a no insertion task scheduling policy. However, we have decided to apply an insertion policy in its design, improving significantly its solutions quality, in order to compare both models in fair conditions.

Definition 4. *The estimated starting time of task t_i on vm_k is defined as:*

$$EST(t_i, vm_k) = avail(i, k, \max_{t_j \in pred(t_i)} (EFT(t_j, vm_l) + dt_{j,i}^{l,k})) \tag{5}$$

where each predecessor task t_j is executed on its corresponding machine vm_l and $avail(i, k, m)$ is the earliest available time of vm_k to compute t_i after time m.

Disk-Network-Computing Processing Model. The DNC model differs from NC model in communications and processing times, because only DNC model considers disk accesses. The computation of tasks is similar but it is necessary to reformulate the main concepts.

Definition 5. *The data transfer time between tasks t_i and t_j mapped on vm_k and vm_l respectively is:*

$$
dt_{i,j}^{k,l} = \begin{cases} \frac{data(i,j)}{ds_k} & : k = l \\[2mm] \frac{data(i,j)}{min(ds_k, nb_k, nb_l)} & : k \neq l \end{cases} \tag{6}
$$

where $data(i,j)$ is the output-data size from t_i to t_j, and vm_k and vm_l are the VMs where tasks are scheduled respectively. In this DNC model, when tasks t_i and t_j are scheduled in the same VM, data input files should be read from local disk.

Definition 6. *The estimated finish time of task t_i executed on machine vm_k involves not only the processing time but also complete input and output data operations. It is defined as:*

$$
EFT(t_i, vm_k) = EST(t_i, vm_k) + input_{i,k} + ct_i^{vm_k} + output_{i,k} \tag{7}
$$

where $input_{i,k}$ is the communication time for input data of t_i on vm_k from all its predecessors. It is defined as:

$$
input_{i,k} = \sum_{t_j \in pred(t_i)} dt_{j,i}^{l,k} \tag{8}
$$

where each predecessor task t_j is executed on its corresponding machine vm_l. The corresponding $output_{i,k}$ is the writing time for all output data of t_i in the vm_k local disk, that is:

$$
output_{i,k} = \frac{\sum_{t_j \in succ(t_i)} data(i,j)}{ds_k} \tag{9}
$$

In DNC model we use an insertion policy which assigns the earliest idle time slot between two already-scheduled tasks on the assigned VM. The length of the time slot should be at least capable of cover not only computation but also data transfer times of the considered task. Additionally, scheduling in this idle time slot should preserve precedence constraints.

Definition 7. *The estimated starting time of task t_i on vm_k is defined as:*

$$
EST(t_i, vm_k) = avail(i, k, \max_{t_j \in pred(t_i)} (EFT(t_j, vm_l))) \tag{10}
$$

where each predecessor task t_j is executed on its corresponding machine vm_l and $avail(i, k, m)$ is the earliest available time of vm_k after m to compute t_i.

When we apply an evaluation model to a workflow problem solution, we get the schedule and its corresponding *a priori* or estimated makespan, but it is only after execution of the workflow - which in this work will be done via IaaS simulations - that we get the actual makespan. We define the robustness of a makespan estimation as the relative error of the a priori makespan with respect to the real makespan (see Eq. 11). Robust a priori makespan will offer scientists a relevant information to take decisions about the computing infrastructure to rent depending on the budget and the urgency of the results.

Algorithm 1. Genetic Algorithm

Require: A Workflow instance, a VMs infrastructure and parameters (pop_{size}, max_{gens}, p_c and p_m)
Ensure: A schedule for workflow and tasks to VMs assignment
 1: Generate a pool P_0 of random solutions. //*initial population*
 2: Evaluate each chromosome of P_0 using DNCevaluator
 3: **for** $t \leftarrow 0$ to max_{gens} **do**
 4:     **Selection:** organize the chromosomes in P_t pairs at random
 5:     **Recombination:** make each pair of chromosomes and mutate both offsprings
         in accordance with p_c and p_m
 6:     **Evaluation:** evaluate offspring chromosomes
 7:     **Replacement:** make a tournament selection 4:2 among every pair of parents
         and their offspring to generate P_{t+1}
 8: **end for**
 9: **return** the best generated solution

---

3   Genetic Algorithm

In this section, we introduce the main components of the genetic algorithm (GA) proposed to solve the Workflow Scheduling Problem, and study the robustness of the solutions using both NC and DNC evaluation models. Algorithm 1 shows a pseudocode of the GA: it is a generational genetic algorithm with random selection and replacement by tournament among parents and offsprings, which confers the GA an implicit form of elitism. The GA uses one of the two evaluation models: NC or DNC. As a result we will have two different genetic algorithms: NC-GA and DNC-GA respectively. Both algorithms require the following parameters: population size (pop_{size}), number of generations (max_{gens}), crossover and mutation probabilities (p_c and p_m).

Coding Schema. The coding schema is based on permutations of tasks [8,9], each one with a specific VM assignment. So a gene is a pair (i,k), $1 \le i \le |T|$ and $1 \le k \le |M|$, and a chromosome includes a gene like this for every task. For example, given an instance with 4 tasks and 2 VMs, a feasible chromosome is the following: chr_1: ((1 2) (4 1) (2 1) (3 2)) which represents the task ordering (t_1, t_4, t_2, t_3) with VMs assignments (vm_2, vm_1, vm_1, vm_2) respectively. We only consider task orders that codify a topological order so every task must be located in a gene after its last predecessor and before its first successor in the chromosome. Therefore, the individuals generated in the initial population and by the genetic operators must be consistent with the task dependencies constraints.

Decoding Schema. The schedule represented by a chromosome is calculated following the selected evaluation model as a decoder. The genes are processed from left to right in the chromosome sequence. For each gene (i,k), the task t_i is scheduled at the earliest free gap of vm_k, after the latest finish time of its predecessors in the workflow, where the processing time of task t_i (computation and communications - depending on the evaluation model) fits. The makespan of the built schedule is the latest finish time of all the workflow tasks.

Crossover. The mating operator should resolve both: the order and VM assignment of the tasks at the generated offspring. A feasible schedule permutation must follow all the dependencies which exists among tasks. For order chromosome mating, we follow [9] and the so called CrossoverOrder algorithm. First the operator randomly chooses a crossover position, which splits each parent sequence into two subsequences. After that, the two first substrings are taken to be the initial sequence of the offspring and then filling the remaining positions with the genes representing the remaining tasks taken from the other parent, while keeping their relative order. The resulting task orders will not cause any dependency conflict since the order of any two tasks should have already be present in at least one parent.

Mutation. The mutation operator should not break the task order dependencies. First, we select a random task T_i. Next, we identify all predecessors and successors of T_i. Then the operator locates the longest subsequence of genes holding T_i that doesn't include any predecessor or successor of T_i. Finally, T_i is moved to a randomly chosen location inside this subsequence. Consequently the assigned VM is mutated to a random index in the set of VMs.

Initial Population. The pop_{size} initial individuals of the population are generated at random but following a topological order of the tasks, and with valid VM index assignments for all tasks.

We start with an empty chromosome, and then we identify as candidate tasks those that have t_{start} as their only predecessor in the workflow. At every step we extract at random a task T from candidate tasks, this task will be appended at the end of the partial chromosome. Then, we update candidate tasks by adding all the successors of T which have all their predecessors in the chromosome. The process is repeated until the set of candidate tasks gets empty. The resulting chromosome tasks sequence follows a topological order.

The initial assignment of virtual machine k is selected at random for every task T_i in range $1 \leq k \leq |VM|$.

4   Experimental Study

The experimental study tries to prove the robustness of the makespan evaluated by the new DNC model, i.e., its makespan estimations should be much more accurate than the estimations of the NC model. Experimental results should expose that these improvements are much more relevant in data-intensive workflow problems. This is the reason to consider both data-intensive and compute-intensive instances in the benchmarks. To validate the a priori makespan outputs of the genetic algorithms we will apply their corresponding solutions to a cloud infrastructure WMS simulator, and then calculate the robustness as the relative error of the simulated makespan with respect to the a priori makespan, defined as:

$$robustness(s) = \frac{makespan_{sim}(s) - makespan_{ga}(s)}{makespan_{ga}(s)} \tag{11}$$

where $makespan_{sim}(s)$ is the actual makespan from the simulation and $makespan_{ga}(s)$ is the a priori makespan from the GA of the solution s.

Benchmark Instances. We selected a repository of real workflows executions called WFCommons [3]. This repository contains a number of real instances of different sizes, from dozens to thousands of tasks. We selected four applications and four instances (two small, one medium and one big) per problem. The selection is the following

- **1000genome**: Data-intensive with a huge ratio of communications vs computations. Data-sets sizes: 82/164/492/738 tasks.
- **cycles**: Compute-Intensive where the DNC and NC model should perform similar because there are not many data transfers. Data-sets sizes: 67/133/437/1091 tasks.
- **montage**: Compute-Intensive but with a significant number of potential parallel transfers too. Data-sets sizes: 58/103/472/1066 tasks.
- **soyKb**: Data-intensive where the DNC model should work better. Data-sets sizes: 96/156/256/546 tasks.

This selection should allow us to test both models in different scenarios, some that are better for the new DNC model: data-intensive problems or workflows with high parallelism; and some where it shouldn't be a significant difference, typically compute-intensive problems.

IaaS Scenarios. In order to evaluate the performance of the model we made several experiments in the four selected data-sets with multiple host configurations. We defined two scenarios 1) Mixed-Disks, the hosts are heterogeneous with the same CPU (441 GFLOPS) and network bandwidth (125 MB/sec) but half the hosts with 20 MB/sec and the other half are 200 MB/sec disk speeds; 2) Homogeneous-Disks, a number of homogeneous hosts with a standard 115 MB/sec disk speed. Each scenario can benefit the different models.

Benchmark Platform. Our GA prototypes and workflow management system (WMS) simulator were coded in C++, and all the experiments were run on a Linux computer with the following specs: Intel Core i7-10700k@3.8 Ghz, 32 GB RAM 3200 MHz MHz, 1TB SSD 2400 MB/sec. We used WRENCH [1] a C++ open-source framework (based on SimGrid) for computation infrastructure, scientific workflows simulation development and downstream data analysis. We have simulated a processes/communications system similar to HTCondor, the High-Throughput Computing environment under the well know Pegasus WMS, where each computing host has direct access to a local disk, and the remote disks from the rest of hosts are accessible by their network interface connections - such as the NFS service in Linux.

Genetic Algorithms Experiments. In all the experiments, GA evolves a population of 100 individuals over 500 generations with mutation probability of 0.1 and crossover probability of 1.0. Both version of the GA (NC-GA and DNC-GA) were run 10 times on each instance and specific infrastructure: 1, 2, 4, 8 and 16 hosts, in both scenarios. Afterwards each solution was tested with the WMS simulator to get the actual makespan.

Table 1. Robustness analysis for each scenario and model - relative errors values are represented as percentages

Problem	Hosts	Mixed-Disks		Homogeneous-Disks	
		NC-GA	DNC-GA	NC-GA	DNC-GA
1000genome	1	131.22	0.00	22.82	0.00
	2	131.19	0.00	23.28	0.00
	4	130.66	0.00	23.08	0.00
	8	125.18	0.01	21.88	0.01
	16	113.93	0.01	20.26	0.01
cycles	1	2.34	0.00	0.41	0.00
	2	2.17	0.01	0.41	0.01
	4	1.54	0.01	0.35	0.01
	8	1.18	0.00	0.30	0.00
	16	1.17	0.00	0.26	0.00
montage	1	21.26	0.02	3.72	0.02
	2	18.66	4.23	5.35	1.62
	4	25.55	5.78	7.75	2.77
	8	33.26	5.47	10.81	3.62
	16	41.72	5.76	13.78	4.28
soykb	1	85.44	0.00	14.86	0.00
	2	65.38	0.00	11.83	0.00
	4	47.39	0.00	8.85	0.00
	8	33.66	0.00	6.64	0.00
	16	25.61	0.00	5.06	0.00

Robustness Study. Table 1 shows the results of our study. We only report robustness values in average, as the deviations are negligible.

In both scenarios DNC-GA is very robust, with minimal percentage errors (<0.02%) in data-intensive (1000genome and soykb) and compute-intensive (cycles) instances. On the contrary, NC-GA has low errors only in compute-intensive instances and presents relevant errors in data-intensive instances, which are strongly increased when moving from the homogeneous to the heterogeneous scenario (>85% in soykb and >131% in 1000genome). Montage differs from cycles (both of them are compute-intensive problems) in its higher I/O operations density, which causes the relative error in NC-GA increases up to 41.72% in the heterogeneous scenario, while DNC-GA error remains below 5.8% in both scenarios. All the previous results makes us conclude that DNC model is considerably more robust in all scenarios.

5   Conclusions

We have studied the importance of an accurate evaluation model for optimizing makespan in the scientific workflow scheduling problem. The sensitivity of data-intensive scheduling problems to disk performance justifies the modelling of these I/O transfers, otherwise the standard evaluation model could drastically underestimate the total execution time. Deviations in the a priori makespan would guide the user to wrong decisions not only in experiment timing, but also in execution costs in a pay-as-you-use infrastructure such as cloud computing. The results from an experimental study show that our approach is successful at showing the robustness of the genetic algorithm schedules in both data and computation intensive instances. As future work, we plan to study robust workflow optimization from a multi-objective perspective where evolutionary algorithms will optimize not only makespan but also cost or energy consumption. Furthermore, introducing the new DNC evaluation model in heuristics such as HEFT [7] for initial population enrichment seems a promising line of research.

Acknowledgement. This research has been supported by the Spanish Government under research grant PID2019-106263RB-I00.

References

1. Casanova, H., et al.: Developing accurate and scalable simulators of production workflow management systems with WRENCH. Future Gener. Comput. Syst. **112**, 162–175 (2020)
2. Chakravarthi, K.K., Neelakantan, P., Shyamala, L., Vaidehi, V.: Reliable budget aware workflow scheduling strategy on multi-cloud environment. Cluster Comput. (2022). https://doi.org/10.1007/S10586-021-03464-4
3. Coleman, T., Casanova, H., Pottier, L., Kaushik, M., Deelman, E., Ferreira da Silva, R.: WfCommons: a framework for enabling scientific workflow research and development. Future Gener. Comput. Syst. **128**, 16–27 (2022)
4. Ghorbannia Delavar, A., Aryan, Y.: HSGA: a hybrid heuristic algorithm for workflow scheduling in cloud systems. Cluster Comput. **17**(1), 129–137 (2014)
5. Juve, G., Chervenak, A., Deelman, E., Bharathi, S., Mehta, G., Vahi, K.: Characterizing and profiling scientific workflows. Future Gener. Comput. Syst. **29**(3), 682–692 (2013)

6. Madni, S.H.H., Abd Latiff, M.S., Abdullahi, M., Abdulhamid, S.M., Usman, M.J.: Performance comparison of heuristic algorithms for task scheduling in IaaS cloud computing environment. PLoS ONE **12**(5), 1–26 (2017)
7. Topcuoglu, H., Hariri, S., Wu, M.Y.: Performance-effective and low-complexity task scheduling for heterogeneous computing. IEEE Trans. Parallel Distrib. Syst. **13**(3), 260–274 (2002)
8. Ye, X., Li, J., Liu, S., Liang, J., Jin, Y.: A hybrid instance-intensive workflow scheduling method in private cloud environment. Natural Comput. **18**(4), 735–746 (2017). https://doi.org/10.1007/s11047-016-9600-3
9. Zhu, Z., Zhang, G., Li, M., Liu, X.: Evolutionary multi-objective workflow scheduling in cloud. Trans. Parallel Distrib. Syst. **27**(5), 1344–1357 (2016)

Compiling Single Round QCCP-X Quantum Circuits by Genetic Algorithm

Lis Arufe[1], Riccardo Rasconi[2], Angelo Oddi[2], Ramiro Varela[1], and Miguel Ángel González[1(✉)]

[1] Department of Computer Science, University of Oviedo, Campus of Gijón, 33204 Gijón, Spain
{arufelis,ramiro,mig}@uniovi.es

[2] Istituto di Scienze e Tecnologie della Cognizione, Consiglio Nazionale delle Ricerche (ISTC-CNR), Via S. Martino della Battaglia, 44, 00185 Rome, Italy
{riccardo.rasconi,angelo.oddi}@istc.cnr.it

Abstract. The circuit model is one of the leading quantum computing architectures. In this model, a quantum algorithm is given by a set of quantum gates that must be distributed on the quantum computer over time, subject to a number of constraints. This process gives rise to the Quantum Circuit Compilation Problem (QCCP), which is in fact a hard scheduling problem. In this paper, we consider a compilation problem derived from the general Quantum Approximation Optimization Algorithm (QAOA) applied to the MaxCut problem and consider Noisy Intermediate Scale Quantum (NISQ) hardware architectures, which was already tackled in some previous studies. Specifically, we consider the problem denoted QCCP-X (QCCP with crosstalk constraints) and explore the use of genetic algorithms to solve it. We performed an experimental study across a conventional set of instances showing that the proposed genetic algorithm, termed GA_X, outperforms a previous approach.

1 Introduction

Quantum computing leverages the properties of quantum physical systems to develop computational models. This paradigm was proposed by R. Feynman

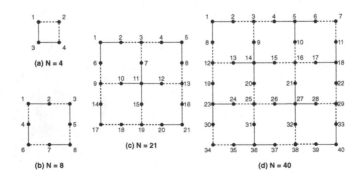

Fig. 1. Four quantum chip designs with different number of qubits.

© Springer Nature Switzerland AG 2022
J. M. Ferrández Vicente et al. (Eds.): IWINAC 2022, LNCS 13259, pp. 88–97, 2022.
https://doi.org/10.1007/978-3-031-06527-9_9

in 1981 and since then a number of approaches has been pursued. There are currently two leading architectures for quantum computers: circuit model (also called gate model) and quantum annealing. One of the most challenging applications of quantum computing is combinatorial optimization. These problems may be naturally framed as energy minimization problems; specifically a problem Hamiltonian H_p is established from the objective function so that its ground state encodes a solution to the problem.

The quantum annealing model requires an initial Hamiltonian H_i that is easy to prepare in a ground state. Then, H_i is transformed through small perturbations towards H_p, which ideally maintains the ground state. One of the most representatives of this type of technology are D-Wave Solvers[1].

In the circuit model, the one we consider herein, a set of quantum logic gates operate on a given state of H_p to obtain finally a ground state. Quantum gates operate on quantum bits (qubits), each qubit representing a quantum state (qstate), i.e., a superposition of the two pure qstates, denoted $|0\rangle$ and $|1\rangle$ respectively. Executing a quantum algorithm on a quantum hardware entails evaluating a set of quantum gates on qubits (one or two in this study), subject to some constraints due to both the algorithm and the hardware.

We consider the hardware technology termed Noisy Intermediate Scale Quantum (NISQ) processors [6,9]. Figure 1 shows four NISQ quantum chip designs with different number of qubits ($N = 4, 8, 21, 40$) inspired by Rigetti Computing Inc. [8]. Each qubit is identified by an integer and it is located in a node. An edge between two qubits represents that a binary gate may operate on them. The type of connection, either dashed or continuous, determines the allowed gates and their processing times. A quantum algorithm may be viewed as a series of quantum gates that must be applied on the qubits over time (see Fig. 2 (b)).

To guarantee adjacency on qstates of a 2-qubits gate, qstates are frequently moved from one qubit to another. This is done by means of *swap* gates, which exchange the qstates on two adjacent qubits. Furthermore, two gates cannot be applied on the same qubit at the same time. These and other restrictions raise the problem of distributing the calculations on the specific hardware, which is known in the literature as Quantum Circuit Compilation Problem (QCCP) and may be formulated in the planning/scheduling framework.

In this work, we explore the use of genetic algorithms to solve a variant of QCCP. We will focus on the class of Quantum Approximate Optimization Algorithm (QAOA) applied to the MaxCut problem [4], which was also considered in [1,3,5,7,10], where the authors present results on the classical benchmark proposed in [10].

QAOA is based on the application of the same set of operators over a number of rounds, but in this paper we restrict our study to only one round. Additionally, we consider the *crosstalk* constraint by which two gates cannot operate simultaneously on adjacent qubits. This problem is denoted QCCP-X; to solve it we propose a genetic algorithm (GA_X) which is inspired in that proposed

---

[1] https://www.dwavesys.com.

in [1] to solve QCCP. In our experimental study, we analyse GA_X and provide results on the set of instances proposed in [10].

The remainder of the paper is organized as follows. In the next section, we give a general description of the QAOA and how it is applied to the MaxCut problem. In Sect. 3 the formal definition of the QCCP-X for MaxCut is given. Section 4 describes the Genetic Algorithm (GA_X) proposed to solve the QCCP-X. Section 5 reports the results of the experimental study. Finally, 6 summarizes the main conclusions and some ideas for future research.

2   QAOA and MaxCut

QAOA [4] is a heuristic algorithm that combines classic and quantum computations to solve combinatorial problems expressed as

$$\text{optimize: } \sum_{\alpha=1}^{m} C_\alpha(\mathbf{z}) \tag{1}$$

where $C_\alpha(\mathbf{z})$ are clauses on a vector of decision binary variables $\mathbf{z} = (z_1, \ldots, z_n)$. So, the goal is to find the assignment of $z_i \in \{0,1\}, 1 \le i \le n$, that optimizes the number of clauses that are satisfied.

To apply QAOA to solve this problem, the user has to translate the clauses $C_\alpha(\mathbf{z})$ into equivalent quantum Hamiltonians $\mathbf{C}_\alpha$, by promoting each variable z_i to a quantum spin, i.e., a qubit, and then select a number of rounds p and two vectors of p angles $\vec{\gamma}, \vec{\beta}, 0 \le \beta_i \le \pi, 0 \le \gamma_i \le 2\pi, 0 \le i \le p$. Then, starting from the n qubits in the qstate $|+\rangle = \frac{1}{\sqrt{2}}|0\rangle + \frac{1}{\sqrt{2}}|1\rangle$, the following state is prepared:

$$|\psi_p(\vec{\gamma}, \vec{\beta})\rangle = \prod_{r=1}^{p} e^{-i\beta_r H_B} e^{-i\gamma_r H_C} |+\rangle^{\otimes n} \tag{2}$$

where H_C is the problem Hamiltonian defined as $H_C = \sum_{\alpha=1}^{m} \mathbf{C}_\alpha$ and H_B a mix Hamiltonian defined as $H_B = \sum_{j=1}^{n} \mathbf{X_j}$, $\mathbf{X_j}$ being the $\mathbf{X}$ Pauli matrix applied to qubit j. This state is measured to obtain an approximate solution to the problem defined in Eq. (1), whose expected value is given by

$$\langle \psi_p(\vec{\gamma}, \vec{\beta})|H_C|\psi_p(\vec{\gamma}, \vec{\beta})\rangle \tag{3}$$

If the values of p, $\vec{\beta}$ and $\vec{\gamma}$ are well selected, the state of the qubits after this transformation will represent a good solution to the problem defined in Eq. (1) with high probability, and the quality of the solution increases with the number of rounds. The selection of $\vec{\beta}$ and $\vec{\gamma}$ is carried out through classic optimization; for example, starting from some initial values and then following simplex or gradient based optimization. For each candidate $(\vec{\gamma}, \vec{\beta})$, the state of Eq. (2) and the expected value in Eq. (3) are calculated on the quantum computer.

2.1 MaxCut Problem

In the MaxCut problem, we are given an undirected graph $G = (V, E)$, where $V = \{1, \ldots, n\}$ is a set of nodes and E is the set of arcs. The goal is to establish a partition of the set V into two subsets V_{+1} and V_{-1} so that the number of arcs in E connecting nodes of the two subsets is maximized, in other words, the goal is[2]

$$\text{maximize:} \quad \sum_{(i,j) \in E} \frac{1}{2}(-\sigma_i \sigma_j), \sigma_k = \begin{cases} -1 \text{ if } k \in V_{-1} \\ 1 \ \ \text{if } k \in V_{+1} \end{cases} \tag{4}$$

The problem is transformed into a minimization one by multiplying the expression above by -1. In this case, we have a Hamiltonian $\mathbf{C}_\alpha$ for each arc (i,j), which depends on just these two variables, so it may be defined as

$$\mathbf{C_{i,j}} = \frac{1}{2}(\mathbf{Z}_i \otimes \mathbf{Z}_j) \tag{5}$$

where $\mathbf{Z_i}$ and $\mathbf{Z_j}$ are the Pauli matrix $\mathbf{Z}$ applied to qubits i and j respectively. Therefore, each one of the m components of the problem Hamiltonian H_C corresponds to the following operator:

$$e^{-i\gamma_r \mathbf{C_{i,j}}} = \begin{pmatrix} e^{-i\gamma_r/2} & 0 & 0 & 0 \\ 0 & e^{i\gamma_r/2} & 0 & 0 \\ 0 & 0 & e^{i\gamma_r/2} & 0 \\ 0 & 0 & 0 & e^{-i\gamma_r/2} \end{pmatrix} \tag{6}$$

which is in fact the $R_{ZZ}(\gamma)$ gate. Every two of these gates commute each other, which means that to organize over time the execution of these gates in one round if two of them share a qubit then they may operate in any order.

In turn, each component of the mix Hamiltonian H_B corresponds to the unitary operator

$$e^{-i\beta_r \mathbf{X_j}} = \begin{pmatrix} \cos(\beta_r) & -i\sin(\beta_r) \\ -i\sin(\beta_r) & \cos(\beta_r) \end{pmatrix} \tag{7}$$

In the next section, the operators (6) and (7) are denoted $p\text{-}s(q_i, q_j)$ and $mix(q_j)$ respectively.

3 Definition of the Quantum Circuit Compilation Problem

In the QCCP, we are given a tuple $P = \langle C_0, L_0, QM \rangle$. QM is the quantum hardware that is represented by an undirected graph $QM = \langle V, E \rangle$, where $V_N =$

---

[2] Note that a single transformation $z = (\sigma + 1)/2$ converts the variables from the $\sigma \in \{-1, +1\}$ space to the $z \in \{0, 1\}$ space.

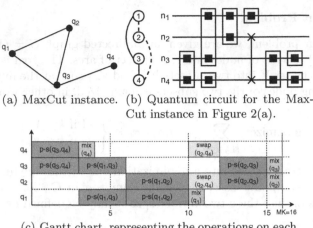

(a) MaxCut instance. (b) Quantum circuit for the Max-
Cut instance in Figure 2(a).

(c) Gantt chart, representing the operations on each
qstate over time.

Fig. 2. Example of MaxCut instance (a) and one possible solution, considering only one round (i.e. $P = 1$), represented by a quantum circuit (b) and a Gantt chart (c).

$\{n_1 \ldots n_N\}$ is the set of nodes (qubits) and E is a set of arcs (n_k, n_l) where the qstates q_i and q_j of p-$s(q_i, q_j)$ or $swap(q_i, q_j)$ gates may be allocated to; mix gates may be executed at any node. The durations of the gates depend on the gate and the type of the arc (continuous or discontinuous).

C_0 is the input quantum circuit, which represents the quantum algorithm to solve the problem at hand. For MaxCut, C_0 includes a set of qstates that are initially mapped to the qubits (as established in L_0) and two sets of quantum gates P-S and MIX including operations of the form p-$s(q_i, q_j)$ and $mix(q_i)$ respectively. In general, the operations in P-S and MIX are applied sequentially over a number of P rounds, but in this work we are considering just one round.

Figure 2(a) shows an example of MaxCut instance for a graph with 4 nodes and the p-s and mix gates that must be executed over a number of rounds. There are some precedence constraints so that a $mix(q_i)$ gate can only be executed after all p-s gates involving the qstate q_i in the same round; however, p-s gates may be executed in any order within each round, provided that no two p-s gates operates on the same qstate at a time.

For p-$s(q_i, q_j)$ gate can be executed, the qstates q_i and q_j must be allocated on a pair of qubits $(n_k, n_l) \in E$. This requires extending the quantum circuit with a number of $swap$ gates to move the qstates towards some pair of adjacent qubits. Therefore, to solve the circuit compilation problem we start from an initial allocation of qstates on the qubits (established in L_0). Then, to distribute the executions of the p-s gates over time, a number of $swap$ gates have to be introduced to ensure the adjacency condition, so that the time required to execute all gates, i.e., the makespan, is minimized. The $mix(q_i)$ gate may be inserted after all p-s gates operating on q_i in each round.

Figure 2(b) shows a compiled quantum circuit that represents a solution for the problem given in Fig. 2(a). In this case only one *swap* gate was introduced to swap the qstates on qubits n_2 and n_4 so that qstates q_3 and q_2 are on adjacent qubits n_3 and n_4; in this setting the gate $p\text{-}s(q_3, q_2)$ may be executed. Rectangles represent *p-s* gates, squares represent *mix* gates and single lines represent *swap* gates. In this example, L_0 establishes that each qstate q_i is on qubit n_i. The quantum hardware is represented on the left. Each horizontal line represents the operations on one qubit over time.

A compiled quantum circuit may also be viewed as a Gantt chart, as we may see in Fig. 2(c). In this solution, the makespan is 16 assuming that a *p-s* gate takes 3 time units on continuous edges and 4 time units on discontinuous ones, and that *swap* gates require 2 time units on all edges, while *mix* gates takes 1 time unit.

The above problem is denoted QCCP in the literature. In this work we consider a restricted version, termed QCCP-X, that considers crosstalk interactions, i.e., two gates cannot be executed in parallel if they operate on adjacent qubits, which strongly limits the parallelisms in the compiled circuit. In particular, in the simple example of Fig. 2, if we consider the QCCP-X, none of the gates could be executed in parallel with any other.

4   The Genetic Algorithm

To solve the one round QCCP-X problem, we propose a Genetic Algorithm (GA_X) that is adapted from the DBGA (Decomposition Based Genetic Algorithm) proposed in [1]. The general structure of GA_X is given in Algorithm 1.

A chromosome is encoded by a pair of chains $(ch1, ch2)$, where $ch1$ is a permutation (initially random) of the set of the *p-s* gates and $ch2$ is a sequence of connections in QM (initially chosen uniformly) of the same length as $ch1$. This encoding must be understood so as the gate $p\text{-}s(q_i, q_j)$ in a position of $ch1$ must be executed on the pair of qubits $\{n_k, n_l\}$ in the same position in $ch2$. To do that, the decoding algorithm has to insert the required *swap* gates to move the qstates (q_i, q_j) from their current qubits towards $\{n_k, n_l\}$. The procedure proposed in [1] guarantees the insertion of the minimum number of *swap* gates for each *p-s* gate.

GA_X iterates until the *Termination Condition* is fulfilled, which in our case is a given number of consecutive generations without improving the best solution found so far. In each iteration, the chromosomes in the population are organized into random pairs to undergo crossover and mutation. The offspring are evaluated and finally, in the replacement step two chromosomes are selected using tournament between each two parents and their two offspring.

To deal with premature convergence, we introduced a diversification step so that after a number of consecutive generations without improvement, all but one of the chromosomes with the same fitness are mutated a number of times in order to introduce diversity in the population.

Algorithm 1: The Genetic Algorithm. It builds a schedule for a one round QCCP-X instance P.

Require: The sets of gates $P\text{-}S$ and MIX. The parameters: $popSize$, P_c, P_m, $noImpr$, $nMutDiv$. The quantum circuit QM.

Ensure: A solution graph SG that represents a compiled quantum circuit for problem P.

    Initial Population: generate $popSize$ initial chromosomes $(ch1, ch2)$, where $ch1$ is a random permutation of the gates in $P\text{-}S$ and $ch2$ is a set of connections in QM, which may be calculated either at random or by some heuristic;

    Evaluation: The decoding algorithm is applied to the initial chromosomes;

    while not *Termination Condition* **do**

        Selection: The chromosomes in the population are organized into random pairs;

        Recombination: Each pair of chromosomes is mated and the offsprings mutated in accordance with probabilities P_c and P_m respectively;

        Evaluation: The decoding algorithm is applied to the offsprings;

        Replacement: for every two parents and its two offspring, the two best ones are selected for the next generation;

        Diversification: After $noImpr$ consecutive generations without improvement, all but one of the chromosomes sharing the same fitness are mutated $nMutDiv$ times;

    return The best solution in the population;

Regarding crossover and mutation, any operator devised for permutation encoding may be adapted. The crossover operates on components $ch1$ and $ch2$ at the same time to generate two offspring. In our experiments, we extended the well-known partial mapping crossover (PMX). We consider a single mutation ($mut1$) that consists in swapping two positions (the gate and the pair of qubits) chosen uniformly. Besides, with the purpose of introducing new genetic material, we use another single mutation ($mut2$) that modifies one of the qubits in a random pair of $ch2$. When a chromosome is mutated, one of the operators is chosen with equal probability.

5   Experimental Study

This section describes the performance obtained with our genetic algorithm proposed in Sect. 4 against the QCCP-X benchmark presented in [2]. In this work, we compare our results with those obtained with the genetic algorithm presented in [7], as they improve those reported in [2]. In particular, the benchmark set we tackle is composed of three benchmarks characterised by instances of three different sizes, based on quantum chips with $N = 8, 21$ and 40 qubits, respectively (see Fig. 1).

All the benchmarks are solved considering $P = 1$ (one pass). In the actual implementation of Algorithm 1 (see previous Sect. 4), we have assigned the following values for the parameters: $popSize = 1000$, $P_c = 100\%$, $P_m = 5\%$,

Table 1. Best and average makespan in 30 independent runs of GA_X $(Best_X/Avg_X)$ and GA_R $(Best_R/Avg_R)$ across each of the Venturelli's instances with size $N = 8, 21, 40$

Inst.	$N = 8$				$N = 21$				$N = 40$			
	$Best_X$	Avg_X	$Best_R$	Avg_R	$Best_X$	Avg_X	$Best_R$	Avg_R	$Best_X$	Avg_X	$Best_R$	Avg_R
1	25	25.0	24	24.5	36	36.9	46	49.6	51	55.1	62	71.4
2	23	23.4	27	27.3	35	37.1	40	45.8	58	63.5	75	84.8
3	24	24.0	24	25.4	37	39.6	41	47.0	52	55.0	72	80.4
4	24	24.0	23	23.0	37	39.3	41	46.4	66	69.5	81	92.2
5	26	26.0	24	25.1	40	41.3	42	48.2	56	62.4	76	83.6
6	23	23.0	25	26.6	38	39.1	43	47.8	61	67.1	78	87.8
7	24	24.0	23	24.9	39	42.6	50	54.4	54	64.1	75	86.1
8	24	24.0	27	27.1	36	38.0	42	47.3	49	55.9	67	75.3
9	25	25.9	27	28.6	37	40.6	42	49.5	57	61.1	74	82.4
10	25	25.0	25	26.3	43	44.2	46	52.4	58	62.5	77	86.6
11	26	26.0	28	28.1	36	38.6	42	46.6	51	58.2	66	77.9
12	25	25.0	25	25.7	39	40.1	46	52.5	56	60.6	75	83.9
13	25	25.0	24	25.4	34	35.9	41	43.4	51	56.7	68	76.2
14	25	25.0	26	26.0	36	39.0	38	47.3	56	62.6	76	82.3
15	27	27.0	25	25.8	35	36.7	42	45.9	53	61.3	72	80.0
16	24	24.0	24	24.7	39	40.6	49	56.5	54	58.0	70	79.2
17	25	25.0	27	28.3	38	40.9	47	51.5	52	54.7	70	77.2
18	23	23.0	22	23.0	41	42.3	45	51.0	55	58.8	75	84.3
19	25	25.0	25	26.5	39	41.2	50	54.1	50	53.7	67	74.5
20	23	23.1	24	25.0	41	44.0	52	56.2	60	65.6	77	87.7
21	22	22.0	21	22.0	41	42.7	52	55.5	59	64.9	76	84.7
22	28	28.0	32	32.1	39	41.0	45	50.1	54	59.6	75	86.1
23	27	27.1	28	28.9	40	42.3	45	50.3	57	61.3	74	81.5
24	24	24.0	22	23.6	38	40.8	45	50.9	52	55.4	65	75.0
25	26	26.0	25	25.5	40	40.8	43	49.1	55	60.8	73	83.3
26	23	23.0	23	23.3	36	37.8	42	46.6	55	58.3	69	79.5
27	26	26.9	28	29.7	44	46.2	49	53.9	56	58.6	67	79.4
28	23	23.0	22	23.1	38	41.6	47	52.3	56	59.0	77	87.7
29	26	26.0	24	24.7	40	41.5	47	51.2	51	53.5	68	72.9
30	24	24.7	24	24.0	39	41.6	44	52.3	55	57.8	70	74.8
31	23	23.9	24	24.0	43	43.6	49	53.2	55	61.1	73	81.5
32	25	25.0	24	25.7	36	36.7	41	45.7	46	49.7	59	66.6
33	26	26.0	28	29.3	37	38.8	46	50.5	52	56.5	73	81.0
34	26	26.0	27	27.6	39	40.9	42	47.5	55	60.1	71	80.8
35	25	25.0	24	24.8	37	39.0	42	46.6	51	57.3	69	76.0
36	24	24.0	23	23.9	40	41.9	44	50.2	55	57.0	78	87.9
37	26	26.0	26	27.6	36	37.2	42	47.7	57	62.5	71	82.4
38	23	23.0	22	22.4	40	41.7	44	51.9	50	53.5	63	71.4
39	23	23.1	22	23.1	39	42.1	44	52.8	53	59.3	71	81.9
40	26	26.3	31	32.7	38	40.6	44	49.0	55	59.6	66	76.0
41	27	27.0	27	27.2	35	36.8	40	43.9	52	55.5	71	79.7
42	25	25.9	24	24.8	36	37.9	42	47.9	53	58.7	74	82.0
43	24	24.0	24	26.5	37	39.5	42	46.8	57	60.9	70	78.6
44	27	27.0	29	29.5	39	39.7	41	48.0	57	63.8	75	82.4
45	23	23.0	24	24.7	37	38.2	40	46.3	53	58.7	71	82.9
46	23	24.8	22	23.6	37	38.8	39	44.3	53	61.5	77	84.4
47	24	24.0	29	29.1	38	42.6	43	48.6	53	59.2	67	75.7
48	25	25.0	25	25.1	37	38.5	44	48.8	54	58.6	70	81.0
49	27	27.0	25	25.8	41	44.6	51	54.8	55	59.2	71	82.0
50	23	23.0	24	24.8	37	39.2	43	47.9	56	58.1	72	82.0

$noImpr = 10$, $nMutDiv = 5$. We set a stop condition of 800 consecutive generations without improving the best solution found so far. The target machine is a 64-bit Windows10 OS running on Intel Core i5-7400 CPU at 3.00 GHz with 16 GB RAM. The results of our experimentation are summarised in Table 1, where we compare our results (GA_X), in columns "$Best_X$" and "Avg_X" with the results of the algorithm presented in [7] (GA_R), in columns "$Best_R$" and "Avg_R". For each instance and method we report the average and the best makespan obtained in 30 runs. For running GA_R a maximum cpu time of 5, 30 and 90 s has been used for the instances of size $N = 8, 21, 40$ respectively, so the computation times are similar to those of GA_X.

The obtained results show that the GA_X clearly outperforms the original counterpart GA_R proposed in [7], which was already improving significantly over the results reported in [2]. In particular, it can be observed that in terms of best makespan, the two algorithms perform rather equally on the $N = 8$ benchmark, with 19 best solutions found by GA_X, against 20 best solutions found by GA_R. In terms of average results however, GA_X seems to perform better than GA_R, producing more solutions of higher quality. Relatively to the $N = 21$ and $N = 40$ benchmarks, GA_X definitely outperforms GA_R on the entirety of the obtained solutions, both in terms of best and average makespan.

Finally, in order to assess the impact of the crosstalk constraint in the solution quality, we have performed experiments with the same instances but without considering that constraint. We have observed that, in average, the makespan increases by 35.7% in $N = 8$ instances, by 39.1% in $N = 21$ instances and by 42.6% in $N = 40$ instances when the crosstalk constraint is considered.

6   Conclusions

In this paper we investigate the performance of a genetic approach to solve the quantum circuit compilation problem applied to a class of QAOA-X circuits. The objective is the synthesis of minimum-makespan quantum gate execution plans that successfully compile idealised circuits to a set realistic near-term quantum hardware architectures. The main contribution of this work is a genetic algorithm that leverages a specific double-chains chromosome encoding, such that the first chain encodes the sequence of gate insertion of the output solution, whereas the second chain encodes the corresponding execution gates in the considered quantum chip. Such encoding is compared with the chromosome encoding proposed in [7], where each gene controls the iterative selection of a quantum gate to be inserted in the solution, over a lexicographic double-key quantum gate ranking returned by a heuristic function. We have performed an experimental study testing our algorithm against a QAOA-X benchmark known in the literature [2,10], proving that the proposed algorithm exhibits very convincing performance.

Acknowledgement. This research was supported by the Spanish Government under project PID2019-106263RB-I00 and by ESA Contract No. 4000112300/14/D/MRP Mars Express Data Planning Tool MEXAR2 Maintenance.

References

1. Arufe, L., González, M.A., Oddi, A., Rasconi, R., Varela, R.: Quantum circuit compilation by genetic algorithm for quantum approximate optimization algorithm applied to maxcut problem. Swarm Evol. Comput. **69**, 101030 (2022)
2. Booth, K.E., Do, M., Beck, J.C., Rieffel, E., Venturelli, D., Frank, J.: Comparing and integrating constraint programming and temporal planning for quantum circuit compilation. In: Twenty-Eighth International Conference on Automated Planning and Scheduling (ICAPS 2018), pp. 366–374 (2018)
3. Chand, S., Singh, H.K., Ray, T., Ryan, M.: Rollout based heuristics for the quantum circuit compilation problem. In: 2019 IEEE Congress on Evolutionary Computation (CEC), pp. 974–981, June 2019
4. Farhi, E., Goldstone, J., Gutmann, S.: A quantum approximate optimization algorithm (2014)
5. Oddi, A., Rasconi, R.: Greedy randomized search for scalable compilation of quantum circuits. In: van Hoeve, W.-J. (ed.) CPAIOR 2018. LNCS, vol. 10848, pp. 446–461. Springer, Cham (2018). https://doi.org/10.1007/978-3-319-93031-2_32
6. Preskill, J.: Quantum computing in the NISQ era and beyond. Quantum **2**, 79 (2018)
7. Rasconi, R., Oddi, A.: An innovative genetic algorithm for the quantum circuit compilation problem. In: Proceedings of the Thirty-Third AAAI Conference on Artificial Intelligence, vol. 33, pp. 7707–7714 (2019)
8. Sete, E.A., Zeng, W.J., Rigetti, C.T.: A functional architecture for scalable quantum computing. In: 2016 IEEE International Conference on Rebooting Computing (ICRC), pp. 1–6. IEEE (2016)
9. Venturelli, D., et al.: Quantum circuit compilation: an emerging application for automated reasoning. In: Bernardini, S., Talamadupula, K., Yorke-Smith, N. (eds.) Proceedings of the 12th International Scheduling and Planning Applications Workshop (SPARK 2019), pp. 95–103 (2019)
10. Venturelli, D., Do, M., Rieffel, E.G., Frank, J.: Temporal planning for compilation of quantum approximate optimization circuits. In: Proceedings of the Twenty-Sixth International Joint Conference on Artificial Intelligence (IJCAI 2017), pp. 4440–4446 (2017)

Elite Artificial Bee Colony for Makespan Optimisation in Job Shop with Interval Uncertainty

Hernán Díaz[1] , Juan José Palacios[1] , Inés González-Rodríguez[2](✉) ,
and Camino R. Vela[1]

[1] Department of Computing, University of Oviedo, Gijón, Spain
{diazhernan,palaciosjuan,crvela}@uniovi.es
[2] Departamento de Matemáticas, Estadística y Computación,
Universidad de Cantabria, Santander, Spain
gonzalezri@unican.es

Abstract. This paper addresses a variant of the Job Shop Scheduling Problem with makespan minimisation where uncertainty in task durations is taken into account and modelled with intervals. Given the problem's complexity, we tackle it using a metaheuristic approach. Specifically, we propose a novel Artificial Bee Colony algorithm incorporating three different selection mechanisms that help in guiding the search towards more promising areas. A parametric analysis is conducted and a comparison of the different selection strategies is performed on a set of benchmark instances. The results illustrate the benefit of using the new guiding strategies, improving the behaviour of the ABC algorithm, which compares favourably to the state-of-the art in the problem. An additional study is conducted to assess the robustness of the solutions obtained under each guiding strategy.

Keywords: Job Shop Scheduling · Makespan · Interval Uncertainty · Artificial Bee Colony

1 Introduction

The job shop scheduling problem (JSP) is considered to be one of the most relevant scheduling problems. It consists in allocating a set of resources to execute a set of jobs under a set of given constraints, with the most popular objective in the literature of minimizing the project's execution timespan, also known as makespan. Solving this problem improves the efficiency of chain production processes, optimising the use of energy and materials [12] and having a positive impact on costs and environmental sustainability. However, in real-world applications, the available information is often imprecise. Interval uncertainty arises as soon as information is incomplete, and contrary to the case of stochastic and

Supported by the Spanish Government under research grant PID2019-106263RB-I00 and by the Asturias Government under research grant Severo Ochoa.

fuzzy scheduling, it does not assume any further knowledge, thus representing a first step towards solving problems in other frameworks [1]. Moreover, intervals are a natural model whenever decision-makers prefer to provide only a minimal and a maximal duration, and obtain interval results that can be easily understood. Under such circumstances, interval scheduling allows to concentrate on significant scheduling decisions and to produce robust solutions.

Contributions to interval scheduling in the literature are not abundant. In [10], a genetic algorithm is proposed for a JSP minimizing the total tardiness with respect to job due dates with both processing times and due dates represented by intervals. In [5] a different genetic algorithm is applied to the same problem, including a study of different interval ranking methods based on the robustness of the resulting schedules. A population-based neighbourhood search for an interval JSP with makespan minimisation is presented in [9]. In [11], a hybrid between PSO and a genetic algorithm is used to solve a flexible JSP with interval processing times as part of a larger integrated planning and scheduling problem. Recently, in [6] a genetic algorithm is applied to the JSP with interval uncertainty minimizing the makespan and achieving the results that are the current state of the art.

Metaheuristic search methods are especially suited for job shop due to its complexity. In particular, artificial bee colony (ABC) is a swarm intelligence optimiser inspired by the intelligent foraging behaviour of honeybees that has shown very competitive performance on JSP with makespan minimisation. For instance, [13] propose an evolutionary computation algorithm based on ABC that includes a state transition rule to construct the schedules. Taking some principles from Genetic Algorithms, [14] present an Improved ABC (IABC) where a mutation operation is used for exploring the search space, enhancing the search performance of the algorithm. Later, [2] propose an effective ABC approach based on updating the population using the information of the best-so-far food source.

In the following, we consider the JSP with makespan minimisation and intervals modelling uncertain durations. The problem is presented in Sect. 2. In Sect. 3 we propose several variants of an ABC algorithm to address this problem. These variants are compared in Sect. 4, where the most successful one is also compared with the state-of-the-art and a robustness analysis is also included.

2   The Job Shop Problem with Interval Durations

The classical *job shop scheduling problem* consists of a set of resources $M = \{M_1, \ldots, M_m\}$ and a set of jobs $J = \{J_1, \ldots, J_n\}$. Each job J_j is organised in tasks $(o(j,1), \ldots, o(j,m_j))$ that need to be sequentially scheduled. We assume w.l.o.g. that tasks are indexed from 1 to $N = \sum_{j=1}^{n} m_j$, so we can refer to task $o(j,l)$ by its index $o = \sum_{i=1}^{j-1} m_i + l$ and denote the set of all tasks as $O = \{1, \ldots, N\}$. Each task $o \in O$ requires the uninterrupted and exclusive use of a machine $\nu_o \in M$ for its whole processing time p_o.

A solution to this problem is a *schedule* s, i.e. an allocation of starting times for each task, which, besides being *feasible* (all constraints hold), is *optimal* according to some criterion, in our case, minimal makespan C_{max}.

2.1 Interval Uncertainty

Following [9] and [5], uncertainty in the processing time of tasks is modelled using a closed intervals. Therefore, the processing time of task $o \in O$ is represented by an interval $\mathbf{p_o} = [\underline{p}_o, \overline{p}_o]$, where $\underline{p}_o$ and $\overline{p}_o$ are the available lower and upper bounds for the exact but unknown processing time p_o.

The interval JSP (IJSP) with makespan mimisation requires two arithmetic operations: addition and maximum. Given two intervals $\mathbf{a} = [\underline{a}, \overline{a}]$, $\mathbf{b} = [\underline{b}, \overline{b}]$, the addition is expressed as $[\underline{a}+\underline{b}, \overline{a}+\overline{b}]$ and the maximum as $[\max(\underline{a},\underline{b}), \max(\overline{a},\overline{b})]$. Also, given the lack of a natural order in the set of closed intervals, to determine the schedule with the "minimal" makespan, we need an interval raking method. For the sake of fair comparisons with the literature, we shall use the midpoint method: $\mathbf{a} \leq_{MP} \mathbf{b} \Leftrightarrow m(\mathbf{a}) \leq m(\mathbf{b})$ with $m(\mathbf{a}) = (\underline{a} + \overline{a})/2$. This is used in [5] and it is equivalent to the method used in [10]. Notice that $m(\mathbf{a})$ coincides with the expected value of the uniform distribution on the interval $E[\mathbf{a}]$.

A schedule s for the IJSP establishes a relative order π among tasks requiring the same machine. Conversely, given a task processing order π the schedule s may be computed as follows. For every task $o \in O$, let $\mathbf{s_o}(\pi)$ and $\mathbf{c_o}(\pi)$ denote respectively the starting and completion times of o, let $PM_o(\pi)$ and $SM_o(\pi)$ denote the predecessor and successor tasks of o in the machine ν_o according to π, and let PJ_o and SJ_o denote the tasks preceding and succeeding o in its job. Then the starting time of o is given by $\mathbf{s_o}(\pi) = \max(\mathbf{s}_{PJ_o} + \mathbf{p}_{PJ_o}, \mathbf{s}_{PM_o(\pi)} + \mathbf{p}_{PM_o(\pi)})$, and the completion time by $\mathbf{c_o}(\pi) = \mathbf{s_o}(\pi) + \mathbf{p_o}$. The makespan is computed as the completion time of the last task to be processed according to π thus, $\mathbf{C_{max}}(\pi) = \max_{o \in O}\{c_o(\pi)\}$. If there is no possible confusion regarding the processing order, we may simplify notation by writing $\mathbf{s_o}$, $\mathbf{c_o}$ and $\mathbf{C_{max}}$.

2.2 Robustness on Interval JSP

When uncertainty is present, solution robustness may become a concern. In fact, makespan values obtained for IJSP are not exact values, but intervals. It is only after the solution is executed on a real scenario that actual processing times for tasks $P^{ex} = \{p_o^{ex} \in [\underline{p}_o, \overline{p}_o], o \in O\}$ are known. Therefore, it is not until that moment that the actual makespan $C_{max}^{ex} \in [\underline{C}_{max}, \overline{C}_{max}]$ can be found. It is desirable that this executed makespan C_{max}^{ex} does not differ much from the expected value of the makespan according to the interval $\mathbf{C_{max}}$.

This is the idea behind the concept of ϵ-robustness first proposed in [3] for stochastic scheduling, and later adapted to the IJSP in [5]. For a given $\epsilon \geq 0$, a schedule with makespan $\mathbf{C_{max}}$ is considered to be ϵ-*robust* in a real scenario P^{ex} if the relative error made by the expected makespan $E[\mathbf{C_{max}}]$ with respect to the makespan C_{max}^{ex} of the executed schedule is bounded by ϵ, that is:

$$\frac{|C_{max}^{ex} - E[\mathbf{C_{max}}]|}{E[\mathbf{C_{max}}]} \leq \epsilon. \tag{1}$$

Clearly, the smaller the bound ϵ, the more robust the interval schedule is.

This measure of robustness is dependent on a specific configuration P^{ex} of task processing times obtained upon execution of the predictive schedule s. In the absence of real data, as is the case with the usual synthetic benchmark instances for job shop, we may resort to Monte-Carlo simulations. We simmulate K possible configurations $P^k = \{p_o^k \in [\underline{p}_o, \overline{p}_o], o \in O\}$ using uniform probability distributions to sample durations for every task and compute for each configuration $k = 1, \ldots, K$ the exact makespan C_{max}^k that results from executing tasks according to the ordering provided by s. Then, the average ϵ-robustness of the predictive schedule across the K possible configurations, denoted $\overline{\epsilon}$, can be calculated as:

$$\overline{\epsilon} = \frac{1}{K} \sum_{k=1}^{K} \frac{|C_{max}^k - E[\mathbf{C_{max}}]|}{E[\mathbf{C_{max}}]}. \tag{2}$$

This value provides an estimate of how robust the solution s is across different processing times configurations.

3 An Artificial Bee Colony Algorithm

The Artificial Bee Colony Algorithm is a bioinspired swarm metaheuristic for optimisation based on the foraging behaviour of honey bees. Since it was introduced in [7] it has been successfully adapted to a variety of problems [8]. In this paper, we adapt it to solve the Interval Job Shop Scheduling problem.

In ABC, a swarm of bees exploit a changing set of food sources with two leading models of behaviour: recruiting rich food sources and abandoning poor ones. In our case, each food source fs encodes an IJSP solution using permutations with repetition [4] and the decoding of a food source follows an insertion strategy, consisting in iterating along the food source and scheduling each task at its earliest feasible insertion position [5]. The richness or nectar amount of each food source is proportional to the makespan of the schedule it represents, so lower makespan values translate into richer food sources.

The ABC starts by generating and evaluating initial pool P_0 of random food sources, so the best food source in the pool is assigned to the hive queen. Then, ABC iterates over a number of cycles, each consisting of three phases mimicking the behaviour of three types of foraging bees: employed, onlooker and scout. In the employed bee phase, each food source is assigned to one employed bee, so this employed bee explores a new candidate food source between its own food source and the queen's one, evaluating the candidate and sharing this information with the rest of the hive. If the new food source is equivalent to queen's (i.e. the best food source found so far), it is discarded for the sake of maintaining diversity in the pool. If it is not discarded and it improves the original food source (i.e. smaller makespan value), it replaces it. Otherwise, the number of improvement trials $fs.numTrials$ of the original food source is increased by one. In the next phase, each onlooker bee chooses a food source and tries to find a better neighbouring one. The new food source receives the same treatment as in the previous phase. Finally, in the scout bee phase, if the number of improvement trials of a food source reaches a maximum number NT_{max}, the scout bee finds a new food source to replace the former one in the pool of solutions. Finally, the algorithm terminates after a number $maxIter$ of consecutive iterations without finding a food source that improves the queen's one. The following subsections provide more detail on each of the phases; the pseudo-code of the resulting ABC is given in 1.

3.1 Employed Bee Phase

Originally, the employed bees search is always guided by the queen's food source. However, this strategy may in some occasions cause a lack of diversity in the swarm and lead to premature convergence [2]. To address this issue, we propose to modify the original algorithm and select the guiding food source from an elite group that will contain the most suitable food sources according to one of the following strategies. In the first strategy, denoted $Elite_1$, it only contains the best-found food source, so it is equivalent to the classical ABC. In the second strategy, denoted $Elite_2$, the elite group contains the food sources with the highest number of improvement trials at the beginning of the iteration and the best food source in the set is selected to guide the employed bee. Finally, in the third strategy, denoted $Elite_3$, the elite group contains the best B food sources in the current swarm and a solution from this group is chosen at random to guide the employed bee. B is a parameter of the algorithm that helps balancing diversity: when $B = 1$, this strategy is equivalent to $Elite_1$, and the larger B is, the more diversity is inserted into the phase.

Once two food sources are selected for each employed bee, a recombination operator is applied with probability p_{emp} to find a new food source to explore. Here, taking advantage of the solution encoding, we propose to use the following operators: Generalised Order Crossover (GOX), Job-Order Crossover (JOX) and Precedence Preservative Crossover (PPX).

3.2 Onlooker Bee Phase

In this phase, food sources are selected from those that have not reached the maximum number of improvement trials. Each selected food source is assigned to an onlooker bee that will explore a neighbouring solution with probability p_{on} to explore a neighbouring solution. Neighbours are obtained by performing a small change on the food source using one of the following operators for permutations: Swap, Inversion or Insertion.

Table 1. Final parameter setup for each variant of ABC

Instance	ABC_{E1}	ABC_{E2}	ABC_{E3}
Recombination operator	JOX	JOX	GOX
Employed probability p_{emp}	0.75	1	1
Neighbourhood operator	Insertion	Insertion	Swap
Onlooker probability p_{on}	0.75	0.75	1
Improvement trials $fs.numTrials$	10	15	20

3.3 Scout Bee Phase

In this last phase, a scout bee is assigned to each food source that has reached the maximum number of improvement trials. Since this food source has not been improved after the given number of attempts, it is discarded and the scout bee is in charge of finding a replacement. To implement this phase, every food source fs having $fs.numTrials > NT_{max}$ is replaced by a random one fs' with $fs'.numTrials = 0$.

4 Experimental Results

The objective of this Section is to evaluate the performance of the three variants of the ABC algorithm in comparison with the state-of-the-art for interval JSP with makespan minimization, which, to our knowledge is the genetic algorithm from [5], referred to as *GA* hereafter.

We consider 12 well-known instances for the job shop problem (in brackets, the size $n \times m$): FT10 (10×10), FT20 (20×5), La21, La24, La25 (15×10), La27, La29 (20×10), La38, La40 (15×15), ABZ7, ABZ8, and ABZ9 (20×15). Processing times are modified to be intervals, so given the original deterministic processing time of a task p_o, the interval time is $\mathbf{p_o} = [p_o - \delta, p_o + \delta]$, where δ is a random value in $[0, 0.15p_o]$. The resulting IJSP instances are available online[1]. We use a PC with Intel Xeon Gold 6132 processor at 2.6 Ghz and 128 Gb RAM with Linux (CentOS v6.10) and a C++ implementation. Every variant of the algorithm is run 30 times on each instance to obtain representative data.

A parameter tuning process has been carried out for the three variants of ABC, namely ABC_{E1}, ABC_{E2} and ABC_{E3}, where ABC_{Ei} incorporates the strategy **Elite**$_i$, $i = 1, 2, 3$, in the employed bee phase. In all cases, the population size is equal to 250 and the stopping criterion consists in $maxIter = 25$ consecutive iterations without improving the best solution found so far. For ABC_{E3}, the size of the elite set is $B = 50$ food sources. The final configuration for the remaining parameters for each variant of ABC is shown in Table 1.

Table 2 summarises the results obtained by the GA from [5] and the three ABC variants. For each algorithm and instance it reports the expected makespan (or midpoint) of the best-found solution ($m(\mathbf{Best})$), the average expected

---

[1] Repository section at http://di002.edv.uniovi.es/iscop.

Table 2. Computational results and times of GA and ABC

	GA				ABC_{E1}				ABC_{E2}				ABC_{E3}			
Instance	m(Best)	Avg.	σ	Time	m(Best)	Avg.	σ	Time	m(Best)	Avg.	σ	Time	m(Best)	Avg.	σ	Time
ABZ7	697.5	738.0	12.87	1.80	703.0	722.3	8.27	**1.66**	691.5	713.0	18.90	6.35	**690.5**	**704.0**	7.27	4.45
ABZ8	718.0	764.2	13.82	**1.76**	721.5	741.7	10.36	2.07	**702.0**	730.9	19.31	7.00	703.0	**722.8**	7.49	4.19
ABZ9	747.0	779.8	15.91	**2.19**	729.5	761.7	19.24	2.27	**715.0**	757.0	19.41	6.59	725.0	**747.8**	10.37	5.97
FT10	947.0	978.6	19.70	**0.48**	945.0	982.1	19.47	0.78	**939.0**	**966.7**	16.73	1.14	940.0	968.2	11.87	1.56
FT20	1182.0	1215.7	15.82	**0.69**	1177.0	1199.0	16.36	0.77	**1173.0**	1190.2	13.17	2.06	**1173.0**	**1185.1**	7.70	2.74
LA21	1079.0	1098.4	13.45	1.13	**1067.5**	1112.6	18.19	**0.90**	1069.5	**1098.4**	15.55	2.54	1073.0	1098.4	13.54	1.82
LA24	973.0	994.3	14.66	0.81	972.0	999.9	14.71	**0.70**	965.0	986.5	15.18	2.06	**956.0**	**982.3**	11.72	2.74
LA25	996.0	1026.9	23.39	0.97	1010.5	1037.5	18.00	**0.71**	**992.0**	1019.5	16.02	3.80	996.0	**1014.9**	8.71	2.44
LA27	1291.5	1361.2	24.67	**1.30**	1281.0	1319.8	16.95	1.38	**1268.5**	1300.5	18.49	4.55	1269.0	**1292.6**	12.25	4.11
LA29	1280.0	1315.9	18.63	**1.08**	1223.0	1281.1	27.14	1.35	**1208.0**	**1250.1**	26.03	5.00	1215.5	1251.6	15.13	4.40
LA38	1268.0	1305.5	27.26	1.41	**1249.5**	1304.5	27.50	**1.27**	1251.5	1289.4	21.17	3.41	1250.0	**1278.3**	17.61	5.96
LA40	1284.0	1328.8	28.50	**1.20**	1252.0	1302.1	21.70	1.43	1256.0	1283.4	17.94	4.04	**1245.0**	**1273.4**	13.81	3.01

makespan across all runs, the standard deviation, and the average CPU time in seconds. The best result for each instance is highlighted in bold. Additionally, ANOVA or Kruskall Wallis statistical tests have been performed on the results depending on the normality of the data, followed by a multi-variable analysis. Grey cells highlight those algorithms with no significant difference w.r.t. the best solution on that instance.

In terms of $m(\textbf{Best})$, GA is outperformed by ABC_{E2} and ABC_{E3} on every instance. ABC_{E2} improves GA 1.82% on average, being up to 5.63% for instance La29. If we pay attention to the average behaviour, ABC_{E3} obtains the best results on 10 out of 12 instances, while it is not significantly different from the best on the remaining 2 instances. On average, its results are 3.02% better than those of GA. However, it is not significantly different than ABC_{E2} on any instance. What is more interesting is that ABC_{E1} is never in the set of best methods, which reinforces the hypothesis that the standard ABC is not adequate for our problem and the proposed alternatives offer a significant improvement both w.r.t. the standard ABC and the state-of-the-art GA.

We can also observe that all ABC variants take longer running times than GA. The reason is that one iteration of ABC takes longer than an iteration of GA and also the dynamic stopping criterion translates into more iterations (hence, longer running times) for ABC. However, the efficiency of ABC_{Ei} per time unit is comparable to if not better than that of GA. Figure 1 depicts the evolution of the midpoint of the best makespan for representative instances La29 and La40. In both cases, ABC_{E1} (red line) and ABC_{E3} (green line) not only outperform GA (black line) in the final result, but also present a better makespan improvement rate per time unit. For ABC_{E2} (blue line) this improvement rate is very similar to that of GA, but ABC_{E2} achieves a better final result by taking longer to converge. This longer time to converge is also observed in ABC_{E3}, the version that achieves better results in average.

Finally, we perform a robustness analysis on the solutions obtained by each method. To do so, for each variant of ABC, each instance and each one of the 30 runs we take the expected makespan according to the obtained solution as well as the associated task processing order. This task order is then executed

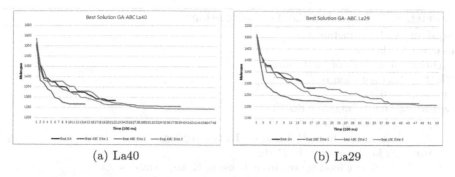

Fig. 1. Evolution along time of the makespan's midpoint for the best schedules obtained with *GA* (in black) and the different variants of *ABC* on instances La40 and La29. (Color figure online)

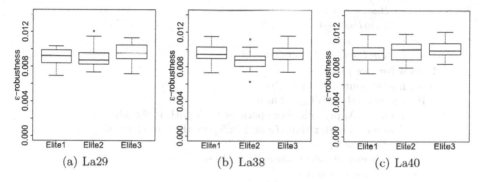

Fig. 2. $\bar{\epsilon}$-robustness of schedules obtained with the different variants of *ABC* on instances La29, La38 and La40.

for $K = 1000$ deterministic realisations of each instance to calculate the $\bar{\epsilon}$ value. Figure 2 shows the boxplots of the resulting $\bar{\epsilon}$ values on three representative instances. Statistical tests on all instances allow to conclude that there is no significant difference between the robustness of the three variants of the ABC. This homogeneity shows that the newly proposed variants ABC_{E2} and ABC_{E3} can obtain better results than a standard ABC (ABC_{E1}) and *GA* without deteriorating the robustness of the solutions.

Algorithm 1. Schema of the ABC Algorithm

Require: An IJSP instance
Ensure: A schedule
  Generate a pool P_0 of food sources
  $Best \leftarrow$ Best solution in P_0
  $numIter \leftarrow 0$
  while $numIter < maxIter$ **do**
    /* Employed bee phase*/
    $E \leftarrow$ Elite group from P_i based on **Elite**$_x$ strategy
    for each food source fs in P_i **do**
      $fs' \leftarrow$ Select food source from E using **Elite**$_x$ strategy
      $new_{fs} \leftarrow$ Apply crossover to (fs, fs') with probability p_{emp}
      if $new_f s$ is better than fs and different than $Best$ **then**
        $fs \leftarrow new_{fs}$
        if new_{fs} is better than $Best$ **then**
          $Best \leftarrow new_{fs}$
          $numIter \leftarrow 0$
      else
        $fs.numTrials \leftarrow fs.numTrials + 1$
    /* Onlooker bee phase*/
    for each food source fs in P_i **do**
      if $fs.numTrials < \mathrm{NT}_{max}$ **then**
        $new_{fs} \leftarrow$ Apply onlooker operator to fs with probability p_{on}
        if new_{fs} is better than fs and different than $Best$ **then**
          $fs \leftarrow new_{fs}$
          if new_{fs} is better than $Best$ **then**
            $Best \leftarrow new_{fs}$
            $numIter \leftarrow 0$
        else
          $fs.numTrials \leftarrow fs.numTrials + 1$
    /* Scout bee phase*/
    for each food source fs in P_i **do**
      if $fs.numTrials > \mathrm{NT}_{max}$ **then**
        $fs \leftarrow$ find new food source
        $fs.numTrials \leftarrow 0$
        if new_{fs} is better than $Best$ **then**
          $Best \leftarrow new_{fs}$;
          $numIter \leftarrow 0$
    $numIter \leftarrow numIter + 1$
  return $Best$

---

5 Conclusions

We have considered the IJSP, a version of the JSP that models the uncertainty on task durations appearing in real-world problems using intervals. We have used an ABC approach as solving method, adapting the general scheme to our problem, and we have tackled the issue of lack of diversity in the swarm by redesigning certain aspects of the employed and onlooker bee phases. This has resulted in three variants of the ABC algorithm. An experimental analysis has shown the potential of these variants, especially those introducing more diversity, ABC_{E2} and ABC_{E3}, which outperform the results of a more standard ABC_{E1} as well as the state-of-the-art from the literature. This improvement is present not only when all methods are allowed to converge and stop after $maxIter$ iterations without improvement, but it would also be the case if the stopping criterion were changed and they were given equal runtime to the state-of-the-art method. Finally, a robustness analysis has shown that the makespan improvement of the new methods is not obtained at the expense of deteriorating the solutions' robustness.

References

1. Allahverdi, A., Aydilek, H., Aydilek, A.: Single machine scheduling problem with interval processing times to minimize mean weighted completion time. Comput. Oper. Res. **51**, 200–207 (2014)
2. Banharnsakun, A., Sirinaovakul, B., Achalakul, T.: Job shop scheduling with the best-so-far ABC. Eng. Appl. Artif. Intell. **25**(3), 583–593 (2012)
3. Bidot, J., Vidal, T., Laboire, P.: A theoretic and practical framework for scheduling in stochastic environment. J. Sched. **12**, 315–344 (2009)
4. Bierwirth, C.: A generalized permutation approach to jobshop scheduling with genetic algorithms. OR Spectrum **17**, 87–92 (1995)
5. Díaz, H., González-Rodríguez, I., Palacios, J.J., Díaz, I., Vela, C.R.: A genetic approach to the job shop scheduling problem with interval uncertainty. In: Lesot, M.-J., et al. (eds.) IPMU 2020. CCIS, vol. 1238, pp. 663–676. Springer, Cham (2020). https://doi.org/10.1007/978-3-030-50143-3_52
6. Díaz, H., Palacios, J.J., Díaz, I., Vela, C.R., González-Rodríguez, I.: Tardiness minimisation for job shop scheduling with interval uncertainty. In: de la Cal, E.A., Villar Flecha, J.R., Quintián, H., Corchado, F. (eds.) HAIS 2020. LNCS (LNAI), vol. 12344, pp. 209–220. Springer, Cham (2020). https://doi.org/10.1007/978-3-030-61705-9_18
7. Karaboga, D.: An idea based on honey bee swarm for numerical optimization, technical report - tr06. Technical report, Erciyes University, January 2005
8. Karaboga, D., Gorkemli, B., Ozturk, C., Karaboga, N.: A comprehensive survey: artificial bee colony (ABC) algorithm and applications. Artif. Intell. Rev. **42**(1), 21–57 (2012). https://doi.org/10.1007/s10462-012-9328-0
9. Lei, D.: Population-based neighborhood search for job shop scheduling with interval processing time. Comput. Ind. Eng. **61**, 1200–1208 (2011)
10. Lei, D.: Interval job shop scheduling problems. Int. J. Adv. Manuf. Technol. **60**, 291–301 (2012)
11. Li, X., Gao, L., Wang, W., Wang, C., Wen, L.: Particle swarm optimization hybridized with genetic algorithm for uncertain integrated process planning and scheduling with interval processing time. Comput. Ind. Eng. **235**, 1036–1046 (2019)
12. Pinedo, M.L.: Scheduling. Theory, Algorithms, and Systems. Springer, New York (2016). https://doi.org/10.1007/978-1-4614-2361-4

13. Wong, L.P., Puan, C.Y., Low, M.Y.H., Chong, C.S.: Bee colony optimization algorithm with big valley landscape exploitation for job shop scheduling problems. In: 2008 Winter Simulation Conference, pp. 2050–2058 (2008)
14. Yao, B., Yang, C., Hu, J., Yin, G., Yu, B.: An improved artificial bee colony algorithm for job shop problem. Appl. Mech. Mater. **26–28**, 657–660 (2010)

Energy Minimization vs. Deep Learning Approaches for Protein Structure Prediction

Juan Luis Filgueiras, Daniel Varela, and José Santos[✉]

CITIC (Centre for Information and Communications Technology Research),
Department of Computer Science and Information Technologies,
University of A Coruña, A Coruña, Spain
{juan.filgueiras.rilo,daniel.varela,jose.santos}@udc.es

Abstract. This article discusses the advantages and problems of different approaches to ab initio protein structure prediction. Recent successful approaches based on deep learning are compared with those based on protein fragment replacements and energy minimization with different search strategies, including ours based on evolutionary algorithms. Selected proteins are considered to analyze the approaches, focusing on the problems of those based on deep learning.

1 Introduction

The native folded structure of a protein determines its function, as it defines interactions with other molecules. The folded structure is resolved by expensive and time-consuming laboratory methods such as X-ray crystallography, nuclear magnetic resonance and electron cryo-microscopy, protein structure information that is deposited in the public Protein Data Bank (PDB) [10]. As an alternative, Protein Structure Prediction (PSP) is one of the main challenges in computational biology, since the prediction of protein structure will enable a fast computational search process for drugs that interact with a given protein involved in a disease, as well as the design of de novo proteins for the same purpose.

Traditional PSP methods rely on finding a resolved protein in PDB with a homologous amino acid sequence, since with high homology the structures are the same. In PSP threading methods, for a target protein and a library of possible folds, these methods search for the fold in which the target sequence best fits. When structural information is not available, "ab initio" PSP is required, which uses only the amino acid sequence information of the protein. This ab initio prediction is based on Anfinsen's dogma, which states that the native structure

This study was funded by the Xunta de Galicia and the European Union (European Regional Development Fund - Galicia 2014–2020 Program), with grants CITIC (ED431G 2019/01), GPC ED431B 2019/03 and IN845D-02 (funded by the "Agencia Gallega de Innovación", co-financed by Feder funds, supported by the "Consellería de Economía, Empleo e Industria" of Xunta de Galicia), and by the Spanish Ministry of Science and Innovation (project PID2020-116201GB-I00).

J. M. Ferrández Vicente et al. (Eds.): IWINAC 2022, LNCS 13259, pp. 109–118, 2022.
https://doi.org/10.1007/978-3-031-06527-9_11

of the protein is determined solely by the amino acid sequence, as well as that the native structure corresponds to the one with the lowest Gibbs free energy.

Therefore, given a protein representation and an energy model associated with protein conformations, PSP becomes a problem of finding the structure that minimizes an energy function. This has been one of the traditional PSP approaches, with simplified lattice models for protein representation [14,16] and with atomic models [6], where metaheuristics play an essential role due to the complexity of the search landscape. In the latter case, Rosetta system [13] is one of the leading methods for PSP. Rosetta ab initio protocol uses small protein fragments (from resolved proteins) and the classical Metropolis criterion to decide whether a structural fragment replaces a part of the current conformational structure of the target protein, with the goal of finding the structure with the minimum energy. Working with the fragment replacement technique, our evolutionary computation solutions (*HybridDE* and *CrowdingDE*) [17,18] outperform Rosetta ab initio protocol when searching for structures with minimal energy and under the same number of conformational energy evaluations.

However, another approach in PSP is to predict the contact map or the interdistance map between amino acids, which is a simpler representation of the three-dimensional structure. This prediction typically uses the information from Multiple Sequence Alignment (MSA) of the target protein sequence as input to deep learning schemes, such as the initial approaches of *trRosetta* [19] and DeepMind's *AlphaFold* [5,15]. DeepMind's recent deep learning-based method, called *AlphaFold2* [8], has shown a very large improvement over previous approaches, as demonstrated by the results in the latest CASP (Critical Assessment of Structure Prediction) competition [4] (CASP14 in 2020).

This paper analyzes the advantages and problems of different ab initio PSP strategies, comparing energy minimization approaches and the recent methods based on deep learning of *AlphaFold2* [8] and *RoseTTAFold* [3], focusing on the problems of the latter with proteins with few homologous sequences. Section 2 provides a brief summary of the main aspects of the PSP approaches considered, Sect. 3 discusses the comparison of PSP alternatives and their problems using selected proteins, while Sect. 4 provides a brief discussion of the results.

2   Methods

2.1   Rosetta Ab Initio Protocol

Two protein representations are used by the Rosetta system: coarse-grained and all-atom. The coarse-grained representation only considers the main atoms of the protein backbone (with their dihedral angles), whereas the side chains are modeled with a pseudo-atom located at their center of mass (Fig. 1).

The Rosetta ab initio PSP protocol [12,13], with the low-resolution protein representation, employs a search technique in which a Monte Carlo procedure decides whether the dihedral angles of small protein fragments can replace the original ones [9,12]. A protein fragment is a group of consecutive amino acids of a resolved protein. Fragments are selected by considering their sequence similarity

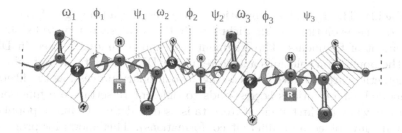

Fig. 1. Rosetta's coarse-grained model for protein representation. It considers only the main atoms of the protein backbone, while pseudo-atoms represent the lateral residues. ω, ϕ and ψ dihedral angles encode each protein conformation.

with respect to the window of consecutive residues of the target protein into which the fragments will be inserted. The decision regarding whether the dihedral angles of a selected fragment replace those of the target protein is based on the Metropolis criterion. This criterion always accepts the changes that improve the energy (lower values), while occasionally accepting dihedral angle changes that worsen the energy, with the probability of accepting the fragment depending on the increase in energy relative to the previous state of the target protein.

The energy of a protein conformation is defined as a weighted linear combination of different energy terms that model the molecular forces acting between the amino acid atoms. For example, steric overlap between backbone and side-chain atoms is penalized, while other Rosetta's energy terms correspond to van der Waals interactions, electrostatics effects and solvation, hydrogen bonding, repulsion and scores related to secondary structure (e.g., helix-strand packing and strand pairing). The detailed definition of the energy terms can be found, for example, in [12], and the weight sets for the individual energy terms for the definition of every Rosetta score are detailed in [13]. The Rosetta score function named *score3* integrates all of the energy components.

In the search for protein conformations with minimum energy, the stochastic Metropolis Monte Carlo procedure is run thousands of times. For this, the Rosetta ab initio protocol is divided into four stages, which use different score functions (progressively incorporating new energy terms) and number of fragment insertion attempts. Rosetta uses the coarse-grained protein representation and its fragment insertion technique (with the Metropolis criterion) throughout these four stages to generate new structural conformations. The final conformations ("decoys") in this ab initio protocol, can be refined in an "Ab initio Relax" procedure using the Rosetta's full atomic model.

2.2 *HybridDE* and *CrowdingDE* PSP Approaches

We defined a memetic combination between Differential Evolution (DE) [11] and the Rosetta's fragment replacement technique for PSP (*HybridDE* approach). The genetic population encodes possible protein conformations using the Rosetta's coarse-grained representation (encoding the dihedral angles for each amino acid). The hybrid combination integrates the advantage of the global search of the evolutionary algorithm with the local search provided by the replacement of fragments. The fragment insertion technique is used in DE to refine the population solutions and to refine the DE candidate or trial solutions. The memetic search follows a three-stage evolutionary process, as the fitness of the encoded conformations corresponds to different Rosetta score functions in each stage, while the first stage of Rosetta is used to define the initial population (with partially folded and different conformations). This allows for progressive structural refinement. The memetic version is detailed in [17,18]. *HybridDE* outperforms the Rosetta ab initio protocol in obtaining conformations with minimum energy and under the same number of conformational energy evaluations.

Nevertheless, obtaining energy-optimized conformations is not the only goal when the energy landscape is deceptive (such as the inaccurate Rosetta's energy model). This occurs when the conformation with the minimum energy does not correspond to the conformation closest to the real native structure. Consequently, one strategy is to obtain a set of optimized conformations (with minimal energy) with structural diversity. For this purpose, we introduced the crowding niching method into the *HybridDE* version, thus forcing the search algorithm to obtain optimized conformations in different niches (with different structural conformations). This increases the chances of obtaining candidate structures close to the native structure. *CrowdingDE* version is detailed in [18].

2.3   *AlphaFold* and *RoseTTAFold*

The recent deep learning-based methods of *AlphaFold2* [8] and *RoseTTAFold* [3] for PSP were considered here.

AlphaFold2 is the latest version of DeepMind's effort in PSP with deep NN architectures, which is an improvement of the first version *AlphaFold* [5,15]. In the case of *AlphaFold2*, the system receives the MSA of a target sequence as input information. MSA algorithms provide the alignment of evolutionarily related protein sequences, with a 2D matrix representation where the horizontal axis represents the residues of the target protein and the vertical axis corresponds to homologous protein sequences with an optimized alignment with respect to the other sequences (alignment that may be suboptimal since heuristics are used).

The idea behind the use of MSA as input information is that correlated mutations between residues indicate their spatial physical interaction. That is, if an amino acid mutates at position i in a homologous sequence (with respect to the target sequence), and a correlated mutation appears at position j in the same homologous sequence, then it is likely that residues i and j are in contact in the tertiary structure, since the correlated mutation tends to maintain the protein structure unchanged.

AlphaFold2's architecture is detailed in [8]. Several self-attention operations are performed in the deep NN architecture. Attention enables the NN to guide the flow of information, by learning to select which aspects of the input information should interact with other aspects of the same input. For instance, MSA representations are processed with consecutive blocks of self-attention in rows and columns. The first generates attention weights for amino acid pairs, allowing identification of which amino acid pairs are most closely related. The second attention process (in the vertical direction of MSA) allows elements belonging to the same target amino acid position to exchange information, i.e., it determines which protein sequences are most informative in the MSA input information.

One of the key modules of the internal architecture of *AlphaFold2* is the main network block called Evoformer, a stack of several NN layers that performs feature embedding. Evoformer works with an embedding of the MSA and with an internal pair representation (a generalized version of a distogram, i.e., a map of interdistances between residues). Both representations exchange information, as updates in the MSA embedding provide new information to change the structural hypothesis in the pair representation, and vice versa.

Evoformer is followed by a NN module or Structure Module that maps the embedding or abstract representation of the Evoformer stack to concrete 3D coordinates of all atoms (as well as the per-residue confidence commented below). In this module, NN attention mechanisms (with invariance to rotations and translations of the protein conformation in space) are used to progressively refine the structure (which includes the side-chain atoms). Finally, the predicted structure information is returned to the Evoformer blocks. Consequently, these two steps (Evorformer and Structural Prediction) are repeated several times in *AlphaFold2* to progressively refine the final and predicted model of the protein.

AlphaFold2 provides two confidence measures of the predicted structures. The first is the predicted local-Distance Difference Test (plDDT), a per-residue measure of local confidence (on a scale from 0–100). This measure estimates how well the prediction would agree with an experimental structure, since it predicts the accuracy of the local distance difference test (lDDT-C_α, considering only the atom C_α in each amino acid) between the predicted and real structures. The second metric is the Predicted Alignment Error (PAE). PAE (x, y) reports the expected position error at residue x, when the predicted and real structures are aligned on residue y. Consequently, it provides a level of confidence about the relative positions of the amino acids (and different domains) of the protein.

RoseTTAFold [3] is also a recent method based on deep-learning and inspired by the DeepMind's framework, as the authors state. It is also an improvement over the previous version of the same group at the University of Washington, called *trRosetta* [19]. *RoseTTAFold* uses a three-track neural network to simultaneously process sequence, distance, and coordinate information. The main new feature in *RoseTTAFold* [3], with respect to *AlphaFold2*, is the incorporation of a third track in the deep NN design, which operates in 3Dcoordinate space. As the authors state [3], this provides a tighter connection between the protein sequence, residue-residue distances and their orientations, as well as the coordinates of all atoms. Therefore, the neural architecture has 1D, 2D and 3D tracks with attention mechanisms. There are connections between the three tracks to allow simultaneous learning of relationships within and between sequences, distances an coordinates. *RoseTTAFold* [3] outperformed other PSP servers with recent structures submitted to PDB. *RoseTTAFold* also provides a per-residue accuracy estimate, based on the predicted lDDT-C_α.

The *AlphaFold2* [1] and *RoseTTAFold* [2] servers were used in the predictions. The commented measures will be used to analyze the results.

3   Results

3.1   Setup of the PSP Approaches

The PSP approaches discussed in the Methods section are used with different proteins. First, taking into account the stochasticity of Rosetta ab initio PSP protocol, it is run 1,000 times to generate 1,000 decoys (candidate conformations). Rosetta parameter *increase_cycles* is set to 10, as recommended on the Rosetta site [13].

Regarding the approaches based on DE (*HybridDE* and *CrowdingDE*), the same setup used in [17,18] was used. DE parameters were experimentally selected to generate candidate conformations in DE with slight variations with respect to their base individual (current conformation in the population), in order to minimize conflicts between atoms in the DE trial or candidate solutions (with a low weigh factor in the mutation operator and a high crossover probability, see [18] for details). These energy minimization approaches use the same number of fitness evaluations (i.e., the same number of energy evaluations of candidate protein conformations) as Rosetta ab initio for generating 1,000 decoys. Note that energy evaluations are synonymous with fragment insertion attempts, since an insertion attempt involves the energy evaluation of the resulting conformation.

For this purpose, *HybridDE* and *CrowdingDE* were run 10 times, with a population of 100 solutions and over 100 generations in the 10 independent runs. Consequently, the 10 runs also generate 1,000 final solutions (joining the final populations of the runs). The fair comparison is obtained since, in *HybridDE* and *CrowdingDE*, parameter *increase_cycles* is set to 0.1 (100 times less than in the case of Rosetta ab initio protocol), because the evolutionary approaches refine 1,000 conformational solutions with the same Rosetta approach based on fragment insertions, but over 100 generations.

For the deep learning-based approaches (*AlphaFold2* and *RoseTTAFold*), the default configuration provided by the servers was used, that is, using the MSA information as input, while the servers provide five candidate models, those with the highest prediction confidence.

3.2   Examples with PDB Proteins

Proteins from PDB [10] were selected, i.e., proteins with known structure. Consequently, these proteins serve to test whether the predictions are close to the folded and resolved structure deposited in PDB. Proteins with shallow MSA information (few sequences homologous to the target protein) were selected in order to test the behavior of deep learning-based approaches. The first example is with protein *1ha8* (pheromone from protozoan E. Raikovi, 51 amino acids).

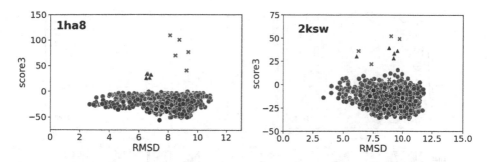

Fig. 2. Energy (*score3*) vs. RMSD (from the native structure, in Å) for proteins *1ha8* and *2ksw*. Gray: Rosetta ab initio. Blue: *HybridDE*. Red: *CrowdingDE*. Green: *AlphaFold2* solutions. Pink: *RoseTTAFold* solutions. (Color figure online)

Figure 2 shows the distribution of solutions generated by the different methods. This is a standard graph in PSP for evaluating the performance of energy minimization methods, as it shows the distribution of the optimized protein decoys (in terms of their distances from the native structure), along with the optimization (in terms of energy) obtained in the optimized solutions. The distances of the optimized conformations from the native structure are calculated with the RMSD (Root Mean Squared Deviation, taking into account the C_α atoms of each amino acid, superimposing each conformation with the native one). The energy of each conformation corresponds to Rosetta's coarse-grained representation (*score3*, which includes all individual energy terms).

With protein *1ha8*, the energy minimization approaches return solutions closer to the native structure with respect to the deep learning approaches. With the former approaches, *HybridDE* and *CrowdingDE* obtain solutions with better energy with respect to Rosetta ab initio, showing the better ability of the evolutionary approaches to sample the conformational space under the same number of energy evaluations. However, *HybridDE* obtains the best solution in energy terms, a solution that is farther away from the native structure with respect to many other solutions. This shows the inaccuracies of the Rosetta's energy model, since the solutions with the best energy do not have to correspond to those closest to the native structure, defining a deceptive energy landscape for the search algorithms. To address this problem, the inclusion of crowding in the memetic evolutionary algorithm (*CrowdingDE*), allows us to obtain a wider distribution of optimized solutions. In fact, *CrowdingDE* presents the closest solution to the native structure.

AlphaFold2 and *RoseTTAFold* present worse solutions in terms of RMSD distance from the native structure. The higher energy (with respect to energy minimization approaches) is due to the fact that some atoms have collisions in the side chains, which can be resolved by further refinement of the structure.

Figure 3 shows information regarding the *AlphaFold2* predictions. With protein *1ha8*, the MSA includes a high number of homologous sequences, although without high sequence identity between the target protein and the homologous

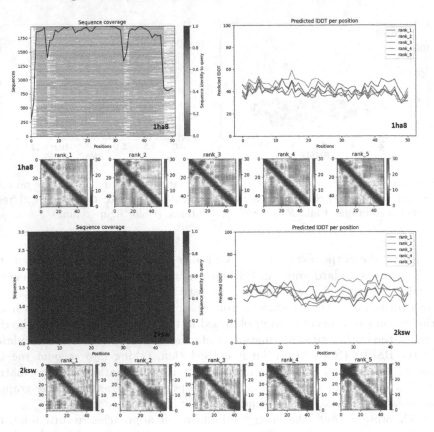

Fig. 3. Information about *AlphaFold2* models with proteins *1ha8* and *2ksw*. For each protein, top left: MSA sequence coverage. Top right: predicted Local Distance Difference Test (plDDT) of the predicted *AlphaFold2* models. Bottom figures: PAE (Predicted Aligned Error) of the five highest-rated *AlphaFold2* models.

ones. This information is not sufficient for fairly high confidence in the predictions. This is shown by the poor confidence in the plDDT per residue, where plDDT > 90 corresponds to predictions modeled with high accuracy, whereas areas where plDDT < 50 should not be considered reliable [8]. Similarly, the PAE graphs for the five best-rated prediction models (considering the average plDDT in the residues) show the low prediction confidence, where the bluer, the lower the estimated error. The analysis with the *RoseTTAFold* solutions would be similar and is not included.

The second example corresponds to protein *2ksw* (46 amino acids, a beetle hemolymph protein). In this case, the MSA map is simple, since there are no homologous sequences found in the genetic databases (except for the sequence itself which was found 3 times). That is, it is an example with no information of proteins with similar sequence. The *AlphaFold2* models present very low confidence at all positions in the protein chain, as can be seen in Fig. 3 with the

PAE plots and with the plDDT measure. Figure 2 shows that the *AlphaFold2* and *RoseTTAFold* solutions present high RMSD values from the native structure and these are worse with respect to the energy minimization approaches. *HybridDE* and *CrowdingDE* provide better average energy of the optimized solutions, although Rosetta ab initio also discovers solutions with low energy.

The final example corresponds to protein *orf8*, a protein component of the SARS-CoV-2 virus with 104 amino acids (protein visualizations of predictions with SARS-CoV-2 proteins can be seen in [7]). This protein has no homologous proteins in the PDB database [10]. Even with the search for homologous sequences in genetic databases, the MSA coverage is poor. The prediction confidence of *AlphaFold2* models is low, as seen in Fig. 4. Neither approach presents accurate solutions, as shown by the distribution of solutions in the energy vs. RMSA plot in Fig. 4.

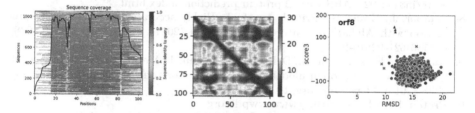

Fig. 4. MSA information input to *AlphaFold2* and *RoseTTAFold* with SARS-CoV-2 protein *orf8*. Left: MSA sequence coverage. Center: PAE (Predicted Aligned Error) of the highest rated *AlphaFold2* model. Right: Energy (*score3*) vs. RMSD with different PSP approaches (same colors as in Fig. 2).

4 Discussion and Conclusions

Predictions with selected proteins show the dependence of deep NN-based approaches on MSA input information. When the MSA information is not detailed enough, deep NN-based approaches can present predictions with low confidence, as show with selected proteins. Energy minimization approaches present better solutions in terms of minimized energy and memetic approaches show better sampling of the energy landscape with respect to the state-of-the-art Rosetta ab initio protocol. However, imperfections in the energy landscape do not allow the best optimized solutions with memetic approaches to correspond to solutions closer to the native structure. In any case, it must be taken into account that proteins with low sequence identity were chosen for the analysis, and the recent approaches based on deep learning present predicted solutions with very low distances to the real native structure in the vast majority of proteins, showing a great leap forward in this problem of computational structural biology.

References

1. AlphaFold2 server. https://colab.research.google.com/github/sokrypton/ColabFold/blob/main/AlphaFold2.ipynb
2. RoseTTAFold server. https://colab.research.google.com/github/sokrypton/ColabFold/blob/main/RoseTTAFold.ipynb
3. Baek, M., DiMaio, F., Anishchenko, I., et al.: Accurate prediction of protein structures and interactions using a three-track neural network. Science **373**(6557), 871–876 (2021). https://doi.org/10.1126/science.abj8754
4. Protein structure prediction center. http://predictioncenter.org/
5. Evans, R., et al.: De novo structure prediction with deep-learning based scoring. In: 13th Critical Assessment of Techniques for PSP, pp. 1–4 (2018)
6. Garza-Fabre, M., Kandathil, S., Handl, J., Knowles, J., Lovell, S.: Generating, maintaining, and exploiting diversity in a memetic algorithm for protein structure prediction. Evol. Comput. **24**(4), 577–607 (2016)
7. Prediction results of the SARS-CoV-2 unsolved proteins. https://www.dc.fi.udc.es/ir/in845d-02/SARS-CoV-2_protein_prediction/index.html
8. Jumper, J., Evans, R., Pritzel, A., et al.: Highly accurate protein structure prediction with AlphaFold. Nature **596**, 583–589 (2021). https://doi.org/10.1038/s41586-021-03819-2
9. Kaufmann, K., Lemmon, G., DeLuca, S., Sheehan, J., Meiler, J.: Practically useful: what the Rosetta protein modeling suite can do for you. Biochemistry **49**, 2987–2998 (2010). https://doi.org/10.1021/bi902153g
10. Protein Data Bank. http://www.wwpdb.org
11. Price, K., Storn, R., Lampinen, J.: Differential evolution. A practical approach to global optimization (2005)
12. Rohl, C., Strauss, C., Misura, K., Baker, D.: Protein structure prediction using Rosetta. Meth. Enzymol. **383**, 66–93 (2004). https://doi.org/10.1016/S0076-6879(04)83004-0
13. Rosetta system. http://www.rosettacommons.org
14. Santos, J., Diéguez, M.: Differential evolution for protein structure prediction using the HP model. In: Ferrández, J.M., Álvarez Sánchez, J.R., de la Paz, F., Toledo, F.J. (eds.) IWINAC 2011. LNCS, vol. 6686, pp. 323–333. Springer, Heidelberg (2011). https://doi.org/10.1007/978-3-642-21344-1_34
15. Senior, A., Evans, R., Jumper, J., et al.: Improved protein structure prediction using potentials from deep-learning. Nature **577**, 706–710 (2020). https://doi.org/10.1038/s41586-019-1923-7
16. Varela, D., Santos, J.: A hybrid evolutionary algorithm for protein structure prediction using the face-centered cubic lattice model. In: Liu, D., Xie, S., Li, Y., Zhao, D., El-Alfy, E.S. (eds.) Neural Information Processing, ICONIP 2017. Lecture Notes in Computer Science, vol. 10634. Springer, Cham (2017). https://doi.org/10.1007/978-3-319-70087-8_65
17. Varela, D., Santos, J.: Crowding differential evolution for protein structure prediction. In: Ferrández Vicente, J.M., Álvarez-Sánchez, J.R., de la Paz López, F., Toledo Moreo, J., Adeli, H. (eds.) IWINAC 2019. LNCS, vol. 11487, pp. 193–203. Springer, Cham (2019). https://doi.org/10.1007/978-3-030-19651-6_19
18. Varela, D., Santos, J.: Protein structure prediction in an atomic model with differential evolution integrated with the crowding niching method. Nat. Comput., 1–15 (2020). https://doi.org/10.1007/s11047-020-09801-7
19. Yang, J., Anishchenko, I., Park, H., Peng, Z., Ovchinnikov, S., Baker, D.: Improved protein structure prediction using predicted interresidue orientations. PNAS **117**, 1496–1503 (2020). https://doi.org/10.1073/pnas.1914677117

Constructing Ensembles of Dispatching Rules for Multi-objective Problems

Marko Đurasević[1(✉)], Lucija Planinić[1(✉)], Francisco J. Gil-Gala[2(✉)], and Domagoj Jakobović[1(✉)]

[1] Faculty of Electrical Engineering and Computing, University of Zagreb, Zagreb, Croatia
{marko.durasevic,lucija.planinic,domagoj.jakobovic}@fer.hr
[2] Department of Computer Science, University of Oviedo, Oviedo, Spain
giljavier@uniovi.es

Abstract. Scheduling represents an important aspect of many real-world processes, which is why such problems have been well studied in the literature. Such problems are often dynamic and require that multiple criteria be optimised simultaneously. Dispatching rules (DRs) are the method of choice for solving dynamic problems. However, existing DRs are usually implemented for the optimisation of only a single criterion. Since manual design of DRs is difficult, genetic programming (GP) has been used to automatically design new DRs for single and multiple objectives. However, the performance of a single rule is limited, and it may not work well in all situations. Therefore, ensembles have been used to create rule sets that outperform single DRs. The goal of this study is to adapt ensemble learning methods to create ensembles that optimise multiple criteria simultaneously. The method creates ensembles of DRs with multiple objectives previously evolved by GP to improve their performance. The results show that ensembles are suitable for the considered multi-objective problem.

Keywords: Genetic programming · Scheduling · Unrelated machines · Dispatching rules · Ensembles · Multi-objective optimisation

1 Introduction

Scheduling is the problem of optimally assigning a set of jobs to a finite number of machines [13]. Such problems have numerous applications in the real world, including manufacturing, universities, airports, hospitals, electric vehicle charging, and the like [8,13]. Since most real-world scheduling problems are NP-hard, they are usually solved using various heuristic methods, most notably metaheuristics. However, metaheuristics are difficult to apply in dynamic environments. Therefore, simple heuristic methods called dispatching rules (DRs) are the method of choice for such problems. DRs construct the schedule online while the system is running by selecting which job to schedule next when a

© Springer Nature Switzerland AG 2022
J. M. Ferrández Vicente et al. (Eds.): IWINAC 2022, LNCS 13259, pp. 119–129, 2022.
https://doi.org/10.1007/978-3-031-06527-9_12

machine becomes available [17]. However, manually constructing such heuristics has proven to be a difficult and time-consuming task, leading to the use of various methods to automatically construct DRs [1].

Genetic programming (GP) is one of the most popular hyperheuristic methods used to develop new heuristics for various combinatorial problems. As such, it is widely used for automatic design of various scheduling problems. In most cases, using such a method, it has been possible to design new rules that outperform various manually developed rules. This led to a large amount of research considering different problem variants and methods for designing better DRs [1].

A key direction in automatic design of DRs is to develop rules that are also suitable for optimising multiple objectives, since most real-world problems usually require optimising multiple objectives [10]. This direction is important because manually developed rules are usually only suitable for optimising a single criterion. This, of course, requires the application of different multi-objective algorithms (MO) to develop rules for different combinations of criteria under consideration. Although previous studies have shown that efficient MO DRs can be designed using GP [16], these rules are limited by the aspect that a single rule still performs poorly in certain situations. One of the most efficient ways to improve the performance of DRs is to combine them into ensembles of rules that make decisions together.

In this study, we are concerned with the application of ensemble learning methods to create ensembles of DRs suitable for simultaneous optimisation of multiple criteria. We are interested in answering the question of whether it is possible to improve the performance of DRs designed for optimising multiple objectives by combining them into ensembles. Therefore, an ensemble learning method is adapted for the MO case and used to create ensembles for a MO problem. The contributions of this study can be summarised as follows:

1. Adapt an ensemble learning method to construct ensembles for MO problems
2. Analyse the performance of the proposed method on a selected MO problem
3. Examine the Pareto fronts obtained by the different MO methods

The rest of the paper is organised as follows. Section 2 provides the overview on the existing literature. The unrelated machines problem and automatic design of dispatching rules for it are described in Sect. 3. The ensemble learning method adapted for MO problems is outlined in Sect. 4. The obtained results are shown in Sect. 5. Finally, the conclusion and future research directions.

2   Literature Review

A MO problem for the job shop environment, where five criteria must be optimised simultaneously, was considered in [9], where several MO algorithms were used. This research was extended in [10], where the authors applied a local search during evolution. In [7], several MO algorithms were used to develop rules for problems involving four and five criteria. In [16], the authors consider several MO problems with 3 to 9 criteria and apply 4 MO GP algorithms to evolve new DRs

for them. In [20], the authors consider the dynamic flexible job shop problem
and apply the NSGA-II and SPEA2 algorithms to construct DRs for multiple
flowtime objective formulations. In [6], the authors analyse how different features
of the job-shop problem affect the performance of a MO GP method.

In [12], the authors apply the cooperative coevolution algorithm to create
ensembles for the job shop environment. In this approach, each subpopulation in
the algorithm represents a rule that is evolved for the ensemble. In [5], a method
called NELLI-GP was proposed for evolving ensembles of DRs, which achieves
better results than the cooperative coevolution from [12]. In [11], four ensemble combination methods were investigated: sum, weighted sum, voting, and
weighted voting. Four ensemble learning methods were compared in [15], including BagCP, BoostGP, cooperative coevolution, and SEC. Since the SEC method
performed the best, the study was extended in [18], where the SEC method was
analysed in more detail. In [14], the ensemble learning methods from [15] were
applied to the resource constrained project scheduling problem. Another type of
ensembles was proposed in [3,4] for the variable capacity one machine problem.
These ensembles use each rule to construct the schedule individually and then
select the best results, making them suitable for static environments.

3   Background

3.1   Unrelated Machines Environment

The unrelated machines environment is a scheduling problem consisting of n
jobs that have to be scheduled on a given set of m machines. Each job i is
defined by its processing time p_{ij} on machine i, its ready time r_j, its due date
d_j, and its weight w_j. The problem is considered under dynamic conditions, i.e.,
it is not known a priori when the jobs will be fed into the system, nor are job
characteristics known before the jobs' ready time. When each job is scheduled,
the completion time C_j and the tardiness of a job T_j can be calculated. The
tardiness represents how much job j spent executing after its due date, and
is defines as $T_j = \max(C_j - d_j, 0)$. Based on the previous properties, several
scheduling criteria can be defined which will be considered in this study:

- C_{max} - maximum completion time of all jobs: $C_{max} = \max_j \{C_j\}$.
- Cw - total weighted completion time: $Cw = \sum_j w_j C_j$,
- Twt - total weighted tardiness: $Twt = \sum_j w_j T_j$,

All of the above criteria need to be minimised simultaneously. Therefore, the
problem considered in this paper can be defined as $R|r_j|C_{max}, Cw, Twt$ using
the standard notation for scheduling problems [13].

3.2   Automatic Design of DRs with GP

DRs are constructive heuristics consisting of a schedule generation scheme (SGS)
and a priority function (PF). The SGS is a procedure that builds the schedule

so that each time a machine becomes available, it selects which job to schedule next. However, the decision of which job to schedule on which machine is not made by the SGS itself; instead, the PF is used to make this decision. The PF is used to assign a numeric value to each job-machine pair, and the pair that received the smallest value is selected for scheduling.

Traditionally, PFs were designed manually, resulting in a plethora of DRs to optimise various criteria. However, another option is to design such PFs using GP. Since PF is a mathematical expression, it can be easily coded as a solution tree in GP. For this purpose, however, a set of terminal and function nodes must be defined that GP can use to construct the expression. The terminal nodes used are listed in Table 1. These nodes represent important values of the system like job processing times, due dates, average execution times, and the like. For the function set, the addition, subtraction, multiplication, protected division (returns 1 if division is by 0), and unary positive operators ($pos(a) = \max(a,0)$). These were selected based on a previous study [19].

Table 1. Terminal set

Terminal	Description
pt	processing time of job j on machine i
$pmin$	minimal processing time (MPT) of job j
$pavg$	average processing time of job j across all machines
PAT	time until machine with the MPT for job j becomes available
MR	time until machine i becomes available
age	time which job j spent in the system
dd	time until which job j has to finish with its execution
w	weight of job j (w_j)
SL	slack of job j, $-max(d_j - p_{ij} - t, 0)$

4 Designing Ensembles for MO Problems

To design ensembles of DRs, two things must be specified: how the ensemble is constructed and how the DRs that make up the ensemble work together.

4.1 Ensemble Construction

Although a variety of ensemble construction methods have been proposed for constructing ensembles of DRs, the simple ensemble combination method (SEC) was chosen. The reason for choosing this method is its inherent simplicity and better results compared to other ensemble learning methods. The idea of the method is that it randomly constructs a set of ensembles from a pool of existing DRs and returns the best ensemble as the result.

Algorithm 1 shows the SEC method adapted for MO optimisation. The method accepts three parameters, the number of ensembles N to construct, the number of rules in ensemble ES, and the set of rules used to construct ensembles R. In each iteration, an ensemble is constructed by randomly selecting ES rules from the set R. When the ensemble is constructed, it is added to the set *constructed* that contains all constructed ensembles. This procedure is repeated N times, resulting in a set containing N ensembles. This set is then nondominately sorted [2] for the specified criteria, and the first front is returned by the SEC method. In this way, a set of solutions that provide different tradeoffs between the considered criteria should be obtained.

Algorithm 1. The simple ensemble combination method

1: **function** SEC(N, ES, R)
2:     *constructed* $\leftarrow \emptyset$
3:     *counter* $\leftarrow 0$
4:     **while** *counter* $< N$ **do**
5:         *counter* $++$
6:         $E \leftarrow \emptyset$
7:         **while** $|E| < ES$ **do**
8:             Select a random DR from $R \setminus E$, and add it to E
9:         **end while**
10:         *constructed* $\leftarrow$ *ensembles* $\cup \{E\}$
11:     **end while**
12:     Perform nondominated sorting on the *constructed* set
13:     **return** first front of *constructed*
14: **end function**

4.2   Ensemble Combination

When a set of rules is chosen to form an ensemble, it is important to specify how these rules will work together, i.e., how their individual decisions will be combined into a single decision. For this purpose, sum and vote combination methods are used [15]. At each decision point, these methods combine the decisions of all the individual rules in the ensembles into a single decision, which is then executed by the SGS. Since each rule computes a numerical priority value for job-machine pairs, the easiest way to aggregate the decisions of the individual DRs is to add the priority values obtained from each rule. Then the job-machine pair with the lowest value is selected and scheduled. This is how the sum combination method works. An obvious pitfall with this method is that the rules in the ensemble can produce very different priority values, which could result in one rule dominating over others. Therefore, the vote combination method uses a simple voting mechanism in which each rule in the ensemble casts a vote for the job-machine pair to be scheduled (the one with the lowest priority value), and the one that received the most votes is eventually scheduled. One problem with this approach is that ties can occur, and while they can be resolved in different ways, they are resolved in such a way that the job that arrived first is selected.

5 Experimental Analysis

5.1 Setup

To test the effectiveness of the adapted SEC method, we evaluate it on the $R|r_j|C_{max}, Cw, Twt$ problem. However, to apply the SEC method, a pool of MO DRs that can be combined into ensembles is required. To obtain this pool of rules, first the considered problem is optimised using the NSGA-II, NSGA-III, HaD-MOEA, and MOEA/D and then all obtained solutions are combined into a single set of nondominated solutions [16]. After this first step, 70 MO DRs were obtained, which are then used by SEC to construct the ensembles.

The SEC method is tested with different parameter values. The values 1000, 5000, and 10000 are used for the number of iterations of the method. Both the sum and vote combination methods are tested with ensemble sizes of 3, 5, and 7. For each parameter combination, the method is executed 30 times and the best Pareto front of each execution is saved. To evaluate the quality of the obtained Pareto fronts, the hypervolume (HV) metric is used [16]. The reason for choosing this metric is that it measures both convergence and diversity of Pareto fronts.

To create and evaluate the ensembles, a set of 120 instances was used [19]. The set was split into two different sets, the training set and test set. The training set was used to develop rules and create ensembles. The test set was then used to evaluate the performance of the constructed rules and ensembles.

5.2 Optimising the $R|r_j|C_{max}, Cw, Twt$ Problem

Table 2 shows the HV values obtained for all tested parameter combinations of the studied SEC method. The row labelled "med" represents the median HV value obtained for each algorithm execution. The line "tot", on the other hand, denotes the HV value of the union of all 30 Pareto fronts obtained in the executions. The last lines denotes the HV value obtained for the set of individual MO rules used by SEC. The best values for each method are in bold. The results illustrate several things. First, the vote combination method clearly achieves better results than the sum method. As for the size of the ensemble, it is difficult to determine which size would be the best. The sum method performs best when 7 is used, but with the vote method, there is no single ensemble size that gives the best results. Second, one can see that the SEC method in a single execution gets Pareto fronts with lower HV values than the front of the MO DRs. However, if we consider the union of these fronts obtained in each execution, SEC always obtained a better Pareto front, at least for the vote method. This seems to indicate that a single execution of SEC is not sufficient to obtain a good approximation of the Pareto front, but rather that multiple executions are required.

To get a better idea of the differences between the Pareto fronts of the MO DRs and the ensembles, the solutions in their respective Pareto fronts are shown in Fig. 1. The figure shows pairwise combinations of the three optimised criteria

Table 2. Results for the HV metric for the $R|r_j|C_{max}, Cw, Twt$ problem

Method			sum			vote	
		3	5	7	3	5	7
SEC-1000	med	0.568	0.565	0.563	**0.588**	0.587	0.586
	tot	0.591	0.593	0.603	**0.649**	0.634	0.622
SEC-5000	med	0.572	0.566	0.567	0.593	**0.596**	0.591
	tot	0.590	0.593	0.597	0.632	0.647	**0.651**
SEC-20000	med	0.571	0.571	0.571	0.598	**0.599**	0.596
	tot	0.589	0.593	0.599	0.622	**0.640**	0.622
MO DRs					0.604		

to better illustrate the Pareto fronts. For the ensemble, the Pareto front of SEC-5000 was used with the vote combination method and an ensemble size of 7 rules, since the best Pareto front was obtained for this parameter combination. For all three combinations, the figure shows that the Pareto front of the ensembles is closer to the origin of the coordinate system, indicating that much better convergence was achieved. However, one problem with this Pareto front could be that more solutions appear to be grouped together, suggesting that the algorithm favours more convergence than diversity.

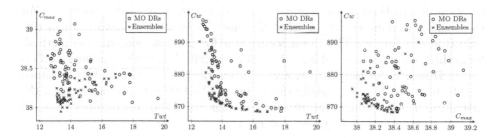

Fig. 1. The Pareto front obtained for the $R|r_j|C_{max}, Cw, Twt$ problem denoted through pairwise combinations of the three optimised criteria

Table 3 shows the descriptive statistics calculated for the obtained Pareto fronts for SEC-5000. The table shows the dominance of the vote combination method, as it obtains better median and minimum values than the sum method for all criteria. Compared to the MO DRs given in the end of the table, the Pareto fronts of the ensembles generally achieve better median and maximum values. For the minimum values, only the sum method achieved better minimum values than the individual MO DRs.

Table 3. Descriptive statistics of the Pareto fronts obtained for the $R|r_j|C_{max}$, Cw, Twt problem

Method		sum			vote		
		min	med	max	min	med	max
E-3	C_{max}	38.13	38.39	39.00	37.95	**38.31**	38.68
	Cw	868.8	872.6	894.8	867.9	**871.8**	894.0
	Twt	13.04	14.16	17.67	12.78	**13.93**	17.04
E-5	C_{max}	38.19	38.33	38.97	37.92	**38.25**	39.11
	Cw	869.2	873.1	885.5	868.2	**870.8**	893.6
	Twt	12.96	**13.85**	16.27	12.58	14.36	17.15
E-7	C_{max}	38.18	38.36	38.88	37.95	**38.16**	38.66
	Cw	868.9	872.2	885.1	868.4	**871.8**	890.2
	Twt	12.94	13.99	16.75	12.49	**13.63**	16.89
MO DRs	C_{max}	38.07	38.46	39.13	38.07	38.46	39.13
	Cw	868.6	880.7	896.9	868.6	880.7	896.9
	Twt	12.70	13.83	19.58	12.70	13.83	19.58

Figure 2 shows the box plots of the optimised criteria for the Pareto fronts obtained by different methods. The results obtained by ensembles are denoted by E-x-y, where "x" stands for "s" or "v" depending on whether the sum or vote combination method is used, and "y" stands for the size of the ensemble. For the C_{max} criterion, we can see that all ensemble variants achieve a better distribution of solutions. This is especially true for the vote combination method. Something similar can be observed for the Cw criterion, with even larger differences. However, for the Twt criterion, in several cases the ensembles obtained Pareto fronts with worse distributions than the MO DRs. In the other cases, the distribution of solutions is mostly similar to the MO DRs, or the values obtained for the criterion are slightly less scattered.

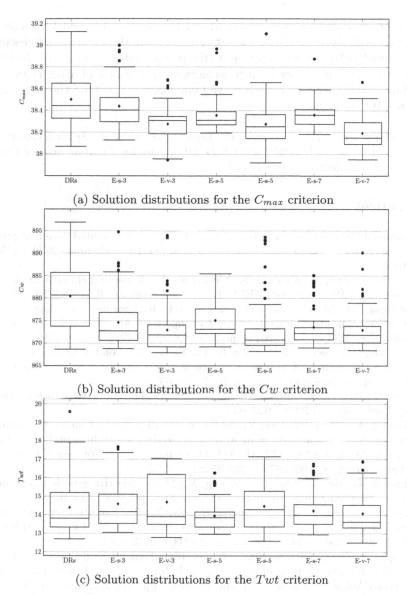

(a) Solution distributions for the C_{max} criterion

(b) Solution distributions for the Cw criterion

(c) Solution distributions for the Twt criterion

Fig. 2. Distribution of solutions for all considered criteria.

6   Conclusion

This study addresses the application of ensemble learning to create ensembles of MO DRs to optimise multiple criteria simultaneously. The SEC method, previously used only for the single objective case, was adapted for multi-objective problems and tested on the $R|r_j|C_{max}, Cw, Twt$. The obtained results show that the constructed ensembles can outperform the results obtained by single MO DRs. The analysis of the Pareto fronts showed that the constructed ensembles achieve much better convergence and still provide good coverage of the search space. In future studies, we plan to explore the possibility of using rules developed for a single target to construct MO ensembles and extend the experiments to more MO problems.

Acknowledgements. This research has been supported by the Spanish Government under research project PID2019-106263RB-I00, and by the Croatian Science Foundation under the project IP-2019-04-4333.

References

1. Branke, J., Nguyen, S., Pickardt, C.W., Zhang, M.: Automated design of production scheduling heuristics: a review. IEEE Trans. Evol. Comput. **20**(1), 110–124 (2016)
2. Deb, K., Pratap, A., Agarwal, S., Meyarivan, T.: A fast and elitist multiobjective genetic algorithm: NSGA-II. IEEE Trans. Evol. Comput. **6**(2), 182–197 (2002)
3. Gil-Gala, F.J., Mencía, C., Sierra, M.R., Varela, R.: Learning ensembles of priority rules for online scheduling by hybrid evolutionary algorithms. Integr. Comput. Aided Eng. **28**(1), 65–80 (2020). https://doi.org/10.3233/ICA-200634
4. Gil-Gala, F.J., Sierra, M.R., Mencía, C., Varela, R.: Combining hyper-heuristics to evolve ensembles of priority rules for on-line scheduling. Nat. Comput., 1–11 (2020). https://doi.org/10.1007/s11047-020-09793-4
5. Hart, E., Sim, K.: A hyper-heuristic ensemble method for static job-shop scheduling. Evol. Comput. **24**(4), 609–635 (2016)
6. Masood, A., Chen, G., Mei, Y., Al-Sahaf, H., Zhang, M.: Genetic programming with pareto local search for many-objective job shop scheduling. In: Liu, J., Bailey, J. (eds.) AI 2019. LNCS (LNAI), vol. 11919, pp. 536–548. Springer, Cham (2019). https://doi.org/10.1007/978-3-030-35288-2_43
7. Masood, A., Mei, Y., Chen, G., Zhang, M.: Many-objective genetic programming for job-shop scheduling. In: IEE CEC, July 2016, pp. 209–216 (2016)
8. Mencía, C., Sierra, M.R., Mencía, R., Varela, R.: Evolutionary one-machine scheduling in the context of electric vehicles charging. Integr. Comput. Aided Eng. **26**(1), 49–63 (2018). https://doi.org/10.3233/ICA-180582
9. Nguyen, S., Zhang, M., Johnston, M., Tan, K.C.: Dynamic multi-objective job shop scheduling: a genetic programming approach. In: Uyar, A.S., Ozcan, E., Urquhart, N. (eds.) Automated Scheduling and Planning, pp. 251–282. Springer, Heidelberg (2013). https://doi.org/10.1007/978-3-642-39304-4_10
10. Nguyen, S., Zhang, M., Tan, K.C.: Enhancing genetic programming based hyper-heuristics for dynamic multi-objective job shop scheduling problems. In: 2015 IEEE Congress on Evolutionary Computation (CEC), pp. 2781–2788 (2015)
11. Park, J., Mei, Y., Nguyen, S., Chen, G., Zhang, M.: An investigation of ensemble combination schemes for genetic programming based hyper-heuristic approaches to dynamic job shop scheduling. Appl. Soft Comput. **63**, 72–86 (2018)
12. Park, J., Nguyen, S., Zhang, M., Johnston, M.: Evolving ensembles of dispatching rules using genetic programming for job shop scheduling. In: Machado, P., et al. (eds.) EuroGP 2015. LNCS, vol. 9025, pp. 92–104. Springer, Cham (2015). https://doi.org/10.1007/978-3-319-16501-1_8

13. Pinedo, M.L.: Scheduling. Springer, Boston (2012). https://doi.org/10.1007/978-1-4614-2361-4
14. Đumić, M., Jakobović, D.: Ensembles of priority rules for resource constrained project scheduling problem. Appl. Soft Comput. **110**, 107606 (2021)
15. Đurasević, M., Jakobović, D.: Comparison of ensemble learning methods for creating ensembles of dispatching rules for the unrelated machines environment. Genet. Program. Evolvable Mach. **19**, 53–92 (2017). https://doi.org/10.1007/s10710-017-9302-3
16. Đurasević, M., Jakobović, D.: Evolving dispatching rules for optimising many-objective criteria in the unrelated machines environment. Genet. Program. Evolvable Mach. **19**, 9–51 (2017). https://doi.org/10.1007/s10710-017-9310-3
17. Đurasević, M., Jakobović, D.: A survey of dispatching rules for the dynamic unrelated machines environment. Exp. Syst. Appl. **113**, 555–569 (2018)
18. Đurasević, M., Jakobović, D.: Creating dispatching rules by simple ensemble combination. Journal of Heuristics **25**(6), 959–1013 (2019). https://doi.org/10.1007/s10732-019-09416-x
19. Đurasević, M., Jakobović, D., Knežević, K.: Adaptive scheduling on unrelated machines with genetic programming. Appl. Soft Comput. **48**, 419–430 (2016)
20. Zhang, F., Mei, Y., Zhang, M.: Evolving dispatching rules for multi-objective dynamic flexible job shop scheduling via genetic programming hyper-heuristics. In: 2019 IEEE Congress on Evolutionary Computation (CEC), pp. 1366–1373 (2019)

Building Heuristics and Ensembles for the Travel Salesman Problem

Francisco J. Gil-Gala[1]([⊠]), Marko Đurasević[2]([⊠]), María R. Sierra[1]([⊠]),
and Ramiro Varela[1]([⊠])

[1] Department of Computer Science, University of Oviedo, Oviedo, Spain
{giljavier,sierramaria,ramiro}@uniovi.es
[2] Faculty of Electrical Engineering and Computing, University of Zagreb,
Zagreb, Croatia
Marko.Durasevic@fer.hr

Abstract. The Travel Salesman Problem (TSP) is one of the most studied optimization problems due to its high difficulty and its practical interest. In some real-life applications of this problem the solution methods must be very efficient to deal with dynamic environments or large problem instances. For this reasons, low time consuming heuristics as priority rules are often used. Even though such a single heuristic may be good to solve many instances, it may not be robust enough to take the best decisions in all situations so, we hypothesise that an ensemble of heuristics could be much better than the best of those heuristic. We view an ensemble as a set of heuristics that collaboratively build a single solution by combining the decisions of each individual heuristic. In this paper, we study the application of single heuristics and ensembles to the TSP. The individual heuristics are evolved by Genetic Programming (GP) and then Genetic Algorithms (GA) are used to build ensembles from a pool of single heuristics. We conducted an experimental study on a set of instances taken from the TSPLIB. The results of this study provided interesting insights about the behaviour of rules and ensembles.

Keywords: Travel Salesman Problem · Heuristics · Ensembles · Hyper-heuristics

1 Introduction

Greedy algorithms guided by single heuristics are usually the best if not the only method suitable to solve large-scale problems or dynamic problems that require solutions in real-time, due to them being able to perform reasonable decisions quickly. In these situations, exact methods or even metaheuristics such as genetic algorithms are not practical because they are very time consuming. Single heuristics as priority rules are often manually designed by experts, but this is also very time consuming and may be a difficult task because the problem features that are relevant for the heuristics are not always evident to the human eye. For this reason, several hyper-heuristic methods have been exploited

© Springer Nature Switzerland AG 2022
J. M. Ferrández Vicente et al. (Eds.): IWINAC 2022, LNCS 13259, pp. 130–139, 2022.
https://doi.org/10.1007/978-3-031-06527-9_13

to automatically design heuristics for various optimization problems, such as the Job Shop Scheduling Problem [16] or the Unrelated Machines Scheduling Problem [7]. In spite of the success of these methods, it is often the case that a single heuristic is not robust enough to produce good solutions to all instances of a given benchmark set. This fact motivates the consideration of ensembles as an alternative that could outperform single heuristics at the cost of a reasonable increment in the computational burden.

Over the last years, there have been some proposals for learning ensembles. For example, Hart and Sim [13] proposed the NELLI-GP method, which is used to create ensembles for the Job Shop Scheduling Problem, where each heuristic is used to solve a particular subset of instances. A different approach was proposed by Gil-Gala et al. [10] for the scheduling problem of a single machine with time-varying capacity; in this case, each of the heuristics in an ensemble is used to solve an instance, the final result being the best of the schedules. The calculation of ensembles is modelled as a set covering problem and solved by means of a genetic algorithm. However, the most common strategy to exploit ensembles is that all the heuristics build a solution collaboratively. This is the approach considered by Durasević and Jakobović in [5], where they remarked that the main decisions that have to be taken to build ensembles are 1) how heuristics are combined and 2) how the heuristics are selected to compose the ensemble. For the first problem, some classic techniques borrowed from machine learning such as summation and voting strategies are of common use, while some methods such as greedy algorithms [4,6] or coevolutionary algorithms [4,5,17] were used for the second.

In this work, we are interested in developing ensembles for solving the Travel Salesman Problem (TSP). In our proposed method, Genetic Programming (GP) [14] is used to evolve a large pool of heuristics for solving the TSP. Then, a genetic algorithm (GA) is used to build ensembles from this pool. We conducted an experimental study across a set of instances taken from the TSPLIB[1].

The remainder of the paper is organised as follows. Firstly, we describe the method used to solve the TSP. Then, in Sect. 3 we present the proposed algorithms designed to evolve heuristics and ensembles. Next, in Sect. 4 we present the experimental analysis and the obtained results. Finally, in Sect. 5 we summarise the main conclusions and outline some ideas for future work.

2   The Travel Salesman Problem and Solving Method

We consider the symmetric Travel Salesman Problem (TSP) that is a well-known NP-hard problem. We are given a matrix $D_{N \times N}$, where d_{ij} denotes the distance between cities i and j and the goal is to obtain an optimal tour, i.e., the shortest path visiting each of N cities exactly once and returning to the starting city. Several algorithms were proposed to find tours, for example genetic algorithms or the well-known Lin-Kernighan Heuristic [15]; however, none of them is actually efficient for large instances or in dynamic environments. In these situations,

---

[1] http://comopt.ifi.uni-heidelberg.de.

greedy algorithms guided by simple priority rules are the most, if not the only, viable solution method.

In this work, we exploit a greedy algorithm that, starting from the initial city, in each iteration selects the next city by means of a priority rule. An example of such rule is the Nearest Neighbour (NN) heuristic: if i is the current city, the priority of the candidate city j is given by $1/d_{ij}$. In general, a priority rule is an arithmetic expression that assigns a priority to each unvisited city, which is calculated from the problem attributes; in the NN heuristic, the only considered attribute is the distance d_{ij}.

A good priority rule usually produces good solutions for a number of instances, but it may produce bad solutions for other instances as well. At the same time, it is clear that different rules may produce quite different solutions for the same instance. For these reasons, it is often the case that a single rule may not be robust enough to produce good solutions for all the instances in a given set. To deal with this issue, a suitable alternative may be to exploit ensembles of rules so that each decision is taken from the aggregated values of the individual rules instead from just a single rule. In this way, a number of rules work together to produce a single solution.

To aggregate the priorities from the rules in the ensemble, we may use the classic summation or voting methods, each one having their own strong and weak points. In our study, we consider the vote combination method proposed in [6], where the priorities given by the rules are normalized so that each rule assigns 1 to the city with highest priority and 0 to the remaining ones. The city with the most votes is the one chosen by the ensemble, breaking ties uniformly.

3   Building Heuristics and Ensembles

The methodology used in this paper is similar to that used in [5,6,9,12] for some scheduling problems. It consists of two steps: 1) a sufficiently large pool of heuristics, i.e., priority rules, is evolved by some hyper-heuristic, in this case Genetic Programming (GP), and 2) from this pool of heuristics, a search algorithm, in our case a Genetic Algorithm (GA), is exploited to build ensembles. In the following subsections we explain the main features of the proposed GP and GA.

3.1   Genetic Programming

Genetic Programming (GP) may be viewed as a hyper-heuristic that is widely used to evolve heuristics for optimization problems. In [2], the authors demonstrated that GP based hyper-heuristics may outperform some other machine learning techniques, such as regression or neural networks, in learning priority rules for a scheduling problem. In this study, we use a generational GP similar to the one proposed in [8], which implements the classical genetic operators proposed by John Koza [14]. They are the one-point crossover, the subtree mutation and the generation of the initial population by means of the ramped half-and-half method. In this paradigm, heuristics are encoded as expression trees [2], which are composed by terminal and function symbols. Terminals are relevant attributes of the problem and function symbols are used to combine the terminals. We have used the following set of terminals for the TSP, which are some of those proposed in [3]:

- D_{cn}: Distance from c to n.
- D_{in}: Distance from i to n.
- D_c: Distance from the centroid of the unvisited cities to n.

where c denotes the current city in the partial tour built so far, i is the initial city and n is a candidate city to be visited next.

D_c is calculated as the distance between c and the point $c\bar{n}$ (centroid of the unvisited cities after n) defined by the coordinates $x = \frac{X-x_n}{N_{rm}-1}$ and $y = \frac{Y-y_n}{N_{rm}-1}$ where N_{rn} is the number of remaining cities to visit, X and Y are the summation of x-values and y-values of the unvisited cities and x_n and y_n are the coordinates of n.

These terminals can be evaluated in $O(1)$, as it is demonstrated in the above work. To do that, X and Y are initialized with the summation of x-values and y-values of the N cities and, when a city is visited, X and Y are updated by subtracting the coordinates of the last visited city.

The function set is the same used in [11] for a scheduling problem of a single machine with time-varying capacity. Additionally, the proposed alphabet includes some numeric constants. The whole set of symbols is summarised in Table 1.

Table 1. Function and terminal sets used to build expression trees. Symbol "-" is considered in unitary and binary versions. max_0 and min_0 return the maximum and minimum of an expression and 0.

Binary functions		+	/	×	max	min	
Unitary functions	-	pow_2	$sqrt$	exp	ln	max_0	min_0
Terminals	Dcn	Din	Dc				
Numeric constants	0.1	0.2	...	0.8	0.9	1.0	

3.2   The Genetic Algorithm

To represent ensembles of maximum size P, we encode a chromosome by a permutation with repetition of heuristics taken P at a time from the pool evolved by GP. Figure 1 shows an example with 3 rules, all of them are different in this case. We consider a generational strategy, similar to that used in [12], with random selection and replacement by tournament among every two mated parents and their two offspring. The initial chromosomes are random variations of heuristics taken uniformly from the pool. As in [12], we use one point crossover and a mutation operator that changes randomly a number of heuristics between 1 and $P/2$ in the chromosome.

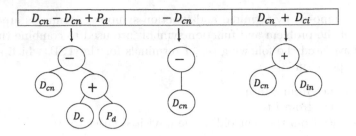

Fig. 1. An example of ensemble composed of three rules. Each rule is represented by the arithmetical expression in each array position.

3.3   The GP and GA Fitness Functions

In both algorithms, GP and GA, the evaluation of a chromosome involves solving a *training set* composed by a number of TSP instances. These instances are solved by each candidate rule in GP and by each candidate ensemble in GA. Therefore, the fitness function calculates the sum of distances produced by all tours created by a heuristic or an ensemble and returns the inverse of this value.

Note that each time a priority must be calculated, the entire tree encoding the heuristic must be traversed to compute the specific values for each terminal. Moreover, ensembles must perform this process with each heuristic and then compute a single priority for each unvisited city. Therefore, we opted to cache all evaluated chromosomes to prevent GP and GA from repeated evaluation.

4   Experimental Study

We conducted an experimental study to analyse the components of the proposed method. To this aim, we implemented a prototype in Java 8 and ran a series of experiments distributed into a Linux machine Dell PowerEdge R740: 2 x Intel Xeon Gold 6132 (2.6 GHz, 28 cores) and 128 GB. The common termination criterion is given by 100 generations, and each configuration of GP and GA is executed 30 times. Additionally, we establish a day (1440 min) as the run-time limit for each execution.

4.1   Preliminaries

The TSPLIB is one of the most used sets of instances to validate solvers for the TSP. We considered the same instances as in [3], 112 in all, but removed those that are not of type EDGE_WEIGTH_TYPE = EUC_2D; so there are 78 left. We select the same 21 instances from them to compose the test set as in [3]. They used another set of 49 instances randomly selected from the remaining instances for training in their genetic program, termed GP-HH, which was parametrised with a population of 200 individuals, 100 generations as termination criterion and a maximum depth of trees of 17. Table 2 summarises the results achieved by heuristics calculated by the GP-HH when solving the test set. As we can see, heuristics evolved by the GP-HH clearly achieves much better results than simple classical heuristics such as Nearest neighbour and Nearest insertion.

Table 2. Average distances produced when solving the test set by some classical heuristic (Nearest neighbour and Nearest insertion) and evolved by the GP-HH proposed in [3].

GP-HH best	Nearest neighbour	Nearest insertion
69705.97	73549.30	73492.49

In this work, our GP approach uses a population size of 200 individuals and crossover and mutation probabilities of 100% and 2%, respectively, which are similar to those reported in [8], the stopping condition and population size are the same as used by the GP-HH in [3]. However, the maximum depth of trees $\mathcal{D}$ that we use is much smaller, being $\mathcal{D} = 8$ instead of $\mathcal{D} = 17$. On the other hand, our terminal set comprises of only three instead of the seven terminals used in [3]. Table 3 shows the run-time (in seconds) necessary for solving the instances berlin52, lin318 and pr2392 with 200 random heuristics generated with $\mathcal{D}$ taken values 4, 8 and 12. As it is observed, the execution time of GP is directly related to the number of cities and the number of symbols in the heuristics.

Table 3. Time (in seconds) for solving three instances with three heuristics of different sizes. These instances have 52, 318 and 2392 cities, respectively. It also reports the average sizes of those heuristics.

	Time (sec.)			Avg. Size
$\mathcal{D}$	berlin52	lin318	pr2392	of heuristics
4	0.12	1.24	64.57	6.93
8	0.38	11.42	645.93	51.89
12	10.84	176.34	9980.31	493.38

In view of the results, we note that our target machine is not powerful enough to execute our GP implementation with large $\mathcal{D}$ values and number of cities. Taking into account that the evaluation of ensembles is much more costly than the evaluation of single heuristics, the GA is parametrised with the population size of 100 individuals and the crossover and mutation probabilities of 80% and 20%, respectively, which correspond to the values used in [12]. We restricted these experiments to construct ensembles composed of 3 heuristics and the stopping condition of 50 generations.

For all the above reasons, in the following experiments, we have limited the number of instances in the training set and the maximum sizes of heuristics for obtaining the results in a reasonable time. The training sets proposed were composed by selecting a maximum number of instances N with less number of cities The instances were picked from the set of 78 instances, disregarding the 21 instances (with a total of 11757 cities) used for testing. Additionally, we removed 8 instances with more than 4000 cities, resulting in a total of 49 instances with a number of cities between 52 (berlin52.tsp) and 3795 (fl3795.tsp), which sum up to a total of 37303 cities. The training sets are summarized in Table 4.

Table 4. The seven training sets proposed that are composed by the N instances with less number of cities.

	Number of cities
N	Cities
7	574
14	1391
21	2595
28	4722
35	10454
42	19756
49	37303

4.2   Results

Table 5 shows the results achieved by heuristics evolved by GP when solving the training and test sets. We observe that when the whole training set is used ($N = 49$), the time taken by GP is prohibitive even though it evaluates half different chromosomes than the other combinations, due to the stopping condition is given by 1440 min execution, which happens before completing 100 generations. When N takes values 7 and 49, training sets with the smallest and largest number of cities respectively, the results in test are worse than other training sets, such as when N takes values 21 and 42, training sets with the best results in test. Specifically, with $N = 42$ the heuristics are better than those calculated by [3]. Furthermore, our GP approach uses fewer training instances, fewer terminals to compose heuristics and smaller maximum size. Thus, we can conclude that our GP approach is able to achieve similar results as GP-HH, but evolving simpler heuristics. From our point of view, the high standard deviation (SD) in the test set with all settings is indicative of the stochastic nature of GP and provides motivation to use more robust methods like ensembles.

To build ensembles, we recorded all heuristics of the last population in each GP execution. Therefore, a total of 6000 heuristics (200 individuals and 30 executions) were collected from each training set. With the seven sets of heuristics,

Table 5. Results achieved by the best **heuristic** evolved in each execution of GP using seven training sets. Results with $N = 49$ are got before complete 100 generations.

	Training			Test			Time	
N	Best	Avg.	SD	Best	Avg.	SD	(min)	Dif.
7	27993.56	28350.12	5038.23	69454.45	71322.78	13087.45	2.80	15434.67
14	35672.09	36262.86	6532.08	68829.59	70295.88	12660.79	8.62	15815.00
21	34398.35	34900.26	6372.18	69527.13	69993.02	12550.59	19.02	15468.60
28	31901.50	32332.86	5756.63	69277.89	70149.60	12841.70	55.42	15499.37
35	52672.88	53312.92	9550.57	69262.11	70190.18	12772.45	317.24	15262.13
42	67907.92	68480.39	12275.50	**68757.23**	**69579.94**	12422.91	976.42	15377.30
49	88598.57	89176.15	15966.83	68900.89	70035.29	12605.37	1440.00	7178.10

Table 6. Results achieved by the best **ensemble** evolved in each execution of GA using seven training sets and focusing on three as the size of ensembles.

	Training			Test			Time	
N	Best	Avg.	SD	Best	Avg.	SD	(min)	Dif.
7	27873.02	28014.24	47.48	69373.19	70445.39	711.62	2.05	2804.17
14	35433.68	35575.04	63.88	69361.87	69940.64	204.93	6.19	2972.60
21	34192.74	34324.42	60.16	69516.05	69848.49	234.67	14.61	2965.13
28	31677.43	31787.73	60.21	69171.82	69831.51	403.42	44.41	3040.57
35	52295.07	52430.72	83.70	68830.68	69835.40	524.95	253.81	3041.53
42	67475.08	67672.47	100.91	68966.14	69567.59	343.50	778.44	2992.97
49	87679.24	87984.75	114.64	**68587.06**	**69493.56**	429.87	1440.00	1639.20

we generated a large pool of heuristics to build ensembles. After eliminating duplicate heuristics (those syntactically equal), 35 296 heuristics compose the set used for building ensembles.

Finally, to assess the viability of ensembles we executed the GA to build ensembles of size 3. The results are summarized in Table 6 and Fig. 2. From our point of view, ensembles are more robust than single heuristics since they are always perform better on average and show lower standard deviation when using the same training set, especially for the smaller sets. However, the best solutions are achieved by single heuristics in some cases. Additionally, there is a considerable gap between the best and average solutions in the test set which motivates further experimentation with alternative combination methods and ensemble sizes, which can help to better predict the behaviour in the test set.

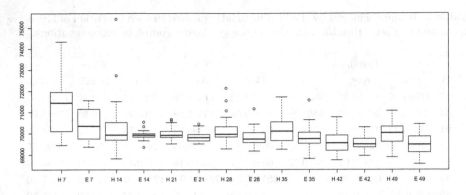

Fig. 2. Boxplots obtained from the results reached on the test set by the heuristics and ensembles evolved from the 7 training sets.

5   Conclusions and Future Work

We have seen that Genetic Programming is a suitable hyper-heuristic to evolve priority rules to solve the TSP that perform better than classic heuristics, as Nearest Neighbour or Nearest Insertion, designed by experts. Even though this is not new, in our experiments we obtained heuristics that are simpler than previous heuristics obtained by other GP implementations. But the main conclusion we may draw from our study is that ensembles obtained combining just a few heuristics (3 in our experiments) are able to improve the results from the best heuristic working alone. At the same time, we consider that there is still room for ensembles to improve. To this end, we will try to devise new methods to exploit them more efficiently.

Acknowledgements. This research has been supported by the Spanish State Agency for Research (AEI) under research project PID2019-106263RB-I00, and by the Croatian Science Foundation under the project IP-2019-04-4333.

References

1. TSP Test Data. http://www.math.uwaterloo.ca/tsp/data/index.html. Accessed 1 Feb 2021
2. Branke, J., Hildebrandt, T., Scholz-Reiter, B.: Hyper-heuristic evolution of dispatching rules: a comparison of rule representations. Evol. Comput. **23**(2), 249–277 (2015)
3. Duflo, G., Kieffer, E., Brust, M.R., Danoy, G., Bouvry, P.: A GP hyper-heuristic approach for generating TSP heuristics. In: IEEE International Parallel and Distributed Processing Symposium Workshops, IPDPSW 2019, pp. 521–529 (2019)
4. Đumić, M., Jakobović, D.: Ensembles of priority rules for resource constrained project scheduling problem. Appl. Soft Comput. **110**, 107606 (2021)

5. Đurasević, M., Jakobović, D.: Comparison of ensemble learning methods for creating ensembles of dispatching rules for the unrelated machines environment. Genet. Program. Evolvable Mach. **19**, 53–92 (2017). https://doi.org/10.1007/s10710-017-9302-3

6. Đurasević, M., Jakobović, D.: Creating dispatching rules by simple ensemble combination. J. Heuristics **25**, 959–1013 (2019)

7. Đurasević, M., Jakobović, D., Knežević, K.: Adaptive scheduling on unrelated machines with genetic programming. Appl. Soft Comput. **48**, 419–430 (2016)

8. Gil-Gala, F.J., Mencía, C., Sierra, M.R., Varela, R.: Evolving priority rules for on-line scheduling of jobs on a single machine with variable capacity over time. Appl. Soft Comput. **85**, 105782 (2019)

9. Gil-Gala, F.J., Mencía, C., Sierra, M.R., Varela, R.: Learning ensembles of priority rules for on-line scheduling by hybrid evolutionary algorithm. Integr. Comput. Aided Eng. **28**(1), 65–80 (2021)

10. Gil-Gala, F.J., Sierra, M.R., Mencía, C., Varela, R.: Combining hyper-heuristics to evolve ensembles of priority rules for on-line scheduling. Nat. Comput., 1–11 (2020). https://doi.org/10.1007/s11047-020-09793-4

11. Gil-Gala, F.J., Sierra, M.R., Mencía, C., Varela, R.: Genetic programming with local search to evolve priority rules for scheduling jobs on a machine with time-varying capacity. Swarm Evol. Comput. **66**, 100944 (2021). https://doi.org/10.1016/j.swevo.2021.100944

12. Gil-Gala, F.J., Varela, R.: Genetic algorithm to evolve ensembles of rules for on-line scheduling on single machine with variable capacity. In: Ferrández Vicente, J.M., Álvarez-Sánchez, J.R., de la Paz López, F., Toledo Moreo, J., Adeli, H. (eds.) IWINAC 2019. LNCS, vol. 11487, pp. 223–233. Springer, Cham (2019). https://doi.org/10.1007/978-3-030-19651-6_22

13. Hart, E., Sim, K.: A hyper-heuristic ensemble method for static job-shop scheduling. Evol. Comput. **24**(4), 609–635 (2016)

14. Koza, J.R.: Genetic Programming: On the Programming of Computers by Means of Natural Selection. MIT Press (1992)

15. McMenemy, P., Veerapen, N., Adair, J., Ochoa, G.: Rigorous performance analysis of state-of-the-art TSP heuristic solvers. In: Liefooghe, A., Paquete, L. (eds.) EvoCOP 2019. LNCS, vol. 11452, pp. 99–114. Springer, Cham (2019). https://doi.org/10.1007/978-3-030-16711-0_7

16. Nguyen, S., Mei, Y., Xue, B., Zhang, M.: A hybrid genetic programming algorithm for automated design of dispatching rules. Evol. Comput. **27**(3), 467–496 (2019)

17. Park, J., Mei, Y., Nguyen, S., Chen, G., Johnston, M., Zhang, M.: Genetic programming based hyper-heuristics for dynamic job shop scheduling: cooperative coevolutionary approaches. In: Heywood, M.I., McDermott, J., Castelli, M., Costa, E., Sim, K. (eds.) EuroGP 2016. LNCS, vol. 9594, pp. 115–132. Springer, Cham (2016). https://doi.org/10.1007/978-3-319-30668-1_8

18. Park, J., Mei, Y., Nguyen, S., Chen, G., Zhang, M.: An investigation of ensemble combination schemes for genetic programming based hyper-heuristic approaches to dynamic job shop scheduling. Appl. Soft Comput. **63**, 72–86 (2018)

Reducing Energy Consumption in Fuzzy Flexible Job Shops Using Memetic Search

Pablo García Gómez[1][(✉)] [iD], Inés González-Rodríguez[1] [iD],
and Camino R. Vela[2] [iD]

[1] Universidad de Cantabria, Santander, Spain
{pablo.garciagomez,gonzalezri}@unican.es
[2] Universidad de Oviedo, Oviedo, Spain
crvela@uniovi.es

Abstract. The flexible job shop is a problem that has attracted much research attention both because of its importance in manufacturing processes and its computational complexity. However, industry is a highly complex environment that is constantly changing, and models and solving methods need to evolve and become richer to stay relevant. A source of complexity is the uncertainty in some parameters, in this work it is incorporated by modeling processing time using triangular fuzzy numbers. We also introduce the objective of reducing energy consumption, motivated by the fight against global warming. To solve the problem, we propose a memetic algorithm, a hybrid method that combines global search with local search. We have put a special focus on the neighborhood functions used to guide the local search since they are key for correct intensification. To assess the performance of the proposed method, we present an experimental analysis that compares the memetic algorithm to a powerful constraint programming solver, and we analyze how the proposed neighborhood functions contribute to increasing the search power of our method.

Keywords: Flexible job shop scheduling · Energy consumption ·
Fuzzy numbers · Memetic algorithm · Neighborhood

1 Introduction

Scheduling has always been a critical problem for most industrial processes, however, the objective has been evolving since the earliest days of industrialization to the present. Historically, the objective was minimizing the maximum completion time, usually known as the makespan, and while it is still relevant it has increasingly been replaced by other production-related measures such as tardiness, as a response to the relocation of factories to different countries. Nowadays the trend is changing again due to newer laws and regulations that seek a reduction in emissions as a countermeasure to global warming. The objective function we propose is framed in this new kind of measures.

© Springer Nature Switzerland AG 2022
J. M. Ferrández Vicente et al. (Eds.): IWINAC 2022, LNCS 13259, pp. 140–150, 2022.
https://doi.org/10.1007/978-3-031-06527-9_14

As the base problem, we use the flexible job shop scheduling problem (FJSP) that tries to model in a generic way problems that consist in planning the execution of a series of operations on a finite set of resources. In order to increase real-life fidelity, we add uncertainty in the processing time of operations, modeling it using triangular fuzzy numbers. This should help to obtain more robust solutions as they consider the whole range of possible events [15].

Even simpler variants of the job shop problem are NP-Hard problems [9] and therefore intractable with exact algorithms. Hence we will make use of metaheuristics in order to find good solutions in a reasonable time. We propose a memetic algorithm that combines an evolutionary method with a tabu search that employs some new neighborhood functions with an emphasis on reducing energy consumption.

Although energy consumption in scheduling problems is a relatively new topic, several papers already can be found in the literature. They can be organized into three different non-exclusive high-level approaches.

The first one consists in scheduling the operations in such a way that the sum of the energy when the resources are processing and where they are kept idle is as low as possible. In [11] a genetic algorithm based on NSGA-II is proposed to solve the job shop minimizing the total electricity consumption and total weighted tardiness. This work is improved in [7] introducing additional components to help the search. In [12] the model is further extended with the addition of crane transportation between machines.

The second approach consists in allowing to turn on and off the resources more than once. This way, if a resource is going to be idle for a long time it can be turned off and the extra energy used in the starting-up process may be compensated with the savings during the off period. This approach is taken in [10], where the model and method from [11] are extended to allow for switching on and off the resources. This is also the energy model in [2], where new job arrivals are considered and a backtracking search algorithm is proposed.

The third approach consists in slowing down resources so that they consume less energy at the cost of taking longer to process the operations. In [18] a multi-objective genetic algorithm incorporated with two problem-specific local improvement strategies is used to reduce total weighted tardiness together with energy consumption in a job shop problem. In [8] the authors consider a job shop with flexibility and they use a shuffled frog-leaping algorithm to reduce total energy consumption and workload.

The choice of one framework over the others depends on the problem under consideration. In [17] all of them are combined in a flexible job shop and a non-dominated sorted genetic algorithm is used to optimize the makespan, the energy consumption and the number of times resources are turned on/off simultaneously.

To this point, all references are for the deterministic case, considering both energy and uncertainty literature is even more scarce. In [16] the authors propose an evolutionary algorithm to reduce the non-processing energy and the total weighted tardiness, and in [1] a memetic algorithm is proposed to minimize the non-processing energy and the makespan.

The main contributions of this paper are the definition of a model to reduce the energy consumption in the fuzzy flexible job shop (FFJSP) and dealing with the issues introduced with uncertainty, together with the definition of the neighborhood structures to improve solutions in a local search procedure.

The rest of the paper is organized as follows. Section 2 formally defines the problem. Section 3 describes the proposed algorithm. In Sect. 4 we report and analyze the experimental results to evaluate the potential of our proposal. Finally, Sect. 5 presents some conclusions.

2   Problem Formulation

The job shop scheduling problem consists in scheduling a set $\mathcal{O}$ of operations (also called tasks) in a set $\mathcal{R}$ of m resources (also called machines) subject to a set of constraints. Operations are organized in a set $\mathcal{J}$ of n jobs, so operations within a job must be sequentially scheduled. Given an operation $o \in \mathcal{O}$, the job to which it belongs is denoted by $\chi_o \in \mathcal{J}$ and the position in which it has to be executed relative to this job is denoted by η_o. The total number of operations in a job j is n_j. There are also capacity constraints, by which each operation requires the uninterrupted and exclusive use of one of the resources for its whole processing time. An operation $o \in \mathcal{O}$ may be executed in any resource from a given set $\mathcal{R}_o \subseteq \mathcal{R}$ and its processing time p_{or} depends on the resource $r \in \mathcal{R}_o$ where it is executed.

We model processing times as triangular fuzzy numbers (TFNs), a particular type of fuzzy numbers [4], with an interval $[a^1, a^3]$ of possible values and a modal value a^2. A TFN can be represented as $a = (a^1, a^2, a^3)$ and its membership function is given by the following expression:

$$\mu_a(x) = \begin{cases} \frac{x-a^1}{a^2-a^1} & a^1 \leq x \leq a^2 \\ \frac{x-a^3}{a^2-a^3} & a^2 \leq x \leq a^3 \\ 0 & x < a^1 \vee a^3 < x \end{cases}$$

For our problem, we need two arithmetic operations, the sum and the maximum. Both operations can be obtained using the extension principle but, unfortunately, the set of TFNs is not closed under the maximum and for this reason we rely on an approximation. This way, the sum of two TFNs a and b is defined as $a+b = (a^1+b^1, a^2+b^2, a^3+b^3)$ and the maximum is approximated as $\max(a, b) \approx (\max(a^1, b^1), \max(a^2, b^2), \max(a^3, b^3))$.

As there exists no natural relation of total order for TFNs, we have to turn to some ranking method. Here, we will use a ranking based on the expected value of TFNs, so $a \leq_E b$ iff $E[a] \leq E[b]$, where $E[a] = \frac{a^1+2a^2+a^3}{4}$.

A solution $(\boldsymbol{\tau}, \mathbf{s})$ to the problem (also called schedule) consists of both a resource assignment $\boldsymbol{\tau}$ and starting time assignment $\mathbf{s}$ to all operations. A solution is said to be feasible if all constraints hold. More formally, let τ_o be the resource assigned to operation $o \in \mathcal{O}$ in this solution and s_o and $c_o = s_o + p_{o\tau_o}$

be its starting and completion times respectively. Then, precedence constraints hold if $\forall i\, c_a^i \leq s_b^i$ when $\eta_a < \eta_b, \chi_a = \chi_b$ and capacity constraints hold if $\forall i\, c_a^i \leq s_b^i \vee \forall i\, c_b^i \leq s_a^i$ when $\tau_a = \tau_b$, for any operation $a, b \in \mathcal{O}$. Notice that the starting time assignment induces a global operation processing order σ and a resource operation processing order δ_r for every $r \in \mathcal{R}$. The position of operation o in σ is denoted by σ_o and the position in which operation o is executed in resource τ_o is denoted by δ_o.

For a feasible solution, the makespan is defined as $C_{max} = \max_{j \in \mathcal{J}} C_j$ where $C_j = c_o$ such that $\chi_o = j, \eta_o = n_j$, denotes the completion time of job j.

To this base problem, we add the concept of energy consumption. We consider two types of energy: active energy and passive energy. Passive energy PE_r is intrinsic to each resource $r \in \mathcal{R}$ and can only be reduced by turning them off. It is the product of the passive power consumption of the resource PP_r and the time it is on. We consider that all resources are turned on at the same time (at instant 0) and turned off when all operations are completed, i.e., resources are on for the entire duration of the makespan. Thus, $PE_r = PP_r C_{max}$. Active energy AE_{or} depends on the power AP_{or} required to execute an operation o in a resource r. This way, $AE_{or} = AP_{or} p_{or}$. Our model is an additive model so the total energy consumption of a resource E_r is the result of summing up the passive energy and the active energy $E_r = PE_r + \sum_{o \in \mathcal{O}, \tau_o = r} AE_{or}$. Given these definitions, the total energy consumption is $E = \sum_{r \in \mathcal{R}} E_r$.

This energy function is equivalent to the first approach we explained in the introduction but it is formulated in a different way. Usually, the states of the resources are disjoint and they can contribute to either the processing energy (the energy consumed when they are executing) or the non-processing energy (the energy consumed when they are idle). However, in the fuzzy job shop this means calculating the idle times of resources, i.e., the time span between the end of an operation and the start of the next one in the same resource, which due to the fact that fuzzy subtraction assumes that ill-known numbers are not interactive, some undesired uncertainty may be introduced. For this reason, inspired by energy models used to reduce energy consumption in data centers, we make use of overlapping states, i.e., an additive model where the two involved energies are aggregated.

3   Memetic Algorithm

To solve the problem we use a memetic algorithm, a hybrid algorithm that combines an evolutionary algorithm with local search, taking advantage of the synergies between both methods.

The evolutionary algorithm is composed of a population of solutions that, in each iteration, is replaced by a new one obtained by combining its individuals. To do so, individuals are randomly matched, giving everyone an equal chance to reproduce, and each pair is combined by means of a crossover operator that generates two offspring. The new population is generated by a tournament such that the best two from each pair of parents and their two offspring are chosen. To encode the solutions, we use the tuple of sequences (τ, σ) and to decode them, we assign to each operation the earliest starting time such that the order defined by σ is not altered. To ensure enough diversity the initial population is generated randomly. A key component here is the crossover operator. We use the extension of the Generalized Order Crossover (GOX) proposed in [5]. Because we use a tournament, this operator is applied unconditionally. We do not make use of any mutation operators because it is incorporated in the local search explained below.

The other component of the memetic algorithm is the local search. In our proposal, offspring generated at each iteration of the evolutionary algorithm are improved using tabu search before the tournament is applied. Tabu search is a local search algorithm that keeps a memory structure, called tabu list, where it stores a trace of the recently visited search space. In particular, to avoid undoing recently made moves, we store in the tabu list the inverse of the moves performed to obtain the neighbors. Our tabu list has a dynamic size, similar to the one introduced in [3], so the size of the list can vary between a lower and an upper bound. When the selected neighbor is worse (resp. better) than the current solution and the upper (resp. lower) bound has not been reached, the list's size increases (resp. decreases) in one unit. If the selected neighbor is the best solution found so far, the list is cleared; this is similar to restarting the search from this solution. We also incorporate an aspiration criterion, so a tabu move can be executed if it improves the best solution found up to this moment. In the rare situation that all neighbors are tabu, we choose the best one, clear the tabu list and slightly change its bounds by picking a random number within a given range.

The neighborhood function is the key component of any local search. In order to describe it we have to introduce some notation. Given a solution $\phi = (\tau, \sigma)$, for an operation o, let JP_o (resp. JS_o) denote its predecessor (resp. successor) in its job, $RP_o(\phi)$ (resp. $RS_o(\phi)$) its predecessor (resp. successor) in its resource and $p_o(\phi)$ its processing time in the resource it is assigned to. Its head $h_o(\phi)$ is its earliest starting time, $h_o(\phi) = \max\{h_{JP_o}(\phi) + p_{JP_o}(\phi), h_{RP_o(\phi)}(\phi) + p_{RP_o(\phi)}(\phi)\}$ with $h_o(\phi) = (0, 0, 0)$ if o has no predecessors, and its tail $q_o(\phi)$ is the time left after o has been processed until all other operations are completed, $q_o(\phi) = \max\{q_{JS_o}(\phi) + p_{JS_o}(\phi), q_{RS_o(\phi)}(\phi) + p_{RS_o(\phi)}(\phi)\}$ with $q_o(\phi) = (0, 0, 0)$ if o has no successors. An operation o is said to be makespan-critical in a solution ϕ if there exists a component i of the fuzzy makespan such that $C_{max}^i = (h_o(\phi) + p_o(\phi) + q_o(\phi))^i$. A makespan-critical block for a component i is a maximal sequence B of operations all requiring the same resource, such that no pair of consecutive operations belong to the same job and where every operation meets $C_{max}^i = (h_o(\phi) + p_o(\phi) + q_o(\phi))^i$.

As our energy function is the addition of two different components, the passive energy and the active energy, we can as well differentiate between two types of neighborhoods.

To reduce passive energy consumption we have to reduce the time the resources are active and to do so we have to reduce the makespan. A neighbor can only improve in terms of makespan, and thus passive energy consumption, if there is some change in makespan-critical operations. Also, if a neighbor is obtained by exchanging the position of two consecutive operations, it can be proved that it can only improve in terms of makespan if the operations lie at the extreme of a makespan-critical block.

This motivates the definition of a neighborhood function for passive energy that is the union of two smaller ones, one that acts on the assigned resources (N_{MCORR}) based on [6] and one that acts on the order of the operations (N_{MCET}) based on [13].

Definition 1. Makespan-critical operation resource reassignment neighborhood (N_{MCORR}). *For a feasible solution $\phi = (\tau, \sigma)$, let $\tau_{(o,r)}$ denote the assignment that results from reassigning operation o to resource r. Then:*

$$N_{MCORR}(\phi) = \{(\tau_{(o,r)}, \sigma) : o \text{ is makespan-critical}, r \in \mathcal{R}_o, r \neq \tau_o\}$$

Definition 2. Makespan-critical end transpose neighborhood (N_{MCET}). *For a feasible solution $\phi = (\tau, \sigma)$, let $\sigma_{(u,v)}$ denote the operation processing order that results from inverting the positions of operations u and v in the same resource. Then:*

$$N_{MCET}(\phi) = \{(\tau, \sigma_{(u,v)}) : u, v \text{ are at the extreme of a makespan-critical block}\}$$

As for active energy consumption, it can only be reduced by moving operations to a more power-efficient resource.

Definition 3. Operation power-efficient resource reassignment neighborhood (N_{OPERR}). *For a feasible solution $\phi = (\tau, \sigma)$, let $\tau_{(o,r)}$ denote the assignment that results from reassigning operation o to resource r. Then:*

$$N_{OPERR}(\phi) = \{(\tau_{(o,r)}, \sigma) : r \in \mathcal{R}_o, r \neq \tau_o, AE_{or} < AE_{\sigma\tau_s}\}$$

The complete neighborhood is the union of the neighborhoods for reducing passive energy N_{MCET} and N_{MCORR} with the neighborhood for reducing active energy N_{OPERR}. It is worth mentioning that, although we have designed N_{MCORR} and N_{OPERR} to reduce one type of energy, they can also alter the other because they move operations between resources. Moreover, there can exist some overlapping between them, i.e., there may be repeated neighbors, that should be removed not to increase execution time. On the other hand, N_{MCET} can only alter passive energy. Later we will make an analysis of how each perturbation affects the search.

As neighbor evaluation is the most time-consuming part of the local search, we make use of a filtering mechanism to discard uninteresting solutions. This mechanism consists in evaluating the neighbors following the order defined by a lower bound, and stopping as soon as this lower bound is bigger than the exact value of any of the already evaluated solutions. We integrated the lower bound described in [5] in our objective function.

4   Experimental Results

To compare the performance of the proposed algorithm we have used the instances proposed in [14] for a fuzzy flexible job shop. As it is usual in benchmark instances, we have completed the missing power consumption values with random values [2]. For passive power we have taken a value in [80, 120] and for active power we have taken [1.5, 2.5] times the passive power.

The experimental analysis is organized as follows. Since the problem definition is new to this work, there are no previous methods or results available for direct comparisons. In consequence, we first present a comparison between our metaheuristic algorithm and those obtained by CP Optimizer, a commercial software developed by IBM known for its outstanding performance in scheduling problems. Then we analyze the effect of the different defined neighborhoods to assess the benefit of combining all of them in the local search.

All results have been obtained in a Linux machine with two Intel Xeon Gold 6132 processors without Hyper-Threading (14 cores/14 threads) and 128 GB RAM using a parallelized implementation of the algorithm in Rust. The source code together with detailed results and benchmark instances can be found at https://pablogarciagomez.com/research

In CP Optimizer we have set a limit of 12 h of real computing time per instance. This limit has been reached in all cases so the solver has returned a lower bound and the best solution found. In the memetic algorithm, after doing a preliminary experimental study, the parameters of the algorithm were set as follows: population size, 100; stopping criterion for the memetic algorithm, 20 iterations without improvement or an average quality of the population equal to the best solution; stopping criterion for the tabu search, 400 iterations without improvement; tabu list lower bound between [20, 30] and tabu list upper bound between [50, 60].

In Table 1 we can see the relative difference between the best and average expected value of the energy obtained by our metaheuristic and the lower bound obtained with CP Optimizer. We also include the relative difference between the best energy found by CP Optimizer and its lower bound. Moreover, we report the time spent by the memetic algorithm in each instance. Our algorithm surpasses CP Optimizer in 11 of the 12 instances and it not only obtains better solutions, but it does so in much less time. In addition, in order to assess that the improvement of our algorithm over CP Optimizer is statistically significant, we have performed Wilcoxon signed-rank test.

To evaluate the performance of the different neighborhoods, we compare the results of executing the memetic algorithm using any possible combination of N_{MCET}, N_{MCORR} and N_{OPERR} as neighborhood in the tabu search. Comparing different neighborhoods can be a tricky task because they can have different characteristics and requisites. In our case, we have opted for only changing neighborhoods and keeping other parameters constant. As we use a dynamic stopping criterion for the tabu search, if one of the neighborhoods happens to be slower to converge, it will be able to use more time while it keeps into the allowed range.

Table 1. Comparison with CP Optimizer

instance	cp optimizer		memetic algorithm			
	lower bound	best(%)	mean(%)	best(%)	real time(s)	cpu time(s)
07a	4827850	9.28	9.08	8.62	39.73	811.93
08a	3771185	16.05	15.21	14.72	58.00	1193.80
09a	3902771	20.01	17.97	17.25	131.60	2689.13
10a	4626061	9.73	9.54	9.04	32.60	670.83
11a	4059000	17.02	15.68	15.10	59.33	1227.27
12a	3572763	20.58	18.72	18.05	107.47	2210.07
13a	6303917	9.27	9.71	9.31	62.90	1324.37
14a	5517284	19.33	17.85	17.28	125.17	2640.53
15a	4668937	23.74	22.62	21.91	254.53	5352.83
16a	5933312	9.84	9.76	9.46	64.47	1363.60
17a	4916945	20.08	18.12	17.57	117.17	2474.97
18a	4731626	23.09	22.02	21.31	219.33	4623.97

To ensure this comparison was fair, after a first execution with the default parameters, we make another one, substantially increasing the stopping criterion. As, by doing this, execution time did not increase significantly, we can conclude that the original dynamic stopping criterion was not halting the search prematurely.

In Fig. 1 we can see the relative difference between the lower bound obtained with CP-Optimizer and the result obtained with the different combinations of neighborhoods. We can conclude that N_{MCORR} is the best standalone neighborhood and this can be explained by looking at the properties of the movements performed by each one. Using N_{MCET} alone only optimizes passive energy because it does not change resource assignment. On the other hand, although N_{MCORR} was designed to reduce passive energy consumption, as it moves operations from one resource to another and the tabu search takes the best not forbidden neighbor, at a side effect it also reduces active energy, but only for a subset of all operations. In the case of N_{OPERR}, it can also reduce the passive energy of a solution, but when used alone it is very limited, as it only finds the most efficient resource for operations. By looking at the graph, it is also clear that the complete neighborhood gives the best results. Although in some instances it is surpassed by other combinations, the Wilcoxon signed-rank test confirms its better performance.

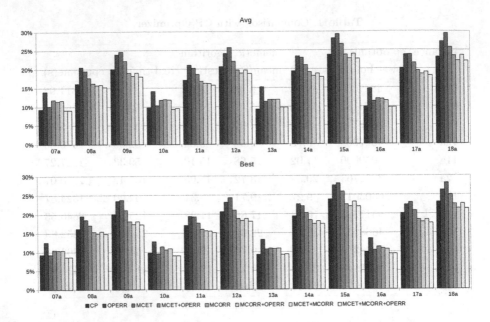

Fig. 1. Comparison between neighborhood functions

5   Conclusions

In this work, we have considered energy consumption minimization in a flexible job shop scheduling problem. The proposed model is based on existing literature for the flexible job shop and the energy function has been built with the objective of fitting into existing proposals both in terms of local search neighborhoods and evolutionary algorithm operators. We have incorporated uncertainty in the problem by considering the processing time of the operations as triangular fuzzy numbers. This way we are solving a problem more similar to real-life situations and improving its applicability. As for the solving method, we have proposed a memetic algorithm, but our focus has been on the neighborhood functions because they determine the intensification power of the local search, the key factor to find the best solutions in the explored search space.

We have carried out an experimental analysis, not only to compare our proposal with a commercial solver in order to check its good performance but also to check how the combination of the different neighborhood functions allows achieving better results.

References

1. Afsar, S., Palacios, J.J., Puente, J., Vela, C.R., González-Rodríguez, I.: Multi-objective enhanced memetic algorithm for green job shop scheduling with uncertain times. Swarm Evol. Comput. **68**, 101016 (2022). https://doi.org/10.1016/j.swevo.2021.101016

2. Caldeira, R.H., Gnanavelbabu, A., Vaidyanathan, T.: An effective backtracking search algorithm for multi-objective flexible job shop scheduling considering new job arrivals and energy consumption. Comput. Ind. Eng. **149**, 106863 (2020). https://doi.org/10.1016/j.cie.2020.106863
3. Dell'Amico, M., Trubian, M.: Applying tabu search to the job-shop scheduling problem. Ann. Oper. Res. **41**(3), 231–252 (1993). https://doi.org/10.1007/bf02023076
4. Dubois, D., Prade, H.: Fuzzy numbers: an overview. In: Readings in Fuzzy Sets for Intelligent Systems, pp. 112–148. Elsevier (1993). https://doi.org/10.1016/b978-1-4832-1450-4.50015-8
5. García Gómez, P., Vela, C.R., González-Rodríguez, I.: A memetic algorithm to minimize the total weighted tardiness in the fuzzy flexible job shop. In: Proceedings of the 19th Conference of the Spanish Association for Artificial Intelligence, CAEPIA 2020/2021, 22–24 September 2021, Málaga, Spain (2021)
6. González, M.A., Vela, C.R., Varela, R.: An efficient memetic algorithm for the flexible job shop with setup times. In: Proceedings of the 23rd International Conference on Automated Planning and Scheduling, ICAPS 2013, 10–14 June 2013, Rome, Italy. AAAI (2013)
7. González, M.Á., Oddi, A., Rasconi, R.: Multi-objective optimization in a job shop with energy costs through hybrid evolutionary techniques. In: Proceedings of the 27th International Conference on Automated Planning and Scheduling, ICAPS 2017, 18–23 June 2017, Pittsburgh, Pennsylvania, USA, pp. 140–148. AAAI Press (2017)
8. Lei, D., Zheng, Y., Guo, X.: A shuffled frog-leaping algorithm for flexible job shop scheduling with the consideration of energy consumption. Int. J. Prod. Res. **55**(11), 3126–3140 (2017). https://doi.org/10.1080/00207543.2016.1262082
9. Lenstra, J., Kan, A.R., Brucker, P.: Complexity of machine scheduling problems. In: Studies in Integer Programming, pp. 343–362. Elsevier (1977). https://doi.org/10.1016/s0167-5060(08)70743-x
10. Liu, Y., Dong, H., Lohse, N., Petrovic, S.: A multi-objective genetic algorithm for optimisation of energy consumption and shop floor production performance. Int. J. Prod. Econ. **179**, 259–272 (2016). https://doi.org/10.1016/j.ijpe.2016.06.019
11. Liu, Y., Dong, H., Lohse, N., Petrovic, S., Gindy, N.: An investigation into minimising total energy consumption and total weighted tardiness in job shops. J. Clean. Prod. **65**, 87–96 (2014). https://doi.org/10.1016/j.jclepro.2013.07.060
12. Liu, Z., Guo, S., Wang, L.: Integrated green scheduling optimization of flexible job shop and crane transportation considering comprehensive energy consumption. J. Clean. Prod. **211**, 765–786 (2019). https://doi.org/10.1016/j.jclepro.2018.11.231
13. Nowicki, E., Smutnicki, C.: A fast taboo search algorithm for the job shop problem. Manage. Sci. **42**(6), 797–813 (1996). https://doi.org/10.1287/mnsc.42.6.797
14. Palacios, J.J., González, M.A., Vela, C.R., González-Rodríguez, I., Puente, J.: Genetic tabu search for the fuzzy flexible job shop problem. Comput. Oper. Res. **54**, 74–89 (2015). https://doi.org/10.1016/j.cor.2014.08.023
15. Palacios, J.J., Gonzalez-Rodríguez, I., Vela, C.R., Puente, J.: Coevolutionary makespan optimisation through different ranking methods for the fuzzy flexible job shop. Fuzzy Sets Syst. **278**, 81–97 (2015). https://doi.org/10.1016/j.fss.2014.12.003
16. González-Rodríguez, I., Puente, J., Palacios, J.J., Vela, C.R.: Multi-objective evolutionary algorithm for solving energy-aware fuzzy job shop problems. Soft. Comput. **24**(21), 16291–16302 (2020). https://doi.org/10.1007/s00500-020-04940-6

17. Wu, X., Sun, Y.: A green scheduling algorithm for flexible job shop with energy-saving measures. J. Clean. Prod. **172**, 3249–3264 (2018). https://doi.org/10.1016/j.jclepro.2017.10.342

18. Zhang, R., Chiong, R.: Solving the energy-efficient job shop scheduling problem: a multi-objective genetic algorithm with enhanced local search for minimizing the total weighted tardiness and total energy consumption. J. Clean. Prod. **112**, 3361–3375 (2016). https://doi.org/10.1016/j.jclepro.2015.09.097

Machine Learning in Computer Vision and Robotics

Enhanced Image Segmentation by a Novel Test Time Augmentation and Super-Resolution

Iván García-Aguilar[1,2(✉)] , Jorge García-González[1,2] ,
Rafael Marcos Luque-Baena[1,2] , Ezequiel López-Rubio[1,2] ,
and Enrique Domínguez-Merino[1,2]

[1] Department of Computer Languages and Computer Science, University of Málaga,
Bulevar Louis Pasteur, 35, 29071 Málaga, Spain
{ivangarcia,jorgegarcia,rmluque,ezeqlr,enriqued}@lcc.uma.es
[2] Biomedical Research Institute of Málaga (IBIMA), C/ Doctor Miguel Díaz Recio,
28, 29010 Málaga, Spain

Abstract. Image segmentation in computer vision applications plays a critical role in the video processing workflow. In real applications, where interesting elements are moving in the presence of moving objects in the background, complex models are required in the segmentation process to obtain better results. In this paper, a methodology based on super-resolution and test time augmentation is proposed to improve the precision and effectiveness of the segmentation process. Our proposal avoids both modification and retraining of the model. Experiments show that our approach can increase the mean average precision of images segmentation in sequences from well-known benchmark datasets with a significant improvement.

Keywords: Image segmentation · Convolutional neural networks (CNN) · Test Time Augmentation (TTA) · Super-resolution (SR)

1 Introduction

The detection of moving objects in image sequences is usually performed using foreground-background segmentation. For this reason, multiple complex probabilistic models have been developed. Maintaining these models was computationally intensive and limited real-time applications for low-resolution sequences. Nowadays, these complex processes are unthinkable without a parallel implementation of such models running on Graphics Processing Units (GPUs). These devices are especially well suited to address segmentation tasks due to the data-parallel computations with high arithmetic intensity. Therefore, many computer vision operations can be run efficiently on modern GPUs, allowing a wide variety of computer vision algorithms to be implemented in real-time applications.

In the field of image segmentation, the application of convolutional neural networks has led to a significant improvement in detecting elements. Given these

© Springer Nature Switzerland AG 2022
J. M. Ferrández Vicente et al. (Eds.): IWINAC 2022, LNCS 13259, pp. 153–162, 2022.
https://doi.org/10.1007/978-3-031-06527-9_15

advances, there are several pre-trained models available for use. One of the most notable being the one known as Mask R-CNN [3]. This model determines a bounding box for each detected object and generates a mask. However, it has many deficiencies related to poor edge segmentation due to the blurred bounding box of the target image and small targets. This fact limits the application of this model in diverse areas.

Several advances attempt to mitigate this problem. *Qijuan Yang et al.* [11] proposes an improved algorithm based on the Mask R-CNN model together with an RPN (Region Proposal Network), which adopts the loss function. Other advances, such as the one established by *Zhang et al.* [12] research the segmentation problem related to the spatial information of the receptive field. For large models, the generated mask will be detailed. However, this mask will be generated from semantic information for small elements. Therefore, a new model is developed, denoted as *Mask-Refined R-CNN* (MR R-CNN). The structure of the network is modified, changing the fully convolutional layer to a new semantic segmentation layer. The layer will be in charge of performing feature fusion. There are other advances based on the modification of the Mask R-CNN model, such as the one developed by *Qifan Wu* [10]. In this case, they focus on aircraft detection in remote sensing images. Therefore, they propose a model denoted as SCMask R-CNN. In this case, a modification is made to one of the convolutional layers based on the network *ResNet101* [4]. This mainly achieves more feature information, as well as an improvement in the segmentation of the detected objects.

The advances established above are based on modifying the base model to improve the segmentation generated for each detected element. In our work, we start from the unmodified base model. Through the application of a Test Time Augmentation (TTA) together with super-resolution processes, we manage to generate a more accurate segmentation. There are several advances related to the application of TTA for the improvement of convolutional neural networks. Works such as [8,9] determine several techniques which improve the performance of the model used. However, they do not consider the application of techniques based on super-resolution. The main principle of this type of technique is based on increasing the number of pixels of the objects to obtain better performance by the network at the time of performing the image segmentation.

Among super-resolution (SR) based methods, there are several models available such as [2,5,6]. Each one of them is made up of a particular structure. For the proposal presented here, we have used *FSRCNN* [2]. This model introduces a deconvolution layer at the end of the network to perform upsampling. The non-linear mapping step in SRCNN is replaced by three steps in FSRCNN. Finally, the smaller filter sizes and a deeper network structure provide better performance and are tens of times faster than other models.

The organization of this paper is structured as follows. In Sect. 2, the proposed methodology is presented and explained in detail. Section 3 is devoted to experimental results. Finally, Sect. 4 gives the conclusions and remarks of this work.

2 Methodology

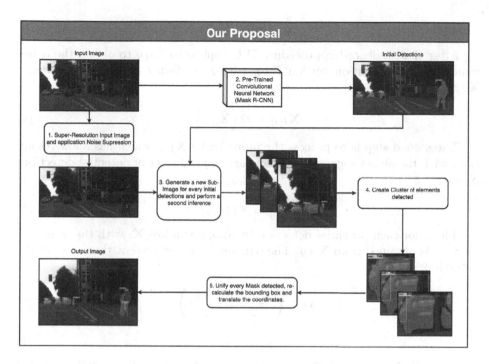

Fig. 1. Workflow of the proposed technique.

The proposed methodology for image segmentation enhancement shown in Fig. 1 is described below. A deep learning neural network for object segmentation is considered that processes an input image $\mathbf{X}$ so that a set of detections S is returned:

$$S = \mathcal{F}(\mathbf{X}) \tag{1}$$

$$S = \{(a_i, b_i, c_i, d_i, q_i, r_i) \mid i \in \{1, ..., M\}\} \tag{2}$$

where M is the number of detections, $(a_i, b_i) \in \mathbb{R}^2$ are the coordinates of the upper left corner of the i-th detection within the input $\mathbf{X}$, $(c_i, d_i) \in \mathbb{R}^2$ are the coordinates of the lower right corner of the i-th detection within $\mathbf{X}$, q_i is the class label of the detection, and $r_i \in \mathbb{R}$ is the class score of the detection. It must be noted that the confidence that an object of class q_i has been detected is measured by r_i. We assume that the coordinate origin is placed at the center of the image.

The first step of our procedure consists in applying a super-resolution network $\mathcal{G}$ to the original low-resolution image $\mathbf{X}_{LR}$ to obtain a high resolution version $\tilde{\mathbf{X}}_{HR}$:

$$\tilde{\mathbf{X}}_{HR} = \mathcal{G}\left(\mathbf{X}_{LR}\right) \tag{3}$$

After that, a denoising procedure $\mathcal{D}$ is applied to $\tilde{\mathbf{X}}_{HR}$ to obtain the noise-removed, high-resolution version $\mathbf{X}_{HR}$ with zoom factor Z of the input image $\mathbf{X}_{LR}$:

$$\mathbf{X}_{HR} = \mathcal{D}\left(\tilde{\mathbf{X}}_{HR}\right) \tag{4}$$

The second step is to process the input image $\mathbf{X}_{LR}$, which has a low resolution, with the object segmentation network to yield a set of potential detections S_{LR}:

$$S_{LR} = \mathcal{F}\left(\mathbf{X}_{LR}\right) \tag{5}$$

Then, for each potential detection in S_{LR}, a window $\mathbf{X}_i$ with the same size as $\mathbf{X}_{LR}$ is obtained from $\mathbf{X}_{HR}$. The window $\mathbf{X}_i$ is centered at the center of the detection:

$$\mathbf{y}_i = \left(\frac{a_i + c_i}{2}, \frac{b_i + d_i}{2}\right) \tag{6}$$

$$\hat{\mathbf{y}}_i = Z\mathbf{y}_i \tag{7}$$

where $\mathbf{y}_i$ is the center of $\mathbf{X}_i$ expressed in coordinates of $\mathbf{X}_{LR}$, while $\hat{\mathbf{y}}_i$ is the center of $\mathbf{X}_i$ expressed in coordinates of $\mathbf{X}_{HR}$. Next, the image segmentation network is run on $\mathbf{X}_i$ in order to obtain a new list of detections:

$$\tilde{S}_i = \mathcal{F}\left(\mathbf{X}_i\right) \tag{8}$$

$$\tilde{S}_i = \left\{\left(\tilde{a}_{i,j}, \tilde{b}_{i,j}, \tilde{c}_{i,j}, \tilde{d}_{i,j}, \tilde{q}_{i,j}, \tilde{r}_{i,j}\right) \mid j \in \{1, ..., M_i\}\right\} \tag{9}$$

where M_i is the number of detections for subimage $\mathbf{X}_i$.

The object detections of $\tilde{S}_i$ are computed in coordinates of $\mathbf{X}_i$. Therefore, they must be translated to coordinates of $\mathbf{X}_{LR}$. The equation to convert a point $\tilde{\mathbf{h}}$ expressed in coordinates of $\mathbf{X}_i$ to coordinates $\mathbf{h}$ of $\mathbf{X}_{LR}$ is as follows:

$$\mathbf{h} = \mathbf{y}_i + \frac{1}{Z}\tilde{\mathbf{h}} \tag{10}$$

Consequently, the set of object detections for window $\mathbf{X}_i$ expressed in coordinates of $\mathbf{X}_{LR}$ is:

$$S_i = \{(a_{i,j}, b_{i,j}, c_{i,j}, d_{i,j}, q_{i,j}, r_{i,j}) \mid j \in \{1, ..., N_i\}\} \tag{11}$$

$$(a_{i,j}, b_{i,j}) = \mathbf{y}_i + \frac{1}{Z}\left(\tilde{a}_{i,j}, \tilde{b}_{i,j}\right) \tag{12}$$

$$(c_{i,j}, d_{i,j}) = \mathbf{y}_i + \frac{1}{Z}\left(\tilde{c}_{i,j}, \tilde{d}_{i,j}\right) \tag{13}$$

$$q_{i,j} = \tilde{q}_{i,j} \tag{14}$$

$$r_{i,j} = \tilde{r}_{i,j} \tag{15}$$

Next, a cluster C_j is computed for each object j by grouping the detections coming from the windows S_i such that the Intersection over Union (IoU) measure computed on their associated segmentation masks is higher than 0.05 (See step 4). After that, each cluster C_j with less than N elements, where N is a tunable parameter, are removed. This is done to filter out possible errors coming from the non max-suppression algorithm integrated in the object segmentation network.

After that, a unified mask is computed for each remaining cluster C_j by adding pixelwise the masks associated to the detections in C_j and marking as true the pixels of the unified mask that correspond to sums greater than zero. Then a unified bounding box is calculated from the unified mask. Finally, a unified class label is obtained by majority voting among the class labels in C_j, and a unified class score is computed as the maximum of the class scores in C_j.

3 Results

This section presents the results of the tests performed to validate our proposal. Therefore, a set of sequences from the dataset known as *Cityscapes* has been selected. [1]. Since these sequences are annotated, they have been used for both quantitative and qualitative studies. We have also tested a series of frames from the dataset named as *VisDrone (Vision Meets Drones)* [13].

A comparison has been made between the original model and our proposal to determine its effectiveness:

- Original Model: The unmodified (RAW) object detection model.
- Proposed: The proposed technique is based on the application of the Test Time Augmentation (TTA) using Super-resolution processes.

Since our proposal is mainly focused on the improvement in terms of image segmentation, *Mask R-CNN Inception ResNet V2 1024 × 1024* has been selected as the base model. This model is a variant of the Mask R-CNN model [3] and has been pre-trained with the Coco dataset [7]. This model is available in the Tensorflow model repository[1].

---

[1] https://github.com/tensorflow/models/blob/master/research/object_detection/g3doc/tf2_detection_zoo.md.

For quantitative results, two metrics have been established to determine the effectiveness of our proposal. First, we make use of the evaluation provided by $COCO$ (Common Objects in Context)[2]. For this purpose, the mAP (mean Average Precision) of the detectors established for each of the selected sequences have been determined. The mAP is divided into a series of groups, determining the efficiency in detecting objects of various sizes. Table 1 shows a comparison of the mean average precision (mAP) obtained for three sequences contained in the validation set of the CityScapes dataset [1] for the class car.

Table 1. Results for every sequence for the Mask-RCNN model used. First, the mAP with different IoU indices is shown. Then, the score obtained according to the size of the detected elements (Small, Medium, and Large) is specified. On the left is the mAP obtained by the base model and on the right of each box is the mAP obtained by our proposal (higher is better). The best results are marked in **bold**.

Sequence	Class	mAP IoU=0.50:0.95	mAP IoU=0.50	mAP IoU=0.75	mAP Small	mAP Medium	mAP Large
Frankfurt	All	0.165 / **0.204**	0.264 / **0.342**	0.175 / **0.199**	0.001 / **0.004**	0.130 / **0.202**	0.469 / **0.513**
	Person	0.102 / **0.183**	0.247 / **0.381**	0.064 / **0.160**	0.000 / **0.008**	0.188 / **0.361**	0.530 / **0.633**
	Bicycle	0.051 / **0.086**	0.154 / **0.232**	0.022 / **0.050**	0.000 / **0.000**	0.086 / **0.187**	0.282 / **0.316**
	Car	0.261 / **0.298**	0.427 / **0.484**	0.277 / **0.307**	0.003 / **0.012**	0.300 / **0.422**	**0.718** / 0.691
Lindau	All	0.226 / **0.279**	0.443 / **0.478**	0.151 / **0.185**	0.009 / **0.018**	0.197 / **0.308**	**0.650** / 0.614
	Person	0.195 / **0.275**	0.377 / **0.498**	0.181 / **0.337**	0.010 / **0.013**	0.301 / **0.512**	**0.700** / 0.666
	Bicycle	0.139 / **0.281**	0.400 / **0.529**	0.043 / **0.116**	0.000 / **0.013**	0.101 / **0.252**	0.567 / **0.699**
	Car	0.388 / **0.412**	0.576 / **0.585**	0.433 / **0.435**	0.027 / **0.048**	0.334 / **0.413**	**0.671** / 0.636
Munster	All	0.153 / **0.207**	0.256 / **0.350**	0.152 / **0.200**	0.001 / **0.009**	0.138 / **0.266**	0.497 / **0.569**
	Person	0.083 / **0.162**	0.195 / **0.323**	0.049 / **0.144**	0.000 / **0.011**	0.237 / **0.453**	0.602 / **0.699**
	Bicycle	0.050 / **0.081**	0.174 / **0.248**	0.008 / **0.031**	0.000 / **0.001**	0.075 / **0.157**	0.319 / **0.360**
	Car	0.281 / **0.320**	0.440 / **0.517**	0.304 / **0.326**	0.003 / **0.017**	0.311 / **0.433**	**0.744** / 0.720

As we can see in Table 1, our proposal obtains a higher mAP in most of the cases. In sequences such as the one denoted as *Munster*, we increase from an overall mAP of 15.3% to 20.7%. This approach is useful in improving detections for medium-sized elements. For example, for the sequence named as *Frankfurt*, it goes from an mAP of 13% for medium-size elements to 20.2% after applying our proposal. Next, the number of elements detected by the model in the sequence, the average number of detections, and the average class inference per frame have been determined. This process has been performed for the three chosen video sequences. This comparison is made in Table 2 on page 7. As we can see, the average number of elements detected for each frame along with their standard deviation is higher compared to the unmodified model. Our proposal increases the total number of elements detected in the entire sequence. Furthermore, we can determine an improvement in terms of the average score obtained, supported by the results provided in the table. For example, the Person class increased from an average score of 89.1% to 93.5%. In addition, the number of items detected improved from 42.71% to 71.53%.

---

[2] https://github.com/cocodataset/cocoapi/blob/master/PythonAPI/pycocotools/cocoeval.py.

Table 2. Number of elements in the sequence, average detections, average class score, and standard deviation for each frame by the unmodified model and our proposal using Mask RCNN model.

Class	Strategy	Total Number Elements	Average Detections	Average Class Score
\multicolumn{5}{Sequence 1: Frankfurt}
Person	Ground Truth	2217	-	-
Person	Original Model	947	4.228 ± 3.547	0.891 ± 0.078
Person	Proposed	**1586**	**6.473 ± 5.583**	**0.935 ± 0.05**
Bicycle	Ground Truth	420	-	-
Bicycle	Original Model	210	1.826 ± 1.265	0.859 ± 0.105
Bicycle	Proposed	**273**	**2.184 ± 1.981**	**0.922 ± 0.065**
Car	Ground Truth	2523	-	-
Car	Original Model	1320	5.41 ± 3.567	0.904 ± 0.064
Car	Proposed	**1772**	**7.174 ± 4.97**	**0.948 ± 0.036**

In order to validate the improvement provided by our proposal, Figs. 2 and 3 of the *CityScapes* dataset [1] and Fig. 4 of the dataset of *Visdrone* [13] are shown.

Fig. 2. Frame *000013_000019* of the sequence denoted as *Lindau* of the CityScapes Dataset [1]. The top image shows the results obtained by the unmodified model while the bottom image shows the detections after applying our proposal.

Fig. 3. Frame *000049_000019* of the sequence denoted as *Munster* of the CityScapes Dataset [1]. The top image shows the results obtained by the unmodified model while the bottom image shows the detections after applying our proposal.

According to Tables 1 and 2, we can conclude that the implementation of the optimized proposal presented improves the accuracy of the elements initially detected by the model. It also detects objects that were not identified a priori. As can be seen in Figs. 2, 3 and 4, the proposed technique results in an increase in the number of detected elements. This approach is appropriate when you want to annotate a dataset more accurately.

Fig. 4. Frame *0000001_05999_d_0000011* of the Visdrone Dataset [13]. The top image shows the results obtained by the unmodified model while the bottom image shows the detections after applying our proposal.

4   Conclusions

In this paper, a method to enhance the performance of an image segmentation procedure has been proposed. The proposal involves two key elements. The first one is the upscaling of the spatial resolution of the input video by a suitable super-resolution neural network. This is aimed to increase the level of detail of the video frame to facilitate subsequent object segmentation. The original low-resolution video frame is processed by an image segmentation neural network to obtain a set of potential detections. Then a window is defined for each potential detection, and the image segmentation network is employed to obtain new detections from each window. Finally, the detections corresponding to the same object are clustered together, and a unified segmentation mask is computed from them. This way, more detections are attained, and with more confidence. Experimental results show that our approach significantly outperforms the base image segmentation procedure, both quantitatively and qualitatively. In particular, it has been found that our proposal detects more objects with an increased mean Average Precision in a variety of real-world scenes from *CityScapes* and *Visdrone* datasets with the advantage of not being necessary to modify the layers that compose the original model.

References

1. Cordts, M., et al.: The cityscapes dataset for semantic urban scene understanding. In: Proceedings of the IEEE Conference on Computer Vision and Pattern Recognition (CVPR) (2016)
2. Dong, C., Loy, C.C., Tang, X.: Accelerating the super-resolution convolutional neural network. CoRR abs/1608.00367 (2016), http://arxiv.org/abs/1608.00367
3. He, K., Gkioxari, G., Dollár, P., Girshick, R.: Mask R-CNN. In: 2017 IEEE International Conference on Computer Vision (ICCV), pp. 2980–2988 (2017). https://doi.org/10.1109/ICCV.2017.322
4. He, K., Zhang, X., Ren, S., Sun, J.: Deep residual learning for image recognition (2015)
5. Kim, J., Lee, J.K., Lee, K.M.: Accurate image super-resolution using very deep convolutional networks. CoRR abs/1511.04587 (2015). http://arxiv.org/abs/1511.04587
6. Kim, J., Lee, J.K., Lee, K.M.: Deeply-recursive convolutional network for image super-resolution. CoRR abs/1511.04491 (2015). http://arxiv.org/abs/1511.04491
7. Lin, T.Y., et al.: Microsoft COCO: common objects in context (2015)
8. Moshkov, N., Mathe, B., Kertesz-Farkas, A., Hollandi, R., Horvath, P.: Test-time augmentation for deep learning-based cell segmentation on microscopy images. Sci. Rep. **10**(1), 5068 (2020). https://doi.org/10.1038/s41598-020-61808-3
9. Nalepa, J., Myller, M., Kawulok, M.: Training- and test-time data augmentation for hyperspectral image segmentation. IEEE Geosci. Remote Sens. Lett. **17**(2), 292–296 (2020). https://doi.org/10.1109/LGRS.2019.2921011
10. Wu, Q., et al.: Improved mask R-CNN for aircraft detection in remote sensing images. Sensors **21**(8) (2021). https://doi.org/10.3390/s21082618. https://www.mdpi.com/1424-8220/21/8/2618
11. Yang, Q., Dong, E., Zhu, L.: An instance segmentation algorithm based on improved mask R-CNN. In: 2020 Chinese Automation Congress (CAC), pp. 4804–4809 (2020). https://doi.org/10.1109/CAC51589.2020.9326740
12. Zhang, Y., Chu, J., Leng, L., Miao, J.: Mask-refined R-CNN: a network for refining object details in instance segmentation. Sensors **20**(4) (2020). https://doi.org/10.3390/s20041010. https://www.mdpi.com/1424-8220/20/4/1010
13. Zhu, P., et al.: Detection and tracking meet drones challenge. IEEE Trans. Pattern Anal. Mach. Intell. (2021). https://doi.org/10.1109/TPAMI.2021.3119563

Encoding Generative Adversarial Networks for Defense Against Image Classification Attacks

José M. Pérez-Bravo[1], José A. Rodríguez-Rodríguez[1],
Jorge García-González[1,2] , Miguel A. Molina-Cabello[1,2(✉)] ,
Karl Thurnhofer-Hemsi[1,2] , and Ezequiel López-Rubio[1,2]

[1] Department of Computer Languages and Computer Science,
University of Málaga, Málaga, Spain
{josperbra,joseantoniorodriguez}@uma.es,
{jorgegarcia,miguelangel,karlkhader,ezeqlr}@lcc.uma.es
[2] Instituto de Investigación Biomédica de Málaga – IBIMA, Málaga, Spain

Abstract. Image classification has undergone a revolution in recent years due to the high performance of new deep learning models. However, severe security issues may impact the performance of these systems. In particular, adversarial attacks are based on modifying input images in a way that is imperceptible for human vision, so that deep learning image classifiers are deceived. This work proposes a new deep neural network model composed of an encoder and a Generative Adversarial Network (GAN). The former encodes a possibly malformed input image into a latent vector, while the latter generates a reconstructed image from the latent vector. Then the reconstructed image can be reliably classified because our model removes the deleterious effects of the attack. The experiments carried out were designed to test the proposed approach against the Fast Gradient Signed Method attack. The obtained results demonstrate the suitability of our approach in terms of an excellent balance between classification accuracy and computational cost.

Keywords: Generative Adversarial Networks · Adversarial attack · Fast Gradient Signed Method attack

1 Introduction

Deep learning (DL) has been widely used during the last decade for many different applications due to its exceptional performance. Particularly, Convolutional Neural Networks (CNNs) have become a standard in most image processing tasks, such as detection [1], segmentation [2], classification [3] or quality enhancement [4]. These deep models outperform classical machine learning methods and provide a powerful tool for scientists and entrepreneurs to develop new solutions.

© Springer Nature Switzerland AG 2022
J. M. Ferrández Vicente et al. (Eds.): IWINAC 2022, LNCS 13259, pp. 163–172, 2022.
https://doi.org/10.1007/978-3-031-06527-9_16

However, there is a security breach in many existing DL models: perturbed input samples that are imperceptible for humans may provoke wrong outputs by the networks. This tentative is called an adversarial attack. DL models learn non-intuitive features that adversarial attacks are able to exploit by using manipulations of the inputs [5]. Focusing on the image classification domain, adversarial examples, i.e., perturbed samples, are designed intentionally to cause false predictions. Sometimes, these adversarial samples generated to disturb one model can be transferred to another target model, which is used to perform what is called a black-box attack [6]. On the other hand, when the adversary has access to all the parts of the intrinsic model, this is referred to as a white-box attack [7]. This paper intends to provide defense mechanisms for this type of attack.

Developing defense mechanisms is of paramount importance since attacks can affect many real-world applications. For example, an adversary can modify traffic signs to cause accidents in autonomous vehicles [8]. Many defensive methods for detecting adversarial samples and providing a correct classification have been proposed. Thus, roughly, these approaches can be categorized into two types: heuristic defenses and provable defenses. The former is only experimentally validated, while the latter is theoretically proved. Creating heuristic defenses is, somehow, easier than proving the effectiveness of a provable defense. In this paper, we will focus on heuristic methods. Some of the most representative heuristic defenses are:

- Adversarial training: fast gradient sign method [9], projected gradient descent [10], generative adversarial training [11].
- Randomization: random input transformation [12], random noising [13], random feature pruning [14].
- Denoising: conventional input rectification [15], Generative Adversarial Networks (GANs) based input cleansing [16], auto encoder-based input denoising [17].

Most of the incorrect classifications of adversarial examples are due to imperceptible modifications of the pixels of an image. This work intends to propose a defensive algorithm to reduce the effect of adversarial attacks employing the combination of a GAN-based input cleansing method and an autoencoder. GANs were proposed by Goodfellow et al. [9], being a model composed of two networks: a generator that learns a mapping between a latent space and a data distribution and a discriminative network that distinguish the proper data. The idea of our method is the use of an encoder to project the input image onto the latent space and then feed the generative adversarial network. Thus, given an adversarial example, the latent vector generated by the encoder would be associated with a benign image learned by the GAN.

Therefore, the contributions of the paper are: 1) a new methodology of defending against adversarial examples is proposed combining GANs and autoencoders, named as EGAN, 2) a practical framework for image classification is implemented with a simple training procedure. The rest of the paper is organized as follows: in Sect. 2 is presented the theory of our proposal, Sect. 3 is devoted for the experimentation, and finally, the conclusions are presented in Sect. 4.

2   Methodology

In this section, our proposed deep learning model is presented. It is called Encoding Generative Adversarial Networks (EGAN) because it contains a Generative Adversarial Network (GAN) that produces an image from a latent vector, and an encoder that produces a latent vector from an image. The encoder is a feedforward deep convolutional neural network.

Let us note G the Generative Adversarial Network:

$$\mathbf{X} = G(\mathbf{z}) \tag{1}$$

where $\mathbf{z} \in \mathbb{R}^L$ is a latent vector, and $\mathbf{X} \in \mathbb{R}^{N \times M \times Q}$ is the generated image with N rows, M columns and Q channels. The latent space dimension L is much smaller than the size of the image, $L \ll NMQ$. On the other hand, let E stand for the encoder:

$$\mathbf{z} = E(\mathbf{X}) \tag{2}$$

As seen, the encoder E performs the inverse operation of the Generative Adversarial Network G. Now, let us assume that G has already been trained on some distribution $P(\mathbf{X})$ of images of interest. In our scheme, G is held fixed so that their parameters are not changed during the training of the encoder E.

The encoder is trained by minimizing the loss function $\mathcal{L}$ given by the mean squared error between the generated image $\mathbf{X}$ and its reconstruction $\hat{\mathbf{X}}$ by the encoder:

$$\hat{\mathbf{X}} = G(E(\mathbf{X})) \tag{3}$$

$$\mathcal{L} = \frac{1}{T} \sum_{i=1}^{T} \left\| \mathbf{X}_i - \hat{\mathbf{X}}_i \right\|^2 \tag{4}$$

where $\|\cdot\|$ stands for the Euclidean norm and T is the number of training images $\mathbf{X}_i$. Please note that in (4) it is assumed that the images are flattened prior to the computation of the Euclidean norm.

The training algorithm for the encoder E reads as follows:

1. Draw T random latent vectors $\mathbf{z}_i \in \mathbb{R}^L$, for $i \in \{1, ..., T\}$.
2. Generate the T associated training images with the GAN: $\mathbf{X}_i = G(\mathbf{z}_i)$.
3. Adjust the trainable parameters of the encoder by stochastic gradient descent on the loss function $\mathcal{L}$ (Eq. 4).
4. If the maximum number of epochs for the training of the encoder has been reached, then halt. Otherwise, go to step 3.

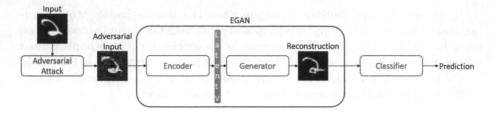

Fig. 1. *EGAN* methodology

In our experiments, the attack applied to the input images is called Fast Gradient Signed Method (FGSM) which consists in propagating $\nabla_{\tilde{\mathbf{X}}} J(\theta, \tilde{\mathbf{X}}, \mathbf{Y})$, where $\tilde{\mathbf{X}}$ is the input image, $\mathbf{Y}$ is the ground truth label for $\tilde{\mathbf{X}}$, and θ stands for the parameters of the attacked classifier, to yield the adversarial sample $\mathbf{X}$:

$$\mathbf{X} = \tilde{\mathbf{X}} + \epsilon * sign(\nabla_{\tilde{\mathbf{X}}} J(\theta, \tilde{\mathbf{X}}, \mathbf{Y})) \tag{5}$$

where ϵ represents the step size in the direction that maximizes the loss, and $J(\theta, \tilde{\mathbf{X}}, \mathbf{Y})$ is the loss used to train the classifier. The higher the value of ϵ, stronger the attack and the easier it is to see with the naked eye.

At test time, a (possibly malformed) test image $\mathbf{X}$ is provided. Then the corresponding reconstructed image $\hat{\mathbf{X}}$ is computed by (3). Finally, the reconstructed image $\hat{\mathbf{X}}$ is passed on to a suitable image classifier.

Figure 1 shows a schema of the proposed method. First, given an adversarial input image, the trained encoder produces a latent vector from that input image. Then, the generator reconstructs the image from that latent vector. And finally, this reconstructed image is supplied as input to the classifier in order to predict its class.

The rationale behind our proposal is that the encoder learns to project an arbitrary input image $\mathbf{X}$ onto a latent vector $\mathbf{z}$ that belongs to the support of the probability distribution $P(\mathbf{z})$ of the latent vectors associated with the probability distribution of images $P(\mathbf{X})$ that was learned by the GAN. This way, if a malformed image from an adversarial attack is provided to the encoder, then the encoder projects the image onto a latent vector that is associated with a corrected image which belongs to the distribution of legitimate images learned by the GAN.

It must be highlighted that our proposed EGAN model is both class-agnostic and classifier-agnostic because the class labels are not used at any time, and there is no flow of information from the image classifier to the EGAN at all. In other words, the EGAN is a fully unsupervised neural model since the class label information is never employed, neither directly nor indirectly. This enhances the robustness of the EGAN as a defense against image classification attacks.

3   Experimental Results

The experiment consists in compare different defense methods against a FGSM adversarial attack, measuring the accuracy of the defense methods across the different values of ϵ (input variation) and the computational time used to complete the experiment by applying these methods as preprocessors.

3.1   Methods

The methods used in the comparison are:

- *Original*: No defense method used.
- *DnCNN* [18]: Convolutional Neural Network trained to predict the noise of a certain sample. It is used for denoising and super-resolution.
- *AutoEncoder* [19]: Convolutional Neural Networks trained to encode and decode an image, making the information pass through a bottleneck and learning the significant features.
- *APE-GAN* [20]: Generative Adversarial Network trained to receive an adversarial sample as input and generate a sample without the adversarial modification.
- *PixelDefend* [21]: Auto-regressive Convolutional Neural Network trained to predict the value of a pixel based on the previous pixels. This network is used to make small changes on the (possibly malformed) sample.
- *Defense-GAN* [16]: Generative Adversarial Network trained to learn the training samples distribution. Then various random latent vectors are generated and optimized to generate reconstructed samples.

3.2   Dataset

The dataset used is the MNIST database (Modified National Institute of Standards and Technology database) which is formed by handwritten digits images and is divided into 60000 training images and 10000 testing images. It was created from another dataset called NIST (National Institute of Standards and Technology), where the training images and the testing images had a different origin. The MNIST was created mixing these images, anti-aliasing and resizing these images to 28×28 pixels.

3.3   Architecture and Parameter Selection

In our experiments, input images of size $28 \times 28 \times 1$ are considered, i.e., $N = 28$, $M = 28$, $Q = 1$; while the ϵ values used in the FGSM attack are from 0 to 1 where 0 means not modifying the input image and 1 means modifying the input image completely.

Regarding the proposed architecture of the encoder E, it is based on the GAN architecture called DCGAN [22], which introduces the use of convolutional layers instead of fully connected layers, in both generator and discriminator networks. This way, the encoder E is composed of four parts. The first part is a convolutional block that comprises a 2D convolutional layer with 3×3 kernel size that increases the number of channels to 100, followed by a batch normalization layer, and a leaky ReLU layer. The second part contains 10 convolutional blocks, each of them with a 2D convolutional layer with 3×3 kernel size that keeps the image size at $28 \times 28 \times 100$, followed by a batch normalization layer, and a leaky ReLU layer. The third part contains 11 convolutional blocks, each of them with a 2D convolutional layer with 3×3 kernel size, followed by a batch normalization layer, and a leaky ReLU layer. Each convolutional block of the third part reduces the image size by two pixels to a final size of $6 \times 6 \times 100$. Finally, the fourth part contains a flatten layer whose output is a vector of size 3600×1, followed by a fully connected linear layer that outputs the latent vector $\mathbf{z}$ of size 30×1. Therefore, the dimension of the latent space is $L = 30$.

According to the classifier used to perform the experiments, it is a convolutional neural network composed of 2 2D convolutional layers with 3×3 kernel size. The first layer increases the number of channels to 20 and uses a stride of 2 while the second layer reduces the number of channels to 10 and uses a stride of 3. The both of this layers are followed by a batch normalization and a ReLU layer. After this the size of the data is $4 \times 4 \times 10$. Then we use 2 linear layers (the first followed by a ReLU layer) with 50 and 10 neurons respectively. Finally, a Log Softmax layer is applied to return the probabilities associated with each class. This trained network classifies no attacked MNIST images with an effectiveness of 99%.

3.4   Results

From a qualitative point of view, our proposed approach $EGAN$ reconstructs images affected by an FGSM adversarial attack, even for highest values of ϵ, as can be observed in Fig. 2.

Regarding the reconstructed images computed by the selected methods for the comparison, Fig. 3 summarizes the visual results for each class of the considered dataset. As it is reported, $EGAN$, $APE\text{-}GAN$ and $Defense\text{-}GAN$ offer a reconstructed image with practically no noise.

In order to compare quantitatively the performance of the selected methods, the considered measure has been the accuracy (also known as detection rate). This measure shows the percentage of hits of the system by providing values in the interval $[0, 1]$, where higher is better.

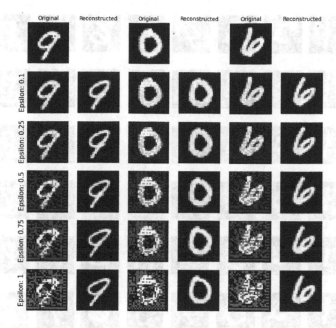

Fig. 2. Original, FGSM adversarial and reconstructed images with *EGAN*

As it can be seen in Fig. 4, most considered methods yield a high similar performance for lower values of Epsilon (ϵ in Eq. 5). However, our proposal *EGAN* is the best method for values of Epsilon higher than 0.25.

Moreover, without loss of generality due to the required computational time of each method is the same independently of the value of ϵ, Fig. 5 shows the computational time against the accuracy performance for $\epsilon = 0.5$. As it can be observed, our proposal is much faster than methods like *Defense-GAN*, that have a similar accuracy. On the other hand, faster methods such as *APE-GAN* do not offer a good performance for higher values of ϵ. This way, the proposed approach *EGAN* offers a good balance between computational time and accuracy.

4   Conclusions

This work proposes a methodology to reconstruct images that have been modified by applying a Fast Gradient Signed Method (FGSM) adversarial attack. This new approach is based on a Generative Adversarial Network (GAN) and an autoencoder. While the GAN produces an image from a latent vector, the encoder performs the inverse operation of the GAN by producing a latent vector from an image. Experiments by considering several well-known methods from the literature indicate that the performance of the proposed approach in terms

Fig. 3. Reconstruction comparison of FGSM adversarial attack with $\epsilon = 0.5$

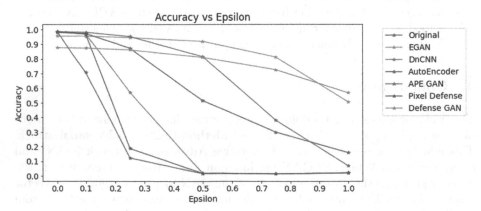

Fig. 4. Average performance of all considered methods. Note that the values of each method are connected together with lines to better compare the results, but this does not mean that the results are related.

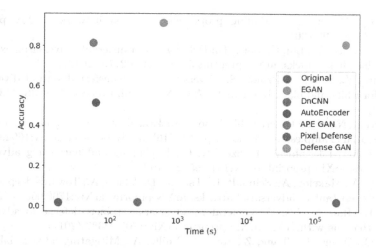

Fig. 5. Accuracy and computational time of different adversarial methods for $\epsilon = 0.5$

of accuracy is suitable to face an adversarial attack. Additionally, the computational cost of the proposal is considerably more reduced than other methods of the same kind with similar yielded accuracy.

Acknowledgments. This work is partially supported by the Ministry of Science, Innovation and Universities of Spain under grant number RTI2018-094645-B-I00, project name Automated detection with low cost hardware of unusual activities in video sequences. It is also partially supported by the Autonomous Government of Andalusia (Spain) under project UMA18-FEDERJA-084, project name Anomalous behaviour agent detection by deep learning in low cost video surveillance intelligent systems. All of them include funds from the European Regional Development Fund (ERDF). The authors thankfully acknowledge the computer resources, technical expertise and assistance provided by the SCBI (Supercomputing and Bioinformatics) center of the University of Málaga. The authors acknowledge the funding from the Instituto de Investigación Biomédica de Málaga – IBIMA and the Universidad de Málaga.

References

1. Ren, S., He, K., Girshick, R., Sun, J.: Faster R-CNN: towards real-time object detection with region proposal networks. IEEE Trans. Pattern Anal. Mach. Intell. **39**(6), 1137–1149 (2016)
2. Sivanarayana, G.V., Naveen Kumar, K., Srinivas, Y., Raj Kumar, G.V.S.: Review on the methodologies for image segmentation based on CNN. In: Satapathy, S.C., Bhateja, V., Ramakrishna Murty, M., Gia Nhu, N., Kotti, J. (eds.) Communication Software and Networks. LNNS, vol. 134, pp. 165–175. Springer, Singapore (2021). https://doi.org/10.1007/978-981-15-5397-4_18
3. Krizhevsky, A., Sutskever, I., Hinton, G.E.: ImageNet classification with deep convolutional neural networks. Adv. Neural Inf. Process. Syst. **25**, 1097–1105 (2012)
4. Steffens, C.R., Messias, L.R., Drews Jr., P.J., Botelho, S.S.d.C.: CNN based image restoration. J. Intell. Robot. Syst., 1–19 (2020)

5. Szegedy, C., et al.: Intriguing properties of neural networks. arXiv preprint arXiv:1312.6199 (2013)
6. Liu, Y., Chen, X., Liu, C., Song, D.: Delving into transferable adversarial examples and black-box attacks. arXiv preprint arXiv:1611.02770 (2016)
7. Tashiro, Y., Song, Y., Ermon, S.: Diversity can be transferred: output diversification for white-and black-box attacks. Adv. Neural Inf. Process. Syst. **33**, 4536–4548 (2020)
8. Papernot, N., et al.: Practical black-box attacks against deep learning systems using adversarial examples, vol. 1, no. 2, p. 3 (2016). arXiv preprint arXiv:1602.02697
9. Goodfellow, I.J., Shlens, J., Szegedy, C.: Explaining and harnessing adversarial examples. arXiv preprint arXiv:1412.6572 (2014)
10. Madry, A., Makelov, A., Schmidt, L., Tsipras, D., Vladu, A.: Towards deep learning models resistant to adversarial attacks. arXiv preprint arXiv:1706.06083 (2017)
11. Lee, H., Han, S., Lee, J.: Generative adversarial trainer: defense to adversarial perturbations with GAN. arXiv preprint arXiv:1705.03387 (2017)
12. Xie, C., Wang, J., Zhang, Z., Ren, Z., Yuille, A.: Mitigating adversarial effects through randomization. arXiv preprint arXiv:1711.01991 (2017)
13. Liu, X., Cheng, M., Zhang, H., Hsieh, C.-J.: Towards robust neural networks via random self-ensemble. In: Ferrari, V., Hebert, M., Sminchisescu, C., Weiss, Y. (eds.) ECCV 2018. LNCS, vol. 11211, pp. 381–397. Springer, Cham (2018). https://doi.org/10.1007/978-3-030-01234-2_23
14. Dhillon, G.S., et al.: Stochastic activation pruning for robust adversarial defense. arXiv preprint arXiv:1803.01442 (2018)
15. Xu, W., Evans, D., Qi, Y.: Feature squeezing: detecting adversarial examples in deep neural networks. arXiv preprint arXiv:1704.01155 (2017)
16. Samangouei, P., Kabkab, M., Chellappa, R.: Defense-GAN: protecting classifiers against adversarial attacks using generative models. In: International Conference on Learning Representations (2018). https://openreview.net/forum?id=BkJ3ibb0-
17. Meng, D., Chen, H.: Magnet: a two-pronged defense against adversarial examples. In: Proceedings of the 2017 ACM SIGSAC Conference on Computer and Communications Security, pp. 135–147 (2017)
18. Zhang, K., Zuo, W., Chen, Y., Meng, D., Zhang, L.: Beyond a Gaussian denoiser: residual learning of deep CNN for image denoising. IEEE Trans. Image Process. **26**(7), 3142–3155 (2017)
19. Wang, W., Huang, Y., Wang, Y., Wang, L.: Generalized autoencoder: a neural network framework for dimensionality reduction. In: Proceedings of the IEEE Conference on Computer Vision and Pattern Recognition Workshops, pp. 490–497 (2014)
20. Jin, G., Shen, S., Zhang, D., Dai, F., Zhang, Y.: APE-GAN: adversarial perturbation elimination with GAN. In: ICASSP 2019–2019 IEEE International Conference on Acoustics, Speech and Signal Processing (ICASSP), pp. 3842–3846. IEEE (2019)
21. Song, Y., Kim, T., Nowozin, S., Ermon, S., Kushman, N.: PixelDefend: leveraging generative models to understand and defend against adversarial examples. In: International Conference on Learning Representations (2018). https://openreview.net/forum?id=rJUYGxbCW
22. Radford, A., Metz, L., Chintala, S.: Unsupervised representation learning with deep convolutional generative adversarial networks. arXiv preprint arXiv:1511.06434 (2015)

Anomalous Trajectory Detection
for Automated Traffic Video Surveillance

Jose D. Fernández[1,2] (iD), Jorge García-González[1,2] (iD),
Rafaela Benítez-Rochel[1,2] (iD), Miguel A. Molina-Cabello[1,2](✉) (iD),
and Ezequiel López-Rubio[1,2] (iD)

[1] Department of Computer Languages and Computer Science,
University of Málaga, Málaga, Spain
josedavid@uma.es, {jorgegarcia,benitez,miguelangel,ezeqlr}@lcc.uma.es
[2] Instituto de Investigación Biomédica de Málaga – IBIMA, Málaga, Spain

Abstract. Vehicle trajectories extracted from traffic video sequences can be helpful for many purposes. In particular, the analysis of detected anomalous trajectories may enhance drivers' safety. This work proposes a methodology to detect anomalous vehicle trajectories by using a vehicle detection, a vehicle tracking and a processing of the tracking information steps. Once trajectories are detected, their velocity vectors are estimated and an anomaly value is computed for each trajectory by comparing its vector with those from its nearest neighbours. The management of these anomaly values allows considering which trajectories are suitable to be potentially anomalous considered. Real and synthetic videos have been included in the experiments to perform the goodness of the proposal.

Keywords: Anomaly detection · Object tracking · Object detection · Video surveillance · Deep learning

1 Introduction

Anomaly detection is an important part of understanding the activities of video surveillance systems [1]. The use of video in computer vision is an important and current research topic that includes autonomous surveillance systems. These systems follow three basic steps: detection of interesting moving objects, tracking of such objects from frame to frame, and analysis of object tracks to detect unexpected situations.

For moving object detection, the latter existing state-of-the-art methods are based on Deep Learning (DL) [2]. This kind of methods have become a powerful technique for object detection due to it is significantly more robust to occlusion, complex scenes, and challenging illumination and, on the other hand, because of the availability of large video data sets and DL frameworks. In fact, the progress of object detection is usually separated into two historical periods (before and after the introduction of DL).

© Springer Nature Switzerland AG 2022
J. M. Ferrández Vicente et al. (Eds.): IWINAC 2022, LNCS 13259, pp. 173–182, 2022.
https://doi.org/10.1007/978-3-031-06527-9_17

Regarding the object tracking, a single method cannot provide good accuracy for different kinds of videos with different situations. The tracking methods can be divided into three categories based on the use of object representations, namely, methods establishing point correspondence, methods using primitive geometric models, and methods using contour evolution. In this work, we have used a method within the first category, that is because we have found that the selected method is very appropriate to the characteristics of the analyzed traffic camera videos and it makes the process of identifying anomalous trajectories easier.

Therefore, the aim of this work is to detect anomalies in vehicle traffic. A deep neural network is used to detect vehicles, then a specific method is described in order to track the vehicles, and finally, a technique to detect anomalous trajectories of vehicles is introduced.

Detection of vehicles that appear in traffic video sequences has been addressed in the literature in order to carry out different tasks. Moreover, the trajectories of the vehicles are determined along the way, so it may be necessary to deal with the tracking of vehicles [3].

Vehicle classification on-road traffic is an important task due to its great potential in traffic management. Different techniques have been used to classify vehicles; an example of a traditional proposal can be found in [4], where it uses a foreground object detection method and a feature extractor to obtain the most significant features of the detected vehicles into several categories such as car, motorcycle, truck or van. However, more recent works [5,6] can do that task by using a neural system based on a Convolutional Neural Network (CNN) architecture, which is a DL network.

Another interesting task related to vehicle detection consists of deriving traffic information. In [7] YOLOv4 algorithm for vehicle detection is used and then the lane-by-lane vehicle trajectories using the detected locations of vehicles are estimated. Based on the estimated vehicle trajectories, the traffic volumes of each lane-by-lane traveling directions and queue lengths of each lane are estimated by matching vehicle locations with HD map.

Latest advances in research related to the field of traffic video surveillance have made possible the study of other relevant problems whose solution arises from the analysis and detection of vehicles along the road. This is the case of the detection of pollution levels of transport vehicles problem which has been addressed in [8,9]. In this works the object detection and classification process is based on a pre-trained Faster-RCNN model [10]. With that recognition and vehicle tracking, the system predicts the pollution of the selected area in real-time. The model which estimates the pollution is based on the frequency of vehicles and their speed.

The rest of the paper is organized as follows. Section 2 describes in detail the methodology used to solve our problem. Section 3 shows several experimental results over several well-known public traffic surveillance sequences. Finally, Sect. 4 outlines the conclusions of the paper.

2 Methodology

To detect anomalous trajectories in video feeds from traffic cameras, we propose a system architecture with the following stages:

1. Vehicle detection: a deep neural network is used to detect vehicles in each image frame of the video.
2. Vehicle tracking: we then keep track of vehicles across multiple frames to get their frame-by-frame positions.
3. Processing of tracking information: for each vehicle, its tracked frame-by-frame positions are processed to highlight possible anomalous trajectories.
4. Thresholding: each possible anomalous trajectory is flagged as anomalous if it surpasses any of several possible thresholds.

Next, each stage is described in detail. The first stage of our proposed system employs an object detection deep convolutional network to obtain tentative detections of vehicles. The output of the object detection network for an input image $\mathbf{X}$ is a set of detections S where each detection consists of an axis-aligned bounding box, an object class label, and a confidence level:

$$S = \mathcal{F}(\mathbf{X}) \tag{1}$$

$$S = \{(a_i, b_i, c_i, d_i, q_i, r_i) \mid i \in \{1, ..., N\}\} \tag{2}$$

where N is the number of detections, $(a_i, b_i) \in \mathbb{R}^2$ are the coordinates of the upper left corner of the i-th detection within the image $\mathbf{X}$, $(c_i, d_i) \in \mathbb{R}^2$ are the coordinates of the lower right corner of the i-th detection within $\mathbf{X}$, q_i is the class label of the detection, and $r_i \in \mathbb{R}$ is the confidence level of the detection.

We threshold the detections at a minimum confidence level of r_{min}, and disregard the object class after we filter out the non vehicle classes. Therefore a filtered set of detections is obtained as follows:

$$S' = \{(a_i, b_i, c_i, d_i, q_i, r_i) \in S \mid r_i \geq r_{min}, q_i \in V\} \tag{3}$$

where V is the set of vehicle classes.

After that, the filtered set S' is passed on the non-maximal-suppression algorithm in order to obtain a further filtered set of detections S'' for the current video frame which is fed to the next stage.

The second stage is object tracking. We pose the tracking problem as a linear sum assignment between the detections at frames $t + 1$ and t contained in the detection sets S''_{t+1} and S''_t, where the cost C_{ij} of matching two detections $s_i, s_j \in S''$ is the Euclidean distance between the centers $\boldsymbol{\mu}_i$, $\boldsymbol{\mu}_j$ of their associated bounding boxes:

$$\boldsymbol{\mu}_i = \left(\frac{a_i + c_i}{2}, \frac{b_i + d_i}{2}\right) \qquad \boldsymbol{\mu}_j = \left(\frac{a_j + c_j}{2}, \frac{b_j + d_j}{2}\right) \qquad C_{ij} = \|\boldsymbol{\mu}_i - \boldsymbol{\mu}_j\| \tag{4}$$

Our algorithm works well only in ideal conditions: when object movements between frames are relatively small, and objects are consistently detected across all frames where they appear. The traffic camera videos we analyze mostly fulfill the former requirement, but even object detectors with very high mAP scores fail the latter requirement for vehicles with small apparent sizes. To make this algorithm more robust under these conditions, we forbid assignments (i.e. recognizing bounding boxes from frames t and $t+1$ as the same tracked object across both frames) that break one of these heuristics:

- The difference in size between both bounding boxes is larger than a given threshold ratio in any of the two dimensions of the axis-aligned bounding boxes. This avoids false tracking instances between objects of very different sizes, and incidentally makes the system more robust in noisy conditions, when the bounding box estimates fluctuate wildly across frames.
- The displacement between the centers of both bounding boxes is larger than a given threshold. Rather than using an absolute threshold, it is relative to the size of the minimum dimension of the bounding box at $t+1$. This avoids false tracking instances where an object is detected at frame t but not at $t+1$, and a nearby object detected at $t+1$ is erroneously assigned to it. This is most useful for distant objects with small apparent sizes in the image, because object detection networks are more prone to fail to detect small objects. While this heuristic is also useful for objects in the foreground with large apparent sizes, it has to be fine-tuned, however, because fast objects on the foreground can show large displacements that are unlikely for distant objects. To address this issue, we apply two different threshold values, depending on the size of the bounding box relative to the size of the image.

When a vehicle detected in frame t is not assigned a detection in frame $t+1$, we do not keep track of it in case we detect it later.

After this stage, we have vehicle trajectories across the camera's field of view. We posit that we can detect vehicles performing anomalous maneuvers by comparing their trajectories with nearby trajectories. To accomplish this in a simple but effective way, we can measure how different is the velocity of a car with respect to the velocity of its nearest neighbors.

To describe this in more detail, we will introduce some formal notation. Let $\boldsymbol{\mu}_i(t) \in \mathbb{R}^2$ be the position (the center of the bounding box) of vehicle i at frame t. If the tracking stage has determined that the same vehicle was in position $\boldsymbol{\mu}_i(t-1)$ for the previous frame, we define its velocity vector $\mathbf{v}_i(t) \in \mathbb{R}^2$ as follows:

$$\mathbf{v}_i(t) = \boldsymbol{\mu}_i(t) - \boldsymbol{\mu}_i(t-1) \tag{5}$$

Here we subsume the frame rate of the camera as a scale factor. If vehicle i is not tracked both at t and $t+1$, its velocity is undefined. For each vehicle i in the current time step with defined velocity $\mathbf{v}_i(t)$, we consider the set of all detections of other vehicles with defined velocities in the last F frames:

$$D_i(t) = \{j \ : \ \exists \mathbf{v}_j(t'), i \neq j, t - t' < F\} \tag{6}$$

Then we select $D_i^N(t) \subseteq D_i(t)$, the subset of the N nearest detections for vehicle i at time t. Proximity is measured between detections of vehicle i at time

t and each vehicle j at time t' as the Euclidean distance between their respective positions $\boldsymbol{\mu}_i(t)$ and $\boldsymbol{\mu}_j(t')$.

After selecting the nearest neighbors $D_i^N(t)$ for each vehicle i, we have to measure how different its velocity vector $\mathbf{v}_i(t)$ is with respect to the velocity vectors of its nearest neighbors $\mathbf{v}_j(t') \in D_i^N(t)$. This can be accomplished by defining the *anomaly value* $A_i(t)$ of vehicle i at frame t as the mean of the moduli of differences among vector velocities:

$$A_i(t) = \text{mean}\left(\|\mathbf{v}_i(t) - \mathbf{v}_j(t')\| \ : \ j \in D_i^N(t)\right) \qquad (7)$$

As a measure of anomaly, $A_i(t)$ has some issues. It is somewhat noisy, with large spikes whenever one-off tracking errors happen. We minimize the impact of these errors using a median filter:

$$A_i'(t) = \text{median}\left(A_i(t), A_i(t-1), A_i(t-2)\right) \qquad (8)$$

such that $A_i'(t)$ is defined only if the three values $A_i(t)$, $A_i(t-1)$ and $A_i(t-2)$ are defined.

Another difficulty is that $A_i'(t)$ is not dimensionless, i.e., it depends on frame rate and distance to the camera, among other considerations. In order to address this inconvenient, we consider $A_i'(t)$ as *potentially anomalous* if its value is equal or higher than the P_k percentile of all anomaly values measured in the last F frames.

Finally, we declare that a potentially anomalous $A_i'(t)$ value is actually anomalous if either of these conditions are met:

- Its value relative the P_k percentile is larger than a specific ratio s: $A_i'(t) \geq s \cdot P_k$.
- The vehicle keeps a consistent record of potentially anomalous values for a large number of consecutive frames. This is somewhat dependent on the characteristic time and size scales of road vehicles.

3   Experimental Results

In order to evaluate the goodness of the proposed methodology, several experiments have been carried out. The following subsections depict the methods and the datasets we have employed, and the obtained results.

3.1   Methods

OpenCV is used to process video snippets, while yolov5 is the object detection network employed for the first stage of our system. Yolov5 is designed to detect objects in still images, so it is used to detect vehicles in each frame. We configure the network to return only the object detections corresponding to vehicles. More specifically, the following COCO classes are included in the vehicle classes set V: *car*, *motorcycle*, *bus*, and *truck*. Also, we disregard object class during non-maximal-suppression since this network occasionally detects truck cabins as standalone cars, even if they are within the bounding box of the whole truck. All other configuration parameters are left unmodified, particularly $r_{min} = 0.25$.

SciPy's implementation is used to solve the linear sum assignment for the tracking stage. Everything else is implemented in Python. Regarding the parameters to detect anomalies, we have found that the size of the set $D_i^N(t)$ (the number of neighbors to check if a trajectory is anomalous) should be small to avoid a long warm-up time, during which comparisons will include lots of vehicles in wildly different trajectories. We use a number of nearest neighbors $N = 5$. Regarding the memory size F, i.e., the number of past frames for which we keep track of past vehicle detections, we have found results to be better for very large values. This amounts to not forgetting any vehicle detection for the duration of each video. With respect to the parameters for trajectory processing, we flag as potentially anomalous all detections at or above the P_k percentile.

3.2   Dataset

Several videos taken from different datasets have been considered in the experiments. These videos allow us to analyze the performance of the system under different anomaly conditions, such as vehicle in the opposite direction or risky fast vehicle. Videos without any anomalous vehicle trajectory are also selected. We used videos from three datasets:

- Two videos from a project [11] which deals with the anomalous trajectory detection in traffic videos offers several real and synthetic sequences. The selected sequences are a real video[1] (noted as *Video1*) that shows a vehicle backing onto a busy road and a synthesized video with CARLA [12] (noted as *Video2*) that depicts a car doing counterflow driving.
- Two videos from the Ko-PER Intersection dataset [13]: the sequences *seq. 1a - SK_4* and *seq. 2 - SK_4*, both cases depicting an intersection with traffic lights. The first video presents no anomalies, while the second video shows a vehicle that waits to turn. In order to test the proposed methodology, we have considered as a potential anomaly that vehicle.
- Two videos from the 2014 CDNET dataset [14]. The sequences *highway* and *streetLight* with no anomalies exhibit a road in a video taken from a camera looking at incoming traffic and from the side, respectively.

3.3   Results

From a quantitative point of view, we have selected several well-known measures in order to test the performance of the proposal. In this work, the spatial accuracy (S) has been considered. This measure provides values in the interval $[0, 1]$, where higher is better, and represents the percentage of hits of the system. True

---

[1] Clip from 02:10 to 02:31 in this Youtube video: https://youtu.be/BF3WuB-7iPo.

Table 1. Performance of the system for sequences *Video1* and *Video2* regarding different values of parameters s scaling factor and P_k percentile. Best results are highlighted in **bold**.

Video1	P_{99}	P_{98}	P_{95}	P_{90}	P_{85}
$s = 3$	0.000	0.000	**1.000**	0.500	0.167
$s = 4$	0.000	0.000	**1.000**	0.500	0.250
$s = 5$	0.000	0.000	**1.000**	0.500	0.250
$s = 6$	0.000	0.000	**1.000**	0.500	0.250

Video2	P_{99}	P_{98}	P_{95}	P_{90}	P_{85}
$s = 3$	**1.000**	**1.000**	0.334	0.077	0.052
$s = 4$	**1.000**	**1.000**	**1.000**	0.200	0.071
$s = 5$	**1.000**	**1.000**	**1.000**	0.500	0.143
$s = 6$	0.000	**1.000**	**1.000**	**1.000**	0.250

Table 2. Performance of the system for tested videos. First row shows the ground truth (GT) which represents the number of anomalous trajectories for each video, while remaining rows depict the performance of the system for the indicated measure.

Measure	*Video1*	*Video2*	*seq. 1a - SK_4*	*seq. 2 - SK_4*	*highway*	*streetLight*
GT	1	1	0	1	0	0
TP	1	1	0	1	0	0
FP	0	0	1	1	1	2
FN	0	0	0	0	0	0

positives or number of hits (TP), false negatives or misses (FN) and false positives or false alarms (FP) are also considered in this work. The spatial accuracy is defined as follows: $S = TP/(TP + FN + FP)$.

First of all, in order to establish the value of parameters P_k percentile of all anomaly values and the ratio s used as thresholds, we have tuned different configurations. With these possible configurations, the system may be more demanding or tolerant with the potential anomalies.

The set of values we have tested are $k = \{85, 90, 95, 98, 99\}$ and $s = \{3, 4, 5, 6\}$ with the sequences *Video1* and *Video2*. The obtained results are shown in Table 1. Due to both videos present only one anomaly, the configuration with fixed values $s = 4$ (or $s = 5$ or $s = 6$) and P_{95} achieves the best performance. This way, we have found that a good strategy to flag a vehicle as actually anomalous is to use either of these heuristics: either its $A_i(t)$ value persists as potentially anomalous for more than a certain number of frames (we have used 60 which corresponding with approximately 2–3 s for the videos we are using), or it is $s = 4$ times larger than the P_{95} percentile.

Table 2 summarizes the performance of the system. As can be observed, our proposal perfectly detects the anomalous trajectories which are in the videos. Additionally, it must be highlighted that there is no false negatives. Nevertheless, several false positives are detected.

Going deeper, Fig. 1 shows the anomaly values $A_i(t)$ for detected vehicles of a selected video plotted by time and a specific frame from that video. It is interesting to observe how real anomalies are well detected in videos *Video1*, *Video2* and *seq. 2, cam. SK_4*. For example, the anomalous trajectory detected in

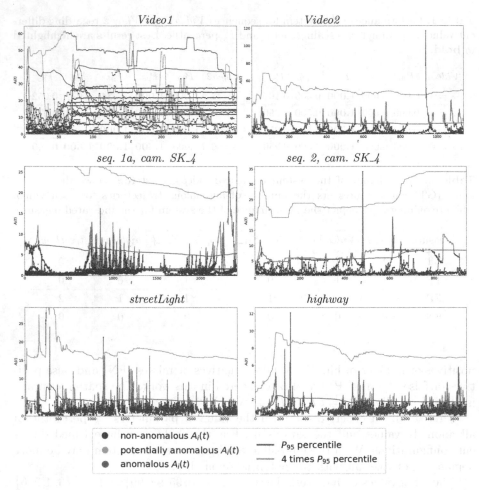

Fig. 1. *Anomaly values* $A_i(t)$ for detected vehicles plotted by time (frame number) in each tested video.

Video1 is predicted as that because the vehicle maintains $A_i(t)$ values above the P_{95} percentile for a long time. Regarding false positives anomalous trajectories, they exhibit a low number of frames with an anomalous *anomaly value* $A_i(t)$ and they are related to tracking errors which can be tackled with better detection and tracking subsystems. From the analysis of the frames where false positives appear, we have deduce that they can be categorize in two possible classes: the first vehicle(s) in a given trajectory is liable to be flagged as anomalous; and, when an area (usually an intersection) accumulates lots of different overlapping trajectories, some vehicles will be flagged as anomalous because their trajectories happen to overlap with very different ones.

The detail of an specific frame showing some vehicles flagged by the system is reported in Fig. 2. Left image shows a vehicle is backing onto a busy road,

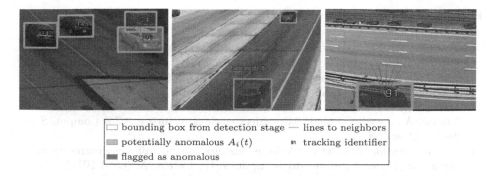

☐ bounding box from detection stage	— lines to neighbors
▨ potentially anomalous $A_i(t)$	⁹¹ tracking identifier
▪ flagged as anomalous	

Fig. 2. Predictions made by the proposal for different videos in an specific instant. From left to right: *Video1* (frame 76), *Video2* (frame 938) and *streetLight* (frame 309).

center image exhibits a vehicle is driving in opposite direction, and right image reports a vehicle which is not actually anomalous, but it is the first vehicle to go through its lane, and it gets compared to vehicles from another lane going in the opposite direction. The $N = 5$ nearest neighbors (detections from the current or past frames) used to compute the anomaly value $A_i(t)$ for that tracked vehicle at time t can be observed for each vehicle.

4   Conclusions

The detection of anomalous vehicle trajectories from traffic video sequences has been addressed in this work. From an input traffic video, the proposed methodology detects the vehicles, tracks them to obtain their trajectory, and then estimates which trajectories can be considered anomalous. Given the fact that we are measuring how different the velocity vector of each vehicle is with respect to the velocity vector of the nearest vehicles, we are considering that a vehicle is anomalous if this difference is very high for a given frame or continuously high for a given length of time. We find that this strategy may detect anomalous trajectories consisting of vehicles going the wrong way in a traffic lane or backing next to a busy lane and works especially well when the vehicle is in the foreground or near the foreground. Experiments with real and synthetic traffic videos demonstrate that the approach assesses appropriately different anomalous vehicle behaviours in different scenarios.

Acknowledgments. This work is partially supported by the following Spanish grants RTI2018-094645-B-I00 and UMA18-FEDERJA-084. All of them include funds from the European Regional Development Fund (ERDF). The authors acknowledge the computer resources, technical expertise and assistance provided by the SCBI (Supercomputing and Bioinformatics) center of the University of Málaga. The authors acknowledge the funding from the Instituto de Investigación Biomédica de Málaga – IBIMA and the Universidad de Málaga.

References

1. Tian, B., Yao, Q., Gu, Y., Wang, K., Li, Y.: Video processing techniques for traffic flow monitoring: a survey. In: 2011 14th International IEEE Conference on Intelligent Transportation Systems (ITSC), pp. 1103–1108 (2011)
2. Zhao, Z.-Q., Zheng, P., Xu, S.-T., Wu, X.: Object detection with deep learning: a review. IEEE Trans. Neural Netw. Learn. Syst. **30**(11), 3212–3232 (2019)
3. Yilmaz, A., Javed, O., Shah, M.: Object tracking: a survey. ACM Comput. Surv. **38**(4), 13–es (2006)
4. Molina-Cabello, M.A., et al.: Vehicle classification in traffic environments using the growing neural gas. In: Rojas, I., Joya, G., Catala, A. (eds.) IWANN 2017. LNCS, vol. 10306, pp. 225–234. Springer, Cham (2017). https://doi.org/10.1007/978-3-319-59147-6_20
5. Molina-Cabello, M.A., Luque-Baena, R.M., López-Rubio, E., Thurnhofer-Hemsi, K.: Vehicle type detection by convolutional neural networks. In: Ferrández Vicente, J.M., Álvarez-Sánchez, J.R., de la Paz López, F., Toledo Moreo, J., Adeli, H. (eds.) IWINAC 2017. LNCS, vol. 10338, pp. 268–278. Springer, Cham (2017). https://doi.org/10.1007/978-3-319-59773-7_28
6. Molina-Cabello, M.A., Luque-Baena, R.M., Lopez-Rubio, E., Thurnhofer-Hemsi, K.: Vehicle type detection by ensembles of convolutional neural networks operating on super resolved images. Integr. Comput. Aided Eng. **25**(4), 321–333 (2018)
7. Tak, S., Lee, J.-D., Song, J., Kim, S.: Development of AI-based vehicle detection and tracking system for C-its application. J. Adv. Transp. (2021). https://doi.org/10.1155/2021/4438861, https://www.hindawi.com/journals/jat/2021/4438861/
8. Molina-Cabello, M.A., Luque-Baena, R.M., López-Rubio, E., Deka, L., Thurnhofer-Hemsi, K.: Road pollution estimation using static cameras and neural networks. In: 2018 International Joint Conference on Neural Networks (IJCNN), pp. 1–7 . IEEE (2018)
9. García-González, J., Molina-Cabello, M.A., Luque-Baena, R.M., Ortiz-de Lazcano-Lobato, J.M., López-Rubio, E.: Road pollution estimation from vehicle tracking in surveillance videos by deep convolutional neural networks. Appl. Soft Comput. **113**, 107950 (2021)
10. Ren, S., He, K., Girshick, R., Sun, J.: Faster R-CNN: towards real-time object detection with region proposal networks (2016)
11. Leiva, G.C.: Videovigilancia de trayectorias anómalas de vehículos en vídeos de tráfico, March 2021
12. Dosovitskiy, A., Ros, G., Codevilla, F., Lopez, A., Koltun, V.: CARLA: an open urban driving simulator. In: Proceedings of the 1st Annual Conference on Robot Learning, pp. 1–16 (2017)
13. Strigel, E., Meissner, D., Seeliger, F., Wilking, B., Dietmayer, K.: The Ko-PER intersection laserscanner and video dataset. In: 17th International IEEE Conference on Intelligent Transportation Systems (ITSC), pp. 1900–1901. IEEE (2014)
14. Wang, Y., et al.: CDnet 2014: an expanded change detection benchmark dataset. In: Proceedings of the IEEE Conference on Computer Vision and Pattern Recognition Workshops, pp. 387–394 (2014)

Defining High Risk Landslide Areas Using Machine Learning

Byron Guerrero-Rodriguez[1], Jose Garcia-Rodriguez[2],
Jaime Salvador[1][(✉)], Christian Mejia-Escobar[1], Michelle Bonifaz[1],
and Oswaldo Gallardo[1]

[1] Central University of Ecuador, P.O. Box 17-03-100, Quito, Ecuador
{bvguerreror,jsalvador}@uce.edu.ec
[2] Department of Computer Technology, University of Alicante, Alicante, Spain

Abstract. Predicting landslides is a task of vital importance to prevent disasters, avoid human damage and reduce economic losses. Several research works have determined the suitability of Machine Learning techniques to address this problem. In the present study, we leverage a neural network model for landslide prediction developed in our previous work, in order to identify the specific areas where landslides are most likely to occur. We have created a dataset that collects an inventory of landslides and geological, geomorphological and meteorological conditioning factors of a region susceptible to this type of events. Among these variables, precipitation is widely recognized as a trigger of the phenomenon. In contrast to related works, we considered precipitation in a cumulative form with different time windows. The application of our model produces probability values which can be represented as multi-temporal landslide susceptibility maps. The distribution of the values in the different susceptibility classes is performed by means of equal intervals, quantile, and Jenks methods, whose comparison allowed us to select the most appropriate map for each cumulative precipitation. In this way, the areas of maximum risk are identified, as well as the specific locations with the highest probability of landslides. These products are valuable tools for risk management and prevention.

Keywords: Landslide · Machine Learning · Susceptibility Map ·
Support Vector Machine · Random Forest · Multi-layer Perceptron

1 Introduction

Landslides may be very dangerous events, hence efforts are made to prevent them and reduce human and economic losses. Availability of quality terrain data, landslide inventories, and recent advances in Machine Learning methods, enable the prediction of landslides [7]. In a previous work, we employed a Multi-layer Perceptron (*MLP*) model for such prediction reaching 99.6% accuracy. Our main contribution was the use of time windows of precipitation for multi-temporal prediction. Rainfall has been widely pointed out as a factor responsible

© Springer Nature Switzerland AG 2022
J. M. Ferrández Vicente et al. (Eds.): IWINAC 2022, LNCS 13259, pp. 183–192, 2022.
https://doi.org/10.1007/978-3-031-06527-9_18

for the occurrence of landslides, both for its durability and intensity [5]. With climate change, precipitation is more extreme and characterized by long duration and high intensity, becoming one of the triggers for landslides [4].

The present work is an extension of the previous one, by complementing the multi-temporal prediction of landslides with the identification and geographic location of the high risk areas by means of a susceptibility map, which is fundamental to formulate disaster prevention actions and mitigate future risk [8,12]. Landslide risk identification and mitigation remains a challenging task [2]. This is a recurrent problem, especially during the rainy season and in places located in the mountains [11]. We have considered a strategic highway in Ecuador known as Aloag-Santo Domingo, frequently affected by small, medium and large-scale landslides, causing fatal accidents as well as the partial and total interruption of transportation. The sinusoidal course, together with the changing slopes, rainfall, and vegetation, make the area a potential permanent risk [9]. Therefore, our research on the estimation of landslide susceptibility and the definition of high risk areas by Machine Learning provides a set of multi-temporal landslide susceptibility maps of the Aloag-Santo Domingo highway, useful for the prevention of damage to people and facilities near the highway. All the inputs used in our work and the products obtained, as well as the source code, are publicly available[1].

The rest of the paper includes the following: Sect. 2 characterizes the geographic area of interest; Sect. 3 describes the methodology employed; Sect. 4 presents the experiments whereas Sect. 5 the results obtained and the corresponding discussion; and Sect. 6 outlines our conclusions and future work.

2   Description of the Study Area

The Aloag-Santo Domingo highway is located in the center-north of the country. It is one of the most important communication arteries, as it connects the Sierra and Coast regions with an approximate length of 110 km (Fig. 1).

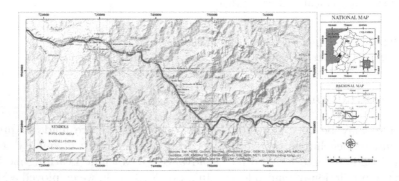

Fig. 1. Location of the Aloag-Santo Domingo highway and study area.

[1] https://github.com/MichelleBV/Landslide_Time_Window_Prediction.

This highway crosses a geographic area of irregular topography with altitudes descending from east to west and fluctuating between 0 and 3730 m. There are strong slopes that correspond to the foothills of the Cordillera Occidental. Plateaus and low hills are found in the lower altitude zones, originating a flat to ondulated relief. The transition between regions results in a wet tropical climate, with annual rainfall of 2000 to 5000 mm mm (INAMHI) and temperatures of 20 to 30 °C. A great variety of botanical species is present, with native and introduced fruit trees, in addition to wood species and 8 forests with special protection status (GAD Santo Domingo, 2016). The Pilaton and Toachi river basins drain surface water from the watersheds responsible for maintaining the area's relative humidity. The action of the dendritic drainage network can erosion riverbanks and contribute to land mass unstability. All of the mentioned aspects determine a potential risk area prone to trigger landslides.

3   Methodology

The definition of high risk landslide areas by Machine Learning comprises the workflow presented in Fig. 2.

Fig. 2. Workflow for multi-temporal susceptibility maps by machine learning.

We started with the delimitation of the geographic area of influence considering the margins of the highway where high mountains, strong slopes and wet tropical climate are prodominant [10]. By using the *buffer* in the GIS, with 1500 m to each side of the highway, the area of influence is 264.92 km². This extension contains all the landslides registered in the inventory provided by the GAD Pichincha, which allowed us to accurately locate a total of 45 landslides with Google Earth (Fig. 5a). The location of landslides on a map of the study area is an important aspect of susceptibility analysis [1]. In our case study, reptation landslides and soil fall predominate with 17.78%, debris flow with 15.56%, rock fall is also frequent with 13.33%. It is alarming that 64.44% of the events involve a very high risk and the rest a high and medium risk.

This delimited area is subdivided into a grid of 20 m × 20 m cells, each being the basic unit of analysis, mapping and susceptibility prediction. This size is based on previous work, reasonable processing speed, and the criteria that smaller sizes cause redundancy and larger sizes cause loss of information. A total of 662303 cells are obtained, each corresponding to one pixel of the image, where the values to each of the conditioning factors of landslides will be stored.

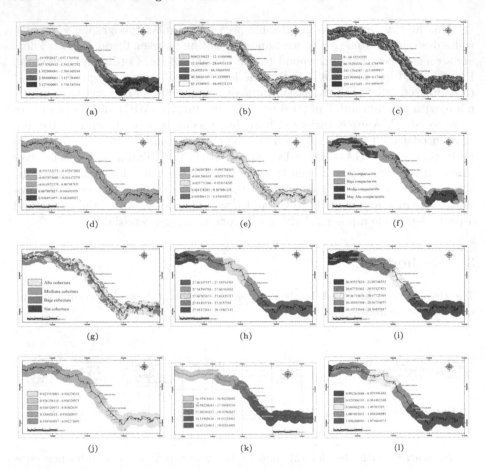

Fig. 3. Maps of conditioning factors: (a) Topography (b) Slope (c) Aspect (d) Profile curvature (e) Plane curvature (f) Vegetation (g) Lithology (h) Max. temperature (i) Min. temperature (j) Relative humidity (k) Solar radiation (l) Wind speed.

The maps of the factors or variables responsible for the occurrence of land-slides are shown in Fig. 3 and were generated with data from several sources [3]. In addition to the inventory of landslides obtained through an official request, the open access web portals allowed us to collect the topographic contour lines [6] and lithological information from the 1:100,000 scale geological sheets published by the IGM; the vegetation cover is provided by the governmental program SIGTIERRAS[2]; and meteorological information registered by Global Weather[3].

---

[2] http://www.sigtierras.gob.ec/.
[3] https://globalweather.tamu.edu/.

Table 1. Summary of the main characteristics of the conditioning factors.

Factor	Category	Source	Range	Description
Topography (DEM)	Geo-morphology	5-m contour lines interpolation	[−18.94; 3730.18]	Decreasing from S-E to N-W, altitudes higher than 1000 m predominate
Slope	Geo-morphology	DEM	[0; 86]	In the central and S-E regions, high values are majority, favoring landslides
Aspect	Geo-morphology	DEM	[0; 360]	Slope direction in which landslides would occur, near the highway 140 to 290 (S-W) predominate
Profile/plane curvatures	Geo-morphology	DEM	−, 0, +	Mainly zero curvature (straight inclined slope), accelerating runoff and landslide flows
Vegetation	Land use	Manually digitized	null, low, mid, high	High and low coverage are mostly distributed along the highway
Lithology	Geology	Manually digitized	low, mid, high, very high	Low compaction predominates in the central zone, and mid compaction in S-E and N-W
Max. temperature	Meteorology	Data interpolation 4 weather stations	[27.46; 28.12]	A small increase from E to W, from the Sierra region to the Coast
Min. temperature	Meteorology	Data interpolation 4 weather stations	[20.16; 21.10]	Decreasing 1°C in W-E direction
Relative humidity	Meteorology	Data interpolation 4 weather stations	[0.92; 0.94]	High values that increase by approximately 2% from E to W direction
Wind speed	Meteorology	Data interpolation 4 weather stations	[0.90; 1.07]	Higher in the Sierra region and decreases towards the Coast by 0.17 m/s
Solar radiation	Meteorology	Data interpolation 4 weather stations	[16.46; 19.03]	Higher values in big mountains (S-E) drying the soil and disfavor landslides

Table 1 summarizes the main characteristics, minimum and maximum values, as well as the behavior of each of the variables. All geomorphological, geological, and land use variables show values that favor the occurrence of landslides. While meteorological variables have less fluctuation of values, they are closely related to precipitation, which is a triggering factor of the phenomenon.

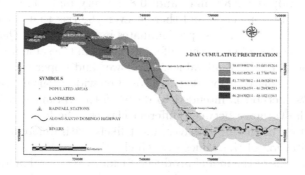

Fig. 4. Map of 3-day cumulative precipitation.

The cumulative precipitation maps are quite similar to each other. Figure 4 presents the 3-day rainfall accumulation, the rest have the same appearance. The rainfall behavior increases in E-W direction but in different ranges: [63.66;

80.35], [89.42; 112.54], [128.46; 160.87], [194.52; 201.64], [260.10; 323.70], for 5, 7, 10, 15, 20, and 30-day, respectively. This could cause a higher landslide risk in the W direction when precipitation days increase and meet the above ranges in mmH_2O.

4   Experimentation

The implementation and execution of the machine learning model for landslide susceptibility prediction was carried out on a laptop computer with Intel Core i5-7200 processor, 2.70 GHz speed, 64-bit architecture, 8 GB RAM, 1TB SSD hard drive, Intel HD Graphics 620 video card, and Microsoft Windows 10 Pro operating system. The development software included Google Earth, R, RStudio, and ArcGIS for the generation of the susceptibility maps.

In our previous work, we performed the evaluation and comparison of the following algorithms: *Support Vector Machine* (SVM), *Random Forest* (RF), and *Multilayer Perceptron* (MLP), the latter being the most suitable prediction model for the estimation of landslide susceptibility. This model receives the dataset of 662303 records, each representing a pixel of the geographic area studied, and calculates the target variable from the predictor variables, yielding a probability value between 0 and 1 for each pixel. These values and the corresponding coordinates are exported to a text file, and imported into the GIS to generate the 20 m × 20 m raster image of the study area. The following classes are defined: null, low, mid, high, and very high, according to the degree of susceptibility to landslides of the Aloag-Santo Domingo highway. The method for distributing values within classes is key to achieve a desired result. We used 3 of the most popular data segmentation methods.

Equal intervals method is the simplest and popular, the range of values for all classes is the same, i.e. the difference between the lower and upper limit. Thus, we have the following intervals: [0.0–0.2[means no susceptibility; [0.2–0.4[: low; [0.4–0.6[: mid; [0.6–0.8[: high; and [0.8–1]: very high. There could be very unbalanced distributions here, and there is even the risk that some classes have no values, or that a certain class predominates in the majority. *Quantile* method tries to distribute the values in the different classes in the same proportion. Each class would contain 20% of all values. The lower and upper limits of each class will depend on the distribution, so there could be widely varying ranges. *Natural breaks of Jenks* method is intended to decrease the variance within each class and increase the variance between different classes. The lower and upper limits will be a function of these objectives, most likely with different ranges and an irregular distribution of the values of each class.

A total of 7 runs of the model produced 21 multi-temporal landslide susceptibility maps. For example, in the 3-day time window map, all geomorphological, geological, land use, and meteorological variables are used for the prediction, including only the 3-day cumulative precipitation and excluding the others: 5, 7, 10, 15, 20, and 30 days of rainfall. The probability values are distributed into 5 classes using equal intervals, quantile and Jenks' methods. The same procedure is followed for the rest of the precipitation time windows.

5   Results and Discussion

In this phase, we visually analyze the resulting maps and select for each cumulative precipitation the one that best fits the conditions that produced the landslides. Each map (prediction) and the distribution of landslides in the inventory (reality) were contrasted. This analysis is performed for each precipitation case in order to select the most appropriate susceptibility map.

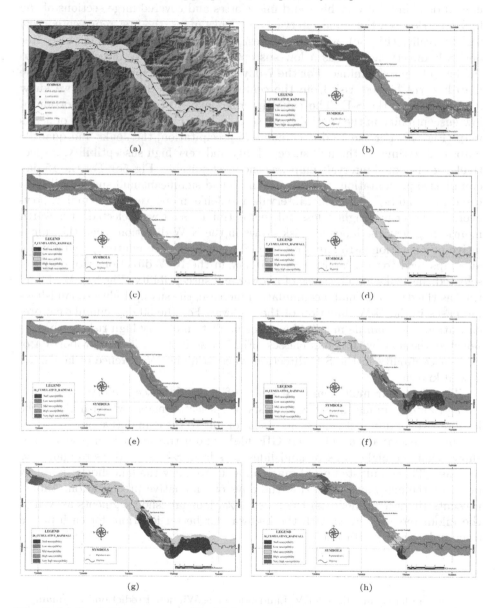

Fig. 5. (a) Landslide inventory; (b)–(h) Susceptibility maps selected for 3, 5, 7, 10, 15, 20, and 30-day cumulative precipitation, respectively.

The landslides in the inventory map (Fig. 5a) are distributed along the highway, with a higher concentration in the center and S-E direction. This is consistent with the map by equal intervals for the 3-day cumulative precipitation (Fig. 5b). The other maps (quantile y Jenks) indicated null susceptibility where landslides generally occur and over-estimation of very high susceptibility, with abrupt change to null and mid susceptibility, which would not be close to reality. For the 5-day cumulative precipitation, the quantile map is discarded because it included only the very high and mid classes and covered large sections of the highway. Between the equal intervals and Jenks maps, the first represented better the reality (Fig. 5c), with the highest probability of landslides in the center and S-E direction, whereas a low susceptibility in the N-W direction, near to the city of Santo Domingo. For the 7-day cumulative precipitation, the quantile map had the highest risk from the center to the N-W direction and we know it should be to the S-E. The equal intervals map included a small portion of low susceptibility in the central zone, so we selected the natural breaks of Jenks map (Fig. 5d). For the 10-day cumulative precipitation, the Jenks and quantile maps over-estimated the null susceptibility and very high susceptibility, respectively, so the equal intervals map was the most suitable (Fig. 5e). For the 15-day cumulative precipitation, the quantile map had significant null susceptibility in the center and S-E. The equal intervals and Jenks maps were very similar, however, the latter has slightly less null susceptibility, so it was selected. It is worth mentioning that the landslide risk grows in the N-W direction when the cumulative precipitation is 15 days (Fig. 5f). For the 20-day cumulative precipitation, all maps tend toward higher susceptibility in the N-W direction. However, we selected the Jenks map because of a lower null susceptibility (Fig. 5g). We found that as the days of rainfall accumulation increase, the susceptibility to landslides increases in the N-W direction of the highway. For the 30-day cumulative precipitation, the quantile map had an over-prediction of very high risk, so that we selected the map with Jenks classes (Fig. 5h) as it has a higher proportion of mid susceptibility in the S-E direction where a higher occurrence of landslides is well-known.

Therefore, our multi-temporal study of landslide susceptibility around the Aloag-Santo Domingo highway consists of 7 selected maps, which indicate the level of risk for different time windows according to the cumulative precipitation. We have generated an animated GIF file[4], whose transition from the 7 maps shows that the higher risk of landslides goes from S-E to N-W as rainfall days increase. These multi-temporal maps allow us to know the landslide risk at any point of the highway considering the days of cumulative precipitation. Table 2 presents (in decimal degrees) the most hazardous landslide segments as well as the kilometers associated with the highway for better location, for each period of cumulative precipitation.

---

[4] https://github.com/MichelleBV/Landslide_Time_Window_Prediction/tree/main/ Gif_Animated_Map.

Table 2. Location of the highest landslide risk for each precipitation time window.

Cumulative precipitation	Risk of landslide	Location-from		km	Location-to		km
3-day	Very high	−0.37961	−78.82371	55	−0.31440	−78.94120	70
	High	−0.44860	−78.56141	41	−0.41954	−78.79244	46
5-day	Very high	−0.37961	−78.82371	55	−0.33892	−78.86701	60
	High	−0.44189	−78.67033	20	−0.37961	−78.82371	55
7-day	Very high	−0.26453	−79.11131	95	−0.257380	−79.12530	97
	High	−0.37687	−78,83014	48	−0.26453	−79.11131	95
10-day	Very high	−0.27634	−79.07719	89	−0.25738	−79.12530	97
	High	−0.38187	−78.82223	45	−0.27634	−79.07719	89
15-day	Very high	−0.31599	−78.95359	73	−0.27634	−79.07719	89
	High	−0.32689	−79.65159	82	−0.27634	−79.16709	93
20-day	Very high	−0.31440	−78.94120	70	−0.27634	−79.07719	89
	High	−0.32409	−78.91820	67	−0.27634	−79.07719	89
30-day	Very high	−0.33309	−78.89530	65	−0.31433	−78.93438	69
	High	−0.44189	−78.67033	20	−0.27634	−79.07719	89

Thus, we can state the most critical segment of the highway, since the risk of landslide is very high from km 55 (and high from km 20) with a time window of precipitation of 3 and 5 days and progresses up to km 97, with a wider time window of precipitation of 7 to 30 days, which indicates a trend of landslide occurrence in an E-W direction as the days of rainfall accumulate.

6 Conclusions and Future Work

In our previous work, we used machine learning models for landslide prediction as a successful alternative to traditional methods. In particular, the multi-layer perceptron exhibited the best performance (99.6% accuracy), being a suitable model to generate susceptibility maps. The prediction outputs values between 0 and 1 as the probability of occurrence of the phenomenon for each cell (pixel) of the study area. With GIS software, these values are distributed into 5 classes of risk (null, low, mid, high and very high) by 3 methods: equal intervals, quantile and Jenks. A total of 21 susceptibility maps were generated, 3 for each of the cumulative precipitation: 3, 5, 7, 10, 15, 20, and 30 days. We contrasted the maps obtained with the historical landslide inventory, to select the one that best fits reality for each cumulative precipitation. The equal intervals and Jenks methods had the best results, forming a group of 7 final maps that show the multi-temporal susceptibility of the study area with respect to the precipitation, one of the most influential variables and triggers of the phenomenon. In addition to estimating the probability of landslide, the geographic areas of highest risk along the highway were also identified. As the days of precipitation increase, the location of the higher landslide risk goes from the S-E to the N-E. Specifically, we identified sites and kilometers of highest risk, being a useful tool for decision making regarding preventive measures in a geographic area characterized by the danger of affecting a strategic route of vial communication. Our study may motivate new research directions in landslide prediction, such as the application of Deep Learning. It is recommended that more weather stations be installed in the area to get a more realistic daily precipitation, verification of the landslide susceptible areas established here by means of periodic site visits, and geotechnical or geophysical studies for the recognition of structures such as faults that favor the occurrence of landslides on the Aloag-Santo Domingo highway.

References

1. Ali, S.A., et al.: GIS-based landslide susceptibility modeling: a comparison between fuzzy multi-criteria and machine learning algorithms. Geosci. Front. **12**(2), 857–876 (2021)
2. Di Napoli, M., et al.: Machine learning ensemble modelling as a tool to improve landslide susceptibility mapping reliability. Landslides **17**(8), 1897–1914 (2020). https://doi.org/10.1007/s10346-020-01392-9
3. Guzzetti, F., et al.: Landslide inventory maps: new tools for an old problem. Earth Sci. Rev. **112**(1), 42–66 (2012). https://www.sciencedirect.com/science/article/pii/S0012825212000128
4. Lee, J.-H., Kim, H., Park, H.-J., Heo, J.-H.: Temporal prediction modeling for rainfall-induced shallow landslide hazards using extreme value distribution. Landslides **18**(1), 321–338 (2020). https://doi.org/10.1007/s10346-020-01502-7
5. Liang, Z., et al.: A hybrid model consisting of supervised and unsupervised learning for landslide susceptibility mapping. Remote Sens. **13**, 1464 (2021)
6. Ma, Z., Mei, G., Piccialli, F.: Machine learning for landslides prevention: a survey. Neural Comput. Appl. **33**(17), 10881–10907 (2020). https://doi.org/10.1007/s00521-020-05529-8
7. Maxwell, A.E., et al.: Slope failure prediction using random forest machine learning and lidar in an eroded folded mountain belt. Remote Sens. **12**(3), 486 (2020)
8. Merghadi, A., et al.: Machine learning methods for landslide susceptibility studies: a comparative overview of algorithm performance. Earth Sci. Rev. **207**, 103225 (2020)
9. Pham, B.T., et al.: A novel ensemble classifier of rotation forest and Naive Bayer for landslide susceptibility assessment at the LUC Yen District, Yen Bai Province (Viet Nam) using GIS. Geomat. Nat. Hazards Risk **8**(2), 649–671 (2017)
10. Rodríguez, B.G., Meneses, J.S., Garcia-Rodriguez, J.: Improving landslides prediction: meteorological data preprocessing using random forest-based feature selection. In: Sanjurjo González, H., Pastor López, I., García Bringas, P., Quintián, H., Corchado, E. (eds.) SOCO 2021. AISC, vol. 1401, pp. 379–387. Springer, Cham (2022). https://doi.org/10.1007/978-3-030-87869-6_36
11. Youssef, A.M., Pourghasemi, H.R.: Landslide susceptibility mapping using machine learning algorithms and comparison of their performance at Abha Basin, Asir region, Saudi Arabia. Geosci. Front. **12**(2), 639–655 (2021)
12. Zhu, Q., et al.: Unsupervised feature learning to improve transferability of landslide susceptibility representations. IEEE J. Sel. Top. Appl. Earth Obs. Remote Sens. **13**, 3917–3930 (2020)

Landslide Prediction with Machine Learning and Time Windows

Byron Guerrero-Rodriguez[1], Jose Garcia-Rodriguez[2],
Jaime Salvador[1]([✉]), Christian Mejia-Escobar[1], Michelle Bonifaz[1],
and Oswaldo Gallardo[1]

[1] Central University of Ecuador, P.O. Box 17-03-100, Quito, Ecuador
{bvguerreror,jsalvador}@uce.edu.ec
[2] Department of Computer Technology, University of Alicante, Alicante, Spain

Abstract. Landslides are among the most destructive natural events, being their prediction necessary to prevent damage to people and infrastructure. This is a problem traditionally addressed with conventional methods, of a deterministic nature, with a limited number of variables and a static treatment of them. In this paper, we propose an approach based on Machine Learning, which has proven to be a successful alternative for dealing with geo-environmental problems. A feature engineering process allowed us to determine the most influential geological, geomorphological and meteorological factors in the occurrence of landslides. These variables together with the landslide inventory, form a dataset to train different machine learning models, whose evaluation and comparison showed the best performance of the multi-layer perceptron with an accuracy of 99.6%. Our contribution consists of treating precipitation dynamically with the use of time windows for different periods. In addition, we determined the ranges of values of the conditioning factors that combined would trigger a landslide for each time window. Both the multi-temporal prediction and the thresholds of the conditioning factors provide technical support for decision making in risk management.

Keywords: Landslides · Machine Learning · SVM · Random Forest · Multilayer Perceptron

1 Introduction

Landslides are highly dangerous nature-related phenomena that can cause loss of life and damage to infrastructure such as roads, buildings and houses [1]. They occur due to the downslope movement of a mass of rock, soil, or materials under the influence of gravity and can be initiated by rainfall, earthquakes and human activity [2]. The analysis and prediction of these events are not only of interest to geologists, but also to local and national authorities and the general public, to establish preventive measures before the disaster and mitigate potential risks to humans and infrastructures. For this reason, it is important

© Springer Nature Switzerland AG 2022
J. M. Ferrández Vicente et al. (Eds.): IWINAC 2022, LNCS 13259, pp. 193–202, 2022.
https://doi.org/10.1007/978-3-031-06527-9_19

to carry out studies that contribute to the prevention [3]. Most research works use conventional methods which are limited to a fixed number of static variables and do not handle the concept of *time windows* (multi-temporality). Our approach aims to address these limitations with *Machine Learning (ML)*, which has proven to be a successful alternative to traditional methods in the geological field [4]. The literature on landslides prediction by *ML* indicates that this is a growing research topic of increasing interest. In the review of related works, we focused on 3 main aspects: geographical area of the study, conditioning factors and types of models. The most studied geographical areas are in Asia, Europe and Africa follow, leaving North and Latin America as the least cited. As a case study, we considered the Aloag-Santo Domingo highway (Ecuador), historically affected by frequent landslides. Our work is thereby one of the first in a region where traditional methods prevail. Once the area of influence has been delimited, it is divided into small square cells of equal size as basic units of analysis and prediction. On the other hand, conditioning factors are a series of variables responsible for the phenomenon. They can be considered stationary and triggering (dynamic) if they vary more over time [5]. We identified variables from several fields, including Geomorphology, Geology, Land Use, Hydrology, and Meteorology. Through a feature extraction process based on the *frequency ratio* technique [6], we determined the most influential geo-environmental factors in occurrence of landslides. These variables, together with the landslide inventory, form an extensive *dataset*. Precipitation, despite being recognized as a triggering factor of the phenomenon, does not appear as one of the most considered variables in previous studies. Its dynamic nature requires special treatment, unlike other variables that do not change over time. Another of our contributions is to handle it in time windows: 3, 5, 7, 10, 15, 20 and 30 days. It is worth mentioning that in the context of climate change, a general increase in extreme precipitation is recognized [7]. Hence we can predict landslide occurrence in a multi-temporal manner, applying learning algorithms. There are many algorithms used, but 3 groups can be distinguished: *SVM* and *RF* notoriously in first place, followed by the *Logistic Regression*, *Multilayer perceptron (MLP)* and *Naive-Bayes*, ending with other less used methods. Thus we selected 3 of the most popular ones: *SVM*, *RF*, and *MLP*. The evaluation and comparison through confusion matrices and *ROC* curves, allows us to select the one with the best performance. The prediction for each time window outputs values between 0 and 1 representing the probability of landslide for each cell or pixel in the image of the study area. Selecting the maximum value (1) and the landslides occurred within the obtained area, we can establish the values of the conditioning factors at which the landslides will occur for each cumulative precipitation. The integration of *Geographic Information System* (*GIS*) and the *R* programming language has provided the best platform for preparing more accurate prediction models [8].

The remaining of the document is organized as follows: Sect. 2 details the work methodology; Sect. 3 presents the experiments, results and their corresponding discussion. Finally, Sect. 4 summarizes conclusions and possible directions for future work.

2 Methodology

Multi-temporal landslide prediction using *ML* follows the workflow depicted in Fig. 1, which was supported by computational tools: *R*, *RStudio*, and *GIS*.

Fig. 1. Workflow for multi-temporal landslide prediction.

Firstly, we delimited the geographic area near a highway in Ecuador known as Aloag-Santo Domingo, where hundreds of landslides have occurred in 60 years of operation [9]. This area is represented as a grid of square cells, which is a simple technique and the matrix format is convenient for various calculations. [10]. The cell (equivalent to a pixel) is the mapping unit and its size is a key aspect for analysis and prediction. We avoided redundancy with smaller sizes or loss of information with larger sizes. In the first case, we would have many cells with the same elevation and slope value, since in a few meters these values do not change significantly; whereas a larger size may imply a significant change in these variables, i.e. two or more values that cannot be included in a single cell. We defined pixels of 20 m × 20 m (Fig. 2) that also allow a reasonable processing time when running the prediction models. A total of 662303 cells are generated, each corresponding to one pixel of the image.

Fig. 2. Equivalence of cells and pixels in the study area.

A landslide inventory map is considered a primary step in the prediction process [11,12]. The importance of this historical record resides in the principle: "the past and the present are the keys to the future" [13], i.e. what happened helps to establish the conditions that produced these events and that would make their occurrence more likely in the future. The landslide inventory was provided by the Consejo Provincial of Pichincha, whose information was collected by the SEG company in the section from km 11.5 to km 77 (Alluriquin village) on the Aloag-Santo Domingo highway, and correspond to the year 2014 (Fig. 3). An accurate inventory includes the date of the event, the spatial extent, and the morphological and geological characteristics [14]. By using Google Earth, we located exactly a total of 45 landslides.

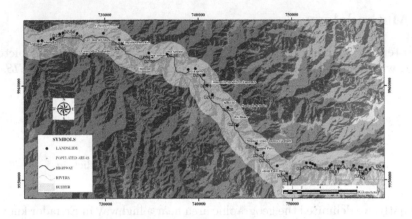

Fig. 3. Landslide inventory map of the study area.

Table 1. Frequency table of conditioning factors.

Factor	Class	N° px. domain	% px. domain	N° px. landslide	% px. landslide	FR
Wind speed	0.929-0.964	86152	13.01	979	60.96	4.69
Solar Radiation	16.38-17.02	110488	16.68	979	69.58	4.17
Max. temp.	27.96 - 28.12	97861	14.78	852	60.55	4.10
Elevation	657.37 - 1392.49	126664	19.07	1228	77.33	4.06
Rel. humidity	0.92-0.93	121762	18.38	979	69.58	3.78
Cum. precip. 10	140.23-147.57	61764	9.33	448	31.84	3.41
Cum. precip. 7	97.91-103.15	62112	9.38	448	31.84	3.40
Cum. precip. 3	41.76-44.05	62192	9.39	448	31.84	3.39
Cum. precip. 20	297.61-311.27	80028	12.08	575	40.87	3.38
Cum. precip. 3	44.05-46.17	80048	12.09	575	40.87	3.38
Cum. precip. 15	222.70-232.97	80056	12.09	575	40.87	3.38
Cum. precip. 5	73.63-77.15	80077	12.09	575	40.87	3.38
Cum. precip. 30	445.53-465.44	80098	12.09	575	40.87	3.38
Cum. precip. 15	211.69-222.70	62672	9.46	448	31.84	3.36
Cum. precip. 20	282.95-297.61	62687	9.47	448	31.84	3.36
Cum. precip. 10	147.57-154.54	80493	12.15	575	40.87	3.36
Cum. precip. 30	424.17-445.53	63022	9.52	448	31.84	3.35
Cum. precip. 7	103.15-108.11	81087	12.24	575	40.87	3.34
Cum. precip. 5	69.79-73.63	63409	9.57	448	31.84	3.33
Plane curv.	-0.280 - -0.091	14114	2.12	92	5.79	2.73
Lithology	Very high	63918	9.62	371	25.46	2.65
Min. temp.	20.93-21.10	195927	29.58	960	59.74	2.02
Aspect	141.17 - 215.99	119102	18.14	523	33.44	1.84
Slope	65.15 - 86.08	86312	13.15	361	23.08	1.76
Lithology	Very low	242076	36.44	917	62.94	1.73
Plane curv.	0.105 - 0.438	13408	2.02	50	3.15	1.56
Slope	28.69 - 46.58	100751	15.34	363	23.21	1.51
Plane curv.	-0.091 - -0.023	64607	9.73	230	14.48	1.49
Slope	46.58 - 65.15	82590	12.58	281	17.97	1.43
Max. temp.	27.667 - 27.817	71512	10.80	193	13.72	1.27
Profile curv.	-0.014-0.0007	537688	80.94	1309	82.43	1.02

The following are the conditioning factors, i.e. the variables responsible for the occurrence of landslides, whose values must be incorporated into the defined mapping units. Most previous studies have used vegetation cover, geomorphological and geological variables, and few have considered meteorological variables, despite the fact that precipitation is one of the main triggers. Once the data for these variables had been collected from various sources and processed by *GIS*, each variable is divided into 5 classes of values using *natural breaks of Jenks*. We carried out a *feature engineering* process to identify the most influential ones by means of the *frequency ratio* (*FR*) [6]. Thus we obtain a ranking of the classes belonging to each one of the conditioning factors. Values of *FR* higher than 1 indicate more influence on landslides, whereas values close to zero indicate no effect on the occurrence of the phenomenon [6]. Table 1 lists the variables and classes that reached the highest values of *FR*, above 1, a criterion used to select the factors as the most influential and relevant for the study. It is noted that precipitation has an intense relation with the occurrence of landslides. It has a dynamic and changing nature with its various accumulations in different periods of time, unlike the static nature of the other variables. Consequently, a multi-temporal analysis can be performed with landslides based on precipitation.

The most influential conditioning factors become the *predictor variables* (explanatory), whereas the occurrence or non-occurrence of landslide (1 or 0) will be the *target variable* (explained), and their values compose our dataset for the learning and prediction process. Table 2 presents its structure and properties.

Table 2. Dataset structure for landslide prediction.

Name	Class	Unit of measure	Type	Field
Landslide	Binary	-	Target	Risk management
Elevation	Quantitative	Meters (m)	Predictor	Geomomorphology
Slope	Quantitative	Grados (°)	Predictor	Geomomorphology
Aspect	Quantitative	Grades (°)	Predictor	Geomomorphology
Profile curvature	Quantitative	Adimensional	Predictor	Geomomorphology
Plane curvature	Quantitative	Adimensional	Predictor	Geomomorphology
Vegetation	Qualitative	-	Predictor	Land use
Lithology	Qualitative	-	Predictor	Geology
Max. Temp.	Quantitative	Grades (°C)	Predictor	Meteorology
Min. Temp.	Quantitative	Grades (°C)	Predictor	Meteorology
Wind speed	Quantitative	m/s	Predictor	Meteorology
Solar radiation	Quantitative	W/m^2	Predictor	Meteorology
Relative humidity	Quantitative	mmH2O	Predictor	Meteorology
3-day cum. precip.	Quantitative	mmH2O	Predictor	Meteorology
5-day cum. precip.	Quantitative	mmH2O	Predictor	Meteorology
7-day cum. precip.	Quantitative	mmH2O	Predictor	Meteorology
10-day cum. precip.	Quantitative	mmH2O	Predictor	Meteorology
15-day cum. precip.	Quantitative	mmH2O	Predictor	Meteorology
20-day cum. precip.	Quantitative	mmH2O	Predictor	Meteorology
30-day cum. precip.	Quantitative	mmH2O	Predictor	Meteorology

The data are organized in a large table, whose columns correspond to each variable (predictors and target); whereas each row is equivalent to one pixel of the study area map. It is noted that the precipitation is multi-temporal, subdivided into: cumulative precipitation of 3, 5, 7, 10, 15, 20, and 30 days, resulting 19 predictor variables. It is necessary a pre-processing to achieve a suitable format by pondering qualitative variables, balancing, and normalizing data.

Lithology and vegetation values must be converted to numbers, so we applied the *one-hot encoding* technique for its numerical representation. There are 4 lithological levels: low, medium, high and very high, according to their favorability for landslide occurrence. These categories are passed to the following value vectors: [1 0 0 0], [0 1 0 0], [0 0 1 0], and [0 0 0 1], respectively, and where the values 1 or 0 indicate the presence or non-presence of a certain class. Similarly for vegetation cover with only 3 categories. During training of the prediction model there should be no bias or preference for a majority class. The geographic extension covered by landslides is much smaller than the area where these events have not occurred. The dataset consists of 662303 registers, 1407 correspond to positive landslide cases. Based on geological criteria such as: low or no slopes, unfavorable lithology and vegetation for the occurrence of the phenomenon, we selected 1407 negative cases. In this way we got a new dataset smaller in size, but balanced. The variables fluctuate in different scales of values and their units of measurement are diverse, so we must put them on the same scale and eliminate the units of measurement. Automatic normalization solves the problem by generating values between 0 and 1.

One of the tasks that characterizes supervised machine learning is to split the dataset into two subsets: training and testing. The first is used to learn from the data and adjust the model parameters, whereas the second is used to evaluate the model's performance. The splitting ratio is 80–20%, respectively, in accordance with recommended practices. Once our dataset is prepared, it will be the main input for the execution of the *ML* algorithms.

3   Experimentation and Results

We have selected 3 algorithms based on previous work that would allow us to associate landslide occurrences with the causal predictors of landslides [15]. Here the *MLP, RF,* and *SVM* models are trained, receiving as input the balanced dataset of 2814 records, 1407 for landslide occurrence and the other half for non-occurrence. This will ensure that each model does not have a bias or preference for one of the two alternatives. Then, the balanced dataset is subdivided in a ratio of 80 and 20% for training and testing. Since it is a multi-temporal prediction with 7 time windows of precipitation, we configured 7 trainings for each model, and in each training we included only one of the cumulative precipitations. First for 3 days, then for 5, 7, 10, 15, 20 and up to 30 days of accumulation. In total, there are 21 experiments performed whose results are analyzed by means of the confusion matrices of each model on the training and test data, considering the label 0 for the absence of landslide and 1 for its occurrence. Performance metrics such as *accuracy, sensitivity* and *specificity* can be calculated to help us evaluate the model. For our prediction problem, we are interested in knowing these 3 indicators. Accuracy is the simplest and measures the percentage of data correctly classified by the model. For a better evaluation we complete it with the model sensitivity, that is, the percentage of successes for the occurrence of landslides exclusively. In contrast, the specificity of the model indicates the percentage of successes only for the absence of landslides. For accuracy, Table 3 summarizes the results for the test data only, as it gives us a better idea of how the models will behave in reality, i.e. with new data not seen during the training. For each model the accuracy values are quite similar. Comparing the 3 models, the neural network presents the highest accuracies, in particular the 20-day cumulative precipitation. Very close is the *RF* model where the same precipitation accumulation stands out. The *SVM* model has the lowest accuracy values, however, they are quite acceptable.

Table 3. Accuracy of the models for each accumulated rainfall.

Cumulative precipitation	MLP accuracy (%)	RF accuracy (%)	SVM accuracy (%)
3-day	99.47	98.31	90.54
5-day	99.47	97.56	90.81
7-day	98.75	97.03	90.90
10-day	99.11	98.18	91.07
15-day	99.29	97.56	91.07
20-day	99.64	99.25	91.07
30-day	99.47	98.00	91.16

In order to know the sensitivity and specificity of the model, we use the *ROC curve*, the area under the curve indicates the performance of the model. In the case of *MLP*, the area under the curve is more and also closer to the vertex (0, 1) suggesting the highest sensitivity and specificity. For *RF*, the specificity of the model is very good but the sensitivity is lower; whereas the specificity of *SVM* is very good but the sensitivity is lower than in the previous models. According to performance metrics and our interest in detecting landslide-positive cases as much as possible, i.e., maximizing sensitivity, we selected the *MLP* model for the multi-temporal prediction of landslide occurrence in the whole study area represented by 662303 cells. For each cell or pixel, we feed the model with the predictor variables and calculate the target variable, which fluctuates between 0 and 1, representing the probability of occurrence of the phenomenon. Then, we selected the cells whose prediction equals the maximum value 1 since they would fit the training data where landslide occurred, recalling that what happened determines the conditions under which these events will occur. The cells or pixels obtained are grouped to form the geographic area of highest landslide risk. Thus, we can identify the inventory landslides within this zone and know the conditions that produce landslides. This procedure is performed for each time window, establishing the range of values (minimum to maximum) of each predictor, including the cumulative precipitation. This combination of ranges determines the features of the terrain and the meteorological conditions that favor the phenomenon. We can plot the maximum and minimum line graphs, with the number of days of rainfall accumulation on the horizontal axis and the conditioning factor on the perpendicular axis (Fig. 4). It is necessary to point out that during the rainfall days considered, the ranges of precipitation obtained were: [39.90–43.48], [66.79–67.84], [105.78–105.79], [134.32–151.35], [217.33–228.16], [302.13–304.39], and [433.70–434.92] in mmH_2O, for 3, 5, 7, 10, 15, 20, and 30-day, respectively.

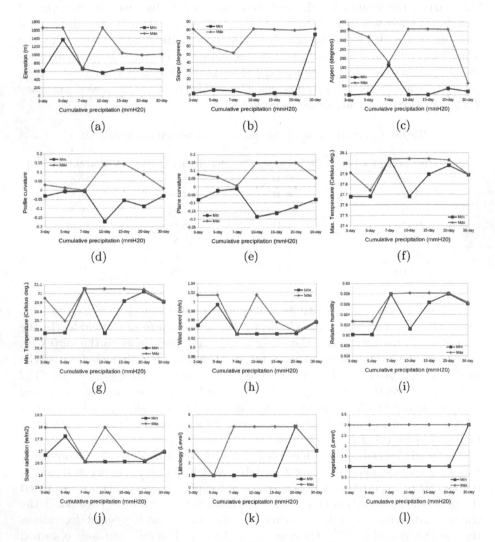

Fig. 4. Line plots for ranges values of: (a) Elevation; (b) Slope; (c) Aspect; (d) Profile curvature; (e) Plane curvature; (f) Max. temperature; (g) Min. temperature; (h) Wind speed; (i) Relative humidity; (j) Solar radiation; (k) Lithology; and (l) Vegetation.

Thus we can predict with what range of values of each factor the landslide will occur in a multi-temporal way based on the cumulative precipitation. For example, considering 3 days landslides will occur if the rainfall accumulates between 39.90 and 43.48 mmH_2O, at elevations between 611.14 and 1657.25 m, slopes from 2.18 to 80.77 °C, any aspect value, on surfaces with straight slope (curvatures tend to zero), maximum temperature between 27.68 and 27.91 $°rmC$, minimum temperature between 20.56 and 20.95 $°rmC$, a wind speed between 0.95 and 1.01 m/s, relative humidity of 0.92, solar radiation between 16.84 and 17.99 W/m^2, with lithologies level 1 to 3, and any type of vegetation. In a similar way, it is possible to perform the prediction for 5, 7, 10, 15, 20, and 30 days, identifying the corresponding ranges of each factor in the Figs. 4a to 4l. In general, we could say that as the number of days of precipitation accumulates, landslides will occur at lower elevations, approximately 600 m is required for landslides to occur (Fig. 4a). The events occur over a wide range of slope values, with the exception of 30-day cumulative precipitation, which would require 73 to 81 °C of slope (Fig. 4b). Landslides can occur in any orientation, except for 30 days of precipitation that would require slopes in N-E direction, between 18 and 63 °C azimuth (Fig. 4c). As rainfall accumulation increases, landslides tend to occur on surfaces with straight slopes, i.e. profile and plane curvatures converge to zero (Figs. 4d, 4e). Both the max. and min. temperatures do not vary significantly, and the values that would favour landslides tend to 28 and 20.9 °C, respectively (Figs. 4f, 4g). As precipitation accumulates, the wind speed favorable to the phenomenon decreases to 0.96 m/s (Fig. 4h). In contrast, the humidity is increasing up to a value of 92.6% (Fig. 4i). Landslides will occur with higher values of solar radiation on few rainy days and with lower solar radiation on many rainy days (Fig. 4j). For lithology (Fig. 4k), the greater accumulation of rainfall makes the soil material more favorable (level 5) for occurrence of landslides. Finally, all vegetation cover classes in the area are prone to landslides (Fig. 4l).

4   Conclusions and Future Work

We have presented the experimentation of 3 machine learning algorithms for the multi-temporal prediction of landslides in a geographic area characterized by the risk of affecting a strategic highway. The results obtained after training and evaluation with test data indicate suitable models, the highest accuracy corresponds to *MLP* with 99.6%, slightly outperforming *RF* by about 2%, and 10% over *SVM*. The *MLP* model allows us to make the prediction for each of the cells (pixels) that compose the study area, resulting in values between 0 and 1, which correspond to the probability of occurrence of the phenomenon. It is possible to know the risk of landslide even at every point of the highway. Precipitation is one of the most influential variables and is dynamic over time, so its treatment was multi-temporal, in contrast to other related works. In addition, we determined the thresholds of each of the variables to know the conditions that a terrain has to trigger a landslide. These products are valuable tools for taking action at certain points of the highway that are more susceptible, such as: ground compaction, protective meshes, or preventive measures. Finally, we can recommend the application of Deep Learning as an extension to our work.

References

1. Achour, Y., Pourghasemi, H.: How do machine learning techniques help in increasing accuracy of landslide susceptibility maps? Geosci. Front. **11** (2019). https://doi.org/10.1016/j.gsf.2019.10.001
2. Mora, R., Vahrson, W., Mora, S.: Mapa de Amenaza de Deslizamientos, Valle Central, Costa Rica. In: Centro de Coordinación para la prevención de desastres naturales en América Central (CEPREDENAC) (1992)
3. Rajakumar, P., et al.: Landslide susceptibility mapping in a hilly terrain using remote sensing and GIS. J. Indian Soc. Remote Sens. **35** (2007). https://doi.org/10.1007/BF02991831
4. Santos, D., Dallos, L., Gaona-García, P.A.: Algoritmos de rastreo de movimiento utilizando técnicas de inteligencia artificial y machine learning. Información tecnológica **31**, 23–38 (2020)
5. Đurić, U., et al.: Machine learning based landslide assessment of the Belgrade metropolitan area: pixel resolution effects and a cross-scaling concept. Eng. Geol. **256**, 23–38 (2019)
6. Arabameri, A., et al.: Landslide susceptibility evaluation and management using different machine learning methods in the Gallicash River Watershed, Iran. Remote Sens. **12** (2020). https://doi.org/10.3390/rs12030475
7. Di Napoli, M., Carotenuto, F., Cevasco, A., Confuorto, P., Di Martire, D., Firpo, M., Pepe, G., Raso, E., Calcaterra, D.: Machine learning ensemble modelling as a tool to improve landslide susceptibility mapping reliability. Landslides **17**(8), 1897–1914 (2020). https://doi.org/10.1007/s10346-020-01392-9
8. Saha, S., et al.: Machine learning-based gully erosion susceptibility mapping: a case study of Eastern India. Sensors **20**(5), 1313 (2020)
9. Rodríguez, B.G., Salvador-Meneses, J., Garcia-Rodriguez, J.: Predicting landslides with machine learning methods using temporal sequences of meteorological data. In: Sanjurjo González, H., Pastor López, I., García Bringas, P., Quintián, H., Corchado, E. (eds.) SOCO 2021. AISC, vol. 1401, pp. 348–357. Springer, Cham (2022). https://doi.org/10.1007/978-3-030-87869-6_33
10. Ba, Q., Chen, Y., Deng, S., Yang, J., Li, H.: A comparison of slope units and grid cells as mapping units for landslide susceptibility assessment. Earth Sci. Inform. **11**(3), 373–388 (2018). https://doi.org/10.1007/s12145-018-0335-9
11. Pham, B.T., et al.: A novel ensemble classifier of rotation forest and Naive Bayer for landslide susceptibility assessment at the Luc Yen district, Yen Bai Province (Viet Nam) using GIS. Geomat. Nat. Hazards Risk **8**(2), 649–671 (2017)
12. Ali, S.A., et al.: GIS-based landslide susceptibility modeling: a comparison between fuzzy multi-criteria and machine learning algorithms. Geosci. Front. **12**(2), 857–876 (2021)
13. Guzzetti, F., et al.: Landslide inventory maps: new tools for an old problem. Earth Sci. Rev. **112**(1), 42–66 (2012). ISSN: 0012-8252. https://doi.org/10.1016/j.earscirev.2012.02.001. https://www.sciencedirect.com/science/article/pii/S0012825212000128
14. Lu, P., et al.: Landslide mapping from multi-sensor data through improved change detection-based Markov random field. Remote Sens. Environ. **231**, 111235 (2019)
15. Merghadi, A., et al.: Machine learning methods for landslide susceptibility studies: a comparative overview of algorithm performance. Earth Sci. Rev. **207**, 103225 (2020)

Live TV Streaming Latency Measurement Using YOLO

Miguel Jose Esteve Brotons[1](✉)(iD), Miguel Angel Santiago Cabello[1](✉),
and José García-Rodríguez[2](✉)(iD)

[1] Telefonica I+D, Madrid, Spain
{miguel.estevebrotons,miguelangel.santiagocabello}@telefonica.com
[2] Computers Technology Department, University of Alicante, Alicante, Spain
jgarcia@dtic.ua.es

Abstract. This paper proposes a simple yet effective approach to measure the e2e latency in the live video streaming pipeline, from when the signal is generated in the production studios until it is played on the client device. The method is based on user-centric behavior by looking at the time the content is produced in the source context and comparing it with the current clock time at the playback device. Given a clock timestamp introduced in the signal at the production stage, we rely on an intelligent streaming latency measurement agent that, first, detects with YOLO that mark at the playout device, then use an OCR to convert the bitmap text in the clock to a string text, and finally, compares it with the real-time clock in the machine, providing real-time end to end streaming latency. Our method, even simple, allows us to measure the latency on any playout device, as it does not rely on any in-band signaling but a human-centric behavior simulated by an intelligent measurement agent.

Keywords: Streaming latency · Object Detection · YOLO · OCR · Measurement

1 Introduction

A lot has been written about the future of internet live TV. Decades ago, families would gather around the TV at the same time every week to watch a show together. Now, TV is available on the go, streaming on smartphones and tablets so that viewers can watch their favorite shows anytime, everywhere.

The evolution of TV intensified last years, and the trend will continue, with technology pushing towards new forms of entertainment. TV will continue to transform into a personalized experience, unlike anything we've ever seen. The personalization of the live TV experience leads to increased consumption of Video on Demand (VoD) like services, but still, live programs such as sports events will hold their space in the pure live streaming scope. However, live sports events require a lower latency to deliver a service that's on par with broadcast or pay-TV while still providing all the benefits of an over-the-top (OTT) distribution and not jeopardizing the viewer experience. DASH Industry Forum

© Springer Nature Switzerland AG 2022
J. M. Ferrández Vicente et al. (Eds.): IWINAC 2022, LNCS 13259, pp. 203–212, 2022.
https://doi.org/10.1007/978-3-031-06527-9_20

(DASH-IF) [4] is adopting a new technology standard to improve the latency in live TV over HTTP protocol. It will not eliminate latency but will for sure make it better. DASH-IF specifies the number of use cases that justify looking for a between architecture in streaming services to minimize the latency. For example, a live event distributed over DASH and regular TV distribution. The event should play out approximately simultaneously on both devices to avoid different perceptions of the same service spread over various platforms. The goal should be to get to a range of delays for the use of the service that is equivalent to cable and Internet Protocol Television (IPTV) services.

Today's live video streaming techniques vary depending on the target applications, use case, and slightly on the used access network technology. From IPTV based technologies, using protocols such as Real Time Streaming Protocol (RTSP) in conjunction with Real Time Protocol (RTP) and User Datagram Protocol (UDP) till more recent developments adopting HTTP as the transport protocol, delegating the video streaming control logic to the clients, first making use of progressive download, taking advantage of the available buffer in the device's memory, and then adding the use of specific adaptive streaming protocols over HTTP. Dynamic Adaptative Streaming over HTTP (DASH) protocol was defined as an attempt to standardize the options that had previously been developed separately using HTTP Live Streaming (HLS), HTTP Smooth Streaming (HSS), and other similar proprietary technologies in a single protocol.

HTTP Adaptative streaming (HAS) dominates OTT-based consumer video distribution today in live and VoD streaming. It is combined with the use of Content Delivery Networks (CDN). In HAS, the video stream is divided into a sequence of short media segments and delivered to the client using standard HTTP servers. With traditional HAS, the segment duration impacts the end-to-end (e2e) latency. One option to reduce e2e latency without shortening segment duration is to use chunked transfer encoding. The data in segments are composed of several chunks, so the encoder can send the different chunks as soon as those are prepared without having to wait to have the entire segment. This schema has led to Low Latency Streaming, which is being standardized in DASH Industry Forum.

In OTT live TV streaming monitoring, a complex problem is to measure the e2e latency of the video stream automatically concerning the contribution signal in the head-end. Several stages introduce latency from the contribution: 1) ingestion, 2) transcoding, 2) storage, 3) Just In Time (JIT) packaging, 4) delivery (CDN), 5) decoding in the end application. Each TV over IP service provider has its ecosystem. How the different stages are integrated is decisive when providing a Live Over Top service with minimum latency. The average e2e latency measurement requires, given a reference frame, identifying its absolute time in the video contribution, and then, once decoded and presented in the user interface, capturing the presentation time again and comparing it with the previously captured time. Given an implemented Low Latency solution, continuous monitoring as a quality parameter becomes essential. We refer to this problem as automatic e2e live streaming latency measurement. In this context, having an automatic end to end latency measurement mechanism acquires relevant importance.

The rest of the paper is then structured as follows. In Sect. 2, we run through the main contributions to date that try to solve the same problem in this or similar contexts. In Sect. 3, we describe the solution we have adopted and the steps we have followed to train the model. Section 4 presents the results obtained based on the number of training iterations, showing specific object detection metrics. Finally, in Sect. 5, we summarize conclusions and possible next steps.

2   Related Work

There are several initiatives that try to measure end-to-end video streaming latency, although in different application scenarios, in addition to the specific one of live TV services. Such is the case of video conference applications and remote control. [10] presents a tool, named vDelay, to measure capture-to-display latency (CDL) and frame rate of real-time video applications such as video chat and conferencing. It measures without modifying the source code of those applications, neither specific hardware. It relies on embedding an EAN-8 barcode-based timestamp in the caller's video and retrieving that timestamp at the called one. Assuming that the machines running the caller and called user agents are time-synchronized within an acceptable error, the CDL latency is the difference between the timestamp retrieved from the caller's video and the current system time at the machine running the called user agent. It utilizes a webcam attached to the caller machine that captures the image on the monitor that includes the timestamp. They use barcode4j [1] as open-source barcode generator. On the receiver side, the application allows selecting the area (top, left, bottom, right coordinates) where the barcode is displayed to grab the barcode image from the frame buffer and pass it to the barcode reader. They utilize zxing [8] as a barcode reader.

Similarly, in [16], the authors present a tool named Avcloack, able to measure several key performance metrics in Video Conference (VC) applications: mouth-to-ear latency and jitter, capture-to-display latency and jitter, and audio-visual synchronization skew. In addition to [10], Avcloack not only generates an EAN-8 barcode but also adds a component for one-way ME (Mouth-to-ear latency) by analogously transmitting timestamps over the VC audio channel. Like in vDelay, the authors assume that NTP synchronizes the sender's clocks and receiver's clock and that clock drift is negligible. They provide measurements on two popular VC applications: Skype and Google+ Hangouts.

In [13], and like in [10,16], the authors focus in measurement of latency in Video Conference applications. For video latency measurement, it also uses a QR-code. As in [10], the author considers to utilizes several timestamp patterns but ends using QR-Code, so it has the advantage of using checksums, with makes the detection robust in the presence of a lossy encoding schema. The paper adds a calibration run to subtract the processing delay introduced from the real measurement. [12] describes a modified codebase of [13] that enables a better user interface and support for audio. [15] extends the results in [14] that dealt only with network latencies in the control and feedback data, with an extensive overview of video delays in video feedback used for marine remote presence applications. They define video latency as the period needed for events in front of a camera sensor to appear on the operator's monitor. This delay is called glass-to-glass delay (G2G). The latency in the targeted application is measured by implementing a controlled scene observed by a camera. The application shows an image periodically changing color signaled with precise timestamps. At the same time, another application accepts a stream from a camera pointed at the screen with the timed changed events and detects the exact time of every change of visual effect. The latency is calculated as the time difference between the application changing the scene (i.e., the color of the image container) and when that change was detected in a video streamed from the camera. The author utilizes FFmpeg to generate the source image events. This method of capture-to-display delay is affected by parameters such as screen refresh and web camera frame rate. [9] presents a video communication chain model where all components that influence e2e latency have been introduced.

In [19] describes a similar approach applied to 360° live video streaming and evaluations setup running in the 5G test network. The experienced e2e latency is measured on different networks as test cases: wired (Ethernet), WLAN (802.11ad), and mobile (LTE-A). Delay measurements were divided into two methods: measurements with network performance indicator Qosim and measurements using screen clock capturing: the streaming video camera captures the current time in milliseconds from screen 1. The player plays the video on screen two that is alongside screen 1. A picture of the screens is taken and calculated the time difference.

A similar approach is followed in [20] where it is described an experimental evaluation setup of the low latency video streaming system for performance measurements using a 5G test network. The paper defines the latency in end-to-end video streaming as the delay between the time a camera captures a video frame until it appears on display. It divides the different steps into capture, encoding, transmission, decoding, and presentation. Each step adds some delay and the sum of the delays is the e2e latency. Like in [19], to evaluate the functionality and performance of low latency video streaming, two methods are used: using screen clock capture and using Qosim The first is considered as an end-to-end latency.

3   System Architecture

In our method, the TV signal must be timestamped on a frame basis with a mark encoding the real-time clock at the production stage. Some TV channels already provide the time clock on a box in the image in the simplest scenario. This is the case of canal 24 h [2] of Spain RTVE [6]. Canal 24 h is a free to air Spanish Television news channel that is produced containing a clock in the bottom right side of the image as shown in Fig. 1

Our approach is composed of two main blocks: a darknet [3] YOLO v3 [18] pretrained with Imagenet to detect that clock in a frame, and pytesseract OCR [7] to convert it to text, to compare that clock with the real-time clock. Figure 2 shows the detailed architecture of our approach.

Fig. 1. TV channel with production clock on the bottom right corner of the Image.

To train our system, we capture several videos, with frame resolution 1068×598, from canal 24 h and annotate those videos using the VOTT tool [5]. The chosen tool labels images or video frames and has an extensible model for exporting labeled data to different suitable formats.

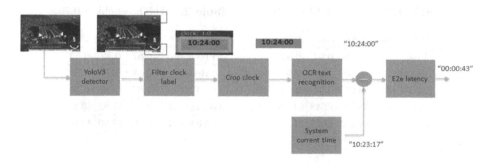

Fig. 2. System architecture

VOTT annotation is produced using csv format. A csv file is generate where each line contains "image", "xmin", "ymin", "xmax", "ymax", "label". There is no single standard annotation format when it comes to image annotation. Some typical object detection annotation formats are: COCO [17], stored in JSON, Pascal VOC [11], stored in XML or YOLO, where a .txt file with the same name that each image is created for each image file in the same directory. We utilize YOLO format, where each .txt file contains the annotations for the corresponding image file, that is <object class>, <object coordinates>, <width> and <heigth>.

As part of the data preprocessing stage, we convert the bounding boxes from format <xmin>, <xmax>, <ymin>, <ymax> to < x>, <y>, <width>, <height>, and then normalize them by diving "x", "width" and "y", "height" by "frame width" and "frame height", respectively.

4   Results

We tested our proposed architecture with a different number of images, but the system got excellent results with just a total of 90 train images and 38 test images. To enrich the annotations for other uses cases, we annotate two classes, the channel's logo, and the clock. The training was executed with 3 x GeForce RTX 3090, Cuda version 11020 (cuDNN 8.1.1). Batch size set to 64. Adam optimizer with learning rate 0.001, momentum 0.9, and decay is 0.00005. We trained up to a maximum number of batches (iterations) of 6000. The initial predicted time to train was 8.5 h.

After training with two classes, class id 0 for the clock and class id 1 for logo, we provide metrics for two Intersection over Union (IoU) thresholds, 0.5 and 0.75, using a confidence threshold of 0.25.

We compare the training results based on the number of iterations for a given dataset. We compare for 6000, 3600, and 1800 iterations, given that the training time is significatively different. Results are showed on Table 1 for IoU threshold 0.5 and on Table 2 for threshold 0.75.

Table 1. IoU Threshold = 0.50

Iterations	6000	3600	1800
Precision	0.99	0.94	0.92
Recall	1.00	1.00	0.97
F1	0.99	0.94	0.92
Average IOU	77.50	62.48	61.29
mAP@0.50	99.82	99.75	95.85

Table 2. IoU Threshold = 0.75

Iterations	6000	3600	1800
Precision	0.67	0.52	0.52
Recall	0.68	0.55	0.59
F1	0.67	0.54	0.56
Average IOU	55.35	41.82	43.23
mAP@0.75	55.77	42.90	43.04

On Fig. 3, 4 and 5 we show the loss and Mean average precision (mAP) curves for 6000, 300 and 1800 iterations respectively, for an IoU threshold 0.5. The convergence of the loss and mAP curves is very similar according to the results provided in Table 1.

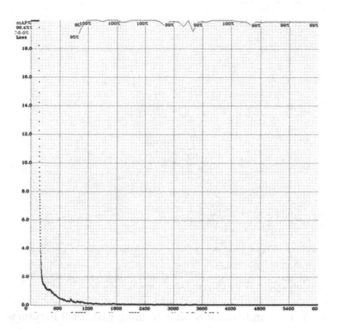

Fig. 3. Loss and accuracy after training with 6000 iterations.

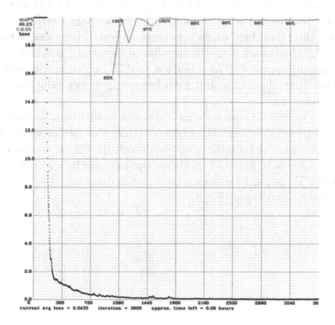

Fig. 4. Loss and accuracy after training with 3600 iterations.

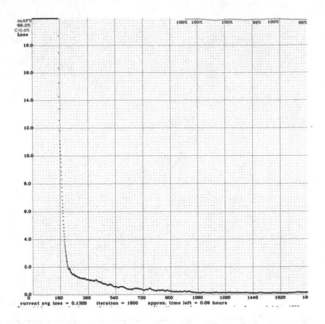

Fig. 5. Loss and accuracy after training with 1800 iterations

It is commonly accepted that if IOU is more significant than 0.5, the prediction is good enough. 0.5 is an arbitrary threshold that can be changed according to our specific problem. For our specific use case, it is better to consider an mAP@0.75 as the clock box mark represents a small fraction of the complete frame. The mAP decreases with the number of iterations but still in acceptable values even though with IoU Threshold set to 0.75, which is a significant threshold considering that the clock and logo bounding boxes relation with regards frame size is about 12.

Empirically, we tried to infer clock detection with image capture focused on different relative positions. We observed that the model works well, which demonstrates the spatial invariance of the detection. Figure 4 shows a mosaic of four inferences in which, for each of them, the capture frame buffer is displaced concerning the TV image. In all cases, the clock is detected, despite being located in different relative positions (Fig. 6).

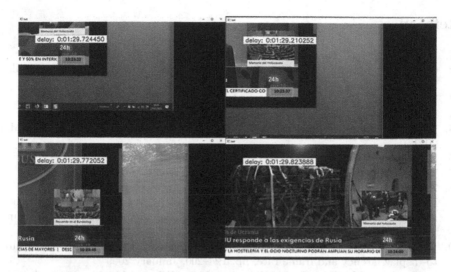

Fig. 6. Mosaic of 4 different captures where the capture frame buffer is displaced with regard the position of the image

5 Conclusions

Despite its simplicity, and to the best of our knowledge, no contribution proposes utilizing object detection to grab the clock timestamp to measure the latency e2e in a scenario of an OTT live TV Service provider. In the context of telecommunications operators providing linear television services by aggregating multiple channels contributed from satellite and cable signals, it is very likely that some of the added media, especially real-time thematic news channels or live sports content, contain a timestamp with the real-time in the broadcast time zone of the country. Our contribution exploits this facility without generating a pilot signal with the clock mark to measure the e2e live streaming latency in a user-centric approach.

To not depend on the fact that within the channel grid, there is a specific channel that shows the time in real-time, one option could be to generate a video signal with FFmpeg that contains a timestamp value and use this signal as a beacon. Also, the timestamp would be incorporated with a precision of milliseconds, instead of seconds, for better measurement accuracy. You could also get the clock reference of the server where FFmpeg is running and compare it with the latency measurement application running to discount the clock drift between the two servers.

Acknowledgement. We would like to thank "A way of making Europe" European Regional Development Fund (ERDF) and MCIN/AEI/10.13039/501100011033 for supporting this work under the MoDeaAS project (grant PID2019-104818RB-I00). This work has also been supported by Telefonica I+D. Furthermore, we would like to thank Nvidia for their generous hardware donation that made these experiments possible.

References

1. Barcode4j. http://barcode4j.sourceforge.net. Accessed 26 Jan 2022
2. Canal 24 horas. https://www.rtve.es/play/videos/directo/informativos/24h/. Accessed 30 Sept 2010
3. Darknet yolo. https://pjreddie.com/darknet/yolo/. Accessed 26 Jan 2022
4. Dashif. https://dashif.org/. Accessed 26 Jan 2022
5. Microsoft vott tool github. https://github.com/microsoft/VoTT. Accessed 12 Mar 2021
6. Rtve. https://www.rtve.es/. Accessed 14 Jan 2022
7. Tesseract. https://tesseract-ocr.github.io/. Accessed 07 Feb 2022
8. Zxing github. https://github.com/zxing/zxing. Accessed 26 Jan2022
9. Bachhuber, C., Steinbach, E., Freundl, M., Reisslein, M.: On the minimization of glass-to-glass and glass-to-algorithm delay in video communication. IEEE Trans. Multimedia, 1 (2017)
10. Boyaci, O., Forte, A., Baset, S., Schulzrinne, H.: vDelay: a tool to measure capture-to-display latency and frame rate, pp. 194–200, January 2009
11. Everingham, M., Gool, L.V., Williams, C.K.I., Winn, J.M., Zisserman, A.: The pascal visual object classes (VOC) challenge. Int. J. Comput. Vis. **88**, 303–338 (2009)
12. Jansen, J.: VideoLat: an extensible tool for multimedia delay measurements, pp. 683–686, November 2014
13. Jansen, J., Bulterman, D.C.A.: User-centric video delay measurements. In: NOSS-DAV 2013 (2013)
14. Kaknjo, A., Omerdic, E., Toal, D.: Measurement of network latency in remote presence applications. IFAC-PapersOnLine **49**(23), 193–198 (2016). 10th IFAC Conference on Control Applications in Marine Systems CAMS 2016
15. Kaknjo, A., Rao, M., Omerdic, E., Robinson, L., Toal, D., Newe, T.: Real-time video latency measurement between a robot and its remote control station: causes and mitigation. Wirel. Commun. Mob. Comput. **2018**, 1–19 (2018)
16. Kryczka, A., Arefin, A., Nahrstedt, K.: AvCloak: a tool for black box latency measurements in video conferencing applications. In: 2013 IEEE International Symposium on Multimedia, pp. 271–278 (2013)
17. Lin, T.Y., et al.: Microsoft COCO: common objects in context, May 2014
18. Redmon, J., Farhadi, A.: YOLOv3: an incremental improvement, April 2018
19. Uitto, M., Heikkinen, A.: Exploiting and evaluating live 360 low latency video streaming using CMAF. In: 2020 European Conference on Networks and Communications (EuCNC), pp. 276–280 (2020)
20. Uitto, M., Heikkinen, A.: Evaluation of live video streaming performance for low latency use cases in 5g, pp. 431–436, June 2021

Analysis of Functional Connectome Pipelines for the Diagnosis of Autism Spectrum Disorders

Clara Jiménez-Valverde[1], Rosa María Maza-Quiroga[1,3] (ID),
Domingo López-Rodríguez[2] (ID), Karl Thurnhofer-Hemsi[1,3](✉) (ID),
Ezequiel López-Rubio[1,3] (ID), and Rafael Marcos Luque-Baena[1,3] (ID)

[1] Department of Computer Languages and Computer Science, University of Málaga,
Málaga, Spain
`clarajimenez@uma.es`, {`rosammq,karlkhader,ezeqlr,rmluque`}`@lcc.uma.es`
[2] Department of Applied Mathematics, University of Málaga, Málaga, Spain
`dominlopez@uma.es`
[3] Instituto de Investigación Biomédica de Málaga - IBIMA, Málaga, Spain

Abstract. This paper explores the effect of using different pipelines to compute connectomes (matrices representing brain connections) and use them to train machine learning models with the goal of diagnosing Autism Spectrum Disorder. Five different pipelines are used to train six different ML models, splitting the data into female, male and all subsets so we can also research the effect of considering male and female patients separately. Our results conclude that pipeline and model choice impact results, along with using general or specific models.

Keywords: Autism · Connectome · Machine learning · Classification

1 Introduction

Autism Spectrum Disorder (ASD) affects the emotional, social, and communication abilities of the patient. Its prevalence among young children is 1–2% [10], but getting the diagnosis is not always easy, and it can require a long process. This is partly due to autism being a spectrum, meaning its characteristics vary between patients and genders. But also because it has been traditionally considered a

This work is partially supported by the Autonomous Government of Andalusia (Spain) under project UMA20-FEDERJA-108, project name Detection, characterization and prognosis value of the non-obstructive coronary disease with deep learning. All of them include funds from the European Regional Development Fund (ERDF). It is also partially supported by the University of Málaga (Spain) under grants B1-2019_01 and B1-2019_02. The authors also thankfully acknowledge the grants of the Universidad de Málaga and the Instituto de Investigación Biomédica de Málaga - IBIMA. Rosa Maza-Quiroga is funded by a Ph.D. grant from the Instituto de Salud Carlos III (ISCIII) of Spain under the i-PFIS program (IFI19/00009).

J. M. Ferrández Vicente et al. (Eds.): IWINAC 2022, LNCS 13259, pp. 213–222, 2022.
https://doi.org/10.1007/978-3-031-06527-9_21

male disease, causing many female patients to be undiagnosed, misdiagnosed, or lately diagnosed [9], which considerably affects their daily lives.

Recently, attention on early diagnosis of ASD through the use of machine learning techniques [3] is increasing. Studies have shown that neurotypical and non-neurotypical brains are wired differently [8], making work on computational modelling of connective differences that can aid in diagnosis important [7].

The study of brain connectivity is based on the construction of the *connectome* [13], a formal representation of the set of brain connections in the form of a weighted graph and its associated adjacency matrix. The graph's nodes generally represent macroscopic regions of the brain, and the weight of its edges indicate the strength of the connection between these regions. This model allows for its management and the application of advanced mathematical and computational techniques. The connectome can be constructed from both anatomical and functional magnetic resonance imaging (fMRI), the latter indicating not the physical connection between brain regions but the intensity of the coactivations between brain regions, i.e., their correlation.

In practice, there are several methods [2,4] to calculate the connectome from an MRI acquisition. This is a problem because (a) there is no standard method for calculation, and (b) the sensitivity of study results to the calculation method used has not been studied. This last point is of great importance, as the possible variability of the results of early diagnostic studies according to the use of different calculation methods is unknown.

This paper aims to analyze the effect of the selection of a particular calculation method on the early diagnosis of ASD using different machine learning methods. In this way, it will be possible to determine whether there is a strong dependence of the results on the *pipeline* of the connectome construction and to discuss how machine learning methods can achieve results comparable to those known in the literature.

The rest of this work is divided into three further sections. We begin by describing the dataset, pipelines, machine learning algorithms and methodology used to create the models. Their results are presented and discussed during the third section, followed by the conclusions.

2   Methodology

The same data has been used on all pipelines to correctly compare their effect on the connectomes produced. While the preprocessed data can be easily obtained for four of the pipelines, the fifth one needs to be executed on the original fMRIs.

Once we have computed the connectomes, all five data sets follow the same process. Firstly, each of them is divided into female, male, and all data sets, which will help us determine the importance of considering each sex separately. For each of these sets (15 in total), we trained six different machine learning (ML) classification models using Cross-Validation and Random Search. A general scheme of the methodology used can be found in Fig. 1.

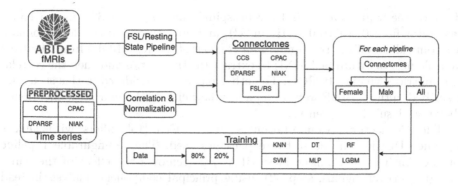

Fig. 1. Scheme of the analysis methodology applied on this study.

2.1   Dataset

The connectomes are computed from the files included in the first edition of the ABIDE project [6], which compiles fMRIs from different entities, totalling 1110 images from both ASD and control patients. The second edition's data has not been used because it is not included on the ABIDE Preprocessed Project [4], which provides time series of four pipelines with several configurations.

- 538 Patients with autism: 65 female and 473 male.
- 572 Patients with autism: 99 female and 473 male.

2.2   Functional Preprocessing Pipelines

A pipeline is a series of steps that, from a raw functional image sequence of a subject, build their correlation matrix (connectome). This work compares five fMRI processing pipelines designed to obtain the connectome. Usually, these pipelines are built from algorithms and functions of standard Neuroimaging processing packages, such as FSL, SPM, ANTs, or FreeSurfer.

The typical steps followed are: S1) basic image pre-processing, correcting artifacts at the beginning or end of the fMRI acquisition, as well as those due to patient motion, slice timing, usually accompanied by a reorientation in a standard coordinate system as well as normalization of the greyscale; S2) removal of signals confusing to process, such as white matter signal, or motion due to the heartbeat and respiration; S3) signal filtering, using, for example, a bandpass filter; S4) transformation (registration) of the image into the standard MNI152 [11] template and labeling to determine a brain parcellation, i.e., the identification of its anatomical regions; S5) calculation of the time series of the average signal (activations) in each anatomical region; S6) construction of the correlation matrix (connectome) between all the time series found in the previous step.

Different pipelines vary on the algorithms used and their parameters. Some add an extra step, usually to eliminate the impact of artifacts in the image.

The first of the pipelines is Duke's Python/FSL Resting State pipeline [2]. It incorporates a non-brain tissue removal stage in step S1), removes the possible effect of the white matter and cerebrospinal fluid signal in S2), uses a band-pass filter from 0.001 to 0.08 Hz in S3), and, in step S4), uses the Automatic Anatomical Labelling [14] standard for Regions of Interest (ROIs) from Montreal Neurological Institute (aal_MNI) to extract the time series and then the correlation matrices within 116 ROIs. The other pipelines considered in this study are described in the ABIDE website [6] and follow closely the four steps mentioned above, with subtle differences.

The Connectome Computation System (CCS) [15] differs with Duke's pipeline (DUKE) on the software packages used. The Configurable Pipeline for the Analysis of Connectomes (CPAC) [5] removes the effect of the white and grey matter signals, step S2), using principal component analysis instead of linear regression. The Data Processing Assistant for Resting-State fMRI (DPARSF) [16] does not normalize the intensity of the image on step S1). The Neuroimaging Analysis Kit (NIAK) [1] does not correct the timing of each slice, possibly inducing incorrect measurements. On step S2), NIAK removes low-frequency drifts using a discrete cosine basis with a 0.01 Hz high-pass cut-off, whereas the rest of the pipelines apply polynomial regression of the signal.

In the ABIDE platform, the results of the latter four pipelines are pre-computed and downloadable according to several preset settings. In our work, we have collected the data from the platform setting the parameters as close as possible to the ones used in Duke's pipeline since its results are not available online and were computed in-house. The main configurations set are: regarding bandpass filtering, the range is 0.01–0.1 Hz; signal regression is performed using the image's global average on every slice, contrary to the mean white matter and spinal fluid signals, more sophisticated; and while Duke's pipeline uses the aal_MNI atlas for ROIs, they use the aal atlas, with the same labels for ROIs, but a different template and a slightly different coordinate system.

For all pipelines, the resulting time series is used to compute the normalized connectomes, as the normalized correlation matrices between them.

2.3   Machine Learning Methods

The six supervised machine learning classifiers used are K-nearest neighbors, Decision Trees, Random Forest, Support Vector Machines, Multilayer Percep-tron, and LightGBM, using the algorithms available on scikit-learn's Python package [12]. Training has been performed separately for each pipeline and dataset (female, male, and both), and 5-fold cross-validation combined with Random Search for each chunk has been used to ensure the models' validity. The search grid for each model has been adjusted individually for each pipeline and dataset to aim at the best possible results.

- **K-Nearest-neighbors** (KNN) is one of the most basic classifiers since it simply stores training data and their class and then compares new data to its k nearest neighbors. The class with the most neighbors is assigned.
- **Decision Trees** (DT) creates models based on rules with higher complexity as the tree's depth increases. These rules are created by dividing training data

into two iteratively, basing divisions on differences between each subset and applying them when certain information gain is achieved.

- **Random Forests** (RF) is an ensemble method, meaning it combines different models to obtain better results. It uses a series of Decision Trees' probabilistic results to reach a verdict.
- **Support Vector Machines** (SVM) create a series of hyper-planes to split training data into its different classes. The best hyperplanes are chosen based on their distance to the nearest points.
- **Multilayer Perceptron** (MLP) belongs to the Neural Networks family. It contains an input and an output layer, with at least one hidden layer in between containing the main weights of the model.
- **LightGBM** (LGBM) uses decision tree-based algorithms seeking better accuracy with higher speed and efficiency while using less memory and therefore handling large-scale data. It achieves this with histogram-based algorithms and best-first growing criteria.

3   Experimental Results

This section presents the experimental results obtained using the six ML methods specified above. The five pipelines analyzed in this paper were compared for each method and each subset of the data (male, female, and all data).

For this purpose, the mean accuracy, sensitivity (True Positive Rate, TPR), and specificity (True Negative Rate, TNR) were computed for train and test data using 5-fold CV combined with random search:

$$Acc = \frac{TP + TN}{TP + FP + FN + TN} \tag{1}$$

$$TPR = \frac{TP}{TP + FN}, \qquad TNR = \frac{TN}{TN + FP} \tag{2}$$

where TP, TN, FP and FN are the true positives, true negatives, false positives, and false negatives, respectively.

First, the results for female data are presented in Figs. 2, 3, and Table 1. KNN and DT models produced the worst trainings, except for the DUKE pipeline using KNN. However, it is probably due to overfitting since the test accuracy is not remarkable. On the other hand, the best results on the training sets were obtained using the MLP and LGBM models, reaching almost 100% accuracy. Now, if we focus on the test sets (Fig. 3), i.e., unseen data, we can have a better overview of the performance of each method. It is shown that SVM and MLP are the best options, specifically for CCS, CPAC, and DPARSF pipelines, reaching accuracies around 70%.

Although CCS and CPAC are the most stable protocols, there is no clear optimum pipeline, meaning that the type of machine learning method used does not matter since they provide the best classification metric for female data. DUKE and NIAK protocols are not recommendable for any method.

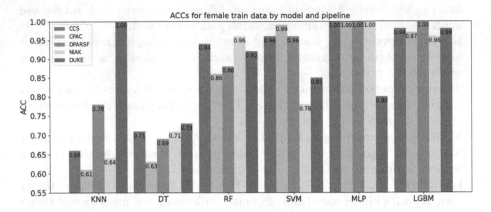

Fig. 2. Mean ACCs for female train data using 5-fold cross-validation.

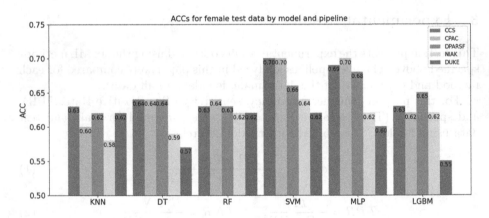

Fig. 3. Mean ACCs for female test data using 5-fold cross-validation.

Table 1. Average Sensitivity (TPR) and Specificity (TNR) measures for female data on the test set using 5-fold cross-validation. Best results are in bold.

	CCS		CPAC		DPARSF		NIAK		DUKE	
	TPR	TNR	TPR	TNR	TPR	TNR	TPR	TNR	TPR	TNR
KNN	0.63	0.72	0.61	0.20	0.62	0.53	0.60	0.07	0.62	0.67
DT	0.66	0.55	0.64	0.16	0.65	0.64	0.64	0.27	0.61	0.26
RF	0.63	0.60	0.63	0.68	0.63	0.51	0.63	0.71	0.62	0.57
SVM	0.70	0.73	**0.72**	0.71	0.66	0.69	0.64	0.70	0.64	0.61
MLP	0.71	0.64	0.70	**0.76**	0.68	0.67	0.65	0.54	0.64	0.51
LGBM	0.65	0.56	0.65	0.54	0.66	0.62	0.65	0.52	0.60	0.40

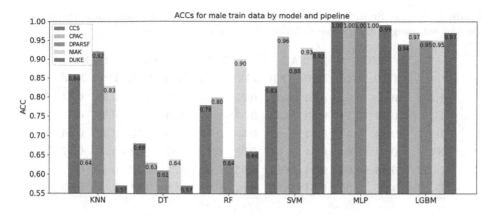

Fig. 4. Mean ACCs for male train data using 5-fold cross-validation.

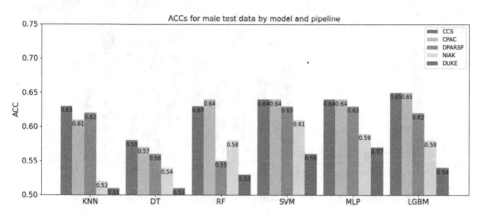

Fig. 5. Mean ACCs for male test data using 5-fold cross-validation.

Table 1 summarizes the TPRs and TNRs obtained by each model and pipeline. As in other medical diagnosis tasks, having a low false negative rate is essential. Thus, a high TNR is an objective. The best measures were achieved using the CPAC pipeline, reaching 72% TPR and 76% TNR for SVM and MLP models, respectively. Specifically, MLP seems to be the most accurate for both measures. CCS pipeline also gives good rates using the SVM model. The rest of the pipelines remain behind, being the KNN model the worst classifier.

Moving on to results for male data (shown in Figs. 4, 5, and Table 2), the overall best training results were obtained once again with MLP and LGBM, while DT gave the worst ones by far. Looking at the test sets, accuracies do not vary too much between models, excepting DT, which has the lowest overall scores. The used pipeline has influence, with CCS and CPAC giving the best results (up to 65% accuracy) and DUKE the worst.

The sensitivities and specificities have decreased a bit concerning female data, reaching a maximum of 65% TPR and 66% TNR. Nevertheless, the larger

Table 2. Average Sensitivity (TPR) and Specificity (TNR) measures for male data on the test set using 5-fold cross-validation. Best results are in bold.

	CCS		CPAC		DPARSF		NIAK		DUKE	
	TPR	TNR	TPR	TNR	TPR	TNR	TPR	TNR	TPR	TNR
KNN	0.63	0.63	0.60	0.63	0.62	0.64	0.52	0.52	0.53	0.54
DT	0.59	0.59	0.58	0.57	0.57	0.56	0.53	0.55	0.50	0.42
RF	0.64	0.62	0.64	0.63	0.59	0.54	0.59	0.57	0.53	0.54
SVM	0.64	0.64	0.64	0.64	0.63	0.64	0.60	0.62	0.56	0.57
MLP	0.64	0.64	0.64	0.65	0.63	0.64	0.58	0.61	0.57	0.57
LGBM	**0.65**	0.65	0.64	**0.66**	0.62	0.63	0.58	0.59	0.54	0.55

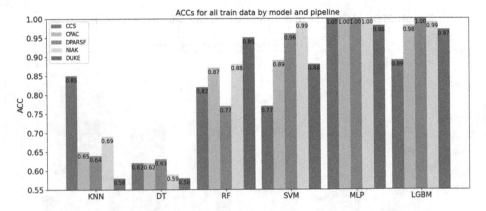

Fig. 6. Mean ACCs for all train data using 5-fold cross-validation.

amount of data (around five times more than female) has provoked a better classification for KNN and DT, giving now reasonable results. Still, CCS and CPAC provide the best rates while DUKE almost does not overcome the 50%.

Results for the subset containing all data are found in 6, 7, and Table 3. Training accuracies show better results for MLP and LGBM and worse ones for DT, once more. MLP offers the best results, reaching 70% accuracy on CPAC preprocessing for the test set. SVM is also close to that score. CCS is again the second-best pipeline, and NIAK and DUKE have inferior performance.

Table 3 shows that CCS pipeline are highly competitive, having the best TNR (68%). This is a more reliable value since we have a big and diverse dataset. MLP and SVM are again the best classifiers, depicting similar sensitivity and specificity (67%). It is also remarkable that a simpler model such as KNN performs better or at least has the same TNR. Clearly, DUKE is the worst pipeline.

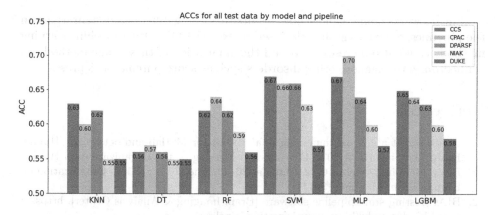

Fig. 7. Mean ACCs for all test data using 5-fold cross-validation.

Table 3. Average Sensitivity (TPR) and Specificity (TNR) measures for all data on the test set using 5-fold cross-validation. Best results are in bold.

	CCS		CPAC		DPARSF		NIAK		DUKE	
	TPR	TNR	TPR	TNR	TPR	TNR	TPR	TNR	TPR	TNR
KNN	0.62	**0.68**	0.58	0.67	0.60	0.67	0.55	0.55	0.57	0.53
DT	0.57	0.57	0.58	0.57	0.58	0.56	0.56	0.43	0.55	0.57
RF	0.61	0.64	0.64	0.66	0.61	0.65	0.58	0.61	0.57	0.55
SVM	0.66	**0.68**	**0.67**	0.66	**0.67**	0.66	0.63	0.63	0.57	0.57
MLP	**0.67**	**0.68**	**0.67**	0.66	0.65	0.63	0.60	0.60	0.58	0.56
LGBM	0.65	0.65	0.64	0.64	0.64	0.62	0.60	0.60	0.59	0.57

4   Conclusions

After analyzing our results, we can extract a series of conclusions. Generally, their accuracies are not great, since the maximum values achieved are 70% for female and all data and 65% for male data. The best TPRs and TNRs are also close to these values, the best combination being 70% TPR and 76% TNR for the MLP model using female CPAC-processed data. It seems like female-oriented models are more specific and sensitive than general models, but when it comes to male patients, using male-specific models worsens the results.

Regarding pipeline choice, it does impact results, with CCS and CPAC pipelines being the most reliable ones, constantly providing results among the best. NIAK and DUKE are the opposite, usually resulting on lower values. The one subset where results are more balanced between pipelines is the female one, with less harsh differences. Model choice also impacts the outcome. SVM and MLP models repeatedly stand out as the ones with better results, with the addition of LGBM on male data and KNN on all data. DT, on the other hand, is consistently the worst one.

Future works could explore how results vary using different configurations on the pipelines, or changing the atlas used to extract ROIs. Other machine learning methods could also be researched and the application of these same methods on connectomes to diagnose other disorders such as schizophrenia or depression.

References

1. Bellec, P., et al.: A neuroimaging analyses kit for Matlab and octave. In: Human Brain Mapping HBM 2011 17th Annual Meeting of the Organization on Human Brain Mapping, Quebec City, Canada, 26–30 June 2011, pp. 1–5. Organization on Human Brain Mapping (2011)
2. BIAC resting state pipeline software [Brain Imaging & Analysis Center]. https://wiki.biac.duke.edu/biac:analysis:resting_pipeline
3. Bone, D., et al.: Applying machine learning to facilitate autism diagnostics: pitfalls and promises. J. Autism Dev. Disord. **45**(5), 1121–1136 (2015)
4. Craddock, C.A., et al.: The neuro bureau preprocessing initiative: open sharing of preprocessed neuroimaging data and derivatives. Front. Neuroinformat. **7** (2013)
5. Craddock, C., et al.: Towards automated analysis of connectomes: the configurable pipeline for the analysis of connectomes (C-PAC). Front. Neuroinform. **42**, 10–3389 (2013)
6. Martino, D., et al.: The autism brain imaging data exchange: towards a large-scale evaluation of the intrinsic brain architecture in autism. Mol. Psychiatry **19**(6), 659–667 (2014)
7. Heinsfeld, A., et al.: Identification of autism spectrum disorder using deep learning and the abide dataset. NeuroImage: Clinical **17**, 16–23 (2018)
8. Hong, S.J., et al.: Atypical functional connectome hierarchy in autism. Nat. Commun. **10**(1), 1–13 (2019)
9. Lockwood Estrin, G., et al.: Barriers to autism spectrum disorder diagnosis for young women and girls: a systematic review. Rev. J. Autism Dev. Disorders (2020)
10. Maenner, M.J., et al.: Prevalence of autism spectrum disorder among children aged 8 Years-Autism and developmental disabilities monitoring network, 11 Sites, United States, 2016. MMWR Surveill. Summ. **69**(4), 1–12 (2020)
11. Mazziotta, J.C., et al.: A probabilistic atlas of the human brain: theory and rationale for its development. Neuroimage **2**(2), 89–101 (1995)
12. Pedregosa, F., et al.: Scikit-learn: machine learning in Python. J. Mach. Learn. Res. **12**, 2825–2830 (2011)
13. Sporns, O., et al.: The human connectome: a structural description of the human brain. PLoS Comput. Biol. **1**(4), e42 (2005)
14. Tzourio-Mazoyer, N., et al.: Automated anatomical labeling of activations in SPM using a macroscopic anatomical parcellation of the MNI MRI single-subject brain. Neuroimage **15**(1), 273–289 (2002)
15. Xu, T., et al.: A connectome computation system for discovery science of brain. Sci. Bull. **60**(1), 86–95 (2015)
16. Yan, C., Zang, Y.: Dparsf: a matlab toolbox for "pipeline" data analysis of resting-state fmri. Front. Syst. Neurosci. **4**, 13 (2010)

A Novel Continual Learning Approach for Competitive Neural Networks

Esteban J. Palomo[1,2](✉)🆔, Juan Miguel Ortiz-de-Lazcano-Lobato[1,2]🆔,
José David Fernández-Rodríguez[1,2]🆔, Ezequiel López-Rubio[1,2]🆔,
and Rosa María Maza-Quiroga[1,2]🆔

[1] University of Málaga, Bulevar Louis Pasteur, 35, 29071 Málaga, Spain
{ejpalomo,jmortiz,josedavid,ezeqlr,rosammq}@lcc.uma.es
[2] Biomedic Research Institute of Málaga (IBIMA), C/ Doctor Miguel Díaz Recio, 28,
29010 Málaga, Spain

Abstract. Continual learning tries to address the stability-plasticity dilemma to avoid catastrophic forgetting when dealing with non-stationary distributions. Prior works focused on supervised or reinforcement learning, but few works have considered continual learning for unsupervised learning methods. In this paper, a novel approach to provide continual learning for competitive neural networks is proposed. To this end, we have proposed a different learning rate function that can cope with non-stationary distributions by adapting the model to learn continuously. Experimental results performed with different synthetic images that change over time confirm the performance of our proposal.

Keywords: Continual learning · Unsupervised learning · Competitive neural networks

This work is partially supported by the Ministry of Science, Innovation and Universities of Spain under grant RTI2018-094645-B-I00, project name Automated detection with low-cost hardware of unusual activities in video sequences. It is also partially supported by the Autonomous Government of Andalusia (Spain) under project UMA18-FEDERJA-084, project name Detection of anomalous behavior agents by deep learning in low-cost video surveillance intelligent systems. It is also partially supported by the Autonomous Government of Andalusia (Spain) under project UMA20-FEDERJA-108, project name Detection, characterization and prognosis value of the non-obstructive coronary disease with deep learning. All of them include funds from the European Regional Development Fund (ERDF). It is also partially supported by the University of Malaga (Spain) under grants B1-2019_01, project name Anomaly detection on roads by moving cameras, and B1-2019_02, project name Self-Organizing Neural Systems for Non-Stationary Environments. The authors thankfully acknowledge the computer resources, technical expertise and assistance provided by the SCBI (Supercomputing and Bioinformatics) center of the University of Málaga. They also gratefully acknowledge the support of NVIDIA Corporation with the donation of two Titan X GPUs. The authors also thankfully acknowledge the grant of the Universidad de Málaga and the Instituto de Investigación Biomédica de Málaga - IBIMA.

J. M. Ferrández Vicente et al. (Eds.): IWINAC 2022, LNCS 13259, pp. 223–232, 2022.
https://doi.org/10.1007/978-3-031-06527-9_22

1   Introduction

Machine learning models are trained from fixed datasets and stationary environments, often overcoming human-level ability. However, these models fail to emulate the process of human learning, which is efficient, robust, and able to learn incrementally, from sequential experience in a non-stationary world [1]. Continual learning is an increasingly relevant area of study that tries to improve the ability of modern learning systems to deal with non-stationary distributions [2]. The main challenge here is the stability-plasticity dilemma: learning requires plasticity for the integration of new knowledge, but also stability in order to prevent the forgetting of previous knowledge. Too much stability will impede the efficient coding of this data, whereas too much plasticity will result in previously encoded data being constantly forgotten [3]. This last problem is also known as catastrophic forgetting, which is defined as a complete forgetting of previously learned information by a neural network exposed to new information [4,5]. Thus, there has been new research interested in the continual learning problem in recent years [6–9]. However, most of these techniques have focused on supervised and reinforcement learning by attempting to learn a series of tasks sequentially, but little attention has been paid to the use of these techniques in unsupervised learning for clustering tasks where input distributions can change over time.

Unsupervised learning aims to analyze a collection of unlabeled data and find structures or patterns without the intervention of a human expert. The information discovered by unsupervised machine learning algorithms is typically used to organize data into meaningful groups based on their similarities or differences [10]. However, it can also be used to establish relationships between features in a dataset [11] or to reduce the dimensionality of data with a large number of characteristics to a new compact data representation in which the features that are redundant or provide little information are not taken into consideration [12].

Competitive neural networks are classical unsupervised models that naturally categorize the input data [13]. They follow the winner-take-all training approach, where the weight vector of each of its processing units, known as neurons, are adapted so that it approximates the mean or centroid of a data cluster. On each training step, only the winning neuron is updated, that is, the neuron with the weight vector that is closest to the current input vector is the only one that change the cluster it represents by taking into account the information provided by the input vector.

Competitive models excel at adaptive vector quantization [14] and have been successfully applied to image processing. Regarding color image segmentation, [15] shows the efficiency of a competitive learning algorithm as a tool for clustering color space whereas [16] trains a competitive network with chromaticity samples of different colors in HSV space and uses it to determine the dominant colors that are used later in the segmentation phase. The ability of a probabilistic competitive neural network to compress multispectral image data is studied in [17]. In addition, in [18] a rival penalized competitive neural network is part of a system designed to recognize human behavior based on body postures in a video sequence.

The reminder of this paper is organized as follows. In Sect. 2, the proposed continual learning competitive model is defined. Experimental results are reported in Sect. 3. Finally, Sect. 4 is devoted to conclusions.

2   The Model

In a competitive learning network composed of K neurons, the training phase can be understood as a sequence of steps during which the network learns to represent the distribution of the input data. Each neuron i has a weight vector $w_i(t)$, which estimates the centroid of the cluster which the neuron represents. In each step t, a sample (data vector) $x(t)$ from the input data is presented to the network, and the selected neuron s is the one with the closest weight vector in the input space, i.e., the neuron whose weight vector is more similar to the input vector. The Euclidean distance is chosen as the measure to estimate the similarity between a neuron weight vector $w_i(t)$ and the input sample $x(t)$ at the training step t:

$$s = winner(t) = argmin_{1 \leq i \leq K} \|x(t) - w_i(t)\|_2 \tag{1}$$

Then, only the winning neuron s is updated according to the updating rule:

$$w_s(t+1) = w_s(t) + \alpha(t)\left(x(t) - w_s(t)\right) \tag{2}$$

In that rule, $\alpha(t)$ is a scalar factor called learning rate that represents the size of the correction, and is monotonically decreasing:

$$\alpha(t) = \frac{\alpha(t-1)}{d(t)} \tag{3}$$

where $d(t)$ is a decay function. Typically, the training phase is divided in two stages. In the first one the neurons are widely but crudely distributed to model the distribution of the input data. For that purpose, the learning rate usually decreases linearly, i.e., $d(t) = 1 + at$, or exponentially, i.e., $d(t) = e^{at}$, with $a \in \mathbb{R}^+$. After that, a second stage is intended to fine-tune the positions of the weight vectors and the learning rate is held constant at a low value.

After the training phase, the weights are fixed and each new input vector is assigned to the cluster corresponding to the neuron with the closest weight vector. If the training was successful, the weights of the neurons are distributed so that they represent the cluster centroids of a Voronoi tesselation.

Our goal is to adapt this model to make it able to learn continuously: after learning a specific input distribution, the neural network should be able to adapt and change the configuration of its weight vectors to represent a different input distribution. We seek to achieve this goal by using a different scaling strategy during training: instead of using a scaling factor α purely dependent on t, a

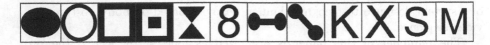

Fig. 1. Binary images used in the experiments, the black pixels in each one representing a rasterized shape.

function that relies on the Euclidean distances between samples and winning neuron weights $\|x(t) - w_s(t)\|_2$ in the last N time steps, from t to $t - N + 1$, is defined. We will note the Euclidean distance as $e(t)$, since it can be seen as the error at each time step t.

The core idea is that if the input distribution changes, the $e(t)$ distances will increase, thus increasing the scaling factor α, which allows the neural model to adapt to the new input distribution and redistribute its neurons more effectively. In order to reduce the effect of noise and outliers, which could hinder the learning process of the network, the median of these distances is proposed as a consensus measure, noted as $C(t)$. Then, that value is used as input for a monotonically increasing function f:

$$\alpha(t) = f(C(t)) \tag{4}$$

Different monotonic function types are considered in the experiments:

- Linear: $\alpha(t) = aC(t)$
- Quadratic: $\alpha(t) = a\left(C\left(t\right)\right)^2$
- Cubic: $\alpha(t) = a\left(C\left(t\right)\right)^3$

Since in the context of the updating rule it only makes sense for $\alpha(t)$ to take values in the $[0 \ldots 1]$ range, the results of these functions are clamped to that interval. All of these functions have been modelled with just a single parameter a in order to limit the parameter space to search, as well as to avoid non-monotonic function shapes. Note that the number of parameters remains the same since parameter a replaces parameter of the same name from (3).

3   Experimental Results

3.1   Dataset

To test the proposed learning system, we use it to model rasterized shapes. Each shape comes from a binary image, as seen in Fig. 1. For each binary image, the normalized coordinates of all black pixels are randomly sampled 10000 times. We perform training tests for sequences of two sampled shapes: in each test, we feed the learning system first 10000 samples from one shape, then 10000 samples from another shape, to test whether it can adapt to different models over time. The system will first adapt to model the input distribution of the first shape, then it will change to attempt to capture the second one.

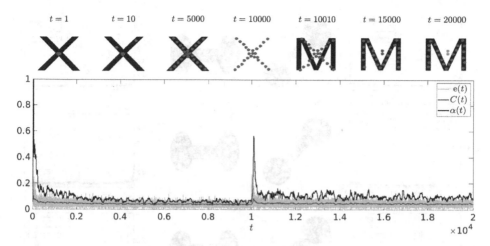

Fig. 2. One of the conducted experiments: from X to M, with $N = 50$, and a cubic function $\alpha(t) = 1000 \cdot C(t)^3$. *Above*: configuration of the neuron weight vectors (red dots) at different training steps, with the shape the samples are coming from in black (no background shape is drawn at $t = 10000$, as this is the time step when we finish feeding samples from the first shape, just before starting feeding samples from the new shape). At $t = 20000$, the neurons marked in green are dead, i.e., no sample is nearer to them than to any other one. *Below*: graph showing the evolution of $e(t)$, $C(t)$ and $\alpha(t)$ through the online training process. (Color figure online)

To quantitatively evaluate the results of each experiment, we measure how good is the system at modeling the samples from the last shape presented to them, using the Mean Quantization Error:

$$\text{MQE} = \frac{1}{K} \sum_{i=1}^{K} \text{qc}_i$$

In the above equation, qe_i is the quantization error of neuron i, defined as the sum of distances between the final weight vector w_i (after training is completed) and the samples of its receptive field R_i, i.e., the $x_1, \ldots, x_j, \ldots x_{R_i}$ input samples that are closer to w_i than to any other weight vector:

$$\text{qe}_i = \sum_{j=1}^{R_i} \|x_j - w_i\|$$

For each sequence of two shapes, we perform an array of tests for all three possible function types (linear, quadratic, cubic), and for each function type a different array of a values, since each function type requires its a parameter to be in a different scale to approximately keep the output of the function roughly at the $[0 \ldots 1]$ range. We have logarithmically spaced (noted as l.s. in the following) the tested values:

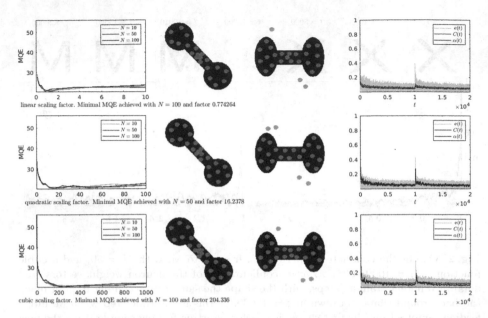

Fig. 3. Results for a sequence of two images: first the inclined dumbbell shape, then the horizontal version. Each row corresponds to a function type (linear, quadratic, cubic). *First column*: each graph shows the results of an array of experiments; we represent the MQE value achieved after the learning phase (one MQE for each experiment); and each line represents the MQE values for an array of experiments, all of them with a specific N and varying scaling factor a. The parameters achieving the best MQE for each function type are recorded below each graph. *Second, third and fourth columns*: in each row, for the experiment with the best MQE for the function type associated to that column, the second and third columns show the neurons (red dots) at $t = 10000$ (right after the samples from the first shape) and at $t = 20000$ (right after the samples from the second shape), respectively. In the third column, neurons marked in green are dead, i.e., they do not represent any sample. The graphs in the fourth column show the evolution of $e(t)$, $C(t)$ and $\alpha(t)$ for each respective experiment with the best MQE. (Color figure online)

- For linear functions, 10 l.s. values between 0.1 and 10.
- For quadratic functions, 20 l.s. values between 0.1 and 100.
- For cubic functions, 30 l.s. values between 0.1 and 1000.

We experiment with three values for N, the size of the time window to compute $C(t)$: 10, 50 and 100. Additionally, we fix the number of neurons at $K = 25$, but please note that (as a result) steady-state mean quantization error (MQE) values will also depend on the area and geometry of the shape: the larger the area, the larger the subsets of samples closer to each neuron, naturally leading to bigger MQE values. We also initialize each neuron's $w_i(0)$ to the mean of a random selection of $10000/K$ samples from the first shape, which in practice tends to cluster together all neurons towards the centroid of the distribution.

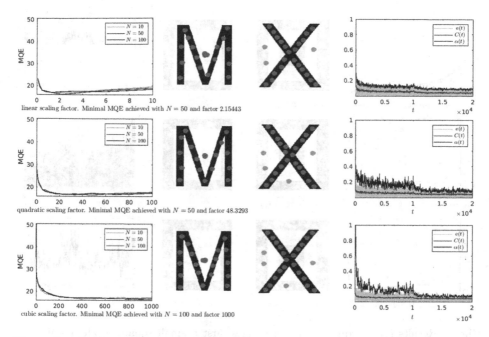

Fig. 4. Results for a sequence of two images: first the shape of the letter M, then the shape of the letter X. The arrangement of the array of results is the same as in Fig. 3. Please refer to the caption of that Figure. In the third column, we have marked in green the neurons that are dead, i.e., no sample from the second image is nearer to them than to other ones. Note that in the examples shown in the second, third and fourth columns, there are no dramatic increases of $\alpha(t)$ after $t = 10000$, but the arrangement of the shapes is such that the neurons rearrange into a good clustering of the second shape with a continuously low $\alpha(t)$.

3.2 Results

The learning system is able to adapt when new distributions are fed to it. For example, in Fig. 2 we can see an experiment where we feed our learning system first the shape of the letter X, then the shape of the letter M. As it can be seen, when the samples fed to the system are switched to the second shape, the value of $e(t)$ significantly increases, leading to an increment of $\alpha(t)$, so that the system adapts to the new shape.

In fact, we have checked that the system is able to adapt to new shapes with experiments testing many parameter combinations and many different sequences of shapes. However, there is no combination of function type, scaling factor a and N that minimizes MQE for all possible sequences of input shapes. Figure 3 shows a summary of the experiments where the system is presented first the inclined dumbbell shape, ($\search$), then the horizontal one ($\leftrightarrow$). The figure is arrayed so each row shows results for experiments with a specific function type (linear, quadratic, cubic). The first column of the figure shows a graph for each function type: summarizing the MQE achieved for experiments with different values for N and

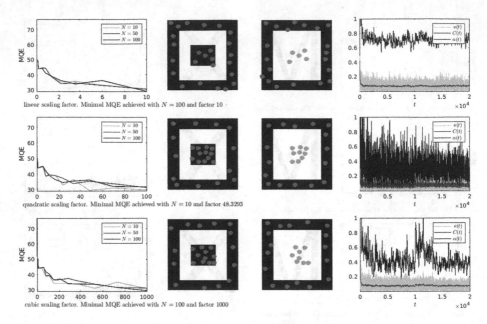

Fig. 5. Results for a sequence of two images: first a small square inside a wall, the just the wall. The arrangement of the array of results is the same as in Fig. 4. Please refer to the caption of that Figure. Since the shapes are such that many neurons end up dead in the center, the best results are achieved by maintaining consistently high $\alpha(t)$ values and thus very jittery movements of neurons. In the experiment shown in the second, third and fourth plots, this behavior enabled one of the neurons inside the inner square to be recruited into modeling the wall of the second shape, lowering the overall MQE.

a. Among those, we select the combination with minimal MQE and we show the state of the neurons for that experiment right after all the samples from the first shape (second column), and after all the samples from the second shape (third column). Note that in the third column, we can see some dead neurons that do not represent any sample from that shape; this is caused because, depending on the specific arrangement of the shapes, some neurons are never selected again in the training process. Finally, the fourth column shows $e(t)$, $C(t)$ and $\alpha(t)$ for that same experiment. Please note that in the middle of these graphs (at $t = 10000$) the learning system has adapted to the first shape and starts to be presented with samples from the second shape, sharply but temporarily increasing $C(t)$ and $\alpha(t)$, which then go again to a background level when the learning system adapts to the new shape.

Our expectation was that the system adaptation to new shapes (i.e. input distribution) would be determined by a significantly increase in the value of $e(t)$, leading to an increment of $\alpha(t)$, in turn enabling the system to adapt to the new shape. However, while this behavior could be observed in some experiments such as the ones shown in Figs. 2 and 3), this did not happen always. Instead, sometimes $\alpha(t)$ would not change significantly, meaning that within the constraints of the parameters of the training process, the system detected that very slow adaptation rates were enough to guarantee the neurons to arrange into a good clustering of the second shape. An example can be seen in Fig. 4. In other cases, the second shape is easy to represent many neurons are not needed. They likely end up as dead and they do not contribute to the clustering because their receptive fields are empty. In theses cases the best $\alpha(t)$ functions induce consistently high $\alpha(t)$ values, which allow the neurons to have initial jittery trajectories that prevent them to be dead during the online training, thus contributing to an overall lower MQE (an example is shown in Fig. 5).

4 Conclusions

In this paper, a novel continual learning approach for competitive neural networks is proposed. The main characteristic of this competitive neural network is the ability to learn continuously by changing the traditional learning rate which decreases linearly for a function of the N most recent $e(t)$ values, so that the learning rate $\alpha(t)$ increases as the $e(t)$ increment when input samples that belong to a different input distribution are presented. Different monotonic function types for the learning rate are considered, namely linear, quadratic, cubic, and exponential.

Experimental results with two-dimensional binary images show that the model is able to adapt to a new input distribution when a different input distribution has been previously presented. Actually, the model is able to find a function to adapt to the new input distribution in the most proper way, which sometimes is a peak and sometimes is similar to a low or a high constant function. However, the best combination of scaling factor a, N, and function type for minimizing the MQE depends on the input distribution. Moreover, we observed dead neurons that do not represent any sample from the input distribution at hand. Nevertheless, this can be solved by using a self-organizing mechanism in addition to a competitive mechanism, which is the research line we plan to follow in future works.

References

1. Hadsell, R., Rao, D., Rusu, A.A., Pascanu, R.: Embracing change: continual learning in deep neural networks. Trends Cogn. Sci. **24**(12), 1028–1040 (2020)
2. Rao, D., Visin, F., Rusu, A.A., Teh, Y.W., Pascanu, R., Hadsell, R.: Continual unsupervised representation learning. In: Advances in Neural Information Processing Systems, vol. 32. Neural Information Processing Systems Foundation, October 2019
3. Mermillod, M., Bugaiska, A., Bonin, P.: The stability-plasticity dilemma: investigating the continuum from catastrophic forgetting to age-limited learning effects. Front. Psychol. **4**, 504 (2013)

4. McCloskey, M., Cohen, N.J.: Catastrophic interference in connectionist networks: the sequential learning problem. In: Psychology of Learning and Motivation - Advances in Research and Theory, vol. 24, no. C, pp. 109–165, January 1989

5. Goodfellow, I.J., Mirza, M., Xiao, D., Courville, A., Bengio, Y.: An empirical investigation of catastrophic forgetting in gradient-based neural networks. In: 2nd International Conference on Learning Representations, ICLR 2014 - Conference Track Proceedings. International Conference on Learning Representations, ICLR, December 2014

6. Shin, H., Lee, J.K., Kim, J., Kim, J.: Continual learning with deep generative replay. In: Advances in Neural Information Processing Systems, vol. 2017. Neural Information Processing Systems Foundation, pp. 2991–3000, May 2017

7. Zenke, F., Poole, B., Ganguli, S.: Continual learning through synaptic intelligence. In: 34th International Conference on Machine Learning, ICML 2017, vol. 8. International Machine Learning Society (IMLS), pp. 6072–6082, March 2017

8. Nguyen, C.V., Li, Y., Bui, T.D., Turner, R.E.: Variational continual learning. In: 6th International Conference on Learning Representations, ICLR 2018 - Conference Track Proceedings. International Conference on Learning Representations, ICLR, October 2018

9. Kirkpatrick, J., et al.: Overcoming catastrophic forgetting in neural networks. Proc. Natl. Acad. Sci. U.S.A. $114(13)$, 3521–3526 (2016)

10. Jain, A.K.: Data clustering: 50 years beyond k-means. Pattern Recogn. Lett. $31(8)$, 651–666 (2010)

11. Chen, M.-S., Han, J., Yu, P.: Data mining: an overview from a database perspective. IEEE Trans. Knowl. Data Eng. $8(6)$, 866–883 (1996)

12. Jolliffe, I.T., Cadima, J.: Principal component analysis: a review and recent developments. Phil. Trans. R. Soc. A. 374, 20150202 (2016)

13. Rumelhart, D.E., Zipser, D.: Feature discovery by competitive learning*. Cogn. Sci. $9(1)$, 75–112 (1985)

14. Ahalt, S.C., Krishnamurthy, A.K., Chen, P., Melton, D.E.: Competitive learning algorithms for vector quantization. Neural Netw. $3(3)$, 277–290 (1990). https://www.sciencedirect.com/science/article/pii/089360809090071R

15. Uchiyama, T., Arbib, M.A.: Color image segmentation using competitive learning. IEEE Trans. Pattern Anal. Mach. Intell. $16(12)$, 1197–1206 (1994). https://doi.org/10.1109/34.387488

16. García-Lamont, F., Cervantes, J., López-Chau, A.: Automatic computing of number of clusters for color image segmentation employing fuzzy c-means by extracting chromaticity features of colors. Pattern Anal. Appl. 23, 59–84 (2020)

17. López-Rubio, E., Ortiz-de-Lazcano-Lobato, J.M.: Dynamic competitive probabilistic principal components analysis. Int. J. Neural Syst. $19(2)$, 91–103 (2009). https://doi.org/10.1142/S0129065709001860

18. Yuan, H., Duo, C., Niu, W.H.: A human behavior recognition method based on latent semantic analysis. J. Inf. Hiding Multim. Signal Process. 7, 489–498 (2016)

SCASA: From Synthetic to Real Computer-Aided Sperm Analysis

Daniel Hernández-Ferrándiz$^{(\boxtimes)}$ ⓘ, Juan J. Pantrigo$^{(\boxtimes)}$ ⓘ,
and Raul Cabido$^{(\boxtimes)}$ ⓘ

Universidad Rey Juan Carlos, Madrid, Spain
{daniel.hernandezf,juanjose.pantrigo,raul.cabido}@urjc.es
http://www.urjc.es

Abstract. Sperm analysis has a central role in diagnosing and treating infertility. Traditionally, assessment of sperm health was performed by an expert by viewing the sample through a microscope. In order to simplify this task and assist the expert, CASA (Computer-Assisted Sperm Analysis) systems were developed. These systems rely on low-level computer vision tasks such as classification, detection and tracking to analyze sperm health and motility. These tasks have been widely addressed in the literature, with some supervised approaches surpassing the human capacity to solve them. However, the accuracy of these models have not been directly translated into CASA systems. This is mainly due to the absence of labelled data, as well as the difficulty in obtaining it. In this work we propose the generation of synthetic semen samples to tackle the absence of labelled data. We propose a parametric modelling of spermatozoa, and show how models trained on synthetic data can be used on real images with no need of further fine-tuning stage.

Keywords: Sperm analysis · Synthetic data · Deep learning

1 Introduction

Infertility affects one in six couples worldwide, and fertility continues to deteriorate globally, partly owing to a decline in semen quality [5]. The last decade has seen significant advances in the analysis of sperm health that have led to new ways of diagnosing and treating infertility. The capability to analyze sperm motility as well as the assessment of their general health is extremely relevant information when selecting the optimal sperm for Assisted Reproductive Technology (ART) [5]. Traditionally, assessment of sperm health was performed by an expert by viewing the sample through a microscope. In order to simplify this task and assist the expert, CASA (Computer-Assisted Sperm Analysis) systems were developed [1]. Thanks to emerging techniques such as deep learning, the accuracy of these systems has been substantially improved in recent years [9,14].

Supported by the Spanish Government research funding ref. RTI2018-098743-B-I00 (MICINN/FEDER) and the Madrid Regional Government research funding ref. Y2018/EMT-5062. In colaboration with Pixelabs.

© Springer Nature Switzerland AG 2022
J. M. Ferrández Vicente et al. (Eds.): IWINAC 2022, LNCS 13259, pp. 233–242, 2022.
https://doi.org/10.1007/978-3-031-06527-9_23

However, nowadays these systems still have limitations and require expert supervision. The quantitative and qualitative analysis of sperm relies on computer vision tasks such as detection, classification and tracking. These tasks have been widely addressed in the literature, with some approaches surpassing the human capacity to solve them [7]. However, the accuracy and precision results of these models have not been directly translated into CASA systems. This is mainly due to the following factors:

- **Highly complex task**. The task to be solved presents a higher complexity than the ones present in general challenges of detection, classification and tracking. The objects (sperm cells) to be detected and tracked are extremely small, very similar, usually blurred, very large in number and frequently occluded. Moreover, semen is often cluttered with debris and cells other than normal mature sperms [14].
- **Small amount of labeled data**. The deep learning systems that perform best for detection, classification and tracking tasks are supervised, so their use relies on obtaining labelled data. Composing a well-balanced and general enough dataset to analyze sperm motility is a highly complex task. Just labeling a video with hundreds of cells moving and maintaining their type and identity between frames is too time-consuming.

Sperm datasets available in the literature [3,11,16] present very specific capture conditions, they are mainly focused on the analysis of animal semen, and the number of samples available is not very high. They are usually made up of hundreds of images that the authors scale up to thousands using data augmentation techniques. Models trained on these datasets offer good performance, but they will not perform well in a general production environment, as the models are over-fitted to the particular conditions of the dataset.

In this paper we propose synthetic data generation as a solution to provide supervised systems with the necessary data to solve the sperm analysis task in a general and robust way. The main contributions of this paper are: (1) we propose a parametric and statistical modelling of spermatozoa, (2) we present the first synthetic sperm sample generator, (3) we show the usefulness of synthetic data for training supervised systems. Models trained on synthetic data can be used on porcine sperm images without previous fine-tuning.

2   Related Work

Sperm health analysis depends on many factors [15]: semen volume, total number of sperm, concentration, vitality, motility, morphology, time to liquefaction, etc. Most major spermatology laboratories and semen processing facilities have a CASA (Computer-assisted sperm analysis) system which automatically calculates these parameters. Although these systems have evolved over the last 40 years [1] they still have limitations, especially in computer vision-related tasks such as detection, classification and tracking of each sperm. In this section we review recent work in the literature focused on solving these problems, present their limitations and propose a potential improvement through synthetic data generation.

In [11] authors propose a framework for the automatic analysis of sperm morphology. In a first stage, sperms are segmented using a Fuzzy C-Means clustering approach. Then, normal/ab-normal sperms are classified using a MobileNet architecture achieving accuracy results of 87%. Authors show good performance using learned features as extracted by MobileNet, and release the SMIDS dataset, which consist of of 3000 patches (normal, abnormal, non-sperm) that were extracted from 200 microscopic images of 17 subjects.

The measurement of sperm health takes into account several factors, including total sperm count, sperm concentration and white blood cell count. All of them require good sperm detection. Solutions to sperm detection based on the use of classical computer vision techniques can be found in the literature [6, 10]. However, machine learning-based solutions currently attain the best results for this problem. Nissen et al. [14] proposed for the first time the use of a Convolutional Neural Networks (CNN) for sperm detection. This CNN generates a probability map that is used to estimate the most probable class for each pixel. As a result, a segmentation mask is generated where each pixel cluster corresponds to a sperm cell. Results report 93% accuracy and 91% precision for a dataset of 765 images. Hidayatullah et al. [9] presented DeepSperm, a deep neural network that uses a specific detection layer to detect small objects. The authors increased the input resolution of the network, used a dropout layer and performed a data augmentation strategy based on saturation and exposure changes. The obtained results outperforms the state of the art in terms of accuracy, speed and requirements of computational resources.

All the works described so far use a set of images or videos to train and test their approach. Datasets used for these papers are not always public [3, 11, 16]. Usually, available datasets are made up of a small number of images or videos (hundreds at best), so that systems trained with them perform very well under the specific conditions set by the dataset itself. But designing a general dataset is not an easy task. The problem is not only to obtain a large volume of data, but also to manually tag it. For this reason, many researchers have recently turned to synthetic data generation as a way to get all the data their supervised systems need to solve a task in a general way [4, 13]. Work such as that proposed by Tremblay et al. [17] demonstrated that synthetic data can work as well as real data for training supervised systems. Authors presented the first work in which a deep neural network trained with synthetic data obtains state-of-the-art results in pose detection with six degrees of freedom.

To the best of our knowledge, there is no previous work in the literature on synthetic data generation to improve the automatic analysis of semen health. All attempts to generate new data are based on the use of data augmentation techniques [2, 8].

3   Our Proposal

In this work we propose a parametric model to generate sperm images and their labels synthetically. To obtain the parametric model of sperm we study some real sperm frames represented in Fig. 1. These frames show a high quantity of spermatozoa with different shapes over a non-uniform background. Due to the high concentration of individuals and the other floating particles, it is common to observe multiple occlusions and agglomerations. The images also show shadows around the different floating elements and the height of each element on the sample affects their size and clarity. One possible decomposition for this kind of images is differentiating three main components: spermatozoa, floating particles and the non-uniform background. To synthesize a spermatozoon we consider its three main parts, namely the head, the middle-piece and the tail, as described in the Fig. 1.

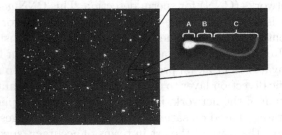

Fig. 1. Sample frame of sperm imaging and schematic zoom of the parts of a normal spermatozoon: Head (a), middle-piece (b) and tail (b).

The classification of the different possible middle-piece and tail shapes bring 6 different categories that affect to their capabilities of insemination. The 6 morphology classes shown in Fig. 2 configure the objective of this study and are described in Table 1.

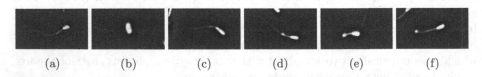

(a)   (b)   (c)   (d)   (e)   (f)

Fig. 2. Spermatozoon morphology classes: (a) Normal, (b) detached head, (c) proximal cytoplasmic droplet, (d) distal cytoplasmic droplet, (e) bent middle-piece with cytoplasmic droplet and (f) terminal cytoplasmic droplet

Establishing a parametric model that fit all this configurations requires to set different parameters to model the constituent parts and classes shown above. The proposed parameter setting models the different parts of a spermatozoon

Table 1. Detailed spermatozoon morphology classes.

Morphology	Tail shape	Droplet position
Normal	Normal	No droplet
Detached head	No tail	No droplet
Proximal cytoplasmic droplet	Normal	Next to the head
Distal cytoplasmic droplet	Normal	Mid tail
Bent middle-piece with cytoplasmic droplet	Reversed or 90 °C after the droplet	Mid tail
Terminal cytoplasmic droplet/coiled tail	Normal/Coiled after mid tail	Tail's end/No droplet

and the droplets that conform the different types. For each morphology class, the head is described by head length h_l and maximum width h_w, the middle-piece is detailed by its length m_l and width m_w as well as the tail, which is also modeled by means of the tail length t_l and width t_w. The droplet, if present, is described by the distance to the head d_x and its diameter d_d. The particular case of coiled tail individuals is also modelled as terminal cytoplasmic droplets, considering the coil as a droplet with a central hole.

Each one of this parameters is measured in a small set of 20 samples for each morphology class. The measurements are taken from the image segmentation, calculated with an adaptive threshold to solve the problem of non-uniform background. This method segments the whole spermatozoa in most cases, except when the tail has extremely low intensity levels compared to the body. To get the measurements, each segmented spermatozoon is rectified by getting the values of the distance transform as shown in the Fig. 3.

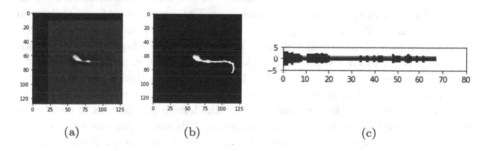

(a)   (b)   (c)

Fig. 3. Spermatozoon crop with extended background (a), segmented image (b) and distance function representation (c).

The mean value and standard deviation are the estimated values for each distribution. The total number of parameters can be calculated as: (mean + std) * (6 classes) * (8 parameters) = 96 parameters, although some of them are zeros due to class particularities 2. The estimation of this parameters is not a critical factor in the model since it is desired to have a greater diversity in sperm to achieve more robust models.

Table 2. Sperm measurements in 20 samples for each morphology.

Morphology	h_l	h_w	m_l	m_w	t_l	t_w	d_x	d_d
Normal	16.2 ± 2.0	7.8 ± 0.8	19.1 ± 3.6	2.3 ± 0.5	43.3 ± 5.4	2.0 ± 0.2	-	-
Detached head	17.1 ± 1.2	7.0 ± 0.6	-	-	-	-	-	-
Proximal cytoplasmic droplet	15.5 ± 1.7	7.7 ± 0.6	18.7 ± 2.8	2.2 ± 0.4	44.6 ± 4.3	2.0 ± 0.1	0.9 ± 1.0	4.8 ± 0.7
Distal cytoplasmic droplet	16.3 ± 1.6	7.2 ± 1.0	16.2 ± 3.0	2.0 ± 0.2	45.0 ± 4.8	2.0 ± 0.1	14.2 ± 3.0	4.6 ± 0.8
Bent middle-piece with cytoplasmic droplet	16.8 ± 1.6	7.0 ± 0.8	13.9 ± 4.9	2.1 ± 0.3	48.7 ± 3.5	2.0 ± 0.1	11.9 ± 4.7	4.5 ± 0.8
Terminal cytoplasmic droplet/coiled tail	16.1± 1.3	7.0 ± 0.4	21.7 ± 4.4	2.2 ± 0.4	-	-	20.1 ± 4.2	3.8 ± 1.8

Once the spermatozoa is modelled, the other components of images are floating particles and background. Floating particles are considered as three different sizes. Big particles to model the agglomerations and traces much larger than spermatozoa heads, and small and very small particles to model the small dots present in the sperm. The background is considered to be similar between the sample images, and it is calculated as the mode image of a small subset of video frames with a low concentration of spermatozoa. Taking the most frequent intensity value of each pixel removes the remaining individuals as they are placed in different positions for each image and keeps the non-uniform distribution of the light. The randomized selection of images allow the generation of different backgrounds.

Generating synthetic images from this parts and parameters is a complex process. First of all the canvas where the rest of components are drawn, the background image, is generated as explained in the above paragraph, with the final image created from the median image of 15 different frames. Floating particles are simplified and created as circles with their different sizes and a small shadow for big and small classes. The number of particles is randomized for each frame between a range of values for each size. The generation of spermatozoon is conditioned by its morphology class. Their parameter values are generated randomly from a Gaussian distribution previously established for each individual. The process follows with the creation of the diameter, angle and intensity vectors. This vectors are generated for the three parts of the spermatozoon and concatenated for the draw process. The diameter vector is generated using the width parameters with the size that describe the length parameters. If the drawn type has a cytoplasmic droplet, the position and diameter parameters are used to change the corresponding vector position. The angle vector is calculated using a sinusoidal function for the middle-piece and tail, with variable amplitude and periods. The bent middle-piece type also includes an inversion of the angle vector with a deviation at this point to generate this particular morphology. The intensity vector is set for each part of the sperm. The final spermatozoon is then drawn segment by segment with circles, starting for the surrounding shadows and following with the actual contour.

4   Experiments

The goal of this experimentation is to prove that models trained with synthetic data are suitable as a training set of a machine learning-based detection system. To this aim, we train a model only with synthetic images and then test it on real images. to determine if this knowledge is properly transferred and the detection model generalizes. Another objective of this process is the identification of problems in the synthetic model to find the optimal parameters.

Training detection models based on convolutional neural networks (CNNs) requires a high amount of labelled data. By using our synthetic generator, we create a new dataset, which is composed by 2500 frames with a range of 130 to 230 spermatozoa with equal probabilities for each morphology. Figures 4 compares some synthetic images with respect to a set of real images.

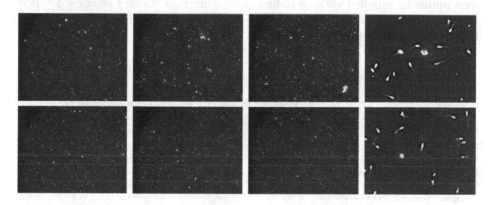

Fig. 4. Sperm image comparison. First row shows real frames and second row shows images from our synthetic dataset. Last column shows the zoom of some samples.

We consider YOLOv5 [12] as a detection model. Specifically, we use the package Ultralytics YOLOv5 running over PyTorch. As we want to accomplish some speed requirements for this project the selected pretrained models are the fastest ones: YOLOv5n, YOLOv5s and YOLOv5m. Table 3 details the characteristics of each model. The metrics used to measure the performance are precision P, recall R and mean average precision mAP. To calculate the metrics it is considered a confidence threshold of 0.6. Furthermore, an IoU value of 0.5 is considered for P, R and mAP@0.5. There is also a range of considered thresholds for IoU, from 0.95 to measure precise detections to 0.5 to measure loosen detections with steps of 0.05 to calculate mAP@0.5:0.95.

To test the model, we have labelled some laboratory images. While some datasets used in sperm focused on searching subcellular structures such as vacuoles use high magnification objectives (over ×100) this dataset is aimed to perform a conventional morphology analysis, where a magnification ratio of ×10 to ×40 is enough to visualise the different parts of the spermatozoon. To record

Table 3. Different characteristics of YOLO models.

Model	Parameters (M)	Speed (ms)	Size (MB)	mAP 0.5:0.95 (on COCO val)
YOLOv5n	1.9	13.0	3.9	0.28
YOLOv5s	7.2	14.5	14.4	0.37
YOLOv5m	21.2	21.4	42.2	0.45

our samples, an Motic Panthera C2 microscope with a total magnification of ×10 and a Blackfly S USB3 camera with a 12.3 MP CMOS Sony sensor are used. To enhance the contrast of the image the camera is configured to have a high gamma value and the backlight enabled. The images are taken as 25 frames videos of the sperm sample with a resolution of 1280 × 1024 and recorded at 25 fps. A small sample of 42 images selected from different sample videos has been manually labelled with an online annotation tool. Table 4 shows a detailed comparison of the morphology distribution for each dataset, finding that the real data is significantly unbalanced.

Table 4. Distribution of individuals per morphology for each dataset.

Morphology	Synthetic dataset (500 images)		Labelled dataset (42 images)	
	Quantity	Percentage	Quantity	Percentage
Normal	14088	16.86%	5549	79.97%
Detached head	13365	15.99%	534	7.69%
Proximal cytoplasmic droplet	13979	16.73%	51	0.73%
Distal cytoplasmic droplet	14229	17.03%	389	5.60%
Bent middle-piece with cytoplasmic droplet	13953	16.07%	232	3.34%
Terminal cytoplasmic droplet/coiled tail	13926	16.67%	183	2.63%
Total	83540	100%	6938	100%

The results for each model are calculated for the different test sets. Figure 5 shows the metrics in each case. Results show a good overall performance with spermatozoa although real images have several particularities, resulting on worse metrics in precision, recall and mean average precision. Recall is reduced due to spermatozoa being hardly detected on agglomerations of individuals with big floating particles and agglomerations of spermatozoa where it is hard to differentiate the head from the rest of the blob. Precision is reduced by false positives produced by floating particles or cytoplasmic droplets with a similar size to smallest spermatozoon heads. Figure 6 displays an example for each one of this cases.

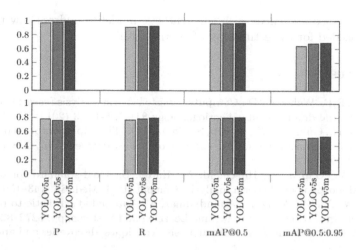

Fig. 5. Bar graphs of metrics for the synthetic dataset (top) and labelled dataset (bottom).

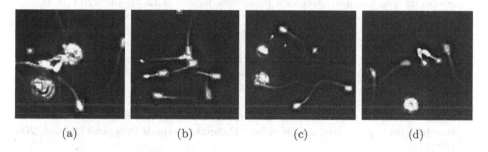

Fig. 6. Problems with detections on real samples: FN on agglomeration with big floating particles (a), FN on agglomeration of spermatozoa (b), FP on small particles with similar size as heads (c) and FP with cytoplasmic droplets (d).

5   Conclusions

We have generated a first parametric model of sperm with the objective of solving the lack of labelled data in this field. To test the performance of our generated synthetic dataset, we trained different models to detect spermatozoa heads. The trained model have proven suitable to detect sperm heads on synthetic images and also to detect most of the spermatozoa heads on the real samples. However, our method still presents problems dealing with agglomerations and false positives on floating particle and cytoplasmic droplets. To address this problems we plan to undertake the following research lines: (1) to include agglomerations and a more detailed model of floating particles, (2) to test a wider range of parameter values to generate an augmented dataset to improve generalization, (3) to compute metrics for the task of classification through crops obtained with the detection results to identify new problems and keep improving the dataset, (4) to generate video sequences with the synthetic model to address new tasks like tracking, needed for the estimation of sperm motility.

References

1. Amann, R.P., Waberski, D.: Computer-assisted sperm analysis (casa): Capabilities and potential developments. Theriogenology **81**(1), 5-17.e3 (2014)
2. Balayev, K., Guluzade, N., Aygün, S., Ilhan, H.O.: The implementation of DCGAN in the data augmentation for the sperm morphology datasets. Eur. J. Sci. Technol. 307–314 (2021)
3. Chang, V., Garcia, A., Hitschfeld, N., Härtel, S.: Gold-standard for computer-assisted morphological sperm analysis. Comput. Biol. Med. **83**, 143–150 (2017)
4. Chen, W., Yu, Z., Wang, Z., Anandkumar, A.: Automated synthetic-to-real generalization. In: Proceedings of Machine Learning and Systems, pp. 8272–8282 (2020)
5. Dai, C., et al.: Advances in sperm analysis: techniques, discoveries and applications (2021)
6. Ghasemian, F., Mirroshandel, S.A., Monji-Azad, S., Azarnia, M., Zahiri, Z.: An efficient method for automatic morphological abnormality detection from human sperm images. Comput. Methods Programs Biomed. **122**(3), 409–420 (2015)
7. He, K., Zhang, X., Ren, S., Sun, J.: Delving deep into rectifiers: Surpassing human-level performance on imagenet classification. In: Proceedings of the IEEE International Conference on Computer Vision (ICCV) (2015)
8. Hidayatullah, P., Mengko, T., Munir, R., Barlian, A.: A semiautomatic dataset generator for convolutional neural network. In: Proceedings of the International Conference on Electrical Engineering & Computer Science (ICEECS 2018), pp. 17–21 (2018)
9. Hidayatullah, P., et al.: Deepsperm: a robust and real-time bull sperm-cell detection in densely populated semen videos. Comput. Methods Programs Biomed. **209** (2021)
10. Hidayatullah, P., Zuhdi, M.: Automatic sperms counting using adaptive local threshold and ellipse detection. In: 2014 International Conference on Information Technology Systems and Innovation (ICITSI), pp. 56–61 (2014)
11. Ilhan, H.O., Sigirci, I.O., Serbes, G., Aydin, N.: A fully automated hybrid human sperm detection and classification system based on mobile-net and the performance comparison with conventional methods. Med. Biolog. Eng. Comput. **58**(5), 1047–1068 (2020). https://doi.org/10.1007/s11517-019-02101-y
12. Jocher, G., Stoken, A., Chaurasia, A.: Ultralytics/yolov5: v6.0 (2021)
13. Nikolenko, S.I.: Synthetic Data for Deep Learning. SOIA, vol. 174. Springer, Cham (2021). https://doi.org/10.1007/978-3-030-75178-4
14. Nissen, M.S., Krause, O., Almstrup, K., Kjærulff, S., Nielsen, T.T., Nielsen, M.: Convolutional neural networks for segmentation and object detection of human semen. In: Sharma, P., Bianchi, F.M. (eds.) SCIA 2017. LNCS, vol. 10269, pp. 397–406. Springer, Cham (2017). https://doi.org/10.1007/978-3-319-59126-1_33
15. World Health Organization: Who laboratory manual for the examination and processing of human semen (2010)
16. Shaker, F.: Human sperm head morphology dataset (hushem). In: Mendeley Data, V3 (2018)
17. Tremblay, J., To, T., Sundaralingam, B., Xiang, Y., Fox, D., Birchfield, S.: Deep object pose estimation for semantic robotic grasping of household objects. In: Conference on Robot Learning (CoRL) (2018)

Inter-session Transfer Learning in MI Based BCI for Controlling a Lower-Limb Exoskeleton

Laura Ferrero[1] , Vicente Quiles[1] , Mario Ortiz[1,2](✉) , Javier V. Juan[1] , Eduardo Iáñez[1] , and José M. Azorín[1,2]

[1] Brain-Machine Interface System Lab, Miguel Hernández University of Elche, 03202 Elche, Spain
{lferrero,vquiles,mortiz,javier.juanp,eianez,jm.azorin}@umh.es
[2] Centro de Investigación en Ingeniería de Elche-I3E, Miguel Hernández University of Elche, 03202 Elche, Spain

Abstract. Motor imagery (MI) brain-computer interfaces (BCI) have a critical function in the neurological rehabilitation of people with motor impairment. BCI are systems that employ brain activity to control any external device and MI is a commonly used control paradigm based on the imagination of a movement without executing it. The main limitation of these systems is the time necessary for their calibration, before using them for rehabilitation. A shorter calibration scheme was proposed for a lower-limb MI based BCI for controlling an exoskeleton. Each subject participated in 5 experimental sessions. Before each session with the exoskeleton, users were guided to perform MI with visual feedback in a virtual reality scenario. Training with virtual reality involves less physical effort and users can have a previous practise on the MI mental task. In addition, transfer learning was employed, so information from previous training sessions was used for the new one. Results showed that the performance of BCI was superior in comparison with baseline methodologies when transfer learning was used.

Keywords: Brain-computer interfaces · Lower-limb · Transfer learning

1 Introduction

Motor imagery (MI) brain-computer interfaces (BCI) have a critical function in the neurological rehabilitation of people with motor impairment. BCIs are systems that employ brain activity to control any external device and MI is a commonly used control paradigm based on the imagination of a movement without actually executing it [8]. When these systems are combined with robotic

Supported by grant RTI2018-096677-B-I00, funded by MCIN/AEI/10.13039/501100011033 and by "ERDF A way of making Europe"; and by the Consellería de Innovación, Universidades, Ciencia y Sociedad Digital (Generalitat Valenciana).

© Springer Nature Switzerland AG 2022
J. M. Ferrández Vicente et al. (Eds.): IWINAC 2022, LNCS 13259, pp. 243–252, 2022.
https://doi.org/10.1007/978-3-031-06527-9_24

exoskeletons, users perform MI to produce the desired changes on the robotic devices.

Rehabilitation therapies can benefit from the usage of BCI in combination with robotic exoskeletons by having longer training sessions and with more reproducible movement patterns. In addition, recovery is greatly enhanced because patients are cognitively engaged on the rehabilitation treatment while performing MI. Therefore, mechanisms of neuroplasticity are augmented [6].

The main limitation of BCI is the amount of time necessary to calibrate the system before its proper usage. Electroencephalography (EEG) is mainly used to record brain activity for BCI due to its high temporal resolution. However, EEG signals are non-stationary, so systems are usually calibrated for each subject and session [16]. This calibration is time consuming and it must be repeated every time they are going to utilize the system which can be exhausting in the case of patients [5,11].

As a solution to long calibration times, previous studies have designed BCIs that are roughly invariant to changes on EEG properties and others have used what is called transfer learning [11]. Transfer learning is defined as the use of information from source domains to improve the performance of a target domain. In a BCI, different domains can be considered as different subjects, days or different devices to control [16].

There are 3 main approaches for transfer learning in BCI: Riemannian alignment of covariance matrices, Euclidean alignment of covariance matrices and regularized common-spatial patterns (CSP). All covariance matrices belong to Riemannian manifold. For Riemannian alignment, covariance matrices of each sample are centered with respect to the reference covariance matrix of the domain [13,15]. Once all samples are aligned,a minimum distance to the mean classifier based on Riemannian Gausssian distributions is trained [7,13,16]. An alternative classification approach consists of transforming these covariance matrices into the Riemannian tangent space so a classifier can be trained in the Euclidean space [14].

Most classifiers are designed for the Euclidean space instead of the Riemannian manifold. Consequently, several studies performed the alignment directly in the Euclidean space. The main advantages of the Euclidean alignment in comparison with the Riemanniann alignment are its simplicity and fast computation [7,16].

A regularized Common Spatial Pattern (rCSP) is a modified version of CSP that creates more reliable spatial filters for the target domain by using labeled samples from source domains. In [2], they designed a regularized CSP framework that tried to reduce the distance between covariance of source domain data and covariance of target domain data, while maximizing the difference of variances of two brain tasks.

For this study, it to was of interest to investigate a new calibration schema for a MI based BCI with a lower-limb exoskeleton. In our previous work [5], we perceived that training with the exoskeleton was fatiguing and at the end of the session, subjects were frequently exhausted. Our approach to solve this problem involves the use of a virtual reality environment for pre-calibration [3]. Training with virtual reality is static, so it involves less physical effort and users can have a previous practise of performing MI with visual feedback, before having to do it in combination with walking with the exoskeleton. In addition, transfer learning was performed based on Euclidean alignment among sessions, so information from previous training sessions was used for the new one. This way, calibration phase can be further shortened. This research shows a comparison of classification results while using transfer techniques and baseline conditions.

2   Material and Methods

2.1   Subjects

Two subjects participated in the study (mean age 21.5 ± 0.71). They did not have movement impairment and did not report any known diseases. They did not have previous experience with BCI nor using a lower-limb exoskeleton. They were informed about the experiments and signed an informed consent form in accordance with the Declaration of Helsinki. All procedures were approved by the Responsible Research Office of Miguel Hernández University of Elche.

2.2   Equipment

EEG was recorded using StarStim R32 (Neuroelectrics, Barcelona, Spain). The electrode setup follows 10–10 international system with 27 electrodes: F3, FZ, F4, FC5, FC3, FC1, FCZ, FC2, FC4, FC6, C5, C3, C1, CZ, C2, C4, C6, CP5, CP3, CP1, CPZ, CP2, CP4,CP6, P3, PZ, P4. Reference and earth electrodes were positioned on the right ear lobe. The sampling frequency 500 Hz.

Participants wore H3 exoskeleton (Technaid, Spain) that assisted their gait by emulating the process of human walking. One operator hold the exoskeleton from the back and subjects used crutches for support. The control of the robotic device was done with commands sent via Bluetooth from a laptop.

Virtual reality environment consisted of VIVE HTC headset (HTC, Taiwan) (2160×1200 resolution, 1080×1200 per eye, 90 Hz refresh rate), two base stations that tracked the location of the headset and Steam software (Valve, United States). Figure 1 shows the equipment setup.

2.3   Experimental Setup

Subjects participated in 5 sessions. Each session was divided in 2 parts: pre-calibration with virtual reality and calibration with the exoskeleton.

Participants performed 10 trials on the first part using the virtual reality environment. They wore the exoskeleton to recreate better the feeling of using it, but it was static and they only received visual feedback. The virtual reality scene consisted of a person walking on a corridor with a first-person perspective. In each trial, they had to perform 3 mental tasks: iddle state, motor imagery

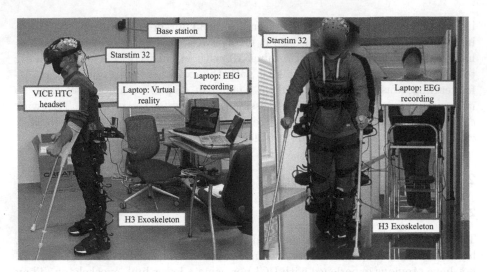

Fig. 1. Equipment setup

of the gait and a regressive count. Schema of a trial can be seen in Fig. 2. For this study, only data from iddle state, motor imagery and their transitions were considered. During half of the trials, the avatar on the environment was not walking and during the other half, it was walking the whole duration of the trial.

For calibration with the exoskeleton, subjects performed 10 trials. They performed the same mental tasks as in pre-calibration (Fig. 2). In this training, there was not a closed-loop control of the exoskeleton. It was commanded by predefined commands. Similar to the protocol design of the previous phase, during half of the trials the exoskeleton was static (full-static) and during the other half it provided walking assistance (full-motion). This training decision was done to train 2 different classifiers: one that could differentiate between brain patterns when users were static and another one that did the same but during the movement. This way, for a test phase as the one presented in [5], classifiers employed can be alternated based on the motion condition of users: static (waiting to start the movement) or in motion (waiting to stop). However, the current research was only focused on the training phase.

2.4   BCI

This subsection provides a detailed description of the BCI. BCI normally have 5 steps: acquisition, pre-processing, feature extraction, classification and evaluation. BCI schema can be seen in Fig. 3.

Acquisition. As aforementioned, the signals of 27 electrodes were acquired 500 Hz sampling frequency. They were processed in 1s epochs with a 0.5 s shift.

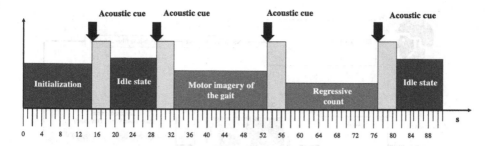

Fig. 2. Description of a trial. It starts with an initialization period in which processing algorithms converge.

Pre-processing. EEG signals were first filtered to suppress unwanted components. They were filtered with a Notch filter 50 Hz to remove the contribution of the power line. Afterwards, a high-pass 2nd order Butterworth filter was applied for the cancellation of DC offset.

The next pre-processing step was the standardization of each EEG channel following the process presented in [1]. It computes the maximum visual threshold of each channel as the mean of the 6 highest values of amplitude. This value is updated for each epoch and the data was standardized as,

$$SV(t)_{ch} = \frac{V(t)_{ch}}{\frac{1}{Ch}\sum_{j=1}^{Ch} MVThreshold_j}, \tag{1}$$

where $V(t)_{ch}$ is the signal of each channel and it is standardized taking into consideration all maximum visual thresholds ($MVThreshold$).

Feature Extraction. This stage is focused on extracting relevant characteristics from EEG data that allow to discriminate between different brain patterns.

The Stockwell transform [12] was applied to each epoch of data in order to obtain a time-frequency representation. It outputs the spectrum of the signal represented as the amplitude with respect to the time and frequency. The amplitudes of frequencies from 5 25 Hz were added (alpha and beta frequency bands). Afterwards, features were averaged in time for each epoch.

Transfer Learning. Euclidean-space alignment (EA) was employed for transfer learning [7]. The principle of this methodology is to make data distribution from different domains more similar. It is based on a reference matrix that is computed as

$$\bar{R} = \frac{1}{n}\sum_{i=1}^{n} X_i X_i^T, \tag{2}$$

where $\bar{R}$ is the reference matrix, X_i is a trial and n is the total number of trials of each domain.

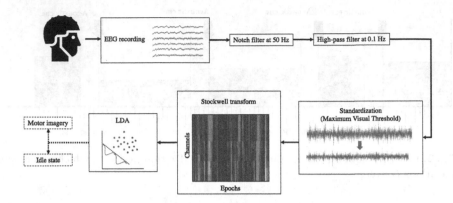

Fig. 3. Brain computer interface schema

The alignment of each trial is done by

$$\tilde{X}_i = \bar{R}^{-1/2} X_i. \tag{3}$$

This way, the mean covariance matrix of all aligned trials of a domain is equal to the identity matrix:

$$\frac{1}{n} \sum_{i=1}^{n} \tilde{X}_i \tilde{X}_i^T = \frac{1}{n} \sum_{i=1}^{n} \bar{R}^{-1/2} X_i X_i^T \bar{R}^{-1/2}$$

$$= \bar{R}^{-1/2} \left(\frac{1}{n} \sum_{i=1}^{n} X_i X_i^T \right) \bar{R}^{-1/2} \tag{4}$$

$$= \bar{R}^{-1/2} \bar{R} \bar{R}^{-1/2} = I$$

Instead of aligning raw EEG signals, data from each frequency band was aligned independently [16].

Classification. Following feature extraction, a leave-one-out cross-validation was performed for each subject and session. Full-static and full-motion trials were evaluated separately. A Linear Discriminant Analysis (LDA) was employed as the classifier.

3   Results

In this section, in order to assess the consequences of transfer learning, three different training schemes have been assessed:

1. *Supervised target domain training*, in which only trials performed within a session with the exoskeleton were used for training the classifier. Thus, one trial was picked each time as the test trial and the rest were used for training.

2. *Supervised source and target domain training*, in which trials from previous sessions with the exoskeleton and the current one were included for training the classifier. However, no trial was transformed with transfer learning. Cross-validation procedure was similar to the previous scheme. Each time one trial of the current session was picked as the test trial, and the remaining trials were used for training.

3. *Pseudo-online supervised transfer learning*, in which trials from previous sessions with the exoskeleton and the current one were first aligned and then, they were employed for training the classifier. Each epoch of the test trial was aligned on-the-fly using information only from training trials.

These 3 approaches were compared in terms of the average classification accuracy from all cross-validation iterations. Table 1 shows the results of subjects S1 and S2. The accuracy was measured as the percentage of correctly classified epochs during idle state and motor imagery periods (%*Rest* and %*MI* respectively) and the total percentage of correct predictions of both periods including the transitions (%*Total*). %*MIRest* was the average of correct predictions for motor imagery and idle state class. Considering full-static trials, the best performance was obtained when transfer learning was applied (*Pseudo-online supervised transfer learning*), followed by *Supervised target domain training* and *Supervised source and target domain training*. The advantages of transfer learning were more evident in S1 than in S2. Regarding full-motion trials, the difference between *Pseudo-online supervised transfer learning* and *Supervised target domain training* was lower than 1%in terms of %*MIRest*. In addition, results with *Pseudo-online supervised transfer learning* were slightly superior than *Supervised source and target domain training*.

4   Discussion

In line with our previous study [4], the average performance during full-static trials and full-motion trials was similar. However, concerning the evolution of accuracy through the sessions, learning effects were more evident for full-static trials [5]. The application of MI based BCI is limited by the difficulties associated with performing imagery tasks [10]. If these brain tasks are combined with the usage of robotic devices, the level of complexity is highly increased. This may explain why each type of training protocol showed a different time tendency.

This research presents a shorter calibration phase than the one employed in our previous works [4,5,9]. To compensate this training reduction, virtual reality was used to provide a first-person scenario to guide the performance of MI task. It has shown promising results increasing the level of performance [10]. Furthermore, the training sample size for each session was increased by using data from previous sessions. However, due to changes on EEG properties through time, differences among sessions can negatively affect the performance of the classifier. The results indicate that performance of the classifier was slightly superior when transfer learning was applied. Overall, these findings are in accordance with [7,16].

On the other hand, by comparing results of EA transfer learning (*Pseudo-online supervised transfer learning*) with baseline conditions (*Supervised target domain training*), the first approach showed greater performance, but it did not deliver better results in all situations. The advantage of transfer learning was more evident for full-static trials than for full-motion. There were some bad trials or outliers that were included in the training that could explain this limitation. Another possible reason is that EA is based on aligning the distribution of independent variables but not the target one, i.e., the predicted class [7].

Table 1. Results from subject S1 and S2

			S1	S2
Pseudo-online supervised transfer learning	Full-static	%Total	55.76±5.05	54.8±2.2
		%MIRest	57.8±7.22	54.57±5.35
		%MI	59.9±14.36	52.86±18.59
		%Rest	55.69±10.28	56.29±14.15
	Full-motion	%Total	52.13±3.78	60.05±2.28
		%MIRest	50.46±3.82	59.93±1.3
		%MI	39.76±14.45	48.29±7.74
		%Rest	61.17±14.16	71.57±9.82
Supervised source and target domain training	Full-static	%Total	50.83±4.41	52.6±2.14
		%MIRest	52.44±5.51	50.43±3.59
		%MI	50.07±11.38	36.29±13.97
		%Rest	54.81±5.36	64.57±12.15
	Full-motion	%Total	50.77±4.31	59.8±2.59
		%MIRest	49.26±4.39	59.14±2.24
		%MI	41.5±6.35	53.29±8.57
		%Rest	57.02±9.23	65±9.11
Supervised target domain training	Full-static	%Total	51.82±4.51	53.2±3.65
		%MIRest	53.73±6.64	53.21±5.7
		%MI	54.64±11.32	49±14.33
		%Rest	52.81±5.31	57.43±6.94
	Full-motion	%Total	52.48±3.96	60.35±2.76
		%MIRest	51.61±5.35	60±2.07
		%MI	45.21±9.78	58±7.38
		%Rest	58±5.28	62±5.83

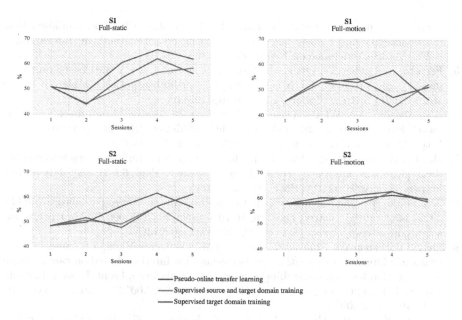

Fig. 4. Average accuracy of MI and idle state class for each subject and session.

5 Conclusion

In summary, this paper presented a shorter calibration scheme for a lower-limb MI based BCI to control an exoskeleton. It was based on previous training with virtual reality, so users were guided to perform MI with visual feedback. In addition, it employed Euclidean alignment transfer learning among sessions. This way, information from previous training sessions was used for the new one. Overall, results when transfer learning was used. It is a preliminary study that was carried out with 2 subjects. However, future research should aim to replicate results in a larger sample.

References

1. Costa, Á., et al.: Decoding the attentional demands of gait through EEG gamma band features. PloS One **11**(4), e0154136–e0154136 (2016). https://doi.org/10.1371/journal.pone.0154136 ,https://pubmed.ncbi.nlm.nih.gov/27115740
2. Feng, Z., Sun, Y., Qian, I., Qi, Y., Wang, Y., Guan, C., Sun, Y.: Design a novel BCI for neurorehabilitation using concurrent LFP and EEG features: a case study. IEEE Trans. Biomed. Eng. **1** (2021). https://doi.org/10.1109/TBME.2021.3115799
3. Ferrero, L., Ortiz, M., Quiles, V., Iáñez, E., Azorín, J.M.: Improving motor imagery of gait on a brain-computer interface by means of virtual reality: a case of study. IEEE Access **9**, 49121–49130 (2021). https://doi.org/10.1109/ACCESS.2021.3068929

4. Ferrero, L., Quiles, V., Ortiz, M., Iáñez, E., Azorín, J.M.: BCI based on lower-limb motor imagery and a state machine for walking on a treadmill. In: International IEEE EMBS Conference on Neural Engineering (2020)

5. Ferrero, L., Quiles, V., Ortiz, M., Iáñez, E., Azorín, J.M.: A BMI based on motor imagery and attention for commanding a lower-limb robotic exoskeleton: a case study (2021). https://doi.org/10.3390/app11094106

6. Gharabaghi, A.: What turns assistive into restorative brain-machine interfaces? Front. Neurosci. **10**, 456 (2016). https://doi.org/10.3389/fnins.2016.00456. https://www.frontiersin.org/article/10.3389/fnins.2016.00456

7. He, H., Wu, D.: Transfer learning for brain-computer interfaces: a euclidean space data alignment approach. IEEE Trans. Bio-Med. Eng. **67**(2), 399–410 (2020). https://doi.org/10.1109/TBME.2019.2913914

8. Jeannerod, M.: Mental imagery in the motor context. Neuropsychologia **33**(11), 1419–1432 (1995). https://doi.org/10.1016/0028-3932(95)00073-C. http://www.sciencedirect.com/science/article/pii/002839329500073C

9. Ortiz, M., Ferrero, L., Iáñez, E., Azorín, J.M., Contreras-Vidal, J.L.: Sensory integration in human movement: a new brain-machine interface based on gamma band and attention level for controlling a lower-limb exoskeleton. Front. Bioeng. Biotechnol. **8**, 735 (2020). https://doi.org/10.3389/fbioe.2020.00735, https://doi.org/10.3389/fbioe.2020.00735

10. Ren, S., Wang, W., Hou, Z.G., Liang, X., Wang, J., Shi, W.: Enhanced motor imagery based brain- computer interface via FES and VR for lower limbs. IEEE Trans. Neural Syst. Rehabilitat. Eng. **28**(8), 1846–1855 (2020). https://doi.org/10.1109/TNSRE.2020.3001990

11. Singh, A., Hussain, A.A., Lal, S., Guesgen, H.W.: A comprehensive review on critical issues and possible solutions of motor imagery based electroencephalography brain-computer interface. Sensors **21**(6) (2021). https://doi.org/10.3390/s21062173. https://www.mdpi.com/1424-8220/21/6/2173

12. Stockwell, R., Lowe, R., Mansinha, L.: Localization of the complex spectrum: the S transform. IEEE Trans. Signal Process. (1996)

13. Wang, F., Ping, J., Xu, Z., Bi, J.: Classification of motor imagery using multisource joint transfer learning. Rev. Sci. Instrum. **92**(9), 94106 (2021). https://doi.org/10.1063/5.0054912

14. Xu, Y., Huang, X., Lan, Q.: Selective cross-subject transfer learning based on Riemannian tangent space for motor imagery brain-computer interface. Front. Neurosci. **15**, 779231 (2021). https://doi.org/10.3389/fnins.2021.779231

15. Zanini, P., Congedo, M., Jutten, C., Said, S., Berthoumieu, Y.: Transfer learning: a Riemannian geometry framework with applications to brain-computer interfaces. IEEE Trans. Biomed. Eng. **65**(5), 1107–1116 (2018). Article no. 779231. https://doi.org/10.1109/TBME.2017.2742541

16. Zhang, X., She, Q., Chen, Y., Kong, W., Mei, C.: Sub-band target alignment common spatial pattern in brain-computer interface. Comput. Methods Programs Biomed. **207**, 106150 (2021). https://doi.org/10.1016/j.cmpb.2021.106150

Autonomous Knowledge Representation for Efficient Skill Learning in Cognitive Robots

Alejandro Romero[1]([✉]), Blaž Meden[2], Francisco Bellas[1], and Richard J. Duro[1]

[1] Integrated Group for Engineering Research, Universidade da Coruña,
A Coruña, Spain
{alejandro.romero.montero,francisco.bellas,richard}@udc.es
[2] Computer Vision Lab, University of Ljubljana, Ljubljana, Slovenia
blaz.meden@fri.uni-lj.si

Abstract. This work explores the effects of the introduction of variational autoencoder based representation learning, and of its resulting latent spaces, within a robotic cognitive architecture to be able to efficiently learn models and policies when raw perceptual dimensionality is very high. The main focus of the paper is on the decision processes of the robots used for action selection. To this end we propose a procedure to obtain from autonomously produced latent state spaces the world and utility models necessary for deliberative operation as a first type of decision process. Additionally, we present a neuroevolutionary based approach to generate policies, for reactive operation, based on the information of the latent state space and using the previously obtained world and utility models to permit offline learning. A set of experiments over a real robot using vision, with the consequent high dimensional raw perceptual space, are carried out in order to validate the proposal.

Keywords: Knowledge representation · Robotics · Action selection

1 Introduction

Lifelong Open-ended Learning Autonomy (LOLA) means that a robot must be able to operate and learn in domains that are unknown at design time [4], reusing knowledge learnt in one domain to facilitate learning in others throughout its lifetime. Robot cognitive architectures provide a path for achieving LOLA [8]. However, when constructing them it is implicitly or explicitly assumed that they were provided with appropriate state space representations by their designers.

This work has been partially funded by the Ministerio de Ciencia, Innovación y Universidades of Spain/FEDER (grant RTI2018-101114-B-I00), Xunta de Galicia (EDC431C-2021/39) and the Centro de Investigación de Galicia "CITIC", funded by Xunta de Galicia and the European Union (European Regional Development Fund- Galicia 2014-2020 Program), by grant ED431G 2019/01, and by the Spanish Ministry of Education, Culture and Sports for the FPU grant of Alejandro Romero.

© Springer Nature Switzerland AG 2022
J. M. Ferrández Vicente et al. (Eds.): IWINAC 2022, LNCS 13259, pp. 253–263, 2022.
https://doi.org/10.1007/978-3-031-06527-9_25

It has recently become clear that to produce robots capable of progressively learning efficiently from their interactions with the world, state spaces [7], as well as the corresponding action spaces [9], need to be learned. The domains and particular goals the robot will have to achieve in them are not known when designing it in LOLA settings, hindering the a priori definition of feature or state spaces without introducing biases. On the other hand, learning directly from observation space is often unfeasible given the large number of sensors required by robots in complex domains and the large dimensions of their data.

On the other hand, the final result of the operation of a cognitive architecture is deciding on the action the robot must apply in a given instant of time to fulfill its goals. In robotics reactive or intuitive action selection or decision processes are fast and automatic and are usually implemented as policies. Traditional policy learning [3,5], however, is based on the idea that the designer provides the goal to be achieved and a state and action space representation. On the other hand, deliberative decision processes require the availability of the corresponding world models to perform prospection, and of utility models for the evaluation of states and these are usually obtained over pre-established state spaces. In other words, both types of decision processes require an appropriate state space representation that allows for feasible learning of goals, models, and policies. However, given the open-ended nature of LOLA, the domains faced by the robot and, thus, the most appropriate state space representation are not known at design time and need to be produced autonomously online.

Inspiration for the autonomous generation of representations can be found in the Reinforcement Learning (RL) literature where they seek to learn the dynamics of the environment where an agent is situated by means of autonomously obtained compact representations In this line, State Representation Learning (SRL) algorithms are constructed to automatically compress high-dimensional observation data into a meaningful low dimensional latent spaces. These algorithms have been applied to different problems such as learning forward [6] or inverse [14] models, or reconstructing observations [1] even in very high dimensional raw perceptual spaces as in Deep Reinforcement Learning (DRL) [11].

In this paper, we present the first steps to integrate SRL strategies within a complete cognitive architecture for robots, in this case the e-MDB cognitive architecture [2]. In particular, we will concentrate on the implications on the two basic approaches to deciding on an action, reactive and deliberative, providing a way to generate reactive policies in the form of ANNs from the deliberative knowledge previously acquired (in latent space) in the form of world and utility models through the interaction of the robot with its environment.

2   e-MDB Cognitive Architecture

The epistemic-Multilevel Darwinist Brain (e-MDB) is a cognitive architecture for lifelong open-ended learning in real robotic systems. It has been under development since the early 2000s s and it allows artificial agents to learn from their experience in dynamic and unknown domains to fulfill their objectives [12]. The e-MDB manages different knowledge nodes. These are the most relevant:

- Drive (Dj): it is a measure of how far the system is from satisfying an internal need (state to achieved or maintained) provided by the designer.
- Goal (G_r): represents states that when reached within a domain reduce the value of, at least, one drive D_j, providing utility.
- Utility Model (UM): function of the probability of reaching a goal G_r starting from a state S_t modulated by the utility achieved (expected utility, $\hat{u}$).

$$\hat{u} = UM(S_t) \tag{1}$$

- World Model (WM): it represents the behavior of the domain. It predicts the state S_{t+1} resulting from applying an action a_i when in state S_t:

$$S_{t+1} = WM(S_t, a_i) \tag{2}$$

- Policy (π_i): A policy is a decision structure associated with a goal G_r that provides the optimal action to be applied when in a perceptual point S_t:

$$a_i = \pi_i(S_t) \tag{3}$$

- P-node: discrete class of (continuous) perceptions that have in common that by applying the same action in the same domain, reach the same state S_{t+1}.
- C-node: product type class that links P-nodes, goals, WMs and the UMs or policies necessary to go from the former to the latter in a domain.

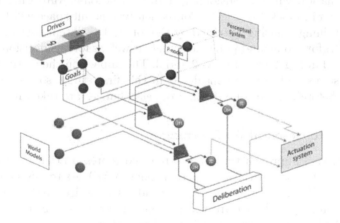

Fig. 1. Schematic of the e-MDB operational structure. (Color figure online)

These knowledge nodes are related to each other through a set of interrelated processes shown in Fig. 1. Starting from the right part, the Actuation System determines the action or policy to be executed. It relies on the most active context (P-node, goal, and WM) through the C-nodes (in red in the Figure). On the left part, we have the initial operational stage, the activation of goals, which will depend on the drives (that are domain independent).

A cognitive architecture for LOLA must be endowed with 4 basic subsystems:

1. A motivational system that manages the robot's drives, selects the active goals, and allows to discover new ones.
2. A learning system that supports the online creation of models and policies.
3. A memory system that allows storing and relating goals, models and all the knowledge that is generated, to support long-term operation.
4. A representational system that allows learning appropriate state space representations, as suggested in this paper.

The first 3 have already been implemented and tested within the e-MDB cognitive architecture in robotic experiments (see [12,13] for information on these motivational, learning and long term memory subsystems). However, until now, the state space representations used by the different components was established by the designer and fixed throughout the e-MDB operation. In this paper we address the problem of obtaining these representations and, more importantly, producing ANN based policies in latent space using the learned representational redescription functions and neuroevolutionary approaches that allow an automatic matching the size of ANNs to the difficulty of the problem.

3   SRL in the e-MDB

To develop a first approach to the representational system of the e-MDB, only visual information will be considered, and a Variational Auto-Encoder will be used, as shown in block 1 of Fig. 2. Consequently, a latent space will be obtained from the raw image sensing obtained by the robot. This latent space will be used in the e-MDB for model and policy learning, as well as for the decision processes, as represented in Fig. 2 with blocks 2 and 3. The impact on the motivational and memory systems will not be considered in this first study, so the goal will be established beforehand and no domain or task changes are taken into account.

3.1   State Representation Learning

The most typical approach to obtain a reduced representation from visual raw observations is to use a variational autoencoder (VAE). As represented in Fig. 2, the Encoder (E) part is the one that provides the desired redescription function. Therefore, $S_t = E(o_t)$ are the perceptions or states (in the appropriate representation) derived from the robot's observation.

The compression level of the VAE is given by the dimensionality of the intermediate layer, which determines the latent space. In the scope of LOLA, the purpose of the representation is not the reconstruction of the image, but rather, the generation of goal directed WMs, UMs and policies. This implies that one can seek higher levels of compression and thus abstraction of the observations.

3.2   World and Utility Model Learning

As displayed in block 2 of Fig. 2, the latent space provided by the Auto-Encoder is stored in a Working Memory and used in the learning system for online WM and

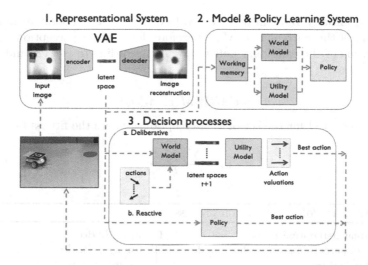

Fig. 2. Processes involved in the SRL of the e-MDB (Color figure online)

UM learning. In this work, the WM is represented as a simple densely connected ANN whose inputs are directly the latent space and the action applied, and whose output is the predicted latent space. To balance network inputs, the input actions are repeated into a tensor of the same size as the latent state space.

This learning process is performed online here, as required by LOLA. Specifically, It uses a temporally ordered series of images as a training set (along with the actions applied between images). The objective in this case is to predict the latent space in $t+1$ and thus be able to reconstruct the image at that point using the error function in (4) to train the WM while the VAE weights remain intact.

In the e MDB, Utility Models are also represented as ANNs, and they can be learned online from the traces experienced by the robot when it reaches a goal. Thus, we can use the information on the trace of states in latent space (perceptions) that were followed to reach the goal as a training set to train an ANN as a UM for that goal.

3.3   Policy Learning

Learning policies directly in open-ended settings is not possible, since we do not know the tasks or the domains that the robot will have to face beforehand. However, they can be learned from the deliberative knowledge (UMs and WMs) acquired by the robot through its interaction with the world. Not knowing in advance the complexity of the task to be solved means that it is also difficult to estimate the necessary network configuration. For this reason, model learning is performed here by means of the NEAT neuroevolutionary algorithm.

The learning process (Algorithm 1) begins with the generation of a population of candidate policies (Π_I), that is, a population of candidate ANNs. These policies are initially random and are evolved using the deliberative models as "simulators of the current reality". Therefore, for a given perception $p_k \in P_n$, the evaluation of the candidate policy $\pi_i \in \Pi_I$ according to (1), (2) and (3) will be:

$$\hat{u}_i^k = UM(WM(p_k, \pi_i(p_k))) \tag{4}$$

This is repeated for the set of P_n perceptions, where the fitness for π_i is:

$$\bar{u}_i = \frac{\sum_{k=0}^n \hat{u}_i^k}{k} \tag{5}$$

Algorithm 1: Policy evaluation process

---

p_k: current perceptual point
P_n: set of perceptions from the P-node
π_i: individual policy
Π_I: population of candidate policies
π^*: optimal policy from Π_I
WM: world model
UM: utility model
$\hat{u}_k$: expected utility for p_k
$\bar{u}_i$: average expected utility for π_i
a_{ik}: action provided by π_i for p_k

for $\pi_i \in \Pi_I$ do
   for $p_k \in P_n$ do
      $a_{ik} \leftarrow \pi_i(p_k)$
      $p_{k+1} \leftarrow WM(a_{ik}, p_k)$
      $\hat{u}_{k+1} \leftarrow UM(p_{k+1})$
      $\bar{u}_i \leftarrow getAverage(\hat{u}_{k+1})$
   end
end
$\pi^* \leftarrow argmax(\bar{u}_i)$

3.4 Decision Processes

Block 3 of Fig. 2 represents the deliberative (a) and reactive (b) decision processes that are executed in the e-MDB. The WM and UM are used in a deliberative process to select the action to be applied by the robot in the environment, while the policy is directly applied in the case of reactive operation. In any case, the chosen action is applied through the robot actuation system, providing a new sensorial state that completes the operational loop. It must be pointed out that decision processes take place after stage 1, because a latent space is required, but learning processes (block 2) run in a different time scale. The learning processes of cognitive architectures are, typically, highly time consuming. Hence, decision processes use the latest available models in an asynchronous fashion.

4   Real Robot Experiment

To analyze SRL and its influence on e-MDB operation, a simple robotic setup was created (see the bottom left image of Fig. 2). It includes a Robobo robot placed on a flat surface, where there is a red area. The goal for the robot is to reach the red area whatever the initial position of both elements. Every time the robot reaches the target, a new trial is started with random positions.

The robot observation is given by an RGB camera placed on the ceiling, which produces 12288 values for each image (height 64 × width 64 × 3 channels). This observation data is input to the VAE in its original range [0, 255]. It will reduce the representation to 64 dimensions (size of the latent space). The structure of this VAE is shown in Table 1. We use ReLU as the activation functions. Network weights are updated using stochastic gradient descent (Adam optimizer). The VAE is trained over 50 epochs with 500 images per epoch (batch size of 32). The VAE parameterization has been studied in [10]. As for the actuation system, the robot moves freely on the table at a constant speed, and the actions control its direction, modifying the robot's orientation by an angle between −180° and 180°.

Table 1. Structure of the VAE.

Layer	Input	Output	Processing	Kernel size	Stride	Padding
1	(64, 64, 3)	(31,31,32)	Convolution	(4,4)	(2,2)	No
2	(31,31,32)	(14,14,64)	Convolution	(4,4)	(2,2)	No
3	(14,14,64)	(6,6,64)	Convolution	(4,4)	(2,2)	No
4	(6,6,64)	(2,2,128)	Convolution	(4,4)	(2,2)	No
5	512	64	Fully connected	–	–	–
6	64	1024	Fully connected	–	–	–
7	(1,1,1024)	(5,5,64)	Deconvolution	(5,5)	(2,2)	No
8	(5,5,64)	(13,13,64)	Deconvolution	(5,5)	(2,2)	No
9	(13,13,64)	(30,30,32)	Deconvolution	(6,6)	(2,2)	No
10	(30,30,32)	(64, 64, 3)	Deconvolution	(6,6)	(2,2)	No

The WM has 128 inputs (64 from the latent space and 64 for the action representation), and 64 outputs (predicted latent space). It consists of 5 convolutional layers with 64 neurons each (the representation dimensionality). The activation function is ReLU in the first 4 layers and Sigmoid in the last one. The ANN-based UM parameterization is shown in Table 2. Again, network weights are updated using an Adam optimizer with a mean square error loss function. In this case, the UM has one output (expected utility) and 64 inputs (state representation in latent space). The value of this expected utility is in the range [0,1]. The parameters of the ANNs that represent the policies were evolved using NEAT, which was configured as shown in Table 2 (the rest of the algorithm parameters have been kept at their default values).

The execution of the experiment (see Fig. 2) can be described as follows: initially, the robot explores the environment driven by an intrinsic exploratory drive that chooses random actions. Therefore, it acquires information related to the domain and generates image sequences in memory that will be used to learn the VAE and the latent space. Once it is learned, the robot continues its intrinsically motivated exploration, obtaining new data in the latent space. This data is used to learn the WM in parallel with the robot operation. When the WM prediction error is below a predefined threshold, this process will end. Once a reliable version of the WM has been learned, the goal is to generate traces that allow reaching the goal and use this information to produce an UM associated with it. In this case, the robot's behavior is oriented towards discovering unvisited states in its latent space. To this end, robot actions are selected using a novelty intrinsic motivation over the candidate states that are prospectively generated with them. Once the UM is learned, policy learning can start. But now the e-MDB already has WM and UM, so the action selection can be carried out using the deliberative process displayed in Fig. 2. To this end, in each time step, 10 random candidate actions are generated within the continuous range of actions, from which the robot chooses the one that provides the highest utility. Finally, once the evolutionary process is finished, the policy obtained will allow the robot to select the optimal action to reach the goal (in latent space). So it is no longer necessary to evaluate candidate actions. This implies a significant reduction in the decision time on which action to perform and more precise actions.

Table 2. Model parameterization.

ANN-based UM		Evolutionary process	
Parameter	Value	Parameter	Value
Input neurons	64	**Generations**	1000
Output neurons	1	**Population**	100
Hidden layers	[64, 16, 6, 2, 1]	**Input neurons**	64
Activation function	tanh	**Output neurons**	1
Batch size	Trace length	**States used for evaluation**	100
Training epochs	10	**Batch size (evaluation)**	30

The results of the complete procedure are displayed in the graphs of Fig. 3. Figure 3(a) shows the robot's performance (number of steps needed to find the goal) during the different stages discussed above in a representative run of the experiment over 5000 time steps. These stages are marked by the different vertical lines in the figure. Thus, the learning of the redescription function, the WM, the UM and the policy can be distinguished. It is possible to see how during the learning of the redescription function and the modeling of the domain, the behavior of the robot is guided by randomly chosen actions. When the WM is learned the robot starts to predict the results of its actions and using novelty reaches the goal more consistently. Similarly, when the robot learns the UM, the average number of steps needed to reach the goal converges (around 5 steps, depending on the initial distance to the goal) as now the robot becomes very efficient in its deliberative selection of actions. This trend is maintained when it learns the policy. The number of steps needed is approximately the same as with the UM, but the computation/decision time lower, as it does not have to evaluate candidate actions. Thus, at the beginning when actions are chosen randomly, the time required is (10^{-6}s), when actions are evaluated in a deliberative process

(WM learned) the time increases $(10^{-3}s)$, however when a policy is learnt, the time decreases again $(10^{-5}s)$.

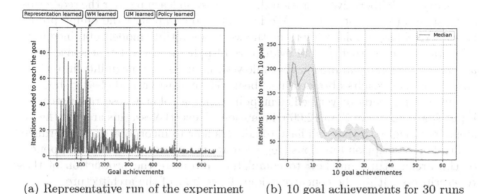

(a) Representative run of the experiment   (b) 10 goal achievements for 30 runs

Fig. 3. Performance analysis of the open-ended learning process.

Figure 3(b) shows the results obtained for 30 independent runs of the experiment. It includes the values of the median and quartiles 1 and 3 resulting from the 30 runs. For clarity, the figure shows intervals with the steps necessary to achieve 10 goals. This graph verifies statistically that the trend shown in Fig. 3(a) is maintained. Finally, to illustrate how optimal the actions provided by the policies were, Fig. 4 shows a couple of robot traces to the goal. In them it can be seen how for the same initial conditions (robot and target in the same place) the actions given by the policy allow reaching the goal in fewer time steps.

Fig. 4. Comparison of robot traces when using UM (top) and policy (bottom).

5   Conclusions

This work addressed the problem of robots making decisions when facing very high dimensional raw perceptual spaces. To this end we have considered state space representation learning through variational autoencoder based redescription functions within a specific cognitive architecture for robots (the e-MDB). In particular, we have provided a procedure to obtain the world and utility models necessary for deliberative operation that is based on learning over the redescribed state spaces (or latent spaces). We have also contemplated the offline production of ANN based policies by using the world and utility models obtained in the first stage to construct virtual evaluators of policies in the latent space within a neuroevolutionary approach that allowed the necessary flexibility in terms of ANN size. The results obtained have been very consistent and clearly show how the procedure leads to very efficient policies for a robot whose raw perceptual input space has more than 12.000 dimensions. Nevertheless, this are just the first steps in a long path that will have to address how to incorporate and coordinate multiple redescription functions (representations) affecting different components of the architecture and how to completely automate the production of these redescriptors within the concurrent knowledge flow of the architecture.

References

1. Alvernaz, S., Togelius, J.: Autoencoder-augmented neuroevolution for visual doom playing. In: 2017 IEEE Conference on Computational Intelligence and Games (CIG), pp. 1–8. IEEE (2017)
2. Bellas, F., Duro, R.J., Faiña, A., Souto, D.: Multilevel Darwinist brain (MDB): artificial evolution in a cognitive architecture for real robots. IEEE Trans. Auton. Ment. Dev. **2**(4), 340–354 (2010)
3. Deisenroth, M.P., Neumann, G., Peters, J., et al.: A survey on policy search for robotics. Found. Trends Robot. **2**(1–2), 388–403 (2013)
4. Doncieux, S., et al.: Open-ended learning: a conceptual framework based on representational redescription. Front. Neurorobot. 59 (2018)
5. Grondman, I., Busoniu, L., Lopes, G.A., Babuska, R.: A survey of actor-critic reinforcement learning: standard and natural policy gradients. IEEE Trans. Syst. Man Cybern. Part C **42**(6), 1291–1307 (2012)
6. Karl, M., Soelch, M., Bayer, J., van der Smagt, P.: Deep variational bayes filters: unsupervised learning of state space models from raw data. arXiv:1605.06432 (2016)
7. Kim, S., Coninx, A., Doncieux, S.: From exploration to control: learning object manipulation skills through novelty search and local adaptation. Robot. Auton. Syst. **136**, 103710 (2021)
8. Kotseruba, I., Tsotsos, J.K.: A review of 40 years of cognitive architecture research: Core cognitive abilities and practical applications. arXiv:1610.08602 (2016)
9. Lesort, T., Díaz-Rodríguez, N., Goudou, J.F., Filliat, D.: State representation learning for control: an overview. Neural Netw. **108**, 379–392 (2018)
10. Meden, B., Prieto, A., Peer, P., Bellas, F.: First steps towards state representation learning for cognitive robotics. In: International Conference on HAIS, pp. 499–510 (2020)
11. Plaat, A., Kosters, W., Preuss, M.: Model-based deep reinforcement learning for high-dimensional problems, a survey. arXiv preprint arXiv:2008.05598 (2020)
12. Romero, A., Bellas, F., Becerra, J.A., Duro, R.J.: Motivation as a tool for designing lifelong learning robots. Int. Comput.-Aid. Eng. **27**(4), 353–372 (2020)

13. Romero, A., Prieto, A., Bellas, F., Duro, R.J.: Simplifying the creation and management of utility models in continuous domains for cognitive robotics. Neurocomputing **353**, 106–118 (2019)
14. Zhang, A., Satija, H., Pineau, J.: Decoupling dynamics and reward for transfer learning. arXiv:1804.10689 (2018)

Autonomous Robot Navigation by Area Centroid Algorithm Using Depth Cameras

Francisco Antonio Marín García(✉)(iD), José Manuel Cuadra Troncoso(✉)(iD),
Félix de la Paz López (✉)(iD), and José Ramón Álvarez-Sánchez(✉)(iD)

Dpto. de Inteligencia Artificial, Univ. Nacional de Educación a Distancia (UNED),
Madrid, Spain
framarin@barbastro.uned.es, {jmcuadra,delapaz,jras}@dia.uned.es

Abstract. This work tries to demonstrate how the use of depth map cameras has considerable advantages compared to laser range measurements. As is known, the laser 2D can only see objects in a single plane, its scanning plane. Then, when using depth map cameras, we have as many planes as the vertical resolution the camera has. In addition, it is possible to derive, with this way of measuring the environment, the height of the objects above the ground, giving the system the 3D characteristic. As we will demonstrate, this 3D feature is not required to navigate a robot under an object (a bridge, for example).

Keywords: Deep camera · Mapping · Robot navigation

1 Introduction

This work is framed in the area of Artificial Intelligence of Perceptual and Autonomous Robotics and more precisely in the navigation control of a robot based on the center of area.

The objective is to improve the obtaining of the advance polygon that configures the laser beams when influencing the obstacles, by means of a depth map camera. The points or image elements of the depth or distance map (matrix) generated by the camera must be projected onto the horizontal plane. It is necessary to pass from the matrix to a vector that contains the relevant "points" of said matrix. These points of the vector will form the vertices of the starry polygon that will be the basis for the calculation of its center of area.

The present work improves the use of laser range measurement that used the technique called 2D $\frac{1}{2}$. The laser only detects objects in its scanning plane. Even the current ones only reach 128 scan planes. With the aforementioned technique, the objects can be in as many planes as the vertical resolution of the camera. The horizontal resolution is equivalent to the number of laser beams and can be a number greater than 180.

Thus, it is proposed to achieve the following objectives:

1. Improve the view of the "world" generated by laser range measurement through the use of depth map cameras.

© Springer Nature Switzerland AG 2022
J. M. Ferrández Vicente et al. (Eds.): IWINAC 2022, LNCS 13259, pp. 264–275, 2022.
https://doi.org/10.1007/978-3-031-06527-9_26

2. Take advantage of the use of cameras to evolve the measurement to 3D.

The rest of the article as follow: 1. *Introduction*, yet viewed. 2. *Problem statement*, main techniques used in reactive robotic navigation up to area center navigation. 3. *Methodology*, an overview of the development of the course of the investigation. 4. *Experiments results*, an explanation of the experiments carried out. 5. *Conclusions and Future Work*, verification of results and future work.

2   Problem Statement

Navigation is the process of determining or maintaining a path to a goal location. One can distinguish between local control strategies and global control strategies [3] The reactive robotics concept was introduced by [5], often referred to as behaviour-based robotics. Different methods have been used for reactive navigation control strategies, i.e. *Potential field, Virtual Forces Field*, VFF [7], VFH or *Vectorial Field Histogram* [4], *Dynamic Window* approach, DWA [6].

The total center of area (CA) qualifier applies to a robot equipped with range sensors that generate measurements in 360° around the robot itself. The center of area is equivalent in two dimensions to the center of mass or gravity. The formula in Cartesian coordinates for the case of a polygon with n vertices $\{(x_j, y_j)\}$ is:

$$x_{CA} = \frac{1}{6A} \sum_{j=1}^{n-1} (x_j y_{j+1} - x_{j+1} y_j)(x_j + x_{j+1}) f(x_j, y_j, x_{j+1} y_{j+1})$$

$$y_{CA} = \frac{1}{6A} \sum_{j=1}^{n-1} (x_j y_{j+1} - x_{j+1} y_j)(y_j + y_{j+1}) f(x_j, y_j, x_{j+1} y_{j+1})$$

where A is the polygon area and f is the commonly used area density function $f \equiv 1$.

In [1] the center of area is used for the first time to achieve a reference system for the integration of sensory data. Later, the center of area was used for robot navigation [2]. The calculated total center of area exerted an attractive force on the robot and as the robot got closer to the center of area the force became repulsive and as a consequence the robot had to look for another center of area. In this way the navigation was produced following successive centers of frontal areas, consequently, this work is based on the strategy called *Partial Area Center*. For simplicity, in the rest of the paper, we will refer partial area center as area center or center of area. In [9] and [8] the ideas about this method are exposed. An advance polygon is built based on the measurements of the sensors (range, depth map cameras). The center of area of the advance polygon is calculated. The robot navigates to the center of area as long as it is accessible. When the calculated area center is not accessible, that is, it is located in an obstacle, a split point is created as an intersection point between the line that joins the robot with the area center and the obstacle itself. This split point splits the actual advance polygon into two sub-polygons. Based on certain criteria, one of them is selected and becomes the advance polygon, calculating its center of area. When the robot passes the split point, it returns to the global polygon. The reach distance of the advancing polygon is a function of its amplitude and this is a function of the split point, the size of the robot is also taken into account.

A modification of the method for reach objectives has been introduced, here the selection of the polygon is made based on the objective to be reached.

3   Methodology

The CoppeliaSim simulator has been used to create the different scenes for the different experiments. But a first scene was created whose objective was how to go from the 3D measurements (pixels) of the camera to the 2D measurements, in other words, to create the algorithm. So, this section tries to express the process that has been carried out to achieve an algorithm that translates the image elements of the depth map into a vector of distances to the objects present in the image from the image plane. Actually, this whole process is a data transformation process. It is based on a distance matrix or depth map and it has been verified how these data change when different objects appear in different positions front to the camera lens. Based on this set of data, the reasoning of this research suggests the idea of how to transform the input data into the output data, which is nothing more than a vector that will contain the distances from the image plane to the objects present in the image plane. At the end, an algorithm is created that performs the transformation of the data.

3.1   Depth Map Camera

The depth map camera delivers a matrix with a number of rows corresponding to its vertical resolution (pixel numbers) and a number of columns corresponding to its horizontal resolution, see Fig. 1. The values of the elements of the array is the distance from the camera to the object displayed in that element. These values are usually normalized in a range from 0.0 to 1.0. The value 0.0 coincides with the so-called "near clipping plane" or close cutting plane (the closest plane of the camera, object close to the lens) and 1.0 coincides with the "far clipping plane" or far cutting plane (the plane from which objects are no longer visible even though they exist). In the experiments it has been set to 0.01 m and 5.0 m respectively. The optimum value of 5 m. has been obtained by experimentation. Another parameter of the camera to take into account is the angle of view that has been established at $86^{\underline{0}}$, which is the value of the RealSense camera of Intel D435 (Depth Field of View (FOV): $86° \times 57°$ ($\pm3°$)).

Distance matrix

1,000	1,000	1,000	1,000	1,000	1,000	1,000	1,000	∘	∘	∘	1,000	1,000	1,000	1,000	1,000	1,000	1,000	1,000
1,000	1,000	1,000	1,000	1,000	1,000	1,000	1,000	∘	∘	∘	1,000	1,000	1,000	1,000	1,000	1,000	1,000	1,000
1,000	1,000	1,000	1,000	1,000	1,000	1,000	1,000	∘	∘	∘	1,000	1,000	1,000	1,000	1,000	1,000	1,000	1,000
1,000	1,000	1,000	1,000	1,000	1,000	1,000	1,000	∘	∘	∘	1,000	1,000	1,000	1,000	1,000	1,000	1,000	1,000
1,000	1,000	1,000	1,000	1,000	1,000	1,000	1,000	∘	∘	∘	1,000	1,000	1,000	1,000	1,000	1,000	1,000	1,000
1,000	1,000	1,000	1,000	1,000	1,000	1,000	1,000	∘	∘	∘	1,000	1,000	1,000	1,000	1,000	1,000	1,000	1,000
∘	∘	∘	∘	∘	∘	∘	∘	∘	∘	∘	∘	∘	∘	∘	∘	∘	∘	∘
∘	∘	∘	∘	∘	∘	∘	∘	∘	∘	∘	∘	∘	∘	∘	∘	∘	∘	∘
∘	∘	∘	∘	∘	∘	∘	∘	∘	∘	∘	∘	∘	∘	∘	∘	∘	∘	∘
0,231	0,231	0,231	0,231	0,231	0,231	0,231	0,231	∘	∘	∘	0,231	0,231	0,231	0,231	0,231	0,231	0,231	0,231
0,230	0,230	0,230	0,230	0,230	0,230	0,230	0,230	∘	∘	∘	0,230	0,230	0,230	0,230	0,230	0,230	0,230	0,230
0,228	0,228	0,228	0,228	0,228	0,228	0,228	0,228	∘	∘	∘	0,228	0,228	0,228	0,228	0,228	0,228	0,228	0,228
0,227	0,227	0,227	0,227	0,227	0,227	0,227	0,227	∘	∘	∘	0,227	0,227	0,227	0,227	0,227	0,227	0,227	0,227
0,226	0,226	0,226	0,226	0,226	0,226	0,226	0,226	∘	∘	∘	0,226	0,226	0,226	0,226	0,226	0,226	0,226	0,226
0,226	0,226	0,226	0,226	0,226	0,226	0,226	0,226	∘	∘	∘	0,226	0,226	0,226	0,226	0,226	0,226	0,226	0,226

↓ ↓ ↓ ↓ ↓ ↓ ↓ ↓ ↓ ↓ ↓ ↓ ↓ ↓ ↓ ↓ ↓ ↓

1,000	1,000	1,000	1,000	1,000	1,000	1,000	1,000	∘	∘	∘	1,000	1,000	1,000	1,000	1,000	1,000	1,000	1,000

Distance vector

Fig. 1. Distance matrix and distance vector

3.2   Images Under Study

The successive sections aim to explain the line of research that has led to the achievement of the algorithm that transforms the distance matrix generated by the camera into a vector of distances that will be used to generate the points of the advance polygon and the calculation of its center of area.

All significant positions of the objects were simulated. The central column of the matrix delivered by the camera has been plotted. First, a scene without objects has been simulated as shown in the Fig. 2a) and its corresponding graph of the central column. As can be seen in this graph shows a succession of values equal to 1.0 and approximately on row 312 (horizon) that value decreases forming a curve. The second scene depicts a suspended object. The Fig. 2b) shows this scene and again the graph of the central column. You can see the position of the object. A scene with an object below the horizon is now simulated. The image in the Fig. 2c) and its corresponding graph. Finally, one object after another, Fig. 2d).

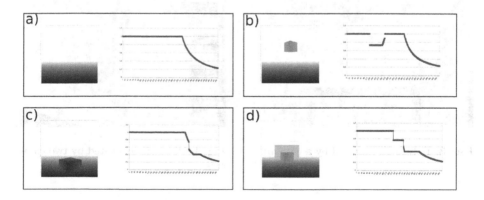

Fig. 2. a) Image without any object, b) Image with a suspended object, c) Image with one object below the horizon, d) Image with one object behind another

3.3   Conclusions of the Imaging Study

After studying the previous images, it could be concluded that objects can be detected if we consider two pixels with the same value. Since we are dealing with calculations in real numbers and in certain circumstances it could happen that two identical consecutive values are not found, but they are very close for an object. For this reason, the criterion of two identical consecutive pixels is changed so that the absolute value of the difference of two consecutive pixels is less than 0.0001. Then, we already have three premises for the possible algorithm:

1. Go through the matrix by columns.

2. Detect objects by the absolute value of the difference of two consecutive pixels being less than 0.0001.

3. In case of detecting several pairs of pixels in a column, the one with the lowest value is taken.

3.4   Advance Polygon Generation

Once a vector has been obtained with the distances to the objects present in the image, these distances must be converted into points of the advance polygon. But in the course of the tests carried out, the problem of using a single depth map camera is manifested. The center of area or centroid calculated was always inside the polygon, never inside an obstacle. See Fig. 3. Using two cameras solves the problem and also covers a circular sector of 172° close to the sector of the 2D laser range measurement scan plane, which, as is known, is 180°. Now the center of area (point) of the advance polygon does not belong to the advance polygon for the same object in Figure above in front of the camera.

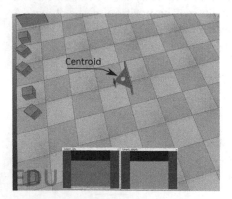
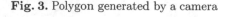

Fig. 3. Polygon generated by a camera   **Fig. 4.** Polygon generated by two cameras

Since the vector of distances are referred to the plane of vision of each camera, these distances must be referenced to the origin of the local coordinates of the robot. Thus, we emulate the beams of the laser range measurement. When using two cameras, the distance vector will be the concatenation of the vectors of both cameras. In the case of laser use, the polygon generated without obstacles is a circular sector. In the case of two cameras it is similar to two isosceles triangles with a common side (the OX axis), which are not suitable for calculating the center of area since the area density function is not constant. Since the laser range measurement is a circular sector where the area density is constant, he suggests constraining the triangles to a circular sector. In other words, the problem is solved by limiting the measurements to a circular sector. Now yes, it is possible to calculate the center of area of the circular sector thus generated.

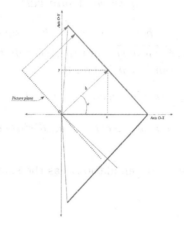

Fig. 5. Calculation of a polygon point

Each point on the slice plane of each camera (thick line in Fig. 5) corresponds to each pixel of horizontal resolution, in the experiments 512 pixels. Since each camera has a certain horizontal viewing angle or perspective angle (remember, for the RealSense D435 Depth Field of View (FOV): 86° × 57° ±3°), the following relationship can be established:

$$degrees\_by\_pixel = {}^{perpective\_angle}\!/_{(camera\_number\_pixels-1)}$$

If the vector of distances is traversed, each pixel will correspond to a certain number of ψ radians.

The theory of navigation by center of area indicates that, depending on the width of the sector of the star polygon, the maximum distance at which the viewing plane is located must be modified. If the center of area is outside the polygon (inaccessible point) a split point is produced and the polygon is divided by this point and as a consequence its width (*angle_width*) will be reduced and the maximum distance (*max_distance*) must be modified:

$$max\_distance = \frac{far\_clipping\_plane \times angle\_width}{2 \times perspetive\_angle}$$

where $far\_clipping\_plane$ is the maximum distance at which the camera can view an object and $perspective\_angle$ is the angle of view of a camera. In the experiments $5\,\mathrm{m}$ and $86\,^\circ\mathrm{C}$ respectively. Now, in order for the polygon to be contained in a circular sector of radius $max\_distance$, the following calculations have to be made:

$\psi = degrees\_by\_pixel \times pixel_n$, $x\_max = max\_distance \times \cos\psi$, $y\_max = max\_distance \times \sin\psi$

The distance d to an object calculated from the $distances\_vector$:

$$d = \frac{far\_clipping\_plane \times (distances\_vector\,[pixel_n] + min\_val)}{(max\_val + min\_val)}$$

Then: $h = \frac{d}{\cos\psi}$, $x = h \times \cos\psi$, $y = h \times \sin\psi$. So, $circular\_sector\_max\_distance = \sqrt{x\_max^2 + y\_max^2}$ and $to\_object\_distance = \sqrt{x^2 + y^2}$

The coordinates of a point(p_x, p_y) shall be:

- if $to\_object\_distance \leq circular\_sector\_max\_distance$ then $p_x = x$ and $p_y = y$.
- if $to\_object\_distance > circular\_sector\_max\_distance$ then $p_x = x\_max$ and $p_y = y\_max$

Now the advance polygon (laser emulation) has the shape shown in Fig. 6.

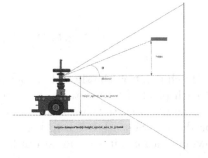

Fig. 6. Polygon laser emulation

Fig. 7. Calculation of the height of objects

But not all the information a depth map camera generates has yet been harnessed. While the polygon has been generated taking into account the distance of any object at any height. Here is the key, the height above the ground of the objects. You can actually extract this information from the camera (Fig. 7). Using this information, the robot can navigate under an obstacle that is a few centimeters (for safety) above the horizontal plane that contains the axis of view of the camera. With this information, a surface would no longer be generated, but a volume, it would be in 3D. For a "world" on the ground there is no need to go to a real 3D, it is enough with what has been called delimited-3D. You won't even need to calculate the height. Discarding all the information from the upper semi-plane of vision (except for a few rows for safety, a few centimeters above the vehicle top) is enough.

4   Experiments Results

Following [9] and [2] as a guide for the experiments carried out, since the aim was to compare the experiments of these articles carried out with the laser range measurement with those carried out in this work with the cameras. There are eight experiments or, to be exact, seventeen experiments if the four variants of three of them are counted. The most relevant are: The first one in the list is called *Successive splits to pass two obstacles*. In *Reach objectives*, see Fig. 8, using the center of area method, the part of the free library for the control of the robot used that deals precisely with reach objectives. In *Trajectories followed by the robot when wandering through a home or office environment*, (Fig. 9) the emergent behaviour of reaching all rooms is shown. On the *Closed circuit* (Figs. 10 and 11), a new feature has been introduced, placing an object on the floor and two bridges, one of them with two levels, in order to verify the delimited-3D feature provided by the use of cameras as opposed to the laser range measurement.

The Fig. 8 shows circles with a number inside them. They will be used to explain the technology of navigation by center of area. The solid line is the path of the robot and the dashed line the successive calculations of the center of area. In 1 the robot follows the calculated center of area. In 2 the calculated point of the center of area is introduced in the obstacle (not shown in the Fig. 8). At this instant a point is obtained which is to be called the split point. An imaginary line is taken that joins the center of the robot with this point. This line divides the advanced polygon into two sub-polygons. One of them is taken at random (except in the case of a reach objective, where the sub-polygon that leads to the target is taken). Once the polygon is selected, the new center of area is calculated: this is the jump from 3 to 4 in the Fig. 8. The maximum viewing distance of the cameras is limited proportionally to the amplitude of the selected sub-polygon. The center of area is followed until at 5 the split point is exceeded. In this time the amplitude will be at its maximum when the maximum amplitude is reached again. At 6 the polygon width is the maximum and continues to follow the center of area.

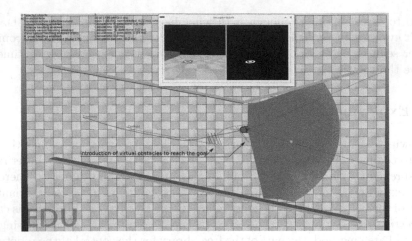

Fig. 8. Reach objectives

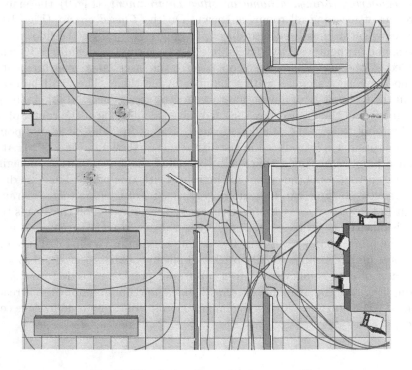

Fig. 9. Wandering through a home or office

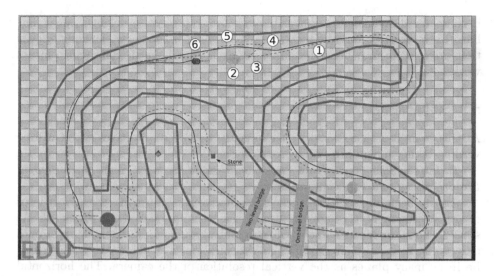

Fig. 10. Closed circuit

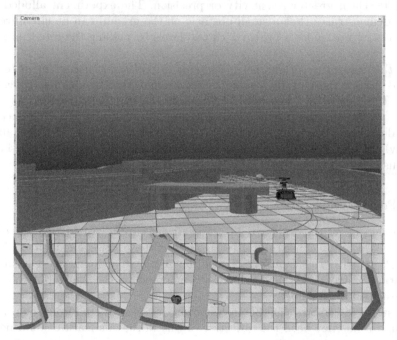

Fig. 11. Snapshot crossing the bridges

5   Conclusions and Future Work

This section will deal with the conclusions. At the beginning of this work, some objectives were set and it is time to verify if it can be concluded that they have been achieved. As usually happens in any research process, problems appear that have been resolved, but the most important thing is that new elements appear that originate or may originate a new research thread that is collected in future works.

5.1 Conclusions

At this point it is necessary to remember the proposed objectives and it will be verified if they have been fulfilled one by one:

1. Improve the view of the "world" generated by laser range measurement through the use of depth map cameras.

At the beginning of this work, the objective of improving the use of laser range measurement through the use of the technique called 2D $\frac{1}{2}$ was set. As stated, the 2D laser only detects objects in its scan plane. Even the current ones only reach 128 scan planes. With the aforementioned technique, the objects can be in as many planes as the vertical resolution of the camera. The horizontal resolution is equivalent to the number of laser beams and can be a number greater than 180. Then, greater sensitivity or precision. The experiment alluded to in Sect. 4 demonstrates that a small obstacle on the ground can be circumvented. You can navigate under a bridge with two levels by passing the robot under the highest bridge.

2. Take advantage of the use of cameras to evolve the measurement to 3D.

The characteristic of 2D $\frac{1}{2}$ cameras can be converted by a simple calculation to 3D. In other words, the height of the objects can be extracted. As stated in 4 a "world" on the ground does not need this 3D feature, what has been called delimited-3D is sufficient. Precisely this characteristic is what has allowed the navigation of the aforementioned experiment *Closed Circuit* in Sect. 4 of the previous objective.

5.2 Future Work

At the time of writing this article, a so-called *Centroid Navigation Device* has already been built, consisting of two Intel Realsense 435 cameras and a Raspberry Pi 4B with the *Centroid Navigation Application* for image capture and navigation control. This device has been mounted on the Amigobot robot and field tests will begin shortly.

As stated in the Sect. 3.4, 3D information can be extracted from the cameras. Although it has not been the objective of this work, this feature could be used in area center navigation in drones.

Acknowlegements. Grant PID2020-115220RB-C22 funded by MCIN/AEI/10. 13039/501100011033 and, as appropriate, by "ERDF A way for making Europe", by the "European Union" or by the "European Union NextGenerationEU/PRTR" .

References

1. Álvarez, J.R., de la Paz, F., Mira, J.: On virtual sensory coding: an analytical model of the endogenous representation. In: Mira, J., Sánchez-Andrés, J.V. (eds.) IWANN 1999. LNCS, vol. 1607, pp. 526–539. Springer, Heidelberg (1999). https://doi.org/10.1007/BFb0100520
2. Álvarez-Sánchez, J.R., de la Paz López, F., Mira, J., Cuadra Troncoso, J.M.: The centre of area method as a basic mechanism for representation and navigation. Robot. Auton. Syst. **55**(12), 860–869 (2007). Robotics and Autonomous Systems in the 50th Anniversary of Artificial Intelligence
3. Arkin, R.C.: Behavior-Based Robotics. MIT Press (1998)
4. Borenstein, J., Koren, Y.: The vector field histogram-fast obstacle avoidance for mobile robots. IEEE Trans. Robot. Autom. **7**(3), 278–288 (1991)
5. Brooks, R.A.: Intellingence without representation. Artif. Intell. **47**, 139–159 (1991)
6. Fox, D., Burgard, W.: The dynamic window approach to collision avoidance. Robot. Autom. Mag. **4**, 23 (1997)
7. Krogh, B.: A generalized potential field approach to obstacle avoidance control. Technical report (1984)
8. Álvarez-Sánchez, J.R., de la Paz López, F., Cuadra Troncoso, J.M., de Santos Sierra, D.: Reactive navigation in real environments using partial center of area method. Robot. Auton. Syst. **58**(12), 1231–1237 (2010)
9. Álvarez-Sánchez, J.R., de la Paz López, F., Cuadra Troncoso, J.M., Rosado Sánchez, J.I.: Partial center of area method used for reactive autonomous robot navigation. In: Mira, J., Ferrández, J.M., Álvarez, J.R., de la Paz, F., Toledo, F.J. (eds.) IWINAC 2009. LNCS, vol. 5602, pp. 408–418. Springer, Heidelberg (2009). https://doi.org/10.1007/978-3-642-02267-8_44

Deep Learning

Data Augmentation Techniques for Speech Emotion Recognition and Deep Learning

José Antonio Nicolás[1], Javier de Lope[1(✉)], and Manuel Graña[2]

[1] Computational Cognitive Robotics Group, Department of Artificial Intelligence, Universidad Politécnica de Madrid (UPM), Madrid, Spain
javier.delope@upm.es
[2] Computational Intelligence Group, University of the Basque Country (UPV/EHU), Leioa, Spain

Abstract. This paper introduces innovations both in data augmentation and deep neural network architecture for speech emotion recognition (SER). The novel architecture combines a series of convolutional layers with a final layer of long short-term memory cells to determine emotions in audio signals. The audio signals are conveniently processed to generate mel spectrograms, which are used as inputs to the deep neural network architecture. This paper proposes a selected set of data augmentation techniques that allow to reduce the network overfitting. We achieve an average recognition accuracy of 86.44% on publicly distributed databases, outperforming state-of-the-art methods.

Keywords: Speech emotion recognition · Data augmentation · Convolutional neural networks · Recurrent neural networks · Long short-term memory · Mel spectrograms

1 Introduction

The nature of emotions [1] has been studied in many scientific disciplines, and psychologists have proposed several models to describe relations among emotion concepts. They tend to agree there is a set of primary emotions that sometimes are arranged in pairs of opposites. Mixtures of two primary emotions lead to new ones. Behaviorists and neurologists would give different interpretations but, independently of theories, emotions are an important part of human relationships and they must be incorporated into the new technology offerings.

Emotion recognition has been one of the most active research fields in the last decade [2]. Human-machine interaction (HMI) trend is to create more natural interfaces between humans and any kind of devices and services. Whatever aspect of the human communication must be emulated.

Speech emotion recognition (SER) has been approached applying many different machine learning techniques [3,4]. Some of these techniques had been

© Springer Nature Switzerland AG 2022
J. M. Ferrández Vicente et al. (Eds.): IWINAC 2022, LNCS 13259, pp. 279–288, 2022.
https://doi.org/10.1007/978-3-031-06527-9_27

successfully utilized in automatic speech recognition (ASR) before being transferred to SER. Examples of such techniques are Gaussian mixture models, hidden Markov models and, support vector machines, which is probably the most used method reported to achieve the best performance [5].

Recently, as in many other research fields, most of the activity is addressed to use deep learning approaches [6,7]. Usually, the input features are extracted as spectrograms, which allows to process them by convolutional neural networks (CNN). Due to the audio signal nature recurrent neural networks and long short-term memory (LSTM) cells have been also proposed for emotion classifying.

Particularly, mel spectrograms [8] are a widely used way of representing audio signals converting them into images [9]. They have been shown to be effective distinguishing features in emotion recognition and facilitate the identification and tracking of timbre fluctuations in sound recordings. The main advantage of mel spectrograms over conventional ones comes from using the mel scale for signal representation. The mel scale is based on the perception of acoustic signals by the human ear and it adjusts the signals by reducing the differences between two close frequencies in the low and high ranges.

The rest of paper is organized as follows. First, we describe the data augmentation techniques to generate new samples, which are used for training the deep neural network model. Section 3 details the network architecture. Section 4 describes the audio emotion database and summarizes the way in which the experiments are performed. Section 5 offers the performance results. Finally, we offer some concluding remarks and directions for future work.

2   Data Augmentation Techniques

Deep network architectures require lots of data to estimate the internal network weights and reduce the overfitting in order to generalize well on unseen data. Usually, most of the speech emotion recognition databases do not contain the number of samples required for deep learning. Some works [10] gather information from several databases. It is a daring approach because the databases have to be created according to specific rules and criteria in order to produce statistically significant results. The most used databases include a rigorous study and they are created by using professional recording techniques.

Data augmentation is a general kind of computational techniques used in deep learning to produce additional data in order to improve learning convergence. Unfortunately most of the methods are designed to work over image databases and, although the proposed model in this paper uses images as input features, many augmentation methods are not applicable here because they modify the images in such a way that they correspond to nonsense audio information. For example, images after rotational or simmetrical operations would not correspond to well formed spectrograms from audio samples.

Thus, we are limiting the use of data augmentation techniques that have been proposed for speech recognition. Although we are working on a different area such as the emotion recognition from audio, we consider it is interesting to verify if those data augmentation techniques are valuable here.

We have applied four different types of data augmentation techniques to the original dataset, which are briefly described in the following subsections.

2.1   Tempo Perturbation

The overlap-add technique based on waveform similarity (WSOLA) [11] was initially proposed to produce high quality speech output for on-line processing with arbitrary time-scaling factors. It applies the concept of waveform similarity for tackling the problem of time-scale modification of speech. We use the WSOLA algorithm to generate a set of new samples to feed the network during the training stage.

Basically, WSOLA streches the duration of the audio signal and leaves unmodified the shape of its spectral envelope. First, it decomposes the time-domain audio signal into short analysis blocks. These blocks are equally spaced along the time axis by H_a (which is the analysis hopsize parameter). Then, it relocates the blocks along the time axis by H_s (which is the synthesis hopsize parameter) to create the new perturbed signal. The blocks relocation is performed according to a perturbation factor α given as:

$$H_s = \alpha \cdot H_a \tag{1}$$

2.2   Vocal Tract Length Perturbation

The vocal tract length normalization [12] is a technique that was initially proposed to minimize the changes in audio signals introduced by the different shapes of the vocal tract between speakers. These variations were counteracted in order to normalize the audio signals, thus improving speech recognition. The algorithm linearly warps the frequency f of the spectrogram of each speaker by a warp factor α to achieve the vocal tract normalization as specified in Eq. (2), where S is the sampling frequency and F_{hi} is a boundary frequency chosen such that it covers the significant formants. The warp factor accounts for the relative length of the individual vocal tract compared to the cannonical mean.

$$f' = \begin{cases} f\alpha & f \leq F_{hi}\frac{\min(\alpha,1)}{\alpha} \\ S/2 - \frac{S/2-F_{hi}\min(\alpha,1)}{S/2-F_{hi}\frac{\min(\alpha,1)}{\alpha}} & \text{otherwise} \end{cases} \tag{2}$$

Posteriorly, the method was reversed and proposed for data augmentation [13] by randomly generating random warp factors for each utterance. Thus, the application was from a normalized database that was used to compare normalized utterances to a database augmented with synthetic utterances that simulate different shapes of vocal tracts. For data augmentation, this technique is usually referred as vocal tract length perturbation.

2.3   Speed Perturbation

The speed perturbation technique [14] was also initially proposed for speech recognition. Given an audio signal $x(t)$, time warping by a factor α produces a warped time signal $x(\alpha t)$. We obtain $\alpha^{-1}\hat{x}(\alpha^{-1}\omega)$ by applying the Fourier transform of the audio signal computed as

$$\hat{x}(\omega) = \int x(t)e^{-i\omega t}dt \tag{3}$$

and it can be seen that the warping factor α produces shifts in the frequency components of $\hat{x}(\omega)$, which correspond approximately to a shift of the spectrum in the mel spectrogram [15].

These changes in the mel spectrogram are similar to those produced using vocal tract length perturbation. In this case, the speed perturbation results in a change in the signal duration that also affects the length of the utterance. However, if the speed of the signal is reduced ($\alpha < 1$), there is a shift in the signal energy towards lower frequencies, which differs from the vocal tract length perturbation from the behavior.

2.4 Additive White Gaussian Noise

Adding noise [16] to the original waveform is one of the most used techniques for data augmentation in speech recognition. Here, we add white Gaussian noise $\mathcal{N}$ to the original audio signal $x(t)$ after normalizing both audio and noise signals. A predetermined signal-to-noise ratio r is used to generate the noise signals.

$$x'(t) = x(t) + \mathcal{N}(0, r) \tag{4}$$

3 Deep Neural Network Architecture

We propose a deep neural network architecture based on an AlexNet [17] network, in which we have removed their last three fully connected layers and added new layers according to our own purposes. As it is well known the original model was formulated to participate in the ImageNet LSVRC-2010 contest [18], where the dataset contained 1.2 million labeled training samples and 1000 different classes. The first two fully connected layers in the original architecture have 4096 neurons. They have been substituted by a LSTM layer with 256 cells, which can learn patterns from temporal data inputs. The third dense layer has been modified to fit to our problem, which requires 8 output neurons, one for each emotion in the dataset as described in the next section, without dropout and a softmax activation function.

Also, we have modified the input layer to reduce the number of channels of the images. In our images, i.e., spectrograms, the color does not contribute with new information. It is mainly used as conventional mechanism to facilitate the human interpretation of such images. Thus, the original first AlexNet network module composed of five convolutional modules is accordingly modified to manage $227 \times 227 \times 1$ grayscale images rather than $227 \times 227 \times 3$ color images.

Each convolutional module uses a similar structure: it is composed by a 2D convolutional layer, which uses relu activation functions, followed by a batch normalization, and only it is not used padding in the first convolutional layer. Table 1 shows the number of convolutional filters, kernel and stride sizes. After the first, second and fifth layers, 2D max-pooling layers are inserted with a 3×3 kernel and stride equals to 2×2. After these eight layers, the LSTM and dense layers are added as explained above.

Table 1. Parameters used by the convolutional layers.

Layer	Conv filters	Kernel	Stride	Padding
1	96	11×11	4×4	No
2	256	5×5	1×1	Yes
3	384	3×3	1×1	Yes
4	384	3×3	1×1	Yes
5	256	3×3	1×1	Yes

4 Design of Experiments and Dataset

We use the RAVDESS database [19] for testing the proposed architecture. The database is composed of 7356 audio and video clips. It provides samples of speech and songs, thus it also allows to train models for the analysis of musical recordings. It is freely available and one of the hardest and most complete corpora that includes also video streams of the samples. This multimodal nature converts this dataset as the perfect testbed for testing and comparing a diversity of classifers and techniques.

The audio dataset contains 1440 samples of speech audio recordings, which are recorded by 24 professional actors (12 male and 12 female) that read two semantically neutral US English phrases. The phrases were selected according the length in syllables and words frequency and familiarity. A total of eight emotions are considered: neutral, calm, happiness, sadness, anger, fear, disgust, and surprise. Each utterance is pronounced in two levels of emotional intensity (only one intensity in the neutral emotion), and there is just one recording for each. The audio files are provided in lossless wave format to avoid the usual artifacts and other alterations added to the original signal by the compression. Each one is about 3 s long.

The *librosa* [20] open software library is used to process the audio files. We 48000 Hz as sampling rate. The initial silence in each recording (about 0.5 s) is removed. Then, we normalize the recordings lengths by padding with zeros when needed in order to achieve a homogeneous format.

The original dataset is randomly partitioned into training (80%), validation (10%) and test (10%) sets. We have carried out the partitioning and selecting process by means of the *scikit-learn* [21] open software library. We define initial seeds for the pseudorandom generator in order to guarantee the experiments reproducibility. Note that we have applied the augmentation techniques commented above to the training set only. Otherwise, we were artificially increasing the model accuracy by adding similar samples in the validation and test sets. After the data augmentation we increase the training dataset size from the 1152 original samples to 10368 samples. We have increased almost ten times the number of samples in the original dataset. The details of generating the new sets of samples by each data augmentation technique are as follows:

Tempo perturbation: As commented above, we use the waveform similarity approach (WSOLA) and generate a new sample by applying the technique to each original sample with $\alpha = 0.8$. It produces 1152 new samples.

Vocal tract length perturbation: Also, we generate a new sample from each original one. We use a sampling frequency $S = 48000$ Hz, $F_{hi} = 4800$ Hz and α is randomly generated by a Gaussian distribution $\mathcal{N}(1, 0.1)$. We obtain 1152 new samples.

Speed perturbation: We use the time strech function provided by *librosa* with strech factors of 0.8, 0.9, 1.1 and 1.2. Those factors are determined from the results by Ko *et al.* [14]. Originally, they generate only two new sets by modifying the speed to 0.9 and 1.1 of the original rate. We have found the optimal results by generating four new sets with the above-mentioned strech factors. We get 4608 new samples.

Additive white Gaussian noise: Since the noise is random we apply this augmentation technique twice with signal-to-noise ratio 15 dB and 30 dB. As noise as audio signals are previously normalized. We obtain 2304 new samples by applying this technique.

Figure 1 shows examples of the original and resulting signals generated by applying the data augmentation techniques. From left to right, (a) original signal, (b) tempo perturbation, (c) vocal tract length perturbation, (d) speed perturbation, and (e) additive white Gaussian noise.

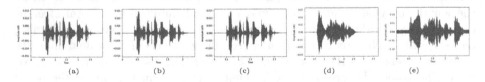

    (a)   (b)   (c)   (d)   (e)

Fig. 1. (a) original audio signal, (b) tempo perturbation augmented signal, (c) vocal tract length perturbation augmented signal, (d) speed perturbation augmented signal, (e) additive white Gaussian noise augmented signal.

Then, we extract the mel spectrograms corresponding to the audio samples. Examples of the mel spectrograms are shown in Fig. 2. We also use the *librosa* open software library for this purpose.

The mel spectrograms are converted to grayscale images. Since the color information is not providing new information to the model we are reducing the required memory to store the images and the time to manipulate them: the grayscale images are represented by 1 channel rather than 3 channels as can be

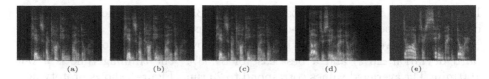

Fig. 2. Mel spectrograms corresponding to (a) original audio signal, (b) tempo perturbation augmented, (c) vocal tract length perturbation augmented, (d) speed perturbation augmented, (e) additive white Gaussian noise augmented.

necessary for color images. Moreover, we transform the amplitude scale to dB to ease the model training. The parameters used to extract the mel spectrogram are summarized in Table 2. They were empirically determined. We have used the default values provided in the software libraries for the rest of parameters.

Table 2. Parameters used to extract mel spectrograms.

Parameter	Value
Sample rate	48000
Length of the FFT window	1024
Window function	Hamming
Window length	512
Samples between successive frames	256
Mel filter banks	128
Max sample rate (filter banks)	24000

Finally, we resize the mel spectrogram images to the appropriate size required by the deep learning neural network (227×227 in the case of the AlexNet-based proposed architecture). To avoid distorted images that can be modified by the data augmentation, we resize them with padding and standardize and normalize them to keep the aspect ratio. These operations are performed by functions provided by the *TensorFlow* [22] open software library.

5   Experimental Results

The network is trained 30 epochs with a stochastic gradient descent (SGD) optimizer. The number of epochs is empirically determined by analysing the model conevrgence. The optimizer is commonly used and recommended for this type of models. The learning rate is 0.001 and the momentum 0.8. The categorical crossentropy provided in *Keras* [23] is used as loss function and batch size is 32 as usually recommended [24] for models as the proposed.

We have used *Google Colaboratory* for the experiments with the following hardware specifications: processor Intel Xeon CPU@2.30 GHz, 20 cores, 35.25 GB

RAM and TPU v2, 180 teraflops, 64 GB High Bandwidth Memory (HBM). We carry out 20 repetitions of hold-out validation experiments.

Averaging over the 20 repetitions, we get an overall accuracy of 86.44% (standard deviation ±3%) and a best case of 89.58%. The training time is about 100 min. The averaged values correspond to 20 runs. Figure 3 shows prototypical training curves. This accuracy outperforms state-of-the-art conventional machine learning and deep learning methods that use the same database. For comparison, the best result reported to date on the RADVESS database is 77.50% [25].

By applying these data augmentation techniques the network is able to generalize and the overfitting is almost completely removed. The overfitting caused by the low number of samples is the main issue when this database is used for speech emotion recognition, which configures it as the one of the hardest audio databases for speech emotion recognition.

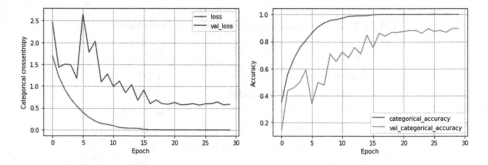

Fig. 3. Loss (left) and accuracy (right) curves in training and validation.

Figure 4 shows the confusion matrix corresponding to one of the training/testing experiments over the original dataset. We can appreciate that the recognition accuracy rates for almost all emotions are over 83%, only fear has recognition rates under that value. In this particular case, the samples in the test set corresponding to that emotion were especially low and unbalanced. The rest of labels are accurately predicted. We do not detect usual misclassifications between emotions in this databases as for example neutral and calm or happiness and fear.

6   Conclusions and Further Work

We have presented a novel computational model for speech emotion recognition based on a deep neural network architecture. The deep neural network model is based on the AlexNet network, which combines a series of convolutional layers plus a layer of long short-term memory cells. The system utilizes mel spectrograms as representative features of samples. We have validated the model with one of the most recent and used speech emotion datasets as is the RAVDESS database. The average recognition accuracy is 86.44%, and the best case is

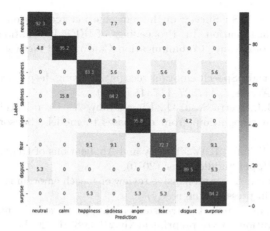

Fig. 4. Confusion matrix corresponding to one of the experiments

89.58%. Those accuracy values outperforms state-of-the-art machine learning methods that use the same database.

The model performance is partially achieved thanks to the selection of data augmentation techniques that have been applied to the original dataset to generate new samples to train the network. The data augmentation has only been used in the training set, otherwise, we were artificially increasing the model accuracy by adding similar samples in the other sets.

Future work may address to apply other data augmentation methods and to analyse the performance increasing by each particular method. The network architecture is also a line of future improving. Although we have achieved good performance indexes we will be finding new architectures to facilitate the use of speech emotion recognition in electronic devices with restricted computational resources such as smartphones or robots.

Acknowledgments. This work has been partially supported by FEDER funds through MINECO project PID2020-116346GB-I00.

References

1. Plutchik, R.: The nature of emotions: human emotions have deep evolutionary roots. Am. Sci. **89**(4), 344–350 (2001)
2. Lieskovská, E., Jakubec, M., Jarina, R., Chmulik, M.: A review on speech emotion recognition using deep learning and attention mechanism. Electronics **10**, 1163 (2021)
3. Anagnostopoulos, C.-N., Iliou, T., Giannoukos, I.: Features and classifiers for emotion recognition from speech: a survey from 2000 to 2011. Springer Sci. **43**, 155–177 (2015)
4. Gangamohan, P., Kadiri, S.R., Yegnanarayana, B.: Analysis of emotional speech—a review. In: Esposito, A., Jain, L.C. (eds.) Toward Robotic Socially Believable Behaving Systems - Volume I. ISRL, vol. 105, pp. 205–238. Springer, Cham (2016). https://doi.org/10.1007/978-3-319-31056-5_11

5. Singh, Y.B., Goel, S.: Survey on human emotion recognition: speech database, features and classification. In: Proceedings of IEEE International Conference on Advances in Computing, Communication Control and Networking, pp. 298–301 (2018)
6. Khalil, R.A., et al.: Speech emotion recognition using deep learning techniques: a review. IEEE Access **7**, 117327–117345 (2019)
7. Abbaschian, B.J., Sierra-Sosa, D., Elmaghraby, A.: Deep learning techniques for speech emotion recognition, from databases to models. Sensors **21**(1249), 1–27 (2021)
8. Rabiner, L.R., Schafer, R.W.: Theory and Applications of Digital Speech Processing. Pearson, Upper Saddle River (2010)
9. Wani, T.M., et al.: A comprehensive review of speech emotion recognition systems. IEEE Access (in press, online ready)
10. Gerczuk, M. et al.: EmoNet: a transfer learning framework for multi-corpus speech emotion recognition. arXiv preprint arXiv:2103.08310 (2021)
11. Verhelst, W., Roelands, M.: An overlap-add technique based on waveform similarity (WSOLA) for high quality time-scale modification of speech. In: 1993 IEEE International Conference on Acoustics, Speech, and Signal Processing, pp. 554–557 (1993)
12. Lee, L., Rose, R.: A frequency warping approach to speaker normalization. IEEE Trans. Speech Audio Process. **6**(1), 49–60 (1998)
13. Jaitly, N., Hinton, G.E.: Vocal tract length perturbation (VTLP) improves speech recognition. In: Proceedings of ICML Workshop on Deep Learning for Audio, Speech and Language, pp. 21–25 (2013)
14. Ko, T., Peddinti, V., Povey, D., Khudanpur, S.: Audio augmentation for speech recognition. Proc. Interspeech **2015**, 3586–3589 (2015)
15. Andén, J., Mallat, S.: Deep scattering spectrum. IEEE Trans. Signal Process. **62**(16), 4114–4128 (2014)
16. Bovik, A.C.: Handbook of Image and Video Processing: Communications. Networking and Multimedia. Academic Press Inc., Orlando (2005)
17. Krizhevsky, A., Sutskever, I., Hinton, G.E.: ImageNet classification with deep convolutional neural networks. Commun. ACM **60**(6), 84–90 (2017)
18. Berg, A., Deng, J., Fei-Fei, L.: Large scale visual recognition challenge (2010). http://www.image-net.org/challenges
19. Livingstone, S.R., Russo, F.A.: The Ryerson audio-visual database of emotional speech and song (RAVDESS): a dynamic, multimodal set of facial and vocal expressions in North American English. PLoS ONE **13**(5), e0196391 (2018)
20. McFee, B. et al.: librosa: Audio and music signal analysis in Python. In: Proceedings of 14th Python in Science Conference, pp. 18–25, Austin, TX (2015)
21. Pedregosa, F., et al.: Scikit-learn: machine learning in Python. J. Mach. Learn. Res. **12**, 2825–2830, e0196391 (2011)
22. Abadi, M. et al.: TensorFlow: large-scale machine learning on heterogeneous systems (2015). https://www.tensorflow.org/
23. Chollet, F., et al.: Keras (2015). https://github.com/fchollet/keras
24. Masters, D., Luschi, C.: Revisiting small batch training for deep neural networks. arXiv preprint arXiv:1804.07612 (2018)
25. Slimi, A., Hamroun, M., Zrigui, M., Nicolas, H.: Emotion recognition from speech using spectrograms and shallow neural networks. In: ACM International Conference on Advances in Mobile Computing & Multimedia, Chiang Mai, Thailand, pp. 298–301 (2020)

Deep Learning Artwork Style Prediction and Similarity Detection

Igor Sorarrain Rebollar and Manuel Graña[⊠]

University of the Basque Country (UPV/EHU),
Manuel Lardizabal 1, 20018 Donostia, Spain
manuel.grana@ehu.es

Abstract. The point of departure of this work is the aim to predict artwork style. The paper presents results retraining some of the most popular deep learning models for image classification, i.e. *ResNet-34, ResNet-50, VGG-16, DenseNet-121*, and a *CNN* model made from scratch over a dataset extracted from *WikiArt* for a *Kaggle* competition. This dataset is composed of 103253 images, categorized into 136 different artwork styles. We select 20 art styles that have enough image samples to allow for network training, achieving accuracy comparable to state of the art results. Moreover, we observe that the structure of the confusion matrix reflects the conceptual relations between the artwork styles, hence points to an induced similarity measure between styles of artwork instances.

Keywords: Artwork style prediction · CNN · Image classification

1 Introduction

This work considers images of digitized fine art, artworks for short. Most online collections of paintings include metadata, i.e. annotations done by art expert that can easily identify the artist, style and genre of a painting using their experience and knowledge of specific features. The aim here is to classify the images of the paintings into different art styles, which would be a very difficult task for a person who is not expert in art.

Deep learning-based models can automatically learn from files such as images, text, or audio, and do not require a previous feature selection. The classification of images is an appropriate task for these models. In this paper, we focus on the application of convolutional neural networks (CNN) to fine art style prediction [3]. This choice is based on the fact that this type of architecture is one of the most effective methods for image classification and has already been reported in state of the art approaches [2]. On the other hand, this type of networks it is also used for audio classification [4] or to classify 3D objects [7].

This paper applies transfer learning to train the ResNet-34, ResNet-50, DenseNet-121, and VGG-16 well known CNN models for style prediction. In addition, we will compare the results obtained by these models with a CNN model trained from scratch.

© Springer Nature Switzerland AG 2022
J. M. Ferrández Vicente et al. (Eds.): IWINAC 2022, LNCS 13259, pp. 289–297, 2022.
https://doi.org/10.1007/978-3-031-06527-9_28

The experimental dataset has been extracted from the WikiArt site[1] to be used in a Kaggle challenge. There are many styles underrepresented, so we have selected 20 art styles having at least 1200 works in the dataset, namely: *"Abstract Expressionism, Art Informel, Art Nouveau (Modern), Baroque, Cubism, Early Renaissance, Expressionism, High Renaissance, Impressionism, Mannerism (Late Renaissance), Naïve Art (Primitivism), Neoclassicism, Northern Renaissance, Post-Impressionism, Realism, Rococo, Romanticism, Surrealism, Symbolism* and *Ukiyo-e"*. After examination of the confusion matrices obtained after training the CNN models, we have reduced the number of styles to 13 fusing some highly confused classes. This reduction on the number of target classes has effectively improved the classification accuracy, obtaining better that state of the art results with some models. The contents of the paper are as follows: Sect. 2 reviews some related works. Section 3 describes our methods and materials. Section 4 describes the experiments and the results achieved. Section 5 gives some conclusions and future work directions.

2   Related Work

There have been many approaches tried to predict distinctive characteristics of the artistic picture. For instance, a technique called *Patch based* is used to predict the media used to paint the work [8]. In essence, it consists of finding the area of the image that contains more information, focusing on different areas (patches or modules) of an image using a multi-column structure. The media to predict is reduced to 4 cases: *"Oil, Pastel, Pencil* and *Watercolor.* They used three datasets, achieving an accuracy of 85%, 93% and 85% respectively. It is true that a great success is achieved, but the set of classes to be predicted is quite small, and the differences between classes are clear. Although it is a method that helps a lot to extract information about the images, it may only be effective when it comes to look for textures or small shapes, which may not be the best case to recognize styles, since the same style can be created with different media; for example, works from baroque could use different media like *oil* or *fresco*.

Deep learning approaches have been proposed. Specifically, various CNN models [6] such as *ResNet-34, ResNet-50* and *AlexNet* were trained to predict 25 art styles following a transfer learning strategy. Another of the techniques used is *Bagging*, which consists of averaging the output of different predictions on various input data variations; and data augmentation, that makes changes to the images (such as rotations, zooms or translations of axes) to create new images from one. Although it is a good idea to increase the input data, *Data Augmentation* has not been performed in this work, due to the possibility of affecting the own style of a work, being able to modify it and losing accuracy.

There are other papers like [1] where several visual descriptors are used to extract information about the artworks, to know more about the art styles. Basically, they recognize art styles using features extracted from deep neural

---

[1] https://www.wikiart.org/.

networks and *PiCoDes (Picture Codes)*. Their descriptors are taken from a CNN trained on *ImageNet*.

3   Methods and Materials

3.1   Dataset

The dataset used for this work was extracted from *WikiArt* to be used for a *Kaggle* competition[2]. It has 103.253 different artworks categorized by experts into 136 art styles. The size of original dataset images is quite big. Due to storage limitations, another dataset with the same pictures, but of reduced size, was used for the experiments. As we can see in Fig. 1, the most frequent 20 styles are very unbalanced; art styles like *Impressionism* have more than 10.000 images, while others like *Art Informel* have about 1200 pictures. To work with a balanced dataset in this preliminary research, all art styles will have the same number of pictures as the style with less pictures, being this 1200. An example of every art style can be seen in Fig. 2.

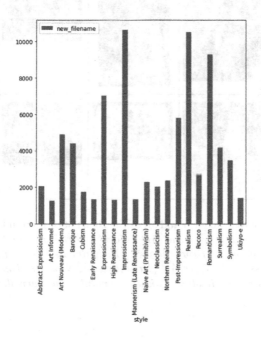

Fig. 1. Number of image samples of the art styles used for the experiments

---

2 The dataset can be download from: https://github.com/somewacko/painter-by-numbers/releases/tag/data-v1.0.

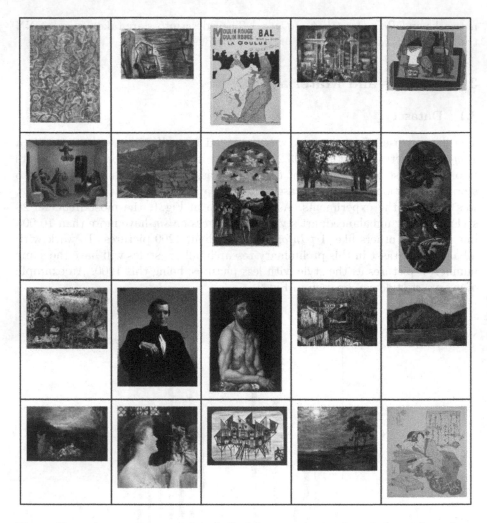

Fig. 2. Example images from each and all of the 20 art styles. From left to right and top to bottom: *"Abstract Expressionism, Art Informel, Art Nouveau (Modern), Baroque, Cubism, Early Renaissance, Expressionism, High Renaissance, Impressionism, Mannerism (Late Renaissance), Naïve Art (Primitivism), Neoclassicism, Northern Renaissance, Post-Impressionism, Realism, Rococo, Romanticism, Surrealism, Symbolism* and *Ukiyo-e"*

3.2 Models

As we mentioned, in this work there will be used 5 different models: *ResNet-34*, *ResNet-50*, *VGG-16*, *DenseNet-121* and a simple CNN model made from scratch. The performance of all of them will be compared, and we will draw some conclusions about the missed cases. All the models except the simple CNN created from scratch, use weights previously calculated for competition in the

ImageNet challenge. Therefore, we are applying a transfer learning approach where the feature extraction layers are given and we retrain the outer layers that provide the final classification.

- Firstly, we have two ResNet architectures with 34 and 50 layers, respectively. The term ResNet comes from *residual neural network*, which is based on pyramidal cell constructs in the cerebral cortex. This type of neural networks uses shortcuts to avoid the problem of *vanishing gradient*. The problem appears when we add too much layers to the network, increasing the training error (instead of decreasing it).
- Secondly, we have *VGG-16*, which is simpler than the two *ResNet* architectures we mentioned above. Its formed of 16 layers, being 13 convolutional layers and 3 dense layers.
- Thirdly, the *DenseNet* [5] layers are narrower, so the number of parameters decreases. Also the network is easier to train. The main reason of this is that *DenseNet* uses *Dense blocks*. In these blocks, each layer takes as input all the previous feature maps, helping the training process by solving the problem of *Vainishing gradient*.
- Finally, we have the simple CNN model made from scratch. The model has 11 layers, 4 of them are convolutional layers with sizes of 32, 32, 64 and 64. There are 3 *MaxPooling* layers of size 2×2. The next are a *Flatten* layer, two *Dense* layers and a *dropout* one. All the activation functions are *ReLU* unless the one for the last *Dense* layer, which is *softmax*. This last layer has a size of 20 (or 13 in the case of merging styles) due to the multi-class classification problem we are facing. Also the model was compiled with the option of *categorical-crossentropy* for the same reason, with a *batch size* of 32. The optimizer used was *RMSprop* with a learning rate of 0.001. In total, this CNN has 2.233.586 parameters.

4   Experiments

Many art styles are historically related to each other, or sometimes one derives from another, or an art style has many variants, hence the dataset has been used in two different ways. Firstly, we try to predict the previously mentioned 20 art styles. Secondly, we merge some styles preserving the overall number of pictures, so that only 13 styles will be predicted. The rationale for merging styles is as follows:

1. **Renaissance:** This is composed of the four variants of *Renaissance* that form the 20 art styles in our dataset: *Early Renaissance, High Renaissance, Mannerism (Late Renaissance)* and *Northern Renaissance.*
   The *Renaissance* was originated in the cultural movement of the fifteenth century in Italy (known as *Quattrocento*), where the *Early Renaissance* was born. Variations like *High Renaissance* were based on the beginning of the sixteenth century (*Cinquecento*). This variant achieves balance and perfection. Years later, *Mannerism (Late Renaissance)* brings the beginning of the

decline and rupture of the balanced and perfect form of classicism. Finally, we have the *Northern Renaissance* which was the variation of the *Renaissance* in the north of Europe.

2. **Abstract-Expressionism-Informel:** In this case, we merged *Abstract Expressionism*, *Art Informel* and *Expressionism*. One the one hand we have *Expressionism*, which was originated in the beginning of the twentieth century in Germany. On the other hand we have both *Abstract Expressionism* and *Art Informel*, which were created after the *WWII*, but the first one was originated in the USA while the second in France, Italy and Spain. The reason of merging *Expressionism* with the other two is that *Abstract Expressionism* is related with *Expressionism*, but the movement of *Expressionism* influenced a lot of different styles like *Cubism* of *surrealism*.

3. **Impressionism:** Here we have merged both *Impressionism* and *Post-Impressionism*. The first one was originated by a group of Parisian artists in the end of the nineteenth century. While *Impressionism* was more centered on details like light an colors, the *Post-Impressionism* tried to accurately reflect the nature with a very subjective view.

4. **Baroque-Rococo:** Finally, we have both *Baroque* and *Rococo*. The *Baroque* was developed in the seventeenth and beginning of eighteenth centuries mainly in Italy. Basically the main feature of this art style is the realism with the use of strong contrasts. The *Rococo* was made in France in the eighteenth century, and its also know as *Late Baroque*, more influenced by nature and mythology.

4.1   Style Prediction Results

In the case of training to predict 20 styles, all the models were trained with 24.000 images, having 1200 per style. Also, every model was trained for 10 epochs because most of them reach their max accuracy in less epochs. This decision was taken to train all the models equally. In Table 1 we can see the train and validation loss with the accuracy of every model. As we can see the model with worst accuracy is the simple CNN model, due to its simple composition. But the worst of the state of the art models is *VGG-16*. The main reason of this may be that *VGG-16* is the simplest network. We also have both *ResNet-34* and *ResNet-50* the first one with less accuracy. The reason could be that *ResNet-34* is composed of less layers, making the training of *ResNet-50* better, gaining more accuracy. Finally, we have the *DenseNet-121* model, with the best accuracy. We have included [2] (predicting only 10 styles) as a state of the art reference in order to give a benchmark value about the quality of the achieved results.

When we predict 13 styles instead of 20, the accuracy achieved is bigger, because the model has less options to predict. The values obtained in this case are showed in Table 2. The results show better accuracy, and the distribution of the models performance is quite similar. Again, the model with the worst accuracy is the simple CNN model. After this we have both *ResNet-34* and *VGG-16* with almost the same accuracy (63.02% and 63.04$ respectively). In the other case, the accuracy of this two was already similar. Again *DenseNet-121* is the network with the best performance, showing that is the best architecture for this work with an accuracy of 66.68% even better than *ResNet-50* with 64.91%. The contrast of [2] with our results is very positive, we have achieved almost always better validation results.

Table 1. Comparison of the performance of the different models recognizing 20 artwork styles. For comparison we include the best result on this dataset reported in [2] trying to recognize 10 styles.

Model name	train_loss	valid_loss	Accuracy
ResNet-34	1.3476	1.4867	0.5072
ResNet-50	1.0799	1.3654	0.5460
VGG-16	1.3402	1.4834	0.5012
DenseNet-121	1.3169	1.3410	0.5625
Simple CNN	2.1852	2.4376	0.3186
[2] 10 styles			0.563

Table 2. Comparison of the performance of the different models with styles merged until we keep 13 artwork styles. For comparison we include the best result on this dataset reported in [2] trying to recognize 10 styles.

Model name	train_loss	valid_loss	Accuracy
ResNet-34	1.2126	1.1422	0.6302
ResNet-50	1.0014	1.0447	0.6491
VGG-16	1.1587	1.1289	0.6304
DenseNet-121	0.9328	1.0095	0.6668
Simple CNN	1.8895	1.9007	0.3799
[2] 10 styles			0.563

4.2   Style Similarity Relations from the Confusion Matrix

Beside the positive prediction accuracy results, the study of the confusion matrix from the best performing model, *DenseNet-121*, when predicting the 20 styles gives provides another insight into the value of CNNs to predict artwork style. In Fig. 3 we plot the confusion matrix as a directed graph. We can see that some art styles are truly related. For example, in the top of the image we can see that the four variants of *Renaissance* are connected, showing the relation between them. We can also see that styles like *Abstract Expressionism* and *Art Informel* are very near, showing that there are very related. As we mentioned above, *Expressionism* influenced a lot of different art styles, that is the reason of being in the centre of the graph connected with several nodes (art styles). Overall, from top to bottom of the figure we appreciate that the styles are organized in their temporal progression, from the early ones to most recent ones. Also, the Japanese Ukiyo-e style appears as a kind of outlier which may have influenced recent styles, specifically the Art Nouveau seems to be the bridge for this influence. It seems that the confusion matrix provides some kind of similarity measure among art styles as a whole, which may be worth more detail examination. Also, this similarity induces an ordering of the art styles which is parallel to their temporal evolution.

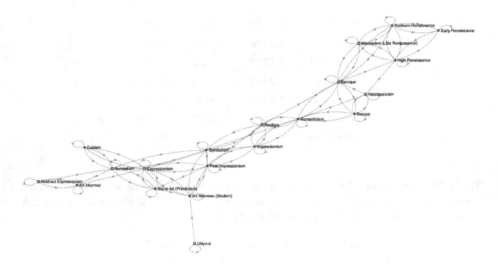

Fig. 3. Directed graph showing the relationship between the 20 art styles induced by the confusion matrix of the *DenseNet-121*.

5   Conclusions and Future Work

After all the experiments, we can conclude that *DenseNet-121* was the model achieving the best accuracy, which is comparable or superior to the state of the art results. Besides, the visual analysis of the confusion matrix, represented as a directed graph, appears to be a map of the relations between styles. Even the temporal evolution of the styles seems to be captured in this representation. We may say that the classification process induces some kind of similarity measure between the art styles, and some ordering that is quite surprising in its parallel with their temporal evolution.

Some improvements for this work could come from using the original dataset with bigger images, though some strategy to scan the images should be defined, because full resolution processing by CNNs is computationally unfeasible. We propose the use of Vision Transformers as an alternative for this task worth exploring. In addition, having more images per style would be an improvement, since the styles we used had 1200 images, which may not be enough for our purpose.

References

1. Bar, Y., Levy, N., Wolf, L.: Classification of artistic styles using binarized features derived from a deep neural network. In: Agapito, L., Bronstein, M.M., Rother, C. (eds.) ECCV 2014. LNCS, vol. 8925, pp. 71–84. Springer, Cham (2015). https://doi.org/10.1007/978-3-319-16178-5_5
2. Cetinic, E., Lipic, T., Grgic, S.: Fine-tuning convolutional neural networks for fine art classification. Expert Syst. Appl. **114**, 107–118 (2018)
3. Ciresan, D.C., Meier, U., Masci, J., Gambardella, L.M., Schmidhuber, J.: Flexible, high performance convolutional neural networks for image classification, pp. 1237–1242 (2011). https://doi.org/10.5591/978-1-57735-516-8/IJCAI11-210
4. Hershey, S., et al.: CNN architectures for large-scale audio classification, pp. 131–135 (2017). https://doi.org/10.1109/ICASSP.2017.7952132
5. Huang, G., Liu, Z., van der Maaten, L., Weinberger, K.Q.: Densely connected convolutional networks (2017)
6. Lecoutre, A., Negrevergne, B., Yger, F.: Recognizing art style automatically in painting with deep learning, vol. 77, pp. 327–342 (2017). https://proceedings.mlr.press/v77/lecoutre17a.html
7. Wang, C., Cheng, M., Sohel, F., Bennamoun, M., Li, J.: NormalNet: a voxel-based CNN for 3D object classification and retrieval. Neurocomputing **323**, 139–147 (2019)
8. Min, Y.: A multi-column deep framework for recognizing artistic media. Electronics **8**, 1277 (2019). https://doi.org/10.3390/electronics8111277

Handwritten Word Recognition
on the Fundación-Osborne Dataset

A. Barreiro-Garrido, V. Ruiz-Parrado, A. Sánchez, and J. F. Velez(✉)

Universidad Rey Juan Carlos, Madrid, Spain
jose.velez@urjc.es

Abstract. Even to this day, offline handwritten text recognition still constitutes a challenging research problem, specially when it comes to perform recognition tasks on historical databases. In this context, the main aim of the present paper is to expound the results obtained after training a deep convolutional Seq2Seq network with attention mechanism using a combination of word training images from both contemporary and historical databases. In the light of the subsequent results, we discuss the effectiveness that different proportions of modern and historical text during the training process have on the final performance of the architecture concerning historical handwritten text recognition.

Keywords: Historical documents · Offline handwriting recognition · Seq2Seq · Osborne dataset · IAM dataset

1 Introduction

Classically, handwriting has been one of the most popular methods to transmit information. At present, there are still a large number of historical documents that have not been transcribed yet. As an example of this, most of the 80 million documents in the Spanish General Archive of the Indies [1] remain without having been properly digitised. Getting a suited transcription of this vast amount of documents is crucial to improve the offline handwritten text recognition (HTR) algorithms, as these are ultimately responsible for automatising the process of converting digital images containing handwritten text, into their appropriate transcriptions [27].

Despite the development of new technologies, thousands of handwritten documents are generated on a daily basis. This constitutes by itself another reason for which the automatic reading, processing and analysing of these type of documents is an interesting branch of research [24] that could eventually reduce costs in many fields, or even be helpful for people with vision-related impairments.

In this context, text recognition and historical document analysis can be considered related but separated problems, as both have their own characteristics and complexities. For instance, historical handwritten characters used to be more uniform than those present in modern texts, as calligraphic styles were more unified among the population. Moreover, back then people also wrote in more

J. M. Ferrández Vicente et al. (Eds.): IWINAC 2022, LNCS 13259, pp. 298–307, 2022.
https://doi.org/10.1007/978-3-031-06527-9_29

than one direction, due to the fact that paper was a scarce resource at the time. As a result of this, some historical manuscripts even contain visible strokes from the other side of the paper sheet (i.e., bleed-through effect) [22].

In recent years, deep learning methodologies have obtained great success while dealing with Artificial Intelligence and Computer Vision problems [29]. For example, these methodologies achieved good results in object recognition [6] and localization [28], natural language processing [31], image generation [12], or domain adaptation [10]. Concerning handwriting recognition, great success has been achieved as well with both modern and historical documents, either with sequencing [24] or word spotting approaches [4, 23].

In particular, attention mechanisms as the one proposed by Chorowski et al. in 2015 [5], have set the state of the art in handwriting recognition when implemented jointly with Seq2Seq models [24,25]. Moreover, it has been seen that combinations of both modern and historical text during the training process of this type of architectures could help to improve the final network performance [11]. In the present work we combine the well-known IAM dataset [18] with the new historical database from The Osborne Foundation, all of it in order to train a Seq2Seq attention model for historical handwritten word recognition purposes.

The rest of this paper is organised as follows: Sect. 2 describes recent works on historical handwriting recognition. Section 3 introduces the material and methods used in our proposal, whereas Sect. 4 describes the experiments and the results achieved. Finally, Sect. 5 draws some conclusions and future works.

2   Related Works

Classical approaches to solve the handwriting recognition problem on modern texts are based on the sequencing of data. More specifically, within these frameworks characters are recognised individually and then the predictions are combined to create words. These characters are typically obtained from an image segmentation or as a result of using a sliding window over the entire original image of text as prior steps to their corresponding identification. Consequently, several works have tried to apply these methods to historical documents. Some of the first attempts to face the handwriting recognition problem in the context of historical texts were based on Hidden Markov Models (HMM). These models were then applied to accomplish automatic recognition tasks on several historical databases such as George Washington [15], Parzival [30], Saint Gall [8], RODRIGO [22], GERMANA [20] and ESPOSALLES [21], respectively, obtaining some good outcomes.

Nevertheless, and even though these algorithms achieved some good results, they were not as good as those obtained on modern texts. From that point on, other strategies based on word spotting tried to face the problem and get better results [27]. In particular, Toledo et al. [27] adapted this methodology to allow recognition of words contained in a specific dictionary. One of the most important advantages of these type of approaches is that they allow to recognise words as entire units, avoiding sequencing of the data.

More recent works on the field include the paper by Sánchez et al. [26], where several configurations of Convolutional Recurrent Neural Network (CRNN) architectures were developed and tested on a set of historical databases, namely the ICDAR-2014, 2015, 2016 and 2017 databases.

Granet et al. [11] trained a CNN-BLSTM-CTC network using different combinations of both modern and historical handwriting databases, namely RIMES, George Washington and ESPOSALLES, obtaining some good results depending on the specific training combination.

Other cutting-edge approaches is the include by Khamekhem et al. [13], which focuses on the use of *Generative Adversarial Networks* (GANs) and on-purpose image degradation of contemporary handwriting datasets such as IAM in order to outperform the current methods devoted to historical handwriting recognition.

3   Material and Methods

In this section we present the architecture employed for the word recognition task. As the conducted experiments detailed in the upcoming sections made use of both the IAM and the Osborne databases, their main features will be briefly reviewed. At the end of this section, we describe the algorithms used for processing the images previous to its input to the proposed model.

3.1   Network Architecture

The selected architecture is based on the Convolutional Seq2Seq with Attention model proposed by Sueiras et al. [24]. Seq2Seq is composed of two parts known as the Encoder and the Decoder. The inputs are the slices (i.e. patches) of an image containing handwritten text, obtained through the use of a sliding window, as we will detail further on. The outputs of the network are the predicted characters of the word image. Figure 1 displays the whole model set up. The code can be downloaded from github.com/jfvelezserrano/HistoricalDocumentRecognition.

The Convolutional Neural Network (CNN): being the first part of the present architecture, it works as a generic feature extractor for the word images. More specifically, the CNN extracts these features from the sequence of patches that constituted the original word.

Regarding the layout of the CNN itself, it has been built upon two groups of alternating convolutional and maxpooling layers followed by a final dense layer. This set up is strongly inspired in the LeNet-5 proposed by LeCun et al. [16].

The CNN is composed of two convolutional layers with 20 and 50 filters, respectively. Both have a fixed kernel size of 5 and the stride of the kernels over the image has been set to 1. We have completed these convolutions with a padding equal to 2 in order to restore the original shape of the image once these filters have been applied. Each of these convolutional layers is followed by a 2×2 maxpooling layer. Finally, the CNN ends up with a dense layer consisting of 1024 neurons with a dropout equal to 0.5.

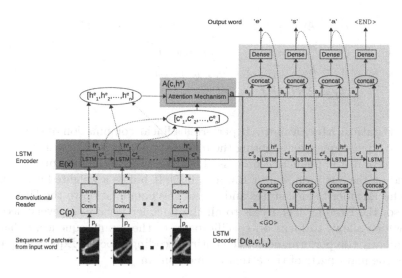

Fig. 1. Detailed set up of the entire Seq2Seq architecture with attention mechanism.

This convolutional reader is ultimately applied to each patch p_i and it outputs a vector x_i that condenses the visual features contained in the patch.

The Encoder: It is composed of two deep Recurrent Neural Networks [25]. In particular, we used two stacked bidirectional LSTM layers that take the sequence of output vectors of features provided by the CNN and try to encode and capture the horizontal relationships between them. The output of the first LSTM layer will ultimately be the input of the second one. At the same time, the bidirectional character of each of these LSTM allows to process the sequence in opposite directions to encode both forward and backward dependencies.

To summarise the encoder procedure, it receives the sequence of vectors x_t that contain the visual features of the patches p_t and then outputs a pair of cell and hidden (i.e. output) state vectors, c_t^e and h_t^e, for every encoder step t.

The Decoder: It consists on a single unidirectional LSTM layer. The goal of it is to generate the target sequence of characters present in the word image. At each time step t, the Decoder generates a pair of cell and hidden (output) state vectors c_t^d, and h_t^d. The latter h_t^d output vector will ultimately yield the predicted target character. To generate the aforementioned output vectors, the Decoder takes as input its own previous character prediction l_{t-1} concatenated with the context vector a_t provided by the attention mechanism.

The Decoder is initialised with the the sum of the backward and forward directions of the Encoder last cell and hidden states (Eq. 1). The initial token of the decoding process is $<START>$. In a similar way, when the prediction is completed, the Decoder outputs the special token $<END>$.

$$\alpha_t = A(c_t^e, h_t^e) < c_t^d, h_t^d >= LSTM(x_t^e, c_{t-1}^e, h_{t-1}^e)$$
$$c_0^d = c_{last,forward}^e + c_{last,backward}^e$$
$$h_0^d = h_{last,forward}^e + h_{last,backward}^e$$
$$l_0 = <START> \tag{1}$$

The Attention Mechanism: It performs a linear combination of the elements from the input sequence, weighting the relative importance that each of them has on the steps of the predictive process. The attention mechanism presented here is based on the one proposed by Bahdanau [5]. It builds a weighted combination of all the Encoder hidden states and passes this combination to the Decoder. In doing so, the Decoder has access to all the Encoder features at every decoding step, which allows to focus on specific parts of the input sequence, enhancing consequently the performance of the entire decoding process. Equation 2 encapsulates the main parts of the attention mechanism.

$$e_{t,l} = w^T \cdot tanh(W_d c_{t-1}^d + W_e h_t^e) \qquad a_{t,l} = \frac{exp(e_{t,l})}{\sum_{k=1}^{l} exp(e_{t,l})} \tag{2}$$

where w, W_d, W_e are trainable parameters, $e_{t,l}$ are the attention scores and $a_{t,l}$ represents a softmax normalisation. These scores will ultimately weight their corresponding encoder outputs to get the context vector of the Decoder.

3.2 Datasets

Granet et al. [11] concluded that historical text recognition usually improves when the historical handwriting text images are trained jointly with larger contemporary handwriting databases. In this subsection we describe the databases used to train and test the model.

IAM. [18] is an English database which first version was published at the ICDAR in 1999 [17]. This dataset is based on the Lancaster-Oslo/Bergen corpus [3]. As of 2022, the last version of the IAM database is made up of 115.320 isolated and labeled words spread over 13.353 text lines from 657 different writers. This was achieved through the scanning of 1.539 pages of text at a 300 DPI resolution. The scanned images were saved in PNG format with 256 gray levels. The IAM partitions used throughout this work consist of 47.926 words for the training set, 7.558 for validation and a total amount of 20.292 words for the test set.

The Osborne Dataset is built upon the Osborne Archive [2], which contains a set of handwritten letters exchanged between distinguished characters of several epochs covering a range that spans from 1830 to 1883 as a byproduct of the importance that the Osborne family held especially during the 19th century in

Puerto de Santa María (Cádiz, Spain) [7]. The corpus of this dataset is made of 200 scanned, RGB-digitised and transcribed documents from the original archive at 400 DPI resolution, and it constitutes an interesting example of a multi-language historical handwritten text database (mostly Spanish, but also English and Italian). The Osborne word image dataset is respectively split into 7,149, 288 and 194 images for training, validation and test.

3.3 Data Preprocessing

The data preprocessing performed is an adaptation of the one developed by Sueiras et al. [24] to the handwriting historical database of Fundación Osborne.

Baseline Detection: This step aims detect and correct the skew of the text lines. The baseline detection of each text line was carried out applying a Random Sample Consensus (RANSAC) regression [9] over the lowest points of each column of pixels (with values above a threshold equal to 20). Similarly, to obtain the corpus line, the procedure was repeated over the highest points of the line image that fulfilled the same condition. Finally, we apply an affine transformation to correct the skew. This preprocessing only was applied to the IAM dataset, because the line information is not present in the Osborne dataset, and because the Osborne dataset does not seem to be affected by this skew.

Slant Correction: In order to account for the slant of the characters, the slant angle α is first identified through the algorithm provided by [14]. Once the slant angle has been obtained, a new affine transformation is applied over the image. Equation 3 displays the adjustment made on the image coordinates whereas equation 4 shows the final affine transformation matrix that has to be applied.

$$x_n = x - y \cdot tan(\alpha)$$
$$y_n = y \qquad (3)$$

$$\begin{pmatrix} 1 & -\alpha & 0.5 \cdot \alpha \cdot w \\ 0 & 1 & 0 \end{pmatrix} \qquad (4)$$

Sliding Window and Patching of the Images: Finally, we perform the splitting of the image into a set of overlapping patches. Each word image is divided in a set of overlapping patches simulating a sliding window that covers it. Two main parameters describe the sliding window configuration: the width of each patch (w); the step size (s), which measures the degree of overlapping. These patches will ultimately be the inputs of the model.

As stated in Sueiras et al. [24], we used $w = 10$ and $s = 2$. Also the word images were resized to 192×48 pixels, yielding a total number of 92 patches per word image.

4 Experiments and Results

The following experiments have been performed over a combination of word images from both IAM and Osborne for train, and only the Osborne images for test. The next subsections are devoted to describe the experiments and their results.

4.1 Implementation Details

The implementation of our handwriting recogniser was coded using the PyTorch library [19] and a GeForce Titan X Pascal GPU. We also set the batch size to 256. A number of 256 units was chosen for both Encoder and Decoder, with a dropout of 0.5 in the cells of the encoder layers. As trainer, we opted for an Adam stochastic optimization algorithm, while the learning rate was initialised to 0.001 but decreased by 2% in every epoch. We also applied an early-stopping criterion of 150 epochs without any improvement in the validation loss.

4.2 Training Process

Even considering the relatively wide sample of 55,075 words that we obtain while combining the training images of IAM and Osborne, we opted to apply a data augmentation algorithm during the training process. This data augmentation performs some minor changes to the images in a random way, all of it in order to obtain a pseudo-infinite sample to train with. This process adds variability to the whole training sample, which is expected to increase the network performance. Firstly, we randomised the order of the training data for each epoch.

As second step, we implemented the data augmentation process proposed in [24] combined with a final salt and pepper background noise, which was applied to half of the training images.

Regarding the character sample, we also decided to keep the IAM characters and discard those in Osborne that were not present in IAM, namely [ñ, ¿, ¡, á, é, í, ó, ú], which were replaced by [n, "", "", a, e, i, o, u], respectively.

Our first experiment consisted in training only with the IAM database (47.926 words in each epoch), whereas our second experiment involved all the available train data (IAM+Osborne datasets = 47.926 + 7,149 words). During the third experiment, we increased the weight of the Osborne dataset during training, duplicating the weight of this database by repeating the Osborne training words (IAM + 2 × Osborne datasets = 47.926 + 14,298 words). Finally, we made a fourth experiment in which we trained only with the Osborne dataset (7,149 words).

4.3 Analysis of Results

This section summarises the results obtained for the four experiments described above for the different proportions between IAM and Osborne data that the network learns during training.

As our main goal is to estimate the effectiveness of the model on historical documents, all the tests have been performed exclusively on the Osborne dataset. We have chosen Word Error Rate (WER) and Character Error Rate (CER) as metrics to estimate the quality of the recognition performance. WER is defined as $1 - accuracy$ at word level, and an analogous definition exists for CER. Table 1 contains both metrics associated to each experiment. Figure 2 shows a graphically the accuracy obtained for experiment 1, where the combination of IAM and Osborne provided our best accuracy results. The left panel describes the accuracy at word level depending on the length of the predicted word, where the right (green) and wrong (red) predictions sum up the total amount. Similarly, the right panel histogram measures the accuracy at character level, displaying the right (green) and wrong (red) predictions for each character in the test sample.

Table 1. Results for the four recognition experiments with different proportions of IAM and Osborne in the batch along the training.

Experiment	Osborne weight during training	WER	CER
1	0%	98.21%	65.69%
2	**13%**	**39.23%**	**16.05%**
3	23%	39.34%	16.87%
4	100%	61.44%	34.87%

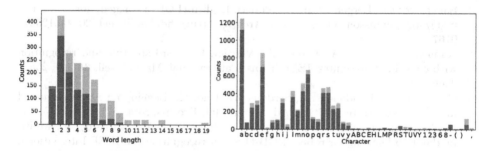

Fig. 2. Detailed results obtained at word (left) and character level (right) for experiment 1. In green/red the number of right/wrong predictions respectively. (Color figure online)

As it can be observed, the recognition results on the Osborne database were significantly improved when the training sample included a major contribution from a contemporary handwritten data set. The Osborne-only experiment exhibited poorer results, but that might well be because of the limited sample variety associated to its training set (only 7149 words). With limited sample sizes, extending and spreading the training results to unseen validation or test data may be a challenging task for any kind of architecture or algorithm.

5   Conclusions

Even though some of the outcomes of the experiments were far from the best results obtained to date for modern handwritten text, we confirm that combinations between modern and historical databases for training have demonstrated to be useful for historical handwriting recognition purposes. Moreover, the best results on tests came with the largest amount of modern text images within the training sample. To improve our results, in future works we plan to incorporate new types of data augmentation techniques. Also, we consider to include special Spanish characters labels into the training set.

Acknowledgements. This work was funded by the Spanish MICINN RTI Project with reference: RTI2018-098019-B-I00. Also, the authors gratefully acknowledge the support of the CYTED Network "Ibero-American Thematic Network on ICT Applications for Smart Cities" (Ref: 518RT0559) and to Fundación SEPI from the Ministerio de Hacienda y Administraciones Publicas. Also we want to give thanks to Fundación-Osborne and to Telefónica Company.

References

1. Archivo General de Indias. https://www.culturaydeporte.gob.es/cultura/areas/archivos/mc/archivos/agi/portada.html. Accessed 09 Feb 2022
2. Fundación   Osborne.   https://www.fundacionosborne.org/es/simple-search. Accessed 08 Feb 2022
3. Lancaster-Oslo-Bergen Corpus of modern English (LOB) : (tagged, horizontal format)/stig johansson. Oxford Text Archive. http://hdl.handle.net/20.500.12024/0167
4. Almazán, J., Gordo, A., Fornés, A., Valveny, E.: Word spotting and recognition with embedded attributes. IEEE Trans. Pattern Anal. Mach. Intell. **36**(12), 2552–2566 (2014)
5. Chorowski, J., Bahdanau, D., Serdyuk, D., Cho, K., Bengio, Y.: Attention-based models for speech recognition. Adv. Neural Inf. Process. Syst. 577–585 (2015)
6. Eitel, A., Springenberg, J.T., Spinello, L., Riedmiller, M., Burgard, W.: Multi-modal deep learning for robust RGB-D object recognition. In: IEEE International Conference on Intelligent Robots and Systems, pp. 681–687 (2015)
7. Terry-Osborne, C., et al.: The Osborne historical archive digitization (in Preparation)
8. Fischer, A., Frinken, V., Fornés, A., Bunke, H.: Transcription alignment of Latin manuscripts using hidden Markov models, pp. 29–36 (2011)
9. Fischler, M.A., Bolles, R.C.: Random sample consensus: a paradigm for model fitting with applications to image analysis and automated cartography. Commun. ACM **24**(6), 381–395 (1981)
10. Glorot, X., Bordes, A., Bengio, Y.: Domain adaptation for large-scale sentiment classification: a deep learning approach. In: Proceedings of the 28th International Conference on Machine Learning, ICML 2011, pp. 513–520 (2011)
11. Granet, A., Morin, E., Mouchère, H., Quiniou, S., Viard-Gaudin, C.: ICPRAM 2018 - Proceedings of the 7th International Conference on Pattern Recognition Applications and Methods, pp. 432–439 (2018)

12. Gregor, K., Danihelka, I., Graves, A., Rezende, D.J., Wierstra, D.: Draw: a recurrent neural network for image generation. In: 32nd International Conference on Machine Learning, ICML 2015, vol. 2, pp. 1462–1471 (2015)
13. Khamekhem Jemni, S., Souibgui, M.A., Kessentini, Y., Fornés, A.: Enhance to read better: a multi-task adversarial network for handwritten document image enhancement. Pattern Recogn. **123** (2022)
14. Kim, G., Govindaraju, V.: Handwritten phrase recognition as applied to street name images. Pat. Recogn. **31**(1), 41–51 (1998)
15. Lavrenko, V., Rath, T.M., Manmatha, R.: Holistic word recognition for handwritten historical documents, pp. 278–287 (2004)
16. Lecun, Y., Bottou, L., Bengio, Y., Haffner, P.: Gradient-based learning applied to document recognition. Proc. IEEE **86**(11), 2278–2324 (1998)
17. Marti, U.-V., Bunke, H.: A full English sentence database for off-line handwriting recognition, pp. 705–708 (1999)
18. Marti, U.-V., Bunke, H.: The IAM-database: an English sentence database for offline handwriting recognition. Int. J. Doc. Anal. Recogn. **5**(1), 39–46 (2003)
19. Paszke, A., et al.: Pytorch: an imperative style, high-performance deep learning library. In: Wallach, H., Larochelle, H., Beygelzimer, A., d' Alché-Buc, F., Fox, E., Garnett, R. (eds.) Advances in Neural Information Processing Systems, vol. 32, pp. 8024–8035. Curran Associates Inc. (2019)
20. Pérez, D., Tarazón, L., Serrano, N., Castro, F., Ramos Terrades, O., Juan, A.: The Germana database, pp. 301–305 (2009)
21. Romero, V., et al.: The Esposalles database: an ancient marriage license corpus for off-line handwriting recognition. Pattern Recogn. **46**(6), 1658–1669 (2013)
22. Serrano, N., Castro, F., Juan, A.: The Rodrigo database, pp. 2709–2712 (2010)
23. Sudholt, S., Fink, G.A.: PhocNet: a deep convolutional neural network for word spotting in handwritten documents, pp. 277–282 (2016)
24. Sueiras, J., Ruiz, V., Sanchez, A., Velez, J.F.: Offline continuous handwriting recognition using seq2seq neural networks. Neurocomputing **289**, 119–128 (2018)
25. Sutskever, I., Vinyals, O., Le, Q.V.: Sequence to sequence learning with NN. Adv. Neural. Inf. Process. Syst. **4**(January), 3104–3112 (2014)
26. Sánchez, J.A., Romero, V., Toselli, A.H., Villegas, M., Vidal, E.: A set of benchmarks for handwritten text recognition on historical documents. Pattern Recogn. **94**, 122–134 (2019)
27. Ignacio Toledo, J., Dey, S., Fornés, A., Lladós, J.: Handwriting recognition by attribute embedding and recurrent NN, vol. 01, pp. 1038–1043 (2017)
28. Tompson, J., Goroshin, R., Jain, A., LeCun, Y., Bregler, C.: Efficient object localization using convolutional networks. In: Proceedings of the IEEE Computer Society Conference on Computer Vision and Pattern Recognition, 07–12-June-2015, pp. 648–656 (2015)
29. Voulodimos, A., Doulamis, N., Doulamis, A., Protopapadakis, E.: Deep learning for computer vision: a brief review. Comput. Intell. Neurosci. (2018)
30. Wüthrich, M., et al.: Language model integration for the recognition of handwritten medieval documents, pp. 211–215 (2009)
31. Young, T., Hazarika, D., Poria, S., Cambria, E.: Recent trends in deep learning based natural language processing. IEEE Comput. Intell. Mag. **13**(3), 55–75 (2018)

Automatic Annotation for Weakly Supervised Pedestrian Detection

Francisco J. Garcia-Espinosa[✉][iD], Antonio S. Montemayor[iD],
and Alfredo Cuesta-Infante[iD]

Escuela Técnica Superior de Ingeniería Informática, Universidad Rey Juan Carlos,
Móstoles, Spain
{franciscojose.garcia,antonio.sanz,alfredo.cuesta}@urjc.es

Abstract. Pedestrian detection is an important task addressed in computer vision given its direct application in video surveillance, autonomous driving and biomechanics among many others. The advent of deep neural networks has meant a breakthrough in its resolution. The major problem is the need for very large labeled datasets, which is usually difficult to obtain, either because it is not publicly available or it is not suitable for the particular problem. To solve it, we design a method capable of self-labeling a detection dataset using only small manually labeled portion of it. Results show an autolabeled dataset of 10342 images from a preliminary set of 1312 manually labeled images.

Keywords: Automatic Labeling · Pedestrian Detection · Weak Labeling

1 Introduction

Convolutional Neural Networks are the bread-and-butter techniques for detection and classification tasks in computer vision due to their inductive bias towards images. However, these good results come at a cost, the need for high computational power and a huge amount of labeled training data. The former can be solved using more efficient network architectures, as MobileNet [4], ShufleNet [5] or EfficientNet [6] to name a few, but the latter is more difficult to deal with.

The cost to get a labeled dataset can not be easily avoided, either using a public released dataset (but maybe it does not fit with the actual problem to be solved) or labeling it manually. With the increasingly size of current used datasets (e.g. ImageNet [3] contains more than 14 million images) manual labeling costs may be unaffordable in terms of time or money.

In this work, we deal with this issue proposing a simple but effective method to automatically label a dataset for pedestrian detection problems. Our method consists of the following iterative process: a detection network is first used to get preliminary pedestrian bounding boxes that are later refined using an iterative algorithm to obtain the final detections. This detection and label refining

© Springer Nature Switzerland AG 2022
J. M. Ferrández Vicente et al. (Eds.): IWINAC 2022, LNCS 13259, pp. 308–317, 2022.
https://doi.org/10.1007/978-3-031-06527-9_30

algorithm improves the overall labeled dataset with a basic and fast manual preliminary supervision.

2 Related Work

In semi-supervised learning, [7–9] used gaussian mixture models to select unlabeled samples of a dataset to be included in the training set. Discriminative models such as SVM had also been used in semi-supervised learning [10]. Other authors propose to add only the examples that contribute to improve the accuracy of the system using a performance-driven approach [11].

In the field of pedestrian detection, research has been done mainly on data augmentation methods. In [12] GANs are used to generate synthetic images of partially occluded pedestrians at different scales. Also, 3D video game engines have been used to generate examples of pedestrian images [13], among others. Since none of them is specifically aimed at dataset autolabeling, we propose a method to deal with it that generates a labeled dataset with a minor manual effort.

3 Experimental Setup

In this section we introduce the dataset, the neural networks architectures used to carry out the experiments and the designed procedure to iteratively label the dataset.

3.1 Dataset

The dataset used in this proposal is the Caltech Pedestrian Detection Benchmark [1]. This dataset provides about 10 h of video sequences taken in urban environments with a camera mounted on a moving vehicle at a resolution of 640 × 480 pixels. Those video sequences provide 250,000 frames containing 350,000 bounding boxes of 2,300 unique annotated pedestrians. Some sample images of the dataset are shown in Fig. 1.

To carry out the experiments, we use the annotated dataset as is (called "d0"), along with two modified versions. In the first one, called "d1", only one annotated pedestrian of each frame is preserved at random. The second version, called "d2", fits with the characteristics of the same named experiment proposed by the original work [1]. That is, only pedestrian labels with bounding boxes taller than 50 pixels are preserved and hardly visible ones are removed from the dataset.

To summarize, the different versions of the dataset are:

- d0: Provided dataset with labeled pedestrians as is.
- d1: Only one pedestrian selected at random is preserved in each frame.
- d2: Only pedestrians with height higher than 50 pixels are preserved.

Fig. 1. Some sample frames from Caltech Pedestrian Detection Benchmark.

3.2   Neural Network Architecture

The proposed method for autolabeling a dataset uses a neural network to detect pedestrians in each frame. Among all the available detection network architectures, we consider some of the best performing ones according to the information provided by MMDetection [2]. MMDetection is one of the main frameworks for PyTorch to use detection networks, pretrained on the ImageNet classification task. The most important detection networks in the MMDetection are Faster RCNN and Cascade RCNN. Moreover, we also consider EfficientDet [6] network (not present in MMDetection) as one of the best performing and lightweight architecture of the state-of-the-art, pretrained in MS COCO. The reported mAP of all networks are shown in Table 1.

Table 1. Reported mAP values of the detection neural networks used.

Network	mAP
Faster RCNN (R-50-FPN 1x)	37.4
Cascade RCNN (R-50-FPN 1x)	40.3
EfficientDet-D0	33.1

3.3   Proposed Method

To bootstrap the automatic labeling process, we need to have a tiny part of the whole dataset labeled. This task must necessarily be performed manually, but it should not be very time consuming. Once this is done, the selected detection

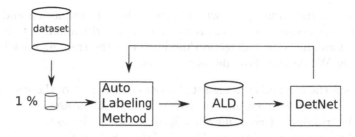

Fig. 2. Workflow of the proposed autolabeling algorithm. ALD stands for Auto Labeled Dataset.

model must be trained using that small fraction of labeled data until the loss value stalls. Next, the whole unlabeled dataset must be evaluated by the trained network. This step will propose multiple bounding boxes containing possible detected pedestrians. Those bounding boxes have an associated value of confidence that can be used to filter false positive detections. Then the remaining bounding boxes are added as annotations in the training set, and the process starts over again. The pseudocode of the process is shown in Algorithm 1 and in Fig. 2.

Algorithm 1. Proposed autolabeling pseudocode

1: **procedure** AUTOLABELING(*labeled, dataset*)
2:     size(labeled) > 0
3:     size(new) $= 0$
4:     **repeat**
5:         labeled = labeled + new
6:         train_detection(labeled)
7:         new = infer_detection(dataset)
8:     **until** $size(new) = 0$

---

4 Experimental Analysis

All the experiments were run using a NVIDIA DGX Station V100 that hosts an Intel Xeon E5-2698 v4 (2.2 GHz) CPU, 256 GB RAM DDR4 and a NVIDIA Tesla V100 GPU. We have carried out 2 analysis; the first one to choose the appropriate detection architecture and the second to test the performance of the proposed method. Before running the experiments, we introduce different versions of the datasets with variations in the amount of data in the training set.

4.1 Dataset Variations

The original dataset is split in three ways: 80% of the data for training, 10% for validation and 10% for test. To simulate an unlabeled dataset, we remove all the labels in the training set while keeping them in validation and test sets for evaluation purposes. Then, we create some reduced training sets in order to test the performance of the detection models when the training data is reduced progressively. We denote those datasets as follows:

- 0.8: This is the original training set. It contains the 80% of the whole dataset.
- 0.1: The training set contains the 10% of the whole dataset.
- 0.05: The training set contains the 5% of the whole dataset.
- 0.01: The training set contains the 1% of the whole dataset.

As previously stated, we also have "$d0$", "$d1$" and "$d2$" versions of the dataset, so in total we have 12 possible combinations.

We test the performance of the detection network when trained using all the versions of the dataset and evaluated on the "$d0$" version of it. The obtained metrics using 1% of the data are shown in Table 2. The results show that the best dataset variation to achieve our objective is "$d0$". We also show the result obtained using 10% of the "$d0$" training data set for completeness.

In view of the results it is interesting to note that the dataset containing only pedestrians of reasonable size performs worse than only using one pedestrian per image, leaving the rest unlabeled. This means that it is more important to label pedestrians of all possible sizes, even if they are not all labeled, than just labeling large pedestrians.

Table 2. mAP, TP, FP and FN scores of the detection network when trained with all the data of "$d0$" and 1% of the images in the train set of each variation of the original dataset. All the tests are performed on the test set of "$d0$".

	mAP	TP	FP	FN
d0	0.445	12716	1992	19694
d0 - 0.01	0.207	10253	6303	22157
d1 - 0.01	0.138	8238	5294	24174
d2 - 0.01	0.112	8492	7445	23918
d0 - 0.10	0.286	4972	9928	25646

4.2   Detection Network Comparison

To determine the best suited architecture for this task, we test the training of all the considered models during 12 epochs, with the "$d0$" versions of the dataset. The results of this experiment are shown in Table 3.

When the training set contains all the data, Cascade RCNN outperforms the rest of the models due to its larger size. This allows to store more information and better generalization in the test set. As the size of the training set diminishes, the performance of all models get worse up to 5%, where EfficientDet takes the lead. This happens because the size of the model is counterproductive when the

Table 3. mAP scores of the different models with "*d0*" datasets. Best values are indicated with green background.

Dataset	EfficientDet	Faster RCNN	Cascade RCNN
d0 - 0.8	0.428	0.546	0.548
d0 - 0.1	0.349	0.373	0.382
d0 - 0.05	0.304	0.286	0.291
d0 - 0.01	0.199	0.138	0.143

training data is scarce due to the large amount of parameters to optimize. As the objective of this work is to use the least possible amount of labeled data, we select the EfficientDet network as the detection architecture.

4.3 Detection Filtering Comparison

In order to add new bounding boxes to the training set, we have to be sure that no false positive samples were added, or at least, minimize them as much as we can. To filter as much false positive detections as we can, we must rely only in the output provided by the detection network taking advantage of the confidence value to be more or less restrictive with the resulting bounding boxes.

Table 4 shows true positive, false positive and false negative samples obtained while varying the confidence threshold of the detection network. In this experiment, we provide the results of training the detection network with only 1% of the dataset, denoted by "*d0 - 0.01*", and with the whole dataset "*d0*", that is the best possible performance that can be achieved with a perfect system output.

Table 4. FP, TP and FN metrics obtained while varying the confidence value threshold from 0.5 to 0.9999.

	Threshold	FP	TP	FN
d0	0.5	3225	96577	177138
d0 - 0.01	0.5	12416	60733	207404
d0	0.9	89	71550	201769
d0 - 0.01	0.9	2729	45006	226919
d0	0.99	1	24690	250444
d0 - 0.01	0.99	393	23957	250357
d0	0.999	0	4912	271328
d0 - 0.01	0.999	17	5245	271404
d0	0.9999	0	403	276155
d0 - 0.01	0.9999	0	95	276465

As expected, the number of false positives decreases as the threshold gets more restrictive, which is our main goal. However, the number of true positives is

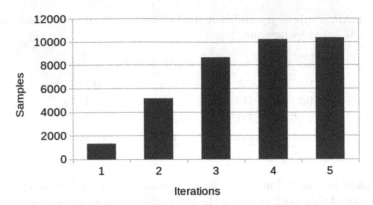

Fig. 3. Training data augmentation in each iteration of the autolabeling algorithm by setting the threshold at 0.999.

also reduced. As the number of true positives (actual pedestrians) is higher than the number of false positives (background bounding boxes), we can assume that the greater amount of correct data dominates the incorrect data, and therefore, the system does not degrade noticeably. We set our threshold to 0.999 and thus, all detections can be added to the training set, progressively improving the size of the training data, as shown in Fig. 3, and system accuracy. Even so, it would be advisable to incorporate auxiliary systems to reduce as much as possible these false positives to further improve the accuracy.

Another problem encountered when evaluating the system is the high number of labeling errors in the dataset. This is a frequent situation in most datasets [17], both public and private. It can be though that errors are only found in specialized datasets, but even in widely used ones, such as ImageNet, errors in labeling have been detected [14–16]. For this reason, the system might behave better than the present work shows, because erroneous and missing labels in the ground truth almost certainly worsen the performance of the network. To illustrate this issue, Fig. 4 shows erroneous false positives reported by the dataset after an iteration of the proposed algorithm. This has two effects on the evaluation. The first one is that the mAP metric worsens noticeably, since a real pedestrian is no longer detected and is also reported as a false positive. The second consequence is that these detections cannot be added to the training set and reduce the performance of the proposed method.

When the process is finished, the system is able to correctly label pedestrians found in the images, as shown in Fig. 5. On the left side of the figure we show the ground truth pedestrian labels in three selected frames, and on the right side we present the same frames with the autogenerated pedestrian labels in red. We can see the autolabel of a second pedestrian in the middle-right image that is not selected even in the provided ground truth of the dataset (and thus implying an incorrect FP). There are also clearly visible pedestrians that are not labeled by the system (FN), as shown in the bottom row.

Fig. 4. Reported erroneous false positives after an iteration of the algorithm. Ground truth labels are shown in green and detections are shown in red. (Color figure online)

5   Conclusions and Future Work

In this work we present a simple and effective method to automatically label a pedestrian dataset for detection tasks. We perform extensive comparison among some state-of-the-art detection architectures to select the most suited one to our objective. We also test the proposed autolabeling algorithm in three different versions of the original dataset to show that it can be used with different types of partial labelings, obtaining reasonable results. However, it is preferable to use data with as much variability in size as possible to obtain better labeling accuracy. As a result, a ×10 increase in the size of the data set has been achieved using a small, manually labeled set.

In future works we will add some auxiliary systems to filter the bounding boxes proposed by the detection network, such as Siamese networks or classical computer vision techniques, to eliminate false positives. We will also explore the effects of Focal Loss in the detection network, because it was designed to be used in datasets with high amount of data. Another possible line of research is to design a custom loss function specially designed to deal with small datasets.

Fig. 5. Labeled pedestrians when the process ends. Ground truth labels are represented in green and generated labels in red. (Color figure online)

Acknowledgements. This research has been supported by the Spanish Government research funding RTI2018-098743-B-I00 (MICINN/FEDER) and the Comunidad de Madrid research funding grant Y2018/EMT-5062.

References

1. Dollár, P.,Wojek, C., Schiele, B., Perona, P.: Pedestrian detection: an evaluation of the state of the Art. PAMI **34** (2012)
2. Chen, K., et al.: MMDetection: Open MMLab Detection Toolbox and Benchmark, arXiv preprint arXiv:1906.07155 (2019)
3. Deng, J., Dong, W., Socher, R., Li, L. J., Li, K., Fei-Fei, L.: ImageNet: a large-scale hierarchical image database. In: CVPR (2009)
4. Howard, A.G., et al.: Mobilenets: efficient convolutional neural networks for mobile vision applications. arXiv preprint arXiv:1704.04861 (2017)
5. Zhang, X., et al.: ShuffleNet: an extremely efficient convolutional neural network for mobile devices. In: CVPR (2018)

6. Tan, M., Le, Q.: EfficientNet: rethinking model scaling for convolutional neural networks. In: ICML (2019)
7. Ramirez, I., et al.: Convolutional neural networks for computer vision-based detection and recognition of dumpsters. Neural Comput. Appl. **32** (2020)
8. Gao, Y., Ma, J., Yuille, A.L.: Semi-supervised sparse representation based classification for face recognition with insufficient labeled samples. IEEE Trans. Image Process. (2017)
9. Paul, M.K., Pal, B.: Gaussian mixture based semi supervised boosting for imbalanced data classification. In: Proceedings of the 2nd International Conference on Electrical, Computer Telecommunication Engineering (ICECTE) (2016)
10. Li, Y.F., Zhou, Z.H.: Towards making unlabeled data never hurt. PAMI (2015)
11. Zhang, R., Rudnicky, A.I.: A new data selection principle for semi-supervised incremental learning. In: ICPR (2006)
12. Liu, S., et al.: A novel data augmentation scheme for pedestrian detection with attribute preserving GAN. Neurocomputing (2020)
13. Huang, S., Ramanan, D.: Expecting the unexpected: training detectors for unusual pedestrians with adversarial imposters. In: CVPR (2017)
14. Hooker, S., Dauphin, Y., Courville, A., Frome, A.: Selective Brain Damage: Measuring the Disparate Impact of Model Pruning. arXiv preprint arXiv:1911.05248 (2019)
15. Northcutt, C.G., Jiang, L., Chuang, I.: Confident learning: estimating uncertainty in dataset labels. J. Artif. Intell. Res. **70**, 1373–1411 (2021)
16. Shankar, V., Roelofs, R., Mania, H., Fang, A., Recht, B., Schmidt, L.: Evaluating machine accuracy on ImageNet. In: International Conference on Machine Learning (ICML) (2020)
17. Northcutt, C.G., Athalye, A., Mueller, J.: Pervasive label errors in test sets destabilize machine learning benchmarks. In: Proceedings of the 35th Conference on Neural Information Processing Systems (NeurIPS 2021) Track on Datasets and Benchmarks (2021)

Explaining CNN Classifications by Propositional Rules Generated from DCT Feature Maps

Guido Bologna$^{(\boxtimes)}$ ⓘ

University of Applied Sciences and Arts of Western Switzerland,
Rue de la Prairie 4, 1202 Geneva, Switzerland
Guido.Bologna@hesge.ch, Guido.Bologna@unige.ch

Abstract. So far, propositional rules have been extracted from Multi Layer Perceptrons to explain how they achieve to classify data. This type of explanation technique is much less prevalent with deep models, such as convolutional neural networks (CNNs). In this work, we propose to transfer the feature maps generated by a CNN to a simpler neural network model from which propositional rules have been generated. To enable the execution of our rule extraction algorithm in a reasonable time, the Discrete Cosine Transform (DCT) was applied to the feature maps retaining a small number of low spatial frequencies. As a proof of concept, this technique was applied to the MNIST benchmark problem. In the frequency domain, for the 60000 training samples, about 1860 unordered rules were generated. The predictive accuracy of the rules was very close to that of a trained CNN, but with about 3% of the testing samples without explanation. In another series of experiments, a slightly lower predictive accuracy was obtained, but with explanations in the form of propositional rules for 99.99% of the testing samples. Finally, we illustrated an example of a propositional rule, for which each antecedent in the frequency domain implies in its variation an incidence on several pixels in the luminosity domain.

Keywords: Model explanation · Rule extraction · CNN

1 Introduction

One of the open research problems with deep models, such as Convolutional Neural Networks (CNNs) is explaining their responses. Specifically, their acquired knowledge is incorporated into the values of the parameters and activations of the neurons, which are at first sight incomprehensible. Before the advent of CNN, a natural way to explain Multi Layer Perceptrons (MLPs) classifications was to use propositional rules [8]. Andrews et al. introduced a taxonomy describing the general characteristics of all rule extraction methods [2]. For Support Vector Machines (SVMs) that are functionally equivalent to MLPs, rule extraction methods were also proposed [6]. More recently, Guidotti et al. presented a survey

© Springer Nature Switzerland AG 2022
J. M. Ferrández Vicente et al. (Eds.): IWINAC 2022, LNCS 13259, pp. 318–327, 2022.
https://doi.org/10.1007/978-3-031-06527-9_31

on black-box models with its "explanators" [7]. In addition, Adadi and Berrada proposed an overview of *Explainable Artificial Intelligence* (XAI), including neural networks [1]. Finally, Vilone et al. review the XAI domain by clustering the various methods using a hierarchical classification with four main clusters [12].

Due to the greater complexity of CNNs compared to MLPs, many recent techniques involve learning interpretable patterns in the local region near a sample [7,10]. However, the main drawback of local algorithms is their difficulty to apprehend a phenomenon in its entirety. Moreover, many other techniques used in image classification visualize areas that are mainly relevant for the outcome [14]. Nevertheless, as stated by Rudin [11]: "it does not explain anything except where the network is looking". Finally, saliency maps could be very similar for several different classes. As with MLPs for which many rule extraction techniques have been defined, it is worth defining new rule extraction algorithms for CNNs.

In this work, the basic strategy is to transfer the feature maps learned by a CNN to the Discretized Interpretable Multi Layer Perceptron (DIMLP) [3]. Unlike MLPs, in DIMLPs the discriminative hyperplanes are precisely localized, which makes it possible to define the antecedents of propositional rules. The neural network models are trained with the MNIST benchmark dataset of digits. After the training of the CNN, the Discrete Cosine Transform (DCT) is applied to CNN feature maps to reduce their size. This approach is general and it can be applied to other classification problems. The simplified feature maps are learned by a DIMLP and finally propositional rules are generated. These rules exhibit in the antecedents the amplitudes of spatial frequencies in the images represented by the feature maps, providing insight in the classification decisions. The obtained predictive accuracy of the extracted rules is similar to that of the original CNN, when the MLP classifications agree with the rule classifications (in about 97% of the testing samples). In the following paragraphs, section two describes the models, in section three we present the experiments with the MNIST dataset, followed by the conclusion.

2 Models

In this on-going project we trained a CNN with two convolutional layers. After training, the feature maps obtained after the two convolutional layers were transferred to an interpretable MLP, which was trained with these maps after compression by DCT. Finally, propositional rules were generated from the MLP.

2.1 CNN Architecture

We describe here a CNN architecture that was trained with the MNIST dataset. We defined:

- a two-dimensional input layer of size 28×28;
- a convolutional layer with 32 kernels of size 5×5;

- a max-pooling layer;
- a convolutional layer with 32 kernels of size 5 × 5;
- a max-pooling layer;
- two fully connected layers; the first with 256 neurons and the second with 10 neurons.

Given a two-dimensional kernel $w_{p,q}$ of size PxQ and a data matrix of elements $x_{a,b}$, the calculation of an element c_{ij} of the convolutional layer is

$$c_{ij} = f(\sum_{p}^{P} \sum_{q}^{Q} w_{p,q} \cdot x_{i+p,j+q} + b_{p,q}); \tag{1}$$

with f a transfer function and $b_{p,q}$ the bias. As a transfer function we use *ReLU* (Rectifier Linear Unit):

$$f(x) = \max(0, x). \tag{2}$$

The max-pooling layer reduces the size of a vector or a matrix by applying a "Max" operator over non-overlapping regions. In this work, the chosen reduction factor along each dimension is equal to two. With this architecture we have 32 feature maps after the first convolutional layer, designated as F_1-maps. Each map in F_1 has size 24×24. Similarly, the 32 maps after the second convolutional layer are denoted as F_2-maps, with size 8×8.

Two fully connected layers of weights follow the second max-pooling layer. The activation function in the first dense layer is a sigmoid function given as

$$\sigma(x) = \frac{1}{1 + \exp(-x)}. \tag{3}$$

Then, within the next dense layer we use a *Softmax* activation function. Specifically, for a number N of s_i scalars it calculates an N-dimensional vector with values between 0 and 1:

$$o_l = \frac{\exp(s_l)}{\sum_k \exp(s_k)}; \tag{4}$$

with o_l as the activation of a neuron in the output layer. Finally, to train the network, the loss function is the cross-entropy [9].

2.2 Discrete Cosine Transform (DCT)

The Discrete Cosine Transform is:

$$(\mathbf{X})_{u,v} = \frac{C(u)}{\sqrt{N/2}} \frac{C(v)}{\sqrt{N/2}} \sum_{i=0}^{N-1} \sum_{j=0}^{N-1} (\mathbf{x})_{i,j} \cos \frac{(2i+1)u\pi}{2N} \cos \frac{(2j+1)v\pi}{2N}, \tag{5}$$

$$C(u) = \begin{cases} \frac{1}{\sqrt{2}} & u = 0 \\ 1 & u > 0 \end{cases}.$$ (6)

Here the DCT is useful for compressing the data provided by the CNN feature maps. Specifically, the values obtained by DCT represent spatial frequency coefficients in the horizontal/vertical direction. Since relevant data of images lies in the low frequencies, we considered 5×5 of lowest frequency coefficients for F_1-maps and 3×3 of lowest frequency coefficients for the F_2-maps.

The size of all the F_1-maps is equal to $24 * 24 * 32 = 18432$. Note that it would have been impractical to use all of them for extracting propositional rules, as the inherent polynomial computational complexity [4] would have resulted in a very long runtime with a very large number of generated rules. After DCT compression, the size of all the F_1-maps and F_2-maps becomes equal to 1088.

2.3 DIMLP Networks

The Discretized Interpretable Multi Layer Perceptron (DIMLP) differs from a standard MLP in the number of connections between the input layer and the first hidden layer. Specifically, any hidden neuron receives only a connection from an input neuron and the bias neuron, while all other layers are fully connected [3]. The activation function in the first hidden layer of DIMLPs is a staircase function, with Q stairs that approximate the sigmoid function; thus it provides quantized values of the sigmoid. With $Q = 1$ we obtain the step function, which is a particular case:

$$\tau(x) = \begin{cases} 1 \text{ if } x > 0; \\ 0 \text{ otherwise.} \end{cases}$$ (7)

The key idea behind rule extraction from DIMLPs is the precise localization of axis-parallel discriminative hyperplanes. In other words, the input space is split into hyper-rectangles representing propositional rules. Specifically, the first hidden layer creates for each input variable a number of axis-parallel hyperplanes that are effective or not, depending on the weight values of the neurons above the first hidden layer. More details on the rule extraction algorithm can be found in [4].

3 Experiments

We performed the experiments with the MNIST dataset [5]. It includes 60000 samples from ten classes in the training set and 10000 samples in the testing set. The same CNN architecture defined in Sect. 2.1 was used. The learning phase was performed with *Keras* libraries. Training parameters had default values, with the "dropout" parameter set to 0.3. Finally, the last 10000 samples of the training set were used as a tuning set for early-stopping [13].

3.1   First Series of Experiments

We first trained a CNN and then we transferred the feature maps with DCT compression to a DIMLP network with a unique hidden layer comprising a number of neurons equal to the number of input neurons (1088). Default learning parameters were utilized [4], along with the same tuning samples used for the CNN. Table 1 illustrates the results. The first row of this Table is related to the original CNN, while the second row provides results obtained by the interpretable CNN, with 25 stairs in the staircase activation function. Columns from left to right designate:

- predictive accuracy on the testing set (%);
- fidelity on the testing set, which is the degree of matching between generated rules and DIMLP classifications (%);
- predictive accuracy of the rules (%);
- predictive accuracy of the rules when rules and DIMLP agree (%);
- number of extracted rules;
- average number of antecedents per rule;
- proportion of default rule activations (%).

Table 1. Results obtained by a trained CNN and a DIMLP. The DIMLP inputs are the feature maps of the CNN.

	Tst. Acc.	Fid.	Rul. Acc. (1)	Rul. Acc. (2)	#Rul.	Avg. #Ant.	Def. R.
CNN	99.50	–	–	–	–	–	–
DIMLP	99.30	97.71	97.41	99.56	1839	9.9	0.64

The predictive accuracy provided by the CNN is higher that measured on DIMLP (99.50% versus 99.30%). Moreover, the predictive accuracy provided by the rules is lower that given by DIMLP (99.30% versus 97.41%). However, it is worth noting that if we only take into account the test samples for which DIMLP and rules provide the same classification (this occurred in 97.71% of the cases), the predictive accuracy of the rules rose up to 99.56%. Hence, explanations as rules were not provided in 2.93% of the testing samples (100 − 97.71 + 0.64 = 2.93%). The value of 0.64% represents the activation of the default rule, which is simply the DIMLP classification without any rule activation.

Objectively, the lack of explanation in a small proportion of the testing set is already a good result. However, a question arising is whether it is possible to obtain an explanation to all the testing samples. In the second series of experiments (see Sect. 3.2) we tried to answer to this question.

The propositional rules generated by DIMLPs are unordered, which means that they are not exclusive and therefore a sample can activate more than one rule. The number of extracted rules may seem high, but with 60000 samples in the training set and over 1000 input neurons, this is not very surprising. The average number of antecedents per rule, which is almost equal to ten shows the complexity of the classification task. Specifically, for the classification of a given sample, the amplitudes of ten frequencies in the original CNN feature maps should be used on average.

Let us illustrate an example of generated rule from the DIMLP trained network; conjunctions of antecedents are represented by symbol F with $F_{4,1}^{1,20}$ indicating the amplitude of the fourth vertical frequency and the first horizontal frequency with respect to the twentieth feature map of the first convolutional layer:

Example 1. $(F_{4,1}^{1,20} \leq -0.167)$ $(F_{1,3}^{1,20} > -0.280)$ $(F_{2,3}^{2,5} \leq 2.691)$ $(F_{2,1}^{2,6} \leq 0.794)$ $(F_{1,1}^{2,8} \leq 3.507)$ $(F_{2,2}^{2,10} \leq 0.992)$ $(F_{3,2}^{2,18} > 0.721)$ $(F_{1,2}^{2,22} \leq 2.402)$ $(F_{3,1}^{2,28} \leq -0.076)$ $\rightarrow$ Class 1.

Figure 1 represents at the top left the centroid of the samples activating the rule shown above, with the DCT coefficients represented at the top right. At the bottom are shown the centroid of the twentieth feature map of the first convolutional layer (left side) and the centroid in the frequency domain (right side). Only the low frequencies of the feature maps were learned by DIMLPs (5×5 upper corner).

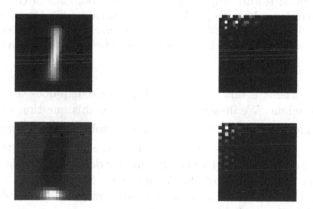

Fig. 1. A centroid of test samples activating a rule (top) and an example of feature map centroid (bottom). Specifically, at the top left is represented the centroid of the samples activating a rule of class "1" (353 samples), the DCT values being represented at the top right. The first two antecedents of this rule concerns the twentieth feature map of the first convolutional layer. At the bottom left is illustrated the centroid in the pixel luminosity domain, while the centroid in the frequency domain is shown at the bottom right.

With respect to the rule given above, pictures of the first and third columns of Fig. 2 show the centroids of the feature maps of the second convolutional layer. The second and fourth columns depict the centroids in the frequency domain.

Only the low frequencies of the feature maps were learned by DIMLPs (3×3 upper corner). The relationship with the feature map in Fig. 1 in which the number "1" is distinguished is less obvious, except for the picture at the bottom of the first column. These feature maps can be considered as specific patterns of activity of the original CNN that are very important in determining the final classification.

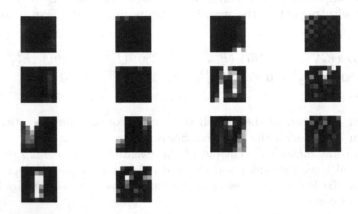

Fig. 2. Centroids of feature maps in the second convolutional layer. Pictures of the first and third columns show the pixel luminosity domain, while the second and fourth columns depict the centroids in the frequency domain. Each couple of pictures is related to the propositional rule given above (for the second convolutional layer).

A question arising is how a centroid of a feature map does vary with respect to a rule antecedent. We illustrate the answer to this question with $F_{4,1}^{1,20}$ and $F_{1,3}^{1,20}$ of the rule given above; note that the centroid is also illustrated in Fig. 1. The centroid value of $F_{4,1}^{1,20}$ is -0.760 and the threshold value of the antecedent is -0.167. Figure 3 depicts in the pixel luminosity domain (after the inverse DCT transformation) the changes of the feature map. Similarly, Fig. 4 is related to $F_{1,3}^{1,20}$. Clearly, the variation of a single antecedent in the frequency domain affects several intensities in the luminosity domain.

Figure 5 illustrates the variation of the centroid of a feature map in the pixel luminosity domain (second convolutional layer). With the picture on the right, we can clearly see the bright pixels that make the corresponding frequency domain antecedent no longer true compared to the left and middle images.

3.2   Second Series of Experiments

Here the key idea is to train several DIMLPs with the feature maps of the original CNN. Since each neural network starts the learning phase with a random configuration of weights (with small values), after training, each network is a little different. Thus, each ruleset extracted from a DIMLP is also different from

Fig. 3. Variation of the centroid of a feature map in the pixel luminosity domain. Here, the antecedent of the rule above is: $F_{4,1}^{1,20} \leq -0.167$. From left to right we have: $F_{4,1}^{1,20} = -0.760$ (the centroid value); $F_{4,1}^{1,20} = -0.167$ (the threshold of the antecedent); $F_{4,1}^{1,20} = 1$ (a value for which the corresponding antecedent is false).

the other extracted rulesets, and the probability that a test sample will activate at least one rule has therefore increased.

We trained up to ten DIMLPs on the same training/tuning/testing data as in the previous experiments. The final classification of the DIMLP ensemble was given by simply adding the activation values of the output neurons of each network. For the rules generated from the neural networks, only the rules in agreement with each classification for each DIMLP were retained. In addition, the final classification by the rules was provided by majority voting. Table 2 illustrates the results obtained, with the number of rules given as an average number over the ten DIMLPs. Fidelity increased to 99.86% and the rules alone correctly classified 99.36% of the testing samples with only a default rule activation (0.01%). Thus, for the ensemble of ten DIMLPs the lack of explanation occurred only in one case out of 10000.

Table 2. Results obtained by a trained CNN and an ensemble of ten DIMLPs. For the rules, their average number is given, as well as the average number of antecedents per rule.

	Tst. Acc.	Fid.	Rul. Acc. (1)	Rul. Acc. (2)	Avg. #Rul.	Avg. #Ant.	Def. R.
CNN	99.50	–	–	–	–	–	–
DIMLP-10	99.33	99.86	99.36	99.33	1860.2	9.8	0.01

Fig. 4. Variation of the centroid of a feature map in the pixel luminosity domain. Here, the antecedent of the rule above is: $F_{1,3}^{1,20} > -0.280$. From left to right we have: $F_{1,3}^{1,20} = 0.445$ (the centroid value); $F_{1,3}^{1,20} = -0.280$ (the threshold of the antecedent); $F_{1,3}^{1,20} = -1.500$ (a value for which the corresponding antecedent is false).

Fig. 5. Variation of the centroid of a feature map in the pixel luminosity domain (second convolutional layer). Here, the antecedent of the rule above is: $F_{2,3}^{2,5} \leq 2.691$. From left to right we have: $F_{2,3}^{2,5} = -0.080$ (the centroid value); $F_{2,3}^{2,5} = 2.691$ (the threshold of the antecedent); $F_{2,3}^{2,5} = 3.500$ (a value for which the corresponding antecedent is false).

4 Conclusion

We transferred the feature maps generated by a CNN to DIMLPs from which propositional rules were generated. To enable the execution of our rule extraction algorithm in a reasonable time, the DCT was applied to the feature maps retaining a small number of low spatial frequencies. Our method was applied to the MNIST benchmark problem. In the frequency domain, for the 60000 training samples about 1860 unordered rules were generated, on average. The predictive accuracy of the rules was very close to that of the CNN, but with about 3% of the testing samples without explanation. In another series of experiments, a slightly lower predictive accuracy was obtained compared to the original CNN, but with explanations in the form of propositional rules for 99.99% of the tested samples.

The antecedents of the extracted rules represent amplitudes of spatial frequencies. We illustrated with several examples that the variation of a single antecedent in the frequency domain affects several pixel intensities in the luminosity domain. Thus, it is possible to determine the relevant locations that contribute to the classification.

We anticipate a number of research questions that will warrant further investigation. Firstly, with the MNIST dataset pictures are considered tiny. In many classification problems, the image size is 224×224; thus, with our current method, we should achieve higher compression ratios with DCT and perhaps lose accuracy. However, by subsampling the images, we could still achieve good predictive accuracy. Finally, Principal Component Analysis (PCA) is another technique capable of performing data compression and should be studied.

References

1. Adadi, A., Berrada, M.: Peeking inside the black-box: a survey on explainable artificial intelligence (XAI). IEEE Access **6**, 52138–52160 (2018)
2. Andrews, R., Diederich, J., Tickle, A.B.: Survey and critique of techniques for extracting rules from trained artificial neural networks. Knowl.-Based Syst. **8**(6), 373–389 (1995)
3. Bologna, G.: Rule extraction from a multilayer perceptron with staircase activation functions. In: Neural Networks, 2000. IJCNN 2000, Proceedings of the IEEE-INNS-ENNS International Joint Conference on, vol. 3, pp. 419–424. IEEE (2000)

4. Bologna, G.: A model for single and multiple knowledge based networks. Artif. Intell. Med. **28**(2), 141–163 (2003)
5. Deng, L.: The MNIST database of handwritten digit images for machine learning research [best of the web]. IEEE Signal Process. Mag. **29**(6), 141–142 (2012)
6. Diederich, J.: Rule Extraction from Support Vector Machines, vol. 80. Springer Science & Business Media, Heidelberg (2008)
7. Guidotti, R., Monreale, A., Ruggieri, S., Pedreschi, D., Turini, F., Giannotti, F.: Local rule-based explanations of black box decision systems. arXiv preprint arXiv:1805.10820 (2018)
8. Holzinger, A., Biemann, C., Pattichis, C.S., Kell, D.B.: What do we need to build explainable AI systems for the medical domain? arXiv preprint arXiv:1712.09923 (2017)
9. Kline, D.M., Berardi, V.L.: Revisiting squared-error and cross-entropy functions for training neural network classifiers. Neural Comput. Appl. **14**(4), 310–318 (2005)
10. Ribeiro, M.T., Singh, S., Guestrin, C.: Why should i trust you? Explaining the predictions of any classifier. In: Proceedings of the 22nd ACM SIGKDD International Conference on Knowledge Discovery and Data Mining, pp. 1135–1144. ACM (2016)
11. Rudin, C.: Please stop explaining black box models for high stakes decisions. arXiv preprint arXiv:1811.10154 (2018)
12. Vilone, G., Longo, L.: Explainable artificial intelligence: a systematic review. arXiv preprint arXiv:2006.00093 (2020)
13. Yao, Y., Rosasco, L., Caponnetto, A.: On early stopping in gradient descent learning. Constr. Approx. **26**(2), 289–315 (2007)
14. Zhang, Q.S., Zhu, S.C.: Visual interpretability for deep learning: a survey. Front. Inf. Technol. Electron. Eng. **19**(1), 27–39 (2018)

Non-analytical Reasoning Assisted Deep Reinforcement Learning

John Schonefeld[⊠]⬤ and Md Karim⬤

Southern Arkansas University, Magnolia, AR 71753, USA
{johnschonefeld,mdkarim}@saumag.edu

Abstract. Addressing the sparse reward problem in Deep Reinforcement Learning (DRL) using human supplied external knowledge or reasoning is a common practice. Such external knowledge and reasoning should not be so complete that a DRL agent does not almost need to perform any exploration questioning its utility. Non-analytical Reasoning could shape an agent's actions sufficiently yet take away minimal credit from the DRL exploration process. We generalize the solution approaches to Non-analytical Reasoning Assisted Deep Reinforcement Learning and present an example solution to "Montezuma's Revenge," a notorious Atari game, applying such reasoning.

Keywords: Reinforcement Learning · Intuition · Insight · Heuristic · Sparse Reward

1 Introduction

In reinforcement learning, an agent interacting in an originally unexplored environment via trial-and-error attempts to maximize its reward. This results in a learned policy that hopefully chooses actions optimally but is practically not achievable when rewards are very sparse since the policy is only updated when the agent successfully reaches a state with an extrinsic reward. The chance to discover a very long sequence of peculiar actions using random exploration is extremely small, necessitating strategies with more directed exploration [12]. A critical issue in reinforcement learning is the task of balancing exploration by sampling actions of its environment to acquire more information and balancing exploitation by making the best decision given current knowledge in order to maximize cumulative rewards. Exploration techniques do have a theoretical guarantee for discovering ideal policies when each state-action is tried a quantity converging towards infinity, so creative exploration techniques are still needed in order to search high dimensional spaces [12].

This material is based upon work supported by the National Science Foundation under Award No. OIA-1946391. Any opinions, findings, and conclusions or recommendations expressed in this material are those of the author(s) and do not necessarily reflect the views of the National Science Foundation.

© Springer Nature Switzerland AG 2022
J. M. Ferrández Vicente et al. (Eds.): IWINAC 2022, LNCS 13259, pp. 328–336, 2022.
https://doi.org/10.1007/978-3-031-06527-9_32

One way to combat this problem is to assist an agent with domain knowledge. For instance, using domain knowledge we, can shape rewards to create more frequent intermediate rewards than the initial sparse rewards and accelerate learning by augmenting the natural rewards with supplementary reward features. For instance, in [10], OpenAI five system achieved the first victory over a professional, world championship eSports team in the game Dota. A shaped reward was given to help alleviate the long-term credit assignment problem based on which humans agreed were beneficial actions giving it a massive edge to observe the game state. This paper contends that truly intelligent agents should be able to solve complex problems with non-analytical reasoning support. We present a DRL solution to the "Montezuma's Revenge" game that uses pixel context-based simple heuristics to achieve successful exploration.

2 Non-analytical Reasoning

We borrow the term "Non-analytical Reasoning" from the clinical literature to refer to the implicit, associative, and automatic reasoning processes that are not derived through a proper analytical foundation. "Intuition and insight are two intriguing phenomena of non-analytical mental functioning (reasoning)" [14]. There are differences of opinion on how best to define intuition or insight. We adopt the definitions presented below.

2.1 Intuition

"Intuition is the ability to understand immediately without conscious reasoning;" intuition is "reached by sensing the solution without any explicit representation of it" [7,14].

Intuition can be presented to an agent as heuristic rules and be used in shaping reward. "Heuristic could refer to any device used in problem solving, be it a program, a data structure, a proverb, a strategy, or a piece of knowledge ... (with) an element of "rule of thumbishness" about the device; ... heuristics fit on a spectrum of devices between those that are random and uninspired and those that (guarantee optimal results)" [11]. Because of the "rule of thumb" nature of intuitions, they are easily translatable as heuristics.

An example of intuition assisted DRL is presented in [4]; the authors used heuristic based reward shaping in the network slice placement problem.

2.2 Insight

"Insight has been understood as the sudden and unexpected apprehension of the solution," usually through restructuring problem representation; Insight depends on previous experience and possibly also on a priori knowledge [6,7,14]. To trigger insight an agent must possess some prior knowledge, be that a priori knowledge (knowledge acquired independently of any particular experience) or earned through some training/experience on a set of tasks that can possibly trigger a "Eureka" moment. To simulate probable insight in an agent (i.e., to shape an agent's action through insight), the agent requires to be trained with some tasks that could possibly be useful in the future.

An example of intuition assisted DRL is presented in [3]; the authors solve the artificial pigeon problem through prior training of the agent on a limited number of sub-tasks.

3   Solving Montezuma's Revenge Using Pixel Context Based Heuristics

We develop a solution to "Montezuma's Revenge," which relies on raw pixels to incorporate prior knowledge to the agent. This technique can be implemented as a reward shaping bonus that can be used with any value or policy optimization algorithm, and it can be efficiently computed while working in high dimensional state spaces. Our technique is established on the theoretical idea that additional rewards can be supplemented through reward shaping, where [9] shows that the original reward function, R, can be substituted with $R' = R + F$, and the idea that humans are capable of detecting objects within the scene while also inferring their relationships, grasping the underlining cause and effect principles. In the game Montezuma's Revenge, humans are able to map the hostile skull to its appropriate pixels, understanding to avoid it. One way to incorporate this domain knowledge is through imitation learning, providing the agent with expert demonstrations of the desired behavior. However, the entire state-space may not be covered. The agent must generalize among states with similarities but not exactly identical. If we can manually extract information in the form of goals and convey them as rewards from raw pixels, then reward features can be acquired through only the representation of high value states. A high value state may be generalized by abstracting background noise and using pixel context based heuristics to suggest whether this state should be rewarded. Therefore, this method bypasses the noisy-TV problem named in [2], and it also uses stationary and persistent rewards. It is also possible to ignore extrinsic rewards and instead replace them with bonus rewards since the density of rewards is very configurable using this method.

One of the difficulties working in high-dimensional state spaces is that input like images increase the complexity [8]. An agent can't observe through the pixel's information like speed, differentiating whether a person is walking or running, or objects like a ladder, understanding to climb it. Human feedback manually could be given to the agent by the person deciding if the agent is on the right track and then shape a reward to convey that to the agent. However, this can't be manually done to billions of frames of images. Thus generalization to unseen states would be necessary from the human feedback. Even with imitation learning the entire state-space will not be covered, resulting in remaining unseen states. In order to fully take advantage of human knowledge, an automatic process must be made. It is usually the case that when generalization is needed, deep neural networks have proven to generalize to previously similar, unseen data. We show that hand-crafted features through the pixels are enough for the agent to isolate and generalize the features to unseen states that may be significantly different with respect to the rest of the image.

3.1 Environmental Setup

The experiments are performed on several well-known games from the Atari Games benchmark [1]. To reduce computational complexity and assess the flexibility of this method alone across several games, a hyperparameter search was not done during experimentation. In the ALE environment for these games, each observation is an RGB image represented as an array with shape (210, 160, 3) where every action is chosen again for a number of frames since they are nearly identical [8]. For preprocessing, the image is converted to grayscale and cropped to a new dimension of (84, 84) [8]. The current frame, along with the last k frames, are mapped into a single observation to give the agent a better understanding of the state of the environment, such as the direction or speed of a moving object [8]. Using k consecutive frames can contain this information within the frames stacked on top of each other to form an observation for the input of the network. The environments used are episodic, therefore termination of an episode is done at the loss of a life or after winning the game. The neural networks were already implemented using the reinforcement learning library, Coach [5]. It implements many state-of-the-art algorithms and provides a python API for neural network packages in Tensorflow. The algorithm of our choosing was the Dueling, Double DQN with Prioritized Experience Replay, and the EGreedy exploration policy. We extended their algorithms to include our own bonus reward and extra features relevant to our experiments. All experiments were run in Google Colab while using the GPU resource option.

3.2 Deep Reinforcement Learning with Reward Shaping

In reinforcement learning, decisions are modelled in an environment through a Markov Decision Process described as a tuple (s, a, r, s', γ) where s symbolizes the observed state, a the action performed, r the reward received, and s' the next state due to previous action performed, and γ is used to discount future rewards [13]. The goal of the MDP is to maximize the future cumulative reward. The rewards at all time steps, t, are aggregated with a discount rate, γ, with a number between 0 and 1 to form the expected return [13].

$$G_t = R_{t+1} + \gamma R_{t+2} + \gamma^2 R_{t+3} + ... = \sum_{k=0}^{\infty} \gamma^k R_{t+k+1} \tag{1}$$

A policy function π will map the distribution of states to actions in the state-action space after the reinforcement agent maximizes the sum expected discounted reward over the policy [13]. This is known as the optimal policy, based on the recursive Bellman equation, which states that the expected return for any state-action pair taken at time t results in the predicted reward formed from the combination of the reward at time t + 1 and the maximum expected discounted reward after that [13].

$$q_*(s,a) = E\left[R_{t+1} + \gamma max_{a'} q_*(s',a')\right] \tag{2}$$

Since it can be difficult to produce the transition probability distributions, a simulator modeling the MDP can be used. In our case, we use the Atari games benchmark.

This paper proposes to integrate reward shaping using prior knowledge decoded through the representation of pixels. This connection is achieved by modifying a pixel-based image of certain states that can dictate whether a state fulfills the hand-crafted requirements suitable to the task. This shaped reward crafted from pixels is added to the environmental reward attaching prior knowledge to the completion of the task in the form of a shaping function $f(s')$ being added to the optimal action-value function in Eq. 2.

3.3   Image to Reward Conversion

Every transition contains the action-state pair and the next state. We use only the next-state that the environment has transitioned into as our input to determine if the state should be rewarded since generalizing over the state-action space itself would be more difficult. We then generalize rewarding states by determining if its next-state contains any relevant features provided by a list of conditions representing the feature through high-level in pixels. By knowing what key features look like, rewarding states can be generalized. Instead of focusing on whether the state is rewarding, we can focus on whether the features of the state are rewarding, allowing greater generalization. Figuring out if a state contains relevant features helps carry the meaning of how a human would play the game but abstracted in the form of pixels so that knowledge can be conveyed. Much like a real human would grasp the optical representations of an object in a scene or character location within the level, any input state that meets the conditions, even significantly different state-action pairs reaching the same next-state can be generalized. This reward shaping technique we used in our experiments proved to be less computationally expensive, yielded greater interpretability, and required no data set. The final optimal action-value function is expressed as Eq. 3.

$$q_*(s,a) = E\left[R_{t+1} + \gamma max_{a'} q_*(s',a') + f(s')\right] \tag{3}$$

Not utilizing prior knowledge in reinforcement learning means a policy will be less sample efficient. By reducing the scope of exploration necessary, the acceleration of agents discovering better policies is possible.

To illustrate the generalization of the method above, imagine a car racing other cars on a track with the goal of finishing in top place. In order to accomplish this, collisions need to be avoided. Therefore, a relevant feature to be considered would be if the car crashed. If it is known that a certain state resulted in a crash, that state could be penalized consequently. By examining the pixels around the car, a condition could be made that for certain pixels values, a crash did indeed happen. By looking at pixels instead of the entire image, states involving a crash can be generalized based on the commonality of containing the feature built to depict a crash (Fig. 1).

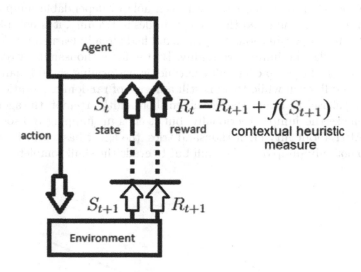

Fig. 1. Reinforcement Learning with Contextual Heuristic Measure

4   Experiments

4.1   Testing

We split the problem into two sub-problems for simplicity. Namely, the agent will attempt to navigate across the level and jump over the skull to reach the key in Montezuma's Revenge. We use the same algorithm without our bonus rewards as a baseline. The training was done until at least a success rate of 90% was achieved for both problems. The average success rates are shown in intervals using episodes gathered from testing time. The chosen number of frames to skip was 4, so for every step, there were four frames. No step limit was used to limit the time frame. The first experiment gives the agent the goal of learning to jump over a dangerous skull without touching it. The second experiment involves navigating across a room to reach a key. The average number of steps per episode for the first experiment is notably smaller, resulting in fewer episodes needed to train the agent.

4.2   Skull Jump with Pixel Based Rewards

The first environment includes a modification of the game Montezuma's Revenge, where the character must learn to jump over a skull to receive a reward. During the initial stages of training, jumping over the skull only occurs infrequently by chance, but throughout training, the agent can consistently jump over the skull to obtain a reward. One reward is given for success, with zero rewards given if unsuccessful. The reward was implemented using only pixels to determine if the character had made the jump.

While the controlled character had been able to dependable jump over the skull after about one hundred thousand episodes in training, it is notable sooner through the testing evaluations that the skull had already learned much of what it needed to make the jump successfully. By the forty thousandth attempt, the agent is making the jump over half the time by performing skillful maneuvering around the skull, even while there is still a degree of random exploration during the training phase. At about the seventeen thousandth attempt, the agent seems to try to make the jump intentionally, but it ends up jumping too soon in the process. After about fifty-eight thousand tries, the agent has learned well-timed actions to not only jump over the skull but to evade the skull completely (Fig. 2).

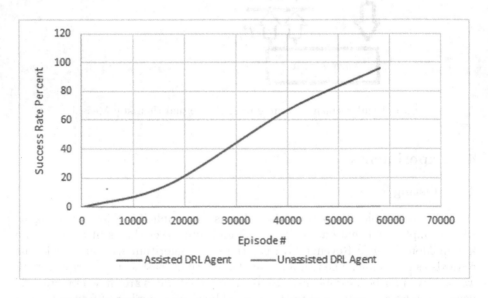

Fig. 2. Testing Average Episodic Reward: Skull Jump Success Rate

4.3   Key-Grab with Pixel Based Rewards

The second environment includes the first level of Montezuma's Revenge, excluding the skull from the first experiment. Starting at the beginning of the room, the agent must utilize ladders and ropes without falling off. In episode eight thousand, five hundred, the agent does not complete the level at all, with a zero success rate. As the number of episodes approaches twelve thousand, the agent escapes local minimum can able to beat the level around half the time. From that point, it comes down to optimization of grabbing the key by the fine-tuning of individual actions with their actual corresponding values. At episode fifty-eight thousand, the average success rate reaches over ninety percent (Fig. 3).

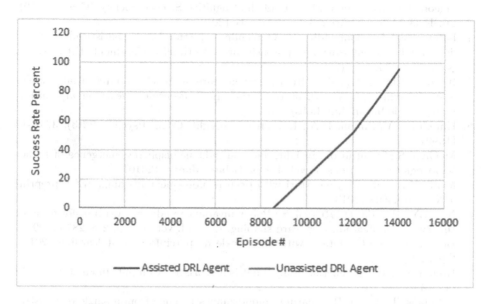

Fig. 3. Testing Average Episodic Reward: Key Grab Success Rate

5   Conclusion

Substantial gains in deep reinforcement learning have been made with increasingly better computational hardware over the years, but very sparse environments in real life applications are still problematic without more advanced exploration techniques. Non-analytical Reasoning can address this problem by maintaining the characteristics of DRL learning. In our experiments we attempt to use a universal deep reinforcement learning algorithm to solve Atari games in combination with adding intermediate rewards through the use raw pixels based intuitive heuristics. The results show that with the addition of pixel based rewards, the agent was able to complete an originally difficult problem that would not have been solved in a time frame any near the same magnitude, with also less robustness. This suggests that manually formulated intuitive input can serve as a reward to guide the agent.

References

1. Bellemare, M.G., Naddaf, Y., Veness, J., Bowling, M.: The arcade learning environment: an evaluation platform for general agents. J. Artif. Intell. Res. **47**, 253–279 (2013)

2. Burda, Y., Edwards, H., Pathak, D., Storkey, A., Darrell, T., Efros, A.A.: Large-scale study of curiosity-driven learning. arXiv preprint arXiv:1808.04355 (2018)

3. Colin, T.R., Belpaeme, T.: Reinforcement learning and insight in the artificial pigeon. In: 41st Annual Meeting of the Cognitive Science Society (CogSci 2019), pp. 1533–1539. Cognitive Science Society (2019)

4. Esteves, J.J.A., Boubendir, A., Guillemin, F., Sens, P.: A heuristically assisted deep reinforcement learning approach for network slice placement. IEEE Trans. Netw. Serv. Manag. (2021)

5. IntelLabs: Intellabs/coach: Reinforcement learning coach by intel ai lab enables easy experimentation with state of the art reinforcement learning algorithms. https://github.com/IntelLabs/coach

6. Kaplan, C.A., Simon, H.A.: In search of insight. Cogn. Psychol. **22**(3), 374–419 (1990)

7. McCrea, S.M.: Intuition, insight, and the right hemisphere: emergence of higher sociocognitive functions. Psychol. Res. Behav. Manag. (2010)

8. Mnih, V., et al.: Playing Atari with deep reinforcement learning. arXiv preprint arXiv:1312.5602 (2013)

9. Ng, A.Y., Harada, D., Russell, S.: Policy invariance under reward transformations: theory and application to reward shaping. In: Icml, vol. 99, pp. 278–287 (1999)

10. Berner, C., et al.: Dota 2 with large scale deep reinforcement learning (2019). OpenAI

11. Romanycia, M.H., Pelletier, F.J.: What is a heuristic? Comput. Intell. **1**(1), 47–58 (1985)

12. Salimans, T., Chen, R.: Learning montezuma's revenge from a single demonstration. CoRR abs/1812.03381 (2018). http://arxiv.org/abs/1812.03381

13. Sutton, R.S., Barto, A.G.: Reinforcement Learning: An Introduction. MIT press, Cambridge (2018)

14. Zander, T., Öllinger, M., Volz, K.G.: Intuition and insight: two processes that build on each other or fundamentally differ? Front. Psychol. **7**, 1395 (2016)

Double-Layer Stacked Denoising Autoencoders for Regression

María-Elena Fernández-García[1]([✉]), Antonio Ros-Ros[2],
Eloy Hontoria Hernández[3], Aníbal R. Figueiras-Vidal[4],
and José-Luis Sancho-Gómez[1]

[1] Tecnologías de la Información y las Comunicaciones, Universidad Politécnica
de Cartagena, Cartagena, Spain
elena.fdez.ga@gmail.com
[2] Iberian Lube Base Oils Company, S.A., 30350 Cartagena, Spain
[3] Economía de la Empresa, Universidad Politécnica de Cartagena,
Cartagena, Spain
[4] Teoría de la Señal y las Comunicaciones, Universidad Carlos III de Madrid,
Avda. Universidad 30, 28911 Leganes, Madrid, Spain

Abstract. A Stacked Denoising Autoencoder (SDAE) is a deep neural
network (NN) model trained and designed in one-by-one stacked layers to reconstruct the non-noisy version of the original input data. It is
an architecture used with great success in statistical pattern recognition
problems.

The objective of this contribution is to determine if an MSDAE can
benefit from the greater capabilities of representation of features obtained
when two layers are introduced in the stacking process instead of a single one. To do this, the design and performance of these machines in
regression problems are presented and analyzed both in terms of error
and calculation cost.

The experimental results underline interesting performance capabilities for specific purposes.

Keywords: Stacked autoencoders · Denoising · Regression · Neural
networks

1 Introduction

An autoencoder (AE) is an artificial neural network (NN) used to learn significant features and new data representations minimizing the reconstruction error
between original and reconstructed data. AEs are composed of an encoder and a
decoder. The encoder performs a feature transformation of the input to a higher
or lower dimensional space. Then, the decoder reconstructs the original data
from the encoder's output by minimizing the reconstruction error. Training the
AE this way, the hidden units try to capture the most appropriate features of
the input data for reconstruction. Common AE applications are: data denoising
[1,2], dimensionality reduction [3,4] and creating generative models [5,6].

© Springer Nature Switzerland AG 2022
J. M. Ferrández Vicente et al. (Eds.): IWINAC 2022, LNCS 13259, pp. 337–345, 2022.
https://doi.org/10.1007/978-3-031-06527-9_33

In particular, denoising autoencoders (DAE) use a noisy version of the original data as input and reconstruct the data without noise. This avoids the DAE from reaching the identity solution, and hence not learning any data features. Trying to undo the noise effect, the DAE can learn statistical dependencies between inputs.

Deep AE can produce more effective feature representations, however training deep AE networks using back-propagation often gets stuck in local minima due to vanishing gradient through the multiple layers. One way of avoiding this problem is by stacking individually trained AEs, i.e. building a deep stacked denoising autoencoder (SDAE) [7].

The contribution of this work is based on a modified version of SDAE (MSDAE) [8] and constitutes a first look at the study of the multilayer design performance of MSDAE. The initial hypothesis of this work is that building a MSDAE by training and stacking multi-layer DAEs will provide better performance compared to a regular MSDAE model. This initial assumption is based on the greater feature extraction capabilities and complex high-dimensional function representation associated with deeper non-linear NN [9,10]. Particularly, we want to test whether using the encoder's feature representation of stacked two-layer DAEs can provide an advantage for regression tasks over a regular MSDAE.

This contribution is divided into four sections. Section 2 presents the architecture and training of the MSDAE-based models under study. Section 3 describes the experiments carried out and shows their results, which are further discussed in Sect. 4. In the final section, we present the general conclusions of this work and lay out future lines of research.

2   Method

The experiments carried out in this study are based on the MSDAE architecture. MSDAE model is composed of a number of Denoising Autoencoders (DAE) which are trained and connected —Stacked— to the network one by one.

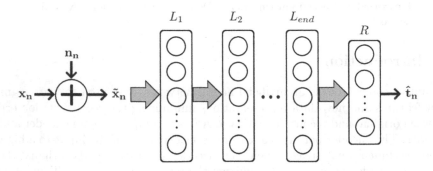

Fig. 1. Scheme of the MSDAE regression machine. The MSDAE input is $\tilde{x}_n$, a noisy version of x_n. The output of the MSDAE feeds a regression layer R trained to produce an estimate $\hat{t}_n$ of the regression label t_n.

Figure 1 shows the scheme of a generic MSDAE regression machine. Its input is a vector composed of a noisy version $\tilde{\mathbf{x}}_n$ of each sample $\mathbf{x}_n$. The input weights of every autoassociative layer, L_1 to L_{end}, are found by MSE minimization training. A final fully connected conventional regression layer R completes the architecture. Afterward, the network is refined for carrying out the regression task, i.e. for obtaining an estimate $\hat{\mathbf{t}}_n$ of $\mathbf{t}_n$.

Taking the MSDAE model from Fig. 1 as a starting point, two variants are proposed —MSDAEdouble and MSDAEdouble1—.

MSDAEdouble is built the same way as a regular MSDAE, but training and stacking two-layer DAEs instead of single-layer DAEs. Figure 2 illustrates the step-by-step training and assembly of a MSDAEdouble model.

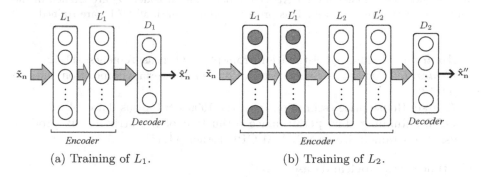

(a) Training of L_1.   (b) Training of L_2.

Fig. 2. Step-by-step training of the MSDAEdouble. Subfigure (a) shows the training of the first double-layer DAE (L_1 and L_1') producing an estimate $\hat{\mathbf{x}}_n'$ of the input $\mathbf{x}_n$. Then the decoder D_1 is discarded, the input weights of L_1 and L_1' are frozen (represented by dark circles) and a new double-layer DAE (L_2 and L_2') and decoder D_2 are trained in the same way, as shown in Subfigure (b). This process continues until all DAEs are trained.

The training of MSDAEdouble1 model is similar to MSDAEdouble. In each step a two-layer DAE is trained, but only the first layer of the DAE is attached to the final network. This difference is shown in Fig. 3 compared to MSDAdouble Fig. 2(b).

3   Experiments and Their Results

3.1   Datasets

To evaluate MSDAE-based designs for regression, seven databases have been used. These datasets have diverse characteristics such as number of samples — sizes— and attributes —dimensions. Four of them are static regression problems and the other three are time series. The static regression problem datasets are:

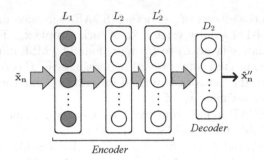

Fig. 3. Training the MSDAEdouble1 model. Starting from Fig. 2(a), then layer L_1' and decoder D_1 are discarded. The input weights of L_1 are frozen (represented by dark circles) and a new double-layer DAE (L_2 and L_2') and decoder D_2 are trained in the same way as the previous step. This process continues until all DAEs are trained.

- **Abalone**: Abalone age estimation from physical measurements, [11,12]
- **Concrete**: Concrete strength estimation from material composition and age [11,13]
- **House**: House price estimation from the 1990 US Census data [14]
- **GPU**: Running time performance estimation of a matrix-matrix product using a parameterizable SGEMM GPU kernel [11,15]

The time series problem datasets are:

- **AirQ**: Temperature estimation from measurements of humidity and air chemicals concentrations using a multi-sensor device [11,16]
- **Weather**: Temperature estimation from meteorological station measures located in Szeged, Hungary [17]
- **Valve**: Valve 3035 opening estimation from ILBOC sensor data of a water temperature regulation system [18].

Table 1 shows the main characteristics of the datasets used for in this contribution.

3.2　Dataset Preprocessing

The datasets' variables have been normalized to zero mean and unity standard deviation.

Time-series datasets *AirQ*, *Weather*, and *Valve* are processed as follows: The estimated variable at the any given instant is predicted from averages of the other 14, 11 and 10 variables respectively. In *AirQ* and *Weather* cases the averages are calculated along 24-hour periods of the last 7 days —producing 98 and 77 input variables respectively—. In *Valve*'s case this is predicted from averages calculated over 6-hour periods of the past 60 h —producing 100 input variables—.

Table 1. Summary of datasets' main characteristics. *: Time series

Dataset	Size	Dimension
Abalone	4177	8
Concrete	1030	9
House	22784	17
GPU	241600	18
*AirQ**	9358	15
*Weather**	96453	12
*Valve**	22182	11

3.3 Machine Design Processes

MSDAE-Based Machines. The three architectures used are based in a MSDAE regression machine, stacking DAEs up to obtain four hidden layers of equal size for each model with one final linear regression layer of size one. DAE layers have hyperbolic tangent activation. DAE size is obtained by validation of those sizes corresponding to an Expansion Factor (with respect to the input size) $EF \in \{1.5, 2, 3, 5, 10, 15, 20, 30\}$ (except for *GPU* dataset where EF was extended with $\{50, 70, 100\}$). The noise influence is chosen by adding a zero-mean Gaussian noise with selectable variance to the values of each sample variable. The Gaussian noise variance is selected by validation among $nv \in \{0.1, 0.2, 0.3, 0.4\}$ times the variance of the sample variables.

All three MSDAE-based machines have the same number of hidden layers. For a four hidden layer architecture, MSDAE and MSDAEdouble1 have to train 4 DAEs —of one and two layers respectively—, and MSDAEdouble model have to train 2 DAEs —keeps both two layers of the trained DAE—.

Validation and Performance Computations. Non-trainable parameters are selected according to the results of a multiple validation process with 50 runs of 60%–20%–20% train–validation–test random partitions of the datasets. Mean Square Error (MSE) is the error criterion for the regression tasks in all cases and the final performance result corresponds to the average of the 50 runs.

Results. Table 2 shows the results of the machine design optimization experiments as described in Sect. 3.3. The best MSE average results are indicated in bold for each dataset. A method is considered better than another when the difference between the means of the corresponding MSEs is at least greater than the average of their standard deviations.

Further study of the EF effect over the results of the three MSDAE-based models was carried out. Figure 4 shows the mean MSE results related to mean MSE value of the MSDAE model —expressed as proportion of MSDAE's mean MSE— for each dataset with increasing EF.

Table 2. Test set MSE mean and standard deviation for each method and dataset. The best results are in boldface as per the criterion described in Sect. 3.3.

Dataset	MSDAE (EF, nv)	MSDAEdouble (EF, nv)	MSDAE-double1 (EF, nv)
Abalone	**0.377**±0.018 (5, 0.2)	**0.376**±0.019 (3, 0.2)	**0.376**±0.016 (2, 0.1)
Concrete	**0.229**±0.026 (5, 0.2)	**0.225**±0.022 (5, 0.1)	**0.231**±0.031 (2, 0.1)
House	**0.300**±0.012 (20, 0.4)	**0.299**±0.011 (20, 0.4)	**0.299**±0.008 (15, 0.4)
GPU	11.80×10^{-3} $\pm 1.10 \times 10^{-3}$ (5, 0.2)	10.52×10^{-3} $\pm 1.05 \times 10^{-3}$ (10, 0.3)	$\mathbf{7.04 \times 10^{-3}}$ $\pm 0.50 \times 10^{-3}$ (30, 0.4)
AirQ	**0.083**±0.008 (2, 0.1)	**0.083**±0.007 (2, 0.1)	**0.082**±0.006 (3, 0.4)
Weather	**0.233**±0.031 (15, 0.4)	**0.244**±0.035 (10, 0.4)	**0.223**±0.038 (10, 0.4)
Valve	**0.009**±0.001 (5, 0.4)	**0.009**±0.001 (5, 0.4)	**0.008**±0.001 (5, 0.4)

4   Discussion of the Experimental Results

The results from Table 2 show that all three MSDAE-based architectures can reach a similar performance in each of the selected regression problems —except for *GPU* where MSDAEdouble1 achieves the best MSE value—.

The advantage of using double-layer MSDAE models for suboptimal selection of the non-trainable parameters is apparent in Fig. 4. MSDAEdouble achieves better results in more complex problems —such as *House*, *GPU* and *Weather*— when the *EF* is very limited compared to their optimum *EF* value form Table 2. With grater *EF* all models reach an equally good mean MSE result, except for *GPU* where MSDAEdouble1 reaches the lowest mean MSE.

Computation cost varies significantly for each model and dataset. Table 3 presents the mean and standard deviation of the training Computation Time (CT) for all datasets. Each machine has the same *EF*, *nv* and number of hidden layers (5, 0.2 and 4 respectively). The CT was obtained running 50 training repetitions on a PC with Intel(R) Core(TM) i7-3770 @ 3.40 GHz CPU and NVIDIA GeForce GTX 1050 Ti GPU.

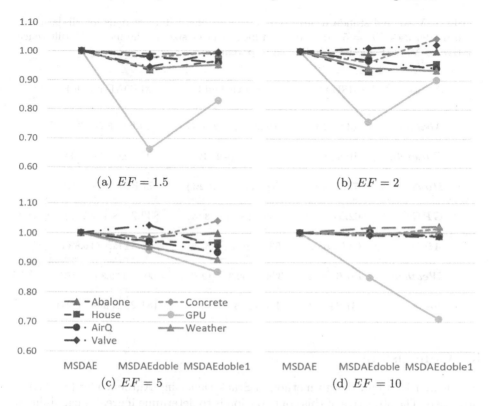

Fig. 4. Evolution with EF increase of the mean MSE results of MSDAEdouble and MSDAEdouble1 machines related to regular MSDAE model's mean MSE value. For every dataset and model nv is 0.3 and hidden layer size is 4.

As shown in Table 3, given the same non-trainable parameters, the CT of training MSDAEdouble machines is the lowest, and training MSDAEdouble1 takes the longest for all datasets. CT differences between models are due to the way each machine's architecture is built during training. MSDAEdouble trains a two hidden layer DAE in every step and adds it to its structure, repeating the process half times the number of hidden layers. While MSDAEdouble1 also trains a two hidden layer AE in each step, only the first layer is added to its structure. MSDAEdouble1 has to repeat the process as many times as the number of hidden layers to get the same size as MSDAEdouble.

Table 3. Mean and standard deviation of the training CT in seconds for all datasets. Each model uses $EF = 5$, $nv = 0.2$ and hidden layer size 4. The mean CT difference relative to MSDAE model is indicated in parentheses.

Dataset	MSDAE	MSDAEdouble	MSDAEdouble1
Abalone	13.6±2.1	10.2±2.5 (−25.0%)	14.6±2.5 (+7.3%)
Concrete	10.4±1.0	8.1±0.6 (−22.1%)	11.4±0.7 (+9.6%)
House	74.2±9.7	58.5±9.1 (−21.2%)	77.8±10.0 (+4.9%)
GPU	662.0±110.2	638.7±83.4 (−3.5%)	842.2±88.4 (+27.2%)
AirQ	63.5±10.2	53.2±10.1 (−16.2%)	67.8±12.1 (+6.8%)
Weather	491.6±99.2	394.5±92.3 (−19.8%)	506.8±79.3 (+3.1%)
Valve	137.8±15.4	130.7±15.1 (−5.2%)	181.2±24.6 (+31.5%)

5   Conclusions

In this article, a new design method of Stack Denoising Autoencoder (SDAE) is proposed. The objective of this contribution is to determine if greater capabilities of feature representation can be obtained when two layers are introduced in the stacking process instead of a single one. In paricular, the design and performance of two different strategies over regression problems are presented and analyzed both in terms of error and calculation cost.

This work constitutes a first look at the study of the multilayer design performance of MSDAE and the obtained results confirm that a reduction of computational cost of 15–20% can be achieved.

Moverover, we think that the use of multi-layer based design of SDAEs can provide an advantage in more complex problems in terms of reducing the estimation error.

Acknowledgements. Thanks to ILBOC, Fundación Séneca (Program 20348/ FPI/17 and Project 20901/PI/18) and Instituto de Salud Carlos III (Project 2018-PI17-00771) for supporting and funding this research work. Part of the experimental results were obtained using the George Mason University Office of Research computing Argo Research Cluster.

References

1. Vincent, P., Larochelle, H., Bengio, Y., Manzagol, P.A.: Extracting and composing robust features with denoising autoencoders. In: Proceedings of the 25th International Conference on Machine Learning, pp. 1096–1103 (2008)

2. Ashfahani, A., Pratama, M., Lughofer, E., Ong, Y.S.: DEVDAN: deep evolving denoising autoencoder. Neurocomputing **390**, 297–314 (2020)
3. Eiteneuer, B., Hranisavljevic, N., Niggemann, O.: Dimensionality reduction and anomaly detection for cpps data using autoencoder. In: 2019 IEEE International Conference on Industrial Technology (ICIT), pp. 1286–1292 (2019)
4. Lin, E., Mukherjee, S., Kannan, S.: A deep adversarial variational autoencoder model for dimensionality reduction in single-cell RNA sequencing analysis. BMC Bioinform. **21**(1), 1 (2020)
5. Lim, J., Ryu, S., Kim, J.W., Kim, W.Y.: Molecular generative model based on conditional variational autoencoder for de novo molecular design. J. Cheminform. **10**(1), 1–9 (2018)
6. Mishra, A., Krishna Reddy, S., Mittal, A., Murthy, H.A.: A generative model for zero shot learning using conditional variational autoencoders. In: Proceedings of the IEEE Conference on Computer Vision and Pattern Recognition Workshops, pp. 2188–2196 (2018)
7. Vincent, P., Larochelle, H., Lajoie, I., Bengio, Y., Manzagol, P.A.: Stacked denoising autoencoders: learning useful representations in a deep network with a local denoising criterion. J. Mach. Learn. Res. **11**, 3371–3408 (2010)
8. Alvear-Sandoval, R.F., Figueiras-Vidal, A.R.: On building ensembles of stacked denoising auto-encoding classifiers and their further improvement. Inf. Fusion **39**, 41–52 (2018)
9. Wang, X., Zhao, Y., Pourpanah, F.: Recent advances in deep learning. Int. J. Mach. Learn. Cybern. **11**(4), 747–750 (2020). https://doi.org/10.1007/s13042-020-01096-5
10. Sen, R., Yu, H.F., Dhillon, I.S.: Think globally, act locally: a deep neural network approach to high-dimensional time series forecasting. Adv. Neural Inf. Process. Syst. **2019**, 32 (2018)
11. Dua, D., Graff, C.: UCI Machine Learning Repository. School of Information and Computer Sci., Univ. California at Irvine (2017). http://archive.ics.uci.edu/ml
12. Clark, D., Schreter, Z., Adams, A.: A quantitative comparison of dystal and backpropagation. In: Proceedings of the 7th Australian Conference on Neural Networks, Australian Nat. Univ., pp. 132–137 (1996)
13. Yeh, I.C.: Modeling of strength of high-performance concrete using artificial neural networks. Cem. Concr. Res. **28**(12), 1797–1808 (1998)
14. Delve database (1995–1996) Univ. Toronto. https://www.dcc.fc.up.pt/~ltorgo/Regression/DataSets.html. Accessed 10 Dec 2021
15. Ballester-Ripoll, R., Paredes, E.G., Pajarola, R.: Sobol tensor trains for global sensitivity analysis. Reliab. Eng. Syst. Saf. **183**, 311–322 (2019)
16. De Vito, S., Massera, E., Piga, M., Martinotto, L., Di Francia, G.: On field calibration of an electronic nose for benzene estimation in an urban pollution monitoring scenario. Sens. Actuators B Chem. **129**, 750–757 (2008)
17. Szeged Weather database (2016) Kaggle. https://www.kaggle.com/budincsevity/szeged-weather. Accessed 10 Dec 2021
18. Fernández-García, M.-E., Larrey-Ruiz, J., Ros-Ros, A., Figueiras-Vidal, A.R., Sancho-Gómez, J.-L.: Machine-health application based on machine learning techniques for prediction of valve wear in a manufacturing plant. In: Ferrández Vicente, J.M., Álvarez-Sánchez, J.R., de la Paz López, F., Toledo Moreo, J., Adeli, H. (eds.) IWINAC 2019. LNCS, vol. 11487, pp. 389–398. Springer, Cham (2019). https://doi.org/10.1007/978-3-030-19651-6_38

Deep Layout Extraction Applied to Historical Postcards

Bruno García, Belén Moreno, José F. Vélez, and Ángel Sánchez(✉)

Escuela Técnica Superior de Ingeniería Informática (ETSII), Universidad Rey
Juan Carlos (URJC), 28933 Móstoles (Madrid), Spain
{bruno.garcia,belen.moreno,jose.velez,angel.sanchez}@urjc.es

Abstract. We describe an experimental study on the layout extraction
problem applied to circulated old postcards. This type of historical documents presents many challenging aspects related with their automatic
analysis as images. For example, their degradation due to passing of
time or the possible overlapping of different elements in a reduced space.
Postcard layout extraction consists in segmenting in regions the various
contained information types present on these images. For the proposed
task, we have used semantic segmentation deep neural networks which
learn to classify the document image pixels into the different considered class categories in postcards (e.g., stamps, postmarks, handwritten
text or illustrations, among others). Our experiments on an annotated
dataset of 100 postcards produced respective global F1-score, Jaccard
and pixel accuracy metrics values of 0.92, 0.85 and 0.92, which endorses
the feasibility of the proposed method. Additionally, to the best of our
knowledge, this paper is one of the first investigation in this problem
applied to historical postcards.

Keywords: Document image analysis · Layout extraction · Historical
postcards · Deep learning · Semantic segmentation networks

1 Introduction

Cultural heritage includes some kind of objects (e.g., ancient documents) that
a society considers as worthy for their conservation [1]. It is actually the matter
of an increasing research and social attention worldwide.

Historical documents are old original documents providing relevant information about a person, place, or past event. The conversion of these documents,
that are originally in paper format, into their digital versions would greatly
help researchers and archivists to have an easy access to their information, to
preserve the documents against the passage of time, and also to apply them
different image processing and machine learning techniques for restoration or
transcription purposes.

With independence from the date in which they were produced, historical documents present other many challenges to their processing. These could

© Springer Nature Switzerland AG 2022
J. M. Ferrández Vicente et al. (Eds.): IWINAC 2022, LNCS 13259, pp. 346–355, 2022.
https://doi.org/10.1007/978-3-031-06527-9_34

include: paper and ink deterioration, complex document structure, bleed-through effect (from the opposite side of the page), illegible handwriting due to the writer, marginal annotations that complicate the transcription, among other difficulties [2].

Old postcards can be considered a category of historical documents that present an increasing interest for museums and for private collectors. These postcards have a historical value and they help us see what life was like at the time when they were printed (e.g., design or photographs of cities, common clothing styles, or architecture of the time).

Automatic analysis of digitized old postcard images has been relatively under-researched. Yen et al. [3] described a method to extract text characters from color postcards printed around 1930. Their proposal followed the following steps: noise preprocessing, irrelevant background removal, threshold binarization, detecting character regions and a post-processing to improve the quality of detected characters. Roc and Mello have researched the problem of restoring digital image of vintage colored postcards [4,5]. For such purpose, the authors employed combined techniques of background segmentation based on edge detection, equalization, color enhancement, and noisy spots removal. The recognition of visual scene categories from historical postcards has been studied by Grzeszick and Fink [6]. The problem has applications related with organizing and tagging postcard collections. Their method included an orientation correction preprocessing, a face detection stage and a classification ensemble based on computed features (including the detected faces). These same authors [7] have also developed a query-by-example word spotting method for grouping historical postcards using a dataset from the period of World War I. After preprocessing the images, the authors compute SIFT descriptors centered on grid image positions creating a visual vocabulary, and using manually-extracted query visual words the postcard groupings are modelled.

In this paper we describe an original method, based on semantic segmentation networks, to effectively solve the problem of layout extraction for old postcards. The paper is organized as follows. Section 2 describes the problem of layout extraction applied on digital images of historical documents. We introduce in Sect. 3 the postcard dataset used in our experiments. Next, the proposed solution based on segmentation networks is presented in Sect. 4. Section 5 shows and analyzes the experimental results achieved. Finally, Sect. 6 outlines the main conclusions of this research.

2   Layout Extraction Applied Historical Document Images

Layout analysis is considered as a fundamental task in document image analysis and understanding [8,9]. A document image is composed different physical regions or entities such as: text components, auxiliary lines, graphical elements, headings, figures, tables, and background. The process of document layout analysis aims to decompose a given document image into its component regions and understand their functional roles and relationships [10,11].

Traditional algorithms for layout analysis can be classified in main two groups depending on their approach [10]. One side, the bottom-up algorithms start with the smallest components of a document (i.e., pixels) and repeatedly group them to form larger homogeneous regions. On the other side, the top-down algorithms start with the complete document image and try to successively divide it to form consistent homogeneous regions. Each approach can work well in specific situations. In addition, one could also use a hybrid method that combines both strategies. With the advent of deep learning, many authors have addressed the problem using different deep network configurations [12]. For example, the application of one-dimensional convolutional neural networks (CNN) to segment image pages into three classes: text, image and tables, respectively [13].

Our approach to the postcard layout problem is based on the semantic segmentation of images, where the goal is to label each pixel of a test image with a predefined class of what is being represented. It is important to remark that we are not separating instances of the same class but what we seek is to predict the class of each pixel of an unknown postcard. Currently, the general document image segmentation problem is being tackled using deep architectures. A good review of deep learning techniques applied to semantic segmentation is presented by García and collaborators [14].

Historical documents presents, in general, relatively complex layouts [15]. In consequence, the employed methods for their segmentation need to be invariant to some inconsistencies in the structures (i.e., document components) and to irregularities in writing styles (i.e., skewing and slants in text lines). Additionally, these methods can also require a certain robustness level to low contrast in the image pages (e.g., faded ink in the handwritten parts). Layout extraction can also be considered as a preprocessing stage required for other related problems with historical document images (e.g., for finding the date of a given document). Different feature extractors (such as SIFT descriptors [15]) and machine learning techniques (such as SVM, MLP or GMM classifiers [16]) have been traditionally applied to solve the problem. More recently, deep learning approaches such as different types of CNNs have been employed [17,18].

To the best of our knowledge, the problem of layout extraction (or segmentation) applied to historical postcards has not been addressed in the literature. Moreover, there is also a need from annotated old postcards datasets which can be used in applications specifically related with this type of historical documents.

3   Historical Postcard Dataset

Our dataset has been created using a total of 100 public random digitized image postcards available from the Bartko Reher antiques onlineshop. For each postcard there are two images available (respectively, the front and the reverse ones); that is, a total of 200 images. The selected postcards are all circulated and they were written approximately in the historical period between 1900 and 1930. Figure 1 illustrates a sample postcard contained in our dataset. From this dataset, a 70% of the images were randomly selected to train the neural models (i.e., semantic segmentation network), a 10% for validation, and the remaining 20% of the images were used for testing, respectively. Note that inside of each three subsets there is the same number of front and reverse postcard images.

Fig. 1. Example of historical postcard from year 1900 in the dataset: (top) front side and (down) reverse side.

To create the ground truth of our dataset, the VGG Image Annotator (VIA) software, developed by the Visual Geometry Group at University of Oxford, was employed. VIA is a simple and standalone manual annotation software for image, audio and video. It runs in a web browser and does not require any installation or setup.

We define the following seven pixel categories in the postcard image layout: background (class = 0), postmark (class = 1), stamp (class = 2), handwritten text (class = 3), printed text (class = 4), auxiliary lines (class = 5), and image or drawing (class = 6), respectively. Note that the number of pixels in each class are highly unbalanced in the images (e.g., there are much more "background" pixels than "auxiliary lines" pixels).

The original spatial resolution of image postcards is a bit variable, with sizes varying between 623×406 pixels and 562×360 pixels. Each complete postcard (i.e., considering both sides) has an average size of 120KB. No pre-processing on the images was carried out, except a size normalization stage of all postcards to fit them to an input resolution of 576×384 resolution, keeping the image aspect ratio. For such purpose, the *resize* OpenCV method was used to perform bilinear interpolation.

4   Semantic Segmentation Architecture

As pointed out, the image semantic segmentation problem (i.e., layout extraction) consists in assigning a class label to each pixel in the postcard test images, such that it will produce grouping together similar parts of the image that belong to the same class. For such purpose, we have analyzed different types of semantic segmentation architectures and finally chose U-Net [19] since its trade-off between performance and inference time is better than other compared model models [20]. We also observed that it also produced very acceptable qualitative results for the tested images. U-Net is a type of encoding-decoding architecture. Another advantage of this model is that it achieves a high accuracy with small datasets (as in our case). Our solution is based on an adapted implementation to that developed by Tsopanidis et al. [21]. For the encoder part, we used a VGG16 network, without including the last two fully connected layers, and the *softmax* activation function. In this VGG16 network we employed a pre-trained model with ImageNet where the pre-trained weights were used as initial weights in the model for its training. The decoder structure is identical, with the only difference being the replacement of the max-pooling operations in the encoder stage with a 2×2 transpose convolutions in the decoder stage. The symmetrical architecture of the network allows the concatenation of the output of each encoder layer with the output of the corresponding decoder layer, before being fed to the next decoder layer [21]. Figure 2 illustrates the architecture of the U-Net network used.

To avoid overfitting during training, an early stopping technique was applied. As a result, the training process is stopped if the validation loss does not improve during 50 epochs. The hyper-paremeters values in the U-Net network training were the following ones:

- Training epochs: 100 (in average)
- Batch size: 8
- Optimizer: RMSprop
- Momentum: 0.9

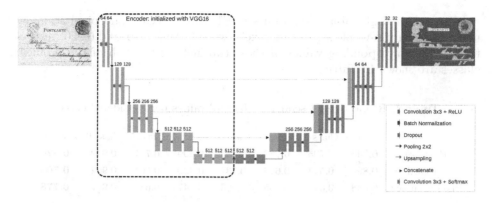

Fig. 2. U-Net architecture with encoder VGG16 used in experiments.

- Learning rate: [0.001–0.0001]
- Epsilon: $1e - 07$

5   Experimental Results

This section describes the achieved results using the whole set of pixels of 20 test postcards (i.e., 40 document images). The labels corresponding to each of these pixels have been predicted by our U-net semantic segmentation network. The total number of test pixels was 8,847,360. These were distributed in the seven considered classes as follows: 50.96% for class 0 (background), 2.19% for class 1 (postmark), 1.69% for class 2 (stamp), 9.98% for class 3 (handwritten text), 3.30% for class 4 (printed text), 2.11% for class 5 (auxiliary lines) and 29.77% for class 6 (image or drawing), respectively. Note that the numbers of test samples in classes are highly unbalanced.

To evaluate the performance of the model, and based on the number of test pixels computed as true positives (TP), false positives (FP) and false negatives (FN), the following metrics were calculated: precision (Pr), recall (Re), F1-score (F1), Jaccard (Jac) and pixel accuracy (P_{acc}), respectively.

$$Pr = \frac{TP}{TP + FP} \qquad\qquad Re = \frac{TP}{TP + FN} \tag{1}$$

$$F1 = 2\frac{Pr * Re}{Pr + Re} \qquad Jac = \frac{A \cap B}{A \cup B} \qquad P_{acc} = \frac{\sum_{i=1}^{K} p_{i,i}}{\sum_{i=1}^{K} \sum_{j=1}^{K} p_{i,j}} \tag{2}$$

where in previous equations A represents the ground truth pixels, B describes the predicted segmentation maps, K represents the total number of pixels in test images, $p_{i,i}$ are the number of correctly predicted pixels as class i, and $p_{i,j}$ are the number of pixels of class i predicted as class j, respectively.

The achieved global average values of F1-score, Jaccard and pixel accuracy metrics, using the whole set of test pixels, were: 0.939, 0.891 and 0.920, respectively. The corresponding values of these two metrics for each of the problem classes are shown in Table 1.

Table 1. Respective F1-score and Jaccard values per considered class.

	Class 0	Class 1	Class 2	Class 3	Class 4	Class 5	Class 6	**Average**
F1-score	0.944	0.705	0.762	0.849	0.809	0.721	0.949	**0.820**
Jaccard	0.893	0.544	0.616	0.737	0.680	0.564	0.902	**0.705**
Pixel accuracy	0.948	0.626	0.655	0.863	0.747	0.637	0.967	**0.778**

Table 2 shows the confusion matrix for the pixels contained in all test postcards.

Table 2. Confusion matrix corresponding to the pixel classification results into the seven classes considered for all test images.

		Predicted						
		class 0	class 1	class 2	class 3	class 4	class 5	class 6
	class 0	**0.964**	0.001	0.000	0.018	0.003	0.003	0.011
	class 1	0.061	**0.683**	0.035	0.090	0.018	0.004	0.110
	class 2	0.023	0.126	**0.723**	0.000	0.000	0.001	0.126
Actual	class 3	0.062	0.000	0.000	**0.906**	0.002	0.011	0.019
	class 4	0.071	0.010	0.002	0.064	**0.806**	0.003	0.044
	class 5	0.103	0.021	0.000	0.126	0.035	**0.713**	0.001
	class 6	0.021	0.000	0.000	0.003	0.000	0.000	**0.975**

We also illustrate in Fig. 3 the qualitative layout results produced by the semantic segmentation network for the same postcard shown by Fig. 1. Different colors have been assigned to the pixels according to their class membership in the postcard layout structure. Note that in our approach each image pixel has been labelled as belonging to only one class.

All of our algorithms were coded in Python using the OpenCV Computer Vision library and the Keras and TensorFlow high-level API for neural networks. The models were trained and tested using an Intel Xeon Processor W-2223 (4C 3.9 GHz Turbo), GPU Nvidia Quadro RTX5000 with 16 GB. Finally, the average layout extraction time per postcard (i.e., the total time to process both front and reverse postcard images) was 157 ms.

It is important to remark that the achieved experimental results are conditioned by some design decisions taken for experiments. In particular, the manual

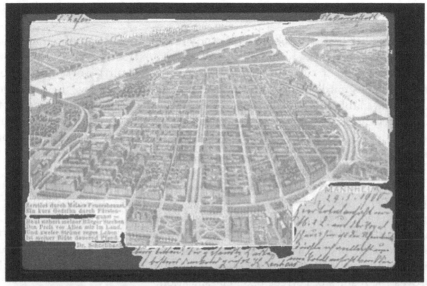

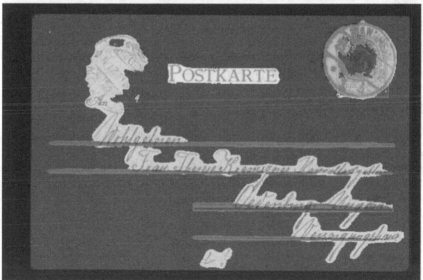

Fig. 3. Result of semantic segmentation for the example historical postcard of Fig. 1.

creation of ground truth in postcard images using the VIA annotator was performed in a simplified form. The threshold for determining TP, FP and FN pixels was set to a fixed value of 0.7. Finally, in this version of the work, each image pixel could only belong to a unique class.

6   Conclusion

This paper described an experimental study on the application of semantic segmentation deep networks to the problem of layout extraction on historical postcards. To the best of our knowledge, this paper is the first work that perform such task on postcards using deep learning. For such purpose, we used a reduced dataset of available images. The considered seven classes to be predicted for the image pixels in the semantic segmentation task are highly unbalanced, which makes the problem more difficult. Experimental results produced approximate promising global average correct pixel prediction results of 0.92, 0.85 and 0.92, respectively, for the F1-score, Jaccard and pixel accuracy metrics.

As future work, we will focus on the classes producing worse prediction results (in particular, "postmark", "stamp" and "auxiliary lines", respectively) in order to improve their detection results. Another interesting aspect consists in modifying the original problem to allow the pixels to belong to several classes at the same time (e.g., pixels that can appear as "postmark" and "stamp" simultaneously). Finally, we will define a method to automatically select a threshold that improves the results of correct pixel classification.

Acknowledgements. The authors gratefully acknowledge the support of the CYTED Network "Ibero-American Thematic Network on ICT Applications for Smart Cities" (Ref: 518RT0559), and also the financial support given by the Spanish MICINN RTI Project with reference: RTI2018-098019-B-100.

References

1. Vecco, M.: A definition of cultural heritage: from the tangible to the intangible. J. Cult. Herit. **11**(3), 321–324 (2010)
2. Philips, J.P., Tabrizi, N.: Historical document processing: a survey of techniques, tools, and trends. In: Proceeding 12th International Joint Conference on Knowledge Discovery, Knowledge Engineering and Knowledge Management (IC3K), INSTICC, Online Event (2020)
3. Yen, S.-H., Chen, M.-F., Lin, H.-J., Wang, C.-J., Liu, C.-H.: The extraction of characters on dated color postcards. In: Proceedings IEEE International Conference on Multimedia and Expo (ICME). vol 2, pp. 1415–1418. IEEE, Taipei (2004)
4. Roe, E., Mello, C.A.B.: Automatic system for restoring old color postcards. In: Proceedings International Conference on Systems. Man, and Cybernetics (SMC), pp. 451–456. IEEE, Seoul (2012)
5. Roe, E., de Mello, C.A.B.: Restoring images of ancient color postcards. Vis. Comput. **31**(5), 627–641 (2014). https://doi.org/10.1007/s00371-014-0988-4
6. Grzeszick, R., Fink, G.A.: Recognizing scene categories of historical postcards. In: Jiang, X., Hornegger, J., Koch, R. (eds.) GCPR 2014. LNCS, vol. 8753, pp. 604–615. Springer, Cham (2014). https://doi.org/10.1007/978-3-319-11752-2_50
7. Fink, G.A., Rothacker, L., Grzeszick, R.: Grouping historical postcards using query-by-example word spotting. In: Proceedings 14th Conference on Frontiers in Handwriting Recognition (ICFHW), pp. 470–475. IEEE, Crete (2014)
8. BinMakhashen, G.M., Mahmoud, S.A.: Document layout analysis: a comprehensive survey. ACM Comput. Surv. **52**(6), 109 (2019)

9. BinMakhashen, G.M., Mahmoud, S.A.: Historical document layout analysis using anisotropic diffusion and geometric features. In: J. Digit. Lib. **21**(3), 329–342 (2020). https://doi.org/10.1007/s00799-020-00280-w

10. Namboodiri, A.M., Jain, A.K.: Document structure and layout analysis. In: Chaudhuri, B.B. (ed.) Digital Document Processing. Advances in Pattern Recognition. Springer, London (2007). https://doi.org/10.1007/978-1-84628-726-8_2

11. Asi, A., Cohen, R., Kedem, K., El-Sana, J., Dinstein, I.: A coarse-to-fine approach for layout analysis of ancient manuscripts. In: Proceedings 14th Conference on Frontiers in Handwriting Recognition (ICFHR), pp. 140–145. IEEE, Crete (2014)

12. Xu, Y., Yin, F., Zhang, Z., Liu, C.-L.: Multi-task layout analysis for historical handwritten documents using fully convolutional networks. In: Proceedings of the 27th International Joint Conference on Artificial Intelligence (IJCAI), pp. 1057–1063. IJCAI, Stockholm (2018)

13. Oliveira, D.A.B., Viana, M.P.: Fast CNN-based document layout analysis. In: Proceedings IEEE International Conference on Computer Vision Workshops (ICCVW), pp. 1173–1180. IEEE, Venice (2017)

14. Garcia-Garcia, A., Orts-Escolano, S., Oprea, S., Villena-Martinez, V., Martinez-Gonzalez, P., Garcia-Rodriguez, J.: A survey on deep learning techniques for image and video semantic segmentation. Appl. Soft Comput. **70**, 41–65 (2018)

15. Garz, A., Sablatnig, R., Diem, M.: Layout analysis for historical manuscripts using sift features. In: Proceedings 11th International Conference on Document Analysis and Recognition (ICDAR), pp. 508–512. IEEE, Beijing (2011)

16. Wei, H., Baechler, M., Slimane, F., Ingold, R.: Evaluation of SVM, MLP and GMM classifiers for layout analysis of historical documents. In: Proceedings 12th International Conference on Document Analysis and Recognition (ICDAR), pp. 1220–1224. IEEE, Washington DC (2013)

17. Corbelli, A., Baraldi, L., Grana, C., Cucchiara, R.: Historical document digitization through layout analysis and deep content classification. In: Proceedings Conference Pattern Recognition (ICPR), pp. 4077–4082. IEEE, Mexico (2016)

18. Trivedi, A., Sarvadevabhatla, R.K.: HInDoLA: a unified cloud-based platform for annotation, visualization and machine learning-based layout analysis of historical manuscripts. In: Proceedings of the International Conference on Document Analysis and Recognition Workshops (ICDARW). IEEE, Sydney (2019)

19. Ronneberger, O., Fischer, P., Brox, T.: U-Net: convolutional networks for biomedical image segmentation. In: Navab, N., Hornegger, J., Wells, W.M., Frangi, A.F. (eds.) MICCAI 2015. LNCS, vol. 9351, pp. 234–241. Springer, Cham (2015). https://doi.org/10.1007/978-3-319-24574-4_28

20. Ahmed, I., Ahmad, M., Khan, F.A., Asif, M.: Comparison of deep-learning-based segmentation models: using top view person images. IEEE Access **8**, 136361–136373 (2020)

21. Tsopanidis, S., Moreno, R.H., Osovski, S.: Toward quantitative fractography using convolutional neural networks. Eng. Fract. Mech. **231**, 106992 (2020)

Detection of Unknown Defects in Semiconductor Materials from a Hybrid Deep and Machine Learning Approach

Francisco López de la Rosa[1]([⊠]), José L. Gómez-Sirvent[1], Corinna Kofler[3], Rafael Morales[1,2], and Antonio Fernández-Caballero[1,2]

[1] Universidad de Castilla-La Mancha, Instituto de Investigación en Informática (I3A), 02071 Albacete, Spain
francisco.lopezrosa@uclm.es
[2] Universidad de Castilla-La Mancha, E.T.S. Ingenieros Industriales de Albacete, 02071 Albacete, Spain
[3] KAI Kompetenzzentrum für Automobil- und Industrieelektronik GmbH, Europastrasse 8, 9524 Villach, Austria

Abstract. Artificial intelligence techniques such as deep learning and machine learning are nowadays implemented in inspection systems in a growing number of industries. These models have reached human-level performance in defect detection and classification tasks when enough data is available. However, most models use supervised learning approaches and, therefore, must have prior knowledge of the number of defect classes that may occur along the production line. This is a major problem in dynamic industries, such as the semiconductor manufacturing industry, where continuous changes in equipment and environment lead to the emergence of new classes of defects. Hence, it is necessary to detect new defect classes and classify them as "unknown" in order to study them meticulously and ensure a good quality of the manufactured semiconductor wafer. This paper presents a novel approach that fuses the ResNet50 convolutional neural network with a Gaussian mixture model for the detection of 100% of the images from the unknown defect class.

Keywords: Convolutional neural network · Gaussian mixture model · Semiconductor materials · Inspection system · Unknown defect detection

1 Introduction

Automation and digitization are enablers in many production areas [7] and thus, also in the semiconductor industry. In there, artificial intelligence is playing an increasingly important role in harnessing the full potential of existing information and knowledge. Information is available along the whole semiconductor production chain in form of many different types of data, such as documents/logs,

© Springer Nature Switzerland AG 2022
J. M. Ferrández Vicente et al. (Eds.): IWINAC 2022, LNCS 13259, pp. 356–365, 2022.
https://doi.org/10.1007/978-3-031-06527-9_35

measurements, or images. One of the image sources are defect density images captured after selected process steps. In the inspections, a laser scans the wafer surface and detects defects via the laser light scattering they cause. This laser scanning measurement provides the coordinates of detected defects on the wafer, as illustrated in Fig. 1, but does not allow drawing conclusions on their defect type. If the detected number of defects exceeds a defined limit, a specified number of these defect positions are randomly selected for a subsequent automatic microscopic inspection. Dependent on the expected defect size, either optical microscopes or scanning electron microscopes (SEM) [9] are used.

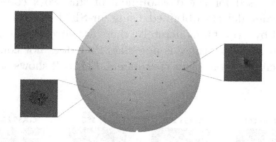

Fig. 1. SEM images from a specified number of detected defects.

Currently, experts manually classify these defect density images by having a look on each picture. This way of proceeding is costly in terms of time and resources. Further, manual classification is error prone and subjective [14,17] and therefore, should be replaced by objective automated procedures. Automated image classification by using artificial intelligence (AI) is a well-known and well performing task [1,2,8,13,18]. In particular, semiconductor defect classification tasks have been successfully carried out by applying deep learning (DL) and machine learning (ML) techniques to SEM images, typically on closed sets [4,15,22]. However, this closed set scenario does not count for semiconductor productions, which are non-stationary and change over time as new manufacturing equipment replaces old one or new products are manufactured where also new defects might appear. From today's perspective, new defects are referred to as "unknowns" in literature [3]. Using a model trained on a closed-set, would classify the unknowns into one of the predefined classes. Therefore, finding a suitable methodology that reliably detects new defects would allow manufacturers to react instantly to changes in production, thereby ensuring the delivery of reliable, high quality products.

This paper presents a hybrid DL and ML model to perform the detection of unknown defects. A commercial CNN, ResNet50, is used to compute feature vectors from the input images. These feature vectors will be used to train and tune a Gaussian mixture model (GMM) [11]. Once tuned, the GMM will determine if the defect image belongs to a "known" or the "unknown" class.

2   Materials and Methods

This section is structured in three subsections. In the first one, the original data and the unknown dataset are presented. The second one introduces the ResNet50 model and details the implementation of the model. Finally, the third subsection describes the GMM algorithm and its implementation to perform the detection of the unknown defects.

2.1   Data

The original data used for the development of this work consist of images of semiconductor wafer defects obtained using an SEM device. These data were manually labeled by experts. Concretely, there are seven different defect classes in the dataset. In addition, there is one class that does not contain any defect, which will be excluded from the experiments. Figure 2 shows samples from the different classes.

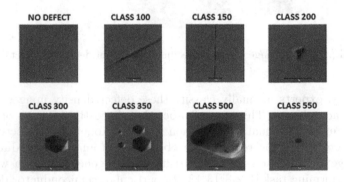

Fig. 2. Samples of the classes of defects considered.

Data preprocessing is crucial step in every work involving computer vision. The images from the original dataset have been preprocessed. First of all, images were resized to 480×480 pixels to standardize the size of all images. The images were then cropped to a size of 400×400 pixels to remove the scale bar at the bottom. Finally, data augmentation techniques based on geometric image transformations (rotation, translation, scaling and flipping) were applied to generate a sufficient number of images to resolve the huge imbalance present in the original dataset and thus allow the proposed algorithm to achieve robust results. The distribution of the dataset before and after the data augmentation is illustrated in Fig. 3, which shows that the imbalance of the original dataset is still noticeable in the augmented dataset. However, the number of images in each class is now adequate to start developing the algorithm.

In addition, a dataset of unknown images has been prepared to perform the first tests with the proposed algorithm. The dataset consists of 80 copyright-free images. The images include everyday objects, animals, plants, etc. These images have been preprocessed as the defect images were previously, adding the same background, size and color model. Some samples of images from the unknown dataset are shown in Fig. 4.

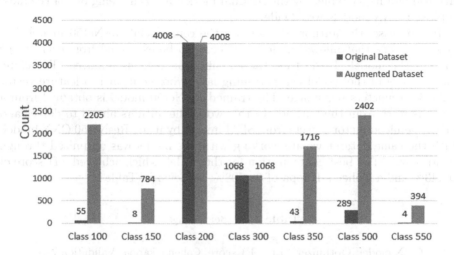

Fig. 3. Distribution of images (original and augmented datasets)

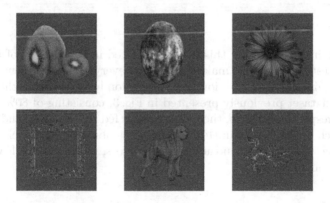

Fig. 4. "Unknown" image samples

The unknown dataset has been divided into two datasets of 40 images each. One of these datasets will be used to fine tune the GMM, while the other shall be used to assess the GMM detection of unknown defects.

2.2 ResNet50

The CNN model that has been chosen for computing the feature vector of the defect images is ResNet50 [5]. ResNet burst onto the scene back in 2015, confirming itself as a real revolution in the CNN field thanks to a novel approach based on residual blocks. These residual blocks introduce a shortcut that skips several layers [19], what allows layer to learn just a residual correction from the previous one rather than modifying the weight of all its neurons. With its depth of 50 layers, ResNet50 combines the high accuracy of such a deep network with the lightness enabled by the residual block approach, being one of the most employed CNN models worldwide.

In this case, the authors do not use the commercial ResNet50 model, but a modified one that allows the feature vector to be extracted from each image fed into the model. To do this, the classification layer is removed. Therefore, the last layer of the model is a flattening layer whose output is a feature vector of 2048 parameters per image. The trained ResNet50 model is obtained from a previous work from the authors. In this work, the authors aimed to detect and classify semiconductor defects from SEM images by using ResNet50 CNN model. With the same dataset we are working with, the model was optimized through a grid search. The best configuration for the model, which achieved a f1-score of 99.443% and a Cohen's Kappa of 98.708%, is shown in Table 1.

Table 1. Model settings.

CNN model	Optimizer	LR	F1-score	Cohen's kappa	Validation loss
ResNet50	SGD	10^{-2}	0.99443	0.98708	0.03031

The training strategy for this model consisted in taking 10% of the original images for testing purposes, making sure that every class is present in this test set. Then, training and validation sets are randomly taking from the rest of the augmented dataset previously presented in Fig. 3, consisting of 80% and 20% of the images respectively. Next, the training set is fed to the model and the feature vector of each of the images in the training set is obtained as model output. The same is done with the test and unknown datasets, obtaining the feature vector of each of their images.

2.3   GMM

In this work, GMM has been chosen to perform the detection of unknown defect classes from the feature vectors obtained with the above-mentioned CNN model. GMM is a probability density model in which each piece of data is understood as a combination of a number of Gaussian distributions [12]. GMM are commonly used as unsupervised clustering methods [16]. In this sense, these models have been used in several works dealing with semiconductor materials [6,20,21].

GMM incorporates a series of configuration parameters. Within these parameters, the most relevant are the number of components and the covariance matrix. The number of components refers to the number of clusters the model will work with. Typically, the larger the number of components, the longer it will take for the model to converge. As for the covariance matrix, it is understood as a constraint on the covariance of the different predicted classes. The most used covariance matrices are "diagonal", "tied", "spherical" and "full" [10].

The feature vectors of the different datasets that were extracted with the CNN model are the input to the GMM. First, as introduced above, the unknown dataset is divided into two sets of 40 images each. The feature vectors from the first set of images is used to fine tune the GMM using a grid search algorithm, while the second set will be used to evaluate the performance of the model. The GMM will be tuned by using a grid search algorithm. This grid search algorithm will handle two different parameters. The first is the number of components, ranging from 1 to 100, while the second is the type of covariance matrix, which can be "spherical", "full", " tied" or "diagonal".

In the training phase, the GMM is fitted to model the probability distribution of the training data (training feature vectors). Once the GMM is fitted, the likelihood of each sample of the training data is measured. In this case, the 1st percentile likelihood is used as a threshold to determine if a sample belongs to a known class. Within the known classes there are some images that present notable differences with respect to the rest of the images. Although this threshold technically introduces a 1% error in the classification, in practice it can improve the performance of the model, since it serves to clean the data. This "classification error" makes the model to classify a small percentage of known images from the test set as unknown. Another term that should be explained is the unknown error, which is the percentage of unknown images classified as known.

The GMM is trained with each of the combinations of the grid search and the mean of the so-called "classification error" and the unknown error is selected as the optimization metric. Finally, once the model is fine tuned, the feature vectors of the second set of unknown images is fed to the tuned GMM model to evaluate the results.

Figure 5 illustrates the methodology that has been explained along this section.

3   Results and Discussion

Every experiment performed in this work has been conducted with a workstation computer with the following hardware specifications: CPU Intel i7-10700KF v8 @ 3.80 GHz, 32 GB RAM, and NVIDIA GeForce RTX 2070 SUPER 8GB. Keras (https://keras.io/), Scikit Learn [10] and TensorFlow (https://www.tensorflow.org/) libraries have been used to train the models, choosing Pycharm (https://www.jetbrains.com/psycharm/) as integrated development environment (IDE) and Python 3.8 (https://www.python.org/) as the programming language.

The first experiment consists in looking for the best parameter combinations for the GMM. The feature vectors from the first set of unknown images are used to tune the model. From the parameter combinations of the grid search with which the GMM is fine tuned, there are several options that offer the same results. The only difference between them is the time the model takes to converge. Table 2 presents the combinations giving the optimal results according to the above metric (average between classification errors and unknowns) and the time taken by the model to converge. The results shown in the table correspond to mean values obtained after ten repetitions.

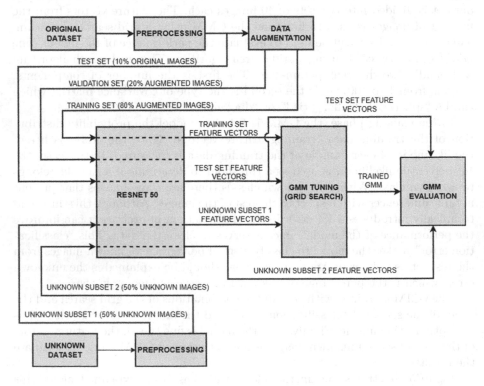

Fig. 5. Methodology.

Table 2. Optimal parameter configuration

N. Comp.	Cov. matrix	Clas. error (%)	"Unk." error (%)	Time (s)
3	Diagonal	0.1818	0	3.8389
4	Diagonal	0.1818	0	4.0690
5	**Diagonal**	**0.1818**	**0**	**3.7791**

Table 2 shows that the difference between times is negligible. However, with the aim of choosing the most efficient parameter combination, the one that requires the lowest computing time has been selected. This combination, which is highlighted in the table, uses 5 components and a "diagonal" covariance matrix, obtaining a classification error of 0.18% and a unknown error of 0%.

Once the optimal configuration has been found, the feature vectors from the second set of unknown images has been used to evaluate the GMM. Figure 6 shows the confusion matrix of the model. This confusion matrix combines the predictions of the ResNet50 model for the known classes and the prediction of the GMM for the unknown classes. It has to be mentioned that, because of the likelihood threshold, some of the images that were previously correctly classified by the CNN model are assigned to the unknown class by the GMM. That is the reason for which some of the images from a known class are classified as unknown in the confusion matrix.

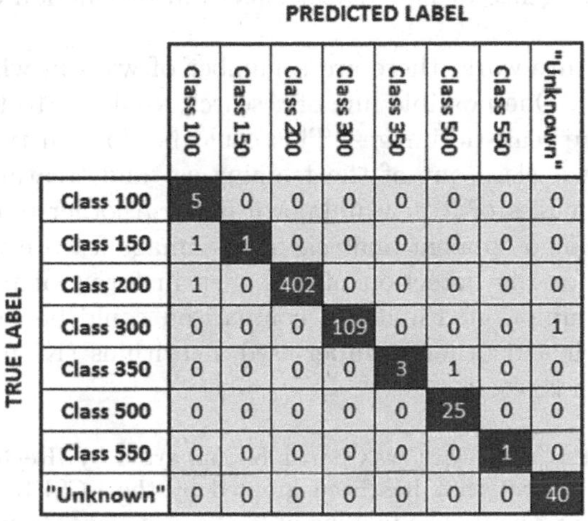

PREDICTED LABEL

	Class 100	Class 150	Class 200	Class 300	Class 350	Class 500	Class 550	"Unknown"
Class 100	5	0	0	0	0	0	0	0
Class 150	1	1	0	0	0	0	0	0
Class 200	1	0	402	0	0	0	0	0
Class 300	0	0	0	109	0	0	0	1
Class 350	0	0	0	0	3	1	0	0
Class 500	0	0	0	0	0	25	0	0
Class 550	0	0	0	0	0	0	1	0
"Unknown"	0	0	0	0	0	0	0	40

TRUE LABEL

Fig. 6. Confusion matrix of the model

The confusion matrix shows that the model is able to correctly classify as unknown every image from the unknown dataset. The 0.18% classification error that presents the model leads to a miss-classification of one image of class 300 as unknown. Nevertheless, the results are quite promising. The proposed combination of ResNet50 CNN and GMM emerges as a feasible solution for the detection of unknown defects in semiconductor materials.

4   Conclusions and Future Work

This work has studied the implementation of a hybrid DL and ML model for the detection of unknown defect classes in semiconductor materials. First, the original imbalanced dataset has been preprocessed and augmented to obtain a sufficient number of images suitable for training the proposed algorithm. The authors have also prepared a dataset consisting of 80 copyright-free unknown images, which have been preprocessed like the original images to obtain images with the same background, size and color model.

A ResNet50 model trained in a previous work by the authors is now modified and used to obtain several feature vectors. The training, test and unknown datasets are fed into the model to obtain the corresponding training, test and unknown feature vectors, which will be the input for the GMM.

Finally, the unknown dataset has been divided in two datasets of 40 images each. The first of these subsets has been used to fine tune the GMM to obtain the optimal settings, while the other one has been used for evaluation purposes. The results are really promising, being the model able to classify the 100% of the unknown dataset images as unknown. Therefore, the proposed model is suitable for the detection of unknown defects in semiconductor materials, helping to react quickly to the emergence of new defect classes in production of semiconductor wafers.

In terms of future work, there are a number of ways in which this research could be extended. One possible line of research would be to test the proposed solution with more realistic images. This could be done in two different ways: by leaving a known class out of the training set and treating it as unknown or by obtaining images of a new unknown class. Another option would be to perform a principal component analysis on the image feature vectors to find an optimal solution for the detection of unknown in terms of performance, time and resource consumption. Finally, a comparison could be made between the proposed approach and other unsupervised algorithms (K- nearest neighbors, K-means, K-medoids, etc.).

Acknowledgments. This work was partially supported by iRel40, a European co-funded innovation project that has been granted by the ECSEL Joint Undertaking (JU) (grant number 876659). The funding of the project comes from the Horizon 2020 research programme and participating countries. National funding is provided by Germany, including the Free States of Saxony and Thuringia, Austria, Belgium, Finland, France, Italy, the Netherlands, Slovakia, Spain, Sweden, and Turkey. The publication is part of grant PCI2020-112001, funded by MCIN/AEI/10.13039/501100011033 and by "NextGeneration EU"/PRTR.

References

1. Abd Al Rahman, M., Mousavi, A.: A review and analysis of automatic optical inspection and quality monitoring methods in electronics industry. IEEE Access **8**, 183192–183271 (2020)
2. Datta, S.: A review on convolutional neural networks. In: Bera, R., Pradhan, P.C., Liu, C.-M., Dhar, S., Sur, S.N. (eds.) ICCDN 2019. LNEE, vol. 662, pp. 445–452. Springer, Singapore (2020). https://doi.org/10.1007/978-981-15-4932-8_50
3. Geng, C., Huang, S.J., Chen, S.: Recent advances in open set recognition: a survey. IEEE Trans. Pattern Anal. Mach. Intell. **43**(10), 3614–3631 (2020)
4. Gómez-Sirvent, J.L., López de la Rosa, F., Sánchez-Reolid, R., Fernández-Caballero, A., Morales, R.: Optimal feature selection for defect classification in semiconductor wafers. IEEE Trans. Semiconduct. Manuf. (2022). https://doi.org/10.1109/TSM.2022.3146849

5. He, K., Zhang, X., Ren, S., Sun, J.: Deep residual learning for image recognition. arXiv preprint arXiv:1512.03385 (2015)
6. Hwang, J., Kim, H.: Variational deep clustering of wafer map patterns. IEEE Trans. Semicond. Manuf. **33**(3), 466–475 (2020)
7. Lin, J., Ma, L., Yao, Y.: A spectrum-domain instance segmentation model for casting defects. Integrat. Comput. Aided Eng. **29**, 63–82 (2022)
8. Modarres, M.H., Aversa, R., Cozzini, S., Ciancio, R., Leto, A., Brandino, G.P.: Neural network for nanoscience scanning electron microscope image recognition. Sci. Rep. **7**(1), 1–12 (2017)
9. Nakamae, K.: Electron microscopy in semiconductor inspection. Measurem. Sci. Technol. **32**(5), 052003 (2021)
10. Pedregosa, F., et al.: Scikit-learn: machine learning in python. J. Mach. Learn. Res. **12**, 2825–2830 (2011)
11. Rasmussen, C.: The infinite gaussian mixture model. Adv. Neural Inf. Process. Syst. **12** (1999)
12. Reynolds, D.A.: Gaussian mixture models. Encyclop. Biomet. **741**, 659–663 (2009)
13. López de la Rosa, F., Sánchez-Reolid, R., Gómez-Sirvent, J.L., Morales, R., Fernández-Caballero, A.: A review on machine and deep learning for semiconductor defect classification in scanning electron microscope images. Appl. Sci. **11**(20), 9508 (2021)
14. Smith, B.: Six-sigma design (quality control). IEEE Spectrum **30**(9), 43–47 (1993)
15. Su, C.T., Yang, T., Ke, C.M.: A neural-network approach for semiconductor wafer post-sawing inspection. IEEE Trans. Semiconduct. Manuf. **15**(2), 260–266 (2002)
16. Wang, J., Jiang, J.: Unsupervised deep clustering via adaptive GMM modeling and optimization. Neurocomputing **433**, 199–211 (2021)
17. Wang, M.J., Huang, C.L.: Evaluating the eye fatigue problem in wafer inspection. IEEE Trans. Semiconduct. Manuf. **17**(3), 444–447 (2004)
18. Wang, P., et al.: The study of defects auto-classification system in semiconductor manufacturing. In: 2020 China Semiconductor Technology International Conference (CSTIC), pp. 1–3. IEEE (2020)
19. Yu, H., Yang, L.T., Zhang, Q., Armstrong, D., Deen, M.J.: Convolutional neural networks for medical image analysis: state-of-the-art, comparisons, improvement and perspectives. Neurocomputing **444**, 92–110 (2021)
20. Yu, J.: Fault detection using principal components-based gaussian mixture model for semiconductor manufacturing processes. IEEE Trans. Semiconduct. Manuf. **24**(3), 432–444 (2011)
21. Yu, J.: Semiconductor manufacturing process monitoring using gaussian mixture model and bayesian method with local and nonlocal information. IEEE Trans. Semiconduct. Manuf. **25**(3), 480–493 (2012)
22. Yuan-Fu, Y., Min, S.: Double feature extraction method for wafer map classification based on convolution neural network. In: 2020 31st Annual SEMI Advanced Semiconductor Manufacturing Conference (ASMC), pp. 1–6. IEEE (2020)

Using Temporal Information in Deep Learning Architectures to Improve Lane Detection Under Adverse Situations

D. Turrado⬚, J. Koloda⬚, and M. Rincón$^{(\boxtimes)}$⬚

Artificial Intelligence Department, UNED, Madrid, Spain
dturrado2@alumno.uned.es,diego.turradoblanco@avl.com, jan@gini.net,
mrincon@dia.uned.es
http://www.ia.uned.es

Abstract. One of the fundamental challenges in the field of autonomous driving is the ability to detect dynamic objects, such as vehicles or pedestrians, and statics ones, such as lanes, in the surroundings of the vehicle. The accurate perception of the environment under the long tale of driving scenarios is crucial for a safe decision making and motion planning.

Mainly, lane detection approaches still function on single-frame basis and do not exploit the (high) temporal correlation of the signals representing the perceived environment. Single-frame detection networks might work well under circumstances where the lanes are perfectly visible, but show a lack of performance under certain situations, like occlusions, shadows, rain, snow, lane degradation, etc. To address the aforementioned problem, this work proves how adding temporal information for lane binary segmentation improves substantially the performance of single-frame architecture under challenging and adverse situations.

Keywords: Lane detection · Recurrent neuronal networks · Adverse situations

1 Introduction

In recent years, the development of computer vision (i.e. new deep learning architectures), sensor technology (i.e. LIDAR) and processors units (i.e. GPU) has made big advances in the field of autonomous driving possible. The ultimate goal of many of these researches is to have a full picture of the environment around the vehicle, detecting dynamic objects such as vehicles or pedestrians, and statics ones such as lanes, and having a semantic understanding of the surroundings which allows a proper motion planning. One of the key and at the same time basic features needed to enable autonomous driving is camera based lane detection. Once the lanes are detected, the vehicle can have a reference to position itself in the surrounding world, so the trajectory planning can calculate where to go, reducing the possibility of collision with vehicles driving in other lanes [4]. Therefore designing robust camera-based real-time lane detection systems is

© Springer Nature Switzerland AG 2022
J. M. Ferrández Vicente et al. (Eds.): IWINAC 2022, LNCS 13259, pp. 366–373, 2022.
https://doi.org/10.1007/978-3-031-06527-9_36

a key milestone for autonomous vehicles (AD) and advanced driver-assistance systems (ADAS).

Most of these systems are based on the information contained in one single frame, and just a few of them take advantage of the information contained in previous frames [6]. This, of course, is not like human drivers work, being able to extrapolate and infer the position of the lanes under challenging situations, like shadows, light reflections, lane occlusion, etc. referring to the information of the past. This can be done because lanes are static, continuous objects on the street, with a huge overlapping between frames, meaning a highly related and temporal correlation of the signals. So the lanes in the actual frame could be partially inferred from the information in the n-last frames, even though the lanes might not be totally visible anymore.

Under those circumstances the performance of the state of-the-art methods decreases, detecting the lanes erroneously, in another direction, or even not detecting it at all like in Fig. 1. The reason might be that with the information contained in the actual frame, is very difficult or even impossible to completely infer the position of all lanes. Due to the fact that modern systems have to work under really variable driving scenarios, working under all possible conditions is crucial to develop robust algorithms. This work shows how including temporal information can dramatically increase the performance of a network under challenging situations.

Fig. 1. Lane detection using LaneNet [6] under driving scenarios with shadows, light reflections and lane occlusions from the TuSimple dataset. Green lanes represent the ground truth and red, the ones inferred by the network.

Therefore, the main hypothesis that tries to prove this work is that the use of recurrent neuronal networks (or, in a more general way, the use of temporal information) improves the performance of neuronal networks under challenging and adverse situations.

2 Methodology

To prove this hypothesis we have selected a state-of-the-art neuronal network, LaneNet [5]. LaneNet is a real time lane detection architecture where the lane edge network is based on a light weight encoder/decoder. To reduce computational cost the encoder is based on the combination of depthwise separable convolutions and pointwise convolutions (1×1 convolutions). On the other hand, to recover input image resolution the decoder is based on sub-pixel convolution layers.

Without modifying this enconder/decoder structure we have incorporated a recurrent neuronal network similar as proposed in [6]. This architecture can therefore be understood as a fully convolutional neuronal network with a recurrent intermediate step to process time information. The encoder abstracts n-input images to n-feature maps which can be seen as time sequence information and be fed into the recurrent neuronal network. These feature maps contain the necessary information to detect the lanes and keep the time related information but have the advantage of its reduced size, which means that they can be handled well by the long short-term memory layers. The output of the ConvLSTM [2] is used as input to the convolutional neuronal network decoder which outputs an array of the same size as the input image containing the probability of each pixel belonging to a lane or not. The complete architecture is shown in Fig. 2.

This idea allows us to compare the same basic encoder/decoder network with just the influence of the recurrent neuronal network gathering temporal information.

3 Training

3.1 Dataset

The TuSimple dataset [1] is used for training and validation. It contains 6408 video clips (3626 for training and 2782 for testing) taken at different daytime and traffic conditions on US highways, under good and medium weather situations. Each video clip is a set of 20 frames with until 5 lanes, where just the last frame is labeled, and with a resolution of 1280×720.

The annotation of each lane is done using polylines, defined by the intersection points between evenly horizontal distributed lines and each lane. On the other hand, because the proposed architecture is conceived to work at pixel level, classifying each one as lane or not lane (binary segmentation). Therefore, using these polylines as basis, ground truth frames have been generated where each pixel belongs to the class 0 (background) or 1 (lane). To do so, each lane has been segmented with a width of 5 pixels.

Since the proposed deep learning architecture is designed to work at pixel level, classifying each pixel as lane or non-lane (binary segmentation), these polylines have been used as a basis to generate a ground truth in which each pixel belongs to class 0 (background) or 1 (lane). For this purpose, each lane has been segmented with a width of 5 pixels.

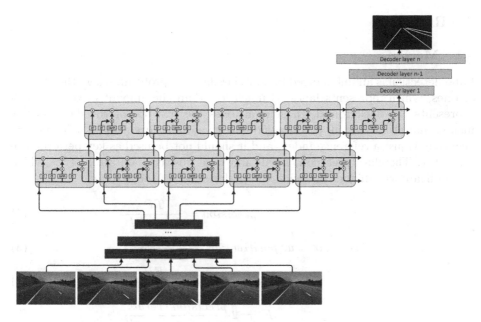

Fig. 2. Network architecture for the special case of 5 frames and ConvLSTM with 2 layers. The basic idea of this architecture for lane detection was proposed in [6], however the encoder/decoder has been adapted to match LaneNet structure.

Table 1. Characteristic of TuSimple dataset [1]. *Just the frame 20th is labeled.

Dataset	Train clips	Test clips	Frames per clip*	Resolution	Lanes
TuSimple	3626	2782	20	1280×720	≤ 5

3.2 Data Augmentation

In order to avoid over-fitting problems and increase performance, data augmentation has been used to train all models. Brightness shifting, gamma correction, adding small amount of noise and random horizontal flip and translation has been implemented.

3.3 Loss and Optimizer

To train the proposed model a binary cross entropy loss function and an ADAM optimizer with a learning rate of 3e-4 has been used. The number of epochs is 500 with a batch size of 15 and 6 for LaneNet and LaneNet-ConvLSTM respectively.

$$binary\ cross\ entropy = \sum_{i=1}^{n} y_i * log(\hat{y}_i) + (1 - y_i) * log(1 - \hat{y}_i) \qquad (1)$$

where y_i is the ground truth value and $\hat{y}_i$ the predicted one.

4   Results

4.1   Metrics

Lane detection is an imbalanced binary classification problem, where the amount of ones, which represents lanes, is much less than the amount of zeros, which represents the background. In general, ones are just 4% of the dataset, this means that classifying all pixels as no-lane gives an accuracy of 96%. Therefore, accuracy is just a reference index, and it should not be used as key performance indicator. Therefore precision, recall and false positive rate are metrics which can indicate with higher precision the performance of the system:

$$precision = \frac{TP}{TP + FP} \tag{2}$$

$$recall\ or\ true\ positive\ rate = \frac{TP}{TP + FN} \tag{3}$$

$$false\ positive\ rate = \frac{FP}{FP + TN} \tag{4}$$

$$F1 = 2\frac{precision \cdot recall}{precision + recall} \tag{5}$$

where TP stands for true positive, TN for true negative, FP for false positive and FN for false negative. Evaluating these metrics under different thresholds, ROC (receiver operating characteristic curve) and PRC (precision recall curve) can be generated. These curves offer the advantage of analyzing the complete classifier behavior instead of selecting an arbitrary threshold, and therefore give a better idea of the overall network performance.

4.2   Performance

The performance of the networks have been analyzed using two different datasets. The first one containing the whole TuSimple validation dataset, so mostly ideal conditions (without occlusions, shadows, etc.). The second one containing exclusively the subset of the original TuSimple validation dataset with challenging situations, adding a further step of complexity to the inference.

Performance Under General Situations: in Table 2, the results for the two different architectures in terms of area under receiver operating characteristic curve, area under precision recall curve, maximum accuracy and its associate F1 are presented. These metrics are the average of five training runs to be able to make better statistical conclusions.

Table 2. Area under ROC (receiver operating characteristic curve), under PRC (precision recall curve), maximum accuracy and its corresponding F1 for the compared state-of-the-art networks.

Network	AUROC	AUPRC	Accuracy	F1
LaneNet	**99.276**	87.616	98.291	78.832
LaneNet-ConvLSTM	99.274	**87.685**	**98.300**	**78.965**

Although, it seems that LaneNet-ConvLSTM outperforms LaneNet in most of the metrics, their performance is quite similar and applying the Student's t-test with 5% significance level revels that there is no statistical difference between both (the p-value for the null hyphotesis $H_0 : \mu_1 = \mu_2$ is 0.40517).

Performance Under Challenging Situations: one important point of this analysis is that the TuSimple dataset has been taken mostly under favorable conditions, with no shadows, no lane occlusions, etc. On the other hand, the discussed methods should outperform single-frame detection algorithms specially under challenging situations, therefore the proposed metrics have been recalculated just for these situations (to do so a manual classification of the validation set has been done). The results of this analysis are presented in Table 3 and show that multi-frame detection algorithms clearly outperform single-frame ones under challenging situations.

Table 3. Area under ROC (receiver operating characteristic curve), under PRC (precision recall curve), maximum accuracy and its corresponding F1 for the compared state-of-the-art networks for only the challenging situations contained in the TuSimple validation set.

Network	AUC-ROC	AUC-PRC	Accuracy	F1
LaneNet	96.487	67.234	96.724	57.437
LaneNet-ConvLSTM	**97.282**	**70.445**	**96.877**	**60.943**

Semantic segmentation architectures should work robustly at a coarse level, identifying the total number of lanes correctly, and at a fine level, detecting solid and robust lanes with a high overlapping with the ground truth. With theses two requirements in mind, the experimental results show visually that ,in general , multi-frame architectures outperform single-frame ones under adverse situations. Figure 3 shows three examples of the predictions of the above mentioned architectures (LaneNet and LaneNet-ConvLSTM) under challenging situations.

Fig. 3. Three examples of images in challenging situations. Top row: LaneNet. Bottom row: LaneNet-ConvLSTM. Green indicates ground truth and red indicates inference.

Multi-frame architectures show a more robust behavior, inferring more solid and robust lanes specially when the contrast is changing rapidly (e.g. entrance of a tunnel). Under these challenging situations, they also show higher capabilities on detecting the lines of the neighboring lanes. The proposed LaneNet-ConvLSTM architecture is also even able to correctly infer complex side lines, which are not in the ground truth, decreasing erroneously the quantitative performance.

5   Conclusions

One key conclusion is that most of the well established datasets in the field of autonomous driving just consider "ideal" conditions, and although two different architectures could show similar performance under those, the long tale influence has to definitely be taken into account. In the analyzed case, the performance of single-frame networks drops more abruptly than multi-frame architectures under challenging situations, leading to the conclusion that temporal information helps under these adverse situations and validating the initial hypothesis.

In future works, the ConvLSTM can be replaced by other types of architectures like transformers [3], which have outperformed RNN in recent years. Another important aspect is that in this work we have focused on 2D segmentation, but this information has to be transformed to 3D in order to be used for motion planning. The use of temporal information for this conversion might be also investigated in further projects.

References

1. https://github.com/TuSimple/tusimple-benchmark/tree/master/doc/lane_detection. Accessed 15 Mar 2022
2. Shi, X., et al.: Convolutional LSTM Network: A Machine Learning Approach for Precipitation Nowcasting. arXiv preprint arXiv:1506.04214 (2015)

3. Vaswani, A., et al.: Attention Is All You Need. arXiv prreprint arXiv:1706.03762 (2017)
4. Wang, W., et al.: A learning-based approach for lane departure warning systems with a personalized driver model. IEEE Trans. Vehicul. Technol. **67**(10), 9145–9157 (2018). https://doi.org/10.1109/TVT.2018.2854406
5. Wang, Z., Ren, W., Qiu, Q.: LaneNet: Real-Time Lane Detec- tion Networks for Autonomous Driving. arXiv preprint arXiv:1807.01726 (2018)
6. Zou, Q., et al.: Robust Lane Detection from Continuous Driving Scenes Using Deep Neural Networks. arXiv preprint arXiv:1903.02193 (2019)

Improvement of Fixation Elements Detection in Aircraft Manufacturing

Leandro Ruiz[1,2], Sebastián Díaz[2], José M. González[2], and Francisco Cavas[3]

[1] Doctorate Program in Industrial Technologies, International School of Doctorate, Technical University of Cartagena, 30202 Cartagena, Spain
leandro.ruiz@mtorres.com
[2] Innovation Division, MTorres Diseños Industriales SAU, Ctra. El Estrecho-Lobosillo, Km 2, Fuente Álamo, 30320 Murcia, Spain
[3] Structures, Construction and Graphical Expression, Technical University of Cartagena, 30202 Cartagena, Spain
francisco.cavas@upct.es

Abstract. The requirements for accuracy and reliability in the manufacturing processes of large aircraft structures are among the most demanding in the industry due to the continuous development of advanced manufacturing processes with tight tolerances and high requirements for process integrity. The main technique for the operation of many of these processes is the detection and precise measurement of fasteners by artificial vision systems in real time, however these systems require adjustment of multiple parameters and do not work correctly in uncontrolled scenarios, which require intervention operations such as manual supervision of the measurement process, leading into a reduction in the autonomy of automated systems.

In this study, a new Deep Learning algorithm based on a Single Shot Detector neural network is proposed for the detection and measurement drills and other fixation elements (such as rivets and temporary fasteners) in an uncontrolled industrial manufacturing environment. The convergence of the new network has been optimized for the detection of elements of a circular nature, instead of the generic anchor boxes usually used. In addition, a fine-tuning algorithm based on a new characterization parameter of the circular geometry is applied to the results obtained from the network. This new metric has made it possible to define a quality parameter with respect to the measurement made.

Keywords: advanced manufacturing · industry 4.0 · neural networks · computer vision

1 Introduction

In recent years the aeronautical sector has undergone a profound transformation of its products and processes of high added value within the framework of environmental sustainability, industry 4.0 and the competitiveness of markets [17].

© Springer Nature Switzerland AG 2022
J. M. Ferrández Vicente et al. (Eds.): IWINAC 2022, LNCS 13259, pp. 374–382, 2022.
https://doi.org/10.1007/978-3-031-06527-9_37

The aeronautical industry has traditionally been conservative about process automation, due to the existence of particular challenges to be addressed, such as the size of an aircraft that is a unique factor in this type of industry or that of large parts that often require simultaneous work by operators and robots. In this scenario, these large dimensions in turn involve robots or machinery with a high spatial mobility to be able to work on the whole of the aircraft part, all while maintaining the high precision characteristics of this type of industry [8].

The recent advances in automation in the framework of Industry 4.0 [2–4,8,13] allow to address these challenges, allowing a greater automation of the manufacturing processes, the increase of production because of the uninterrupted operation of the automated processes, and improved process quality control by reducing the scope for potential human error and early identification of potential problems.

One of the most important phases of aeronautical manufacturing processes is the correct identification and positioning of the part to be machined (drilling or riveting) within the work volume of the machine, Therefore, it is necessary that the machine can detect and measure the actual position of the part to be able to adjust the CNC program [8].

Machine vision systems are widely used as a reference system in industrial manufacturing processes [1,5,6,13,18,20], and specifically in the aeronautical sector they are used for verification [13], metrology [3] and quality analysis [6,20], however, their use remains a challenge due to the high demands in terms of machining performance required by this type of industry. These high manufacturing precisions require a correct detection and measurement of the elements in uncontrolled industrial scenarios, with changing lighting, shadows, chips, etc., therefore could lose reliability as the captured scenes vary. Likewise, the casuistry of the fixing elements to be detected is quite wide, distinguishing between drills, blind drills, countersinks, rivets of different types, temporary fasteners, etc. In these situations, two possible scenarios of malfunction can be given:

The system is unable to correctly detect the drill. In these cases, the image is presented to the machine operator to manually select the correct position of the drill. This is a situation in which the productivity of the machine is severely impacted, punctually interrupting the overall flow of the process.

The system erroneously identifies any intruding object as a reference element. This failure in detection can lead to incorrect positioning of the part, or to out-of-position drilling.

In both cases these errors cause a serious economic impact on the manufacturing process, since in many cases it is necessary to repair or even dispose of the corresponding part [1].

One solution to this problem is the use of machine learning (ML) algorithms that are known to detect the underlying patterns in the data without requiring explicit instructions in their programming. In the scientific literature there are multiple examples of systems capable of understanding or emulating human responses such as natural language processing or vision [16]. Since the introduction of the so-called convolutional neural networks (CNN) these systems have shown great potential in artificial vision tasks, in tasks such as segmentation, classification and detection of images [1,2,13]. In addition, the introduction of deep learning algorithms based on convolutional neural networks is expected to improve the reliability of the machine vision systems currently used, reducing both the need for manual intervention and the rate of incorrect measurements, and thus increasing the productivity of the manufacturing process while reducing its costs.

The objective of this research work is to design and validate a CNN network with which to detect and classify the different mechanical fasteners present in an aeronautical manufacturing process in an uncontrolled industrial scenario.

2   Materials and Methods

2.1   Dataset

The experiments carried out have employed a set of images obtained from several manufacturing and assembly machines of aircraft components, with different lighting conditions and scene complexity. Out of focus, erroneous images and those that do not contain any detectable element have been discarded from this set. Figure 1 shows some examples of this dataset, in which images from drilling and riveting machines predominate.

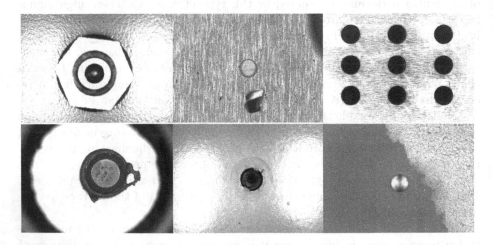

Fig. 1. Sample of images from the dataset

Image Processing and Labelling. The elements present in the images have been categorized into 8 classes: Drill, Countersink, Rivet, Protruding Rivet, Temporary Fastener 1, Temporary Fastener 2, Hexagonal and Screws. The prevalence of elements in each category is different, being the Drill category the most abundant.

The labeling of images has been carried out semi-automatically, using an algorithm for potential region proposal based on connected region labeling (blobs), which have then been classified by a neural network [19]. Finally, this proposed labeling has been validated by experts to correct identification errors.

2.2 Proposed Approach

For the development of the detection neural network, several state-of-the-art architectures have been evaluated [11], such as R-CNN, SSD and RetinaNet, finally developing an architecture based on SSD networks [15], using a very lightweight backbone, with only 7 layers, inspired by MobileNet architectures [9]. The location of the elements will be carried out through values relative to the anchor boxes (represented in Fig. 2). Since the elements to be detected will always be of circular nature, their size is characterized using only the value of their height h, and therefore simplifying the network.

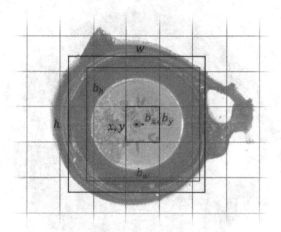

Fig. 2. Element true bounding box relative to the nearest anchor box

The structure of the neural network can be divided into 3 sections:

- An input layer, where a normalization of the image is carried out, which maps it into the interval $v \in [-1, 1]$. The configured image size is 480×343 px.
- Next, the data passes through a convolutional section (network backbone), composed of 7 convolutional blocks, which use Batch Normalization [10] and ELU activation signal.
- Finally, feature maps are extracted from the last 4 convolutional blocks, which information is fed into the prediction section, which contains convolutional blocks for both category and location prediction.

In this work, it has been decided to train the network using the Focal Loss function (with parameters $\alpha = 0.25$ and $\gamma = 2$) [14] instead of Hard Mining scheme, due to its better management of the imbalance in the number of "positive" cases (element detection) and "negative" cases, much more abundant.

Measurement of the Fixation Elements. For the accurate adjustment of the center and diameter of the referencing elements (of a circular nature), a detection and optimization algorithm has been designed, called Spoke.

The algorithm starts from the circle proposed by the detection neural network (Fig. 3), on which a set of radii (or spokes) is defined and the values of the image over them are analyzed. These profiles are analyzed in search for the point of greatest contrast.

Fig. 3. Accurate measurement algorithm "spoke"

A least squares fit is performed on the detected points in order to obtain the circle that best models said set of points [7]. Using the new adjusted circle as starting point, a new iteration of the algorithm is executed, in which the search area is restricted by shortening the length of the evaluation radii. This process is repeated until the mean squared error of the fit is less than a set threshold.

2.3 Experimental Setup

A total of 24k images has been used, which have been randomized and divided into training and validation sets following a proportion of 85%–15%. Various data augmentation transformations have been randomly applied to the set of images for training:

- Horizontal and vertical symmetry and 180° rotation
- Image scaling and translation
- Brightness and contrast transformations.

The model has been trained with Tensorflow 2 and Keras, using an Adam optimizer [12], during 400 epochs of 100 iterations each. Said training has been executed on a PC with 32GB of RAM and a GTX1070Ti model GPU.

Quality Parameter for Result Evaluation. For the evaluation of the neural network performance when it comes to correctly measuring the detected elements location, an *ad hoc* metric has been designed, which allows to assign a score in the interval [0, 1] according to the quality of the detection made. To achieve this, two dimensionless error values are calculated for each detected element, taking into account center and diameter deviation, respectively:

$$\epsilon_c = \frac{\sqrt{(x - x_0)^2 + (y - y_0)^2}}{d_0}$$

$$\epsilon_d = \frac{|d - d_0|}{d_0}$$

Finally, the detection quality parameter is defined from the expression

$$Q = q_c \cdot q_d = e^{-a\epsilon_c} \cdot e^{-b\epsilon_d}$$

where the coefficients take the values $a = 3$ and $b = 2$. Quality parameter values are shown in Table 1 for several sizes and deviations.

Table 1. Location and diameter quality factors: q_c (left) and q_d (right)

Error (mm)	Diameter (mm)				Error (mm)	Diameter (mm)			
	4	6	8	10		4	6	8	10
0.01	99%	100%	100%	100%	0.01	100%	100%	100%	100%
0.02	99%	99%	99%	99%	0.02	99%	99%	100%	100%
0.05	96%	98%	98%	99%	0.05	98%	98%	99%	99%
0.1	93%	95%	96%	97%	0.1	95%	97%	98%	98%
0.2	86%	90%	93%	94%	0.2	90%	94%	95%	96%
0.5	69%	78%	83%	86%	0.5	78%	85%	88%	90%
1	47%	61%	69%	74%	1	61%	72%	78%	82%

In both cases, 3 categories have been defined for the quality of the detected elements: Very good ($q > 97.5\%$), medium (95%) and poor ($q < 95\%$). Considering the product of both values, the corresponding ranges for the quality parameter can be estimated: Very good ($q > 95\%$), medium (90%) and poor ($q < 90\%$).

3 Results

Network performance has been evaluated for different detection thresholds. Specifically, the maximum F1-value is reached for a threshold of 0.60. However, for this application, given the greater seriousness of a false positive in detection (which could lead to erroneous drilling of the part) compared to false negatives, a higher detection threshold of 0.70 is selected. With this configuration the false positive and negative rates are 0.45% and 2.78% respectively.

On the other hand, the quality factor for location and diameter measurement has been also evaluated, both for the raw output of the network and after the refinement achieved by the Spoke algorithm (Table 2).

Table 2. Quality parameter values for validation images

	Center (q_c)	Diameter (q_d)	Global (Q)
Network raw output	92.7%	94.0%	87.3%
Spoke refinement	98.4%	97.4%	96.0%

Finally, some neural network detection examples are shown in Fig. 4.

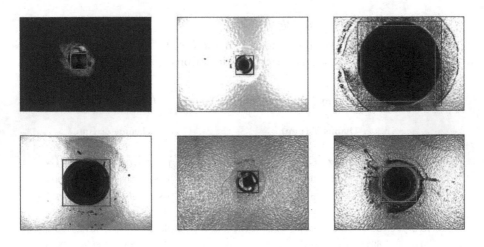

Fig. 4. Referencing elements detection sample

4   Discussion and Conclusions

With the chosen configuration, with a global false positive and negative rates of 0.45% and 2.78% respectively, the classification rates are also very high, exceeding 90% in all categories. The accuracy of the system in terms of element location yields an average quality factor of 98.4% in location and 97.4% in diameter measurement, equivalent to errors of 0.04 mm and 0.11 mm (for an 8mm diameter element) respectively, sufficiently accurate for the manufacturing processes mentioned. With this configuration, it is observed that the prediction of an image takes the system about 4.5 ms, while the execution of the Spoke algorithm requires 24 ms.

A novel system has been developed for the accurate detection and measurement of reference elements in industrial environments of aeronautical manufacturing processes, thus improving the reliability of inspection processes compared to conventional systems: on one hand, the need for manual interventions is reduced, and on the other hand the number of erroneous operations is reduced. The developed system has been integrated into a real production environment, with a rate of manual intervention by operators of 13.3% (due to detection errors of the previous algorithm, based on detection and filtering through blobs), achieving a drastic reduction of errors and reaching a new rate of manual interventions of only 0.6%.

Funding. This publication has been carried out in the framework of the Project "Nuevas Uniones de estructuras aeronáuticas" reference number IDI-20180754. This Project has been supported by the Spanish Ministry of Ciencia e Innovación and Centre for Industrial Technological Development (CDTI).

References

1. Bauer, J., Bas, G., Durakbasa, N., Kopacek, P.: Development trends in automation and metrology. IFAC-PapersOnLine **48**(24), 168–172 (2015)
2. Bevilacqua, M.G., Caroti, G., Piemonte, A., Terranova, A.A.: Digital technology and mechatronic systems for the architectural 3D metric survey. In: Ottaviano, E., Pelliccio, A., Gattulli, V. (eds.) Mechatronics for Cultural Heritage and Civil Engineering. ISCASE, vol. 92, pp. 161–180. Springer, Cham (2018). https://doi.org/10.1007/978-3-319-68646-2_7
3. Carmignato, S., De Chiffre, L., Bosse, H., Leach, R., Balsamo, A., Estler, W.: Dimensional artefacts to achieve metrological traceability in advanced manufacturing. CIRP Annal. **69**(2), 693–716 (2020)
4. Cavas-Martinez, F., Fernandez-Pacheco, D.G.: Virtual simulation: a technology to boost innovation and competitiveness in industry (2019)
5. Conesa, J., Cavas-Martínez, F., Fernández-Pacheco, D.G.: An agent-based paradigm for detecting and acting on vehicles driving in the opposite direction on highways. Exp. Syst. Appl. **40**(13), 5113–5124 (2013)
6. Elgeneidy, K., Al-Yacoub, A., Usman, Z., Lohse, N., Jackson, M., Wright, I.: Towards an automated masking process: a model-based approach. Proc. Inst. Mech. Eng. Part B: J. Eng. Manuf. **233**(9), 1923–1933 (2019)

7. Ghilani, C.D.: Adjustment Computations: Spatial Data Analysis. Wiley, New York (2017)
8. Gramegna, N., Bonollo, F., Della Corte, E., Grosselle, F., Cocco, M.: Innovative and integrated technologies for the development of aeronautic components (2010)
9. Howard, A.G., et al.: Mobilenets: efficient convolutional neural networks for mobile vision applications. arXiv preprint arXiv:1704.04861 (2017)
10. Ioffe, S., Szegedy, C.: Batch normalization: accelerating deep network training by reducing internal covariate shift. In: International Conference on Machine Learning, pp. 448–456. PMLR (2012)
11. Jiao, L., Zhang, F., Liu, F., Yang, S., Li, L., Feng, Z., Qu, R.: A survey of deep learning-based object detection. IEEE Access **7**, 128837–128868 (2019). https://doi.org/10.1109/ACCESS.2019.2939201
12. Kingma, D.P., Ba, J.: Adam: a method for stochastic optimization. arXiv preprint arXiv:1412.6980 (2014)
13. Kupke, M., Gerngross, T.: Production technology in aeronautics: upscaling technologies from lab to shop floor (2018)
14. Lin, T.Y., Goyal, P., Girshick, R., He, K., Dollár, P.: Focal loss for dense object detection. In: Proceedings of the IEEE International Conference on Computer Vision, pp. 2980–2988 (2013)
15. Liu, W., et al.: SSD: single shot multiBox detector. In: Leibe, B., Matas, J., Sebe, N., Welling, M. (eds.) ECCV 2016. LNCS, vol. 9905, pp. 21–37. Springer, Cham (2016). https://doi.org/10.1007/978-3-319-46448-0_2
16. Lozano, R., Leandro: Detección y clasificación de elementos de fijación aeronáutica mediante técnicas de machine learning (2021). https://doi.org/10.31428/10317/9465
17. Maria Fernanda Barbato, S., Carlos Henrique Pereira, M., Eduardo Gomes, S.: Prioritization of product-service business model elements at aerospace industry using analytical hierarchy process. Acta Scientiarum. Technology **41**(1) (2019). https://doi.org/10.4025/actascitechnol.v41i1.37934, https://periodicos.uem.br/ojs/index.php/ActaSciTechnol/article/view/37934
18. Rocha, L., Bills, P., Marxer, M., Savio, E.: Training in the aeronautic industry for geometrical quality control and large scale metrology. In: Majstorovic, V.D., Durakbasa, N. (eds.) IMEKOTC14 2019. LNME, pp. 162–169. Springer, Cham (2019). https://doi.org/10.1007/978-3-030-18177-2_16
19. Ruiz, L., Torres, M., Gómez, A., Díaz, S., González, J.M., Cavas, F.: Detection and classification of aircraft fixation elements during manufacturing processes using a convolutional neural network. Appl. Sci. **10**(19) (2020). https://doi.org/10.3390/app10196856
20. Wang, Z., Zhou, Y., Li, G.: Anomaly detection for machinery by using big data real-time processing and clustering technique. In: Proceedings of the 2019 3rd International Conference on Big Data Research, pp. 30–36

A New Artificial Intelligence Approach for the Radiographic Classification of Sacroiliitis

Esther Fernandez[1], Javier Garrigos[2], Jose Javier Martinez[2], Irene Cases[3], Manuel Jose Moreno[1], Luis Francisco Linares[1], Angel García[4], Jose Manuel Ferrandez[2(✉)], and Eduardo Fernández[5,6] (iD)

[1] Division of Rheumatology, Virgen de la Arrixaca, University Clinical Hospital, Murcia, Spain
[2] Department of Electronics, Computer Architecture and Projects, Technical University of Cartagena, Murcia, Spain
jm.ferrandez@upct.es
[3] Division of Radiology, Virgen de la Arrixaca, University Clinical Hospital, Murcia, Spain
[4] Division of Rheumatology, University Hospital Torrevieja, Alicante, Spain
[5] Bioengineering Institute, Universidad Miguel Hernandez, Elche, Spain
e.fernandez@umh.es
[6] CIBER Research Center on Bioengineering, Biomaterials and Nanomedicine (CIBER BBN), Madrid, Spain

Abstract. Radiographs of the sacroiliac joints are commonly used as the first imaging methods for the diagnosis of Sacroileitis in patients with back pain. This study aims to develop and validate a new artificial intelligence approach for the automatic classification of the grade of sacroiliitis on conventional radiographs. We included a total of 267 patients with chronic back pain and clinical suggestion of Axial Spondyloarthritis who presented in a specialized center. Radiographs of sacroiliac joints were evaluated by 3 rheumatologists and 1 radiologist according to the modified New York criteria. For training the network, labeled sacroiliac joints images were resized and then several artificial neural networks were tested. Better results were achieved using the CNN-XGBoost architecture, which provided good generalizability and a high specificity with acceptable sensitivity in the detection of the grade of sacroiliitis, except for class 1. Although more studies are still needed, these artificial intelligence algorithms could potentially assist medical clinicians for the detection of radiographic sacroiliitis.

Keywords: Artificial intelligence · Deep Learning · Sacroiliitis

1 Introduction

Axial Spondyloarthritis (axSpA) is a chronic inflammatory disease that involves predominantly the enthesis of the sacroiliac joints (SIJs) and the spine. It is caused by different rheumatic diseases, most commonly ankylosing spondylitis

© Springer Nature Switzerland AG 2022
J. M. Ferrández Vicente et al. (Eds.): IWINAC 2022, LNCS 13259, pp. 383–390, 2022.
https://doi.org/10.1007/978-3-031-06527-9_38

(AS) but also psoriatic arthritis, reactive arthritis and spondylitis with inflammatory bowel disease [15]. axSpA is prevalent in young adults and is related to an important decreased quality of life, causing great socioeconomic impact. It usually presents with inflammatory pain and stiffness in the lower back. If early diagnosis and early treatment are not achieved this disease may evolve and present complications as complete fusion of the spinal vertebrae and sacroiliac joints leading to an important reduced mobility and increased risk of fractures.

Traditionally, imaging of the sacroiliac joints (SIJs) starts with conventional radiographs of SIJs, and this technique is recognized as the first imaging technique in patients with suspected axSpA. However, the diagnosis of sacroiliitis may be difficult in many patients and the reliability of sacroiliitis detection with an X-ray is usually low, especially in the early stages of sacroiliitis [5,11,13,17]. In addition, despite efforts to standardize the evaluation, the diagnosis performed by expert radiologists and rheumatologists still remains subject to significant intrapersonal and interpersonal variation.

Deep learning has produced remarkable results in the classification of medical data [7,12], and the ability to identify meaningful patterns in large data sets makes machine learning very attractive for screening of diseases such as Axial Spondyloarthritis (axSpA). In this framework a recent work has shown that a deep convolutional neural network (CNN) can detect sacroiliitis in patients with suspected axial spondyloarthritis [1]. However, this approach is unable to assess the stage or grade of sacroiliitis, which is a need for the treatment and following up of the patients. Therefore, the main goal of this work is to develop and validate a new approach based on artificial intelligence techniques for the automatic classification of the grade of sacroiliitis on conventional radiographs.

2   Methods

This retrospective study was approved by the Institutional Review Board (IRB) at the University Hospital. We included 267 patients with chronic back pain and clinical suggestion of Axial Spondyloarthritis who presented to a rheumatologist in a specialized center (Division of Rheumatology, Virgen de la Arrixaca, University Clinical Hospital Murcia, Spain) from 2011 until 2020. Pelvic radiographs were collected and anonymized.

X-ray images were reviewed by 3 rheumatologists and 1 radiologist regarding the presence or absence of sacroiliitis findings in each sacroiliac joint. They graded in consensus the severity of sacroiliitis according to the New York criteria: grade 0, normal sacroiliac joints with well-defined margins; grade 1, suspicious changes (incipient sclerosis with some blurring of the joint margins); grade 2, loss of definition of the articular margins with areas of reactive sclerosis but without alteration of the joint width; grade 3, unequivocal abnormality, evidence of sclerosis, widening, narrowing, or partial ankylosis; grade 4, complete ankylosis [10]. Figure 1 shows an anteroposterior radiograph showing normal sacroiliac joints and some representative examples of each grade according to New York criteria.

2.1 Imaging Pre-processing

Pelvic radiographs of the sacroiliac joints in DICOM (Digital Imaging and Communications in Medicine) format varied in size, resolution and quality. We used Fiji, an open-source platform for biological-image analysis [14] to adjust the greyscale levels of all images. Afterwards, we selected manually each sacroiliac joint and performed a pre-processing to reduce the noise component present in the x-ray images and to normalize the images. Noise reduction was performed using a median filter. To further improve the quality of the sacroiliac joint radiograph image we performed image normalization and contrast equalization using Fiji. Then we converted every image to the Tagged Image File Format (TIFF). These preprocessing steps allow to improve efficiency of deep learning models with less amount of data.

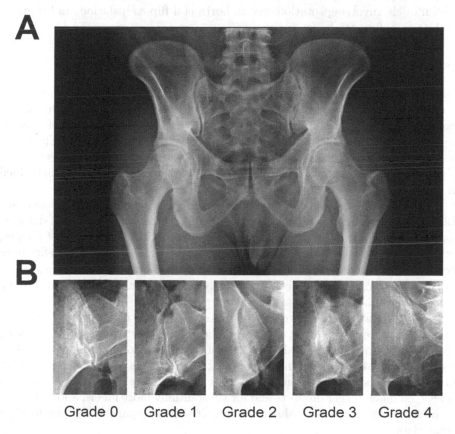

Fig. 1. Examples of X-ray images. A, Normal pelvis radiograph. B, Representative images of sacroiliac joints according to the New York criteria.

2.2 Model Training

After the image dataset have been pre-processed, the next step was to train the artificial neural network models for the classification of the grade of sacroiliitis. The dataset consisted of 534 grayscale images of variable size (101 for Class0, 72 for Class1, 158 for Class2, 119 for Class3, 84 for Class4). For the conventional hold out training approaches, 80% of the images were used for training and 20% were reserved for testing. For the cross-validation approaches, 10-fold stratified cross-validation was used to enforce the same distribution of samples between classes in each fold.

Images were resized to 244×244 pixels for the ResNet50 [8,18] and EfficientNetV2S backbones [16], and 299×299 pixels for the Xception [4] backbone. Grayscales images were expanded to 3 identical channels to make them RGB compatible. Data augmentation was included as a preprocessing stage for the CNN models, involving rotation, zoom, horizontal flip, translation, and contrast random transformations for each epoch.

2.3 Model Architecture

Many artificial neural networks for X-Ray radiographs classification have been proposed in the last years. However, instead of developing a new model, it is a common approach using a well-known architecture and applying transfer learning [18] to customize the network parameters to the new application. Therefore, most of these architectures are derived from openly available deep neural networks (frequently constructed around a CNN-based core) that have been trained on large image datasets such as ImageNet [6].

This technique has at least two advantages. First, it minimizes the undesirable effect of overfitting, which often occurs due to the relatively small datasets available in the case of radiographic images (hundreds or thousands of images, versus several million in the case of generic datasets). Secondly, it benefits from the excellent feature extractors developed by these models, whose architectures and hyper-parameters have been extensively tuned to obtain the best results on datasets of millions of images.

In [2], the authors compare sixteen different architectures of CNN that have marked the state-of-the-art in image classification of chest radiographs datasets. Their results show that more shallow networks (typically older ones) may achieve results comparable to their more complex counterparts with shorter training times. The author assumption is that these models have been trained on color images, on much bigger datasets and for substantially more labels, and often represent more complex relationships than required for comparably simpler medical image data.

Therefore, our first strategy was to use transfer learning technique by combining a base CNN model as feature extractor, with a top dense stack customized for the sacroiliitis application. A classifier composed of several dense layers was instantiated on top of the selected convolutional backbone. Specifically, the classifier was composed of a global average pooling layer, a dense layer with 128 or

256 neurons (64 for the EfficienNetV2S) with ReLU activation, 0.5 dropout rate, and a final dense layer for classification with 5 neurons and softmax activation. Sparse categorical cross entropy was used for the loss function, and Adam or RMSprop as optimizers, with an adaptive learning rate.

For the base model, several flavors of Resnet [8], EfficienNet [16] and Inception [4] architectures were used, besides a custom designed CNN core for basic comparison. Combined, a total of 10 architectures, each with several sets of hyperparameters, more than 150 different models were fitted to the sacroiliitis dataset. We also used XGBoost, an advanced gradient boosting algorithm with several improvements over other gradient tree boosting algorithms that extended the method for multibillion samples and parallel computing [3].

3   Results

First results were disappointing, since no model obtained outstanding marks using conventional metrics (accuracy, precision, sensitivity, f1-score). In addition, small variations in the hyperparameters, or the training procedure, caused models that had obtained a relatively significant accuracy of around 50% to obtain accuracies of around 25–30% (close to a random guess for a 5-class problem), which showed the lack of stability of the classifiers, and the complexity of the dataset. The poor metrics indicated that our dense classifiers where highly interfered by image noise, despite the demonstrated effectiveness of CNNs in extracting spatial features, resulting in low classification accuracy.

To improve performance, we used Ensemble learning which is a technique that combines multiple classifiers that process different hypotheses to construct a combined space that a single classifier cannot afford in presence of diverse and complex data features. Kearns and Valiant [9] showed that an ensemble of weak classifiers can generate more accurate predictions than a single classifier, as long as data is sufficient. Several ensemble methods have been developed since then, mainly based on decision trees. Chen proposed XGBoost [3], an advanced gradient boosting algorithm with several improvements over other gradient tree boosting algorithms that extended the method for multibillion samples and parallel computing. The results of a single XGBoost model increased the classification rate to an average of 47% accuracy (Fig. 2).

Then, we moved to an alternative approach to work with the sacroiliitis dataset, which consisted in combining the most powerful feature extractors based on CNN architectures, with one of the most advanced ensemble classifier architectures like XGBoost. Thus, we develop and trained a combined CNN-XGBoost model. For the CNN we used the ResNet50 architecture, which had shown the best feature extraction capabilities during the precedent tests. We kept the convolutional kernel, trained on the ImageNet dataset and eliminated the top classifier. The kernel was used to predict features for the full sacroiliitis dataset, which transformed the input image space of (534, 224, 224, 3) into a feature space with dimensionality (534, 7, 7, 2048). Using this approach the feature tensor for each image was reduced to a single dimension, resulting in a tensor of

class	precision	recall	f1-score	support(samples)
0	0.68	0.50	0.58	30
1	0.29	0.15	0.20	13
2	0.42	0.70	0.53	27
3	0.32	0.35	0.33	20
4	0.64	0.41	0.50	17
metric avg	0.47	0.42	0.43	107
weighted avg	0.49	0.47	0.46	107

Fig. 2. Results using a single XGBoost model to fit the sacroiliitis dataset.

shape (534, 100352) that was used as the input for the XGBoost model. A grid search was used to find the optimum set of hyperparameters for the XGBoost, which finally obtained an accuracy of 57%, improving the basic XGBoost approach (Fig. 3). The sensitivity (recall) for all classes but Class 1 was over 60%. Thus, we found that Class 1 was completely misclassified (the 13 samples of this class were classified as belonging to Class 0 or to Class 2).

class	precision	recall	f1-score	support(samples)
0	0.64	0.60	0.62	30
1	0.00	0.00	0.00	13
2	0.47	0.63	0.54	27
3	0.58	0.70	0.64	20
4	0.80	0.71	0.75	17
metric avg	0.50	0.53	0.51	107
weighted avg	0.54	0.57	0.55	107

Fig. 3. Results using a combined CNN-XGBoost model to fit the sacroiliitis dataset.

4   Discussion

The ability of deep learning models to search for subtle patterns show promise for screening of diseases such as axial spondyloarthritis (axSpA), a spectrum of chronic conditions characterized by inflammation in the axial skeleton that can cause pain, joint damage, and disability. Our trained model successfully detected the grade of sacroiliitis with an accuracy over 60%. With further improvement and validation, we hope that this approach could be helpful to aid the detection of radiographic sacroiliitis and reduce the frequency of delayed diagnosis.

Since the available number of images per class was relatively low, we used imaging pre-processing to improve the classification performance. Furthermore, the images were augmented prior to training through various transformations consisting of rotation of up to 10°, flipping, magnification of up to 1.1, lighting variations and warping. This approach allowed us to achieve significant classification results with less data than using standard methods. Thus, the model can perform more efficiently since it does not need to learn which part of the image should be considered.

Our results suggest that machine learning tools may be used for automatic classification of the severity of sacroiliitis on conventional radiographs. However, we need more data to improve the robustness and performance of the classification. Thus, in further implementations we plan to detect the sacroiliac joints and perform all the preprocessing stages automatically. Therefore, now that we confirmed the potential of this approach, we plan to conduct a further study with larger datasets from multiple institutions.

5   Conclusions and Future Development

We developed and validated a new approach based on artificial intelligence techniques for the automatic classification of the grade of sacroiliitis on conventional radiographs.

The artificial neural network showed good generalizability and a high specificity with acceptable sensitivity in the detection of the grade of sacroiliitis. Although more studies are still needed, machine learning techniques for computer-aided classification could be used by non-expert medical clinicians to aid the detection of radiographic sacroiliitis.

Acknowledgements. This project has received funding by grant RTI2018-098969-B-100 from the Spanish Ministerio de Ciencia Innovación y Universidades and by grant PROMETEO/2019/119 from the Generalitat Valenciana (Spain).

References

1. Bressem, K.K., et al.: Deep learning for detection of radiographic sacroiliitis: achieving expert-level performance. Arthritis. Res. Ther. **23**(1), 106 (2021)
2. Bressem, K.K., Adams, L., Erxleben, C., Hamm, B., Niehues, S.M., Vahldiek, J.L.: Comparing different deep learning architectures for classification of chest radiographs. arXiv preprint arXiv:2002.08991 (2020)
3. Chen, T., Guestrin, C.: XGBoost: a scalable tree boosting system. In: Proceedings of the 22nd ACM SIGKDD International Conference on Knowledge Discovery and Data Mining (KDD 2016), pp. 785–794. ACM, New York (2016). https://doi.org/10.1145/2939672.2939785
4. Chollet, F.: Xception: deep learning with depthwise separable convolutions. arXiv preprint arXiv:1610.02357 (2016)
5. Christiansen, A.A., et al.: Limited reliability of radiographic assessment of sacroiliac joints in patients with suspected early spondyloarthritis. J. Rheumatol. **44**(1), 70–77 (2017)

6. Deng, J., Dong, W., Socher, R., Li, L.J., Li, K., Fei-Fei, L.: Imagenet: a large-scale hierarchical image database. In: 2009 IEEE Conference on Computer Vision and Pattern Recognition, pp. 248–255 (2009). https://doi.org/10.1109/CVPR.2009.5206848

7. Getty, N., Brettin, T., Jin, D., Stevens, R., Xia, F.: Deep medical image analysis with representation learning and neuromorphic computing. Interf. Focus **11**(1), 20190122 (2021)

8. He, K., Zhang, X., Ren, S., Sun, J.: Deep residual learning for image recognition. arXiv preprint arXiv:1512.03385 (2015)

9. Kearns, M., Valiant, L.: Cryptographic limitations on learning Boolean formulae and finite automata. J. ACM **41**(1), 67–95 (1994)

10. van der Linden, S., Valkenburg, H.A., Cats, A.: Evaluation of diagnostic criteria for ankylosing spondylitis. A proposal for modification of the New York criteria. Arthritis. Rheum. **27**(4), 361–368 (1984)

11. Poddubnyy, D., et al.: Rates and predictors of radiographic sacroiliitis progression over 2 years in patients with axial spondyloarthritis. Ann. Rheum. Dis. **70**(8), 1369–1374 (2011)

12. Raza, K., Singh, N.K.: A tour of unsupervised deep learning for medical image analysis. Curr. Med. Imaging **17**(9), 1059–1077 (2021)

13. Rodriguez, V.R., et al.: Assessment of radiographic sacroiliitis in anteroposterior lumbar vs. conventional pelvic radiographs in axial spondyloarthritis. Rheumatology (Oxford) **60**(1), 269–276 (2021)

14. Schindelin, J., Arganda-Carreras, I., Frise, E., Kaynig, V., Longair, M., Pietzsch, T., Preibisch, S., Rueden, C., Saalfeld, S., Schmid, B., Tinevez, J.Y., White, D.J., Hartenstein, V., Eliceiri, K., Tomancak, P., Cardona, A.: Fiji: an open-source platform for biological-image analysis. Na.t Methods **9**(7), 676–682 (2012)

15. Sieper, J., Poddubnyy, D.: Axial spondyloarthritis. Lancet **390**(10089), 73–84 (2017)

16. Tan, M., Le, Q.V.: Efficientnetv2: smaller models and faster training. arXiv preprint arXiv:2104.00298 (2021)

17. Ulusoy, H., Kaya, A., Kamanli, A., Akgol, G., Ozgocmen, S.: Radiological scoring methods in ankylosing spondylitis: a comparison of the reliability of available methods. Acta Reumatol. Port. **35**(2), 170–175 (2010)

18. Zhuang, F., et al.: A comprehensive survey on transfer learning. arXiv preprint arXiv:1911.02685 (2019)

Deep Reinforcement Learning in Agents' Training: Unity ML-Agents

Laura Almón-Manzano[✉][iD], Rafael Pastor-Vargas[iD],
and José Manuel Cuadra Troncoso[iD]

Universidad Nacional de Educación a Distancia (UNED), Madrid, Spain
lalmon1@alumno.uned.es, rpastor@scc.uned.es, jmcuadra@dia.uned.es

Abstract. Video games are an area where Artificial Intelligence has multiple application scenarios, allowing to add improvements that can be applied to provide greater realism in the game experience, accelerate its development (even automate it) and save costs, among other benefits. Beyond the commercial vision and from a research point of view, different strategies and algorithms are applied in certain facets/applications that pose a significant challenge in terms of the development of these algorithms and their applicability (in this area and others). These applications include the creation of intelligent agents (which can be cooperate or adversarial), the automatic generation of content (structures, characters, scenarios, etc.), the modeling of player behavior and habits, and particular rendering techniques. This paper focuses on the use of the open source project Unity ML-Agents Toolkit to train different intelligent agents using Deep Reinforcement Learning techniques and associated learning algorithms applied to this scenario of Artificial Intelligence use.

Keywords: Deep Reinforcement Learning · Intelligent Agents · Video Game

1 Introduction

Video games have always been an ideal vehicle for AI research in the development or improvement of new algorithms, especially in the Reinforcement Learning branch, since, generally, at any given moment, there is a game state and a number of possible actions from which the player and/or the enemies must select the one most likely to lead to their victory.

From an economic point of view, the video game industry has been generating more economic activity than the rest of the cultural and digital content sectors for several years and that continues to grow exponentially and constantly.

Last years have seen tremendous progress in computer graphics. However, the behavior of Non-Player-Characters or NPCs is still ruled by old Artificial Intelligence techniques such as finite state machines, navigation grids and behavior trees, which tend to achieve inflexible and unrealistic behaviors. The greater this gap between graphics and behavioral realism, the more evident becomes the

© Springer Nature Switzerland AG 2022
J. M. Ferrández Vicente et al. (Eds.): IWINAC 2022, LNCS 13259, pp. 391–400, 2022.
https://doi.org/10.1007/978-3-031-06527-9_39

need for research into new Machine Learning techniques to achieve more realistic NPC behaviors.

In addition, the usual techniques are time and effort consuming, as each of the particular situations in which the agent may be encountered must be taken into account, which may also introduce unexpected errors.

For all these reasons, the objective of our work is to research about the training of intelligent agents in video games using Deep Reinforcement Learning and use the open source project Unity ML-Agents to train agents for different use cases, developing our own algorithm and comparing our results with those obtained with the Unity's algorithm.

Section 2 describes the evolution of AI in video games, Sect. 3 shows the development of our example using Reinforcement Learning in a game scenario, and Sect. 4 presents the conclusions drawn and some ideas for future work.

2 AI and Games

AI, and, in particular, intelligent agents, has been an important area of research for games since their beginning [11]. In early games, as board games, developers tried to get an opponent as close to human-like as possible. In fact, Alan Turing was the first to develop an algorithm to play chess around 1948 [10]. A decade later, in 1959, Arthur Samuel used Reinforcement Learning for the first time to create a program that learned to play checkers by playing against itself [7]. In 1992, Gerald Tesauro built on Samuel's work, adding an Artificial Neural Network, to create the TD-Gammon software, which learned to play backgammon playing against itself several milion times and was able to reach the level of the best players [9]. In 1994 and 1997, Chinook and IBM's Deep Blue software beat the world checkers champion Marion Tinsley and the chess grandmaster Garri Kaspárov, respectively [5,8].

In non-symmetric games, where the opponent or opponents do not have the same strategy to follow to win as the player, the goal of developers is not always to achieve a human-like behavior, but a more or less realistic one that is entertaining to compete against. To this end, in the late 1970s, Space Invaders (Toshihiro Nishikado 1978) and Galaxian (Namco 1979) added complexity to the game by introducing hash functions that "learned" from the player's actions, being considered the first learning systems introduced in the world of video games. In the 1980s some games such as Pac-Man (Namco 1980), Karate Champ (Technōs Japan 1984) and Madden Football (Electronic Arts 1988) added different "personalities" to characters, so that they had different behaviors.

The 1990s and 2000s introduced characters' behaviors based on player's actions with games such as Creatures (Creature Labs 1996), Golden Eye 007 (Rare 1997) and Black and White (Lionhead Studios 2001), and, with Half-life (Valve Corporation 1999), the concept of cooperation between enemies to take cover, search for the player, flank the opponent, etc. Also, Halo: Combat Evolved (Bungie Studios 2001) introduced recognition of threads from enemies; Far Cry (Crytek 2004) used learning methods to guess the player's behavior and use military tactics against them using the player's last known position in which the enemies have seen them, adding more realism to the game experience; and F.E.A.R. (Monolith Productions 2005) was the first game to include real-time goal-oriented action planning to adapt dynamically to the events of the environment.

In recent years, online games in which a team of players have to cooperate to face the opposing team have become increasingly important. In the practice mode against AI in this type of game, the AI of the enemies needs to simulate as much as possible the behavior of a human player in order to prepare the players for a normal game against human enemies. Thus, there are a multitude of competitions to create the most victorious AI possible for different games, and research in this area has focused on this.

An important milestone for the field of agent AI research was reached in 2014, when algorithms developed by Google DeepMind, using Artificial Neural Networks, learned to play different games of the classic game console Atari 2600 at a level higher than human from only flat pixels as input [4]. The same company also developed the AlphaStar AI system, which beat two professional gamers playing StarCraft II: Wings of Liberty (Blizzard Entertainment 2010) in January 2019, thus becoming the first AI to beat a professional gamer [1]. In April of the same year, the AI OpenAI Five beat the world-winning Dota 2 (Valve Corporation 2013) team OG in the finals, becoming the first AI to beat the world champions in an e-sport [2].

However, it is relevant to note that this type of AIs that use Artificial Neural Networks, despite continuing to be an important area of research, are not being used by almost any commercial game. Moreover, even the research is practically focused on symmetric games, ignoring other types of both enemy and companion AI behaviors.

Reinforcement Learning algorithms are very suitable (and common) for the development of this type of AIs, since, at each instant there is a state of the game composed of all the information the agent knows and a set of actions that it can take and that will have a direct consequence in the game that can be measured to give the agent a certain (positive or negative) reward that it can try to predict to choose at each moment the correct action that will bring it closer to achieving its goal. In addition, Neural Networks are also very practical for training agents with complex behaviors, since they are an approximation of a nonlinear function and can act as a function that converts complex input data into a final integer that can represent the optimal action to be taken by the agent to maximize the reward obtained.

3   Game Scenario as Environment for Reinforcement Learning

As an environment for the development of the example shown in this paper, we have chosen the Unity engine and its ML-Agents Toolkit. Unity is a real-time

3D development platform created by Unity Technologies that has a free personal version. It consists of a rendering and physics engine, as well as a graphical user interface called Unity Editor. Unity has received wide adoption in the video game, AEC (Architecture, Engineering, Construction), automotive and film industries, and is used by a large community of game developers. In addition, Unity is a very convenient tool for AI research, as it is a general purpose and cross-platform engine and allows rapid prototyping of complete simulated environments. To this end, the open source project Unity ML-Agents Toolkit[1] allows researchers and developers to create training scenarios for intelligent agents using the Unity Editor and interact with them through a low-level Python API using a ML library such as Tensorflow [3]. Agents can be trained with the (PyTorch based) implementations of RL algorithms included in this tool, or by using any other algorithm or implementing one using the low-level Python API.

With Unity ML-Agents, a training scenario is a Unity scene that contains one or more agents that continuously receive updated information and interact with other entities according to the decisions they have made based on that information. An agent is an autonomous actor that performs actions depending on its observations of its state in the environment. It observes its environment, and passes its observations to its policy, which decides the best course of action using these observations and passes the chosen actions back to the agent, which executes those actions within its environment.

As a case study, it has been decided to create a typical RPG scene in which the player character faces multiple enemies. Since this is a complex scenario for training, with many possible actions by the agents and sparse rewards, it has been proceeded to simplify the scenario as much as possible in the first place, in order to train increasingly intelligent agents in an increasingly complex scenario.

3.1 Enemy Training Using the PPO Algorithm Implementation of ML-Agents

First of all, it has been started by training the enemy agent, whose goal is to reach and defeat the player, using the PPO algorithm implementation included in the ML-Agents Toolkit.

In this case, the actions that the agent will be able to perform will be to move forward, rotate to change direction and attack, so a discrete action space of size equal to 3 branches is more appropriate: 1. Attack (equal to 0 for not attacking and equal to 1 for attacking), 2. Move (equal to 0 for not moving and equal to 1 for moving), and 3. Rotate (equal to 0 for not turning, equal to 1 for turning to the left and equal to 2 for turning to the right).

A penalty (a negative reward) that the agent receives at each step has been added to incentivize it to attack the character as soon as possible. When the agent attacks, if it hits the character it receives a positive reward equal to 1 and the episode is over, while if it misses its attack it receives a small negative reward to prevent it from attacking continuously without having the character

---

[1] https://github.com/Unity-Technologies/ml-agents.

in its attack range. In addition, in case the agent cannot attack yet (since there is a minimum time between attacks, or cooldown), the action mask of branch 0 (the attack branch) is modified, preventing it from taking the value 1 in its next action decision; that is, preventing the agent from attacking at that moment.

As for the observations, choosing what information the agent will receive at each step is one of the most important decisions to achieve the desired behavior after learning, and, generally, several trial and error attempts are necessary to find the optimal case. The agent's objective is to find and reach the character to attack it, so it needs to know the distance between them, to know if it is in its attack range, and the direction it should take to go towards it.

Calculating the distance between two points is very simple, and Unity provides a function for this purpose. To check if the agent is oriented towards the character, the dot product between the direction the agent is facing and the direction from the agent to its target normalized has been used. Thus, if the agent is facing its target, the angle between them is zero, then their dot product is equal to 1. If the angle between both vectors is less than 90°, then their dot product is positive. If the angle is equal to 90°, then their dot product is 0. If the angle is greater than 90° (obtuse), then their dot product is negative. Lastly, if the agent is facing the opposite direction of its target, the angle is equal to 180°, so their dot product is equal to −1.

Therefore, the observations added to the agent at each training step are the dot product between the direction the enemy is facing and the direction to its target normalized, and a boolean indicating whether the character is in its attack range. In addition, the agent relies on the observations it collects thanks to its Ray Perception Sensor 3D component, in which the "Character" and "Wall" tags have been set as "Detectable Tags" to detect the character and the walls (to avoid walking against them). It has been decided to use 10 rays around the enemy, with a full 180 °C angle, so that it can detect characters and walls located anywhere around it, avoiding unintelligent situations, such as it keeps walking looking for the character when it is behind the agent.

To ensure that the enemy can find and attack the character from different initial positions, and to avoid learning for the previous specific case only (overfitting), both the enemy and the character have been placed in random positions at the beginning of each episode, and the training has been repeated. As expected, it took the agent longer to reach the ideal behavior, being able to adapt to different situations. The final results are shown in Table 1.

3.2 Enemy Training Using a Custom Algorithm

It has been decided to use the low-level Python API to implement a DQN and export the resulting model in an ONNX file that can be used in Unity for inference. It was decided to implement a DQN specifically because it is a simple algorithm to implement and not already contained in the Unity ML-Agents package. Moreover, since the action space in this scenario is discrete, it is a suitable solution. For this purpose, the PyTorch library has been used. The constructed network consists of three Linear layers (which apply a linear transformation to

Table 1. Final results obtained in enemy training using the PPO algorithm implementation of ML-Agents.

Step	Time Elapsed (seconds)	Mean Reward	Std of Reward
50000	57.968	-104.536	73.474
100000	107.268	-16.478	17.195
150000	157.762	-0.094	1.266
200000	209.697	0.801	0.317
250000	262.190	0.949	0.109
300000	315.356	0.969	0.064
350000	369.035	0.974	0.056
400000	420.642	0.978	0.039
450000	474.507	0.979	0.040
500000	529.359	0.980	0.034

the data passed as input); the first two (the hidden layers), making use of the ReLU (Rectified Linear Unit) activation function. This network takes as input the state of the game known by the agent and returns as output a 3-dimensional action vector (since the agent's action space consists of 3 branches) with as many values in each one as possible actions for the corresponding branch, where the index of the element with the highest value corresponds to the optimal action for the current policy.

To update the policy and make the agent learn, two neural networks have been created with this architecture: a main Local network and a Target network. When updating the policy, the Q values for the current states of the scenario are calculated with the Target model using the Bellman Equation, and the expected Q values with the Local model, and the weights of the Local neural network are updated trying to minimize the loss between the expected and Target Q values. Then, a "soft update" of the Local neural network weights is performed.

To handle the exploration/exploitation trade off, the epsilon-greedy strategy has been used to choose the action to be taken by the agent at each decision making. With this method, a random number is generated within the semi-open range [0.0, 1.0). If this number is greater than the epsilon parameter (which starts equal to 1, and decreases in each episode, until reaching a minimum or until the end of the training), the optimal action is selected according to the current policy ("exploitation"). Otherwise, a random action is selected ("exploration").

The first training attempt proved to be totally unstable, since the positive rewards were too "sparse", which is a common problem in training scenarios. To solve this problem, the reward signals have been modified: instead of giving the agent a constant negative reward at each iteration, this reward has been modified to vary according to how close the agent is to the target (the closer the agent is to the target, the closer to 0 this reward will be).

After this change, the agent appeared to learn in the first iterations, until it stuck, "unlearning", and the training became unstable again. As Roderick [6] explains, this is a common problem in DQNs, for which there are some solutions that minimize it, such as using the experience replay technique, limiting the rewards in the range $[-1, +1]$, and limiting as much as possible the number of both inputs and outputs of the neural network.

Adding experience replay is very simple: the agent's experiences are added to a buffer that discards the oldest ones when its maximum size is exceeded, and, when updating the policy, a random sample of experiences contained in this buffer is taken into account. Thus, the agent's old experiences also have an influence when updating the policy, not only the newest ones. However, this is not enough to achieve stable training.

To bound the rewards in the range $[-1, +1]$ and, at the same time, reduce the number of outputs of the neural network, the agent's action space has been modified. First, the branch with the possible actions of attacking or not attacking has been eliminated, since the agent can only attack when it has already reached its target, so this decision is not relevant in decision making. With this change, the output of the neural network has been reduced to a 2-dimensional action vector. In addition, the reward signals have been modified by adding a negative reward and interrupting the episode if the agent hits a wall, to avoid this erroneous behavior.

To reduce the output of the neural network as much as possible to a one-dimensional action vector, the two remaining branches have been merged into one of size 6 (2×3) containing all possible decisions (all combinations between movement and rotation). In addition, to minimize the neural network inputs too, the parameters of the Ray Perception Sensor 3D component have been modified, reducing the number of rays per direction to 3 and the maximum ray degrees to 90, which is equivalent to 28 numerical observations. Then, counting the 2 separate ones, the total size is 30.

After these changes, the neural network has 30 input units and 6 output units, and 2 hidden layers with 64 units by default. The previous problems were solved and the training remained stable, achieving the desired behavior of the agent after a few training episodes.

Another difficulty encountered is that, as the Unity ML-Agents documentation warns: "The ML-Agents Toolkit only supports the models created with our trainers. Model loading expects certain conventions for constants and tensor names." Due to this limitation, the inputs and outputs of the neural network have been modified to match in form and name those required by Unity, adding a new input and several constant outputs and setting the exact names required when exporting the model to ONNX. In this way, the resulting model can be used in Unity for inference.

Due to the large number of hyperparameters (12), finding the optimal combination is a time-consuming task and requires many comparisons. In this work, some of the possible combinations have been tested by modifying the most relevant hyperparameters that can influence the training process the most.

Tables 2 and 3 show the final training results obtained using the PPO algorithm implementation of the Unity ML-Agents package and those obtained using the custom implementation of the DQN algorithm with the chosen hyperparameters, respectively. To make as fair a comparison as possible, the previously created Side Channel has been used to set the same configuration parameters used by Unity (as well as the same simplified training scenenario with only one agent). The most important one is the time scale, with a value equal to 20, which greatly speeds up the training process with very little effect on the results.

Table 2. Final training results obtained using the PPO algorithm implementation of the Unity ML-Agents package.

Step	Time Elapsed (seconds)	Mean Reward	Std of Reward
50000	626.849	-0.275	1.041
100000	1251.742	-0.233	1.045
150000	1974.158	0.283	0.927
200000	2599.288	0.316	0.904
250000	3348.597	0.627	0.637
300000	4040.563	0.686	0.551
350000	4825.220	0.796	0.334
400000	5517.882	0.816	0.266
450000	6007.860	0.837	0.205
500000	6401.993	0.854	0.102

Table 3. Final training results obtained using the custom DQN algorithm implementation with the chosen hyperparameters.

Episode	Step	Time Elapsed (seconds)	Mean Reward	Std of Reward
300	10136	50.477	-0.259	1.041
600	24956	123.890	0.092	1.026
900	35166	174.095	0.680	0.492
1200	42837	211.606	0.800	0.264
1500	50081	246.931	0.796	0.296
1800	56655	279.044	0.846	0.107
2100	63084	310.291	0.845	0.167
2400	69188	339.953	0.860	0.079
2700	76236	374.318	0.840	0.174
3000	82057	402.552	0.861	0.158

As can be seen from these tables, training using the custom DQN algorithm implementation is much faster and also requires far fewer steps to reach high reward values. With this implementation, a fairly high mean reward value (equal to 0.846) and low standard deviation (equal to 0.107) are reached after 1800 episodes, which in this case consisted of 56655 training steps and took 279.044 s (4.65 min). Thereafter, training remained more or less stable, ending, after 3000 episodes, consisting of 82057 steps and taking 402.556 s (6.71 min), with a mean reward value equal to 0.861 and standard deviation equal to 0.158. On the other hand, with the implementation from ML-Agents, after 50000 steps, which took 626.849 s (10.45 min), the mean reward was negative, with a very high standard deviation. After 500000 steps, a high mean reward (equal to 0.854) and low standard deviation (equal to 0.102) was achieved, but taking 6401.993 (106.7 min).

The difference in time elapsed between the two trainings is so large (as can also be seen in Fig. 1) that it can be concluded that, in this case, it has been worthwhile to create a custom implementation of the DQN algorithm using the low-level Python API.

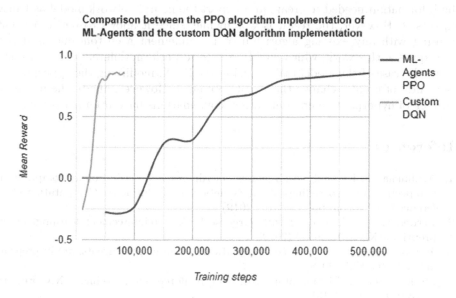

Fig. 1. Comparison between the PPO algorithm implementation of ML-Agents and the custom DQN algorithm implementation.

4   Conclusions and Future Work

With the study of the state of the art, it has been reaffirmed that video games are a very useful vehicle to test new AI techniques and that, in turn, these techniques can also be very useful for the different applications of AI in the field of video games. Both AI and game development have come a long way in recent years. However, there is very little research that focuses specifically on AI techniques applied to video games, despite the many benefits.

The Unity ML-Agents Toolkit has proven to be a very large project that offers many possibilities and lines of research to explore. The enormous amount of features included in this toolkit exceeds the scope of this work. Nevertheless, they are all interesting, and some of them very useful, so they can be studied in future work.

Implementing the DQN using the low-level Python API of Unity ML-Agents has been the major difficulty encountered working on this project, due to the lack of documentation. The only documentation provided by Unity on this API consists of a description of the components that make up a UnityEnvironment and its methods. Due to the novel (and advanced) nature of this project, there is no bibliography, examples or tutorials about it either (while there are plenty of tutorials on how to train agents using the ML-Agents algorithm implementations). Therefore, the code itself has had to be used as a "substitute for documentation". In addition, Unity does not provide support for using externally trained models for inference, so again, the repository code itself has been searched for the information needed to create and export the neural network model as Unity expects it. However, the result is worthwhile, since it allows to perform agent training with any existing algorithm or to implement a custom one as it has been done in this work, which could be used to perform different comparisons.

In the case of the model trained using the DQN, modifying the hyperparameters did not greatly change the results obtained. However, due to the immense number of hyperparameters, only a few combinations have been performed.

References

1. Arulkumaran, K., Cully, A., Togelius, J.: Alphastar: an evolutionary computation perspective. In: Proceedings of the Genetic and Evolutionary Computation Conference Companion, pp. 314–315 (2019)
2. Berner, C., et al.: Dota 2 with large scale deep reinforcement learning. arXiv preprint arXiv:1912.06680 (2019)
3. Juliani, A., et al.: Unity: a general platform for intelligent agents. arXiv preprint arXiv:1809.02627 (2018)
4. Mnih, V., et al.: Playing atari with deep reinforcement learning. arXiv preprint arXiv:1312.5602 (2013)
5. Newborn, M.: Deep blue's contribution to AI. Ann. Math. Artif. Intell. **28**(1), 27–30 (2000)
6. Roderick, M., MacGlashan, J., Tellex, S.: Implementing the deep q-network. arXiv preprint arXiv:1711.07478 (2017)
7. Samuel, A.L.: Some studies in machine learning using the game of checkers (1959). https://doi.org/10.1147/rd.33.0210
8. Schaeffer, J., Lake, R., Lu, P., Bryant, M.: Chinook the world man-machine checkers champion. AI Magaz. **17**(1), 21 (1996)
9. Tesauro, G.: Temporal difference learning and td-gammon. Commun. ACM **38**(3), 58–68 (1995)
10. Turing, A.M.: Digital computers applied to games. Faster than thought (1953)
11. Yannakakis, G.N., Togelius, J.: Artificial Intelligence and Games, vol. 2. Springer, Cham (2018). https://doi.org/10.1007/978-3-319-63519-4

Artificial Intelligence Applications

Basic Arithmetic Calculations Through Virus-Based Machines

Antonio Ramírez-de-Arellano[1($\boxtimes$)], David Orellana-Martín[1] (ID),
and Mario J. Pérez-Jiménez[1,2] (ID)

[1] Research Group on Natural Computing, Department of Computer Science
and Artificial Intelligence,Universidad de Sevilla, Avda. Reina Mercedes s/n,
41012 Seville, Spain
{aramirezdearellano,dorellana,marper}@us.es
[2] SCORE Lab, I3US, Universidad de Sevilla, 41012 Seville, Spain

Abstract. In Natural Computing, several models of computation based
on processes occurring in nature exist. While some of them are well-
established computing framework, there are some types of devices that
are underdeveloped. This is the case of Virus Machines, framework
inspired by the movement of viruses between hosts, and how can they be
replicated while certain events happen. The relevance of this work lies in
the formal definition of the framework and both the insights presented
about the formal verification of the different designs and the possible
new research lines.

In this work, Virus Machines are studied from a numerical point of view.
In this sense, five different devices regarding the four basic arithmetic operators are created, and some insights about the proofs of their correctness
are stated. While addition, subtraction and multiplication require only of
one device, for division two different machines will be designed: one for the
quotient of the division and the other for the remainder.

Keywords: Natural computing · Virus machine · Arithmetic
calculator · Information fusion

1 Introduction

This work can be considered as a contribution to the area of *Natural Computing*,
which is a field of research that investigates both human-designed computing
inspired by nature and computing that occurs in nature.

In virology, a virus is a parasitic biological agent that can only reproduce after
infecting a host cell. Every animal, plant, and protist species on this planet has
been infected by viruses. Viruses can transmit from one host to another through
various routes (e.g., conjunctival route, mechanical route, etc.). For additional
details on viruses, refer to [2].

In this study, a new computing paradigm, introduced in [1], based on the
transmissions and replications of viruses, is introduced. This paradigm provides
non-deterministic computing models that consist of several cell-like *hosts* connected to one another by *channels*. Viruses are placed in the hosts and can

© Springer Nature Switzerland AG 2022
J. M. Ferrández Vicente et al. (Eds.): IWINAC 2022, LNCS 13259, pp. 403–412, 2022.
https://doi.org/10.1007/978-3-031-06527-9_40

transmit from one host to another by passing through a channel, and can replicate itself while transmitting. These processes are controlled by several instructions, which are attached to the channels. These systems can be considered as a heterogeneous network that consists of:

- A *virus transmission network*: a weighted directed graph, wherein each node represents a *host* and each arc represents a *transmission channel* through which viruses can transmit between hosts or exit to the environment. In addition, each arc has associated a weight (natural number $w > 0$), which indicates the number of viruses that will be transmitted.
- An *instruction transfer network*: a weighted directed graph, wherein each node represents a *control instruction unit* and each edge represents an optional *instruction transfer path* with a positive integral weight.
- An *instruction-channel control network*: an undirected graph, wherein each node represents either a *control instruction* or a *transmission channel* and each edge represents a relationship between an instruction and a channel.

The computing models of this paradigm are universal (equivalent in power to Turing machines) when there is no limit on the number of viruses present in any host during a computation. The paper is organized as follows. Next section, the computing paradigm of virus machines is presented. In Sect. 3, the different modules concerning the basic arithmetic operators are presented. The paper ends with some open problems and concluding remarks.

2   Virus Machines

In what follows we formally define the **syntax** of the *Virus Machines*.

Definition 1. *A Virus Machine of degree* $(p,q), p \geq 1, q \geq 1$ *is a tuple* $\Pi = (\Gamma, H, I, D_H, D_I, G_C, n_1, \ldots, n_p, i_1, h_{out})$, *where:*

- $\Gamma = \{v\}$ *is the singleton alphabet;*
- $H = \{h_1, \ldots, h_p\}$ *and* $I = \{i_1, \ldots, i_q\}$ *are ordered sets such that* $v \notin H \cup I$, $H \cap I = \emptyset$ *and* $h_{out} \notin I \cup \Gamma$: *either* $h_{out} \in H$ *or* h_{out} *represents the environment (denoted by* h_0*);*
- $D_H = (H \cup \{h_{out}\}, E_H, w_H)$ *is a weighted directed graph, where* $E_H \subseteq H \times (H \cup \{h_{out}\})$, $(h, h) \notin E_H$ *for each* $h \in H$, *out-degree*$(h_{out}) = 0$ *and* w_H *is a mapping from* E_H *onto* $\mathbb{N} \setminus \{0\}$;
- $D_I = (I, E_I, w_I)$ *is a weighted directed graph, where* $E_I \subseteq I \times I$, w_I *is a mapping from* E_I *onto* $\mathbb{N} \setminus \{0\}$ *and the out-degree of each node is less than or equal to 2;*
- $G_C = (V_C, E_C)$ *is an undirected bipartite graph, where* $V_C = I \cup E_H$ *being* $\{I, E_H\}$ *the partition associated with it: every edge connects an element from* I *with, at most, an arc from* E_H;
- $n_j \in \mathbb{N} (1 \leq j \leq p).$

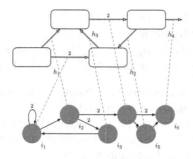

Fig. 1. Structure of a *Virus Machine*

A *Virus Machine* (VM, for short) $\Pi = (\Gamma, H, I, D_H, D_I, G_C, n_1, \ldots, n_p,$
$i_1, h_{out})$ of degree (p, q), can be viewed as an ordered set of p hosts labelled with
$h_1, \ldots, h_p$, where host h_j initially contains exactly n_j *viruses*, and an ordered
set of q *control instruction units* labelled with $i_1, \ldots, i_q$. Symbol h_{out} represents
the *output region*: it can be a host in the case that $h_{out} \in H$ or h_{out} can refer
to the environment in the case that $h_{out} = h_0$. Arcs from the directed graph
D_H represent *transmission channels* through which viruses can transmit from
one host h_s (different from h_{out}) to another different host $h_{s'}$, or to the environment. If $s' = 0$, viruses may exit to the environment. In any moment, at
most one instruction is *activated* and then the channel $(h_s, h_{s'})$ (arc in G_C)
with weight $w_{s,s'}$ attached with it, will be *opened*. Then, $w_{s,s'}$ viruses will be
transmitted/replicated from h_s to $h_{s'}$. By default, each channel is *closed*.

Arcs from the directed graph D_I represent *instruction transfer paths*, and
they have associated within a weight. Finally, the undirected bipartite graph
G_C represents the *instruction-channel network* by which an edge $\{i_j, (h_s, h_{s'})\}$
indicates a control relationship between instruction i_j and channel $(h_s, h_{s'})$.

Graphically, a virus machine of degree $(4, 6)$ with 4 hosts and 6 control
instructions can be represented as a heterogeneous network consisting of three
graph, as illustrated in Fig. 1. Each host is depicted as a rectangle and each
instruction is depicted as a circle. Each arrow is either a virus transmission
channel linking the hosts (or pointing to the environment), or an instruction
transfer path linking the instructions; in both cases, each arrow is assigned with
a positive integral weight (the weight 1 is not marked for simplicity). The control
relationships between instructions and channels are represented as dotted lines.

In what follows, the **semantics** associated with the computing model
of the virus machines is described. An *instantaneous description* or a *configuration* C_t at an instant t of a virus machine is described by a tuple
$(a_{0,t}, a_{1,t}, \ldots, a_{p,t}, u_t)$ where $a_{0,t}, a_{1,t}, \ldots, a_{p,t}$ are natural numbers, $u_t \in I \cup \{\#\}$,
where $\# \notin H \cup h_0 \cup I$ is an object for characterizing halting configura-
tions. The meaning of C_t is the following: at instant t the environment contains exactly $a_{0,t}$ viruses and the host h_s contains exactly $a_{s,t}$ viruses, and
if $u_t \in I$, then the instruction u_t will be activated at step $t + 1$ (otherwise, if $u_t = \#$, then no instruction will be activated). The initial config-

uration of the system $\Pi = (\Gamma, H, I, D_H, D_I, G_C, n_1, \ldots, n_p, i_1, i_{out})$ is $C_0 = (0, n_1, \ldots, n_p, i_1)$. A configuration $C_t = (a_{0,t}, a_{1,t}, \ldots, a_{p,t}, u_t)$ yields configuration $C_{t+1} = (a_{0,t+1}, a_{1,t+1}, \ldots, a_{p,t+1}, u_{t+1})$ in one *transition step* if we can pass from C_t to C_{t+1} if we can pass from C_t to C_{t+1} in the following form.

(a) First, given that C_t is a non-halting configuration we have $u_t \in I$. Then the control instruction unit u_t is activated.

(b) If u_t is attached to a channel $(h_s, h_{s'})$ then the channel will be opened and:
   - If $a_{s,t} \geq 1$ then only one virus is consumed from host h_s and $w_{s,s'}$ copies of v are produced in the region $h_{s'}$.
   - If $a_{s,t} = 0$ then no virus is consumed from host h_s and no virus is produced in the region $h_{s'}$.

(c) If u_t is not attached to any channel then there is no transmission of viruses.

(d) Object $u_{t+1} \in I \cup \{\#\}$ is obtained as follows:
   - If *out-degree*$(u_t) = 2$ then there are two different instructions $u_{t'}$ and $u_{t''}$ such that $(u_t, u_{t'}) \in E_I$ (with weight $w_{t,t'}$) and $(u_t, u_{t''}) \in E_I$ (with weight $w_{t,t''}$).
      • If instruction u_t is attached to a channel $(h_s, h_{s'})$:
         * If $a_{s,t} \geq 1$ then u_{t+1} is the instruction corresponding to the *highest* weight path ($max\{w_{t,t'}, w_{t,t''}\}$). If $w_{t,t'} = t_{t,t''}$, the next instruction is selected in a non-deterministic way.
         * If $a_{s,t} = 0$ then u_{t+1} is the instruction corresponding to the *lowest* weight path ($min\{w_{t,t'}, w_{t,t''}\}$). If $w_{t,t'} = w_{t,t''}$, the next instruction is selected in a non-deterministic way.
      • If instruction u_t is not attached to a channel, then the next instruction u_{t+1} ($u_{t'}$ or $u_{t''}$) is selected in a non-deterministic way.
   - If *out-degree*$(u_t) = 1$ then the system behaves deterministically and u_{t+1} is the instruction that verifies $(u_t, u_{t+1}) \in E_I$.
   - If *out-degree*$(u_t) = 0$ then $u_{t+1} = \#$, and C_{t+1} is a halting configuration.

Definition 2. *A Virus Machine with input, of degree* $(p, q, r), p \geq 1, q \geq 1, r \geq 1$ *is a tuple* $\Pi = (\Gamma, H, H_r, I, D_H, I, D_H, D_I, G_C, n_1, \ldots, n_p, i_1, h_{out})$, *where:*

   - $(\Gamma, H, I, D_H, D_I, G_C, n_1, \ldots, n_p, i_1, h_{out})$ *is a Virus Machine of degree* (p, q).
   - $H_r = \{h_{i_1}, \ldots, h_{i_r}\} \subseteq H$ *is the ordered set of* r *input hosts and* $h_{out} \notin H_r$.

If Π is a virus machine with input of degree $(p, q, r), p \geq 1, q \geq 1, r \geq 1$ and $(\alpha_1, \ldots, \alpha_r) \in \mathbb{N}^r$, the *initial configuration* of Π with input $(\alpha_1, \ldots, \alpha_r)$ is $(0, n_1, \ldots, n_{i_1} + \alpha_1, \ldots, n_{i_r} + \alpha_r, \ldots, n_p, i_1)$. Thus, each r-tuple $(\alpha_1, \ldots, \alpha_r) \in \mathbb{N}^r$, is associated with an initial configuration $(0, n_1, \ldots, n_{i_1} + \alpha_1, \ldots, n_{i_r} + \alpha_r, \ldots, n_p, i_1)$.

A computation of a virus machine Π with input $(\alpha_1, \ldots, \alpha_r)$, denoted by $\Pi + (\alpha_1, \ldots, \alpha_r)$, starts with configuration $(0, n_1, \ldots, n_{i_1} + \alpha_1, \ldots, n_{i_r} + \alpha_r, \ldots, n_p, i_1)$ and proceeds as stated above. The result of a halting computation of $\Pi + (\alpha_1, \ldots, \alpha_r)$ is the total number of viruses sent to the output region during the computation.

Next, a particular kind of virus machines providing function computing devices, is introduced.

Definition 3. *Let $f : \mathbb{N}^k - \to \mathbb{N}$ be a partial function. We say that function f is computable by a virus machine Π with k input hosts if for each $(x_1, \ldots, x_k) \in \mathbb{N}^k$ we have the following:*

- *If $(x_1, \ldots, x_k) \in dom(f)$ and $f(x_1, \ldots, x_k) = z$, then every computation of $\Pi + (x_1, \ldots, x_k)$ is a halting computation and the output is z.*
- *If $(x_1, \ldots, x_k) \in \mathbb{N}^k \setminus dom(f)$, then every computation of $\Pi + (x_1, \ldots, x_k)$ is a non-halting computation.*

3 Arithmetic Operation Modules

In this section, we provide different modules for the different basic arithmetic operations; that is, addition, substraction, multiplication and division (both quotient and remainder). In these types of machines, the encoding of natural numbers will be given by an unary encoding; that is, the input number $n \in \mathbb{N}$ will be encoded by v^n; that is, n copies of the object v. In what follows, we introduce the different modules and some of their properties.

3.1 Add Module

This module is a Virus Machines with two input hosts, where the two terms of the addition are introduced as an input. The Virus Machine

$$\Pi_{add} = (\Gamma, H, H_r, I, D_H, D_I, G_C, n_1, n_2, i_1, h_{out})$$

of range $(2, 3, 2)$ where:

1. $\Gamma = \{v\}$, $H = H_r = \{h_1, h_2\}$, $I = \{i_1, i_2, i_3\}$;
2. $D_H = (\{h_0\} \cup H, E_H, w_H)$, where $E_H = \{(h_1, h_0), (h_2, h_0)\}$ and $w_H(h_1, h_0) = w_H(h_2, h_0) = 1$;
3. $D_I = (I, E_I, w_I)$, where $E_I = \{(i_1, i_1), (i_1, i_2), (i_2, i_2), (i_2, i_3)\}$ and $w_I(i_1, i_1) = w_I(i_2, i_2) = 2, w_I(i_1, i_2) = w_I(i_2, i_3) = 1$;
4. $G_C = (I \cup E_H, E_C)$, where $E_C = \{\{i_1, (h_1, h_0)\}, \{i_2, (h_2, h_0)\}\}$;
5. $n_i = 0, i \in \{1, 2\}$;
6. $h_{out} = h_0$.

A visual representation of this Virus Machine can be found in Fig. 2a. The idea is that all the viruses present in the initial configuration to the environment (i.e. the output region). Let (a, b) be the input of Π; then the following invariants hold in this machine.

$\phi(k) \equiv \mathcal{C}_k = (k, a - k, b, i_1)$, for $0 \leq k \leq a$

In the first k steps, a viruses go from h_1 to the environment. Then, in configuration a no viruses are available in h_1, therefore the next instruction is i_2.

$\phi'(k) \equiv \mathcal{C}_{a+1+k} = (a + k, 0, b - k, i_2)$, for $0 \leq k \leq b$

From configuration $\mathcal{C}_{a+1}$, instruction i_2 is executed until no more viruses are available in the host h_2, and thus i_3 will be selected as the next instruction.

Finally, in configuration $\mathcal{C}_{a+b+2}$, instruction i_3, that is not attached to any channel, thus next instruction is $\#$ and the computation halts. Therefore, $\mathcal{C}_{a+b+3} = (a + b, 0, 0, \#)$.

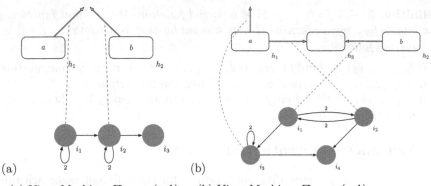

(a) Virus Machine $\Pi_{add} + (a, b)$ (b) Virus Machine $\Pi_{sub} + (a, b)$

Fig. 2. Virus Machines for addition and subtraction operations

3.2 Sub Module

The Virus Machine presented computes the reduced difference, represented with the symbol $\overset{\bullet}{-}$ operation; that is, $a \overset{\bullet}{-} b = a - b$ if $a \geq b$, 0 otherwise. The Virus Machine
$$\Pi_{sub} = (\Gamma, H, H_r, I, D_H, D_I, G_C, n_1, n_2, n_3, i_1, h_{out})$$
of range $(3, 4, 2)$ where:

1. $\Gamma = \{v\}$, $H = \{h_3\} \cup H_r$, where $H_r = \{h_1, h_2\}$, $I = \{i_1, i_2, i_3, i_4\}$;
2. $D_H = (\{h_0\} \cup H, E_H, w_H)$, where $E_H = \{(h_1, h_3), (h_1, h_0), (h_2, h_3)\}$ and $w_H(h_1, h_0) = w_H(h_2, h_0) = 1$;
3. $D_I = (I, E_I, w_I)$, where $E_I = \{(i_1, i_2), (i_1, i_3), (i_2, i_1), (i_2, i_4), (i_3, i_3), (i_3, i_4)\}$ and $w_I(i_1, i_2) = w_I(i_2, i_1) = w_I(i_3, i_3) = 2, w_I(i_1, i_3) = w_I(i_2, i_4) = w_I(i_3, i_4) = 1$;
4. $G_C = (I \cup E_H, E_C)$, where $E_C = \{\{i_1, (h_2, h_3)\}, \{i_2, (h_1, h_3)\}, \{i_3, (h_1, h_0)\}\}$;
5. $n_i = 0, i \in \{1, 2, 3\}$;
6. $h_{out} = h_0$.

A visual representation of this Virus Machine can be found in Fig. 2b. The idea is that viruses from h_1 are "countered" by viruses from h_2 and, if any virus remains in h_1, then goes to the environment. Let (a, b) be the input of Π, and let $mod(a, b)$ be the *modulus* operator; then the following invariants hold in this machine.

$\phi(k) \equiv C_k = (0, a - \lfloor \frac{k}{2} \rfloor, b - \lceil \frac{k}{2} \rceil, k, i_{1+mod(k,2)})$, for $0 \leq k \leq min\{2(a+1) - 1, 2b)\}$.

Here, two different cases can arise. If $a < b$, then the first $2(a + 1) - 1$ steps, instructions i_1 and i_2 will alternate one after the other, in order to send to h_3 (a "garbage" host) one virus each host alternaly. As h_1 will run out of viruses before h_2, in the configuration $C_{2(a+1)-1}$, since no more viruses are available in host h_1, instruction i_4 is selected as the next instruction, and configuration

$\mathcal{C}_{2(a+1)+1}$ is a halting configuration. Otherwise, if $a \geq b$, then the first $2b$ steps, instructions i_1 and i_2 will alternate one after the other. In this case, h_2 will run out of viruses before h_1, thus in the configuration $\mathcal{C}_{2b}$, instruction i_3 will be the next instruction. Then, from that point, the following invariant holds:

$\phi'(k) \equiv \mathcal{C}_{2b+k} = (k, a - b - k, 0, k, i_3)$, for $0 \leq k \leq a - b$

After $a - b$ steps, $a - b$ viruses will be sent to the environment and, since no more viruses are available in host h_1, next instruction is i_4, that will lead to a halting configuration $\mathcal{C}_{2b+a-b+2}$.

3.3 Mul Module

A Virus Machine capable of returning the multiplication of two given numbers is given below. The Virus Machine

$$\Pi_{mul} = (\Gamma, H, H_r, I, D_H, D_I, G_C, n_1, n_2, n_3, n_4, i_1, h_{out})$$

of range $(4, 5, 2)$ where:

1. $\Gamma = \{v\}$, $H = \{h_3, h_4\} \cup H_r$, where $H_r = \{h_1, h_2\}$, $I = \{i_1, i_2, i_3, i_4, i_5\}$;
2. $D_H = (\{h_0\} \cup H, E_H, w_H)$, where $E_H = \{(h_1, h_3), (h_2, h_4), (h_3, h_1), (h_3, h_0)\}$ and $w_H(h_1, h_3) = 2, w_H(h_2, h_4) = w_H(h_3, h_1) = w_H(h_3, h_0) = 1$;
3. $D_I = (I, E_I, w_I)$, where $E_I = \{(i_1, i_2), (i_1, i_5), (i_2, i_2), (i_2, i_3), (i_3, i_1), (i_3, i_1), (i_4, i_3)\}$ and $w_I(i_1, i_2) = w_I(i_2, i_2) = w_I(i_3, i_4) = 2, w_I(i_1, i_5) = w_I(i_2, i_3) = w_I(i_3, i_1) = w_I(i_4, i_3) = 1$;
4. $G_C = (I \cup E_H, E_C)$, where
   $E_C = \{\{i_1, (h_2, h_4)\}, \{i_2, (h_1, h_3)\}, \{i_3, (h_3, h_1)\}, \{i_4, (h_3, h_0)\}\}$;
5. $n_i = 0, i \in \{1, 2, 3, 4\}$;
6. $h_{out} = h_0$.

We can see the idea of this Virus Machine in Fig. 3. Let (a, b) the the input of Π. The following invariant holds:

$\phi(k) \equiv \mathcal{C}_{k(3a+3)} = (a \cdot k, a, b - k, 0, k, i_1)$, for $0 \leq k \leq b$

From the first configuration, viruses from h_2 will be sent to host h_4 (a "garbage" host) in order to "count" the number of times that viruses from h_1 must be sent to the environment. Then, instruction i_2 will send two times the number of viruses in h_1 to h_3 in a steps. When it finishes, it goes to instruction i_3, that will be executed alternately with i_4 until no viruses remain in h_3. This will happen in $2a + 1$ steps. When this happens, the next instruction selected is, again, i_1. This process will go on until no viruses remain in h_2, where instruction i_5 is selected and leads to a halting configuration in the next step, in configuration $\mathcal{C}_{b(3a+3)+2}$.

3.4 Quotient Module

The division operation can be seen as a function $f : \mathbb{N}^2 \rightarrow \mathbb{N}^2$, such that $f(D, d) = (q, r)$, fulfilling the following requirement: $D = d \cdot q + r$. q is said

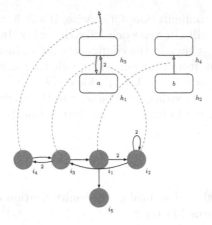

Fig. 3. Virus Machine $\Pi_{mul} + (a, b)$

to be the *quotient* of the division, while r is the *remainder*. The device returning the *quotient* is the Virus Machine

$$\Pi_{quo} = (\Gamma, H, H_r, I, D_H, D_I, G_C, n_1, n_2, n_3, n_4, i_1, h_{out})$$

of range $(4, 5, 2)$ where:

1. $\Gamma = \{v\}$, $H = \{h_3, h_4\} \cup H_r$, where $H_r = \{h_1, h_2\}$, $I = \{i_1, i_2, i_3, i_4, i_5\}$;
2. $D_H = (\{h_0\} \cup H, E_H, w_H)$, where
   $E_H = \{(h_1, h_3), (h_2, h_4), (h_3, h_0), (h_4, h_2)\}$ and $w_H(h_2, h_4) = w_H(h_1, h_3) = w_H(h_3, h_0) = w_H(h_4, h_2) = 1$;
3. $D_I = (I, E_I, w_I)$, where $E_I = \{(i_1, i_2), (i_1, i_3), (i_2, i_1), (i_2, i_5), (i_3, i_4), (i_4, i_1), (i_4, i_4)\}$ and $w_I(i_1, i_2) = w_I(i_2, i_1) = w_I(i_4, i_4) = 2, w_I(i_1, i_3) = w_I(i_2, i_5) = w_I(i_3, i_4) = w_I(i_4, i_1) = 1$;
4. $G_C = (I \cup E_H, E_C)$, where
   $E_C = \{\{i_1, (h_2, h_4)\}, \{i_2, (h_1, h_3)\}, \{i_3, (h_1, h_0)\}, \{i_4, (h_4, h_2)\}\}$;
5. $n_i = 0, i \in \{1, 2, 3, 4\}$;
6. $h_{out} = h_0$

This Virus Machine can be depicted as in Fig. 4a

By definition, we will say that $a/0 = 0, a \in \mathbb{N}$. Let (a, b) be the input of Π. Then the following invariant holds:

$\phi(k) \equiv C_{k(3b+3)} = (k, a - b \cdot k, b, b \cdot k - k, 0, i_1)$, for $0 \le k \le \lfloor \frac{a}{b} \rfloor$

From the first configuration, instructions i_1 and i_2 will alternately be executed until h_1 or h_2 go out of viruses. If h_2 goes out of viruses first, then it means that we can add 1 to the temporary quotient (i.e. the number of viruses in the environment). If this is the case, from i_1, the instruction i_3 is selected, and one virus is sent from h_3 to the environment (taking into account that viruses in h_3 are not useful in any other sense, therefore we use them as "counters"). When h_1 runs out of viruses, and instruction i_2 is executed, the instruction selected is i_5, leading to a halting configuration in $C_{\lfloor a/b \rfloor \cdot (3b+3)+2}$. Let us recall that in this case we say that, by definition, $a/0 = 0, a \in \mathbb{N}$.

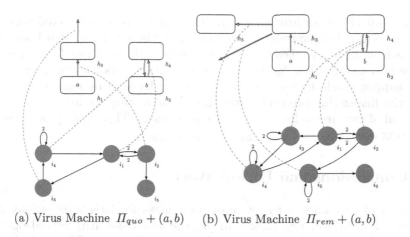

(a) Virus Machine $\Pi_{quo} + (a, b)$ (b) Virus Machine $\Pi_{rem} + (a, b)$

Fig. 4. Virus machines for the quotient and remainder of division operations

3.5   Remainder Module

While in the previous subsection, the Virus Machine answering the *quotient* of the division of two given numbers was given, below is presented one returning the *remainder* of such operation. The Virus Machine

$$\Pi_{rem} = (\Gamma, H, H_r, I, D_H, D_I, G_C, n_1, n_2, n_3, n_4, n_5, i_1, h_{out})$$

of range $(5, 6, 2)$ where:

1. $\Gamma = \{v\}$, $H = \{h_3, h_4, h_5\} \cup H_r$, where $H_r = \{h_1, h_2\}$, $I = \{i_1, i_2, i_3, i_4, i_5, i_6\}$;
2. $D_H = (\{h_0\} \cup H, E_H, w_H)$, where
   $E_H = \{(h_1, h_3), (h_2, h_4), (h_3, h_5), (h_3, h_0), (h_4, h_2)\}$ and $w_H(h_1, h_3) = w_H(h_2, h_4) = w_H(i_3, i_5) = w_H(h_3, h_0) = w_H(h_4, h_2) = 1$;
3. $D_I = (I, E_I, w_I)$, where
   $E_I = \{(i_1, i_2), (i_1, i_3), (i_2, i_1), (i_2, i_5), (i_3, i_3), (i_3, i_4), (i_4, i_1), (i_4, i_4), (i_5, i_5), (i_5, i_6)\}$ and $w_I(i_1, i_2) = w_I(i_2, i_1) = w_I(i_3, i_3) = w_I(i_4, i_4) = w_I(i_5, i_5) = 2$, $w_I(i_1, i_3) = w_I(i_2, i_5) = w_I(i_3, i_4) = w_I(i_4, i_1) = w_I(i_5, i_6) = 1$;
4. $G_C = (I \cup E_H, E_C)$, where
   $E_C = \{\{i_1, (h_2, h_4)\}, \{i_2, (h_1, h_3)\}, \{i_3, (h_4, h_2)\}, \{i_4, (h_3, h_5)\}, \{i_5, (h_3, h_0)\}\}$;
5. $n_i = 0, i \in \{1, 2, 3, 4, 5\}$;
6. $h_{out} = h_0$

This Virus Machine is represented visually in Fig. 4b.

In order to fulfil the basics of the division, that is, $D = d \cdot q + r$, we say that the remainder of the division $a/0, a \in \mathbb{N}$ is equal to a. Let (a, b) be the input of Π. Then the following invariant holds:

$$\phi(k) \equiv C_{k(4b+3)} = (0, a - b \cdot k, b, 0, 0, b \cdot k, i_1), \text{ for } 0 \leq k \leq \lfloor \tfrac{a}{b} \rfloor$$

The idea is similar to the quotient module. First, we alternate between instructions i_1 and i_2, until one of them run out of viruses. On the one hand, if

h_2 runs out of viruses first, then it means that b can be subtracted once again from a. When this happens, instruction i_5 is selected, that takes back all the viruses from h_4 to h_2, when this process finishes, all the viruses from h_3 are sent to the host h_5, that is a "garbage" collector, and it goes back to instruction i_1. This happens each $4b + 3$ steps. On the other hand, if h_1 runs out of viruses first, the finalization protocol starts, first by activating the instruction i_5, that sends all of the viruses from h_3 to the environment. This whole process leads to a halting configuration $\mathcal{C}_{\lfloor a/b \rfloor \cdot (4b+3) + remainder(a,b) + 3}$.

4   Conclusions and Future Work

The idea of this work is to establish some ideas for later applications in the framework of information fusion. In [3], the four basic arithmetical operators are used to give an explicit basic probability assignment (BPA) calculator by means of Spiking Neural P systems. Since the encoding is totally different in this framework, some changes must be introduced in order to obtain such kind of calculator.

Apart from that, and since the framework is in a very early stage, several research lines are open, as well as some ideas for extension of the model, in a similar way to extensions in the framework of Membrane Computing.

Acknowledgements. This work was supported by "Junta de Andalucía (Consejería de Economía, Conocimiento, Empresas y Universidad)" (P20_00486) – Desarrollo de modelos computacionales de especies invasoras en el Guadalquivir: herramientas de gestión para su control y prevención. D. Orellana-Martín also acknowledges Contratación de Personal Investigador Doctor. (Convocatoria 2019) 43 Contratos Capital Humano Línea 2. Paidi 2020, supported by the European Social Fund and Junta de Andalucía.

References

1. Chen, X., Pérez-Jiménez, M.J., Valencia-Cabrera, L., Wang, B., Zeng, X.: Computing with viruses. Theoret. Comput. Sci. **623**, 146–159 (2016)
2. Dimmock, N.J., Easton, A.J., Leppard, K.: Introduction to Modern Virology. Blackwell Publication, Malden (2007)
3. Zhang, G., Rong, H., Paul, P., He, Y., Neri, F., Pérez-Jiménez, M.J.: A complete arithmetic calculator constructed from spiking neural P systems and its application to information fusion. Int. J. Neural Syst. **31**(1), 2050055 (2001)

An Efficient and Rotation Invariant Fourier-Based Metric for Assessing the Quality of Images Created by Generative Models

J. Gamazo, J. M. Cuadra, and M. Rincón[✉]

Artificial Intelligence Department, UNED, Madrid, Spain
mrincon@dia.uned.es
http://www.ia.uned.es

Abstract. Recent progress in generative image modeling is leading to a new era of high-resolution fakes visually indistinguishable from real life images. However, the development of metrics capable of discerning whether images are synthetic or not runs behind the race of achieving the best generator, thus bringing potential threats. We propose a rotation invariant metric capable of distinguishing real and generated image datasets and we call it CSD (Circular Spectrum Distance) due to its circular nature and its inherent relation to the Fourier Spectrum. Its performance is analysed on a whole brain MRI dataset. CSD has similar behavior to FID during training but requires smaller batch sizes and is faster to compute.

1 Introduction

Since their introduction, generative adversarial networks (GANs) [7] have dominated the state of the art in image generation tasks. It has been demonstrated that GANs are capable of learning very different distributions, producing images that are indistinguishable from the real ones [14,15]. However, the question of how to assess their performance remains open. The subjectivity of this assessment, bound to the high variety of domains in which an image generator could be trained, makes the effort of developing a universal metric, valid for all image generation models, a tremendously hard task. Therefore, even though possible quantification metrics have been proposed (see [2] for a review), to this day, subjective image quality assessment is the most reliable way to evaluate the visual quality of generated images. Reliable quantitative metrics, objective and automatic, can be used to compare generative models, but also to assist during the training process. Additionally, a good metric could help to detect fake images or videos generated with deep learning methods.

The evaluation of GANs has been widely treated in the literature [2,10,16, 18,19]. An efficient evaluation metric should not only favor models that achieve high fidelity samples, agreeing with humans' subjective perception, but also be

J. M. Ferrández Vicente et al. (Eds.): IWINAC 2022, LNCS 13259, pp. 413–422, 2022.
https://doi.org/10.1007/978-3-031-06527-9_41

sensitive to image distortions and favor models that generate diverse samples (detecting different overfitting situations such as mode collapse, mode drop, or memorization) and provide disentangled representation spaces [2]. In the last years, Inception Score (IS) [18] and Frechet Inception Distance (FID) [10] have led all benchmarks on GAN evaluation. However, these two metrics are potentially flawed because they use the Inception Network trained on ImageNet as a basis, so it is not clear whether these metrics could be used for classes outside the scope of this dataset or they would lead to misinterpretations [2], as it is not clear whether the features resulting from an ImageNet pre-trained model are meaningful outside their domain [17]. Another branch of GAN metrics research relies on using the discriminator part of the GAN to assess the performance of the generator [12,16]. However, these methods do not provide a way to compare between different models, as they use discriminators trained for the specific task.

To the authors' knowledge, all proposed metrics use either pixel or latent spaces generated with neural networks. However, none of them has delved into the goodness of spectral representations and the inherent difficulty for GANs to reproduce the high frequencies of real samples [22,25]. Some works [8,20,23] have outlined the advantages of introducing complex filters in CNNs due to their rotation invariance, an ability that is "learnt" in real-valued CNNs by feeding them with rotated images obtained with data augmentation [11]. Rotation invariant CNNs, a case of Group Equivariant Convolutional Networks [3], yield better results than usual CNNs when applied to medical image segmentation [21].

Zhang et al. [25] describe how the up-sampling modules, present in the generator of GANs, produce artifacts that are barely visible as a checkerboard pattern in the spatial domain but are definitely noticeable in the frequency domain. In order for the generator to get rid of those patterns, the learned convolution cores must behave like low-pass filters, rendering the generator unable to learn high-frequency characteristics correctly. In [22] they also compare the frequency domain results of a series of GAN models, showing that some of them are more prone to present artifacts than others. In [5], the authors show the differences in the Fourier spectra of real and generated images by first reducing their dimensionality, averaging circular bins of the spectrum, fitting an exponential decay function to highlight differences in high-frequency characteristics, and later training an SVM to detect the spurious dataset.

This work contributes to the state-of-the-art with a new metric for GAN evaluation that draws on Fourier spectral images for both real and generated datasets to quantify their differences and evaluate the performance of the generator. It has a similar behavior to that of FID during training but needs smaller batch sizes and is faster to compute.

2   Methods

We use the idea of dimensionality reduction by binning [5] to develop a rotation invariant metric that uses the Fourier spectrum of the dataset to evaluate the performance of the generator of a GAN. The process has three steps: 1) obtain a one-dimensional measurement from the image spectrum; 2) integrate this measurement across the real and synthetic datasets; and 3) quantify the distance between them.

Let f be the value of the pixels of an image with dimensions $W \times H \times C$, defined by $f : \mathbb{R}^3 \to [0,1]$. Constraining the values of $\mathbb{R}^3$ to (x, y, z), where x and y take discrete values in the range $[1, W]$ and $[1, H]$ respectively, and z is a discrete variable that spans $\{1, C\}$. Let us denote by $\hat{f}'(k_r, \theta, z)$ the Fourier transform (spectrum) of f in polar coordinates, where k_r, θ and z are the distance to the center, the angle and the channel number respectively. This Fourier transform is applied to axes (x, y) and z remains unchanged. We reduce the dimensionality of the Fourier spectrum summing over the continuous variable θ, and obtain the reduced spectrum as in Eq. 1:

$$m'(k_r, z) = a \int_0^{2\pi} |\hat{f}'(k_r, \theta, z)| d\theta, \tag{1}$$

where a represents an image-dependent normalization factor such that the condition $\max\{m'(k_r, z)\} = 1$ is fulfilled, and the values of the components of m' are constrained to the interval $[0, 1]$. Given that the number of channels is discrete, we can further reduce the dimensionality again by taking the L_2 norm through that axis and normalizing accordingly (Eq. 2):

$$m(k_r) = \frac{1}{\sqrt{C}} \sqrt{\sum_{i=1}^{C} m_i'^2}, \tag{2}$$

where $m_i' \equiv m'(k_r, i)$.

We could obtain the *histogram-based spectral group average*, $M(k_r)$, by discretizing k_r into k uniform bins and averaging over each element for a group of N images. However, in order to reduce the computational cost, we have reversed these two steps: computing the spectrum of the dataset average image first ($\hat{f}(k_r, \theta, z)$), and then calculating $\hat{M}(k_r)$ by taking its L_2 norm (Eq. 3) over the C channels. Figure 1 shows a graphical illustration of the steps followed to obtain the histogram-based spectral group average.

$$M'(k_r, z) = a \int_0^{2\pi} |\hat{f}(k_r, \theta, z)| d\theta \quad \Longrightarrow \quad \hat{M}(k_r) = \frac{1}{\sqrt{C}} \sqrt{\sum_{i=1}^{C} M_i'^2} \tag{3}$$

This expression has an associated error ($M = \hat{M} \pm \Delta$) that stems from two sources: 1) the averaged spectrum and 2) the norm through the channels' dimension. The first error is computed as the sampling variance $\sigma^2(k_r, \theta, z)$, and is propagated to the integral. Then, the second source of error can also be propagated assuming that $M_i' \equiv M'(k_r, i)$ is statistically independent to M_j' for every $i \neq j$:

$$\Delta'(k_r, z) = \sqrt{\int_0^{2\pi} \sigma^2(k_r, \theta, z) d\theta} \quad \Longrightarrow \quad \Delta(k_r) = \frac{1}{\sqrt{C}} \sqrt{\frac{\sum_i M_i'^2 \Delta_i'^2}{\sum_i M_i'^2}} \tag{4}$$

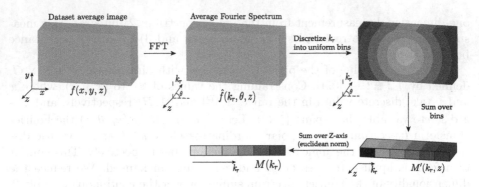

Fig. 1. Graphical illustration of the methodology followed to obtain $M(k_r)$.

Taking an original dataset and building another one with generated images, one can compute $M_o = \hat{M}_o \pm \Delta_o$ and $M_g = \hat{M}_g \pm \Delta_g$ (original and generated respectively), and calculate the distance between the curves. Assuming that errors are distributed normally and that k_r has k discrete points, and therefore both curves are polygonal, it has been proved that discrete Fréchet distance is a good measure of the similarity between them [1].

Following the definition of the discrete Fréchet distance in [6], we define a new metric, which we call *Circular Spectrum Distance* (CSD), as the minimum coupling of M_o and M_g (Eq. 5).

$$\text{CSD} = d_{\text{F}}(M_o, M_g) = \min_{i=1,\ldots,k} \left\{ \max_{j=1,\ldots,k} \{ d_e(\hat{M}_{o_i}, \hat{M}_{g_j}) + \Delta_{o_i} + \Delta_{g_j} - 2\sqrt{\Delta_{o_i} \cdot \Delta_{g_j}} \} \right\} \quad (5)$$

where d_F represents the Fréchet distance and $d_e()$, the Euclidean distance in $\mathbb{R}$. Therefore, since CSD follows the same principles as Fréchet distance, the conditions for considering CSD a suitable metric are met. Algorithm 1 shows that the use of this metric during training is straightforward.

3 Experimental Setup

To analyse CSD metric behavior, we use StyleGAN [14] to learn and generate synthetic images. This architecture is not constrained to any predefined distribution, but this is learned during the training process, which allows for a more linear entanglement and a higher capacity to detect features in the latent space $\mathcal{W}$. On the other hand, uncorrelated Gaussian noise is added after every convolutional layer in order to achieve a stochastic component that lets the architecture produce finer details.

Algorithm 1: Implementation of the Circular Spectrum Distance (CSD)

Function mean_var(μ, σ^2, B):

> **Result:** M' and Δ' as defined in Eqs. 3 and 4
>
> **Input:** $\mu \rightarrow$ Average 2D spectrum of the data
>
> $\qquad$ $\sigma^2 \rightarrow$ Variance of the 2D spectrum
>
> $\qquad$ $B \rightarrow$ Number of bins used to discretize the radial dimension
>
> **while** $i < B$ **do**
>
> $\quad$ | $\quad$ $M'_i \longleftarrow$ mean($\mu[i]$) $\qquad\qquad\qquad\qquad$ // Radial mean
>
> $\quad$ | $\quad$ $\Delta'_i \longleftarrow \sqrt{\mathrm{sum}(\sigma^2[i])}$ $\qquad\qquad\qquad$ // Radial variance
>
> **end**
>
> **return** M', Δ'

return

Function Main:

> **Result:** Circular Spectrum Distance as given by Eq. 5
>
> $\mu_o, \sigma_o^2 \longleftarrow$ Avg Fourier spect(original dataset)
>
> $M', \Delta' \longleftarrow$ mean_var(μ_o, σ_o^2, B)
>
> $M_o, \Delta_0 \longleftarrow$ Eqs. 3 and 4
>
> **foreach** *epoch* **do**
>
> $\quad$ | $\quad$ $g \longleftarrow$ generator()
>
> $\quad$ | $\quad$ $\mu_g, \sigma_g^2 \longleftarrow$ Avg Fourier spectrum(g)
>
> $\quad$ | $\quad$ $M', \Delta' \longleftarrow$ mean_var(μ_g, σ_g^2, B)
>
> $\quad$ | $\quad$ $M_g, \Delta_g \longleftarrow$ Eqs. 3 and 4
>
> $\quad$ | $\quad$ CSD $\longleftarrow$ Eq. 5
>
> **end**

We used the publicly available dataset from the MICCAI WMH Challenge, consisting of 168 cases with two brain MR image modalities (T1-weighted and FLAIR) from three different MR scanners. We have chosen this dataset because of its underlying rotation invariance, as brain images do not have a preferred orientation per se. Images were independently bias field corrected, coregistered and finally T1-weighted volume was resampled to FLAIR space [4]. We used a brain extraction tool [13] to remove uninteresting structures, such as the skull. 3D images were then cropped to the region of interest and resized with linear interpolation to $(57, 256, 256)$. The neural network was then fed with the axial planes of this volume. Black images were removed from the dataset. As a result, the final dataset comprised 3,420 two channel images (T1-weighted and FLAIR).

A StyleGAN with Exponential Moving Average was trained on the 3,420 MRI dataset, each being $256 \times 256 \times 2$. No other data augmentation techniques were applied. The generator networks consists of seven style blocks as defined in [14], with an input latent space of 512 dimensions. Model hyperparameters were as follows: batch size: 8, mixing regularization: random style mixing, learning rate: 4 times larger for the discriminator to stabilize training [10]. We did not used any progressive growing method in the generator and trained the architecture using WGAN loss with gradient penalty (WGAN-GP) [9]. No feedback from CSD was added to the loss function, but we used Exponential Moving Average to prevent cycling around the optimal solution [24].

4   Evaluation

To evaluate the behavior of CSD, we analyse 1) its response to different distortions of the original dataset (Sect. 4.1), 2) its behaviour during training (Sect. 4.2), and 3) its computational performance (Sect. 4.3).

4.1   Response to Image Distortions

A metric for quality assessment in image generation tasks is only valid if it can evaluate the level at which images degrade. We carried out distortion experiments on the original dataset and calculated the CSD for each of them. Figure 2 shows that CSD responds appropriately to different distortions, increasing its value with the magnitude of the distortion in all cases but "patches", presumably due to its nature: when many patches are added, the image transforms into a meaningless zero image, and CSD cannot assess its quality.

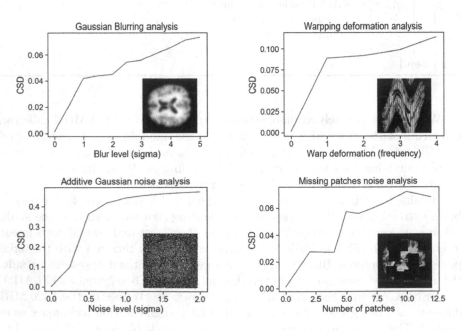

Fig. 2. CSD response to different image distortions.

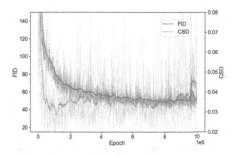

Fig. 3. Evolution of FID and CSD metrics during training.

4.2   Behaviour During Training

A valid way to understand what a metric is measuring is to pay attention to its behaviour during training and compare it to a well-known benchmark. Figure 3 shows FID and CSD during training over three runs with a sample of 10,000 MRI each. It shows that CSD is noisier but keeps a clear tendency: after a period of stabilisation in the first epochs, it increases and stagnates at a higher value, approximately 60% over the first stabilised value. FID, however, declines constantly with lower slope and with lighter variations during the whole training, thus bringing very little feedback on how the training is performing. This exact behaviour has been shown in all runs.

4.3   Performance Analysis

CSD metric was implemented in Tensorflow2 and its performance was compared to that of FID varying the batch size. This study was carried out on a system with 2 Intel (R) Xeon (R) Silver 4210 CPU@2.20 GHz and one GPU Tesla V100 with 32 GB RAM. The results displayed in Fig. 4 show that CSD outperforms FID in terms of speed for small batch sizes. While time for CSD rises linearly with batch size, FID resembles a logarithmic behaviour. As these measurements are very system-dependent, we can only claim that in this specific architecture, CSD is faster for small batch sizes and slowly approaches the speed of FID (potentially exceeding it) when the batch size is greatly increased to non-practical values.

On the other hand, it is a well known problem that FID needs on the order of 10k images to function properly, which heavily increases its computation time. Therefore, we analysed this dependence for CSD. We used a fully trained generator to produce a variable number of images (1 to 5,000) and computed CSD. This process was repeated five times for every batch to draw conclusions on consistent results. Figure 5 shows that CSD remains fairly constant and with a minor variance with an order of magnitude of 10^2 images. Therefore we can claim that we shall be in the range where CSD is faster than FID and yet obtain meaningful results.

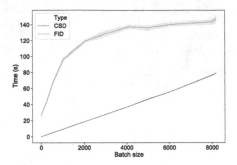

Fig. 4. Computational cost analysis.

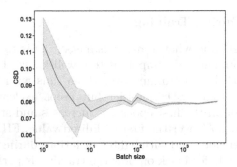

Fig. 5. Correlation of CSD with the number of images.

Even though FID (and IS) has proved to be very powerful, one of its biggest drawbacks is its reliance on pretrained models. This can be considered a disadvantage in terms of reliability when facing outside the scope of the training set (generally ImageNet). Furthermore, feeding images through a neural network to get its latent representation is memory expensive when increasing the batch size. Batch sizes in FID should be on the order of 10^4 images, which represents roughly 4 GB RAM in half-precision floating point format. We conducted two experiments to demonstrate that CSD was less expensive than FID. It was concluded that 1) CSD needed far less data, as it produced meaningful, accurate results with only 10^2 images (Fig. 5); and 2) within this range it was faster (Fig. 4).

5 Conclusions and Future Work

We have introduced CSD, a metric based on the distance between original and synthetic Fourier spectra that can be used to assess the performance of the generator of GANs and that does not depend on pretrained models to operate. The hypothesis underlying this metric is that the generators of GANs tend to work as low-pass filters and hence the generated images present a high deviation from the original images in the high frequencies.

To the authors' knowledge, there are no other works that delve into the use of Fourier Spectrum to create metrics valuable for GANs. The use of Fourier spectra is residual in the literature of generative deep learning, limiting itself to subjective analyses and architecture comparisons. With this work, we demonstrate that even the easiest usages of this tool are beneficial. In-depth study of complex-valued networks might be profitable especially in classification tasks due to their rotational invariance. Moreover, as future work, it could be worthwhile to experiment with different norms and analyze the metric behavior.

Acknowledgments. The authors gratefully acknowledge research project PID2019-110686RB-I00 of the State Research Program Oriented to the Challenges of Society.

References

1. Alt, H., Godau, M.: Computing the Fréchet distance between two poligonal curves. Int. J. Comput. Geom. Appli. (1995). https://doi.org/10.1142/s0218195995000064
2. Borji, A.: Pros and cons of GAN evaluation measures. Comput. Vis. Image Underst. (2019). https://doi.org/10.1016/j.cviu.2018.10.009
3. Cohen, T.S., Welling, M.: Group equivariant convolutional networks. In: 33rd International Conference on Machine Learning, ICML 2016, vol. 6, pp. 4375–4386, February 2016
4. Duque, P., Cuadra, J.M., Jiménez, E., Rincón-Zamorano, M.: Data preprocessing for automatic WMH segmentation with FCNNs. In: Ferrández Vicente, J., Álvarez-Sánchez, J., de la Paz López, F.,Toledo Moreo, J., Adeli, H. (eds.) From Bioinspired Systems and Biomedical Applications to Machine Learning, IWINAC 2019. LNCS, vol 11487, pp. 452–460. Springer, Cham, (2019). https://doi.org/10.1007/978-3-030-19651-644
5. Dzanic, T., Shah, K., Witherden, F.: Fourier spectrum discrepancies in deep network generated images, November 2019
6. Eiter, T., Mannila, H.: Computing discrete Fréchet distance. Tech. rep. (1994)
7. Goodfellow, I.J., et al.: Generative adversarial nets. In: Advances in Neural Information Processing Systems (2014). https://doi.org/10.3156/jsoft.29.5_177_2
8. Guberman, N.: On complex valued convolutional neural networks, February 2016. http://arxiv.org/abs/1602.09046
9. Gulrajani, I., Ahmed, F., Arjovsky, M., Dumoulin, V., Courville, A.: Improved training of wasserstein GANs. In: Advances in Neural Information Processing Systems (2017)
10. Heusel, M., Ramsauer, H., Unterthiner, T., Nessler, B., Hochreiter, S.: GANs trained by a two time-scale update rule converge to a local nash equilibrium. In: Advances in Neural Information Processing Systems (2017)
11. Goodfellow, I., Yoshua Bengio, A.C.: Front Matter. In: Linear Algebra, pp. i–ii. Elsevier (2014). https://doi.org/10.1016/B978-0-12-391420-0.09987-X
12. Im, D.J., Kim, C.D., Jiang, H., Memisevic, R.: Generating images with recurrent adversarial networks, February 2016
13. Isensee, F., et al.: Automated brain extraction of multisequence MRI using artificial neural networks. Hum. Brain Mapp. (2019). https://doi.org/10.1002/hbm.24750
14. Karras, T., Laine, S., Aila, T.: A style-based generator architecture for generative adversarial networks. In: 2019 IEEE/CVF Conference on Computer Vision and Pattern Recognition, CVPR, pp. 4396–4405. IEEE, June 2019, https://doi.org/10.1109/CVPR.2019.00453

15. Karras, T., Laine, S., Aittala, M., Hellsten, J., Lehtinen, J., Aila, T.: Analyzing and improving the image quality of StyleGAN. In: 2020 IEEE/CVF Conference on Computer Vision and Pattern Recognition, CVPR, pp. 8107–8116. IEEE, June 2020. https://doi.org/10.1109/CVPR42600.2020.00813

16. Olsson, C., Bhupatiraju, S., Brown, T., Odena, A., Goodfellow, I.: Skill rating for generative models, August 2018. http://arxiv.org/abs/1808.04888

17. Raghu, M., Zhang, C., Kleinberg, J., Bengio, S.: Transfusion: understanding transfer learning for medical imaging. In: Proceedings of the 33rd International Conference on Neural Information Processing Systems. Curran Associates Inc. (2019). https://papers.nips.cc/paper/2019/hash/eb1e78328c46506b46a4ac4a1e378b91-Abstract.html

18. Salimans, T., Goodfellow, I., Zaremba, W., Cheung, V., Radford, A., Chen, X.: Improved techniques for training GANs. In: Advances in Neural Information Processing Systems (2016)

19. Shmelkov, K., Schmid, C., Alahari, K.: How good is my GAN? pp. 218–234, July 2018. https://doi.org/10.1007/978-3-030-01216-8_14

20. Tygert, M., Bruna, J., Chintala, S., LeCun, Y., Piantino, S., Szlam, A.: A mathematical motivation for complex-valued convolutional networks. Neural Comput. **28**(5), 815–825 (2016). https://doi.org/10.1162/NECO_a_00824, https://direct.mit.edu/neco/article/28/5/815-825/8157

21. Veeling, B.S., Linmans, J., Winkens, J., Cohen, T., Welling, M.: Rotation equivariant CNNS for digital pathology. In: Frangi, A., Schnabel, J., Davatzikos, C., Alberola-López, C., Fichtinger, G. (eds.) Medical Image Computing and Computer Assisted Intervention–MICCAI 2018. LNCS, vol. 11071, pp. 210–218. Springer, Cham (2018). https://doi.org/10.1007/978-3-030-00934-2_24

22. Wang, S.Y., Wang, O., Zhang, R., Owens, A., Efros, A.A.: CNN-Generated images are surprisingly easy to spot... for now. In: 2020 IEEE/CVF Conference on Computer Vision and Pattern Recognition, CVPR, pp. 8692–8701. IEEE, June 2020. https://doi.org/10.1109/CVPR42600.2020.00872

23. Worrall, D.E., Garbin, S.J., Turmukhambetov, D., Brostow, G.J.: Harmonic networks: deep translation and rotation equivariance. In: 2017 IEEE Conference on Computer Vision and Pattern Recognition, CVPR, pp. 7168–7177. IEEE, July 2017. https://doi.org/10.1109/CVPR.2017.758

24. Yazıcı, Y., Foo, C.S., Winkler, S., Yap, K.H., Piliouras, G., Chandrasekhar, V.: The unusual effectiveness of averaging in GAN training. In: 7th International Conference on Learning Representations, ICLR 2019, June 2018

25. Zhang, X., Karaman, S., Chang, S.F.: Detecting and simulating artifacts in GAN fake images. In: 2019 IEEE International Workshop on Information Forensics and Security, WIFS, pp. 1–6. IEEE, December 2019. https://doi.org/10.1109/WIFS47025.2019.9035107

A First-in-Class Block-Based Programming Language Distance Calculation

Luis-Eduardo Imbernón Cuadrado[1] , Ángeles Manjarrés Riesco[2] ,
and Félix de la Paz López[2(✉)]

[1] Hipoo, Madrid, Spain
[2] Department of Artificial Intelligence, Universidad Nacional de Educación a
Distancia, Madrid, Spain
{amanja,delapaz}@dia.uned.es

Abstract. Due to the rising interest in Computer Science (CS) in primary school, block-based programming languages have gained much significance. Within this article, we provide a first insight of our research into the identification of help needs of primary school children, when they are performing Scratch exercises. A first-in-class distance calculation method has been defined that takes into account the block-based programming languages idiosyncrasy.

Keywords: Automatic hint generation · Distance calculation ·
Block-based programming language · Teaching with Scratch

1 Introduction

In the last decade, online learning environments have gained attention, even more since the start of the lockdown in 2020 caused by the recent coronavirus (SARS-CoV2 or CoVid-19) pandemic [15]. Additionally, CS is experiencing an exponential growth, and Scratch, a graphical block-based programming language, is a promising approach to improve students' Computational Thinking (CT) skills in primary school [4,9].

In education, feedback is an important factor as it allows students to assess their learning progress. Identifying when a student has a mental block and providing personalized feedback can be difficult when teachers and learners are separated by space and time such as in online learning settings [6]. As concluded in [1], automatic feedback provided by the software, improves students' performance in programming activities.

As learning programming could be hard for novices, there are some next-step hint generators that provide support to the students, and also help to reduce the instructor effort [1]. The most common approach for generating next-step hints, is to identify the best solution candidate for the task, and then generate the next-step suggestion that moves the student closer to the selected solution.

© Springer Nature Switzerland AG 2022
J. M. Ferrández Vicente et al. (Eds.): IWINAC 2022, LNCS 13259, pp. 423–432, 2022.
https://doi.org/10.1007/978-3-031-06527-9_42

The selection of the best solution candidate is made by calculating the distance between the student's workspace and the different solutions. However, we have realized that the different existing distance calculation approaches take into account the name and the position of the program blocks, ignoring other attributes like the block family, or the value of their inputs.

To our knowledge, since not all the students have the same skills in CT, it may not be effective for the conditions under with the helping hints are shown to be the same for each student. Based on the above considerations, the goal of the current work is to present the first-in-class distance calculation for block-based programming languages.

The context of this work is robot tutoring systems research for block-based programming language teaching in primary school [7,8]. The suggested distance function will be used to train an artificial intelligence model, that will allow the system to identify when a student needs help while performing exercises of block-based programming languages. This will allow the robot tutor to know the moment when to carry out an optimal pedagogical intervention.

The rest of the paper is structured as follows. In Sect. 2, we present the research context and the technological choices, we explain the user experience carried out to evaluate our proposal, and we detail the distance calculation for block-based programming languages. In Sect. 3 we report on the results of our research. Finally, in Sect. 3 we include a discussion of our work and outline some future research lines suggested by our experience.

2   Materials and Methods

2.1   Research Context and Technological Choices

Throughout this section, we present the current state in the research areas of interest for this paper. Such areas are: block-based programming interfaces in primary school education, hint generators in pedagogical software and distance calculation methods.

Block-Based Programming Interfaces in Primary School. Programming learning is beneficial for primary school children, giving them the required tools to improve problem-solving, as in [13] where students have been engaged to solve arithmetic sequences, and geometric sequences and series using block-based programming codes instead of using algebra. There are other benefits such as improvement in efficiency and learning, an increase of enthusiasm, motivation, sense of fun and CT [3,14]. Block-based programming interfaces, compared to text-based programming are useful in reducing the complexity of programming, and they are also effective at creating interest towards programming in primary school [16].

Our experiment is based in Scratch, which is a free web-based programming tool focused on young people, that allows games, interactive stories and animations [4] to be created. This tool has been used in many CT research projects where primary school children were involved, as in [4,9,10].

Hint Generators. Learning programming with Scratch can be difficult, and students may get stuck in an exercise step. It could be advisable to generate some help that shows the next steps to the students who are stuck. This feedback must be individual, and it is desirable for it to be automatically created [12].

There are different approaches to generating hints, such as Next-Step (NS) hints and Waypoint (WP) hints. In [2] NS hints and WP hints are compared within a higher proficiency and a lower proficiency group. In this study, NS hints helped students to become quicker, more accurate and more efficient in resolution for both higher and lower proficiency groups than WP hints.

Distance Calculation Methods in Block-Based Programming Languages. When we have to identify how "far" or "close" is a block-based program from its solution, we have to measure in some way, the distance between this program and the solution. Because of its structure, block-based programming programs could be transformed into Abstract Syntax Trees (ASTs). There are several methods that can be used to measure the "closeness" between two different ASTs, such as pg-gram implented in [12], Edit Distance (TED) applied in [5] or Tree Inherited Distance (TID) as defined in [11]. Though these methods measure the distance between two ASTs, they just consider two dimensions: the position and the label of the node. In block-based programming as we will further explain, there are different dimensions that could affect the distance calculation.

2.2   User Experience with Scratch

The purposes of the user experience were:

– Testing our novel method for calculating the distance in a block-based programming language.
– Collecting data to assist the development of an intelligent model for identifying when a primary school student has need of pedagogical assistance, through the use of machine learning techniques.

Because our final goal is to assist students in a real learning environment while they are performing Scratch exercises, data collection must be done in a real learning environment. For that purpose, we have reached a collaboration agreement with two learning centers, and we have designed 10 scratch exercises that students must carry out, from lower to higher difficulty. Finally, the definition and validation of the distance function is a secondary objective to add value to the aforementioned final goal.

Since not all students have the same knowledge of Scratch, they will need help at different points of the process, so the model must be customized based on each knowledge level. To evaluate this, we have also designed 3 level assessments, ordered from lower to higher difficulty, that must be completed prior to executing the aforementioned exercises. These assessments measured the student's prior knowledge of Scratch.

The complete user experience process is described below:

- We first send the informed consent to the parents or legal custodians of the students. Before the students participate, both parents or legal custodians have enough time to consider participation.
- Then, the students whose parents have authorized their participation start by filling in a questionnaire.
- After that, they start the experience by carrying out the assessments. During them, they can't request any kind of help to evaluate the real prior knowledge of Scratch, but they can exit from the assessment at any time. Once the students have completed or exited from all the assessments, the knowledge level is set.
- Finally, the students can start doing the Scratch exercises in their preferred order. In those exercises they can ask for help and also switch to another exercise at any time they want.

From the first interaction with Scratch, up to the end of the exercises, all the interactions have been recorded in a database with the aim of analyzing them later. All this information is anonymous, by previously giving a random number to each participant. The stored information of this experiment is hereunder listed:

- Student data: student number, gender, mother_tongue, age and competence.
- Exercise data: name, description, skills, is_evaluation and solution_distance data.
- Interaction data: date_time, request_help, seconds_help_open and last_login.
- Workspace data: elements.

2.3   Distance Calculation for Block-Based Programming Languages

In programming learning activities there may be multiple solutions for a single task. The learning progress could be measured by calculating the distance between the student's workspace and the best candidate solution, i.e. the solution with the smallest distance with respect to the student's workspace.

In a block-based programming language, there are block families that depict a common functionality for their blocks. Each block can have, in turn, an input, and each input can contain one or many fields in which to input values. When designing a program in a block-based programming language, blocks could be placed in a single block for a sequential execution, or in different groups for a parallel execution.

In summary, the dimensions that influence the distance in a block-based programming language are:

1. Block family
2. Block
3. Block position
4. Block inputs values

Block-Family Distance Calculation. Let A be the block-family set of the student's workspace, and B the block family set of the exercise solution. The difference between both family groups is fixed as the symmetric difference between the set A and the set B.

We consider the correct family set as the block families in the student's workspace, that are also present in the exercise solution; and the wrong family set as the block families in the student's workspace, that didn't exist in the exercise solution. The distance calculation is carried out as follows: Being:

$F_c = \{x \mid \forall x \in A \cap B\}$, the correct family set.
$F_i = \{x \mid \forall x \in A \triangle B\}$, the wrong family set.

If x is a set of elements, and $n(x)$ is the function returning the number of elements in x, the distance between the families of the solution and the families of the student's workspace is translated into:

$$d_f = n(F_i) \tag{1}$$

Block Distance Calculation. As mentioned previously, blocks are grouped by families, which means that blocks are elements of these families. We consider the correct block set as the block elements in the student's workspace, that are also present in the exercise solution; and the wrong block set as the block elements in the student's workspace that are not present in the exercise solution. Let:

$E_{fc} \subset F_c$, the block set belonging to the correct families sets.
$E_{fs} \subset B$, the exercise solution block set.
$E_{fi} \subset F_i$, the block set belonging to the wrong families sets.
$E_c = \{x \mid \forall x \in E_{fc} \cap E_{fs}\}$, the correct block set.
$E_i = \{x \mid \forall x \in E_{fc} \triangle E_{fs}\}$, the wrong block set.

The distance calculation between the solution block set and the student's workspace block set is defined by:

$$d_e = n(E_i) + n(E_{fi}) \tag{2}$$

Block Position Distance Calculation. As noted above, blocks can be organized sequentially, establishing an order for the execution of each of them. Once we get the correct block set in the student's workspace, it is important to check that those blocks are executed in the proper order. To ensure this, we compare the position of each block in the student's workspace with the position of the same block in the solution.

Let $A_o = \{block, position\}$ the set of the existing blocks and positions in the student's workspace, and $B_o = \{block, position\}$ the set of blocks and positions existing in the solution. Assuming the position is a natural number higher than zero we get:

$$A_{oc} = x, pos_a \mid \forall x, pos_a \in A_o \cap E_c$$
$$B_{oc} = y, pos_b, x \mid \forall x \in A_{oc}, \forall y, pos_b \in B_o \cap E_c, y = x$$
$$n_a = n(A_{oc})$$

The distance calculation of the position in the correct blocks sets, is carried out by subtracting from the position of each block in the student's workspace, the position of those same blocks in the solution. We use the term correct block position for the position of a block in the student's workspace term that coincides with the same position of the same block in the exercise solution; and the term wrong block position for the position of a block in the student's workspace that does not coincide with the position of the same block in the exercise solution. Therefore, the distance of the correct block positions is calculated as follows:

$$d_{E_c} = \sum_{i=1}^{n_a} |pos_{a_i} - pos_{b_i}|$$

In the same way, the value of the wrong block positions E_i is also taken into account. To do this, the value of each position of the blocks belonging to E_i is added, as follows:

$$C_{E_i} = z, pos_c \mid \forall z, pos_c \in A_o \cap E_i$$
$$n_c = n(C_{E_i})$$
$$d_{E_i} = \sum_{i=1}^{n_c} pos_{c_i}$$

The final position distance will be the sum of the correct block position distance and the wrong block position distance:

$$d_p = d_{E_c} + d_{E_i} \tag{3}$$

Block Inputs Values Distance Calculation. As mentioned in Sect. 2.3, blocks can have alphanumerical and numerical inputs. The input distance calculation is made in two steps: In a first step, we compare the input values of the correct blocks (E_c) in the student's workspace and the solution, and in a second step, we add the input values belonging to the wrong block set (E_i).

Because there can be both alphanumerical and numerical inputs, we defined two different ways to calculate the distance based on the input typology.

Let E_c the correct block set, $A_i = \{block, input\}$ the set of blocks and inputs belonging to the student's workspace, $B_i = \{block, input\}$ the set of blocks and inputs belonging to the solution, and $C_i = \{block, input\}$ the set of blocks and inputs belonging to the wrong block set. It's defined:

$A_{ic} = x, input_a \mid \forall x, input_a \in A_i \cap E_c$
$B_{ic} = x, input_b, y \mid \forall x \in A_{ic}, \forall y, input_b \in B_i \cap E_c, y = x$
$n_a = n(A_{ic})$
$C_{ii} = z, input_c \mid \forall z, input_c \in C_i$
$n_c = n(C_{ii})$

The distance calculation of the input values in the correct block set, between the student's workspace and the solution, is done in two different ways: On the one hand, if it's an alphanumerical value, and there is some difference between the student's workspace and the solution, we set 1 as difference value. On the other hand, if it's a numerical input, we calculate the numerical difference between the student's workspace input value and that of the solution one:

$$d_{ic} = \sum_{i=1}^{n_a} \begin{cases} \frac{|input_{a_i} - input_{b_i}|}{input_{b_i}}, \text{ if the input is numerical} \\ 1, \text{ if the input is alphanumerical, and if } input_{a_i} \neq input_{b_i} \end{cases} \tag{4}$$

As in Eq. 4, the distance calculation of the input values in the wrong block set is also done in two different ways as follows:

$$d_{ii} = \sum_{i=1}^{n_i} \begin{cases} input_{c_i}, \text{ if the input is numerical} \\ 1, \text{ if the input is alphanumerical} \end{cases} \tag{5}$$

The final input distance is calculated as the sum of the distance of the input values existing in the correct block set (d_{ic}), and the distance of the input values existing in the wrong block set (d_{ii}):

$$d_i = d_{ic} + d_{ii} \tag{6}$$

Total Distance. As outlined above, there is an order of relevance in the parameters when determining the distance between the workspace and the solution.

So the total distance is calculated as the weighted sum of each of the Eqs. 1, 2, 3 and 6.

The total distance between the student's workspace and the solution is defined as follows:

$$d_t = d_f + \left(\frac{1}{2} \cdot d_e\right) + \left(\frac{1}{4} \cdot d_p\right) + \left(\frac{1}{8} \cdot d_i\right) \tag{7}$$

3   Results

To test our distance function, on one hand we have made different unit tests to verify that the program calculates the distance correctly, and on the other hand, an expert scored different programs based on their solution. This score, goes from

Table 1. Score comparison.

Exercise	Calculated Distance	Score set by the teacher
1	0	10
1	55.25	4
1	2.25	8
2	75.125	7
2	23	8
2	176.875	3
3	12.125	6
3	0	10
3	3	8
4	1.125	9
4	123	1
4	0	10
5	226	0
5	98.25	5
5	6.375	7

0 to 10, and has been compared with the distance calculated by our function. We have chosen 5 exercises from those mentioned above, and have randomly chosen 3 programs for each exercise from the user experience. In Table 1 we show the distance calculations and the scores given by the teacher for each program.

In Table 2 we show a summary of the data collected during the user experiences.

Table 2. Data collection.

Interactions	Help Requests	Students	Average Age	Boys	Girls
7526	323	41	13.6	26	15

4   Discussion

In this research, we have developed a method for calculating the distance between the workspace and the closest solution, during the realization of block-based programming exercises.

One important reason for this distance calculation, is to ensure that the students will be properly guided to reach the closest solution to the exercise. To achieve this goal, the distance calculation method must be able to correctly calculate the distance of the different solutions and return the smallest of them. This has been verified by carrying out unit tests in the developed distance function.

The other important aspect is to confirm that the distance calculations are appropriate for measuring how far or close to the solution the student is. Therefore, we have randomly taken 5 exercises with 1 solution for each exercise, and we have asked an expert to score from 0 to 10 three different situations of each exercise with respect to the given solution. These scores are then compared to the distances calculated by our function. In Table 1, we can observe that the greater the distance, the lower the score the expert has assigned, hence the calculated distance by our function is inversely proportional to the score. Therefore, we think that it is a good first approach for the distance calculation.

We consider that this first approach, including the data collection and the distance calculation, is relevant, because there are no repositories in the literature containing user interactions in a block-based programming software, and solution distance metrics could help to build a model that will predict when a primary school student needs help.

As future work, we intend to perform new user experiences to collect more data, and explore feature selection methods, as well as Recurrent Neural Network (RNN) architectures to generate a help model. Finally, we will refine and validate more rigorously the distance calculation, implement this model in Scratch, and we will validate it in a real learning environment.

Acknowlegements. Grant PID2020-115220RB-C22 funded by MCIN/AEI/10.130 39/501100011033 and, as appropriate, by "ERDF A way for making Europe", by the "European Union" or by the "European Union NextGeneration EU/PRTR".

References

1. Cavalcanti, A.P., et al.: Supporting teachers through social and emotional learning. In: Computers and Education: Artificial Intelligence, vol. 2, pp. 100027 (2021). ISSN: 2666920X, https://doi.org/10.1016/j.caeai.2021.100027
2. Cody, C., Maniktala, M., Lytle, N., Chi, M., Barnes, T.: The impact of looking further ahead: a comparison of two data-driven unsolicited hint types on performance in an intelligent data-driven logic tutor. Int. J. Artif. Intell. Educ., 1–34 (2021). https://doi.org/10.1007/s40593-021-00237-3
3. Chiu, J.-I., Tsuei, M.: Meta-analysis of children's learning outcomes in block-based programming courses. In: Stephanidis, C., Antona, M., Ntoa, S. (eds.) HCII 2020. CCIS, vol. 1294, pp. 259–266. Springer, Cham (2020). https://doi.org/10.1007/978-3-030-60703-6_33
4. Fagerlund, J., Häkkinen, P., Vesisenaho, M., Viiri, J.: Computational thinking in programming with Scratch in primary schools: a systematic review, In: Computer Applications in Engineering Education, vol. 29, pp. 12–28 (2021). ISSN: 10990542, https://doi.org/10.1002/cae.22255
5. Fahid, F.M.: Progression trajectory-based student modeling for novice block-based programming, In: UMAP 2021 - Proceedings of the 29th ACM Conference on User Modeling, Adaptation and Personalization, pp. 189–200 (2021). ISBN: 9781450383660, https://doi.org/10.1145/3450613.3456833
6. Howard, N.R.: How Did I Do?: giving learners effective and affective feedback. Education Tech. Research Dev. **69**(1), 123–126 (2020). https://doi.org/10.1007/s11423-020-09874-2

7. Imbernón Cuadrado, L.-E., Manjarrés Riesco, Á., de La Paz López, F.: ARTIE: An integrated environment for the development of affective robot tutors, In: Frontiers in Computational Neuroscience, vol. 10 (2016). https://doi.org/10.3389/fncom.2016.00077

8. Imbernón Cuadrado, L.-E., Manjarrés Riesco, Á., de la Paz López, F.: FER in primary school children for affective robot tutors. In: Ferrández Vicente, J.M., Álvarez-Sánchez, J.R., de la Paz López, F., Toledo Moreo, J., Adeli, H. (eds.) IWINAC 2019. LNCS, vol. 11487, pp. 461–471. Springer, Cham (2019). https://doi.org/10.1007/978-3-030-19651-6_45

9. Jiang, B., Li, Z.: Effect of scratch on computational thinking skills of Chinese primary school students. J. Comput. Educ. 8(4), 505–525 (2021). https://doi.org/10.1007/s40692-021-00190-z

10. Jo, Y., Ju Chun, S., Ryoo, J.: Tactile scratch electronic block system: expanding opportunities for younger children to learn programming. Int. J. Inf. Educ. Technol. 11, 319–323, (2021). ISSN: 20103689, https://doi.org/10.18178/ijiet.2021.11.7.1529

11. Mlinaric, D., Milasinovic, B., Mornar, V.: Tree inheritance distance. IEEE Access 8, pp. 52489–52504 (2020). ISSN: 21693536, https://doi.org/10.1109/ACCESS.2020.2981260

12. Obermüller, F., Heuer, U., Fraser, G.: Guiding next-step hint generation using automated tests. In: Annual Conference on Innovation and Technology in Computer Science Education, ITiCSE, pp. 220–226 (2021). ISBN: 9781450382144, ISSN: 1942647X, https://doi.org/10.1145/3430665.3456344

13. Ng, O.-L., Cui, Z.: Examining primary students' mathematical problem-solving in a programming context: towards computationally enhanced mathematics education. ZDM – Mathematics Education 53(4), 847–860 (2020). https://doi.org/10.1007/s11858-020-01200-7

14. Sáez López, J.M., Buceta Otero, R., De Lara García-Cervigón, S.: Introducing robotics and block programming in elementary education, In: RIED. Revista Iberoamericana de Educación a Distancia, vol 24, pp. 95 (2020). ISSN: 1138–2783, https://doi.org/10.5944/ried.24.1.27649

15. Uddin, I., Shariq Imran, A., Muhammad, K., Fayyaz, N., Sajjad, M.: A systematic mapping review on mooc recommender systems. IEEE Access 9, 118379–118405 (2021). ISSN: 21693536, https://doi.org/10.1109/ACCESS.2021.3101039

16. Wang, J.: Use hopscotch to develop positive attitudes toward programming for elementary school students. Int. J. Comput. Sci. Educ. Sch. 5, 48–58 2021. https://doi.org/10.21585/ijcses.v5i1.122

17. Yu,W., Yong Kim, I., Mechefske, C.: Analysis of different RNN autoencoder variants for time series classification and machine prognostics, vol. 149. Academic Press (2021). ISSN: 10961216, https://doi.org/10.1016/j.ymssp.2020.107322

An Approach to Emotions Through Lexical Availability

Pedro Salcedo-Lagos[1], Pedro Pinacho-Davidson[2], J. M. Angélica Pinninghoff[2],
G. Gabriela Kotz[3], and A. Ricardo Contreras[2(✉)]

[1] Department of Educational Informatics, Universidad de Concepción,
Concepción, Chile
psalcedo@udec.cl
[2] Department of Computer Science, Universidad de Concepción, Concepción, Chile
{ppinacho,mpinning,rcontrer}@udec.cl
[3] Department of Foreign Languages, Universidad de Concepción, Concepción, Chile
gkotz@udec.cl

Abstract. People are able of transforming emotions into words, as a mechanism to communicate it. Additionally people are able to express emotions which can be grouped around specific interest centers. These two elements are considered as the basis for this work, which analyzes how people react when exposed to similar concepts. Different human groups are able to express themselves about a common phenomenon, by using different lexical elements. This work collects information from different geographic regions, considering an heterogeneous population. We present in this work the way people using a common language represent concepts which describe emotions depending on location and other variables, like educational level, gender and age, among others. The collection of the available lexicon is achieved through the use of the lexical availability methodology, supported by using neural networks.

Keywords: Emotions · Lexical availability · Lexicon · Neural networks

1 Introduction

Emotions are important in the daily life of people. An emotion is an affective state which can serve to motivate a particular behavior. Examples of emotions include sadness, joy, safety, loneliness and fear. In recent years emotions have arose as a relevant issue in social sciences, because of the impact they have in daily life of people. This fact has open a new dimension for research, by recovering emotions from the lexicon. The above is based on the fact that the lexicon is a linguistic component which reflects different situations that people deal with, and as a consequence it allows emotions to be expressed. The previous assessment suggests that speakers belonging to a specific community may use the lexicon that the specific community handles to reflect, express, describe or even name emotions.

© Springer Nature Switzerland AG 2022
J. M. Ferrández Vicente et al. (Eds.): IWINAC 2022, LNCS 13259, pp. 433–442, 2022.
https://doi.org/10.1007/978-3-031-06527-9_43

This work is aimed to detect a set of emotions which are described with different lexicons, depending on different regions. To allow this classification, the key issue is to collect the available lexicon through the use of lexical availability methodology, supported by the use of neural networks.

There is a lot of literature devoted to lexical analysis, lexical availability and to the use of mathematical concepts to carry very interesting approaches. However, the combination of emotions and lexical availability is an open path that deserves to be explored. The work of [9] analyzes the role of the lexicon in the cultural and mental constructions to express an emotional message in a population of young people. The target sample consists of university students which accepted to participate by answering two surveys. The analysis considered the fundamentals of cognitive linguistic, specifically from the metaphor, image schemes and prototype categories. Among the most relevant results, the recovered lexicon may be classified into expressive terms, descriptive terms and figurative terms. A more specific work [2] deals with the relationships between lexicon and emotions in the student context. Authors combine lexical availability with graph theory, showing that students verbalize their emotions and that these relate to certain centers of interest.

The scope of initiatives such as those mentioned above, has important projections. In the context of human and robots interaction, the work of Val-Calvo et al. [19], deals with face emotions recognition, aiming to build intelligent systems which can adapt to the changing mood of users. This challenging work points to affective HRI (Human-Robot Interaction), as a tool to improve communication human-robot in real-time [8]. Emotions are described in a theory developed by Plutchik [13], characterizing an emotion as a reaction an individual presents according to the needs of adaptation to the surrounding environment the individual requires. Emotions may be described by using a particular lexicon, which is linked to the individual behavior.

This article is structured as follows; first section consists of the current introduction. Second section presents the model developed for this work. Third section describes the scope of the work, while fourth section presents the results obtained. Finally, section five presents the conclusions.

2   The Model

Plutchik [13] proposes that emotions present an adaptive characteristic, in which emotions are produced when an individual is able to adapt to their surrounding environment, which is particularly complex because of the evolutive property. He presents his structural model as a colored wheel, in which emotions are distributed according to their neighborhood, similarity or contraposition. Emotions which are in contraposition are separated (in the grayscale colored wheel) by $180^{c}irc$. It means these emotions are pictured in opposed locations in the wheel. This structural model identifies eight primary emotions: disgust, joy, surprise, trust, fear, sadness, anger and anticipation. The model identifies also emotions resulting from the combination of two primary emotions, defined as secondary emotions.

Emotions are associated with a color. According to the intensity of an emotion, the corresponding color intensifies. Emotions are more intense when they approach to the center of the wheel. In the same sense, emotions may evolve from a particular state to a different one. If trust intensifies, then it can turn into admiration. On the other hand, if trust diminishes, it may turn into acceptance. Figure 1 shows the emotions wheel in the structural model.

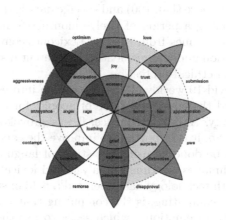

Fig. 1. Plutchik wheel

According to Reeve [14], emotions are triggered as a response to specific situations, and relates an adaptive function to a primary emotion. We are interested in how the available lexicon allows us to express an emotion.

3 Scope of the Work

Given the previous framework, this research analyzes, from the point of view of lexical availability, how emotions in general, and the Covid-19 pandemic, in particular, have impacted a large number of people which initially considers 22 different countries in Ibero America. This universe was reduced to the 8 countries with the most significant data. The emotional expressiveness of people, in different geographic locations, is studied through the use of Lexical Availability as a technique which provides useful information, according to data collected from people living in different environments and having different formation level in a wide age range. This work is a step ahead on the work focused on teachers and students interaction during pandemic [15].

Lexical Availability is a lexical-statistical methodology used to recover lexical units grouped into semantic fields called *interest centers*. The resulting lexicon, called *available lexicon*, is part of the speaker's mental lexicon, available to be activated when communications needs so require [7]. The knowledge of the mental lexicon of a group of speakers, is useful for several lines of research, because having the set of answers as a starting point, it is possible to create a multidimensional image which represents the semantic relationships among the available lexical units.

This work analyzes how the lexical availability influences the ability to express emotions on a universe which considers people from 8 countries, and 11 interest centers. The sample use in the study considered 13918 individuals, 8729 female, 4966 male, and 223 other. The countries considered are those with higher number of individuals (more than 100) and specific data is shown in Table 1. Data has been collected during a period of twelve months (from September 2020 to September 2021). Data comes from the site Lexicones.com which provides free access to the information under agreement with different institutions, and taking into account legal and ethical protection.

The spread of Covid-19 worldwide has caused an impressive change in daily habits. It has affected the emotional state of people, for example experiencing higher levels of anxiety. As a consequence, it has provoked a different way of expressing emotions. So, it is important to improve the capability of recognizing emotions, and it can be done by using the study of language with natural language processing techniques, sentiment analysis and lexical availability [2]. The study of emotions with technology has generated a field of study called Affective Computing. Affective computing, is the computing that relates to, arises from, or deliberately influences emotion - which seeks to use the power of emotions in different environments. One of the objectives of affective computing is the development of infrastructure and tools to allow handling emotionally charged information [12]. Affective computing could also be applied to the stress reduction and early detection of mental illness.

From an academic point of view, although the pandemic is a global tragedy, it also offers an opportunity to a better understanding of human behavior. The consumption of information has been modified during the Covid-19 pandemic, specially in the phase of strict confinement. Citizens are informed more and more frequently with respect to the time prior to the health crisis. Despite the above, it is necessary to maintain a critical attitude regarding the information provided by the media, which carry out coverage conditioned by the editorial line, in a sensationalist manner, generating unnecessary social alarm [11] and, in the worst case, affecting the quality of the data (lexical) collected.

Expected results, in this work, include a global perception on how people having different living environment which exhibit different characteristics deal with different emotions through language.

Variables this initiative takes into account include: professional degree, type of work, gender, age, city and country. Additionally, 11 interest centers are considered: joy, love, anticipation, aversion, trust, rage, fear, anger, surprise, and sadness. For analytical considerations, Covid-19 is labelled as an interest center. We have included two *new* emotions, because of the impact they represent in the data collected: love and rage. The procedure is as follows:

- As a first step, after obtaining lexicons from Lexicones.com for the eight countries and the 11 interest centers, natural language processing (NLP) techniques have been used to establish tokens and for lemmatize the database [1]. It allows grouping the similar words as a unique one, for not to count it as the expression of a different emotion. It has been realized in Python using the FreeLing 4.2 library. Also, the dataset was cleansed of stopwords using the NLTK library.
- As a second step, specific tools called Dispogen [4] and Dispografo [5] are used to process lexical data. It allows to compute the average of words by subject (XR), the cohesion index in each interest center, the lexical availability index (IDL) for each word, and the personal lexical availability index of each person (IDLp) [4,5]. It allows to validate the utility of the proposal to acquire emotions concepts.
- Having the same objective of the previous step, during the third step, it is analyzed the degree of emotion contained in the lexicon of every person considered (a list of words associated to every interest center). It is implemented by using Python and the SentimentAnalysisSpanish library, which uses a convolutional neural network to predict the degree of a sentiment in Spanish sentences. It allows to detect that there exist significant differences in the degree of emotions when interest centers for different countries are considered.
- Finally, in the fourth step, a neural network has been trained to predict the interest center in terms of the lexicon collected for every country. For this, we used the software SPSS 25, trying different architectures, with different number of hidden layers and different number of neurons per layer. Then we used Google Cloud (AutoML), which automatically determines the best configuration. The next stage in our research is to predict emotions for every separated country, in terms of the available lexicon. For now, this objective is beyond the scope of this presentation.

4 Results

For analyzing the available lexicon, the first step is to compute the average of words for every interest center. This is shown in Table 2. Cohesion index is a relationship between words which makes the word signify identical o semantically related concepts in common knowledge.

In the average, Covid-19 trigger the highest value. Although Covid-19 is not an interest center as defined by Plutchik, it is interesting to note that it is the item with a highest global average. Even so, we considered to include it because it is currently impacting a great number of emotions.

Table 1. Countries and considered individuals

Country	Number of individuals
Argentina	2472
Chile	4792
Colombia	1837
Ecuador	575
Spain	911
Mexico	2035
Peru	718
Venezuela	578

Table 2. Average words for every interest center

Center of interest	Words average (XR)	Cohesion index
Rage	9.0	0.0057
Surprise	9.2	0.0070
Love	12.1	0.00080
Joy	10.17	0.0072
Fear	9.30	0.0064
Sadness	9.05	0.0077
Disgust	7.82	0.0063
Covid-19	13.21	0.057
Anger	9.23	0.0090
Trust	9.13	0.0098
Anticipation	6.76	0.0076

From the IDL for every word, it is possible to compute the individual IDL as indicated in [3]. It allows to know how the individual lexicon impact the lexicon of a group. In this work it is important to understand which emotions are more relevant in a specific context. This variable is then considered in the process of training the neural network.

Next table (Table 3) shows the degree of emotion for each country. The value is an index in the interval [0,1], where 0 stands for an absolute negative emotion and 1 stands for an absolute positive emotion. Although it does not exist a significative difference for emotions in different countries, the observed average for interest centers indicates a negative value for Covid-19. On the other hand, the interest center **joy** exhibits the most positive value. IC denotes Interest Center.

We tried two machine learning approaches to determine the IC from a set of single words. The first one was the application of a simple Multilayer

Table 3. Emotion degree

IC	Argentina	Chile	Colombia	Ecuador	Spain	Mexico	Peru	Venezuela	Average
Joy	0.51	0.54	0.53	0.55	0.58	0.52	0.59	0.50	0.54
Love	0.46	0.48	0.48	0.38	0.42	0.44	0.45	0.40	0.44
Anticipation	0.42	0.42	0.41	0.52	0.39	0.38	0.43	0.49	0.43
Aversion	0.19	0.20	0.19	0.22	0.20	0.23	0.14	0.24	0.20
Trust	0.35	0.34	0.36	0.32	0.35	0.40	0.40	0.39	0.36
Covid-19	0.13	0.14	0.12	0.11	0.12	0.11	0.11	0.14	0.12
Rage	0.20	0.21	0.17	0.26	0.31	0.18	0.23	0.14	0.21
Fear	0.15	0.16	0.13	0.13	0.11	0.17	0.17	0.16	0.15
Anger	0.21	0.24	0.18	0.22	0.23	0.18	0.27	0.20	0.22
Surprise	0.46	0.48	0.50	0.53	0.56	0.56	0.50	0.49	0.51
Sadness	0.20	0.25	0.20	0.18	0.20	0.22	0.23	0.22	0.21

Perceptron (MLP) developed with SPSS used for a primary exploration of a simple Machine Learning (ML) approach. Meanwhile, the second approach applied Google AutoML for testing a most robust technique over the same problem.

4.1 Primary Exploration of ML over the Problem

MLP is a classic ML technique very used today because of its simplicity and good results for variates regression and classifications problems [6,10,21]. MLP is a feedforward artificial neural network. MLP has at least three layers: an input layer, a hidden layer, and an output layer. Typically, MLP implements one hidden layer (not a deep network) and utilizes supervised learning. For our configuration, the input layer has one neuron for each word in the dataset (10915), and the output layer is defined by one neuron for each interest center considered (7). It is important to note that only 7 of the 11 available interest centers were considered because of the limitation of computing resources for this stage, a laptop equipped with a CPU Core i7-1065G7 and 12 GB for RAM. The number of hidden layers, the number of neurons by layer, and the activation function for hidden and output layers were the hyper-parameters explored using SPSS v.25 [17]. Thus, the best setup is shown in Table 4.

Table 4. Best setup for the neural network

Parameter	Best configuration
Number of hidden layers	1
Number of neurons in the hidden layer	19
Activation function for the hidden layer	hyperbolic tangent
Activation function for the output layer	Softmax

The model was trained with 70% of available records in the dataset. The other 30% was used for testing purposes. Cross-entropy loss was the cost function used to optimize the model during training. Meantime, the training process was stopped when two consecutive training steps did not decrease the model's error. As a result, the testing of the model raises a main classification error of 20.9%, supporting the use of a more sophisticated technique for tackling the problem.

4.2   Use of AutoML over the Problem

Automated Machine Learning (AutoML) is a new approach for applying machine learning to real-world problems. AutoML concept allows these tools to automatize all the stages of the model construction, from the preprocessing of raw data to the tuning of the hyper-parameters and model training. Exists multiple commercial platforms for AutoML like Dataiku, DataRobot, H2O Driverless AI, RapidMiner, and TIBCO. However, these are mainly oriented to corporative decision takers without experience in ML topics. Beyond these corporative approaches, AutoML features can be found in developing libraries like Auto-Sklearn, Auto-Keras, and H2O AutoML for coding purposes, being a very active research area today [16,20,22]. Also, some of these tools are integrated with Cloud computing services, improving exploration and training models' support. Examples are Microsoft Automated Machine Learning, Amazon SageMaker Automatic Model Tuning, and Google AutoML [18]. This last one was chosen to tackle our classification problem. We Use the automatic text classification feature of Google AutoML to tackle the same problem of the primary exploration. Thus, the dataset was shuffled and split into three parts 80% for training, 10% for validation, and 10% for testing. As a result, the model achieved a mean precision of 0.93 for classifying all 11 different labels. In this case, it is possible to use all the datasets (all labels) because the service of the Google Cloud clears the hardware problems for exploring and training the model.

4.3   MLP Vs AutoML Comparison

We compare both approaches regarding their precision, understanding precision as the rate of correct labeled word by interest center. In these terms, MLP achieves a precision of 79.1% in the testing stage and AutoML 93% showing a remarkable performance for AutoML, which also tackle the complete problem with the 11 labels. Table 5 presents a complete comparison in terms of precision for both approaches. The label n/a represents the impossibility of processing, in a reasonable time, the entire database.

Table 5. MLP vs AutoML comparison

Interest center	MLP Precision	AutoML Precision
Covid-19	0.88	0.97
Love	0.82	0.95
Joy	0.82	0.95
Fear	0.69	0.94
Anticipation	0.5	0.94
Surprise	n/a	0.93
Sadness	n/a	0.93
Trust	n/a	0.89
Rage	0.9	0.89
Aversion	0.59	0.85
Anger	n/a	0.81
Mean precision	0.79	0.93

5 Conclusions and Future Work

The combination of lexical availability and neural networks shows interesting results when predicting emotions in diverse environments, considering different social parameters. The number of individuals and the number of different locations included give us an important base line for future research. The capability of determining differences in emotions detected in a specific location in a specific context or historical reality, is an important achievement of this work, pointing to the objectives that affective computation pursues, with respect to the adaptability of emotions.

Acknowledgement. This study has been partially supported by Project Fondecyt 1201572, National Agency for Research and Innovation.

References

1. Bird, S., Loper E., Klein, E.: Natural Language Processing with Python. O'Reilly Media Inc. (2009)
2. Blanco, O., Salcedo, P., Kotz, G.: Lexical analysis of emotions: an approach using lexical availability and graph theory (in Spanish). Lingüística y Literatura **78**, 56–84 (2020)
3. Cellealta Barroso, F., Gallego Gallego D.: Medidas de disponibilidad léxica: comparabilidad y normalización (in Spanish). Boletín de Filología, vol. 511, Santiago, Chile (2016)
4. Echeverría, M., Urzúa, P., Figueroa, I.: Dispogen II. Programa computacional para el análisis de la disponiblidad léxica (in Spanish), Universidad de Concepción (2005)

5. Echeverría, M., Vargas, R., Urzúa, P., Ferreira, R.: Una nueva herramienta computacional para el análisis de relaciones semánticas en el léxico disponible (in Spanish). RLA, Revista de Lingüística Teórica y Aplicada **46**, 81–91 (2008)
6. Li, F., Zhang, X., Lu, A., Xu, L., Ren, D., You, T.: Estimation of metal elements content in soil using x-ray fluorescence based on multilayer perceptron. Environ. Monit. Assess. **194**, 95 (2022)
7. Carmen, F.J., Natividad, H.M.: Revista electrónica de estudios hispánicos: Lexical and socionomastics availability (in Spanish). Ogigia. **25**, 185–2010 (2018)
8. Górriz, J.M.: Artificial intelligence within the interplay between natural and artificial computation: advances in data science, trends and applications. Neurocomputing **410**, 237–270 (2020)
9. Grunewald, U., Osorio, J.: To feel, to say, to do: expressive variety and emotion prototypes in the youth vocabulary. Onomazein **22**, 125–163 (2010)
10. Kolagati, S., Priyadharshini, T., Mary Anita Rajam, V.: Exposing deepfakes using a deep multilayer perceptron - convolutional neural network model. Int. J. Inf. Manage. Data Insights **2**(1), 100054 (2022)
11. Masip, D., Aran-Ramspott, S., Ruiz-Caballero, C., Suau, J., Almenar, E., Puertas-Graell, D.: Consumo informativo y cobertura mediática durante el confinamiento por el Covid-19: sobreinformación, sesgo ideológico y sensacionalismo (in Spanish). El Profesional de la información **29**(3), 1–12 (2020). https://doi.org/10.3145/epi.2020.may.12
12. Picard, R.: Affective Computing for HCI. The MIT Press (1997)
13. Plutchik, R.: The nature of emotions: human emotions have deep evolutionary roots, a fact that may explain their complexity and provide tools for clinical practice. Am. Sci. **89**(4), 344–350 (2001)
14. Reeve, J.: Understanding Motivation and Emotion, 7th edn. Wiley (2018)
15. Salcedo, P., Morales-Candia, S., Fuentes-Riffo, K., Rivera-Robles, S., Sanhueza-Campos, C.: Teachers' perception analysis on students' emotion in virtual classes during covid-19 pandemic: a lexical availability approach. Sustainability **13**(6413), 2021 (2021)
16. Kanti Karmaker, S., Hassan, M., Smith, M.J., Xu, L., Zhai, C., Veeramachaneni, K.: AutoML to date and beyond: challenges and opportunities. ACM Comput. Surv. **54**(8), 1–36 (2022)
17. https://www.ibm.com/cl-es/products/spss-statistics. (visited January 2022)
18. https://cloud.google.com/automl. (visited January 2022)
19. Val-Calvo, M., Alvarez-Sánchez, J.R., Ferrández-Vicente, J.M., Fernández, E.: Affective-robot story-telling human-robot interaction: exploratory real-time emotion estimation analysis using facial expressions and physiological signals. IEEE Access **8**, 134051–134066 (2020)
20. He, X., Zhao, K., Chu, X.: AutoML: a survey of the state-of-the-art. Knowl. Based Syst. **212**, 106622 (2021)
21. Xu, Y., Li, F., Asgari, A.: Prediction and optimization of heating and cooling loads in a residential building based on multi-layer perceptron neural network and different optimization algorithms. Energy **240**, 122692 (2022)
22. Zoeller, M.-A., Huber, M.F.: Benchmark and survey of automated machine learning frameworks. J. Artif. Intell. Res. **70**, 122692 (2021)

A Bacteria-Based Metaheuristic as a Tool for Group Formation

A. Ricardo Contreras[(✉)], P. Valentina Hernández, Pedro Pinacho-Davidson, and M. Angélica Pinninghoff J.

Department of Computer Science, University of Concepción, Concepción, Chile
{rcontrer,valenthernandez,ppinacho,mpinning}@udec.cl

Abstract. Groups of students develop and enhance their learning capabilities based on the opportunities and the challenges they face. Within each group particular capabilities are identified for the different members. This allows for the identification of individual studying styles. Based on previous developments supported by artificial intelligence techniques, we develop a new approach, which combines diversity and efficiency. Our approach allows for critical improvements when compared to similar proposals based on genetic algorithms techniques.

Keywords: Group formation · Bacteria-based algorithms

1 Introduction

Group work is currently seen as a need when dealing with the search of solutions for complex problems. Group formation is not a new strategy for solving problems. As history shows, the strength of groups may be used to force a social or political set of rule through a conquest process. Bigger armies increase the probability of conquer a region by using the simple strategy of brute force. However, some exceptional examples show that less numerous group leaded by an intelligent strategy may not only resist, but also defeat massive groups. The question arises immediately: what characterizes such exceptional groups?

It seems natural to explain the success of such groups by taking into account the characteristics of some specific individuals, which can lead an effective group solver. In the same line of thinking, it seems that the existence of a unique leader is not enough to guarantee the successful accomplishment of a particular task. Nowadays it is best understood the idea of task force, which in short words describes the collection of a set of particular abilities. The existence of different points of view allows to detect, as a group, some warnings that could affect the achievement of the goal for that group.

The problem of group formation has been addressed by using different approaches. The idea of grouping individuals to reach good solutions is based on the key idea that combination of diverse abilities may help to solve problems which an isolated individual can not successfully accomplish.

© Springer Nature Switzerland AG 2022
J. M. Ferrández Vicente et al. (Eds.): IWINAC 2022, LNCS 13259, pp. 443–451, 2022.
https://doi.org/10.1007/978-3-031-06527-9_44

In this work we are interested in groups of students to improve their performance in the teaching-learning processes.

In order to deal with group formation strategies, there are different approaches to be considered. Having in mind the idea that homogeneity among different groups and heterogeneity inside groups are key elements. One of the approaches uses genetic algorithms to generate groups, as shown in [5]; where different individuals are labelled according to specific characteristics. Based on the combination of these characteristics a decision on how to assign a specific individual to a particular group is realized through the use of genetic algorithms. In [7], authors develop a statistical approach trying to find the best solution through an exhaustive search. As expected, it works when the set of individuals is reduced but does not apply for bigger groups.

The benefits of collaborative learning as presented in [3], support the proposal for working with groups of students, to improve learning processes according to specific characteristics of individuals. Based on the existence of a common goal students not only work together; they also improve their academic benefits and obtain social and psychological improvements. To enhance group interactions may help to reach the group success; problems arise when the work to be done is not properly distributed among the students. In [1] authors present the results of applying collaborative groups to online courses, focused on features a course should exhibit, as a guide to allow the students form the groups according to their own preferences. In [8] we can see the results of implementing a system for collaborative groups assignment in a massive online course, forming groups by using two criteria: a random approach and the use of k-means. According authors, it is possible to obtain a higher participation level and a higher satisfaction level when students are grouped by using k-means.

In this work a new algorithm for students group formation is presented. The behavior of the proposed algorithm is compared with results obtained on the same problems by using genetic algorithms [2,5,6].

This article is structured as follows; first section consists of the current introduction. Second section describes the problem to solve. Third section is devoted to introduce the key concepts of bacteria algorithm. Fourth section is devoted to the implementation issues, while section five describes the results. Finally, section six presents the conclusions.

2   The Problem

The problem this proposal attacks is a problem of balancing groups of students in such a way that groups can be characterized according to specific features, and then measured and rearranged, if necessary, to obtain a set of resulting groups with similar capabilities, i.e., we are dealing with an optimization problem. This work considers two approaches: the first one based on specific tests an a second one based on lexical availability.

2.1 Collaborative Groups Based on Specific Tests

This type of groups focuses on the learning process, obtaining benefits because of the collaborative approach of students helping each others to solve a common task. However, not every group works in exactly the same way. Some of the will work efficiently while other will not achieve this behavior. To obtain similar groups, which means homogeneous groups with respect to the features the individual exhibit, it is necessary to consider characteristics which are measured by means of four specific tests: Multiple intelligence test (T_1), Learning style (T_2), Leadership (T_3) and Assertiveness (T_4).

T_1 considers seven types of intelligence: Linguistic, Mathematical/Logical, Visual/Spatial, Kinesthetic, Musical, Interpersonal and Intrapersonal.

T_2 considers four different learning styles: Active, Theoretical, Pragmatic and Reflexive.

T_3 takes into account three different leadership types, which are associated to decision making: autocratic leadership, democratic leadership and *laissez-faire* or liberal leadership.

For assertiveness (T_4) the student is asked to qualify 30 elements (in a range 1 to 7) considering seven different assertiveness types.

These tests allow to characterize every student to have a criteria when deciding which student is assigned to which group. The idea is to have a higher level of diversity inside each group, which in turns helps to have more homogeneous groups.

2.2 Collaborative Groups Based on Lexical Availability

These groups focuses on lexical knowledge of students, which is taken as a personal characterization. Every group presents similar characteristics in terms of available lexicon. To obtain this information, it is applied a lexical availability test which covers different topics. In this work, the considered topics are: i) Numeric systems and algebra, ii) Calculus, iii) Algebraic structures, iv) Geometry and, v) Data and Probability. In a limited period of time, students create a list, for each topic, with a set of words (representing concepts or objects) the students think are related with the topic. This approach allows to numerically compute the *distance* between the vocabulary of two students.

The groups consider students belonging to 10 pedagogy courses, five in the University of Concepción (UdeC), considering 130 students, and five in the University of BioBio (UBB), considering 233 students.

3 The Model

The proposal is inspired by the survival in a bacterial population, on how this population evolves and develop a resistance to antibiotics, i.e., bacteria are no more affected by the application of antibiotics. In real life, infections caused by resistant microorganisms often fail to respond to conventional treatment, resulting in prolonged illness and greater risk of death. Antibiotic resistance is a type of drug resistance where a microorganism is able to survive exposure to an antibiotic [4].

Bacteria are unicellular organisms of microscopic size capable of living in oceans, land, space and even in the human intestine. The relationship between humans and bacteria is complex; sometimes the bacteria behavior may be beneficial to human beings, and sometimes may trigger dangerous diseases.

For bacteria, there are four mechanisms for genetic variation and recombination. These are:

- Mutation. A change in the genetic information of an organisms, which occurs with a probability and is the result of an error in the process of DNA replication.
- Conjugation. A transference of genetic material among bacteria belonging to the same generation.
- Transformation. The process in which a bacteria may capture pieces of genetic material that can be found free in the environment. This material has been released by another bacteria at the time of death.
- Transduction. Is the transference of genetic material with the help of a bacteriophage, for example, a virus. The current implementation of the algorithm does not consider this mechanism.

The development of a resistance to antibiotics may be a serious problem for humans, however for bacteria it represents an evolutive improvement, increasing their survival capability. From this point of view, bacteria behavior represents a new paradigm for dealing with evolving individuals (a common strategy for solving optimization problems). This work emphasizes the collaborative behavior of bacteria and considers biological issues as a source of inspiration to develop the proposed mechanism:

- The capability to develop antibiotic resistance through a collaborative strategy. This capability is achieved as a result of genetic transfer by using conjugation, transformation and mutation.
- The *horizontal* transfer, which is the process of sharing genetic material with the neighborhood, i.e., with the neighbors which belong to the same generation

4   Bacteria Algorithm

The bacteria algorithm is based on a set of iterations, each one of them realizing genetic variation operations, aimed to iteratively improve the quality of the population. In the following, it is defined the concept of bacteria from the algorithmic point of view.

The problem to deal with is the process of group formation. A bacteria, is a solution, which represents a valid answer to the problem. A bacteria contains group members (students), and every student is linked to a specific group. Coding of a bacteria consists in assigning an identification number to each student, avoiding repetitions. In doing so, a bacteria is represented as a sequence of numbers, which are ordered from left to right as shown in Fig. 1. This figure represents a coding example for a bacteria, containing 9 students which are labelled with numbers from 0 to 8. An interpretation for this figure is that numbers 6, 2, 8 represent group number 1; numbers 4, 0, 1 represent group number 2 and numbers 7, 5, 3 represent group number 3.

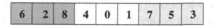

Fig. 1. A bacteria showing groups of individuals

Algorithm 1. Bacteria algorithm

Data: iterations, parameters for genetic variation and free genetic
    variation
Result: Final bacteria population
P ⟵ Population initialization;
it ⟵ 0 ;
while *it < iterations* **do**
    F ⟵ Evaluation(P);
    A ⟵ Antibiotic creation(F, P);
    P_{DR} ⟵ Classification(P, F, A);
    P ⟵ Genetic variation(P_{DR});
    P_{DR} ⟵ Classification(P, F, A);
    P_D ⟵ Antibiotic application(A, P_{DR});
    P ⟵ Regeneration(P_D);
    if *min(F) = max(F)* **then**
        | P ⟵ Free genetic variation(P);
    end
    it ⟵ it+1 ;
end

Population Initialization. Population is randomly created, taking into account that an individual cannot belong to more than one group. The quantity of generated bacteria is based on a parameter which indicates the minimum number of bacteria a population can hold. A bacteria population contains a set of individual bacteria, each one of them with the structure shown in Fig. 1.

Evaluation. The quality of a bacteria is measured by using an evaluation function. The value of the measure is the evaluation of the bacteria, i.e., a value which represents how fit is a bacteria in terms of survival.

For group generation based on specific tests, we use the evaluation function proposed in [5].

For group generation based in lexical analysis, we use the evaluation function proposed in [7].

Antibiotic Creation. Antibiotics are the elements in charge of bacteria eliminations. From the biological point of view, this objective can be achieved in two different ways: eliminating bacteria or inhibiting the grow of the population. Different bacteria need to be attacked with different antibiotics. For antibiotics creation there is a random selection of two bacteria pairs; for every pair, the bacteria with the best evaluation is selected, and between both winning bacteria, the poor evaluation is selected. The idea supporting this mechanism points to generate an antibiotics with a medium value. If the best evaluation is selected, then it should eliminate a great amount of bacteria losing the genetic variability it is expected to maintain.

Classification. Once the antibiotic is represented together with their associated evaluation, the entire bacteria population is classified into two groups: receptors and donors. This classification considers the evaluation of the antibiotics, which acts as a barrier between these two groups in such a way that every bacteria whose evaluation is less or equal to the antibiotic evaluation is considered strong enough to survive to the antibiotic effect, and are labelled as donors. On the other hand, receptors bacteria are those with an evaluation higher than the antibiotic evaluation, and hence are considered the weakest individual in the population and then prone to be eliminated by the effect of the antibiotic. In other words, this a minimization problem.

Genetic Variation. Changes in the genetic material of a bacteria may help to improve their evaluation to increase the probability of survival. Three different genetic variations are considered:

- Conjugation. Every receptor bacteria has a probability p_c of interaction with a donor bacteria, mixing their genetic material. It produces a modification in the receptor bacteria.
- Transformation. Receptor bacteria can capture, with a probability p_t, a piece of genetic material (results of a previously dead bacteria) which remains in the environment. It is similar to conjugation, except that the genetic material does not come from a living bacteria, but the rest of a bacteria which was not able to survive the antibiotic on a previous step.
- Mutation. Donors and receptors bacteria are able to mutate, with a probability p_m. However, a donor bacteria mutation is accepted only if the bacteria evaluation improves.

Antibiotic Application. It consists in the elimination of every bacteria labelled as receptor, i.e., the weakest bacteria in the population. Once a bacteria dies, it has the capability, with a probability p_f to release into the environment a piece of their genetic material, which can be captured by another bacteria during the transformation process.

Regeneration. After the elimination step, it may occur that the bacteria population is drastically reduced. If this situation occurs a threshold level of bacteria is defined avoid a critically small population.

A possible consequence of the population elimination and regeneration is to reach a state in which every individual in the population exhibit identical evaluation. This condition is called *stagnation*. It means there is only one group of identical individuals and hence it is not possible to realize a classification. The effect of this is that the population entire survive or the entire population dies when an antibiotic is presented. It is an undesirable behavior, because it means the algorithm does not find better solutions.

Free Genetic Variation. This step is the solution to stagnation. Here is implemented the genetic variation process, including conjugation, transformation and mutation, as above, but taking into account both, donors and receptors bacteria.

The bacteria algorithm deals with an important number of parameters. In process of searching for the ideal values, the algorithm may become unstable. Hence, the different percentages used in the steps of genetic variations may be determinant in the performance of the algorithm. To deal with this problem, it is necessary to introduce elitism, which is implemented for controlling the bacteria population, maintaining in the population the individuals which present a good evaluation. It is achieved by using three alternative mechanisms: i) delete from the population an important number of individuals with bad evaluation (about 90% of the total population); ii) keep alive the bacteria with the current best evaluation, and iii) keep alive only bacteria with no repeated value of evaluation, to maintain genetic variability.

After choosing any of the above alternatives, a minimum population size must be guaranteed. If the population size is below the minimum, bacteria are created randomly until this minimum is reached. The goal of these steps is to restore the genetic variability of the population.

5   Results

To provide a comparison, experiments consider two class of problems, as indicated in Subsects. 2.1 and 2.2.

Specific Tests Criteria. To illustrate the obtained results, we show the evaluation function evolution for a small class, approximately 20 students, considering the strategy of specific tests. The algorithm behavior is shown in Fig. 2. The genetic algorithm reach the best solution after 50 iterations approximately. In this case, the evaluation does not improve, reaching a steady state value. For the bacteria-based algorithm, it is reached a better value for evaluation, but increasing the number of iterations to approximately 110.

Figure 2 shows the evaluation evolution of both; the strategy which uses genetic algorithm (denoted as GA) and the strategy which uses an algorithm based on bacteria with elitism (denoted as BE).

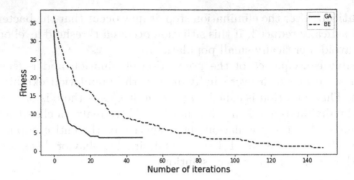

Fig. 2. A comparison between the GA-based and the Bacteria-based algorithms (specific tests criteria)

Lexical Availability Criteria. If we consider the characterization of students according to lexical availability, for a big class (over 55 students), it is shown in Fig. 3 the algorithm behavior. It is possible to observe that in this case, the bacteria based algorithm obtains better results than the genetic algorithm after 250 iterations.

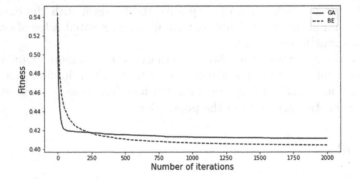

Fig. 3. A comparison between the GA-based and the Bacteria-based algorithms (lexical availability criteria)

It is important to note that for both criteria, the genetic algorithm appears a good alternative, but, when the number of iteration is increased, the bacterial algorithm behave, at least, as well as the genetic algorithm, improving the value of the evaluation function. In the second example (see Fig. 3) we can see that the difference in favor of bacterial algorithm increases slightly as the number on iterations increases.

A very interesting issue is that for bacteria-based algorithms, we employ a unique set of parameters. It means the bacteria based algorithm reach good results which are independent of the size of the population or the size of the problem. When testing genetic algorithms, the best performance is reached by modifying the values of the parameters considered for every different case. Even so, the results obtained with algorithms based on bacteria exhibit a better performance than those based on genetic algorithms.

6   Conclusions

In this work, we presented an algorithm based on bacteria behaviour. We have shown that genetic algorithms quickly evolve to a local optimum evaluation value, and are not able to improve that value.

We introduce the concept of elitism as a mechanism to control the way in which an evaluation evolves. This key element is crucial to constrain random behaviour during the evaluations. This randomness is particularly serious when high value parameters.

Finally, in this work we have shown that the use of a unique set of parameters in bacteria algorithms performs better when compared to genetic algorithms. This holds even adjusting parameters for the different scenario configurations. Once the set of parameters for the bacteria algorithm are defined, no further changes are needed. Even with changes in population.

References

1. Brindley, J.E., Blashke, L.M., Walti, C.: Creating effective collaborative learning groups in an online environment. Int. Rev. Res. Open Distrib. Learn. 10(3) (2009)
2. Górriz, J.M.: Artificial intelligence within the interplay between natural and artificial computation: advances in data science, trends and applications. Neurocomputing 410, 237–270 (2020)
3. Laal, M., Ghodsi, S.M.: Benefits of collaborative learning. Procedia Soc. Behav. Sci. 31, 486–490 (2012)
4. Odonkor, S.T., Addo, K.K.: Bacteria resistance to antibiotics: recent trends an challenges. Int. J. Biol. Med. Res. 2(4), 1204–1210 (2011)
5. Pinninghoff, M.A., Contreras, R., Salcedo, P.: Genetic algorithms as a tool for structuring collaborative groups. Natural Comput. 16(2), 231–239 (2017)
6. Pinninghoff J., M.A., Orellana M., J., Contreras A., R.: Bacterial resistance algorithm. An application to CVRP. In: Ferrández Vicente, J.M., Álvarez-Sánchez, J.R., de la Paz López, F., Toledo Moreo, J., Adeli, H. (eds.) IWINAC 2019. LNCS, vol. 11487, pp. 204–211. Springer, Cham (2019). https://doi.org/10.1007/978-3-030-19651-6_20
7. Rojas, D.; Zambrano, C., Salcedo, P.: A method for collaborative group formation by using lexical availability. REDIE: Revista Electrónica de Investigación Educativa 21(21), 17 (2019). (in Spanish)
8. Sans-Martínez, L., et al.: Creating collaborative groups in a MOOC: a homogeneous engagement grouping approach. Behav. Inf. Technol. 38(11), 1107–1121 (2019)

KANT: A Tool for Grounding and Knowledge Management

Miguel Á. González-Santamarta[1(✉)], Francisco J. Rodríguez-Lera[1],
Francisco Martín[2], Camino Fernández[1], and Vicente Matellán[1]

[1] Universidad de León, León, Spain
{mgons,fjrodl,cferl,vmato}@unileon.es
[2] Universidad Rey Juan Carlos, Madrid, Spain
francisco.rico@urjc.es

Abstract. The roboticist community divides the knowledge representation and decision-making in the symbolic and sub-symbolic fields. Thus, real-world robotics grounded representation requires specific software techniques for landing continuous and discrete state variables in both fields. This research designs and develops an Open Source tool called KANT (Knowledge mAnagemeNT). It will be used to translate sub-symbolic properties and attributes from the robot environment to a symbolic paradigm in the Knowledge Base, in particular to PDDL. Based on Python, KANT includes mechanisms to enhance the process of knowledge manipulation in real-world scenarios through the use of in-memory or non-SQL databases, which would mean a time enhancement of around 30% of total time in middleware such as ROS 2.

Keywords: Robotics · Knowledge management · Grounding · PDDL · ROS 2

1 Introduction

Future directions of social robotics point out to long-term tasks in highly dynamic environments. Thus, it is a cornerstone to define how to correlate the physical world which is sensed and changed by robots for any internal representation. However, this process relies on different challenging pieces: Software Engineering, Artificial Intelligence and robotics. Thus, this paper presents KANT a new open software tool[1] to simplify the translation process between symbolic and sub-symbolic world.

The idea of dealing with the robot state, its status and its environmental situation, among others, implies knowledge and its manipulation over time. This means software that allows interacting with different representations of robot knowledge. KANT provides a set of features to roboticist: 1) simplifying the technical process of interacting with knowledge storage; 2) easing the use of high-level languages such as Planning Domain Definition Language (PDDL) and 3) using the standard de facto "ROS 2" middleware for its integration in real robots. It also helps developers to recognize PDDL

---

[1] https://github.com/uleroboticsgroup/kant.

© Springer Nature Switzerland AG 2022
J. M. Ferrández Vicente et al. (Eds.): IWINAC 2022, LNCS 13259, pp. 452–461, 2022.
https://doi.org/10.1007/978-3-031-06527-9_45

objects by their names and attributes and provides an abstraction to save robot knowledge in practically any scenario given the right driver.

In this paper, we present KANT, a solution for PDDL knowledge management for robots. The tool can interpret the sub-symbolic information and generate convenient symbolic information that can be understood by a planner. Practically, it allows manipulating PDDL from Python code. As a result, scalability, flexibility and decoupling are improved. Besides, developers do not have to worry about the implementation of the storage implementation of the Knowledge Base.

The rest of this paper is organized as follows. Section 2 explores the state of the art. Section 3 describes the engine from a high level and development level. Section 4 report the description and results of our experiment. The paper shows the discussion of our approach in Sect. 5 and conclusions are presented in Sect. 6.

2 Related Work

There are several software alternatives facing the problem of using different software components for storing the knowledge of robots using PDDL. However, KANT provides adaptability, flexibility and scalability based on software patterns.

PlanSys [10] presents advanced approaches using C++ features as well as command-line options to interact with the knowledge. Besides, it also presents a code approach to manipulate PDDL. However, it has a certain grade of coupling due to the use of ROS communications mechanisms to manipulate the PDDL knowledge.

Thinking in deliberative options, ROSPlan [3], the most popular planning solution because it is based on the Robot Operating System - ROS [14], provides a pool of tools to work with robot planning. It provides a ROS node-based Knowledge Base that allows managing the PDDL knowledge with ROS communication mechanisms. For instance, ROSPlan uses the ROS communication interfaces, which involves creating the proper messages and using the right clients in each case. As a result, its solution is again very coupled to the whole tool. Our approach proposes a disconnected solution that allows its integration not only with ROS but also with databases.

The work presented in [6] uses the entity-component-system (ECS) to create actions similar to the PDDL actions. Then, those actions can be translated into PDDL to be used by a planner. Nevertheless, this is never measured and compared with other techniques, as using directly the PDDL language.

The authors in [8] introduce Tool Ontology and Optimization Language (TOOL), which is based on OWL 2 [12]. TOOL has a domain-specific language (DSL) whose elements are offered as Kotlin types that are created using the Factory Method design pattern. The elements of this DSL are translated into an OWL ontology, which is classified. Finally, the ontology is used to generate the PDDL domain that can be solved. This means an extra step for knowledge manipulation. Other alternatives such as OARA architecture [4] defines a specific language (DSL) to create robot skills that are the actions a robot needs to perform to achieve a mission. Then, using this language, the PDDL domain can be generated to be used in a planner. However, the OARA approach based on DSL requires knowledge of this language which makes it highly coupled to the architecture itself and KANT would be used standalone just using in Python.

3   Knowledge Management Engine

KANT presents a straightforward approach for grounding robot models into a Knowledge Base. This mechanism enhances reusability, scalability and inter-operability of robot knowledge along the time using a programming language and would be used in other reviewed grounding tools.

Representing knowledge using software patterns should be encouraged by new software developers focused on robotics. DTO, which stands for Data Transfer Object [11], aims to transfer the data between software components. DTO pattern is used to encapsulate PDDL information that can be shared between robotic components.

DAO is an abbreviation for Data Access Object [13]. It aims to use a software component to abstract and encapsulate all access to the data source. The DAO handles the connection to the data source to obtain and store data so it should encapsulate the logic for retrieving, saving and updating data in your data storage (a database, a file system, whatever). In this case, the data source will be the Knowledge Base where PDDL is stored. There can be a DAO family for each storage type treated.

The next step defines the storing treatment to the Knowledge Base, as a temporary element working as an in-memory option or something permanent as a database. The use of an Abstract Factory [5] as a creational artifact lets you produce families of related objects without specifying their concrete class, this means that it is transparent for developers to the final treatment of the knowledge. However, to interact easily with the methods of each family, it is proposed to use the Factory Method pattern. This last pattern allows substituting direct object construction (for instance the calls for the new operator) for the ones established into the factory method.

KANT is represented as K in Fig. 1. Any robot component can use it to access the Knowledge Base. As a result, any component can query and modify knowledge in the same way and without caring about how it is stored. Besides, updating the knowledge of a robot from sensors data is more simple thanks to it.

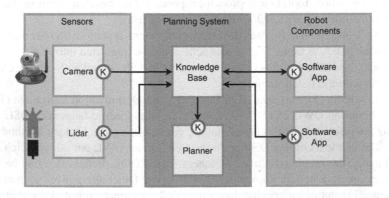

Fig. 1. Kant modules in a generic robotic framework for grounding and manipulating knowledge.

3.1 PDDL Abstractions in KANT

The PDDL planning domain model used in this research is the PDDL 2.1 [7] and is defined by the next tuple $\langle T, O, P, P, A \rangle$:

- Types: represent something and restrict what can form the parameters of an action.
- Objects: is a set of typed objects, allow to declare objects that are present in the world with a twofold: name-type.
- Predicates: represent something that can be true in the world. It can involve several objects.
- Propositions: is a set of features that describe current the world.
- Actions: define the transformation between the states of the world.

The PDDL elements have been encapsulated into DTO elements. Following this, we have developed a DTO for each PDDL element. The structure of each PDDL element modeled with the DTO pattern is the following:

- Types: A type is composed of only one string attribute, which represents its name.
- Objects: An object is composed of one Type DTO attribute, which represents its PDDL type; and one string attribute, which represents its name.
- Predicates: A predicate is composed of one string attribute, which represents its name; and one Type DTO List attribute, which represents its arguments.
- Propositions: A proposition is composed of one string attribute, which represents its name; and one Object DTO List attribute, which represents its PDDL objects. It also has a boolean attribute, which represents if it is a goal.
- Actions: An action is composed of the following attributes:
  - A string attribute, which represents its name.
  - A boolean attribute, which represents if it is a durative action.
  - An integer attribute, which represents its duration.
  - An Object DTO List attribute, which represents its parameters.
  - A Condition/Effect DTO List attribute, which represents its conditions. The Condition/Effect DTO is similar to the Proposition DTO but it also has a string attribute, which represents the moment the condition or effect must occur; and a boolean attribute, which represents if it is a negative condition or effect.
  - A Condition/Effect DTO List attribute, which represents its effects.

On the other hand, the DAO instances can be used to interact with the PDDL knowledge in the Knowledge Base. Three main functions can be used:

- *get*: this function returns a DTO from the Knowledge Base. It provides access to the current PDDL that the robot has to all robot components. In the case of PDDL types, objects, predicates and actions, this function takes their names to search for them. However, in the case of the PDDL propositions, there are three get functions: get_by_predicate, to search for a list of propositions with a given predicate name; get_goals, to search for the propositions that are goals; and get_no_goals, to search for the propositions that are not goals.
- *save*: this function is used to save a DTO. If the knowledge exists, it is updated. As a result, all robot components can produce knowledge for the robot.

– *delete*: this function is also implemented in all DAO and is used to delete a DTO from the Knowledge Base.

Since the roboticist would have many DAO families such as SQL-database, non-SQL databases, and in-memory for storing robot knowledge, KANT deploys the Abstract Factory Pattern. With this pattern, it is encapsulated different factories that have something in common, that is the creation of DAO.

When combining DTO and DAO patterns, a robot component can query, save, edit and delete the data from the Knowledge Base without having to worry about the type and the implementation of the data source. That means that the DAO implementation acts like an interface between the source code of the developers and the Knowledge Base. Besides, the DTO pattern allows encapsulating the PDDL independently of the type of storage used. The resulting architecture is presented in Fig. 2. As a result, developers can manipulate and manage knowledge from source code enhancing reusability, scalability and flexibility.

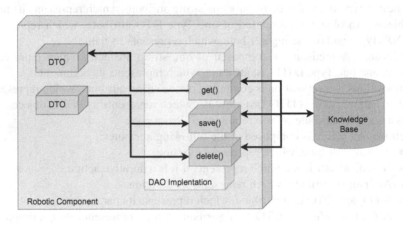

Fig. 2. KANT architecture

3.2   Implementation Overview

This section presents a practical guide for applying KANT to manage PDDL knowledge. To this end, the software approach for managing a simple robot task, the navigation between waypoints, using Code Listings (CL onwards), is schemed.

Task and Knowledge. A simple robot task is proposed as an example to illustrate how the developer interacts with PDDL. The task consists of moving a robot called rb1; from its current way-point, named wp1; to another way-point, labeled as wp2 in a period of time of 10 s.

Translating the Task to PDDL from the Source Code. The roboticist and the AI researcher need to focus on a single point, generating and managing a PDDL Domain file. The PDDL domain file presents two types, robot and wp (waypoint); one predicate, robot_at that implies if a robot is in a waypoint (wp); and one durative-action, navigation, that models the navigation between waypoints for a time period and involves a robot in a new waypoint from a previous waypoint. Besides, there are three objects in the initial problem that are a robot named rb1 and two wp, wp1 and wp2. Finally, the goal that wants to be achieved is to have the rb1 robot in wp2.

Using PDDL from the Source Code. Firstly, the DTO classes are used. These classes store the PDDL information. As a result, the PDDL types previously mentioned are instantiated in Python using the *PddlTypeDto* class with the name of each type. This is presented in CL 1.1.

Code Listing 1.1. Python PDDL Types DTO Example.

```
1 robot_type  = PddlTypeDto("robot")
  wp_type     = PddlTypeDto("wp")
```

Predicates are created with the *PddlPredicateDto* class. The robot_at predicate is presented in 1.2. This predicate is created with its name and the *PddlTypeDto* instances of the necessary PDDL types.

Code Listing 1.2. Python PDDL Predicates DTO Example.

```
  robot_at = PddlPredicateDto(
2     "robot_at", [robot_type, wp_type])
```

The creation of a PDDL object is similar to predicate creation. As it is presented in 1.3, a PDDL object can be created using the *PddlObjectDto* class that needs its name and a *PddlTypeDto* instance. On the other hand, the PDDL proposition is created using the *PddlPropositionDto* class with a *PddlPredicateDto* instance and its *PddlObjectDto* instances. Besides, a proposition can be marked as a goal using the is_goal argument (CL 1.4).

Code Listing 1.3. Python PDDL Objects DTO Example.

```
1 rb1 = PddlObjectDto(robot_type, "rb1")
  wp1 = PddlObjectDto(wp_type, "wp1")
3 wp2 = PddlObjectDto(wp_type, "wp2")
```

Code Listing 1.4. Python PDDL Propositions DTO Example.

```
  pddl_proposition_dto = PddlPropositionDto(
2     robot_at, [rb1, wp1])

4 pddl_goal_dto = PddlPropositionDto(
      robot_at, [rb1, wp2], is_goal=True)
```

PDDL actions are created using the *PddlActionDto* class. As it is shown in CL 1.5, parameters, conditions and effects must be created.

Code Listing 1.5. Python PDDL Navigation Action DTO Example.

```
   r = PddlObjectDto(robot_type, "r")
 2 s = PddlObjectDto(wp_type, "s")
   d = PddlObjectDto(wp_type, "d")

 4
   condition_1 = PddlConditionEffectDto(
 6     robot_at,
       [r, s],
 8     time=PddlConditionEffectDto.AT_START)

10 effect_1 = PddlConditionEffectDto(
       robot_at,
12     [r, s],
       time=PddlConditionEffectDto.AT_START,
14     is_negative=True)

16 effect_2 = PddlConditionEffectDto(
       robot_at,
18     [r, d],
       time=PddlConditionEffectDto.AT_END)
20
   pddl_action_dto = PddlActionDto(
22     "navigation",
       [r, s, d],
24     [condition_1],
       [effect_1, effect_2])
```

The action parameters are *PddlObjectDto* while conditions and effects are created with a new class, *PddlConditionEffectDto*. The *PddlConditionEffectDto* instances are created like *PddlPropositionDto* instances but with the possibility of selecting the time, if the action is durative. Conditions and effects can also be negative. The available times for conditions and effects are AT_START, AT_END and OVER_ALL. Then, an action can be created with its name, its parameters, a list of *PddlObjectDto* instances; and its conditions and effects, two lists of *PddlConditionEffectDto* instances. In addition, an action can be durative or not using the durative argument, which is True by default.

4 Evaluation Procedure

For evaluating our proposal, it is proposed a high-level task extracted and adapted from ERL-SciRoc 2019 Deliver coffee shop orders chapter [1]. This task presents a robot that will assist people in a coffee shop. The robots will take care of customers, by taking orders and bringing objects to and from tables.

Because this competition domain is quite deterministic and dynamic, these tasks are representative of real-world performance. During the performance, the robot needs a considerable number of objects, actions, and propositions that are queried, created, edited and deleted during execution.

These tasks are discretized and it is proposed temporal metric for modeling the environment. This experimental process evaluates the completion time of these five consecutive tasks that include PDDL manipulation using KANT.

1. Time to reset PDDL (TtR): this is the time spent to delete all the knowledge from the Knowledge Base.
2. Time to load initial PDDL (TtL): this is the time spent to load the initial PDDL elements.
3. Time to check tables (TtC): this is the time spent to simulate the task of checking several tables.
4. Time to serve an Order (TtS): this is the time spent to simulate the task of serving an order.
5. Time to guide a Person (TtG): this is the time spent to simulate the task of guiding a person.

It is implemented two DAO families to be able to store PDDL: 1) MongoDB [2] and 2) Knowledge Base in-memory using ROS 2. These families are deployed together with the three-layer cognitive architecture MERLIN [9] and everything has been simulated using a ROS 2 Foxy environment. An extended explanation of the experiment is presented in the public GitHub Repository.

4.1 Results

After running 3000 times each test in a regular computer (laptop with 32 GB RAM and an Intel(R) Core(TM) i7-8750H CPU @ 2.20 GHz), the results presented in Table 1 and Table 2 are obtained.

DAO in-memory approach presents an execution time of almost one hundred twenty-two minutes. The mean time of each iteration is 2.432 s with a median of 2.385 s. The time to load the PDDL gets 52 min, resetting knowledge takes 13 min, and the other tasks are performed in 23, 18 and 14 min in TtC, TtS and TtG tasks.

DAO MongoDB family defines an execution time of seventy-six minutes for the same 3000 iterations. From the total time, 3.5 min were used for resetting the database.

Table 1. Manipulating PDDL using in-memory.

	TtR	TtL	TtC	TtS	TtG	Total
Mean	0.263	1.051	0.465	0.364	0.29	2.432
Std Dev.	0.124	0.285	0.18	0.152	0.137	0.446
Min	0.039	0.527	0.218	0.16	0.114	1.312
Max	0.805	3.041	2.065	1.618	1.489	4.722
Sum	787.571	3152.132	1393.824	1093.036	869.431	7295.995

Table 2. Manipulating PDDL using MongoDB.

	TtR	TtL	TtC	TtS	TtG	Total
Mean	0.069	0.612	0.329	0.288	0.216	1.514
Std dev	0.002	0.014	0.008	0.007	0.006	0.027
Min	0.063	0.569	0.299	0.262	0.194	1.446
Max	0.1	0.756	0.411	0.344	0.264	1.815
Sum	206.676	1835.754	987.505	865.309	646.987	4542.231

Approximately 31 min were devoted to loading the PDDL information. When dealing with the tasks we found that during the experiment, it spent 16 min for the Checking the tables task, then 14 min for the Serving an Order and finally 10 min for the time to guide a person. Tables 1 and 2 present the descriptive statistics of the overall experiment measured in seconds.

5 Discussion

Open-source science and software development impacts, not only on society, but also on scientific research. The mechanisms for grounding processes should be generalized and based on Open Source libraries.

The processes involved in knowledge management should present exactly what is happening behind the scenes in order to guarantee Explainable reasoning in robotics. Besides, the use of ROS 2 as the based middleware, simplifies the use of KANT in state-of-the-art robots and amplifies its impact on the overall community. This would avoid breaking the rule "Don't reinvent the Wheel".

The results collected also present the quality difference when the model is managed by the right approach. KANT as a tool for easily using different database systems, and the figures present the differences between databases, where the same experiment would be carried out in a smaller period of time. For instance, TtR spends a 70% less time in MongoDb, consuming 35% lower of time for the full experiment. However, the inclusion of databases is not always possible, leaving the selection at the discretion of the researcher deploying the solution that fits better to their robotic scenario.

6 Conclusions

In this paper, a novel approach for manipulating PDDL using software design patterns has been proposed. Our aim is, on the one hand, to simplify the methods for interacting with knowledge in run-time from a software engineer perspective. This approach would attract the interest in deliberative and planning fields from the software developers in the robots community and formalize the process of working with PDDL in any kind of robot.

Authors believe that the models based on well-known software patterns together with the implemented solution in Python 3 would simplify the adoption of PDDL as a language for the Knowledge Base.

Under current robotics competition scenarios, we plan to evaluate the performance of this approach using a real robot as well as educationally understand how new researchers interact with PDDL more comfortably. Finally, KANT needs to be upgraded with more PDDL elements such as Numeric Fluents, in order to encompass modern versions of PDDL.

References

1. Basiri, M., Piazza, E., Matteucci, M., Lima, P.: Rulebook of the European robotic league for consumer service robots (2018). https://eu-robotics.net/robotics_league/erl-consumer
2. Bradshaw, S., Chodorow, K., Brazil, E.: MongoDB: the Definitive Guide: Powerful and Scalable Data Storage. The Expert's Voice in Open Source, O'Reilly Media, Incorporated (2019). https://books.google.es/books?id=ohGAvgAACAAJ
3. Cashmore, M., et al.: ROSplan: planning in the robot operating system. In: Proceedings International Conference on Automated Planning and Scheduling, ICAPS, vol. 2015, pp. 333–341, January 2015
4. Charles Lesire, D.D., Grand, C.: Formalization of robot skills with descriptive and operational models. IEEE (2020)
5. Ellis, B., Stylos, J., Myers, B.: The factory pattern in API design: a usability evaluation. In: 29th International Conference on Software Engineering (ICSE 2007), pp. 302–312. IEEE (2007)
6. Fischbach, M., Wiebusch, D., Latoschik, M.E.: Semantic entity-component state management techniques to enhance software quality for multimodal VR-systems. IEEE Trans. Vis. Comput. Graph. **23**(4), 1342–1351 (2017). https://doi.org/10.1109/TVCG.2017.2657098
7. Fox, M., Long, D.: PDDL2. 1: an extension to PDDL for expressing temporal planning domains. J. Artif. Intell. Res. **20**, 61–124 (2003)
8. Gavran, I., Mailahn, O., Müller, R., Peifer, R., Zufferey, D.: Tool: accessible automated reasoning for human robot collaboration. In: Proceedings of the 2018 ACM SIGPLAN International Symposium on New Ideas, New Paradigms, and Reflections on Programming and Software, Onward! 2018, pp. 44–56. Association for Computing Machinery, New York (2018). https://doi.org/10.1145/3276954.3276961
9. González-Santamarta, M.Á., et al.: MERLIN a cognitive architecture for service robots. Appl. Sci. **10**(17), 5989 (2020). https://doi.org/10.3390/app10175989
10. Martín, F., Ginés, J., Rodríguez, F.J., Matellán, V.: PlanSys2: a planning system framework for ROS2. In: IEEE/RSJ International Conference on Intelligent Robots and Systems, IROS 2021, Prague, Czech Republic, 27 September–1 October 2021. IEEE (2021)
11. Monday, P.B.: Implementing the data transfer object pattern. In: Monday, P.B. (eds.) Web Services Patterns: Java™ Platform Edition, pp. 279–295. Apress, Berkeley (2003). https://doi.org/10.1007/978-1-4302-0776-4_16
12. Motik, B., et al.: OWL 2 web ontology language: structural specification and functional-style syntax. W3C Recomm. **27**(65), 159 (2009)
13. Nock, C.: Data Access Patterns: Database Interactions in Object-oriented Applications. Addison-Wesley, Boston (2004)
14. Quigley, M., et al.: ROS: an open-source robot operating system. In: ICRA Workshop on Open Source Software, Kobe, Japan, vol. 3, p. 5. (2009)

Clustering of COVID-19 Time Series Incidence Intensity in Andalusia, Spain

Miguel Díaz-Lozano[1]([⊠])(iD), David Guijo-Rubio[2](iD), Pedro Antonio Gutiérrez[2](iD), and César Hervás-Martínez[2](iD)

[1] Fundación Pública Andaluza Progreso y Salud, 41092 Sevilla, Spain
i42dilom@uco.es
[2] Department of Computer Science and Numerical Analysis, University of Córdoba, 14071 Córdoba, Spain
{dguijo,pagutierrez,chervas}@uco.es

Abstract. In this paper, an approach based on a time series clustering technique is presented by extracting relevant features from the original temporal data. A curve characterization is applied to the daily contagion rates of the 34 sanitary districts of Andalusia, Spain. By determining the maximum incidence instant and two inflection points for each wave, an outbreak curve can be described by six intensity features, defining its initial and final phases. These features are used to derive different groups using state-of-the-art clustering techniques. The experimentation carried out indicates that $k = 3$ is the optimum number of descriptive groups of intensities. According to the resulting clusters for each wave, the pandemic behavior in Andalusia can be visualised over time, showing the most affected districts in the pandemic period considered. Additionally, in order to perform a pandemic overview of the whole period, the approach is also applied to joint information of all the considered periods.

Keywords: COVID-19 contagions · Clustering · Curve characterization

1 Introduction

In order to mitigate the effects of the COVID-19 pandemic, a wide variety of research studies have been carried out. More specifically, regarding the data collected from this pandemic and from an analytical point of view, several Machine Learning (ML) techniques have been applied in order to propose solutions and mechanisms supporting experts in the subject [10]. The research works in this field include deep learning models for early diagnosis using chest images, obtaining accurate diagnostic models, and the prediction of several pandemic parameters. These data can be treated as time series, as the data is collected chronologically over time. Many different techniques can be applied to time series. One attracting special attention these days is unsupervised classification, also known as clustering [1]. More specifically, time series clustering tasks are unsupervised

© Springer Nature Switzerland AG 2022
J. M. Ferrández Vicente et al. (Eds.): IWINAC 2022, LNCS 13259, pp. 462–471, 2022.
https://doi.org/10.1007/978-3-031-06527-9_46

ML descriptive methods whose goal is to discover different categories in time series dataset [8]. Hence, clustering algorithms divide an initial set of time series into k different clusters or groups, in such a way that patterns belonging to the same group are as similar as possible to patterns in the same cluster, and as different as possible to patterns organized in other groups. In this sense, the objective is to maximize the inter-cluster distance while minimizing the intra-cluster distance.

This study is focused on the pandemic development behavior of Andalusia, the most populated autonomous community of Spain. This region is administratively divided into 34 sanitary districts, for which COVID-19 stats are reported and publicly available.

In this article, the main novelty is twofold: 1) proposing a detailed characterization of the contagion curve by identifying the maximum incidence and two inflection instants for each outbreak, in different sanitary districts of Andalusia. Moreover, by measuring the intensity between these events, the different waves are characterized by means of six intensity features. And 2) the application of different clustering techniques to this novel representation of the outbreaks, aiming to group the different districts according to their intensity rates of each wave. Furthermore, the geographical cluster variation over time is graphically presented.

2   Data Description and Processing

In this study, time series data belonging to the 34 Andalusian (Spain) sanitary districts[1] have been used to analytically describe the behavior of the COVID-19 pandemic in Andalusia. The information has been obtained from the official Andalusian government[2], with daily COVID-19 statistics. The information about positive diagnoses, cured and deceased people is available since February 26, 2020. In this study, 5 different waves are identified, each one defined by an increment and followed by a decrease in the contagion rate. Therefore, the following temporal limits for the different waves are considered:

1. The first wave spans from March 12, 2020, to April 15, 2020.
2. The second wave spans from July 31, 2020, to December 15, 2020.
3. The third wave spans from December 15, 2020, to March 13, 2021.
4. The fourth wave spans from March 13, 2021, to June 15, 2021.
5. The fifth wave spans from June 15, 2021, to September 15, 2021.

However, the first and fourth waves have been excluded from this study. The main reason behind these exclusions is that during the first wave, the shortest and least intense one, the reporting systems were not prepared and the provided

---

[1] Andalusian sanitary districts: https://www.sspa.juntadeandalucia.es/servicioanda luzdesalud/el-sas/servicios-y-centros/mapa-centros.

[2] The number of infections in Andalusia is daily reported at https://www.juntade andalucia.es/institutodeestadisticaycartografia/badea/operaciones/consulta/anual/ 42249.

information was erratic. Moreover, regarding the fourth wave, it is characterized by the beginning of the vaccination campaign, resulting in a set of heterogeneous contagions rates for all the districts where similarities are difficult to find, precisely due to the differences in the pace of vaccination and the different decisions of the provinces.

The information reported regarding daily contagions on the 34 districts presents a weekly pattern in which fewer diagnoses are recorded appropriately during weekends. This effect is common in most countries [14], and it is due to differences in testing timings, i. e. fewer patients are tested on Saturdays and Sundays, thus, presenting reporting delays. With the aim of reducing the time series noise produced by this weekly pattern, the original time series are preprocessed by applying the Savitzky-Golay (SG) smooth filter [16]. Concretely, this filter is applied with a window size $w = 5$ and using a 3-degree polynomial. For instance, Fig. 1 shows both the original daily contagions time series and the resulting smoothed time series after applying the SG filter in the district of Córdoba, from July 15, 2020, to September 15, 2021.

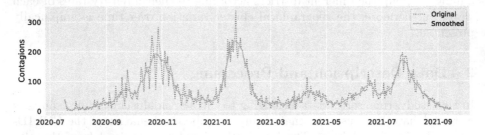

Fig. 1. Original and SG-smoothed daily contagions time series in the district of Córdoba from July 15, 2020 to September 15, 2021.

The shape of all the curves, regardless the outbreak number and the sanitary district, is defined by a soft initial growth. Then, when a sufficiently high number of infected people is reached, an exponential increment occurs due to the high contagion rate. The stabilization phase begins when the maximum incidence instant takes place. After that, contagions slow down and the outbreak becomes under control. In this sense, three relevant points are identified for each wave and district: t_b (inflection point where the transmission rate accelerates), t_s (inflection instant of stabilization of the outbreak) and t_m (instant of highest incidence). The two first points are identified according to the percentage change of the number of infections with respect to the previous day, so that t_b and t_s occur when the maximum and minimum percentage change takes place, respectively. Moreover, t_m is reached when the maximum number of daily contagions for each wave is reached. For instance, Fig. 2 shows the two inflection points and the maximum incidence instant during the third wave of the district of Córdoba.

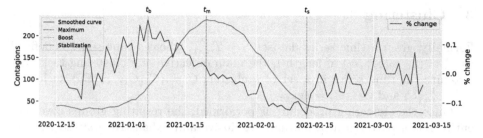

Fig. 2. Inflection and maximum incidence points during the third wave of the district of Córdoba.

These three points allow the characterization of the curve by measuring the intensity between pairwise points. This intensity is calculated as the slope of the linear regression between a pair of points of the curve. In this sense, six different intensities features are calculated for each wave and district using different periods of the wave: growth (I_G, from the beginning of the wave to t_m), rise (I_R, from the beginning of the wave to t_b), boost (I_B, from t_b to t_m), decrease (I_D, from t_m to t_s), ending (I_E, from t_s to the end of the wave) and stabilization (I_S, from t_m to the end of the wave). For instance, Fig. 3 shows the intensity features extraction for the third wave of the district of Córdoba.

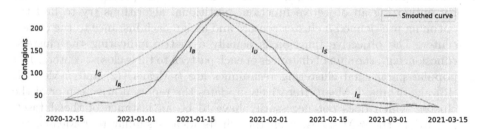

Fig. 3. Features extraction for the third wave of the district of Córdoba.

By applying this methodology, each wave of a single Andalusian district is now characterized by these 6 intensity features, 3 of them represent the first phase of the wave (i.e. before the wave contagion peak is reached), whereas the remaining 3 features characterize the second phase, where the wave begins to stabilize after the maximum incidence point. Additionally, with the aim of building a general characterization of the considered pandemic period in Andalusia, patterns are built using all the features from the three waves, resulting in a dataset of 18 intensities features per sanitary district. Therefore, a total of 4 datasets will be assessed (one for each wave individually and the general dataset, combining the three waves). Finally, regarding the number of patterns, a total of 34 instances are considered in this study, one per sanitary district.

3   Clustering

Formally, given a time series dataset $S = T_i{}_{i=1}^N$, where a time series is defined as $T_i = (v_1, v_2, \ldots, v_l)$ of length l, the main objective of a clustering task is to organize the time series in a set of k clusters $C = \{C_0, C_1, \ldots, C_k\}$ such that $C = \cup_{i=1}^k C_i$ and $C_i \cap C_j = \emptyset \forall i \neq j$.

Once the clustering procedure is performed, the resulting groups cover the entire set of patterns in a mutually exclusive and exhaustive way, so that an instance is assigned just to one group. There are a wide amount of clustering techniques in the literature. They have been categorized in several ways, depending on the way in which the algorithm builds the groups. In this study, we focus on two types of well-known clustering methods [7], hierarchical and partitional methods:

1. **Hierarchical** clustering methods build the groups partitioning the instances in either top-down (divisive clustering) or down-top (agglomerative) fashion. In the first case, the whole dataset is associated to a cluster that is iteratively divided according to the dissimilarities between instances. On the other hand, agglomerative clustering initially assigns a group to each instance, and similar clusters are merged recursively. In both cases, the similarity between groups should be measured using a distance metric and a linkage criterion. Hierarchical clustering results in a dendrogram representing the clustering structure.
2. **Partitional** clustering methods aim to find a unique partition of the data. By optimizing an objective function, partitional algorithms try to find the optimum pre-defined k cluster centers and assign each instance to the closest center. The objective function is usually a metric indicating the clusters' cohesion, e.g., the sum of distances of each pattern to their closest center. Most popular partitional clustering techniques are k-Means [12] and k-Medoids [13] algorithms. k-Means iteratively updates the representative center of the cluster, which does not necessarily have to be an instance of the dataset. Regarding the k-Medoids, even though its idea is similar to k-Means, the main difference is that k-Medoids updates the centers choosing an instance as the representative center of a cluster.

The criteria to evaluate the quality of a clustering algorithm are divided into two categories [2]: **external**, making use of grown-truth labels, and **internal**, used when no external information is available, as is the case of this study. Internal metrics measure the intra-cluster homogeneity and inter-cluster separability. Several internal metrics have been proposed to validate clustering results [11]. In this article, four popular internal evaluation metrics have been used: Silhouette Index (SI) [15], Calinski-Harabasz (CH) index [4], Dunn Index (DI) [6] and Davies-Bouldin (DB) index [5]. The first three metrics (SI, CH and DI) have to be minimized to represent better clustering results, whereas the last index (DB) has to be minimized.

4   Experimental Settings and Results

In this section, the parameters used for the different clustering techniques are detailed, as well as the results achieved by these methods.

4.1   Experimental Settings

k-Means, k-Medoids and agglomerative hierarchical techniques have been applied in this study. These techniques have been run with the following parameters: for the agglomerative clustering, the distance between two clusters or patterns is computed by the Euclidean distance. Also, Ward's linkage [9] has been chosen as linkage criterion. The k-Means method has been executed 20 times as it is an stochastic technique. The best result is chosen according to the sum of distances between the patterns and their corresponding centroid. The initial centroids are set using k-means++ initialisation [3]. For the k-Medoids technique, the Euclidean distance is used as the dissimilarity measure. Finally, for the computation of the internal SI metric, the Euclidean distance has been used.

4.2   Results

The nature of partitional clustering algorithms requires that a number of clusters k is specified. On the other hand, the hierarchical method requires selecting a value of k from the generated output. Aiming to find the appropriate k, the k-Means technique has been run with $k = 1, 2, \ldots, 9$, measuring the distortion D for each execution. The distortion D is computed as the sum of squared distances from the patterns to the closest centroid:

$$D = \sum_{j=1}^{k} \sum_{i=1}^{n_j} \|\mathbf{x}_{i,j} - \mathbf{c}_j\|^2, \tag{1}$$

where n_j is the number of patterns assigned to cluster j, $\mathbf{x}_{i,j}$ is the i-th pattern of the j-th cluster, and $\mathbf{c}_j$ is the centroid of cluster j. Figure 4 shows the evolution of the distortion with respect to the number of clusters using the three waves individually and the general dataset (combining the three waves), previously defined in Sect. 2. As expected, distortion decreases as the number of clusters increases. Hence, the objective is to find the elbow of the curve, i.e., the minimum number of clusters in which the distortion reduction is no longer significant. In this case, as can be seen, the elbow of the curve is found at $k = 3$.

Table 1 presents the internal quality metrics detailed in Sect. 3 for the three resulting clusters using the three clustering approaches and the four generated datasets (one for each wave individually and the complete one, combining the three waves).

According to Table 1, it can be seen that the best values for the metrics are concentrated in the results obtained by the k-Means technique. These three clusters are defined by their intensities values. In this way, three different COVID-19 incidence groups are identified for each pandemic period: major, high and

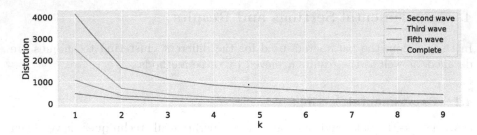

Fig. 4. Evolution of the distortion for the k-means clusters using $k = 1, 2, \ldots, 9$.

Table 1. Quality measures for the three clustering techniques using $k = 3$.

Wave	Agglomerative				k-means				k-medoids			
	SI	CH	DB	DI	SI	CH	DB	DI	SI	CH	DB	DI
2	**0.68**	*39.11*	**0.59**	**0.34**	*0.62*	**45.46**	*0.75*	*0.16*	0.46	28.62	0.92	0.09
3	0.64	73.59	**0.63**	0.13	*0.66*	**75.81**	*0.64*	**0.13**	0.67	*75.12*	*0.64*	*0.12*
5	**0.58**	*52.95*	0.80	0.15	0.58	**54.77**	*0.81*	0.12	*0.40*	47.34	0.82	*0.12*
Complete	*0.66*	*34.05*	0.83	0.33	**0.68**	**42.26**	0.80	**0.44**	0.41	31.59	0.98	0.14

Best value for each metric, wave and algorithm is highlighted in **bold**, whereas the second best result is in *italics*

moderate incidence. In Table 2, the mean values for all the intensity features of the three groups obtained with the k-Means technique are presented for all the datasets. For the complete dataset, mean values for each of the six intensity features for the three waves is calculated.

Table 2. Intensity mean values of the clusters obtained by the k-Means method.

Wave	Major incidence						High incidence						Moderate incidence					
	I_R	I_B	I_G	I_D	I_E	I_S	I_R	I_B	I_G	I_D	I_E	I_S	I_R	I_B	I_G	I_D	I_E	I_S
2	0.50	4.80	4.61	−9.45	0.15	−6.63	0.56	1.99	1.62	−4.75	−0.29	−2.84	0.19	0.92	0.60	−1.70	0.14	−1.05
3	3.12	17.90	9.94	−13.26	−1.86	−7.36	1.58	8.18	4.54	−6.02	−0.65	−3.29	0.12	3.24	2.02	−2.24	−0.11	−1.41
5	6.36	12.33	9.51	−9.36	−2.10	−6.98	1.30	4.83	2.89	−3.83	−1.36	−3.15	0.39	2.16	1.27	−1.58	0.00	−1.27
Complete	4.33	11.65	7.60	−10.26	−1.60	−6.34	1.36	7.56	4.43	−6.94	−1.00	−4.39	0.46	2.97	1.84	−2.73	−0.13	−1.74

These three clusters are spatially represented in Figs. 5 and 6, where black lines delimit the 8 Andalusian provinces and white lines delimit the 34 sanitary district borders. In Fig. 5 the three waves intensities features have been jointly considered for determining the three groups. Furthermore, in Fig. 6, the temporal evolution of the clusters is represented by using the specific wave intensity features. Red, orange and gray colors represent major, high and moderate incidence clusters, respectively.

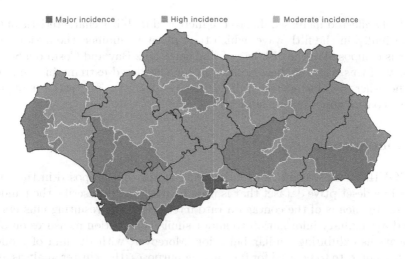

Fig. 5. Results achieved by the k-means clustering technique using $k = 3$ and the three waves together. (Color figure online)

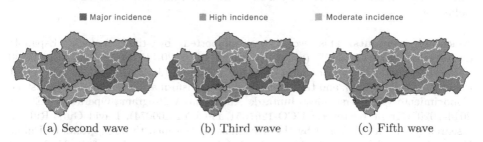

(a) Second wave   (b) Third wave   (c) Fifth wave

Fig. 6. Results obtained by the k-means clustering approach using $k = 3$ on the second (a), third (b) and fifth (c) wave. (Color figure online)

4.3   Discussion

According to Table 2, the resulting clusters represent three sorts of intensities. In this regard, intensities magnitudes are clearly segregated into the different classes. These magnitudes depend on the considered pandemic period, and they increase with respect to the time at which the outbreak occurs. In the temporal overview of the considered pandemic periods shown in Fig. 5, it can be appreciated that those areas where the virus spread was major are the districts of Málaga, Costa del Sol and Granada, possibly due to the high tourist affluence and the presence of a considerable number of students that increase population mobility. Districts that include province capitals except Jaén, where population density is higher, or are close to the province capital, exhibit high intensity.

Furthermore, in Fig. 6, the geographical evolution of the three clusters' distribution is visible. During the second wave, only three districts were very intensely affected. During the third wave, which coincided with the Christmas holidays, several coastal districts showed major intensity, and the number of districts intensively affected increased due to the increased mobility characteristic of these dates. Finally, in the fifth wave, which took place in summer, the major intense cluster is composed of the districts of Málaga, Cádiz Bay and Costa del Sol. The intensity of this wave in these zones can be considered extreme in comparison with the other two clusters (see Table 2) as a result of the concentration of people in these coastal zones during summer.

5   Conclusions

The COVID-19 daily contagions curve characterization proposed in this article results in a descriptive dataset that is used to analytically describe the pandemic situation by means of the contagion rate intensities. The resulting clusters may be used as auxiliary information to adopt similar prevention measures on different locations exhibiting similar behavior. Moreover, with the aim of modeling the contagion rate to be used for forecasting purposes, this cluster analysis allows the possibility of reducing the number of models required to forecast the transmission rate in all the districts by using joint information from areas with similar behavior.

Acknowledgements. This work was supported by the "Agencia Española de Investigación (España)" (grant reference: PID2020-115454GB-C22/AEI/10.130 39/501100011033); the "Consejería de Salud y Familia (Junta de Andalucía)" (grant reference: PS-2020-780); and the "Consejería de Transformación Económica, Industria, Conocimiento y Universidades (Junta de Andalucía) y Programa Operativo FEDER 2014-2020" (grant references: UCO-1261651 and PY20_00074). David Guijo-Rubio's research has been subsidised by the University of Córdoba through grants to Public Universities for the requalification of the Spanish university system of the Ministry of Universities, financed by the European Union - NextGenerationEU (grant reference: UCOR01MS).

References

1. Aghabozorgi, S., Seyed Shirkhorshidi, A., Ying Wah, T.: Time-series clustering - a decade review. Inf. Syst. **53**, 16–38 (2015). https://doi.org/10.1016/j.is.2015.04.007

2. Arbelaitz, O., Gurrutxaga, I., Muguerza, J., Pérez, J.M., Perona, I.: An extensive comparative study of cluster validity indices. Pattern Recognit. **46**(1), 243–256 (2013). https://doi.org/10.1016/j.patcog.2012.07.021

3. Arthur, D., Vassilvitskii, S.: K-means++: the advantages of careful seeding. In: Proceedings of the Eighteenth Annual ACM-SIAM Symposium on Discrete Algorithms, SODA 2007, USA, pp. 1027–1035. Society for Industrial and Applied Mathematics (2007)

4. Caliński, T., JA, H.: A dendrite method for cluster analysis. Commun. Stat. Theory Methods **3**, 1–27 (1974). https://doi.org/10.1080/03610927408827101

5. Davies, D.L., Bouldin, D.W.: A cluster separation measure. IEEE Trans. Pattern Anal. Mach. Intell. **PAMI-1**(2), 224–227 (1979). https://doi.org/10.1109/TPAMI.1979.4766909

6. Dunn, J.C.: Well-separated clusters and optimal fuzzy partitions. J. Cybern. **4**(1), 95–104 (1974). https://doi.org/10.1080/01969727408546059

7. Fraley, C., Raftery, A.E.: How many clusters? Which clustering method? Answers via model-based cluster analysis. Comput. J. **41**(8), 578–588 (1998). https://doi.org/10.1093/comjnl/41.8.578

8. Guijo-Rubio, D., Durán-Rosal, A.M., Gutiérrez, P.A., Troncoso, A., Hervás-Martínez, C.: Time-series clustering based on the characterization of segment typologies. IEEE Trans. Cybern. **51**(11), 5409–5422 (2021). https://doi.org/10.1109/TCYB.2019.2962584

9. Ward Jr., J.H.: Hierarchical grouping to optimize an objective function. J. Am. Stat. Assoc. **58**(301), 236–244 (1963). https://doi.org/10.1080/01621459.1963.10500845

10. Khan, M., et al.: Applications of artificial intelligence in COVID-19 pandemic: a comprehensive review. Expert Syst. Appl. **185**, 115695 (2021). https://doi.org/10.1016/j.eswa.2021.115695

11. Liu, Y., Li, Z., Xiong, H., Gao, X., Wu, J.: Understanding of internal clustering validation measures. In: 2010 IEEE International Conference on Data Mining, pp. 911–916. IEEE (2010)

12. MacQueen, J., et al.: Some methods for classification and analysis of multivariate observations. In: Proceedings of the fifth Berkeley Symposium on Mathematical Statistics and Probability, Oakland, CA, USA, vol. 1, pp. 281–297 (1967)

13. Park, H.S., Jun, C.H.: A simple and fast algorithm for k-medoids clustering. Expert Syst. Appl. **36**(2, Part 2), 3336–3341 (2009). https://doi.org/10.1016/j.eswa.2008.01.039

14. Ricon-Becker, I., Tarrasch, R., Blinder, P., Ben-Eliyahu, S.: A seven-day cycle in COVID-19 infection, hospitalization, and mortality rates: do weekend social interactions kill susceptible people? medRxiv (2020). https://doi.org/10.1101/2020.05.03.20089508

15. Rousseeuw, P.J.: Silhouettes: a graphical aid to the interpretation and validation of cluster analysis. J. Comput. Appl. Math. **20**, 53–65 (1987). https://doi.org/10.1016/0377-0427(87)90125-7

16. Savitzky, A., Golay, M.J.E.: Smoothing and differentiation of data by simplified least squares procedures. Anal. Chem. **36**(8), 1627–1639 (1964). https://doi.org/10.1021/ac60214a047

Triage Prediction of a Real Dataset of COVID-19 Patients in Alava

Goizalde Badiola-Zabala[1](✉), Jose Manuel Lopez-Guede[1,2], Julian Estevez[1,3], and Manuel Graña[1,3]

[1] Computational Intelligence Group, Basque Country University (UPV/EHU), Vitoria-Gasteiz, Spain
goizalde.badiola@ehu.eus
[2] Department of Systems and Automatic Control, Faculty of Engineering of Vitoria, Basque Country University (UPV/EHU), Nieves Cano 12, 01006 Vitoria-Gasteiz, Spain
[3] Department of Computer Science and Artificial Intelligence, Faculty of Informatics, Basque Country University (UPV/EHU), Paseo Manuel de Lardizabal 1, 20018 Donostia-San Sebastian, Spain

Abstract. The COVID-19 pandemic has increased the pressure on developing clinical decision-making systems based on predictive algorithms, potentially helping to reduce the unmanageable strain on healthcare systems. In an attempt to address this challenging health situation, we attempted to provide a contribution to this endeavour with an in-depth study of a real-life dataset of covid-19 patients from a local hospital. In this paper, we approach the problem as triage prediction problem, formulated as multi-class classification problem, with special care on the age normalization of physiological variables. We report experimental results obtained on a data sample covering COVID-19 patients assisted in a local hospital. To do this, we tried to emulate the triage decisions of the physicians recorded in a dataset containing the measurements of physiological variables and the triage decision. We obtained results that provide encouragement for a real-life application development of the data balancing and classification in the prediction of the triage that the medical doctors will assign the critical patients.

Keywords: COVID-19 · Modeling · Machine Learning

1 Introduction

Machine Learning (ML) is a part of data science and it has the capability to solve data-related problems by understanding and analyzing large data sets. While solving a problem with ML, the problem will be categorized into suitable groups so that the best ML algorithm can be applied to solve it. The main focus of the article is the search of predictive models of the risk levels of COVID-19 patients entering ED. These risk levels are determined by a "triage" process, coded by numbers from 1 to 5, with 5 being the mildest and 1 the most severe.

© Springer Nature Switzerland AG 2022
J. M. Ferrández Vicente et al. (Eds.): IWINAC 2022, LNCS 13259, pp. 472–481, 2022.
https://doi.org/10.1007/978-3-031-06527-9_47

The structure of the paper is as follows, Sect. 2 gives some background information and a short review of the state-of-the-art of data analysis and prediction algorithms addressing the covid-19 pandemic. Section 3 discusses the different ways we have explored in order to normalize the dependent variables in order to make them uncorrelated respect the age. Section 4 describes the computational experiments performed to predict triage level of each patient. Section 5 provides results of these performed experiments. Finally, Sect. 6 concludes the article.

2 Related Work

Many ML-based models have been developed to predict COVID-19 patients outcomes, preventing progression in time to minimize individual, medical, and social costs. Chen et al. [3] proposed a multimodality machine learning-based method to differentiate sever and nonsevere COVID-19 clinical patients. Feng et al. [4] developed a diagnostic model to aid in the early identification of suspected COVID-19 pneumonia patients. The performed model was able to perform with a 100% recall score the identification of COVID-19 on admission in fever clinics. Sun et al. [2] focused on the classification of different severity levels for COVID-19 patients. Wu et al. [7] developed a RF-SMA-SVM model to differentiate the severity of COVID-19 based on 26 blood routine indicators and several demographic features, exhibiting a high prediction accuracy. Liang et al. [5] utilized an online calculation tool for patient triage to identify the severe cases as early as possible. Soltan et al. [6] presented the application of a machine-learning-based classifier to exclude patients regarding their severity within 1h of hospital admission. Benito-Leon et al. [1] studied the detection of severity subgroups among COVID-19 patients based on clinical data and laboratory tests obtained during patient examination in ED.

3 Methods

3.1 Ethical Approval and Patient Consent

The ongoing project has been arisen because of the needs in the Health care field that have been emerged as a result of the current pandemic. Specifically, obtaining predictive models based on AI to help health-care employees improving the management and treatment of each patients individually is the main focus of the study. Making special emphasis on the specific characteristics of the population of the Historical Territory of Alava. The current study was approved by BIOARABA Health Research Institute, a relevant agent in the Basque scientific research area.

The demographic, vital, drug supply and laboratory data needed for this study come from the University Hospital of Alava (HUA) between October 2020 and March 2021. All ethical standards and preoccupation for patients privacy have been respected during the performance of the study. The ethics committee validated the present study and granted an exemption for patient data collection informed consent due to the retrospective character of the study, and its anonymization.

3.2 Normalization of the Age Dependent Variables

Age is an important variable in this casuistry, as many physiological variables are strongly dependent of it. For example, whereas heart rate usually decreases with age, blood pressure typically increases with age. Figure 1 gives a more detailed view of the distribution of the patients age variable.

To evaluate the dependence pf physiological variables on age, we show the scatter plots and regression lines of Heart Rate, Diastolic Blood Pressure and Systolic Blood Pressure versus Age in Figs. 2, 3 and 4, respectively, separating the plots by each Triage value. It can be observed that the younger patients show a higher Heart Rate than the older patients. Both blood pressure variables reflect an increase with age. For this reason, it is necessary to normalize these variables by removing their age dependency.

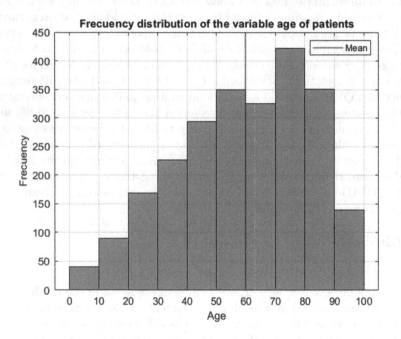

Fig. 1. Frequency distribution of the variable age of patients

Considering the age dependency of physiological variables, prior to apply the classification models, we normalized the variables Heart Rate, Diastolic Blood Pressure and Systolic Blood Pressure to obtain age-independent classifiers. We have tried five normalization methods.

1. The first approach, denoted *Norm1* in the results below, and known by z-score, measure the distance of a data point from the mean in terms of the standard deviation. The standardized data set has mean 0 and standard deviation 1, and retained the shape properties of the original data set (same skewness

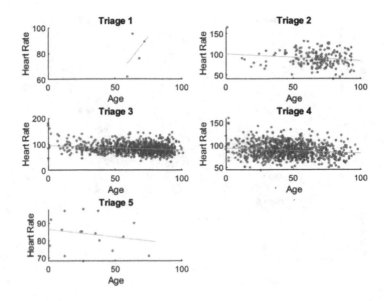

Fig. 2. Scatter plots of Heart Rate versus Age for each pf the triage values

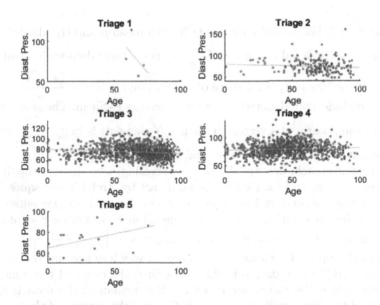

Fig. 3. Scatter plots of Diastolic blood pressure versus Age for each of the triage values

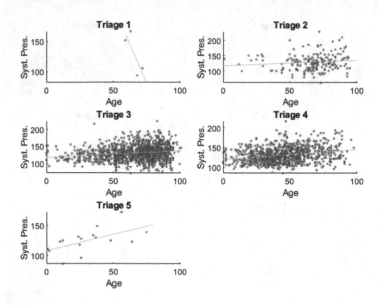

Fig. 4. Scatter plots of Systolic blood pressure versus Age for each of the triage values

and kurtosis). For a random variable $\mathbf{X}$ with mean μ and standard deviation σ, the z-score of a value x is $z = \dfrac{(x - \mu)}{\sigma}$. For sample data with mean $\overline{X}$ and standard deviation S, the z-score of a data point x is $z = \dfrac{(x - \overline{X})}{S}$.

2. The second method, denoted *Norm2*, is known as P-Norm. The general definition for the ρ-norm of a vector v that has N elements is $||v||_p = \left[\sum\limits_{k=1}^{N} |v_k|^p \right]^{1/p}$ where p is any positive real value, Inf, or -Inf.

3. The third approach, denoted *Norm3*, is re-scaling, who changes the distances between the min and max values in a data set by stretching or squeezing the points along the number line. The z-scores of the data are prevented, so the shape of the distribution remains the same. The equation for re-scaling data X to an arbitrary interval $[a, b]$ is $X_{rescaled} = a + \left[\frac{X - min_X}{max_X - min_x} \right] (b - a)$.

4. The fourth approach, referred to as *Norm4*, takes into account the interquartile range (IQR) of a data set which described the range of the middle 50% of values when the values are sorted. If the median of the data is $Q2$, the median of the lower half of the data is $Q1$, and the median of the upper half of the data is $Q3$, then $IQR = Q3 - Q1$.

5. The fifth approach, denoted *Norm5*, consider the median absolute deviation (MAD) of a data set which represents the median value of the absolute deviations from the median $\tilde{X}$ of the data: $MAD = \text{median}\left(|x - \tilde{X}| \right)$. Therefore, the MAD describes the variability of the data in relation to the median.

3.3   Class Balancing

The case at hand, as mentioned above, is a clear example of imbalance problem, which can be clearly seen in the Fig. 3, where the number of samples in one class is much higher than the other classes. Most cases with this problem of bias towards the majority class, usually achieve high classification accuracy but low sensitivity in the minority class, which is usually the interesting one, and in this case, represents the most severe cases, which are the ones we are most interested in detecting. There are different ways to deal with the imbalance class problem and in this case we will deal with two different methods.

1. Synthetic Minority Over-sampling Technique (SMOTE). Involves random linear interpolation between nearest neighbor samples of the minority class.
2. The over-sampling (OVER) of the minority class, which is the random repetition of some of the samples.

Figure 3 shows how the classes have been fully balanced after the application of the two balancing methods explained above.

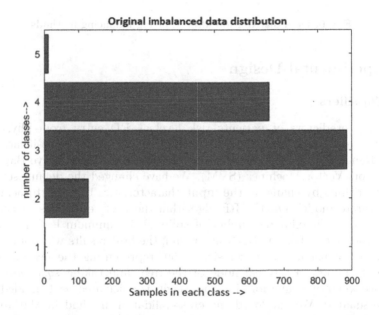

Fig. 5. Original imbalance data distribution regarding Triage variable

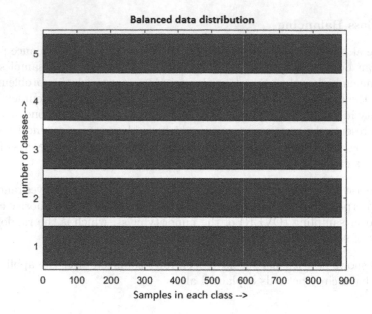

Fig. 6. Data distribution after applying balancing methods

4   Experimental Design

4.1   Classifiers

To develop predictors of patients risk level at ED entry from physiological and demographic characteristics, we attempted four types of classification algorithms: Random forest (RF), K-Nearest Neighbours (KNN), Naive Bayes (NB) and Support Vector Machines (SVM). We have changed the default settings of these algorithms by changing the input characteristics in order to achieve the most accurate model. On the RF algorithm the best result was reached with learning ratio 1, maximum number of splits of 8, minimum leaf size of 4 and 2048 decision trees. For the KNN algorithm, the best results was obtained with one number of neighbor, bucket size of 50 (representing the maximum number of data points in the leaf node of the tree) and taking *squaredinverse* as a distance weighting function, i.e. the weight is calculated as 1 divided by the distance squared. We employed the cross-validation method in Matlab Development Environment to perform k-fold cross-validation, in our case k = 10. We have repeated the experiments with each normalization procedure in relation to the age variable described in the previous section and to the balancing methods, in order to assess which combination of normalization, classification and balancing method is best for our casuistry.

4.2   Process

Figure 4 shows the process of distributing the dataset into training and test datasets to avoid circular effects and biasing of test results by training data misuse. The process starts with the collection of risk level data, i.e. triage level, and proceeds to randomly divide the data into 70%/30% subsets, which are used for training and testing, respectively. Training includes the application of data balancing techniques, normalization of the three age-dependent variables and classifier training, the last two of which are applied to the test data.

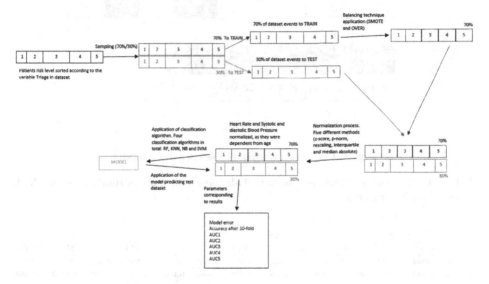

Fig. 7. Distribution of the dataset into training and test datasets in order to avoid circular effects and biasing of test results by training data misuse.

5   Results

The average accuracy obtained by the cross-validation experiments with each feature independently is presented in Table 1. It can be observed that the only algorithm that provides a result higher than 0.80 accuracy is KNN. Random forest is the second best classifier, SVM the third and NB the last. Furthermore, the best normalization methods are *Norm2* and *Norm5*, as they have obtained each three of the best values in their respective rows. It is noticeable that the best result, in terms of accuracy, is the KNN classifier with *Norm3* and oversampling. In order to make it clearer, Fig. 5 shows the confusion matrix with the model with the highest accuracy in Table 1. It can be seen that in the most severe cases (triage level 1 for very severe and triage level 2 for severe) the level of discrimination is very high.

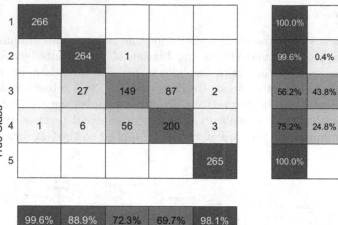

Fig. 8. Confusion matrix of best accuracy model

Table 1. Average accuracy of the data balancing and data normalization methods across classifier training

	Classifiers											
	RF			KNN			NB			SVM		
	w/o S	SMOTE	OVER	w/o S	SMOTE	OVER	w/o S	SMOTE	OVER	w/o S	SMOTE	OVER
w/o N	**0,6944**	0,7614	0,7473	0,5911	0,8378	0,8661	0,6801	0,6279	**0,5988**	0,6605	0,6605	0,6356
Norm1	0,6884	0,7569	0,7315	0,5094	0,8395	0,8703	0,6664	**0,6357**	0,5975	0,6765	**0,6717**	**0,6488**
Norm2	0,6808	0,7643	**0,7518**	**0,8418**	0,8324	0,8658	0,6759	0,6308	0,5837	0,6495	0,6085	0,5988
Norm3	0,6817	0,7508	0,7470	0,6487	0,8314	**0,8745**	0,6727	0,6353	0,5895	0,6706	0,6653	0,6446
Norm4	0,6713	0,7592	0,7405	0,6195	0,8224	0,8696	0,6727	0,6353	0,5895	**0,6816**	0,6485	0,6253
Norm5	0,6664	**0,7595**	0,7399	0,5758	**0,8436**	0,8654	**0,6844**	0,6295	0,5982	0,6791	0,6682	0,6446

Note. Without normalization (w/o N), Without sampling (w/o S), Random interpolation (SMOTE), Over-sampling minority class (OVER). Bold values are maximum values per column.

6   Conclusions

An important detection point for COVID-19 cases is the hospital ED. This is where the most severe cases requiring immediate attention should be detected. To this end, the triage method, which aims to identify the most seriously ill patients, has been taken into account. Early identification of patients, who are at high risk of being weak and who are likely to need hospitalization, would enable to accelerate delays in ED when there are multiple simultaneous admissions. It is a system for selecting and classifying patients on entry to the ED, based on their therapeutic needs and the resources available to care for them. In predictive algorithms, commonly, the number of instances in different classes is expected to be similar. For many real-life classification problems, however, the number of instances can be heavily skewed. For algorithms that try to predict the severity level of the patient at ED entry, as is in the case, the given dataset is unbalanced. This mismatch can lead to inaccuracies in model performance since training will be done with a high amount of very urgent and standard levels, and a insignificant amount of data from other levels. Therefore, corrective measures and procedures have been applied to deal with class imbalance. A clear dependence of certain variables on age has also been detected, which is why normalization methods have been applied to eliminate this condition.

The original records of the dataset are quite noisy, with many missing values and some erroneous values. Direct recording of physiological sensors and storage without human intervention would improve the quality of the data. The aim is to detect as many of the most serious cases as possible in order to provide a direct and immediate service, to avoid future complications and to give priority to the patients who need the quickest attention. From our experiments we would recommend the utilisation of k-nearest neighbor as a classification method, the third normalization method and over sampling as a class balancing method.

Acknowledgments. The authors would like to express their gratitude to Fundación Vital for the financial support to the project "Aportaciones de Modelos Predictivos para COVID-19 basados en Inteligencia Artificial específicos para el Territorio Histórico de Alava - COVID19THA". In addition authors thank to the group "Nuevos desarrollos en salud" of Bioaraba and to Osakidetza-Servicio Vasco de Salud for their collaboration.

References

1. Benito-Leon, J., del Castillo, M.D., Estirado, A., et al.: Using unsupervised machine learning to identify severity subgroups among covid-19 patients in the emergency department. J. Med. Internet Res. **23**(5), e25988 (2020)
2. Sun, C., et al.: Accurate classification of covid-19 patients with different severity via machine learning. Clin. Transl. Med. **11**(3), e25988 (2021)
3. Bao, F., Chen, Y., Ouyang, L., et al.: A multimodality machine learning approach to differentiate severe and nonsevere covid-19: model development and validation. J. Med. Internet Res. **23**(4), e23948 (2021)
4. Chen, X., Feng, C., Wang, L., et al.: A novel artificial intelligence-assisted triage tool to aid in the diagnosis of suspected covid-19 pneumonia cases in fever clinics. Ann. Transl. Med. **9**(3), 201 (2021)
5. Liang, W.: Early triage of critically ill covid-19 patients using deep learning. Nat. Commun. **11**(1), e25988 (2020). https://doi.org/10.1038/s41467-020-17280-8
6. Soltan, A.A.S.: Rapid triage for covid-19 using routine clinical data for patients attending hospital: development and prospective validation of an artificial intelligence screening test. Lancet Digit. Health **3**(2), e78–e87 (2021)
7. Wu, P., Ye, H., Cai, X., et al.: An effective machine learning approach for identifying non-severe and severe coronavirus disease 2019 patients in a rural Chinese population: the Wenzhou retrospective study. IEEE Access **9**, 45486–45503 (2021)

Vision-Based Human Posture Detection from a Virtual Home-Care Unmanned Aerial Vehicle

Andrés Bustamante[1], Lidia M. Belmonte[1,2], António Pereira[3,4],
Pascual González[1,5,6], Antonio Fernández-Caballero[1,2,6],
and Rafael Morales[1,2(✉)]

[1] Instituto de Investigación en Informática de Albacete, Unidad Multidisciplinar en Neurocognición y Emoción, 02071 Albacete, Spain
[2] Universidad de Castilla-La Mancha, E.T.S. Ingenieros Industriales de Albacete, 02071 Albacete, Spain
Rafael.Morales@uclm.es
[3] Polytechnic Institute of Leiria, Computer Science and Communications Research Centre, School of Technology and Management, 2411-901 Leiria, Portugal
[4] INOV INESC INOVAÇÃO, Institute of New Technologies—Leiria Office, 2411-901 Leiria, Portugal
[5] Universidad de Castilla-La Mancha, Escula Superior de Ingeniería Informática de Albacete, 02071 Albacete, Spain
[6] Biomedical Research Networking Centre in Mental Health (CIBERSAM), 28016 Madrid, Spain

Abstract. Monitoring is essential to provide assistance to people who require home care due to their age or health condition. This paper presents the vision-based detection of three postures of a person (standing, sitting and laying down) from an unmanned aerial vehicle. The proposal uses the MediaPipe Pose Python module, considering only seven skeleton points and a set of trigonometric calculations. The work is evaluated in a Unity virtual reality (VR) environment that simulates the monitoring process of an assistant UAV. The images acquired by the UAV's on-board camera are sent from the VR visualiser to the Python module via the Message Queue Telemetry Transport (MQTT) protocol. The simulation shows very promising results for the detection of a person's postures.

Keywords: Unmanned aerial vehicle · Home assistance · Computer vision · Human posture · Virtual reality

1 Introduction

The elderly represent the population group with the highest level of dependency and need for care. They are prone to physical and mental disability or deterioration [7]. Moreover, they need adequate supervision in case of an accident or any other need. However, continuous supervision leads to work overload for carers, both in specialised centres and at home. In addition, due to the high costs of specialised care, family members often have to take care of the dependent persons

© Springer Nature Switzerland AG 2022
J. M. Ferrández Vicente et al. (Eds.): IWINAC 2022, LNCS 13259, pp. 482–491, 2022.
https://doi.org/10.1007/978-3-031-06527-9_48

themselves. All this has led to research of strategies to reduce the work overload of caregivers [8].

Several research projects have focused on supporting caregivers through the use of various technologies for monitoring dependent persons. Among them is the use of computer vision in real time. One such project was to detect whether a person was eating, observing or taking their medication, and to notify the caregiver of the occurred events [21]. This proposal demonstrates the usefulness of image processing where objects and actions are distinguished through the use of colour-based computer vision algorithms.

Other works have focused on the search for human activity recognition using different devices, from smartphones, wearables, video and electronic components to more innovative systems based on WiFi or assistance robots [19]. Interestingly, 60% of the technological monitoring solutions are based on computer vision through different camera types. Although visual monitoring has proven to be a viable and popular option, its implementation within a home would require a large number of cameras. Innovative approaches are therefore emerging in which unmanned aerial vehicles (UAVs) using robust trajectory planning to fly safely in indoor environments are able to monitor dependent people via an on-board camera [5].

Conducting these kinds of experiments indoors with drones can be dangerous in real environments. For this reason, research has initially focused on 3D environments through the development of a virtual reality (VR) platform [2,3]. Thanks to this approach, the benefits of using drones as assistant robots for monitoring dependent people in a realistic and safe virtual environment can be evaluated. The platform is based on real-time communication through the Message Queue Telemetry Transport (MQTT) protocol of the various modules implemented to recreate the behaviour of an autonomous vision-based UAV for monitoring dependent people. One of the main modules is the computer vision module in charge of processing the images captured by the UAV's on-board camera to detect various states of the person [12]. This article complements previous research, focusing on image processing to detect postures of the monitored person. We also use the MQTT protocol to transfer the images from the virtual environment to image processing in Python.

2   Monitoring Dependent People at Home from UAVs

Our research revolves around the use of small vision-based UAVs to assist dependent people at home [2–6,12]. The main objective is to monitor the person in order to determine their condition and possible required assistance. Another alternative for monitoring would be the use of static cameras. However, this would require deploying multiple cameras in the home to avoid dead spots and, in addition, the ability to detect the person would be reduced as the person moves away from the camera. Therefore, a moving aerial robot has the potential to cover a larger area and monitor more closely and efficiently than a number of static cameras.

Fig. 1. The three postures to be identified (standing, sitting and laying down).

UAVs are useful tools that have been used in conjunction with image processing in various research areas. For instance, UAVs have been used with image processing based on colour detection algorithms in outdoor environments for human body detection [18]. However, in indoor scenarios people monitoring is problematic when using only colour-based algorithms due to the complexity and large number of objects and colours found in a house. On the other hand, through image processing it is possible to detect objects based on colour [21] or recognise mood on faces [12], but the detection of human posture is more complex.

In addition to cameras to effectively monitor a person, some hardware devices incorporating different senors have been used. For example, the Microsoft Kinect has a depth sensor that allows a more optimised tracking of the person human skeleton [13,20]. Some UAVs currently carry depth sensors to avoid obstacles and even track people, as is the case of the DJI drones [22]. However, for the detection and estimation of human poses solutions solely using conventional cameras have also been proposed. This is the case of a model for suspicious movements detection in people through posture estimation. The algorithm takes 3.4 s for the detection of a single person, without considering the extra time required to process and estimate the postures [15].

For an efficient monitoring of dependent people less time is required. This is why our proposal focuses on using a promising algorithm for human detection and pose estimation that was born from a very recent research [23]. The ultimate objective is to determine if a person is standing, sitting or laying down though only processing colour images captured by a UAV's camera. Figure 1 illustrates the three postures to be identified during the monitoring process in the VR platform. It should be noticed that dependent people are sitting or laying down most of the time. Having a system that allows the person to be detected efficiently and differentiated from other objects and recognise their current posture is an advance in monitoring, supervision and alarm of elderly or dependent people through affordable devices.

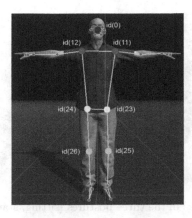

Fig. 2. Landmarks highlighting the relevant joints: nose = id(0); left shoulder = id(11); right shoulder = id(12); left hip = id(23); right hip = id(24); left knee = id(25); right knee = id(26).

3 Computer Vision Algorithms

This section describes the computer vision algorithms implemented to detect whether the person is standing, sitting or laying down. First, the MediaPipe framework used to obtain the required key points of the human skeleton is introduced. Then, the key points are used to detect the human avatar in the images obtained from the virtual scene in Unity. Finally, we describe how the three different postures are identified.

3.1 MediaPipe

MediaPipe is a framework for building multimodal applied machine learning pipelines. It provides solutions for different kinds of applications like face detection [11], hand bones detection and tracking [10] and so on. In this paper, the Pose library of MediaPipe is used to map the 3D pose landmarks which estimate the joints of the human skeleton. The library generates up to 33 landmarks, each one with a unique id. But, in our solution only seven relevant joints are used to determine one of the three searched postures of the human being (standing, sitting and laying down). The landmarks used are illustrated on the human avatar of Fig. 2.

3.2 Human Detection

The VR visualiser module developed in Unity as part of the VR simulation platform of the assistant UAV transmits the images captured by the UAV's on-board camera via MQTT to the new computer vision module. This module programmed in Python processes each image with MediaPipe and obtains the relevant points on the skeleton of the human avatar. The recognition of the

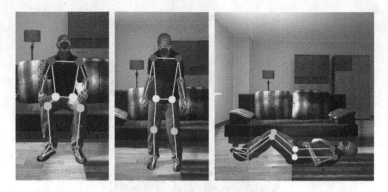

Fig. 3. Skeleton landmarks in the three postures (sitting, standing, and laying down).

avatar skeleton is shown in Fig. 3 for the three different positions to be estimated. It should be noted that the algorithm perfectly scans and generates the avatar skeleton in each of the positions evaluated in this work in a room that has several background colours. This would represent an obstacle for any algorithm where false positives could be generated [9], requiring additional processing to reduce these false alarms [16]. The efficiency of the visual computation in the MediaPipe algorithm is remarkable, as complex systems or multi-camera scanning are usually utilised to achieve this type of complete human mapping [17].

Figure 4 shows a block diagram of the solution implemented in Python to detect the position of the avatar from an image received from the UAV camera monitoring the avatar at the virtual house. Once the image captured in Unity reaches Python, it is scanned by the MediaPipe algorithm where the skeleton reference points are obtained. Of these, only seven relevant points are considered to estimate the posture of the avatar corresponding to shoulders, hips, knees and nose. From the appropriate identifiers, the (x, y) position of these points in the 2D image plane is calculated. These coordinates are used to determine the posture of the avatar, as will be detailed in the next section.

3.3   Posture Detection

Once the coordinates of each point in the 2D plane are obtained, it is possible to estimate the avatar's posture from the position of the selected points and the angles generated among all the points by using simple trigonometry, which represents an enormous simplicity compared to the use of more advanced algorithms or classifiers [1,14].

Firstly, the height of the shoulder points, id(11) and id(12), are used to determine the direction of the avatar, since with a slight rotation both shoulders differ in height in the 2D plane. The direction of the avatar determines the points in the left or right side of the avatar that are used in the remaining calculations: left points (ids 11, 23, 25) when the avatar is turned to its right (left of the

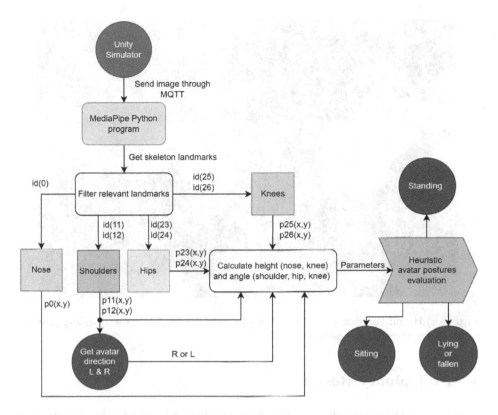

Fig. 4. Block diagram of the implemented solution.

image), or right points (ids 12, 24, 26) when the avatar is turned to its left (right of the image).

Secondly, the difference in height between the points of the nose and the knee on the side of the skeleton as determined by the avatar's direction is analysed. After trial and error adjustment, it has been determined that if the distance is less than 20 pixels, the person will be laying down (see Fig. 5a). However, if this distance is greater or equal than 20 pixels, the person will be in a standing or sitting posture. It should be noted that the tests have been carried out when the person is laying down with a horizontal direction of the body (the imaginary line that would join the head with a foot). When this direction changes and approaches vertically, the laying posture looks very similar to the standing posture in a 2D image (see Fig. 5b), leading to estimation errors that will need to be resolved in future work. Finally, between the standing and sitting positions, the angles formed among the shoulder-hip-knee points are very noticeable (see Fig. 5b and 5c). Therefore, the differentiation of these postures is possible by simply measuring this angle. If the angle formed is higher than 140 °C, the avatar's posture is standing while if the angle is less than 140 °C, the avatar's posture is sitting.

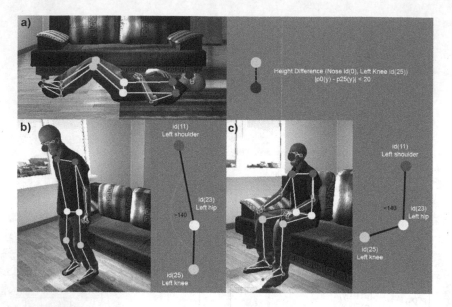

Fig. 5. a) Height condition in laying down posture. b) Angles in the standing posture. c) Angles in the sitting posture.

4 Preliminary Results

This section introduces some preliminary results of the solution implemented to detect the human pose from the monitoring process of the assistant UAV. The tests have been performed on the VR platform, where the images from the UAV camera in the virtual scenario in Unity are sent via MQTT to the computer vision module programmed in Python. Here, the objective is to first determine the direction of the avatar in the 2D image captured by the camera, meaning the side to which the avatar's body is turned, either to the left or to the right. Then, considering this direction and the angles formed by the three points of the shoulder, knee and hip joints, as well as the height of the nose in relation to the knee, the aim is to determine and differentiate the avatar's posture.

In order to evaluate the performance of the computer vision solution, different tests have been carried out considering the three possible positions of the avatar, and also considering that the avatar is turned and placed on opposite sides of the room, where its direction and skeletal points change. The results in all cases have been positive, as it has been possible to correctly determine the direction and posture of the avatar, as shown in Fig. 6. This figure shows the windows generated by the OpenGL library from the Python program. In the upper part you can see the result of the avatar in the three positions in which it is slightly turned to its left, and in the lower images the same result is shown, but in another side of the room in which it is turned to its right.

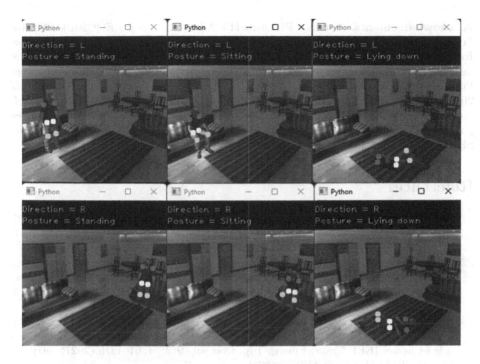

Fig. 6. Posture detection results

5   Conclusions

This article has introduced a computer vision solution for the detection of a person's posture monitored by a UAV for home care. The developed solution is based on the use of the Pose library of MediaPipe and allows differentiating between three possible postures: standing, sitting and laying down. It performs a series of trigonometric calculations by considering relevant reference points in the human skeleton. The solution has been implemented in the computer vision module programmed in Python for the VR platform, which simulates the process of monitoring a dependent person from a small drone in a virtual home.

The first evaluation results of the programmed solution are satisfactory. Furthermore, it should be noted that MediaPipe Pose library promises an optimal and fast recognition of the human body and can therefore be implemented in real-time systems. In addition, the skeleton is generated progressively as the human body is displayed on the camera, which prevents the algorithm from stopping due to incomplete visualisation of the body. The points obtained from the library cover the entire human skeleton and can be used in future work for more extensive posture recognition. One of the main areas for improvement is to extend the recognition of the laying position to other situations where the direction of the body is not horizontal. Another future work will be the estimation of the distance of the person with respect to the UAV's camera in order to use this information for the drone's trajectory planner.

Acknowledgements. Grants PID2020-115220RB-C21 and EQC2019-006063-P funded by MCIN/AEI/10.13039/501100011033 and by "ERDF A way to make Europe". This work was also partially supported by CIBERSAM of the Instituto de Salud Carlos III. This work has also been partially supported by Portuguese Fundação para a Ciência e a Tecnologia - FCT, I.P. under the project UIDB/04524/ 2020 and by Portuguese National funds through FITEC - Programa Interface, with reference CIT "INOV - INESC Inovação - Financiamento Base". This work has also been partially supported by Junta de Comunidades de Castilla-La Mancha/ESF (grant No. SBPLY/21/180501/000030).

References

1. Belagiannis, V., Zisserman, A.: Recurrent human pose estimation. In: 2017 12th IEEE International Conference on Automatic Face Gesture Recognition, FG 2017, pp. 468–475 (2017). https://doi.org/10.1109/FG.2017.64

2. Belmonte, L.M., García, A.S., Morales, R., de la Vara, J.L., López de la Rosa, F., Fernández-Caballero, A.: Feeling of safety and comfort towards a socially assistive unmanned aerial vehicle that monitors people in a virtual home. Sensors **21**(3) (2021). https://doi.org/10.3390/s21030908

3. Belmonte, L.M., García, A.S., Segura, E., Novais, P., Morales, R., Fernández-Caballero, A.: Virtual reality simulation of a quadrotor to monitor dependent people at home. IEEE Trans. Emerg. Top. Comput. **9**(3), 1301–1315 (2021). https://doi.org/10.1109/TETC.2020.3000352

4. Belmonte, L.M., Morales, R., García, A.S., Segura, E., Novais, P., Fernández-Caballero, A.: Assisting dependent people at home through autonomous unmanned aerial vehicles. In: Novais, P., Lloret, J., Chamoso, P., Carneiro, D., Navarro, E., Omatu, S. (eds.) ISAmI 2019. AISC, vol. 1006, pp. 216–223. Springer, Cham (2020). https://doi.org/10.1007/978-3-030-24097-4_26

5. Belmonte, L.M., Morales, R., García, A.S., Segura, E., Novais, P., Fernández-Caballero, A.: Trajectory planning of a quadrotor to monitor dependent people. In: Ferrández Vicente, J.M., Álvarez-Sánchez, J.R., de la Paz López, F., Toledo Moreo, J., Adeli, H. (eds.) IWINAC 2019. LNCS, vol. 11486, pp. 212–221. Springer, Cham (2019). https://doi.org/10.1007/978-3-030-19591-5_22

6. Belmonte, L.M., Morales, R., Fernández-Caballero, A.: Computer vision in autonomous unmanned aerial vehicles - a systematic mapping study. Appl. Sci. **9**(15) (2019). https://doi.org/10.3390/app9153196

7. Carretero, S., Garcés, J., Ródenas, F.: Evaluation of the home help service and its impact on the informal caregiver's burden of dependent elders. Int. J. Geriatr. Psychiatry **22**(8), 738–749 (2007). https://doi.org/10.1002/gps.1733

8. Carretero, S., Garcés, J., Ródenas, F., Sanjosé, V.: The informal caregiver's burden of dependent people: theory and empirical review. Arch. Gerontol. Geriatr. **49**(1), 74–79 (2009). https://doi.org/10.1016/j.archger.2008.05.004

9. Dalal, N., Triggs, B., Schmid, C.: Human detection using oriented histograms of flow and appearance. In: Leonardis, A., Bischof, H., Pinz, A. (eds.) ECCV 2006. LNCS, vol. 3952, pp. 428–441. Springer, Heidelberg (2006). https://doi.org/10.1007/11744047_33

10. Halder, A., Tayade, A.: Real-time vernacular sign language recognition using MediaPipe and machine learning. Int. J. Res. Publ. Rev. **2**, 9–17 (2021)

11. Lugaresi, C., et al.: MediaPipe: a framework for building perception pipelines (2019)
12. Martínez, A., Belmonte, L.M., García, A.S., Fernández-Caballero, A., Morales, R.: Facial emotion recognition from an unmanned flying social robot for home care of dependent people. Electronics **10**(7) (2021). https://doi.org/10.3390/electronics10070868
13. Moon, S., Park, Y., Ko, D.W., Suh, I.H.: Multiple kinect sensor fusion for human skeleton tracking using Kalman filtering. Int. J. Adv. Rob. Syst. **13**(2), 65 (2016). https://doi.org/10.5772/62415
14. Newell, A., Yang, K., Deng, J.: Stacked hourglass networks for human pose estimation. In: Leibe, B., Matas, J., Sebe, N., Welling, M. (eds.) ECCV 2016. LNCS, vol. 9912, pp. 483–499. Springer, Cham (2016). https://doi.org/10.1007/978-3-319-46484-8_29
15. Penmetsa, S., Minhuj, F., Singh, A., Omkar, S.: Autonomous UAV for suspicious action detection using pictorial human pose estimation and classification. ELCVIA Electron. Lett. Comput. Vis. Image Anal. **13**(1), 18 (2014). https://doi.org/10.5565/rev/elcvia.582
16. Pietraszek, T.: Using adaptive alert classification to reduce false positives in intrusion detection. In: Jonsson, E., Valdes, A., Almgren, M. (eds.) RAID 2004. LNCS, vol. 3224, pp. 102–124. Springer, Heidelberg (2004). https://doi.org/10.1007/978-3-540-30143-1_6
17. Puwein, J., Ballan, L., Ziegler, R., Pollefeys, M.: Joint camera pose estimation and 3d human pose estimation in a multi-camera setup. In: Cremers, D., Reid, I., Saito, H., Yang, M.-H. (eds.) ACCV 2014. LNCS, vol. 9004, pp. 473–487. Springer, Cham (2015). https://doi.org/10.1007/978-3-319-16808-1_32
18. Rudol, P., Doherty, P.: Human body detection and geolocalization for UAV search and rescue missions using color and thermal imagery. In: 2008 IEEE Aerospace Conference, pp. 1–8. IEEE (2008)
19. Sanchez-Comas, A., Synnes, K., Hallberg, J.: Hardware for recognition of human activities: a review of smart home and AAL related technologies. Sensors **20**(15), 4227 (2020). https://doi.org/10.3390/s20154227
20. Schwarz, L.A., Mkhitaryan, A., Mateus, D., Navab, N.: Human skeleton tracking from depth data using geodesic distances and optical flow. Image Vis. Comput. **30**(3), 217–226 (2012). Best of Automatic Face and Gesture Recognition 2011. https://doi.org/10.1016/j.imavis.2011.12.001
21. Seint, P., Zin, T., Tin, P.: Intelligent monitoring for elder care using vision-based technology. Int. J. Innov. Comput. Inf. Control **17**(3), 905–918 (2021). https://doi.org/10.24507/ijicic.17.03.905
22. Watkins, L., Fairbanks, K.D., Li, C., Yang, M., Robinson, W.H., Rubin, A.: A black box approach to inferring, characterizing, and breaking native device tracking autonomy. In: 2020 11th IEEE Annual Ubiquitous Computing, Electronics Mobile Communication Conference (UEMCON), pp. 0303–0308 (2020). https://doi.org/10.1109/UEMCON51285.2020.9298163
23. Xu, H., Bazavan, E.G., Zanfir, A., Freeman, W.T., Sukthankar, R., Sminchisescu, C.: GHUM & GHUML: generative 3d human shape and articulated pose models. In: 2020 IEEE/CVF Conference on Computer Vision and Pattern Recognition (CVPR), pp. 6183–6192 (2020). https://doi.org/10.1109/CVPR42600.2020.00622

Development and Validation of a Novel Technology for Postural Analysis and Human Kinematics

Rocío López Peco[1]([✉]) [iD], Roberto Morollón Ruiz[1] [iD],
Cristina Soto-Sánchez[1,2] [iD], and Eduardo Fernández[1,2] [iD]

[1] Bioengineering Institute and Cátedra Bidons Egara, University Miguel Hernández,
Elche, Spain
rocio.lopezp@umh.es
[2] CIBER Research Center on Bioengineering, Biomaterials and Nanomedicine
(CIBER BBN), Madrid, Spain

Abstract. In this study we have implemented and validated the Azure Kinect system for the acquisition and analysis of the human kinematics to be applied to the practical clinic for physiotherapy and rehabilitation, as well as in research studies. The progressive increase in the ageing of the world population in the first world countries, increasingly demands the need to find new, more automated, and versatile technological systems for the acquisition and analysis of human movement data that help us to diagnose, track the evolution of the pathologies and determine how our movements influence the development of the musculoskeletal pathologies. In this work, we were able to develop a measurement technology and validate the ability of the system based on Deep Learning (DL) and Convolutional Neural Networks (CNN), to make precise and fast measurements in real-time compared to the gold standard goniometry used by clinicians. Its precision has allowed verifying its validity for the measurement of large body joints.

Keywords: Applications on Biology and Medicine · Behavior based computational methods · Applications on Health Biotechnology

1 Introduction

Human kinematics refers to the study of the movement of the human body and it is based on the physical laws that determine static and dynamic body positions. Movement is a consequence of the contraction of the muscles which displace the bones around their joints [9]. The study of the human postures and movements gave rise to disciplines such as bio-mechanics and ergonomics, which are being widely applied within healthcare to prevent the development, and to treat with higher efficacy, musculoskeletal diseases. To do so, several methods have been used to capture and analyse human static body position and kinematics. The first, and most classic, method used to study the static and articular range of

© Springer Nature Switzerland AG 2022
J. M. Ferrández Vicente et al. (Eds.): IWINAC 2022, LNCS 13259, pp. 492–504, 2022.
https://doi.org/10.1007/978-3-031-06527-9_49

body joints was goniometry [11]. But despite being a highly accurate technology, it is also a tedious and time-consuming method.

More recently, new technologies based on video analysis were developed to observe and take measurements from images from the human body to analyze posture and kinematics. Nonetheless, the data collected by these means is still manual and therefore laborious, and the information obtained has the limitation of the two-dimensional environment which cannot solve measurement distortions introduced by the capture angle on the image. On the other hand, *digital human modelling (DHM)* and virtual ergonomics methods are based on a modelling of the body postures in a three-dimensional virtual environment, but still, the image capture is conventional photography, and it is not a real-time method. Thus, so far, the most complete technology to register human kinematics, are the so-called *motion capture methods (MOCAP)* [6]. These technologies use sensors such as cameras for optical detection and magnetic or inertial sensors to capture the spatio-temporal pattern of human movement in digital display systems. Unfortunately, these methods have major limitations such as an elevated cost, time-consuming set up and rigorous control of the environment, which makes them inappropriate for their applications in small clinics or the industrial sector [10].

Nowadays, major improvements are being implemented to develop capture body motion systems without markers. These systems acquire the data by tomography through a set of cameras or through an RGB-Depth system, which infers the depth data with the help of an infrared (IR) camera. Recent improvements in the performance of the IR cameras and the computational power analysis, are allowing these systems to acquire a great acuity for the capture of human movement [13]. One of the most widespread RGB-IR systems is the Microsoft Kinect originally launched for the Xbox in 2010. The most recent launch of this product is the Azure Kinect system in 2019 by Microsoft, which runs in Windows 10 by a software development kit (SDK) and provides real-time three-dimensional virtual visualization of the entire body.

Recently, several research groups proposed the Kinect system as a versatile and powerful tool to be applied to areas such as rehabilitation, ergonomics, or computer vision, due to the capability to capture the image of the human body in 3D in real time [13]. Other studies implemented the code of the system to provide postural information of the human body with assessments for ergonomic scales [3]. Thus, *Manghisi, V. et al.* implemented an evaluation method of the "Rapid Upper Limb Assessment" (RULA scale) in the Kinect 2 system that showed a good correlation of scale scores in comparison to a motion capture system based on optical markers [8]. In this context, these techniques could be very helpful to evaluate the functional assessment of the patient for the identification of the pathologies prior to any kind of rehabilitation treatment. *Cukovic, S. et al.* [4] developed a diagnostic technique for scoliosis using the Azure Kinect DK system hardware and the "Unity 3D" program.

Nowadays, motion capture and biomechanics records of the human movement is also widely used as tools for therapy in rehabilitation to achieve the immersion

of the patient in a virtual reality and to work on rehabilitation through entertaining videogames, as in *Chang, C. et al.* that previously proposed as rehabilitation method based on virtual reality and the Azure Kinect capture system for
patients with spinal cord injury [3]. Based on this background and given that
ergonomics is considered the most useful way to fight against musculoskeletal
disorders [7], the new techniques related to digital human modelling and motion
capture, will become an extremely useful tool to plan and design new ergonomics
for rehabilitation and preventive healthcare. In this context, the implementation
of new efficient, accurate, fast, affordable, and user-friendly methods to perform
these kinds of analyses acquires importance to approach this important health
and social problem. Consequently, the objective of this work is to develop and
validate, based on the gold standard goniometry for physiotherapy and rehabilitation, an innovative-technology based on the Azure Kinect system to perform
human postural and kinematics studies to prevent, detect, and treat pathologies.

2   Materials and Methods

Eight healthy participants male 62.5% and female 37.5%, average age of 37.75 ±
11.76 years, body mass of 22.72 ± 3.81, weight of 66.75 ± 16.65 kg, and height
of 170.0 ± 0.08 cm were enrolled in this pilot study designed to compare the
measurements taken with the goniometer and the Azure Kinect system for six
joints positions in two different movements.

2.1   Manual Goniometry

The manual measurements of the six joint positions were manually measure with
a digital goniometer *(Neoteck Digital Angle Finder TL792, US)* taken as reference the classic gold standard method [11], placing the fulcrum of the goniometer on the axis of the joint and the arms aligned with the body segments to
be measured. The measurement of the angle shown on the digital screen of the
goniometer was collected for further analysis. The joint positions were measured
as follow:

- Ankle flexion: resting position corresponds to 90°, with goniometer's fulcrum
  on the external malleolus, the fixed arm aligned with the longitudinal midline
  of the leg and the mobile arm aligned with the fifth metatarsal midline.
- Hip abduction: resting position corresponds to 90°, with goniometer's fulcrum
  on the hip, the fixed arm aligned with the contralateral anterosuperior iliac
  spine and the movable arm along the femur longitudinal midline.
- Shoulder abduction: resting position corresponds to 0°, placing the goniometer's fulcrum on the acromion and with the fixed arm aligned with the midax-
  illary line, parallel to the sternum, and the movable arm aligned with the
  humerus longitudinal line.

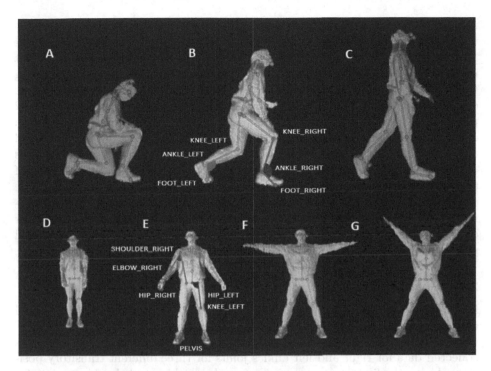

Fig. 1. Image of the transitory positions for each movement: A) first, B) second and C) third, position for movement 1; B), 3 joints selected to assess data angles for left (orange) and right (red) ankles overwritten on the image; D) first, E) second, F) third and G) fourth position in movement 2. E) 3 joints selected to assess data angles for shoulder (pink) and hip (blue) overwritten on the image. (Color figure online)

2.2 Automatic Measurements

Automatic data acquisition was taken continuously at 30 frames/s. Then, for analysis, we selected the time point at which the manual measurement was taken as reference for the automatic measurement, and then, selected the 150 frames recorded around that second.

Image Capture

Hardware. We used the 3D data acquisition capture Azure Kinect system connected to a PC to track the body positions of participants. The system includes a 12 MP RGB camera (BGRA; 720 px; 16:9) and a 1 MP IR (depth) camera (NFOV unbinned mode) [5]. The Kinect sensor was connected to the USB port of an Intel Core i9 3.60 GHz processor desktop computer (64 GB RAM), running Windows 10 ultimate (64 bits), a motherboard Gigabyte Technology H370 HD3-CF and a graphic card GeForce RTX 2080 Ti. The sensor was placed at a distance of 1.5 m away from the patients, in the operation range of the depth sensor.

Software. We used the software development kit *Azure Kinect SDK 1.3.0* (k4a.dll) to interact with the hardware and manage the basic functioning and the *Azure Kinect body tracking SDK 0.9.5* (k4abt.dll) to visualise the three-dimensional point map on the body person representation. This process is based on Deep Learning (DL) and Convolutional Neural Networks (CNN) that detects and identify some corporal locations, where the points are then placed. The system generates 32 points (x, y, z data coordinates) which are identified in the virtual representation of the person and the AI assign them to an associated corporal region and named them as joints. During the acquisition of the coordinates the software also assigns an automatic value of confidence to the measurement that values the reliably of the camera to detect the joints (0 = great certainty, 1 = insecure and unrealistic capture, 2 = unable to locate the point). We use an application programming interface *Azure-Kinect-python* library from Github to export this data to Python for data processing. As entry data for data collection, we used the three-dimensional positions of joints, which were identified by the body tracking system.

2.3 Data Collection

Informed consent was given by the participants before data collection. Manual and automatic data acquisition were taken simultaneously given that the software was able to track independently the participant and the researcher. We collected data for right and left ankles joints for three different transitory positions during the first movement, and left and right hips and shoulders joints for four different transitory positions during the second movement.

- First movement: the participant stand up from an initial position in which the left knee was sitting on the floor and the right knee was 90° flexed. At the final standing position, the left foot was sitting behind the right one. We took measurements at each of the 3 states shown in Fig. 1 A, B C.
- Second movement: from basal standing to bilateral abduction of legs and arms. We took measurements at each of the 4 states shown in Fig. 1 D, E, F, G.

Automatic Joint Angular Degree Assessment. For the constitution of the physiological joints, we selected groups of three points from the body map "joints" generated by the program. With the three joints selected we assessed the angular degree in each of the different transitional positions. The joints created by the system did not always match with the physiological human ones, so we designed a function we called *angle_btw_3_points* which took the coordinates of the three selected points corresponding to joints to build 2 vectors and assess their angle according to the formula:

$$\theta = \arccos\left(\frac{\vec{A} * \vec{B}}{|\vec{A}||\vec{B}|}\right) \tag{1}$$

The ankle joints were selected as a representative example of a medium size joint and the shoulder and hips joints as a representative example of a big size joint, to be tested in our study.

2.4   Statistical Analysis

Statistical analysis was performed on Python 3.8. A T-Student Test was carried out to assessed significant differences between manual and automatic methods. Graphics and plot representations were performed with *Matplotlib* and *Numpy* libraries.

3   Results

3.1   Software Joint Position Stability

In this section, we first evaluated the tracking performance of the Azure Kinect sensor compared with the goniometry methodology. Specifically, we evaluated the spatial agreement of the placement of the joints assigned by the Azure Kinect, to evaluate the reliability of our records. For that, we evaluated the differences in precision between the spatial axes of the system by selecting the coordinates of all the joints automatically created in all the seven transitionary positions and assessed the mean and standard deviations for each of the three spatial axes. Since the system infers the z-axis data with a mechanism different from those of the x and y axes, we first check if the data corresponding to the z axis presented a greater bias degree.

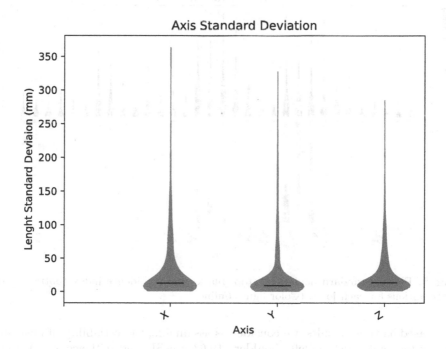

Fig. 2. Plot of standard deviation distributions on x, y, z axes for all the samples.

Figure 2 shows the probability density (violin diagram) of the media and standard deviations for each of the axes and for all the measurements (joints, participants and postures). The largest amount of data showed a standard deviation ranging from 0 to 25 mm, been the z-axis the one with the greatest deviations and the y-axis the one with the lower one (X = 12.85 mm, Y = 9.35 mm, Z = 13.48 mm).

Then, to refine the analysis, we grouped the data to assess the media value of the x, y, z, values and represented the standard deviation and confidence index individually for the different joints. Figure 3 (top) shows the distribution of standard deviations for each joint, and the confidence index (bottom) for those values, combining the measurements of the three axes, for all the positions and participants. The results show small standard deviations and accurate confidence measurements for joints such us pelvis, navel, chest, neck, clavicles, hips, head, nose, eyes and ears showed, with standard deviations values of 13.52 mm ± 2.13 and confidences values of 0.01 ± 0.01. Shoulders, elbows, knees, ankles and feet showed higher values of standard deviations and confidence but still under 33.56 mm ± 11.89 and 0.04 ± 0.03 values respectively. Only the measurements corresponding to the joints located in the hands, had values of standard deviation higher than 50 mm, 58.67 mm ± 9.56 and very low confidence values, 1.34 ± 0.55 (unconfident measurements) resulting in non-optimal measurements for posterior analysis.

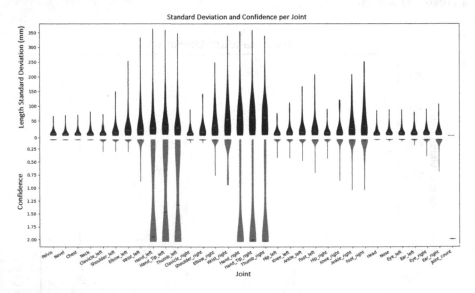

Fig. 3. Plot of standard deviations (top, black) and confidence index (bottom, red) distributions for each joint. (Color figure online)

Based on these results, we consider as assumable, the variability of measurements for joints such as left shoulder (19.63 mm SD and 0.01 accuracy), right shoulder (22.68 mm SD and 0.01 accuracy), left hip (15.96 mm SD and 0.01 accuracy), right hip (13.64 mm SD and 0.01 accuracy), left ankle (29.99 mm SD and

0.02 accuracy) and right ankle (45.70 mm SD and 0.09 accuracy) to be compared with the goniometry technique and assess the global performance of the system.

Results on Fig. 3 also show a pattern of axial symmetry for media values and standard deviation distributions for left and right regions for all the participants, but the values were lower for the left hemibody. After this result and even though the system has the ability to infer hidden joints from the hemibody or corporal region less accessible to the camera, we wanted to check if the data obtained were less precised given that in the first movement the left hemibody was less accesible to the camera. Then we analyzed movement 1 and 2 separately (Fig. 4) and observed that for movement 1, when a hemibody was less accessible to the camera, measurements were less precise, and for movement 2, when both hemibodies were equally accessible to the camera, no differences were detected for the different body members.

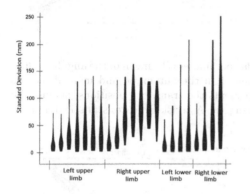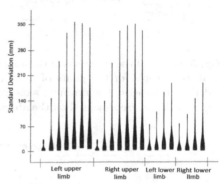

Fig. 4. Plot of standard deviation distributions of joints by body regions (left upper limb, right upper limb, left lower limb and right lower limb) for movement 1 (left) and movement 2 (right).

Table 1. Data and statistical analysis (I): mean and standard deviations of manual and automatic measurements for the first movement, expressed as mean $\pm$ standard deviation. "p" values obtained with the "Student's T". Statistical significance in $p <$ 0.05.

Pose State		Joint Angle	
		L Ankle	R Ankle
1	Manual	$74,79 \pm 16,24$	$81,63 \pm 11,25$
	Automatic	$114,20 \pm 12,60$	$107,56 \pm 6,12$
	p	$<0,01$	$<0,01$
2	Manual	$84,62 \pm 9,86$	$66,85 \pm 8,61$
	Automatic	$118,43 \pm 4,33$	$115,63 \pm 4,29$
	p	$<0,01$	$<0,01$
3	Manual	$101,34 \pm 6,17$	$91,47 \pm 7,42$
	Automatic	$119,07 \pm 9,39$	$108,74 \pm 13,58$
	p	$<0,01$	$<0,01$

Performance of the Automatic Method to Measure the Joint Positions. In this section, we present the evaluation of the measurements taken with the automatic method and compared them to the gold standard goniometry to determine if we can validate it as a viable method to use in the clinical

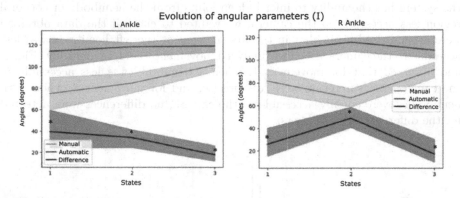

Fig. 5. Graph of the evolution of the angular parameters (I): mean of the angular values of all the people for the joints of movement 1 in the automatic and manual records and the differences. The ordinate axis represents the transitory positions, against the angles in degrees represented on the abscissa axis. Asterisk indicates statistic difference

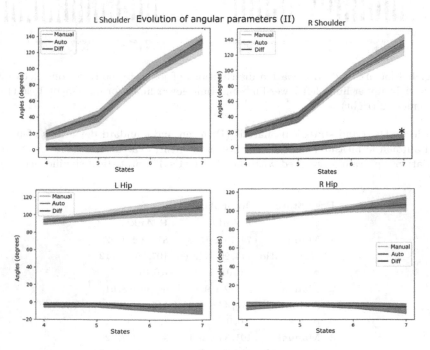

Fig. 6. Graph of the evolution of the angular parameters (II): mean of the angular values of all the people for the joints of movement 2 in the automatic and manual records and the differences. Asterisk indicates statistic difference.

Table 2. Data and statistical analysis (II): mean and standard deviations of manual and automatic measurements for the second movement, expressed as mean ± standard deviation. "p" values obtained with the "Student's T". Statistical significance in $p <$ 0.05.

Pose State		Joint Angle			
		L Shoulder	**R Shoulder**	**L Hip**	**R Hip**
1	Manual	$74,79 \pm 16,24$	$81,63 \pm 11,25$	$94,11 \pm 4,5$	$41,54 \pm 14,84$
	Auto	$114,20 \pm 12,6$	$107,56 \pm 6,120$	$91,23 \pm 1,9$	$118,89 \pm 4,10$
	p	0,1	0,82	0,13	0,09
2	Manual	$36,66 \pm 8,03$	$39,17 \pm 7,61$	$97,31 \pm 1,63$	$99,90 \pm 3,72$
	Auto	$42,03 \pm 6,84$	$40,06 \pm 5,44$	$42,03 \pm 6,84$	$96,24 \pm 1,33$
	p	0,17	0,79	0,17	0,26
3	Manual	$89,98 \pm 3,53$	$91,43 \pm 4,09$	$104,08 \pm 2,95$	$107,60 \pm 5,21$
	Auto	$95,80 \pm 11,81$	$97,55 \pm 7,87$	$101,54 \pm 3,58$	$102,72 \pm 4,36$
	p	0,22	0,08	0,14	0,06
4	Manual	$127,80 \pm 10,39$	$128,04 \pm 9,03$	$110,14 \pm 7,5$	$112,62 \pm 9,769$
	Auto	$135,90 \pm 7,69$	$138,59 \pm 9,09$	$106,21 \pm 8,71$	$108,38 \pm 10,87$
	p	0,1	0,04	0,35	0,43

routine. We assessed the mean and standard deviation of the automatic measurements and the angular degree obtained with the goniometry and through our *angle_btw_3_points* function for each joint and each transition state for movement 1 and movement 2.

Figure 5 shows the changes in the angular degrees along the first movement for the left ankle and the right ankle, shown as mean values (continuous line) and standard deviation (dashed areas) at each transitory position (A, B, C). Goniometry data is depicted in blue, automatic data in red and the difference in violet. The measurements for the left ankle showed significative differences ($p < 0,05$) for both systems in all the joint positions measured along the first movement (Table 1). The greatest difference was at the first position where both measurements differed up to almost 40°. In addition, the evolution of both manual and automatic records followed the same slope tendency in the first transition but opposite for the second one. For the right ankle the greatest difference was measured at the second position and increased up to almost 49°, while the evolution of the measurement followed opposite slope tendency.

Figure 6 shows the changes in the angular degrees for the left and right shoulder and left and right hips at the four reference positions (D, E, F, G) of the second movement. Equally, as in Fig. 5, the blue line represents the goniometry data measurements, the red line the automatic data and the violet line the difference between them. The maximum difference of degrees for the left shoulder was 10° at position 4, for the right shoulder 8° at position 4, for the right hip 5° at position 3 and for the left hip 4° at position 4. Table 2 shows no significant differences in any of the joint's measurements along the second movement in all the positions. In this case, the evolution of both manual and automatic records followed the same slope tendency for the entire movement.

4   Discussion

The results obtained with this work show that the Azure Kinect system can be used as an automatic fast, economic, and friendly user system to efficiently detect and measure the positions of big joints of the human body for its application in the physiotherapist and rehabilitation environment.

We first have shown that the depth measurement (z axes) of the Azure Kinect system based on IR technology is as efficient as the mechanism to assess the x and y coordinates based on the RGB system. Other studies had previously reported the accuracy of the Kinect camera, thus, [13] analyzed the accuracy and performance of Kinect 1 and Kinect 2 cameras (predecessors of the Azure Kinect) compared to other motion capture methods. They concluded that the Kinect 2 camera had higher accuracy than the Kinect 1, however, the Kinect 2 depth showed large measurement deviations in the detection of the lower legs due to the infrared technology. Those problems were improved in the new Azure Kinect system as shown in [12] but unfortunately, not completely solved.

Yeung, L. et al. [14] also studied the depth sensor acuity of the Azure Camera Kinect applied to the study of gait from different viewing angles. Their experiments showed a high accuracy of the gait for the hip and knee joints recorded from the sagittal plane in comparison to the frontal plane. These differences were also evident in the measurements made in our study for movements 1 and 2, in which the left hemibody was partially hidden during movement 1 compared to movement 2, whose position was frontal and both hemibodies were equally available. These results indicate that before a practical application of the system, it is essential to place the camera at an appropriate visual angle for accurate capture and measurement. This is also the case for the goniometry studies in which it is essential to locate the goniometry in the correct position and place the fulcrum of the goniometer on the axis of the joint for the movement required, and the arms of the goniometer aligned with the body segments to be measured.

Furthermore, in Tölgyessy, M et al. [12] also studied the acuity of the Azure Kinect and Kinect 1 and Kinect 2 cameras. They observed that the measurements presented some limitations in open and sunny spaces due to interferences with the infrared depth capture system. Therefore, we must consider the environmental conditions for future experiments when transferring to our clinic by taken in account the illumination conditions of our room, the distance to the patient and the sensor as previously mentioned, as well as any other external factor which might interfere with data collection.

4.1   Validation Method

It is important to mention that the joints studied in this work have been proposed as representative examples of what we expect to find in other joints. Still, in future studies, we intend to extend the study to the rest of the joints in a wider range of postures.

The statistical analysis for shoulders and hips showed no statistical differences ($p > 0.05$) between the automatic and manual methods (Table 2; Fig. 6). These data show that the average differences between both methods are very close to zero, which makes an error of negligible clinical significance, and therefore, an appropriate system to use in the physiotherapy or rehabilitation practical environment.

Regarding the ankle joints, the results of the T Student test showed statistical differences ($p < 0.05$) between the automatic and manual methods for all the positions measured, which means that at least for this join, the automatic systems is not an optimal technology to apply without optimization. We also realized that in the case of the ankles, the different transitional positions we asked the participants to maintain can be more variable than the positions for the hips and shoulder given that the ankles can move very differently in different persons as they progress from an asymmetric bent knee position to an asymmetric standing position. These differences can be a source of variability when averaging the measurements from all the patients, so we should improve our study by asking the patients to always keep the same angle with both ankles and then measure the angle with the Azure Kinect system. Figure 5 showed how these data follow different statistical distributions showing that the behaviour of the automatic system differed completely from the standard method.

We conclude that the Azure Kinect system is an easy and fast system that constitutes an accurate and viable tool to be applied in the clinical setting for the measurement of several body joints such as hips, knees, shoulders, and elbows, that is, the big body joints. Future improvements will be needed to apply the measurements in smaller joints with less precise measurements such as ankles, neck, and small joints from the hands and feet.

4.2   Advantages and Applications

A great advantage of this automatic system is the absence of markers and additional instrumentation applied to the patient body, avoiding problems such as poor placement of the goniometer, especially during movements. It also allows the patient to move freely and feeling more comfortable and gives faster measurements avoiding the patient to maintain uncomfortable positions during measurements. Also, this technology can be easily integrated in virtual rehabilitation to allow the patient to interact with a virtual environment such as in immersive video-games. In the near future, we would like to implement this technology and develop an automatic ergonomic scale to determine improper posture that affect the development of musculoskeletal pathologies due to maintenance of certain postures. Given that records are obtained and viewed in real-time, it is also an ideal candidate for interaction and feedback for the study of sport activities and gestures. In addition this technology obtains almost any parameter of human kinematics desired, without limitations, its characteristics can be modelled according to the needs and its price is more economical than any other video capture system in the market.

Acknowledgements. This project has received funding by grant RTI2018-098969-B-100 from the Spanish Ministerio de Ciencia Innovación y Universidades, by grant PROMETEO/2019/119 from the Generalitat Valenciana (Spain) and by grant agreement No. 899287 (project NeuraViPer), and by the Ayudas a la Investigación from the University Miguel Hernandez (2021).

References

1. Alaoui, H., et al.: AI-enabled high-level layer for posture recognition using the azure kinect in unity3D. In: IEEE 4th International Conference on Image Processing, Applications and Systems, pp. 155–161 (2020)
2. https://azure.microsoft.com/es-es/services/kinect-dk/#industries (2021)
3. Chang, C., et al.: Towards pervasive physical rehabilitation using Microsoft Kinect. In: 6th International Conference on Pervasive Computing Technologies for Healthcare and Workshops, pp. 159–162 (2012)
4. Cukovic, S., et al.: Supporting diagnosis and treatment of scoliosis: using augmented reality to calculate 3D spine models in real-time - ARScoliosis. In: IEEE International Conference on Bioinformatics and Biomedicine, pp. 1926–1931 (2020)
5. https://docs.microsoft.com/es-es/azure/kinect-dk/hardware-specification (2021)
6. Gómez Echeverry, L.L., et al.: Human motion capture and analysis systems: a systematic review. Prospectiva **16**(2), 24–34 (2018)
7. Hussain, M., et al.: Digital human modeling in ergonomic risk assessment of working postures using RULA analysis of working postures among workers of lime stone quarry, cutting and polishing units view project. In: International Conference on Industrial Engineering and Operations Management, Bangkok, pp. 2714–2725 (2019)
8. Manghisi, V., et al.: Real time RULA assessment using Kinect v2 sensor. Appl. Ergon. **65**, 481–491 (2017)
9. Rueda, L.: Principios de biomecánica. Apunts Sports Medicine **148**, 39–43 (2005)
10. Scano, A., et al.: Analysis of upper-limb and trunk kinematic variability: accuracy and reliability of an RGB-D sensor. Multimodal Technol. Interact. **4**(2), 14 (2020)
11. Taboadela, C.H.: Goniometría, una herramienta para la evaluación de las incapacidades laborales. 1a ed. Asociart ART (2007)
12. Tölgyessy, M., et al.: Evaluation of the Azure Kinect and its comparison to kinect V1 and kinect V2. Sensors **21**(2), 413 (2021)
13. Wang, Q., et al.: Evaluation of pose tracking accuracy in the first and second generations of Microsoft Kinect. In: IEEE International Conference on Healthcare Informatics, pp. 380–389 (2015)
14. Yeung, L., et al.: Effects of camera viewing angles on tracking kinematic gait patterns using Azure Kinect, Kinect v2 and Orbbec Astra Pro v2. Gait Posture **87**, 19–26 (2021)

Multi-agent LoRaWAN Network for End-of-Life Management of Electric Vehicle Batteries

Celia Garrido-Hidalgo[1]([✉]), Luis Roda-Sanchez[1,2], Teresa Olivares[1],
F. Javier Ramírez[3], and Antonio Fernández-Caballero[1]

[1] Instituto de Investigación en Informática de Albacete and Departamento de
Sistemas Informáticos, Universidad de Castilla-La Mancha, 02071 Albacete, Spain
celia.garrido@uclm.es
[2] NEC Ibérica S.L., 28108 Madrid, Spain
[3] E.T.S. Ingenieros Industriales, Departamento de Administración de Empresas,
Universidad de Castilla-La Mancha, 02071 Albacete, Spain

Abstract. The LoRaWAN standard has become one of the most
extended Internet-of-Things technologies in both academia and industry
due to its long communication range and high energy efficiency. Given the
fast-growth expectations of the reverse logistics sector —partly caused
by an imminent number of electric-vehicle batteries to be disposed of in
the coming years—, the adoption of wireless machine-type communications promises several benefits towards products' end-of-life monitoring
and diagnosis. While LoRaWAN seems a suitable technology for this purpose, its scalability limitations need to be first resolved. To shed light
on this matter, this work presents a multi-agent approach to support
an efficient allocation of network resources in time-slotted communications running on top of LoRaWAN's MAC layer. By considering different
slot-length computation strategies, the multi-agent network components
interact with joining LoRaWAN devices and assign them to the most
convenient transmission schedule which, in turn, depends on both application and hardware-specific constraints. Our results point to network
scalability improvements ranging from 43.22% to 86.54% depending on
the slot-length computation strategy being applied.

Keywords: Multi-Agent System · LoRaWAN · Scheduling · Resource
Allocation · End-of-Life · Electric Vehicle Batteries

1 Introduction

Low-Power Wide-Area Networks (LPWAN) are finding their way into the
Internet-of-Things (IoT) ecosystem as a means of enabling machine-type communication under negligible energy cost, with the LoRaWAN standard having
become a popular solution in both academia and industry [14]. The recent growth
of the logistics sector —and more specifically, *reverse* logistics (RL)— opens
great opportunities for the development of the LPWAN market, where end-of-life

© Springer Nature Switzerland AG 2022
J. M. Ferrández Vicente et al. (Eds.): IWINAC 2022, LNCS 13259, pp. 505–514, 2022.
https://doi.org/10.1007/978-3-031-06527-9_50

(EoL) assessment of products to be reconditioned or remanufactured is currently hindered by uncertainties about their health condition or location [8]. In this context, the EoL management of electric-vehicle batteries (EVBs) has already become a global concern, not only because of the high value associated to their raw materials but their risk of becoming hazardous for the environment [17]. Moreover, as worldwide electric vehicle sales continue to grow, an enormous number of EVBs are expected to be disposed of in a short-term basis [13].

As a result, the design of wireless battery management systems is gaining special interest in the literature [13]. These aim to enable health-condition monitoring, lifetime prognostics, fault detection and prediction of individual EVBs during their life cycle and recovery stages [4, 11]. It is in this domain where the use of machine-type IoT communication standards, such as LoRaWAN, can bring several benefits in terms of cost, power consumption, communication range, and infrastructure availability [9]. Nonetheless, one of the key drawbacks of LoRaWAN lies in an inefficient use of the shared spectrum caused by its ALOHA-like nature, which leads to a poor reliability in large-scale deployments [18]. In order to alleviate such scalability concerns, different time-slotted scheduling algorithms were proposed in the literature, with recent real-world results pointing to reliability improvements of up to 29% under high network loads [7]. However, in most cases, scheduling metrics are computed offline so as to reduce network-management complexity which, in turn, limits the network's scalability by not considering the actual communication requirements of end nodes in the network. While lightweight service management contributes towards sustaining the overall network's scalability in real-time, agent-based approaches can bring several benefits in resource-constrained environments given their relatively low computational load [2, 3].

To shed light on this matter, a multi-agent system (MAS) approach is presented in this work, where the co-existence of different data-reporting periods, payload sizes, or hardware specifications (e.g., clock skew) in the same network is considered towards EoL management of EVBs. For this, a set of distributed agents interact with LoRaWAN scheduling entities as well as with joining end nodes to support on-demand resource allocation. This paper addresses the design, development, and network scalability evaluation of the solution, for which different resource-allocation criteria are tested within an EVB-recovery scenario.

2   Multi-agent LoRaWAN Network Management

This section introduces the MAS proposal for resource allocation in time-slotted LoRaWAN networks. For this, not only LoRaWAN fundamentals as well as the system's design and logic are addressed, but the scheduling algorithm that builds on top of both the end nodes and network server is described.

2.1   LoRa and LoRaWAN

The LoRaWAN standard is built on top of the LoRa modulation technology [14]. It provides medium access control (MAC) for LoRa transmissions in which end devices communicate with a set of gateways (uplink communication) through a star-of-stars topology. Despite both uplink and downlink communication being available, only the former is encouraged to as to sustain the network's scalability given the gateways' half-duplex capacity. LoRaWAN gateways are responsible for forwarding received LoRa frames to a specific network server through a backhaul such as Ethernet or 4G/5G using TCP/IP, where these are de-duplicated and processed.

LoRa is based on chirp spread spectrum (CSS) modulation technique, where the achieved data rate will depend on the coding rate, bandwidth, and spreading factor (SF). The latter can vary from SF7 to SF12 so as to increase communication ranges at the expense of longer transmission airtime. As SFs are known to be quasi-orthogonal to one another, transmissions from different devices using the same bandwidth but different SFs are not expected to collide. The number of chirps used per symbol is determined by 2^{SF}, while transmission airtime can be obtained according to Semtech's design guide [16]. For instance, a 5-byte-payload frame using a bandwidth of 125 kHz and coding rate of 4/5 requires a transmission airtime of 61.7 ms when using SF7, while this time increases up to 1482.8 ms when SF12 is used.

In Europe, the LoRaWAN technology operates in the unlicensed frequency bands of 433, 868 and 915 MHz, being the European Telecommunications Standards Institute (ETSI) responsible for regulating air-time usages in the different frequency bands [5]. While the ones destined for LoRaWAN end devices are restricted to 1-% duty cycles (setting a maximum channel occupation of 36 s per hour and device) the band where gateways operate has a limit of 10% so as to support a fair use of downlink capabilities.

2.2 Architecture and Components

In this work, following an algorithm recently presented [12], end devices are responsible for triggering uplink communication with the so-called Network Synchronization and Scheduling Entity (NSSE) in order to get a set of available time slots to perform communication with their associated gateway. While the multi-agent network management algorithm proposed in the current work (presented throughout this section) is built on top of such logic, the required architectural components are described in the following lines.

The architecture of the MAS is shown in Fig. 1, which consists of seven software agents that interact with the LoRaWAN network (network server, gateway, and several co-located end devices), and the NSSE (responsible for launching the specific-purpose instances that handle synchronization and scheduling tasks). The proposed agents collaborate to reduce the use of resources in the network —e.g., *uplink channel occupancies* and *downlink usages*— by computing the required length of slots of each of the NSSE instances and assigning the most suitable SF and synchronization period to the joining nodes. The individual roles of each agent are described in the following lines:

(i) *Frame FWD*. It is responsible for filtering and forwarding LoRaWAN packets to the multi-agent components upon devices' join and periodic data reports, and to the already-deployed NSSE instance after synchronization.

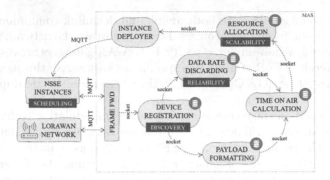

Fig. 1. Multi-agent components for time-slotted LoRaWAN resource allocation.

(ii) *Device registration.* It gathers information about devices that join the network for the first time and add them to a device database.

(iii) *Payload formatting.* It extracts data fields from frame payloads such as uplink periodicity needs or clock skew upon device's join, and sensed magnitudes upon periodic reports.

(iv) *Data rate discarding.* It implements reliability criteria based on the received signal strength of joining nodes and the current transmission strategy.

(v) *Time on air calculation.* It computes the required transmission time of LoRaWAN frames according to the magnitudes end devices aim to report.

(vi) *Resource allocation.* It is responsible for implementing scalability-oriented criteria to assign resources to joining end nodes. For instance, minimizing downlink usages in single-gateway deployments.

(vii) *Instance deployer.* Based on information provided form previous agents, it triggers a new NSSE instance for new SF-scheduling channels or assigns end nodes to an existing one when already launched.

2.3   Resource-Allocation Algorithm

The implementation of the previous MAS-based architecture enables the dynamic allocation of resources in the network based on its current status as well as on the needs of joining end devices for different SFs. For this, the proposed network management approach leverages SF orthogonality while performing a slot-allocation mechanism that considers the half-duplex capabilities of LoRaWAN gateways to support reliable downlink communication and assigns physical-layer parameters to end nodes on demand according to their needs. Figure 2 shows a state machine describing the stages agents go through to allocate new devices.

Three goal-oriented stages are proposed, where agents will collaborate to provide end nodes with a valid series of transmission slots not to interfere with one another: (i) *warm-up period*, during which agents collect information from the network relying on their ALOHA-like nature given low-traffic conditions; (ii) *launching stage*, in which agents deploy the required NSSE instances for

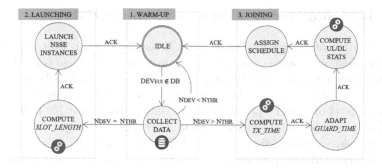

Fig. 2. State machine of the resource-allocation algorithm performed by agents.

each SF based on the available information; and (iii) *joining stage*, during which agents assign end nodes to a specific schedule based on their communication requirements and physical constraints.

During the *launching* stage, the agents compute *slot lengths* based on devices' *clock skew* and *payload length* for each of the SFs. Note that, while *slot lengths* should be the same for each SF-based NSSE instance, the internal division of times per slot —*guard time* plus *transmission time*— may be different for each device. First, the *transmission time* depends on *payload lengths* and the selected SF which, in turn, is conditioned by the end device's location based on the available gateway coverage. Second, the *guard time* is conditioned by the adopted *synchronization period* and device's *clock skew*, which is used to prevent overlapped transmissions. Based on the two selectable parameters (*synchronization period* and *SF*), agents collaborate to balance, as far as possible, traffic over the different NSSE instances so as to delay network congestion and to guarantee downlink communication at gateway level. This is done by first computing the required *transmission time* and then, adapting the resulting *guard time*. Finally, uplink (UL) and downlink (DL) occupancies are computed for decision-making.

Once agents shift to the third goal-oriented stage, at least one NSSE instance will be already deployed for each possible SF. Given gateway downlink constraints imposed by ETSI band-usage regulations, the priority for new joining end devices will be to adapt their time slot sub-fields (*guard time* and *transmission time*) to already existing slot lengths at NSSE instances in order to avoid the re-allocation of co-located devices. For this, the *Resource allocation agent* will select the most suitable SF based on:

(i) *Uplink occupancy.* Percentage of time that needs to be reserved in all the concurrent SF-based schedules for a specific node's communication.
(ii) *Downlink usage.* Time percentage that downlink will be unavailable at the gateway-side due to an on-going transmission or its associated time-off period in compliance with ETSI [5].

The proposed system, in addition, can be used for benchmarking resource-allocation strategies in time-slotted LoRaWAN networks through the modification of agents' goals according to the available context information.

3   EoL Management of Electric Vehicle Batteries

The integration of accurate sensors in EVB packs is key to protect them from damage caused by adverse operation, transportation or storage conditions. Cell-based data generated are used to estimate the state-of-health (SoH) and state-of-charge (SoC) of the battery. These indicators are useful to determine the aging and charge level of battery packs, which in turn provide valuable information to adapt EoL operational strategies for product recovery [15].

The wireless transmission of the EVB's SoH and SoC is raising interest among reverse logistics providers as a means to expedite testing and grading operations [4,6]. However, despite these being typically computed on-board, the complexity of estimation methods is negatively influenced by high quantities of battery cells to be monitored. Hence, there is also growing interest in the transmission of raw sensor data for remote server-side fault detection and preventive maintenance in order to improve decision-making [1,13].

A series of interviews with third-party logistics providers and recyclers conducted by Prevolnik and Ziemba point to *collection* as a key phase in the reverse supply chain of EVBs [19]. As volumes of EoL battery packs are quite low these days, non-critical ones are transported to consolidation points and remain stored for long periods of time until a certain quantity is reached. However, monitoring the individual conditions of each EVB during storage in compliance with local authorities is vital. These typically include standard distances between rows of pallets (from 6 to 2 m), height of stacks (up to 2 stacked EVBs), space between layers (more than 1 m), and supervised battery temperature or voltage, among others. Therefore, the large size of consolidation facilities increases the difficulty of individual product monitoring.

A practical approach to LoRaWAN-enabled EoL monitoring of EVBs is addressed in this section. As a proof-of-concept, a set of devices are emulated and report periodically *temperature, voltage, location,* and *discharge current* data, which are involved in remote SoH and SoC estimation of battery packs [10]. With the focus being put on their *storage* stage, the target application scenario consists of a set of end nodes whose geographic spread will determine a set of possible SFs to initiate communication with their associated gateway.

3.1   System Setup and Results

The payload format used for device registration consists of three fields: *device data* (hardware specifications of end nodes such as their *clock skew*), *application data* (application-specific constraints such as *uplink periodicity*), and *generic payload* (contains the sensed magnitudes to be periodically reported).

Both end nodes and gateways were emulated using the *ChirpStack device emulator* in order to inject high loads of traffic in the network. Data payloads and SF distributions were randomized according to scenarios shown in Table 1. These are connected to *ChirpStack network server*, following the standard LoRaWAN architecture, which runs an MQTT integration with the *frame forwarder* component. While the NSSE are executed using *Click Router Framework*, the remaining

Table 1. Device emulator setup.

Parameter	Description	Distribution	Value
t_s	Simulation time	Constant	8000 s
N_{dev}	Number of LoRaWAN nodes	Constant	2500 nodes
T_{sk}	Clock skew of devices	Random linear	$[5, 75]$ ppms
T_{UL}	Data reporting period (uplink)	Random linear	$[5, 30]$ minutes
PL	LoRaWAN frame payload size	Constant	6 bytes

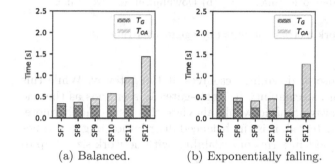
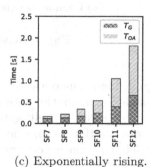

(a) Balanced.   (b) Exponentially falling.   (c) Exponentially rising.

Fig. 3. Guard-time (T_G) distributions and transmission time on airs (T_{OA}) for setups 1 (a), 2 (b), and 3 (c).

software agents were developed using *Python* and connected to the same *PostgreSQL* database. Finally, agent-based communication was implemented using *TPC sockets* following a distributed approach.

In order to test the improvements in scalability, three *launching* strategies were considered for setting up slot lengths: *Setup 1* (all SF-schedules have the same guard-time length); *Setup 2* (the sum of all the previous guard times is distributed following a decreasing exponential distribution); and *Setup 3* (the guard-time sum follows an exponential distribution). Figure 3 shows the resulting time slots upon launching the schedules following each of the strategies.

The previous setups were tested under three application scenarios, which vary the geographic distribution of end nodes with respect to the gateway. The following weights for randomized SF distributions were emulated: *Scenario 1* (30% of devices join with SF7, 20% with SF8 and SF9, and 10% with SF10-SF12); *Scenario 2* (all the SFs have the same probability of being used during join); *Scenario 3* (10% of devices join with SF7-9, 20% with SF10 and SF11, and 30% with SF12). The *joining* strategy was, in all cases, to assign the node to the SF schedule which implies the lowest use of uplink plus downlink resources.

Figure 4 shows the resulting uplink occupancy and downlink usage computed by agents over time for each of the setups shown in Fig. 3. As can be seen, downlink usages limit the network's scalability in all cases. This can be caused by excessively short slot lengths, which force more frequent resynchronization events

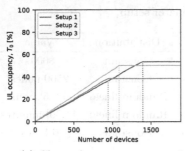
(a) Channel occupancy over time.

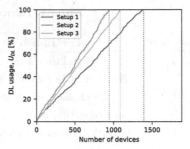
(b) Downlink usage over time.

Fig. 4. Network metrics computed by agents over time.

and, hence, increase the use of downlink resources at the gateway. While this behavior limits the network's scalability in single-gateway scenarios as the one being tested, a multi-gateway scenario would alleviate this issue. Furthermore, from the three setups being tested, it is the balanced distribution of guard times (*Setup 1*) which performs best in terms of scalability, with network size of up to 1393 end devices.

Finally, Table 2 shows the resulting number of end nodes reached for all the slot-length computation *setups* and application *scenarios* proposed. It can be noticed how, depending on the end nodes' distribution within the application scenario, a different slot-length computation setup performs best.

Table 2. Maximum number of devices for each *scenario* and *setup*.

		Devices	Allocation breakdown [%]					
			SF7	SF8	SF9	SF10	SF11	SF12
Scen. 1	Setup 1	**1393**	31.08	19.17	20.82	8.90	10.77	9.26
	Setup 2	943	18.13	29.06	23.33	9.12	7.85	12.51
	Setup 3	1086	8.93	20.17	12.62	38.21	10.87	9.21
Scen. 2	Setup 1	919	15.02	18.72	18.06	16.43	14.91	16.87
	Setup 2	671	9.09	24.74	21.16	15.50	9.24	20.27
	Setup 3	**961**	4.27	14.88	11.13	37.67	14.67	17.38
Scen. 3	Setup 1	628	9.55	10.51	8.76	19.27	23.09	28.82
	Setup 2	416	4.81	13.70	9.86	21.39	14.42	35.81
	Setup 3	**776**	4.12	8.51	3.87	32.86	21.91	28.74

In addition, the SF allocation breakdown is provided, where the one from *Setup 1* always corresponds to the input SF distribution being emulated (*Scenario 1* to *3*) since the minimum use of uplink/downlink resource always is always equivalent achieved using the lowest-possible SF (shortest slot lengths).

Setup 2 and *3*, conversely, allocate end devices when possible to other SFs seeking for a lower use of resources. For instance, agents configured under *Setup 3* reach the highest network size when the end nodes' distribution of *Scenario 2* is emulated by changing devices from lower SFs to higher ones (SF10 in this case).

In view of the results, it is clear how deployments where nodes are located distant to the gateways should compute slot lengths based on the strategy from *Setup 3*, while balancing guard times among all SF schedules (*Setup 1*) is preferable in scenarios where nodes are located nearby. This can be explained according to Fig. 3, since a higher proportion of SF12 nodes will benefit from longer guard times (*Setup 3*) by delaying synchronization periods. On the whole, network-size improvements achieved by multi-agent network components range from 43.22% (*Scenario 2*) to 86.54% (*Scenario 3*).

4   Conclusions

This work has addressed the design, implementation, and testing of an agent-based network manager to support application-oriented resource allocation in multi-SF time-slotted LoRaWAN networks. For this, an application scenario within the scope of EoL collection and management of EVBs has been presented, with three different spread distributions of LoRaWAN nodes being tested.

Our results point to the benefits of integrating resource-allocation components in the network, which should select a suitable slot-length computation strategy depending on their individual hardware specifications or communication requirements, as well as their geographic distribution. Specifically, the three strategies tested in the current implementation differ in terms of network scalability when the geographic distribution of LoRaWAN nodes changes, with an exponential distribution of guard times within time slots reaching the highest network size when end nodes are located far from the gateway.

Acknowledgments. Grant RTI2018-098156-B-C52 funded by MCIN/AEI/10.130 39/501100011033 and by "ERDF A way to make Europe". Grant 2021-GRIN-31042 funded by Universidad de Castilla-La Mancha. Grant 2019-PREDUCLM-10703 funded by Universidad de Castilla-La Mancha and by "ESF Investing in your future". Grant DIN2018-010177 funded by MCIN/AEI/10.13039/501100011033.

References

1. Adhikaree, A., Kim, T., Vagdoda, J., Ochoa, A., Hernandez, P.J., Lee, Y.: Cloud-based battery condition monitoring platform for large-scale lithium-ion battery energy storage systems using Internet-of-Things (IoT). In: 2017 IEEE Energy Conversion Congress and Exposition (ECCE), pp. 1004–1009. IEEE (2017)
2. Bordel, B., Alcarria, R., Martín, D., Sánchez-de Rivera, D.: An agent-based method for trust graph calculation in resource constrained environments. Integr. Comput. Aided Eng. **27**(1), 37–56 (2020)
3. Bordel, B., Alcarria, R., Robles, T., Sánchez-de Rivera, D.: Service management in virtualization-based architectures for 5G systems with network slicing. Integr. Comput. Aided Eng. **27**(1), 77–99 (2020)

4. Chen, M., et al.: Recycling end-of-life electric vehicle lithium-ion batteries. Joule **3**(11), 2622–2646 (2019)
5. European Telecommunications Standards Institute (ETSI): Short Range Devices (SRD) operating in the frequency range 25 MHz to 1 000 MHz, rev. 3.1.1, February 2017
6. Friansa, K., Haq, I.N., Santi, B.M., Kurniadi, D., Leksono, E., Yuliarto, B.: Development of battery monitoring system in smart microgrid based on Internet of Things (IoT). Procedia Eng. **170**, 482–487 (2017)
7. Garrido-Hidalgo, C., et al.: LoRaWAN scheduling: from concept to implementation. IEEE Internet Things J. **8**(16), 12919–12933 (2021)
8. Garrido-Hidalgo, C., Olivares, T., Ramirez, F.J., Roda-Sanchez, L.: An end-to-end Internet of Things solution for reverse supply chain management in Industry 4.0. Comput. Ind. **112**, 103127 (2019)
9. Garrido-Hidalgo, C., Ramirez, F.J., Olivares, T., Roda-Sanchez, L.: The adoption of Internet of Things in a circular supply chain framework for the recovery of WEEE: the case of lithium-ion electric vehicle battery packs. Waste Manage. **103**, 32–44 (2020)
10. Haq, I.N., et al.: Development of battery management system for cell monitoring and protection. In: 2014 International Conference on Electrical Engineering and Computer Science (ICEECS), pp. 203–208. IEEE (2014)
11. Harper, G., et al.: Recycling lithium-ion batteries from electric vehicles. Nature **575**(7781), 75–86 (2019)
12. Haxhibeqiri, J., Moerman, I., Hoebeke, J.: Low overhead scheduling of LoRa transmissions for improved scalability. IEEE Internet Things J. **6**(2), 3097–3109 (2018)
13. Li, W., Rentemeister, M., Badeda, J., Jöst, D., Schulte, D., Sauer, D.U.: Digital twin for battery systems: cloud battery management system with online state-of-charge and state-of-health estimation. J. Energy Storage **30**, 101557 (2020)
14. LoRa Alliance: LoRaWAN^{TM} 1.0.3 Specification, rev. 1.0.3, June 2018
15. Noura, N., Boulon, L., Jemeï, S.: A review of battery state of health estimation methods: hybrid electric vehicle challenges. World Electr. Veh. J. **11**(4), 66 (2020)
16. Semtech: SX1272/3/6/7/8: LoRa Modem, rev. 1, July 2013
17. Slattery, M., Dunn, J., Kendall, A.: Transportation of electric vehicle lithium-ion batteries at end-of-life: a literature review. Resour. Conserv. Recycl. **174**, 105755 (2021)
18. Van den Abeele, F., Haxhibeqiri, J., Moerman, I., Hoebeke, J.: Scalability analysis of large-scale LoRaWAN networks in NS-3. IEEE Internet Things J. **4**(6), 2186–2198 (2017)
19. Ziemba, A., Prevolnik, F.: The reverse logistics of electric vehicle batteries: challenges encountered by 3PLs and recyclers. Jönköping University, May 2019

Spatial Frames of Reference and Action: A Study with Evolved Neuro-agents

Nicola Milano[1] and Michela Ponticorvo[2]([⊠])

[1] Institute of Cognitive Sciences and Technologies, National Research Council, Rome, Italy
[2] Department of Humanistic Studies, University of Naples "Federico II", Naples, Italy
michela.ponticorvo@unina.it

Abstract. Solving spatial tasks is crucial for adaptation and is made possible by the representation of space. It is still debated which is the exact nature of this representation that can rely on egocentric and allocentric frames of reference.

In this paper, a modelling approach is proposed to complement research on humans and animal models. Artificial agents, simulated mobile robots ruled by an artificial neural network, are evolved through Evolutionary strategies to solve a spatial task that consists in locating the central area between 2 landmarks in a rectangular enclosure. This is a non-trivial task that requires the agent to identify landmarks' location, spatial relation between landmarks and landmark position relative to the environment.

Different populations of agents with different spatial frames of reference are compared. Results indicate that both egocentric and allocentric frames of reference are effective, but allocentric frames gives advantages and leads to better performance.

Keywords: Spatial tasks · Evolutionary Strategies · Spatial frames of reference · Action · Embodied agents

1 Introduction

Dealing with spatial tasks, such as remembering landmark locations or exploiting relations between conspicuous objects is a key ability to assure adaptation for animals [45, 46, 49, 50].

Since the seminal work of Tolman [48], it is accepted that spatial abilities are connected to some representation of space. The concept of cognitive map introduced by Tolman and still a cornerstone in cognitive studies [3, 10, 15], was originally intended as a representation of location and objects according to Euclidean geometry, but it is now meant, in a more general way, as a mean of organizing spatial information on precise dimensions, based on an allocentric point of view.

N. Milano and M. Ponticorvo—Authors contributed equally.

© Springer Nature Switzerland AG 2022
J. M. Ferrández Vicente et al. (Eds.): IWINAC 2022, LNCS 13259, pp. 515–523, 2022.
https://doi.org/10.1007/978-3-031-06527-9_51

The term allocentric [8,33,35,42] is traditionally and widely used to discriminate between different frames of spatial reference, in opposition with egocentric [26,30]. Indeed, an allocentric reference frame is based on a coordinate system that represents spatial information, as landmark's location and the relations between objects in the environment, adopting a point of view that is independent from the subject, whereas an egocentric reference frame is centered on the subject body, also considering part of it. This means that egocentric representations change depending on the subject point of view.

These representations are different also if we consider their neural substrates [11,39]. Allocentric, world-centered representations of the environment are associated with the hippocampal formation including the hippocampus and the entorhinal cortex [6,14,37]. Egocentric representations or image spaces [4] are analogs of self-centered spatial relationships and are prevalently associated with the parietal cortex [28,43] and frontoparietal networks, which are involved, in humans if lesioned, in impairment of spatial attention [2,47].

Most authors recognize the role of both kind of representations to allow navigation [9]: they can be used switching between one and the other in a flexible way, depending on the navigation task features. Along the last years, many cognitive models have been suggested to explain how these processes interact [1]. Nonetheless, there is still a debate on the relation between allocentric and egocentric representations, on what determines if one or the other is used, under which circumstances, which are the functional relations between them etc. [16,21, 23,40]. Relying on these frames depends on different factors and it can change in different species, in different tasks and along individuals' lifetime too. In humans, there is also an interindividual variability for the preferential use of egocentric and allocentric strategies [29]: some use the more flexible cognitive map-like strategy whereas others tend to rely on a more rigid creature-of-habit approach.

At ontogenetic level, the allocentric frame, which is more flexible, emerges later [5,34] and in recent studies it emerged that these spatial frames decline differently with age (for reviews [24,27]). With ageing the egocentric strategies are maintained and the impairment in the use of allocentric and switching abilities is observed [12].

Moreover, some observations indicate that allocentric representations, which are more flexible and adaptable, indeed have an egocentric substrate [17,51, 52]. The paper by Filimon [17] poses this issue explicitly, reviews evidence for allocentric frame of reference and concludes that "all spatial representations may in fact be dependent on egocentric reference frames". It seems that there is a hierarchical organization between egocentric and allocentric frame of reference, with the first one on the base, as it emerges before and is more resilient and the second one more advanced and flexible but weaker too.

In this paper, to verify if these representations emerge allow to solve the task. Moreover, we will try to understand the role of sensorimotor mechanisms, that according to Avraamides and Kelly [1] can have a facilitation or interference role. In this study we explore this issue employing artificial neuro-agents; this approach complements the study on humans and animal models, highlighting what are the core mechanisms involved in solving spatial tasks with different frame of reference and allowing a thorough manipulation at behavioral and neural level [38].

2   Material and Method

2.1   The Task

The task is designed as a spatial problem consisting in a simulated Khepera robot that has to find, and then stay, in a particular area of the arena, identified as the middle point between two landmarks. The robot is located in a flat rectangular arena of variable dimensions, surrounded by walls, with height and width variable in size between 0.5 and 0.8 m. Inside the arena two cylindrical objects, with the diameter of 0.03 m, acting as landmark are placed randomly. The circular area with the center between the two landmarks and radius 0.05 m is our target area (Fig. 1).

The robot, which has a circular shape and a diameter of 0.06 m, is provided with two motors controlling the desired speed of the two corresponding wheels, a ring of lidar lasers is located around the robot body covering the 360° spectrum, with a laser every 10° for a total of 72 laser sensors. The lasers cover a maximum distance of 0.5 m and return the precise distance between the robot and the environment surrounding him.

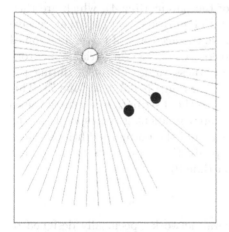 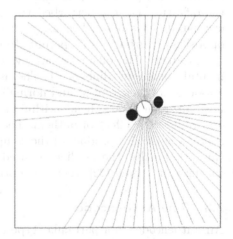

Fig. 1. Graphical visualization of the task: the robot is the white circle and its goal is to spend as long as possible in the nest area, identified as the middle point between the two cylindrical landmarks. The robot and the landmarks are randomly placed in the arena at the beginning of new episodes. Blue rays are the lidar laser forming the sensory apparatus of the robot, giving distance information from the walls and the landmarks.

To solve the problem the robot have to navigate and locate the target area between the two landmark and spend more time possible in it. Each run last 500 timesteps and the reward is +1 for each timestep spent in the target area and 0 otherwise, the fitness is the sum of the rewards. The robot only gets fitness if it is able to find exactly the target with no information about the distance, the fitness is so very sparse and the task is not trivial.

The robot is controlled through a three layer feed forward neural network: the input layers is composed by the sensory information returned by the each laser, for a total of 72 input neuron; the hidden layer consists in 30 neuron with a hyperbolic tangent activation function; finally the output motor layer is formed by two neurons directly controlling the speed of the wheels. The connection weights of the neural network controllers are encoded in a vector of floating point values and evolved through the evolutionary algorithm described in the following section.

2.2   The Evolutionary Algorithm

We selected the OpenAI-ES method since it is one of the most effective evolutionary methods for continuous control problems [36]. The algorithm operates on a population centered on a single parent θ, uses a form of finite difference method to estimate the gradient of the expected fitness, and update the center of the population distribution with the Adam stochastic optimizer [22].

The pseudo-code of the algorithm is reported below (Fig. 2). At each generation, the algorithm generates the Gaussian vectors ε that are used to make the offspring, i.e. the perturbed versions of the parent (line 4), which are then evaluated (lines 5–6). The usage of couples of mirrored samples that receive opposite perturbations [7] permits to improve the accuracy of the estimation of the gradient. The offsprings are evaluated for N episodes in variable environmental conditions (lines 5–6). The average fitness values obtained during the episodes are then ranked and normalized in the range $[-0.5, 0.5]$ (line 7). This normalization makes the algorithm invariant to the distribution of fitness values and reduce the effect of outliers. The estimated gradient g corresponds to the average of the dot product of the samples ϵ and of the normalized fitness values (line 8). Finally, the gradient is used to update the parameters of the parent through the Adam [22] stochastic optimizer (line 9).

2.3   The Autoencoder

An autoencoder is a particular type of neural network, specifically designed to encode inputs into a compressed and meaningful representation, also called latent space, and then decode it back such that the reconstructed inputs are similar as possible to the original one. Autoencoders have been first introduced in the work by Rumelhart [41] as a neural network trained to reconstruct its input. During these years many different types of autoencoder have been proposed and they have found applications in different domains, i.e. dimensionality reduction, anomaly detection, clustering, generative model [18,20,25,44]. Recently autoencoders have been used as latent space extractor to find meaningful and more informative representations of the features for control problem [19,32].

The OpenAI-ES algorithm

$\sigma = 0.02$: mutation variance

$\lambda = 20$: half population size (total population size = 40)

θ: connection weights

$f()$: evaluation function

optimizer = Adam

η: number of evaluation episodes

φ: method used to select the environmental conditions

1 initialize θ_0

2 **for** $g = 1, 2, \ldots$ **do**

3   **for** $i = 1, 2, \ldots \lambda$ **do**

4   sample noise vector: $\varepsilon_i \sim N(0, I)$

5   evaluate score: $s_i^+ \leftarrow f(\theta_{t-1} + \sigma * \varepsilon_i, \eta, \varphi)$

6   evaluate score: $s_i^- \leftarrow f(\theta_{t-1} - \sigma * \varepsilon_i, \eta, \varphi)$

7   compute normalized ranks: $u = \text{ranks}(s)$, $u_i \in [-0.5, 0.5]$

8   estimate gradient: $g_t \leftarrow \frac{1}{\lambda} \sum_{i=1}^{\lambda} (u_i * \varepsilon_i)$

9     $\theta_g = \theta_{g-1} + \text{optimizer}(g)$ ts.

Fig. 2. Pseudo-code for Evolutionary algorithm

Here we define an autoencoder that has to reconstruct the robot Euclidean distance from the landmark and from the vertex of the arena, plus his Cartesian coordinate (x,y) for a total of 8 inputs. Following Milano and Nolfi [32], we use a latent layer to encode the inputs of 32 neuron, augmenting the dimensionality of the problem to retrieve more useful information from our inputs. The autoencoder is trained with 20'000 input data collected from random exploration of different environments, with different arena size and landmark position. Then the latent vector is used as input of the controller network along the sensory information.

3 Results

We define two setups for the problem: i) base setup, where the robot has only sensory information about the environment coming from its lidar sensor; ii) autoencoder setup where along with sensory information we have the latent information coming from the autoencoder.

Figure 3 shows the average fitness curve and the boxplot distribution for the two distributions. The autoencoder setup outperforms the base version of the problem (Wilcoxon non-parametric test p-value < 0.01) being able to find on average robots that navigate better in the environment and spend more time in the reward area.

Encoded information about the spatial reference of the robot appears to solve some local minima problem arising in the base setup problem, augmenting the perception of the environment of evolved robot.

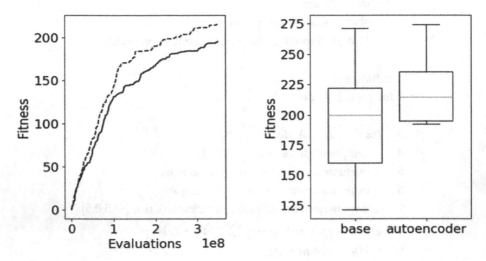

Fig. 3. Left: Average fitness curve of 10 replications of the experiments, dashed line curve represents the autoencoder setup, solid curve the base setup. Right: Boxplot showing the best results obtained in 10 replications. Boxes represent the inter-quartile range of the data and horizontal lines inside the boxes mark the median values. The whiskers extend to the most extreme data points within 1.5 times the inter-quartile range from the box

4   Conclusions and Future Directions

Representing flexibly spatial information is a powerful mean of adaptation. Counting on richer information can lead to better performance. The results we have described on artificial organisms indicate that the proposed task, which is not trivial, can be solved relying on sensory information coming directly from the environment the artificial agent acts in.

The autoencoder provides the artificial agent with a representation of the environment that, as it is allocentric works as a map. In this case, the performance is higher and more stable between the different agents (different solutions). This is in accordance with the reflection on active exploration of the environment is the basis of the egocentric spatial frame of reference which is built on embodiment and situatedness. In this study we have explored this issue employing artificial neuro-agents; this approach complements the study on humans and animal models, highlighting what are the core mechanisms involved in solving spatial tasks with different frame of reference and allowing a thorough manipulation at behavioral and neural level [31, 38].

In next studies we will address the issue of the hierarchical organization between egocentric and allocentric frame of reference, with the first one on the base, verifying if the egocentric one emerges before and is more resilient and the allocentric one is more advanced and flexible but weaker too.

Additional Materials

More details about the model and the related code can be provided to whom is interested by emailing the authors Nicola Milano (nicola.milano@istc.cnr), or Michela Ponticorvo (michela.ponticorvo@unina.it).

Acknowledgements. This paper is heartly dedicated to Orazio Miglino who shared with authors ideas, discussion and suggestions on the approach and methods for artificial agents.

References

1. Avraamides, M.N., Kelly, J.W.: Multiple systems of spatial memory and action. Cogn. Process. **9**(2), 93–106 (2008)
2. Bartolomeo, P.: Visual neglect. Curr. Opinion Neurol. **20**(4), 381–386 (2007)
3. Behrens, T.E., et al.: What is a cognitive map? Organizing knowledge for flexible behavior. Neuron **100**(2), 490–509 (2018)
4. Bottini, R., Doeller, C.F.: Knowledge across reference frames: cognitive maps and image spaces. Trends Cogn. Sci. **24**(8), 606–619 (2020)
5. Bremner, J.G., Bryant, P.E.: Place versus response as the basis of spatial errors made by young infants. J. Exp. Child Psychol. **23**(1), 162–171 (1977)
6. Broadbent, N.J., Squire, L.R., Clark, R.E.: Spatial memory, recognition memory, and the hippocampus. Proc. Natl. Acad. Sci. **101**(40), 14515–14520 (2004)
7. Brockhoff, D., Auger, A., Hansen, N., Arnold, D.V., Hohm, T.: Mirrored sampling and sequential selection for evolution strategies. In: Schaefer, R., Cotta, C., Kołodziej, J., Rudolph, G. (eds.) PPSN 2010. LNCS, vol. 6238, pp. 11–21. Springer, Heidelberg (2010). https://doi.org/10.1007/978-3-642-15844-5_2
8. Bures, J., Fenton, A.A., Kaminsky, Y., Zinyuk, L.: Place cells and place navigation. Proc. Natl. Acad. Sci. **94**(1), 343–350 (1997)
9. Burgess, N.: Spatial memory: how egocentric and allocentric combine. Trends Cogn. Sci. **10**(12), 551–557 (2006)
10. Burles, F., Liu, I., Hart, C., Murias, K., Graham, S.A., Iaria, G.: The emergence of cognitive maps for spatial navigation in 7-to 10-year-old children. Child Dev. **91**(3), e733–e744 (2020)
11. Buzsáki, G., Tingley, D.: Space and time: the hippocampus as a sequence generator. Trends Cogn. Sci. **22**, 853–869 (2018)
12. Collett, T.S., Graham, P.: Animal navigation: path integration, visual landmarks and cognitive maps. Curr. Biol. **14**(12), R475–R477 (2004)
13. Colombo, D., et al.: Egocentric and allocentric spatial reference frames in aging: a systematic review. Neurosci. Biobehav. Rev. **80**, 605–621 (2017)

14. Danjo, T.: Allocentric representations of space in the hippocampus. Neurosci. Res. **153**, 1–7 (2020)
15. Epstein, R.A., Patai, E.Z., Julian, J.B., Spiers, H.J.: The cognitive map in humans: spatial navigation and beyond. Nat. Neurosci. **20**(11), 1504–1513 (2017)
16. Fabroyir, H., Teng, W.C.: Navigation in virtual environments using head-mounted displays: allocentric vs. egocentric behaviors. Comput. Hum. Behav. **80**, 331–343 (2018)
17. Filimon, F.: Are all spatial reference frames egocentric? Reinterpreting evidence for allocentric, object-centered, or world-centered reference frames. Front. Human Neurosci. **9**, 648 (2015)
18. Guo, X., Liu, X., Zhu, E., Yin, J.: Deep clustering with convolutional autoencoders. In: Liu, D., Xie, S., Li, Y., Zhao, D., El-Alfy, E.S. (eds.) Neural Information Processing, ICONIP 2017. LNCS, vol. 10635, pp. 373–382. Springer, Cham (2017). https://doi.org/10.1007/978-3-319-70096-0_39
19. Ha, D., Schmidhuber, J.: "World models." arXiv preprint arXiv:1803.10122 (2018)
20. Hasan, M., Choi, J., Neumann, J., Roy-Chowdhury, A.K., Davis, L.S.: Learning temporal regularity in video sequences. In: 2016 IEEE Conference on Computer Vision and Pattern Recognition (CVPR), pp. 733–742 (2016)
21. Jordan, K., Schadow, J., Wuestenberg, T., Heinze, H.J., Jäncke, L.: Different cortical activations for subjects using allocentric or egocentric strategies in a virtual navigation task. Neuroreport **15**(1), 135–140 (2004)
22. Kingma, D.P., Ba, J.: Adam: a method for stochastic optimization. arXiv preprint arXiv:1412.6980 (2014)
23. Klatzky, R.L.: Allocentric and egocentric spatial representations: definitions, distinctions, and interconnections. In: Freksa, C., Habel, C., Wender, K.F. (eds.) Spatial Cognition. LNCS (LNAI), vol. 1404, pp. 1–17. Springer, Heidelberg (1998). https://doi.org/10.1007/3-540-69342-4_1
24. Ladyka-Wojcik, N., Barense, M.D.: Reframing spatial frames of reference: what can aging tell us about egocentric and allocentric navigation? Wiley Interdisc. Rev. Cogn. Sci. **12**(3), e1549 (2021)
25. Le, L., Patterson, A., White, M.: Supervised autoencoders: improving generalization performance with unsupervised regularizers. In: Bengio, S., Wallach, H., Larochelle, H., Grauman, K., Cesa-Bianchi, N., Garnett, R. (eds.) Advances in Neural Information Processing Systems, vol. 31, pp. 107–117. Curran Associates, Inc. (2018)
26. Lei, X., Mou, W.: Updating self-location by self-motion and visual cues in familiar multiscale spaces. J. Exp. Psychol. Learn. Memory Cogn. **47**(9), 1439–1452 (2021)
27. Lester, A.W., Moffat, S.D., Wiener, J.M., Barnes, C.A., Wolbers, T.: The aging navigational system. Neuron **95**(5), 1019–1035 (2017)
28. Marchette, S.A., Bakker, A., Shelton, A.L.: Cognitive mappers to creatures of habit: differential engagement of place and response learning mechanisms predicts human navigational behavior. J. Neurosci. **31**(43), 15264–15268 (2011)
29. Marchette, S.A., Vass, L.K., Ryan, J., Epstein, R.A.: Anchoring the neural compass: coding of local spatial reference frames in human medial parietal lobe. Nature Neurosci. **17**(11), 1598–1606 (2014)
30. McNamara, T.P., Rump, B., Werner, S.: Egocentric and geocentric frames of reference in memory of large-scale space. Psychonomic Bull. Rev. **10**(3), 589–595 (2003)
31. Miglino, O., Ponticorvo, M., Bartolomeo, P.: Place cognition and active perception: a study with evolved robots. Connection Sci. **21**(1), 3–14 (2009)

32. Milano, N., Nolfi, S.: Autonomous learning of features for control: experiments with embodied and situated agents. PLOS ONE **16**(4), 1–12 (2021). https://doi. org/10.1371/journal.pone.0250040
33. Mou, W., McNamara, T.P., Valiquette, C.M., Rump, B.: Allocentric and egocentric updating of spatial memories. J. Exp. Psychol. Learn. Memory Cogn. **30**(1), 142 (2004)
34. Newcombe, N.S.: Navigation and the developing brain. J. Exp. Biol. **222**(Suppl 1), jeb186460 (2019)
35. O'Keefe, J.: An allocentric spatial model for the hippocampal cognitive map. Hippocampus **1**(3), 230–235 (1991)
36. Pagliuca, P., Milano, N., Nolfi, S.: Efficacy of modern neuro-evolutionary strategies for continuous control optimization. Front. Robot. AI **7**, 98 (2020)
37. Parslow, D.M., et al.: Allocentric spatial memory activation of the hippocampal formation measured with fMRI. Neuropsychology **18**(3), 450 (2004)
38. Ponticorvo, M., Miglino, O.: Encoding geometric and non-geometric information: a study with evolved agents. Anim. Cogn. **13**(1), 157 (2010)
39. Poucet, B., Cressant, A.: On the spatial information used by the neural substrates of navigation. Curr. Psychol. Cogn. **17**, 901–920 (1998)
40. Rinaldi, A., et al.: Flexible use of allocentric and egocentric spatial memories activates differential neural networks in mice. Sci. Rep. **10**(1), 1–15 (2020)
41. Rumelhart, D.E., Hinton, G.E., Williams, R.J.: Parallel distributed processing: explorations in the microstructure of cognition. In: Learning Internal Representations by Error Propagation, Chap. 1, pp. 318–362. MIT Press, Cambridge, MA, USA (1986). http://dl.acm.org/citation.cfm?id=104279.104293
42. Shelton, A.L., McNamara, T.P.: Multiple views of spatial memory. Psychonomic Bull. Rev. **4**(1), 102–106 (1997)
43. Schindler, A., Bartels, A.: Parietal cortex codes for egocentric space beyond the field of view. Curr. Biol. **23**(2), 177–182 (2013)
44. Song, C., Liu, F., Huang, Y., Wang, L., Tan, T.: Auto-encoder based data clustering. In: Ruiz-Shulcloper, J., Sanniti di Baja, G. (eds.) CIARP 2013. LNCS, vol. 8258, pp. 117–124. Springer, Heidelberg (2013). https://doi.org/10.1007/978-3-642-41822-8_15
45. Thinus-Blanc, C.: Animal spatial cognition. In: Weiskrantz, L. (ed.) In Thought without Language, pp. 371–395. Oxford University Press, Oxford (1988)
46. Thinus-Blanc, C., Save, E., Poucet, B.: Animal spatial cognition and exploration. In: A Handbook of Spatial Research Paradigms and Methodologies, vol. 2, pp. 59–86 (1998)
47. Toba, M.N., et al.: Common brain networks for distinct deficits in visual neglect. A combined structural and tractography MRI approach. Neuropsychologia **115**, 167–178 (2018)
48. Tolman, E.C.: Cognitive maps in rats and men. Psychol. Rev. **55**, 189–208 (1948)
49. Tommasi, L., Laeng, B.: Psychology of spatial cognition. Wiley Interdisc. Rev. Cogn. Sci. **3**(6), 565–580 (2012)
50. Waller, D.E., Nadel, L.E.: Handbook of Spatial Cognition. American Psychological Association (2013)
51. Wang, R.F., Spelke, E.S.: Updating egocentric representations in human navigation. Cognition **77**(3), 215–250 (2000)
52. Wang, R.F.: Theories of spatial representations and reference frames: what can configuration errors tell us? Psychonomic Bull. Rev. **19**(4), 575–587 (2012). https://doi.org/10.3758/s13423-012-0258-2

Multi-Agent Systems in Support of Digital Twins: A Survey

Elena Pretel[1] , Elena Navarro[1,2(✉)] , Víctor López-Jaquero[1,2] ,
Alejandro Moya[1] , and Pascual González[1,2]

[1] LoUISE Research Group, I3A, University of Castilla-La Mancha, Albacete, Spain
{mariaelena.pretel,elena.navarro,victormanuel.lopez,alejandro.moya,
pascual.gonzalez}@uclm.es
[2] Computing Systems Department, University of Castilla-La Mancha,
Albacete, Spain

Abstract. The joint use of technologies such as IoT, Artificial Intelligence, Cloud Computing or Virtualization has fostered the development of digital twins (DT). A DT is described as a physical entity, its virtual counterpart and the data connections between both. Digital twins are increasingly being used to enrich physical entities by exploiting different computational approaches, which are applied to the virtual twin part. One of such approaches is the multi-agent systems (MAS) paradigm. It is claimed they resemble DT in many features. In order to analyse the suitability of MAS for DT, this paper presents the results of a systematic literature review focused on the analysis of current proposals exploiting MAS to support the design of digital twins. We found that the integrating the multi-agent paradigm with digital twins can be challenging, because the distinction among them is sometimes blurry. Moreover, it has been detected that MAS are generally the interaction environment for the DTs, and data of the DTs allow agents' better decisions to be made in real time. That is, the massive volume of data stored by the DT allows agents to make decisions based on these data, and on the other hand, MAS shapes the environment where the DTs operate and interact.

Keywords: Digital Twin · Multi-Agent systems

1 Introduction

In recent decades, the development of technologies such as the Internet of Things (IoT), Artificial Intelligence, Cloud Computing or Virtualization have contributed to the digitization of different assets, systems and processes [26]. The integration of these technologies has given origin to digital twins (DTs), which are likely to be one of the most important developments in the field of technology in the next years. A digital twin (DT) is often described as a physical entity, a virtual counterpart, and the data connections between the two. They

This paper is part of the R+D+i project PID2019-108915RB-I00 funded by MCIN/
AEI/10.13039/501100011033.

are gaining more and more interest due to their significant potential in many applications fields [2].

One of the approaches that has many similarities to DT is Multi-Agent Systems (MAS) [26]. MAS are agent-based systems that act as an external entity operating in a specific environment while scanning and collecting data [7]. Although some authors have already sketched the idea of exploiting MAS for developing DT [14,26], no previous work has been proposed up to now that focuses on investigating the relationship between these two concepts: "Digital Twin" and "Multi-agent". This paper analyzes whether this relationship exists or not and how they may complement each other.

The rest of the paper is organized as follows: Sect. 2 describes DTs technology and MAS. Then, Sect. 3 describes the methodology used for the study. Next, Sect. 4 shows the analysis carried out to answer the stated research question. Finally, Sect. 5 presents both the conclusions drawn and our future work.

2 Related Works

The Digital Twin (DT) concept was originally coined by Grieves and Vicker in 2003 [11]. The DT model proposal was made up by three elements: i) a real space with physical objects, ii) a virtual space with virtual objects, and iii) a link between the two spaces for the bi-directional flow of data between real and virtual spaces allowing the convergence of physical and virtual systems.

Up to now, a widely accepted definition of DT has not been achieved, neither a process for developing and deploying DT. Several attempts can be found in the literature that pursue this purpose. For example, [2,14,25] gather different definitions extracted from other proposals as well as the main characteristics that a DT should feature. These authors do converge, at a high level, in defining a Digital Twin as a computer model that simulates the life of a physical entity, such as an object, a process, a person, or some of these characteristics. However, as claimed in [2], a DT is more than a simple simulation, a DT is a living, intelligent and evolving model. It follows the lifecycle of its physical twin to monitor, control and optimize its functions, continuously predicting its future states. A DT is continuously interacting with its physical twin and its environment, exchanging data in real time. This definition does consider the three elements proposed by Grieves: i) physical entity, ii) virtual entity and iii) relationship between both.

During the last years DTs have widely attracted the attention from both academia and industry. They are being used in a wide variety of domains such as manufacturing [31], agriculture [20], healthcare [23], etc. This explains why it is considered a strategic trend whose market is expected to grow at a 38% annually to reach $16 billion by 2023 [9].

According to [32] this massive growth is caused by advances in the key enabling technologies that can be exploited for DT such as Internet of Things (IoT), Artificial Intelligence, Big Data, Cloud Computing, real-time sensors, virtualizations, multi-agents, etc. It is worth highlighting that one of such technologies, multi-agent systems, resemble DT in many features. Multi-Agent Systems

(MAS) are agent-based systems that act as an external entity operating in a specific environment while exploring and collecting data [7,25]. These agents are widely used to simulate complex environments where they coordinate and cooperate or compete to achieve common goals [22,30]. Normally, the agents have the following properties [39]: i) *autonomy*: agents operate without the direct intervention of humans, ii) *reactivity*: agents perceive their environment and respond in a timely manner to the changes that occur in it, iii) *proactivity*: agents are able to make decisions to achieve their goals, and iv) *social competence*: agents interact with other agents, and perhaps with humans as well and their interaction patterns evolve throughout the time.

The exploitation of MAS is thus a good approach to develop software entities that can represent and mimic the behavior of real-world entities. These features offered by MAS make them proper candidates for the development of DT. Some authors have already sketched this idea. For instance, Minerva et al. [25] comment on the direct correlation that exists between an agent and a logical object (the digital part of the DT) as both represent physical entities. These authors also highlight that MAS can be used to simulate the behaviour of a specific environment, which is one of the most relevant functions of the DT. On the other hand, as Grieves described [11], a DT consists of multiple entities and virtual environments, where each one has an objective to fulfil. Jones et al. [14] highlights the potential of MAS to integrate and control the DTs. As can be seen, there are several similarities between agents and DTs, so many of the issues addressed in the development of MAS should be considered as valuable contributions to the development of DT.

In the literature, there are some relevant papers that explore the DT field. Some papers [2,8,14,25] have elaborated literature reviews with the aim of reviewing the definitions of Digital Twin published so far in the literature, as well as the main characteristics that a DT must have or which areas DT applications have been developed for. However, our paper differs from those works in different ways. Firstly, regarding the methodology of the study, a systematic review has been carried out without establishing any specific time frame. Then, the papers analyzed do not belong to any specific field of application, so that different domains have been considered in this work. And finally, it is important to highlight that this study focuses on DTs as a concept linked to MAS. We are fully aware of the influence that other technologies may have on DT, but they are out of the scope of this work.

3   Methodology

In order to conduct this study, the guidelines proposed by Kitchenham et al. [18] have been applied. Therefore, we first defined the research question to be answered with this work:

RQ: How do current proposals exploit multi-agent systems to support those features expected in a digital twin?

Then, we defined as search string "Digital twin", as well as two alternative wordings to find any work related to MAS, "Multi-agent" or "Multiagent". We used Scopus as search engine, as it is the one that provides more detailed information about the papers. The query was conducted in November 2021 and resulted in a corpus of literature related to DT and MAS. The corpus, made up by 74 papers, was stored for their review. From these results, we excluded articles that were not written in English, non-peer-reviewed papers, or inaccessible papers. While we included all those with proposals for multi-agent systems to address the development of Digital Twins. Finally, the corpus used for the study has 27 papers.

4   Discussion

To answer the RQ defined, this Section presents the outcomes of the analysis of the papers related to the use of MAS for the design of DTs. This analysis has been conducted using the set of essential properties that DTs must have according to Minerva et al. [25]. These properties can be classified into two groups: i) fundamental characteristics of DTs and ii) characteristics that add value to DT. The first set of fundamental characteristics ensures that the DTs adequately represent the physical asset and behaves in the same way as the physical assets in a given context. This set consists of three properties:

- *Representativeness and contextualization*: The DT should be as close as possible to its physical twin; however, it is difficult to fully represent it and sometimes it may be even unnecessary. Therefore, the DT should have only those attributes that are actually relevant for its context of use.
- *Reflection*: this property indicates that all relevant attributes of the physical entity must be represented in a timely manner in the DT. The DT updates its state after collecting data from the physical world, being its state complete when all the data has been updated.
- *Entanglement*: it is a fundamental property of DTs since it refers to the communication relationship between the digital and the physical twin. The exchange of information among them must be instantaneous (in real time).

The properties that provide added value to the DT are the following:

- *Replication*: This property refers to the ability to clone a physical entity in the digital world depending on the context.
- *Persistency*: the DT must be persistent and resistant over time, so that it is always available.
- *Memorization*: this property refers to the ability of the DT to store all past and present data of the physical twin. This data reflects the dynamics of the object itself and the context in which it operates.
- *Composability*: this property refers to the ability to group several objects into a composite, so that the behavior of the composite object, as well as that of the individual components, can be observed and controlled.

- *Accountability/Manageability*: this property refers to the ability to manage DTs accurately and completely. For example, in case of failure in the physical part, the DT must provide solutions to that failure by helping its recovery.
- *Augmentation*: the DT initially contains the relevant attributes of its physical twin for the context in which it works, but if the context changes, new attributes and functionality could be added as needed.
- *Ownership*: there are two types of ownership, on the one hand, the one that refers to the owner of the DT data, and on the other hand, the one that refers to the owner of the DT and the physical twin, which may not be the same.
- *Servitization*: the DT provides services to the physical world to be able to control the physical twin and operate in the real environment using actuators, for example.
- *Predictability*: this property refers to the ability of the DT to simulate the behavior of its physical twin in a specific environment and interact with other objects in that environment.

In the following, we analyze whether the DT proposed in the papers identified in Sect. 3 support the properties described above. Table 1 shows a summary of this analysis, identifying which properties are supported by each paper. It has not been possible to determine which properties of DTs are supported by papers [3,13,24,28,40]. This is because these papers focus their research on the design of an architecture that enables the integration of these technologies in industry, but they do not describe their own DTs. On the other hand, Minerva et al. [25] discuss all the properties that a DT should have and suggest the use of MAS for its development, but does not describe how to use them for constructing DTs.

Table 1. Properties of DTs, extracted from [25], supported by the selected papers.

Properties	[1]	[5]	[6]	[10]	[12]	[15]	[16]	[17]	[19]	[20]	[21]	[26]	[27]	[29]	[31]	[34]	[35]	[33]	[36]	[37]	[38]
Context	✓	✓	✓	✓	✓		✓	✓	✓	✓	✓	✓	✓	✓	✓	✓	✓	✓	✓	✓	✓
Reflection	✓		✓	✓	✓		✓				✓					✓	✓	✓	✓	✓	
Entanglement	✓	✓	✓	✓	✓	✓	✓	✓	✓	✓	✓		✓	✓	✓				✓	✓	✓
Replication		✓		✓			✓		✓	✓						✓	✓	✓			
Persistency						✓															
Memorization	✓	✓	✓	✓	✓		✓	✓			✓	✓	✓	✓		✓	✓	✓	✓	✓	✓
Composability																					
Accountability																					
Augmentation						✓			✓						✓						
Ownership								✓													
Servitization	✓		✓	✓	✓																
Predictability	✓	✓	✓	✓	✓	✓	✓	✓	✓	✓	✓		✓			✓	✓	✓	✓	✓	✓

From Table 1 the first conclusion that can be drawn is that not all the properties defined in [25] are supported by the DTs proposed in the papers analyzed. However, the three features that form the set of fundamental properties (*representativeness and contextualization*, *reflection*, and *entanglement*) are supported by most of the proposals. This indicates that when defining and modeling a DT using MAS it is essential to have good connectivity between the physical world and cyberspace so that the data exchange between the DT (or agent) and the physical part is instantaneous. And it should also be noted that the DT should be as similar as possible to the physical twin, with all the relevant attributes of the physical twin being represented in a timely manner in the DT for each context.

On the other hand, we argue below why we believe that some of the properties of the second subset, defined in [25] as value added, are more accepted than others. Regarding the *memorization* property, it is logical that many proposals consider it because massive volumes of data are generated with these technologies, and these data are used by agents to make better decisions based on them in real time. Moreover, the *predictability* property refers to the interaction among DTs as well as between DT and other objects. Given that DTs are being studied jointly with MAS, it was expected that this property was included in most of the proposals, since multi-agent systems are characterized by the easy interaction both among agents as well as between agents and other objects of the environment.

Other properties are considered in few proposals. The first one, *replication*, is included in those papers where the authors needed to have more than one DT for the same physical asset, because they have to be used in different contexts. For example, in [33] authors develop DTs of plants for precision agriculture management. Since authors consider that the context of the plant changes according to its development stage, they create a different DT for the same plant for each one of such stages. The *augmentation* property is included in those papers, where they propose that, in the future, their DTs will be enriched to consider other characteristics or other functions that may be needed in new contexts. For example, manufacturing industries are moving towards mass customization, where each customized product is represented by a DT [29]. In these cases, new features or functions may be added in the future to the DT to further personalize the product. Finally, in some papers, their DTs can act on the physical world, so they comply with the *servitization* property. For example, also in the field of manufacturing, in [10] they describe how real objects are turned into intelligent objects that incorporate self-management capabilities. This facilitates that if the DT detects an anomaly in its behavior, it can address it, for example, by stopping the production and, thus, avoiding further losses.

The *persistency* and *ownership* properties are each one considered in just one paper. As aforementioned, *persistency* states that the DT must be always available throughout time. In [12] authors discuss a case study of DTs in the healthcare domain. DTs act when an anomaly is detected in the patient's medical parameters alerting the user so that he can take the appropriate measures. Therefore, in this paper they emphasize the importance of the DT being always available over time. Regarding *ownership*, in [17] they refer to the second type by analyzing how personal DTs can replace a person in some activities. The authors provide some facilities that can be used by a person to create his own DT, so that the owner of such DT is his creator. Finally, the properties *composability* and *accountability/manageability* are not supported by any of the proposals analyzed.

Additionally, the same set of 27 papers are also analyzed from the point of view of the characteristics expected for multi-agent systems as discussed in [39]. As can be observed, people do not participate in the decisions made by the agents defined in the analyzed papers, in other words, the agents they use have *autonomy*, and the physical-cybernetic convergence is complete. This is also achieved thanks to the use of DT. In the proposals studied, the data captured from the physical world by the sensors deployed are essential for the agents to be *reactive* and *proactive*. All these data are collected by the DT, justifying why the memorization property of DT was included in most of the proposals, as we pointed out above. Finally, it is worth highlighting the existing relationship between the property of predictability of DT and the property of *social competence* of the agents, since both refer to the interaction between themselves, and even with people so it was expected that all the papers analyzed satisfy such property.

After analyzing the DT and MAS proposals by using the properties identified in [25] and [39], we also analyzed how both technologies interplay in these papers. But first of all, we would like to emphasize that integrating MAS with DTs can be a challenging task because the distinction is sometimes blurred. Considering this issue several conclusions can be drawn: i) some papers ([3,10,20,24,31,33–35,37]) use ontologies (key semantic component of the MAS) to organize the knowledge of the physical asset in the cyberworld, which is fed by real data obtained by the DT. In these cases, ontologies are used as a tool to digitize the knowledge of the environment and of the physical twins needed by the agents to make decisions, ii) in other papers ([6,16,19,27]), DTs are seen just as a database. In these cases, DTs of the various physical entities constitute large knowledge databases that the agents can observe, making decisions based on such information as well as also acting on the DT, iii) other papers ([4,5,17]) comment that when a DT has an objective to fulfill, then such DT is developed as an agent, being modeled the environment in which all the DT operate as a multi-agent system, and iv) finally, other papers ([1,15,26]) need to define different types of DTs that must interact in a specific environment. Then, such environment is provided by a multi-agent system where DTs can interact with each other. In general, digital twins and multi-agent systems are in essence integrated in two ways: i) DTs get real-time data from physical entities and these data is used by agents to make better decisions, and ii) multi-agent systems are the interaction environment of DTs.

5   Conclusion and Future Work

In this paper we report the results of a literature review about DTs and their interplay with multi-agent systems in order to understand and deepen the synergies between them. The systematic process followed led us to identify a collection of 74 papers related to DTs and MAS in Scopus database. Once these papers were filtered a final corpus of 27 papers was selected. It is undeniable that DTs and MAS are two terms that have attracted the interest of the research community in recent years.

In the analysis of the corpus, we first discussed whether the current proposals for DTs feature the properties a DT should have according to [25] and then the same has been done for the characteristics of MAS indicated in [39]. After this initial analysis was done, synergies between both were studied, two of which stand out: on the one hand, the DT memorization property, which refers to the ability of the DT to store all the data of the physical twin, is used by the agents of the MAS to exploit these data to make better decisions. This helps the agents in becoming both reactive and proactive. On the other hand, the predictability property of the DTs, related to the interaction between DTs and humans, is equivalent to the social competence of agents. This enables MAS to provide an interaction environment for the DTs.

Regarding our future work, it would be interesting to identify which extensions to current MAS proposals would be necessary to provide a comprehensive proposal for DT. The proposals identified in this paper that offer most of the properties desirable in the implementation of DTs are our starting point. On the other hand, given that there is an upward trend in the number of publications related to DT and MAS, the work could be updated in the coming years to see how the proposals evolve. Also, we are considering exploiting other search engines using the same query and replicate the work done to try to identify a larger number of papers.

References

1. Bakliwal, K., Dhada, M.H., Palau, A.S., Parlikad, A.K., Lad, B.K.: A multi agent system architecture to implement collaborative learning for social industrial assets. IFAC-PapersOnLine **51**(11), 1237–1242 (2018)
2. Barricelli, B.R., Casiraghi, E., Fogli, D.: A survey on digital twin: definitions, characteristics, applications, and design implications. IEEE Access **7**, 167653–167671 (2019)
3. Borangiu, T., Morariu, O., Răileanu, S., Trentesaux, D., Leitão, P., Barata, J.: Digital transformation of manufacturing. Industry of the future with cyber-physical production systems. Roman J. Inf. Sci. Technol. **23**(1), 3–37 (2020)
4. Bremer, J., Gerster, J., Brückner, B., Sarstedt, M., Lehnhoff, S., Hofmann, L.: Agent-based phase space sampling of ensembles using Ripley's K for homogeneity. In: De La Prieta, F., El Bolock, A., Durães, D., Carneiro, J., Lopes, F., Julian, V. (eds.) PAAMS Workshops 2021. CCIS, vol. 1472, pp. 191–202. Springer, Cham (2021). https://doi.org/10.1007/978-3-030-85710-3_16
5. Clark, T., Barn, B., Kulkarni, V., Barat, S.: Language support for multi agent reinforcement learning. In: Proceedings of the 13th Innovations in Software Engineering Conference on Formerly known as India Software Engineering Conference, pp. 1–12. ACM, New York, NY, USA, February 2020
6. Croatti, A., Gabellini, M., Montagna, S., Ricci, A.: On the integration of agents and digital twins in healthcare. J. Med. Syst. **44**(9), 1–8 (2020). https://doi.org/10.1007/s10916-020-01623-5
7. Dorri, A., Kanhere, S.S., Jurdak, R.: Multi-agent systems: a survey. IEEE Access **6**, 28573–28593 (2018)
8. Errandonea, I., Beltrán, S., Arrizabalaga, S.: Digital twin for maintenance: a literature review. Comput. Ind. **123**, 103316 (2020)

9. Gartner: Gartner Top 10 Strategic Technology Trends for 2019. Technical report (2019). https://www.gartner.com/smarterwithgartner/gartner-top-10-strategic-technology-trends-for-2019

10. Gorodetsky, V.I., Kozhevnikov, S.S., Novichkov, D., Skobelev, P.O.: The framework for designing autonomous cyber-physical multi-agent systems for adaptive resource management. In: Mařík, V., et al. (eds.) HoloMAS 2019. LNCS (LNAI), vol. 11710, pp. 52–64. Springer, Cham (2019). https://doi.org/10.1007/978-3-030-27878-6_5

11. Grieves, M., Vickers, J.: Digital twin: mitigating unpredictable, undesirable emergent behavior in complex systems. In: Kahlen, F.-J., Flumerfelt, S., Alves, A. (eds.) Transdisciplinary Perspectives on Complex Systems, pp. 85–113. Springer, Cham (2017). https://doi.org/10.1007/978-3-319-38756-7_4

12. Hafez, W.: Human digital twin: enabling human-multi smart machines collaboration. Adv. Intell. Syst. Comput. **1038**, 981–993 (2020)

13. Havard, V., Sahnoun, M., Bettayeb, B., Duval, F., Baudry, D.: Data architecture and model design for Industry 4.0 components integration in cyber-physical production systems. Proc. Inst. Mech. Eng. Part B J. Eng. Manuf. **235**(14), 2338–2349 (2021)

14. Jones, D., Snider, C., Nassehi, A., Yon, J., Hicks, B.: Characterising the digital twin: a systematic literature review. CIRP J. Manuf. Sci. Technol. **29**, 36–52 (2020)

15. Jung, T., Shah, P., Weyrich, M.: Dynamic co-simulation of Internet-of-Things-components using a multi-agent-system. Procedia CIRP **72**, 874–879 (2018)

16. Jung, Y., Han, C., Lee, D., Song, S., Jang, G.: Adaptive volt-var control in smart PV inverter for mitigating voltage unbalance at PCC using multiagent deep reinforcement learning. Appl. Sci. **11**(19), 8979 (2021)

17. Kazakov, V.V., et al.: Personal digital twins and their socio-morphic networks: current research trends and possibilities of the approach. CEUR Workshop Proc. **2569**(February), 29–34 (2020)

18. Kitchenham, B., Pearl Brereton, O., Budgen, D., Turner, M., Bailey, J., Linkman, S.: Systematic literature reviews in software engineering - a systematic literature review. Inf. Softw. Technol. **51**(1), 7–15 (2009)

19. Kostromin, R., Feoktistov, A.: Agent-based DevOps of software and hardware resources for digital twins of infrastructural objects. In: The 4th International Conference on Future Networks and Distributed Systems (ICFNDS), pp. 1–6. ACM, New York, NY, USA, November 2020

20. Laryukhin, V., Skobelev, P., Lakhin, O., Grachev, S., Yalovenko, V., Yalovenko, O.: Towards developing a cyber-physical multi-agent system for managing precise farms with digital twins of plants. Cybern. Phys. **8**(4), 257–261 (2019)

21. Latsou, C., Farsi, M., Erkoyuncu, J.A., Morris, G.: Digital twin integration in multi-agent cyber physical manufacturing systems. IFAC-PapersOnLine **54**(1), 811–816 (2021)

22. Liu, X., Yu, S., Li, Q., Zheng, L., Wang, X., Sun, H., Wang, F.: MAS-based parallel intelligence communities. In: 2021 IEEE 1st International Conference on Digital Twins and Parallel Intelligence (DTPI), pp. 426–429. IEEE, July 2021

23. Liu, Y., et al.: A novel cloud-based framework for the elderly healthcare services using digital twin. IEEE Access **7**, 49088–49101 (2019)

24. Massel, L.V., Massel, A.G.: Development of digital twins and digital shadows of energy objects and systems using scientific tools for energy research. E3S Web of Conf. **209**, 02019 (2020)

25. Minerva, R., Lee, G.M., Crespi, N.: Digital twin in the IoT context: a survey on technical features, scenarios, and architectural models. Proc. IEEE **108**(10), 1785–1824 (2020)

26. Niati, A., Selma, C., Tamzalit, D., Bruneliere, H., Mebarki, N., Cardin, O.: Towards a digital twin for cyber-physical production systems. In: Proceedings of the 23rd ACM/IEEE International Conference on Model Driven Engineering Languages and Systems: Companion Proceedings, pp. 1–7. ACM, New York, NY, USA, October 2020

27. Ocker, F., Urban, C., Vogel-Heuser, B., Diedrich, C.: Leveraging the asset administration shell for agent-based production systems. IFAC-PapersOnLine **54**(1), 837–844 (2021)

28. Park, K.T., Son, Y.H., Noh, S.D.: The architectural framework of a cyber physical logistics system for digital-twin-based supply chain control. Int. J. Prod. Res. **59**(19), 5721–5742 (2021)

29. Ramesh, A., Qin, Z., Lu, Y.: Digital thread enabled manufacturing automation towards mass personalization. In: Volume 2: Manufacturing Processes; Manufacturing Systems; Nano/Micro/Meso Manufacturing; Quality and Reliability. American Society of Mechanical Engineers, September 2020

30. Roda, C., Rodríguez, A.C., López-Jaquero, V., Navarro, E., González, P.: A multi-agent system for acquired brain injury rehabilitation in ambient intelligence environments. Neurocomputing **231**, 11–18 (2017)

31. Roque Rolo, G., Dionisio Rocha, A., Tripa, J., Barata, J.: Application of a simulation-based digital twin for predicting distributed manufacturing control system performance. Appl. Sci. **11**(5), 2202 (2021)

32. Singh, M., Fuenmayor, E., Hinchy, E.P., Qiao, Y., Murray, N., Devine, D.: Digital twin: origin to future. Appl. Syst. Innov. **4**(2), 36 (2021)

33. Skobelev, P.O., et al.: Development of models and methods for creating a digital twin of plant within the cyber-physical system for precision farming management. J. Phys. Conf. Ser. **1703**(1), 012022 (2020)

34. Skobelev, P., Laryukhin, V., Simonova, E., Goryanin, O., Yalovenko, V., Yalovenko, O.: Developing a smart cyber-physical system based on digital twins of plants. In: 2020 Fourth World Conference on Smart Trends in Systems, Security and Sustainability (WorldS4), pp. 522–527. IEEE, July 2020

35. Skobelev, P., Laryukhin, V., Simonova, E., Goryanin, O., Yalovenko, V., Yalovenko, O.: Multi-agent approach for developing a digital twin of wheat. In: 2020 IEEE International Conference on Smart Computing (SMARTCOMP), pp. 268–273. IEEE, September 2020

36. Temkin, I., Myaskov, A., Deryabin, S., Konov, I., Ivannikov, A.: Design of a digital 3D model of transport-technological environment of open-pit mines based on the common use of telemetric and geospatial information. Sensors **21**(18), 6277 (2021)

37. Wan, H., David, M., Derigent, W.: Design of a multi-agent system for exploiting the communicating concrete in a SHM/BIM context. IFAC-PapersOnLine **53**(3), 372–379 (2020)

38. Wan, H., David, M., Derigent, W.: Modelling digital twins as a recursive multi-agent architecture: application to energy management of communicating materials. IFAC-PapersOnLine **54**(1), 880–885 (2021)

39. Zambonelli, F., Jennings, N.R., Wooldridge, M.: Developing multiagent systems. ACM Trans. Softw. Eng. Methodol. **12**(3), 317–370 (2003)

40. Zheng, X., Psarommatis, F., Petrali, P., Turrin, C., Lu, J., Kiritsis, D.: A quality-oriented digital twin modelling method for manufacturing processes based on a multi-agent architecture. Procedia Manuf. **51**, 309–315 (2020)

Automatic Selection of Financial Ratios by Means of Differential Evolution and for Predicting Business Insolvency

José Santos[1(✉)], Óscar Sestayo[1], Ángel Beade[2], and Manuel Rodríguez[2]

[1] CITIC (Centre for Information and Communications Technology Research),
Department of Computer Science and Information Technologies,
University of A Coruña, A Coruña, Spain
{jose.santos,oscar.sestayo}@udc.es
[2] Business Department, University of A Coruña, A Coruña, Spain
{a.beade,manuel.rodriguez.lopez}@udc.es

Abstract. Differential evolution was used for the automatic selection of financial ratios for the prediction of business insolvency. A sample of companies from the Galician economy is used to predict the insolvency of a company a year in advance. The genetic population encodes possible sets or combinations of financial ratios, and the quality of each encoded solution is determined by the classification accuracy provided by a KNN classifier that uses the selected encoded ratios. Finally, the selected and relevant ratios are used with a more robust classifier, a classical multilayer perceptron, which provides greater sensitivity in the prediction results.

1 Introduction

Prediction of business insolvency is a classification problem that attempts to determine insolvency from the available information of the financial statements of a company. Machine learning methods provide suitable approaches to obtain financial decision support systems that can help in monitoring the financial health of a company. This is especially important for finance companies and any other that take credit risk on business loans. However, given the large number of features that can be considered from that financial information for the learning models, automatic selection of features is an appropriate alternative to be considered. In classification problems, the objective of feature selection is to discover the most relevant characteristics, trying to reduce the dimensionality of a (typically) high feature space without compromising the classifier performance.

Feature selection methods are commonly categorized based on whether the selection criterion depends on the classifier and its associated learning algorithm [4]: i) The *filter approach*, which does not depend on the classifier/learning algorithm. Features are usually selected on the basis of statistical measures and

This study was funded by the Xunta de Galicia and the European Union, with grants CITIC (ED431G 2019/01), GPC ED431B 2019/03, and by the Spanish Ministry of Science and Innovation (project PID2020-116201GB-I00).

J. M. Ferrández Vicente et al. (Eds.): IWINAC 2022, LNCS 13259, pp. 534–544, 2022.
https://doi.org/10.1007/978-3-031-06527-9_53

information content. ii) The *wrapper approach*, which depends on the specific classifier model employed. One possibility is to train the classifier with different subsets of characteristics, selecting the features that provide the best classification performance. Another possibility is that the trained classifier (with all the features) can select the most relevant ones for the classification, such as the sensitivity analysis in trained Artificial Neural Networks (ANNs) [13].

Filter methods are typically faster than wrapper methods. However, the former ignore the possible interaction of features and the performance of the characteristics in a specific classification algorithm. On the other hand, the usual drawback of the wrapper methods is their high computational burden [14].

In this work, an Evolutionary Algorithm (EA) was used for the automatic selection of the most relevant features (financial ratios) in predicting (1-year ahead) business insolvency. Differential Evolution (DE) [8] was selected as evolutionary algorithm to automatically determine that subset of relevant features. DE was selected because is a well-established, contrasted and robust method with proven advantages over other evolutionary methods [6].

In previous works, DE was used with both categories of feature selection. For example, Chakravarty et al. [3] used DE to automatically find out the most important features with a filter approach. The DE genetic population encodes possible feature subsets and the fitness function considers the intra-class and inter-class variation of the feature values. On the contrary, Zhao et al. [14] used DE in combination with both feature selection approaches in a biomarker discovery task. First, three filter methods (Fisher Score, T-statistic and Information Gain) were used to generate the feature pool as input to DE. A Support Vector Machine (SVM) is then used as the classifier to set the fitness of each feature subset. Serrano-Silva et al. [12] used metaheuristic algorithms (including DE) for automatic feature weighting in different classification problems, including bankruptcy prediction (only with six attributes or features). Similarly, Salcedo-Sanz et al. [11] used, for the prediction of insolvency in non-life insurance companies, a Simulated Annealing search hybridized with an SVM to find the most relevant ratios from a limited set of 21 financial ratios.

In the field of business insolvency prediction, traditional approaches used statistical methods such as discriminant or logit analysis [1], including the use of machine learning in the last decades [7]. To determine the differentiating characteristics between companies, financial ratios were mainly used as discriminative variables in the prediction/classification models. Financial ratios are defined as relative magnitudes of two selected numerical values taken from financial statements (balance sheet, income statement and cash flow statement) to gain meaningful information about a company. These ratios are related to, e.g., liquidity, leverage, growth, margins, profitability, rates of return and valuation.

In our work, DE [8] was used for the automatic selection of the relevant financial ratios. The DE genetic population will encode solutions that specify the selected ratios from an ample set of predefined financial ratios. The fitness associated with each encoded solution or subset of selected ratios will be determined by how well that subset of ratios solves the classification task with a simple classifier model (K-Nearest Neighbors - KNN). The evolutionary algorithm obtains an optimized selected subset for the classification task. Therefore, it is a wrapped method, since the selection depends on the classifier used.

The importance of the method relies on the fact that the evolutionary algorithm performs a global search over the space of possible solutions (subsets of selected ratios). The EA automatically determines the number of selected ratios, without a priori decision about the appropriate number of ratios. Moreover, the method can be combined with filter methods if the initial set of ratios is chosen taking into account the relevance provided by classical statistical filter methods. Consequently, experiments that use this alternative are considered, comparing the classification accuracy when a first selection of the pool of ratios is employed. In addition, a test is considered to analyze the performance of the selected subset of ratios (using KNN) with a more robust classifier such as an ANN.

The rest of the paper is structured as follows. Section 2 details the methods used: the EA employed (DE), how the solutions are coded, their fitness using the KNN classifier and the data selection. Section 3 expounds the experiments performed, with the comparison of different alternatives regarding the initial set of ratios, as well as a comparison with the results of a trained ANN with the selected ratios. Finally, Sect. 4 includes a brief discussion of the main results.

2 Methods

2.1 Differential Evolution

DE [8] is a population-based search method. DE creates new candidate solutions by combining existing ones according to a simple formula of vector crossover and mutation, and then keeping whichever candidate solution has the best fitness.

Apart from the population size, DE has only two defining parameters: F (differential weight) and CR (crossover probability). The weight factor F (usually in $[0, 2]$) is applied over the vector resulting from the difference between (randomly chosen) pairs of vectors (x_2 and x_3 in Algorithm 1). CR is the probability of crossing over a given vector of the population (target vector x) and a "mutant" vector created from the weighted difference between two vectors ($x_1 + F(x_2 - x_3)$) (line 10 in the pseudo-code). The "binomial" crossover (specified in Algorithm 1) is used for defining the value of the "trial" or "candidate" vector (y). The index R guarantees that at least one of the vector components will be changed in the generation of the trial solution (line 9 in the pseudo-code).

Finally, the fitness of the trial vector ($f(y)$) and that of the target vector ($f(x)$) are compared to select the one that survives in the next generation (line 16 in the pseudo-code). Thus, the fitness of the best solution of the population is improved or remains the same through generations.

The DE scheme that chooses the base vector x_1 randomly was used (variant $DE/rand/1/bin$ [8]), which provides the lowest selective pressure. The fundamental idea of DE is to adapt the step length in the mutant vector ($F(x_2 - x_3)$) intrinsically along the evolutionary process. As the evolution goes on, the population converges and the step length becomes smaller and smaller, providing

Algorithm 1. Differential Evolution algorithm.

```
1: Initialize the population randomly
2: Evaluate solutions (KNN accuracy with the encoded selected ratios)
3: repeat
4:    for all solutions x in the population do
5:       Let x₁, x₂, x₃ ∈ population, randomly obtained {x₁, x₂, x₃, x different from each other}
6:       Let R ∈ {1, ..., n}, randomly obtained {n is the dimension of the search space}
7:       for i = 1 to n do
8:          Pick rᵢ ∈ U(0, 1) uniformly from the open range (0,1).
9:          if (i = R) ∨ (rᵢ < CR) then
10:             yᵢ ← x₁ᵢ + F(x₂ᵢ − x₃ᵢ)
11:          else
12:             yᵢ = xᵢ
13:          end if
14:       end for{y = [y₁, y₂...yₙ] is a new generated candidate solution}
15:       Evaluate fitness f(y) of candidate y (KNN accuracy with its encoded selected ratios)
16:       if f(y) ≤ f(x) then
17:          Replace solution x by y
18:       end if
19:    end for
20: until termination criterion is met
21: return z ∈ population \∀t ∈ population, f(z) ≤ f(t)
```

an automatic exploration/exploitation balance in the search. This standard DE version is appropriate for our purpose focused on its combination with a simple classifier to perform the feature selection process, without requiring modern DE versions [6] with, for example, self-adaptation of its defining parameters.

Encoding of Solutions. Each DE genetic population solution encodes a subset of selected features. We used a real-valued encoding and, therefore, the standard DE operators can be used, without requiring binary DE versions [5].

Given a complete set of D features (financial ratios), every encoded solution is a D real-value vector, with values in the range $[-1, 1]$. Positive or zero values denote that the corresponding features are selected, while the negative values indicate that the feature is not considered. Therefore, a given phenotype (selected subset of features) can be represented by different genotypes, since each selection/non-selection of a feature can be represented with different real values. In the generation of the mutant vector, if a value exceeds such bounds ($[-1, 1]$), the resulting value is set as a random value in the range [8]. These aspects help to maintain diversity in the population.

Note also that the coding allows to automatically determine the most appropriate number of selected features, i.e., it is not necessary to establish how many relevant features should be selected.

KNN Classifier and Fitness Definition. The fitness is given by the classification accuracy provided by a KNN classifier with the subset of selected ratios that encodes each population solution. This accuracy is considered with a test set (next subsection), different from the training set, the latter with a priori correct classifications. Since the most appropriate value for the parameter K largely depends on the classification problem, we employ two values in the ranges normally considered ($K = 3$ and $K = 15$). The Euclidean distance between the values of the selected financial ratios was considered as measure of distance in the KNN classifier (with all ratios normalized in [0, 1], taking into account their lowest and highest values).

2.2 Financial Ratios and Dataset of Companies

An ample initial set of fifty-nine financial ratios was used, selected based on the popularity of each ratio in the accounting literature and business insolvency. The selected ratios have been obtained from the balance sheet and the annual income statement. The ratios are grouped into different financial measures. Below is a brief description of each group (detailed definition in [2]):

- Activity-related (ACT01-ACT05): These type of ratios are linked to the volume of operations carried out by a company.
- Leverage (LEV01-LEV04):
  - Operating leverage: It measures how the operating income of a company will change in response to a change in sales.
  - Financial leverage: Unlike operating leverage, financial leverage takes into account financial costs (taxes, fees, etc.).
- Debt (DEB01-DEB03): These measure the volume of external financing.
- Structure (STR01-STR09): Percentage structure of assets and liabilities.
- Liquidity (LIQ01-LIQ13): These provide an idea of whether a company will be able to pay its debts when due.
- Profitability (PRF01-PRF06): Describe whether the company generates sufficient income to cover costs and remunerate its owners.
- Turnover (TUR01-TUR08): Performance in a specified period of time.
- Solvency (SOL01-SOL09): Ability to meet financial obligations.
- Treasury (TRS01-TRS02): Ability to meet short-term financial obligations.

The selected companies correspond to small and medium companies (SMEs) located in the Autonomous Community of Galicia (Spain). A wide range of SMEs is used, whose data were obtained from the Iberian Balance Sheet Analysis System (SABI) [9]. This is a dataset that provides information on the balance sheets of more than 2.5 million Spanish companies. The criterion for categorizing a company as failed was the legal declaration of suspension of payments, which is the concept most used in business bankruptcy studies.

The available business population was divided into two subsets:

- A training set, which is made up of 136 failed (insolvent) companies, whose 1 year prior to insolvency was in the interval [2007, 2012]. The same number (136) of non-failed companies was included in this set, matched with those failed by: 1) accounting year, 2) volume of asset and 3) activity sector.

- A test set formed by another 136 failed companies and 2,389 non-failed companies. However, for the evaluation of the fitness of each encoded solution, a reduced test set was considered, with the same number (136) of failed and non-failed companies (and the same matching criteria as in the case of the training set). Thus, this reduced set has balanced data for an easier interpretation of the results of the classification, in addition to the lower computational time required when the fitness is calculated for each encoded solution.

Moreover, with the whole test set, many more input patterns or records are considered. A "record" consists of the data of a company in a fiscal year (with its failure category 1 year in the future). In other words, the same company can provide different records corresponding to different years. In this way, the whole test set provides 18,360 records (136 belonging to companies that fail and 18,224 obtained from the 2,389 non-failed companies in different fiscal years). This complete test set is used for comparisons of results between different approaches.

3 Results

3.1 Setup of the Experiments

With the DE/KNN automatic selection of ratios, different "test variants" are considered. Two variants initially select the 30 most relevant ratios according to the Fisher Score and T-statistic filters (filter definitions can be found, for example, in [14]). These 30 preselected ratios are the ones that the DE process will consider in the evolutionary selection process. Consequently, the genotypes encode the selection or not of these 30 ratios. The third test variant considers the complete set of 59 ratios without any prior selection, that is, the EA selects the appropriate ratios from the full set. Moreover, these three variants were tested with two values of the parameter K in the classifier ($K = 3$ and $K = 15$).

The setup of DE was: population size $= 100$, low crossover probability ($CR = 0.1$), whereas the F parameter takes a random value in the interval $[0,9]$ every time a candidate solution is defined (Sect. 2.1), and the DE process was run over 500 generations. These parameters were experimentally tuned to provide the best results in most of the test variants, avoiding also premature convergence.

With each test variant, the EA was run 30 times to select the ratios most appropriate for the classification process. The selected ratios in each test variant were those selected in the best solution and in all the 30 independent runs.

3.2 Classification Accuracies in the Different Test Variants

Table 1 shows a summary of the results with the three test variants considered. Table 1 specifies, for each test variant and value of K in the KNN classifier, the average value of the best result (best solution) in the independent DE runs, as well as the best value of such independent runs. These values correspond to the fitness (accuracy) considering the (reduced) test set, that is, the accuracy or correct classified companies of the reduced (and balanced) test set.

Taking into account the results in Table 1 it is not possible to establish which is the best value of K since, using the 59 ratios (in the initial pool of ratios) and $K = 3$, slightly better values are obtained (with respect to $K = 15$). However, in the other two test variants, the best values are obtained with $K = 15$.

The number of final selected ratios varies from 2 to 9 in the different tests. Figure 1 shows the percentage of times (normalized in $[0, 1]$) that the different

Table 1. Classification accuracy (fitness) in the different test variants (using the reduced test set).

	3NN		15NN	
Test variant (starting pool of ratios)	*Average*	*Best*	*Average*	*Best*
59 ratios	88,48	90,77	88,17	89,63
30 best ratios with Fisher Score	86,23	88,6	88,40	89,70
30 best ratios with T-statistic	85,87	87,20	87,69	89,44

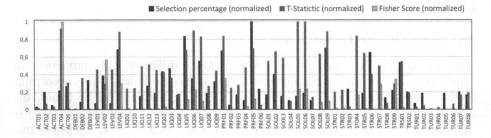

Fig. 1. Percentage of times that a ratio has been selected in the different tests. The T-statistic and Fisher Score values are also included for the 59 financial ratios. All values are normalized in [0, 1].

ratios have been selected (in the best solution) in all the tests performed with the EA, that is, considering the six different variants included in Table 1. Therefore, Fig. 1 illustrates the number of times each ratio has been selected (in the best solution) in the EA runs and in the different test variants, regardless of whether it has been finally selected in each test variant. Figure 1 also includes the values of the T-statistic and Fisher Score measures for all ratios.

In many cases, there is a correlation between the selection rate of a ratio and the value of the T-statistic or the Fisher Score value. For example, ratios such as ACT01, ACT03, DEB01, TUR03, TUR04 and TUR06 were never selected and also these ratios have low values with the two filtering measures. Few examples, such as STR04 and STR07 have never been selected despite the vales in the filters. Finally, ratios such as DEB03, STR03 and TUR05 were sometimes selected but these ratios present very low values in the filter methods. However, it must be taken into account that the graph does not give information regarding whether the ratios provide a high capability for the classification by themselves or in combination with other selected ratios.

Using the complete test set, Table 2 shows the classification results (using the selected ratios with DE) in the three test variants and with standard classification measures. The class "insolvency" corresponds to the "positive" examples, whereas the class "non-insolvency" (healthy companies) corresponds to the "negative" examples.

Table 2. Classification measures (in percentages) using the complete test set with the three test variants.

Test variant	K	Accuracy	Precision	Sensitivity	Specificity
30 best ratios with Fisher Score	3NN	87.45	4.60	80.88	87.50
	15NN	92.67	8.28	88.23	92.71
30 best ratios with T-statistic	3NN	89.25	5.90	90.44	89.25
	15NN	91.32	7.32	91.92	91.32
59 ratios	3NN	94.62	10.42	82.35	94.72
	15NN	95.72	12.80	82.35	95.81

The "sensitivity" measure ($TP/(TP+FN)$, True positive rate) is emphasized here. This is more important from an application point of view. This measure is improved lowering the number of false negatives (FN), that is, minimizing the number of companies that are predicted not to fail, but actually fail.

The most remarkable aspect is that, with the second test variant, when the initial set of ratios to be selected by the EA is given by the 30 best ratios according to the T-statistic filter, the sensitivity is higher or slightly higher compared to the other two test variants. On the contrary, the accuracy is better with the third variant, when the EA can select from the full set of ratios. Regarding the value of K in the classifier, it is clear that with $K = 15$ the results are higher, slightly higher or equal in all cases. The low values in "precision" ($TP/(TP + FP)$) are due to the imbalance between the companies that fail (positive class) and those that are healthy (negative class). A small proportion of False Positives in the 18,224 patterns of healthy companies produces the low precision values.

Finally, without applying the evolutionary selection of the most relevant ratios, when the KNN uses the full set of 59 ratios, for example with $K = 3$, the classification measures are: Accuracy: 83.52%, Precision = 3.44%, Sensitivity = 78.67% and Specificity = 83.56%. The comparison of these results with those obtained by the evolutionary selection of ratios (Table 2, starting with 59 ratios, $K = 3$), shows a better result applying the evolutionary selection of ratios, since, for example, the sensitivity increases from 78.67% to 82.35%.

3.3 Accuracies with an ANN Model and the Selected Ratios

The selected ratios with the simple KNN classifier can now be tested with more powerful classifiers. A simple feedforward ANN model was used for this purpose. Matlab [10] was used to train multilayer perceptrons to perform the binary classification with the same training and test data used in the previous experiments.

Using the same setup specified in [2], different ANNs were trained (with the Scaled Conjugate Gradient backpropagation variant) to select some with a given criterion. 10,000 ANNs were trained, since 10 parameter combinations (modifications in the number of neurons in each hidden layer) were considered and, additionally, with each parameter combination, the ANN training was performed 1,000 times (that is, repeating 1,000 times the training process).

To narrow down the number of selected trained ANNs, only a limited set of trained ANNs was saved, those in which the "accuracy" did not drop below 90%, both in the whole test and in the training set and, additionally, when the companies with false negatives were less than a low number (12). This ANN selection is because our objective in these ANN trainings is to obtain a result with the minimum number of FNs, that is, to be as accurate as possible in predicting insolvent companies. In other words, the ANN prediction models are chosen from the conservative point of view of an investor or credit officer.

Table 3 shows the classification results with two selected ANN parameter combinations and different number of selected ratios. The first one corresponds to a trained ANN when 3 relevant ratios are used as input for the ANN, and this has two hidden layers with 3 and 2 nodes, with an output node that determines the classification (topology 3-3-2-1). The ratios chosen for the inputs of the ANN are the three most selected by the EA considering all the test variants (Fig. 1). The second ANN configuration corresponds to a structure 10-7-3-1, that is, when using the 10 most frequently selected ratios. Therefore, high accuracy is obtained with the ANNs, in addition to a high sensitivity (both higher than 90%), since only 10 or 9 of the 136 insolvent companies are incorrectly classified.

Table 3. Confusion matrices with the complete test set.

		ANN topology 3-3-2-1		ANN topology 10-7-3-1	
		Prediction		Prediction	
		Insolvency	Non-Insolvency	Insolvency	Non-Insolvency
Class	Insolvency	126 (TP)	10 (FN)	127	9
	Non-Insolvency	1761 (FP)	16463 (TN)	1751	16473

These results are slightly better, in terms of sensitivity, than those obtained with an ANN with inputs selected from an ANN sensitivity analysis [2,13], using the same training and test sets. That is, the results show that the relevant ratios obtained with KNN serve to obtain better results in a more powerful classifier.

4   Discussion and Conclusions

Our study focused on two main objectives: to obtain a significant reduction of the input parameters in a predictive model, without losing the quality of the results obtained, and to reduce the error of the classifier/predictor in companies classified as non-failed that, in reality, end up being insolvent companies.

The classification models were designed to predict the insolvency of a company in the following year. This prediction can be considered as a warning to take action and change the economic course of the company, before reaching a critical point in the financial situation. For the feature selection process, a wrapper method was considered, combining differential evolution and a simple classifier (KNN), in addition to a previous filtering of ratios based on classical univariate analyses (Fisher Score and T-statistic). Future work should also consider other feature selection strategies.

The results obtained show a high percentage of classification success in predicting the insolvency one year in advance. Most of the tests performed present around 90% (accuracy) of success. The results achieved by a basic KNN classifier, using the complete set of 59 ratios, are worse than those achieved by using the KNN with the selected ratios by the hybrid DE/KNN feature selection process.

Since the ratios were selected with a simple classifier, the selected ratios were tested using a more powerful classifier such as a connectionist model. The trained ANNs, with the features selected by the DE/KNN process, were chosen to achieve the best possible results, not so much in terms of the percentage of successes in the global prediction, but in minimizing the failures in which the prediction of a failed company is contrary to reality. That is, sensitivity is the most important aspect from the investor's point of view. Since the selected trained ANNs obtain results with very low values regarding false negatives, this indicates that these classifiers can be used as a fairly reliable model for predicting insolvency.

References

1. Altman, E., Marco, G., Varetto, F.: Corporate distress diagnosis: comparisons using discriminant analysis and neural networks (the Italian experience). J. Bank. Finance **18**, 505–529 (1994)
2. Beade, A., Santos, J., Rodríguez, M.: Selección automática de ratios financieros significativos en modelos conexionistas de predicción de la insolvencia empresarial mediante análisis de sensibilidad. In: XVII Encuentro AECA (Asociación Española de Contabilidad y Administración de Empresas) 138b, pp. 1–28 (2016). http://www.aeca1.org/xviiencuentroaeca/comunicaciones/138b.pdf
3. Chakravarty, K., Das, D., Sinha, A., Konar, A.: Feature selection by differential evolution algorithm - a case study in personnel identification. In: Proceedings IEEE Congress on Evolutionary Computation, pp. 892–899 (2013)
4. Chandrashekar, G., Sahin, F.: A survey on feature selection methods. Comput. Electr. Eng. **40**(1), 16–28 (2014)
5. Doerr, B., Zheng, W.: Working principles of binary differential evolution. Theoret. Comput. Sci. **801**(1), 110–142 (2020)
6. Eltaeib, T., Mahmood, A.: Differential evolution: a survey and analysis. Appl. Sci. **8**(10), 1945 (2018)
7. Jayasekera, R.: Prediction of company failure: past, present and promising directions for the future. Inter. Rev. Financ. Anal. **55**, 196–208 (2018)
8. Price, K.V., Storn, R.M., Lampinen, J.A.: Differential Evolution. A Practical Approach to Global Optimization. NCS, Springer, Heidelberg (2005). https://doi.org/10.1007/3-540-31306-0
9. Iberian Balance Sheet Analysis System (SABI). https://www.informa.es/en/business-risk/sabi

10. Matlab. https://www.mathworks.com/products/matlab.html
11. Salcedo-Sanz, S., Deprado-Cumplido, M., Segovia-Vargas, M., Pérez-Cruz, F., Bousoño-Calzón, C.: Feature selection methods involving support vector machines for prediction of insolvency in non-life insurance companies. Intell. Syst. Acc. Financ. Manag. **12**, 261–281 (2004)
12. Serrano-Silva, Y., Villuendas-Rey, Y., Yáñez-Márquez, C.: Automatic feature weighting for improving financial decision support systems. Decis. Support Syst. **107**, 78–87 (2018)
13. Yeung, D., Cloete, I., Shi, D., Ng, W.: Sensitivity Analysis for Neural Networks. Natural Computing Series, 2010th Edition. Springer, Heidelberg (2010). https://doi.org/10.1007/978-3-642-02532-7
14. Zhao, X., Bao, L., Ning, Q., Ji, J., Zhao, X.: An improved binary differential evolution algorithm for feature selection in molecular signatures. Mol. Inf. **37**(4), e1700081 (2018)

Feature Ranking for Feature Sorting and Feature Selection: FR4(FS)²

Paola Santana-Morales[1], Alberto F. Merchán[1], Alba Márquez-Rodríguez[1],
and Antonio J. Tallón-Ballesteros[2(✉)]

[1] University of Huelva, Huelva, Spain
{paola.morales,alberto.fernandez320,alba.marquez139}@alu.uhu.es
[2] Department of Electronic, Computer Systems and Automation Engineering,
University of Huelva, Huelva, Spain
antonio.tallon.diesia@zimbra.uhu.es

Abstract. This paper proposes a methodology to feature sorting as
well as feature selection in the context of supervised machine learning
algorithms. Feature sorting has been revealed as a step which may play
a paramount role in machine learning. Nonetheless, the scalability is an
important drawback. This paper proposes to add a further stage in order
to only retain attributes with a positive influence (att+) and limiting
them in a predefined percentage of att+ set. This contribution aims at
introducing a new methodology where all attributes are not included in
the data mining task but also the positive influence ones till a certain
limit. We have followed two different types of sorting by means of different feature ranking methods. The approach has been assessed in three
binary problems with a number of features between 1000 and 10000, and
a number of instances from 200 to 7000; the test-bed includes challenging data sets from NIPS 2003. According to the experimental results for
InfoGain and GainRatio the 90% of the attributes with positive influence
are enough to get results in most of the cases comparable to the results
with raw data taking into account that the required time to train the
classifiers is shorter and hence in the non-required time we may be able
to process more instances.

Keywords: Big data mining · feature sorting · feature ranking ·
feature selection · data pre-processing · DMME

1 Introduction

Data pre-processing requires significant effort in the scheduling of any data-
driven project and is an essential activity before creating any model capable of
making predictions using the data. In order to reduce the volume of samples,
instance selection is an essential [22] task which is a horizontal data selection.
Moving on to the vertical data selection, one of the main problems with large
amounts of data is an ensuing large number of attributes, which may turn the

© Springer Nature Switzerland AG 2022
J. M. Ferrández Vicente et al. (Eds.): IWINAC 2022, LNCS 13259, pp. 545–550, 2022.
https://doi.org/10.1007/978-3-031-06527-9_54

data set impractical for any learning machine [17]. There are many methodologies to create prediction systems such as CRoss Industry Standard Process for Data Mining (CRISP-DM) [21] and its extended version called Data Mining Methodology for Engineering applications (DMME) which also includes the data pre-processing stage [7]. Feature engineering has an outstanding function in data analytics; it encompasses many fields such as feature transformation, feature generation, feature selection, feature analysis and many others [19]. By its part, feature construction has been successfully combined with ontologies to improve the classification performance in the context of daily living activities [14].

From some years ago till now, we are living in data science era [1] and the interactivity is slowly becoming a crucial ingredient of any system [9]. The lifestyle has changed and a qualitative thinking is in some moments almost mandatory [20]. Of course, social networks are on the rise and hence legal regulations should be developed and fulfilled by the companies [6].

This paper applies feature selection procedures based on feature ranking to obtain an initial arrangement of the characteristics and then only from those features with a positive weight a percentage of them are retained to build a decision-making model. Particularly, the performance of the original and proposed percentage is analysed in order to shed light on the recommendation about the preferable feature ranking method with certain classifiers which differ in the way to represent the knowledge. The remaining of this paper is organised as follows. Section 2 reviews different concepts about attribute selection. Section 3 describes the proposed approach. Then, Sect. 4 depicts the experimental results. Lastly, Sect. 5 draws some conclusions.

2   Attribute Selection

Attribute selection is a process to determine from the training set which attributes are more relevant to predict or explain the data, and conversely which attributes are redundant, meaning that they do not provide significant information [12]. Attribute selection methods can be classified into three categories: attribute ranking [11], attribute subset selection and extended attribute subset selection [16]. The first is based on getting a list of attributes ranked according to an evaluation measure, the second chooses a minimum subset of characteristics that satisfy an evaluation criteria [4] whereas the third applies the procedure described in the second approach more than once. There are many criteria to create a taxonomy within the feature selection field. According to the usage or not of a learning algorithm in the data preparation step of feature selection, three methods may be distinguished such as filters [15], semi-wrappers [18] and wrappers [8]. Filters score the features, individually, or a subset, according to an inner measure in the data such as the correlation or any type of statistical measure; semi-wrappers compute the performance of the feature set with a supervised machine learning method which is different from the target learner while in the wrappers the supervised strategy to evaluate the potential solution is exactly the same as the target machine learning algorithm.

3   The Proposed Methodology

Feature Selection (FS) is one of the possible approaches to reduce the dimensionality of the data. It picks up among the original variables those that are better suited for the problem at hand [5]. There are various kinds of methods to contend with feature selection [10]. FS involves two phases: the first, to get a list of attributes according to an attribute evaluator and the second, to carry out a hunt on the original list. All candidate lists would be evaluated using a measure evaluation and the best one will be returned. The rationale of this proposal is to keep in the attribute space only the potentially beneficial attributes selected by InfoGain (IG) or by GainRatio (GR) [13] in an independent way. IG assesses the value of an attribute by measuring the information gain with respect to the class while the GR assesses the value of the attribute by measuring the gain ratio with respect to the class.

The proposal of the contribution is to take a sample of the database in such a way that a percentage of the attributes that have a positive incidence in the dataset is taken, that is, when we apply the ranking method to the selection of attributes, the threshold 0 should be taken. In this case, we will apply the methods named above, InfoGain($p\%$) and GainRatio($p\%$), where p is the percentage that we want to study, to databases that have at least 1000 attributes. In particular, we will apply the above for a percentage of 90%.

4   Experimental Results

In this paper we apply attribute selection based on feature ranking to three databases, which are shown in Table 1.

Table 1. Description of the binary data sets

Database	# Instances	# Attributes
Arcene	200	10000
Dexter	600	20000
Gisette	7000	5000
Mean ± SD	2600 ± 3815.76	11667.67 ± 7637.63

Classification methods are strategies used to predict the response variable of a database. In the project we have used three of these methods: J48, JRip and IBk. The J48 classifier is an implementation of the C4.5 algorithm proposed by Quinlan. It is a classifier based on decision trees [2]. On the other hand, the JRip classifier is the *RIPPER* algorithm based on reduced incremental pruning to reduce the error. Finally, the IBk classifier is the k-nearest neighbour classifier [3]. To evaluate the effectiveness of these classifiers on the different databases we will use three metrics: Accuracy (Acc), confusion matrix and Cohen's kappa. The first of these, Acc, represents the percentage of observations that are correctly classified. Likewise, in the confusion matrix, each column represents the number of predictions in each class, while each row represents the instances in the actual class. Thus, the diagonal of the matrix will consist of the instances that have been correctly predicted. Cohen's kappa coefficient measures the degree of agreement based on comparing the observed agreement in a data set.

The results we have obtained are shown in Tables 2, 3 and 4. For Arcene the results concerning accuracy and Cohen's kappa show a relationship between a classifier and a feature ranking method whereas considering the confusion matrix for those supervised machine learning algorithms which maximise the sum of the main diagonal elements, the errors whose values are in the secondary diagonal the position with the highest value (worst case) may be in the first or in the second row affecting a different class. The situation for Gisette is on the other way round which has sense according to the No-Free Lunch theorem by Wolpert; now the differences between cells in the secondary diagonal are more abrupt. Dexter data set is the highest dimensionality problem which is included in this contribution and according to the results the straightforward conclusion is that C4.5 operates better than the remaining classification algorithms including data pre-processing, followed by RIPPER and 1NN.

Table 2. Results of Arcene's Dataset

Dataset		Accuracy			Cohen's kappa			Confusion Matrix					
		C4.5	1NN	RIPPER	C4.5	1NN	RIPPER	C4.5		1NN		RIPPER	
Arcene	FULL	82	80	68	0.62	0.59	0.32	14 1	8 27	16 4	6 24	10 4	12 24
	GainRatio	76	76	76	0.51	0.50	0.52	16 6	6 22	13 3	9 25	17 7	5 21
	InfoGain	76	80	72	0.51	0.58	0.42	16 6	6 22	14 2	8 26	13 5	9 23
	Average ± SD	78 ± 3.464	78.667±2.309	54±36.148	0.547±0.064	0.557±0.049	0.42±0.1	15.3±1.2 4.3±2.9	6.7±1.2 23.7±2.9	14.3±1.5 4±1	7.7±1.5 25±1	13.2±3.5 5.3±1.5	8.7±3.5 22.7±1.5

Table 3. Results of Gisette's Dataset

Dataset		Accuracy			Cohen's kappa			Confusion Matrix					
		C4.5	1NN	RIPPER	C4.5	1NN	RIPPER	C4.5		1NN		RIPPER	
Gisette	FULL	93.6	95.31	94.8	0.90	0.91	0.90	812 49	63 826	818 25	57 850	843 59	32 816
	GainRatio	94.29	96.97	94.29	0.89	0.94	0.89	824 49	51 819	842 20	33 855	831 56	44 819
	InfoGain	94.69	96.69	95.26	0.89	0.93	0.91	831 49	44 826	837 20	38 855	820 28	55 847
	Average ± SD	94.193±0.551	96.323±0.889	95.783±0.485	0.893±0.006	0.927±0.015	0.9±0.01	822.3±9.6 49±0.00	52.7±9.6 823±4.1	832.3±12.7 21.7±2.9	42.7±12.7 853.3±2.9	831.3±11.5 47.7±17.1	43.7±11.5 827.3±17.1

Table 4. Results of Dexter's Dataset

Dataset		Accuracy			Cohen's kappa			Confusion Matrix					
		C4.5	1NN	RIPPER	C4.5	1NN	RIPPER	C4.5		1NN		RIPPER	
Dexter	FULL	90	62.67	86.67	0.8	0.25	0.73	66 6	9 69	43 24	32 51	62 7	13 68
	GainRatio	85.33	82.67	82	0.71	0.65	0.64	64 11	11 64	60 11	15 64	58 10	17 65
	InfoGain	88	80	84	0.76	0.6	0.76	64 7	11 68	50 5	25 70	60 9	15 66
	Average ± SD	87.778±2.343	75.113±10.859	84.23±2.343	0.757±0.045	0.5±0.218	0.71±0.062	64.7±1.2 8±2.6	10.3±1.2 67±2.6	51±8.5 13.3±9.7	24±8.5 61.7±9.7	60±2 7±4.4	15±2 66.3±1.5

5 Conclusions

This paper presented a new approach to feature sorting under the umbrella of supervised machine learning problems in order to re-arrange the initial feature space according to the ranking achieved by a good number of feature selection procedures by only keeping a percentage of the potentially beneficial attributes under the hypothesis that positive weights, id est, greater than 0 as a threshold may have a positive effect in the classification model and may be able to help to distinguish instances from different classes. The empirical study comprised a test-bed of three binary data sets with problems of special difficulty like three challenges from NIPS 2003. There is not a clear winner which represents that the considered percentage of a ninety per cent is a good choice for GainRatio and InfoGain where attribute subset selection may be impractical due to combinatorial explosion issue which is a typical characteristic of NP problems.

Acknowledgments. This work has been partially subsidised by the project US-1263341 (*Junta de Andalucía) and FEDER funds.*

References

1. Cao, L.: The data science era. In: Data Science Thinking. DA, pp. 3–28. Springer, Cham (2018). https://doi.org/10.1007/978-3-319-95092-1_1
2. Taborda, C.H.C., García, N.G., Rozo, J.J.P., et al.: Análisis de datos mediante el algoritmo de clasificación J48, sobre un cluster en la nube de AWS. Redes de Ingeniería, 3–15 (2016)
3. Díaz-Barrios, H., Alcmán-Rivas, Y., Cabrera-Hernández, L., Morales-Hernández, A., Chávez-Cárdenas, M.C., Casas-Cardoso, G.M.: Algoritmos de aprendizaje automático para clasificación de Splice Sites en secuencias genómicas. Revista Cubana de Ciencias Informáticas 9(4), 155–170 (2015). Universidad de las Ciencias Informáticas
4. Guyon, I., Elisseeff, A.: An introduction to variable and feature selection. J. Mach. Learn. Res. **3**, 1157–1182 (2003)
5. Han, J., Pei, J., Kamber, M.: Data Mining: Concepts and Techniques. Elsevier (2011)
6. Hod, S., Chagal-Feferkorn, K., Elkin-Koren, N., Gal, A.: Data science meets law. Commun. ACM **65**(2), 35–39 (2022)
7. Huber, S., Wiemer, H., Schneider, D., Ihlenfeldt, S.: DMME: data mining methodology for engineering applications - a holistic extension to the CRISP-DM model. Procedia CIRP **79**, 403–408 (2019)
8. Kohavi, R., John, G.H.: Wrappers for feature subset selection. Artif. Intell. **97**(1–2), 273–324 (1997)
9. Kraska, T.: Northstar: an interactive data science system. Proc. VLDB Endow. **11**(12), 2150–2164 (2021)
10. Langley, P.: Selection of relevant features in machine learning. Defense Technical Information Center (1994)
11. Narendra, P.M., Fukunaga, K.: A branch and bound algorithm for feature subset selection. IEEE Trans. Comput. **9**, 917–922 (1977)

12. Olafsson, S., Li, X., Wu, S.: Operations research and data mining. Eur. J. Oper. Res. **187**(3), 1429–1448 (2008)
13. Quinlan, J.R.: Induction of decision trees. Mach. Learn. **1**(1), 81–106 (1986)
14. Salguero, A.G., Medina, J., Delatorre, P., Espinilla, M.: Methodology for improving classification accuracy using ontologies: application in the recognition of activities of daily living. J. Ambient. Intell. Humaniz. Comput. **10**(6), 2125–2142 (2018)
15. Sánchez-Maroño, N., Alonso-Betanzos, A., Tombilla-Sanromán, M.: Filter methods for feature selection – a comparative study. In: Yin, H., Tino, P., Corchado, E., Byrne, W., Yao, X. (eds.) IDEAL 2007. LNCS, vol. 4881, pp. 178–187. Springer, Heidelberg (2007). https://doi.org/10.1007/978-3-540-77226-2_19
16. Tallón-Ballesteros, A.J., Cavique, L., Fong, S.: Addressing low dimensionality feature subset selection: ReliefF(-k) or extended correlation-based feature selection(eCFS)? In: Martínez Álvarez, F., Troncoso Lora, A., Sáez Muñoz, J.A., Quintián, H., Corchado, E. (eds.) SOCO 2019. AISC, vol. 950, pp. 251–260. Springer, Cham (2020). https://doi.org/10.1007/978-3-030-20055-8_24
17. Tallón-Ballesteros, A.J., Correia, L., Leal-Díaz, R.: Attribute subset selection for image recognition. Random forest under assessment. In: Sanjurjo González, H., Pastor López, I., García Bringas, P., Quintián, H., Corchado, E. (eds.) SOCO 2021. AISC, vol. 1401, pp. 821–827. Springer, Cham (2022). https://doi.org/10.1007/978-3-030-87869-6_78
18. Tallón-Ballesteros, A.J., Riquelme, J.C., Ruiz, R.: Semi-wrapper feature subset selector for feed-forward neural networks: applications to binary and multi-class classification problems. Neurocomputing **353**, 28–44 (2019)
19. Tallón-Ballesteros, A.J., Tuba, M., Xue, B., Hashimoto, T.: Feature selection and interpretable feature transformation: a preliminary study on feature engineering for classification algorithms. In: Yin, H., Camacho, D., Novais, P., Tallón-Ballesteros, A.J. (eds.) IDEAL 2018. LNCS, vol. 11315, pp. 280–287. Springer, Cham (2018). https://doi.org/10.1007/978-3-030-03496-2_31
20. Tanweer, A., Gade, E., Krafft, P.M., Dreier, S., et al.: Why the data revolution needs qualitative thinking. Harvard Data Sci. Rev. **3** (2021)
21. Wirth, R., Hipp, J.: CRISP-DM: towards a standard process model for data mining. In: Proceedings of the 4th International Conference on the Practical Applications of Knowledge Discovery and Data Mining, pp. 29–39. Citeseer (2000)
22. Zhang, X.-W.: A Study of Novel Instance Selection Methods Based on Support Vector Regression with Model Selection. Ph.D. thesis (2023)

A Computational Drug Repositioning Method for Rare Diseases

Belén Otero-Carrasco[1,2] ⓘ, Lucía Prieto Santamaría[1,2] ⓘ,
Esther Ugarte Carro[1] ⓘ, Juan Pedro Caraça-Valente Hernández[2] ⓘ,
and Alejandro Rodríguez-González[1,2(✉)] ⓘ

[1] Centro de Tecnología Biomédica, Universidad Politécnica de Madrid,
28660 Boadilla del Monte, Madrid, Spain
alejandro.rg@upm.es
[2] ETS Ingenieros Informáticos, Universidad Politécnica de Madrid,
28660 Boadilla del Monte, Madrid, Spain

Abstract. Rare diseases are a group of unusual pathologies in the world
population, hence their name. They are considered the great neglected
field of pharmaceutical research. To date, over 6,000 rare diseases have
been identified and most of them lack treatment. The fact that they are
so rare in the population does not encourage research efforts since their
treatments are not in high demand. This work aims to analyze potential
drug repositioning strategies that could be applied to these types of diseases. That is, discovering if existing drugs currently used for treating
certain diseases can be employed to treat rare diseases. This process has
been carried out using computational methods that compute similarities
between rare diseases and other diseases, considering biological characteristics such as genes, proteins, and symptoms. The obtained potential
drug repositioning hypotheses have been contrasted with related clinical
trials found in scientific literature published to date.

Keywords: Rare diseases · Orphan diseases · Drug repositioning ·
Computational biology

1 Introduction

Rare diseases affect a small proportion of the population (usually less than
1/1,500 in USA or 1/2,000 in Europe) when considered individually [1]. However, more than 55 million people suffer from a rare diseases in Europe and in
USA [2]. A large number of these diseases have a genetic etiology, around 70%
[3]. The average time to diagnose a rare disease is more than seven years. Half of
the rare diseases affect children. Over one-third of children with a rare disease
will not live more than five years, and about 35% of these children will die within
the first year of life [4].

Universidad Politécnica de Madrid.

According to the European Organization for Rare Diseases (EURORDIS[1]) statistics, and every year around 250 new ones are described. This makes it very difficult to approach de novo drug development for this huge number of diseases, mainly due to research and development costs [5]. *De novo* drug development costs between $2 and to $3 billion for each disease and the total development time is at least 13 to 15 years [6]. In addition, since the Orphan Drug Act of 1983, only 600 treatment options have been available to rare diseases [1].

The use of drug repositioning for rare diseases is an alternative that has gaining popularity in recent years. Drug repositioning is the process of redeveloping a compound for its use in a different disease. This procedure is effective and a potential alternative to *de novo* drug development. The process of repurposing drugs for new indications, compared with the development of novel orphan drugs, is a time-saving and cost-efficient method [7]. Investment by pharmaceutical companies to apply costly traditional drug development processes to rare diseases is limited. This is mainly due to the small number of people affected by each case and the lack of information on these diseases. In this manner, the application of drug repositioning to rare diseases is highly promising [8].

The continuous advances in computer science and artificial intelligence have favored the use of the drug repositioning process over the years. Different studies have generated new hypotheses of the computational repositioning of drugs using different computational techniques of machine learning or artificial intelligence, where techniques such as logistic regression [9], support vector machine [10], neural network [11], and deep learning [12] have stood out. It is worth highlighting a recent study that has presented a new methodological pipeline for the potential generation of new drug repositioning hypotheses by means of integrating biomedical knowledge [13]. In addition, one of the most innovative applications within the field of drug repositioning has been its application to COVID-19 where there are numerous studies through which potential treatments for this disease have been proposed [14].

Focusing on rare diseases, drug repositioning in these cases is usually more complicated, mainly due to the scarcity of data [15]. However, various computational tactics have been developed based mainly on similarities between biological characteristics of diseases and omics data [1]. A new drug repositioning strategy in rare diseases is being developed through the (GCAN) [16].

An analysis has been carried out to propose possible hypotheses for drug repositioning in rare diseases through the DISNET[2] platform [17], which holds information about the relationship between diseases and genes, diseases and symptoms, symptoms and drugs, drugs and targets, among others. The used drug repositioning method considers the genetic and symptomatologic associations of a disease of interest to find reusable drugs [14]. Furthermore, information on rare diseases has been collected from the Orphanet website[3].

---

[1] https://www.eurordis.org.
[2] https://disnet.ctb.upm.es.
[3] https://www.orpha.net.

The manuscript is organized as follows: Sect. 2 explains the methods used for the analysis, Sect. 3 presents the obtained results and Sect. 4 details the conclusions.

2   Methods

2.1   Data Acquisition and Integration

To perform drug repositioning in rare diseases, information on these diseases was extracted from the Orphanet website. The rare disease name, geographical prevalence and prevalence value were retrieved. This information was obtained specifically from Orphadata, the Orphanet section in which all the public and private data is registered and can be queried. Firstly, we downloaded the complete Orphanet database in an XML file. Then, we parsed it via Python[4] (The code is available online as a FOOTNOTE to the GIT) to extract the information for those rare diseases present in the DISNET platform. DISNET integrates knowledge about biomedical diseases extracted from public sources in the form of textual and structured data, and it includes, among other things, diseases, related symptoms, genes, drugs, and drug targets [17].

From this platform, the genes and symptoms associated with the rare diseases considered for the study were selected (the extraction and unification of these data was carried out on 08/05/2021).

Fig. 1. Workflow followed to integrate and pick data from DISNET and Orphanet platforms.

Orphanet contains information on 6,043 rare diseases, but only 3,785 were available in the DISNET database. Since we needed diseases with associated genes and symptoms and no-related drugs, the final number of rare diseases was reduced to 519 (see Fig. 1). To develop the analysis, a more limited list of rare diseases was needed. For that purpose, several pathways hereafter explained were followed.

2.2   Methodological Analysis

2.3   Pathways for Disease Selection

The number of rare diseases present in the databases consulted (Oprhanet and DISNET) that met the criteria for this study was very high. For this reason, we

---

[4] https://medal.ctb.upm.es/internal/gitlab/b.otero/dr-for-rare-diseases.

decided to make a smaller selection of rare diseases to continue with the next steps of the process. The final list of rare diseases was constructed based on: (i) the number of associated genes, (ii) the number of associated symptoms, (iii) the geographical prevalence and (iv) the prevalence value itself.

In the current research, the most interesting, rare diseases had a global prevalence so the future results could have a greater scientific- social impact. Furthermore, it would be important to find potential treatments for diseases with a very low prevalence value (1/1,000,000) because these diseases are considered "excessively rare" within this type of pathology and therefore, finding treatment for them is more complicated, mainly due to the lack of cases. Finally, rare diseases must have an optimum number of associated genes and symptoms from a computational cost point of view.

Considering these points, a final set of 13 rare diseases was chosen to carry out the analysis. Table 1 shows them along with the number of associated genes and symptoms. Diseases have a unique code for their identification extracted from the Unified Medical Language System (UMLS)[5] and called Concept Unique Identifiers (CUIs). This code allows the normalization of the data for its query in different databases.

2.4   Drug Repositioning

Computational drug repositioning approaches employ modern heterogeneous biomedical data to identify new indications for already existing drugs. In this work, we present four different computational drug repositioning strategies to propose potential drug repositioning hypotheses for the selected 13 rare diseases.

Table 1. List of the considered rare diseases along with their number of genes and symptoms.

CUIs	Disease name	N.Genes	N.Symptoms
C0011195	Dejerine-Sottas syndrome	31	10
C0023944	Locked-In Syndrome	1	17
C0024054	Lown-Ganong-Levine syndrome	1	6
C0024901	Diffuse cutaneous mastocytosis	1	237
C0027877	Congenital neuronal ceroid lipofuscinosis	38	52
C0036391	Schwartz-Jampel syndrome	23	5
C0265202	Seckel syndrome	15	4
C0268059	Neonatal hemochromatosis	1	43
C0549463	X-Linked Lymphoproliferative Disorder	11	1
C0751337	X-Linked Emery-Dreifuss Muscular Dystrophy	44	32
C0869083	Dahlberg-Borer-Newcomer syndrome	12	2
C1852146	Vibratory urticaria	1	11
C0796280	Acromegaloid facial appearance syndrome	1	90

---

[5] https://www.nlm.nih.gov/research/umls/index.html.

1) Triplets' Approach. The first computational drug repositioning strategy was the use of triplets. Triplets are similarity associations between a non-rare disease and a rare disease through a biological characteristic. In this study, five different types of triplets have been constructed based on five essential biological factors:

o Non-rare disease - Gene - Rare disease
o Non-rare disease - Symptom - Rare disease
o Non-rare disease - Protein interaction - Rare disease
o Non-rare disease - Pathway - Rare disease
o Non-rare disease - Variant - Rare disease

To calculate the similarity centered on a biological characteristic between both diseases, the Jaccard similarity index was utilized:

$$Jaccard(A, B) = \frac{|A \cap B|}{|A \cup B|} \tag{1}$$

First, every rare disease in the final list was paired with all the non-rare diseases. In this manner, the similarity value for all the "Non-rare disease - Rare disease" pairs were obtained based on the aforementioned five biological characteristics. For each biological property, the pairs were ordered from the highest to the lowest similarity score. Subsequently, the top 5 non-rare diseases associated to the specific rare disease were selected in each biological feature group. Therefore, we had the top 5 non-rare diseases derived from the gene, symptom, protein interaction, pathway and variant similarities for each rare disease. The next step consisted in extracting the drugs associated to the top non-rare diseases.

To identify the drug repositioning candidates to treat the corresponding rare disease, we searched the common drugs among those associated to the top 5 five non-rare diseases in each biological set. Afterwards, we checked what drugs matched between all the feature groups. These drugs would be potentially repositioned as treatments for the rare disease in study.

2) Triplets with Associated Target Approach. In this computational drug repositioning method, the triplets linked the non-rare disease to a rare disease by a biological characteristic and were imposed that the drugs of the selected non-rare diseases had as their target a protein encoded by a gene associated to the rare disease under study. Once this filter had been made, the drug identification process was performed as explained in the previous approach.

3) Direct Drug Repositioning Approach. The rare disease was associated to a gene that encoded the protein target of a drug. Hence, there was a direct relationship between the rare disease and the drug, being possible to use it as a potential treatment for it.

4) Paths' Approach. Another method that has been followed to achieve drug repositioning in rare diseases has been to develop 6 strategies that are based on different biological characteristics of the diseases and their associated drugs. These have been called "paths" due to the existence of 6 paths to follow until the repositioning of drugs for these diseases.

1. Rare disease-symptom-drug: From the symptoms of the rare disease, we obtained the drugs that were directly indicated for them.
2. Rare disease-symptom-disease-drug: From the rare disease symptoms, we extracted the diseases that were related to those symptoms. The drugs related to these diseases were then identified.
3. Rare disease-symptom-gene-target-drug: From the symptoms associated with rare disease, we remove the diseases that share these symptoms. From these symptomatologically similar diseases, we extract the associated genes. Afterwards, the targets associated with these genes and, finally, drugs related to these targets were identified.
4. Rare disease-gene-disease-drug: Identifying genes associated with rare disease allowed us to identify diseases that also share gene associations with them. These diseases led to the identification of drugs that are indicated for these diseases.
5. Rare disease-gene-protein-target-drug: From the genes associated with the disease, their proteins and associated targets were extracted. Finally, drugs acting on these targets were obtained.
6. Rare disease-gene-protein- protein interaction -target-drug: From the genes associated with the disease, their proteins were extracted, the high quality protein-protein interactions data, and the associated target from which the corresponding drugs are obtained.

3   Results and Discussion

3.1   Computational Drug Repositioning

After completing the four proposed computational drug repositioning methods, all the generated results were put together to create a final set of drugs shared by all the approaches for each pathology in study. Drug repositioning candidates were identified for 9 out of 13 rare diseases through the computational methods. However, if we do not consider the triplets' approach (1) due to its more general filtering from a biological standpoint, potential repurposable drugs are detected for 11 out of the 13 rare diseases (Table 2).

Table 2. Summary of the results for the four developed computational drug repositioning approaches. The numbers in the table represent the number of drugs resulting in each case.

Disease name	Triplets	T.Target	Direct DR	Paths	All	TT.DDR.P *
Dejerine-Sottas syndrome	6	17	17	2	0	2
Locked-In Syndrome	46	0	0	80	44	80
Lown-Ganong-Levine syndrome	0	0	0	965	965	965
Diffuse cutaneous mastocytosis	7	0	0	4	2	4
Congenital neuronal ceroid lipofuscinosis	2	0	0	48	2	48
Schwartz-Jampel syndrome	533	0	30	15	10	14
Seckel syndrome	6	2	2	0	0	2
Neonatal hemochromatosis	2	0	0	91	0	0
X-Linked Lymphoproliferative Disorder	0	0	7	1	1	1
X-Linked Emery-Dreifuss Muscular Dystrophy	10	0	0	126	10	126
Dahlberg-Borer-Newcomer syndrome	1	8	0	0	0	8
Vibratory urticaria	2	0	0	0	2	0
Acromegaloid facial appearance syndrome	35	2	2	0	2	2

* TT = Triplets target DDR = Direct Drug Repositioning P = Paths

If we combine the results obtained in ALL with the results of TT.DDR.P, 12 out of 13 diseases have computational repositioning. The diseases with no associated drugs only had a single gene. For the next steps of the analysis, two diseases were discarded: (i) Neonatal hemochromatosis (because no drug repositioning candidates were obtained via computational repositioning) and (ii) Lown-Ganong-Levine (due to the high number of potentially repurposable drugs that was obtained for it). Therefore, these diseases will not be considered for verifying the results in clinical trials and scientific literature.

3.2   Validation of Results in Clinical Trials

Once the drug candidates were identified via computational drug repositioning strategies, we checked whether these drugs were related or not in the scientific literature to the rare diseases as their potential treatments. 289 possible candidate drugs have been found to be possibly repositioned to 11 (out of 13) of the rare diseases studied. This represented a significant number of treatments that could be effective for these diseases. Since research in rare diseases is scarce, only 52 drugs had a described relationship with any of the rare diseases in the scientific literature (see Fig. 2).

The drugs found in the scientific literature related to the pathologies under study can refer to treatments for these diseases or just the opposite: substances that produce or favor the appearance of it. In our case, 24 out of 52 were depicted as effective treatments for these rare diseases (Table 3).

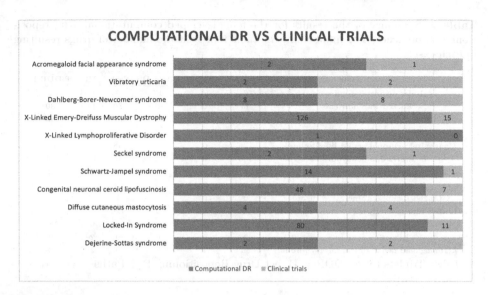

Fig. 2. Verification of the results achieved by computational drug repositioning through published clinical trials.

An example of the in-depth study that has been carried out to complete Table 3 is shown below with the disease Diffuse cutaneous mastocytosis. In this pathology, the four drugs that were obtained by repositioning are found in the scientific literature. One of the drugs obtained was alcohol, this in the literature indicates that it should be avoided by patients with the diagnosis of this disease [18]. Silversulfadiazine is a cream that is applied in areas with erosion by this disease [19]. Dexamethasone is a glucocorticoid; it has been seen in the scientific literature that corticosteroids and glucocorticoids are used to treat this disease [19,20]. Acetaminophen was used by postoperative patients [20].

Searching the scientific literature and the clinical trials, 9 out of 11 rare diseases had a described relationship with the drug repositioning candidates proposed through the computational methods. Delving into the clinical trials compiled for potential repurposable drugs for these rare diseases, it has been observed that only 2 present toxic drugs, that is, they would cause this disease. In this manner, potential repurposable drugs have been detected via computational methods and proven in the scientific literature for 7 rare diseases.

Table 3. Based on the scientific literature, drug effects on the rare diseases studied are detailed below.

Name disease	Drugs Clinical trials	Drugs effects	Drugs toxic
Dejerine-Sottas syndrome	2	1	1
Locked-In Syndrome	11	2	9
Diffuse cutaneous mastocytosis	4	3	1
Congenital neuronal ceroid lipofuscinosis	7	5	2
Schwartz-Jampel syndrome	1	1	0
Seckel syndrome	1	0	1
X-Linked Lymphoproliferative Disorder	0	0	0
X-Linked Emery-Dreifuss Muscular Dystrophy	15	11	4
Dahlberg-Borer-Newcomer syndrome	8	0	8
Vibratory urticaria	2	0	2
Acromegaloid facial appearance syndrome	1	1	0

4   Conclusions

Considering the number of existing rare diseases, the appearance of new ones every year, and the large number of people affected worldwide, drug repositioning is proposed as an useful and effective strategy to find treatments. Based on the results obtained in this study, it can be concluded that the use of the DISNET platform as a tool and data source together with the computational techniques developed can lead to potential time-saving treatments for these diseases.

Within our selection of diseases, for 92% of the cases repositioning has been found computationally and of these, in 83% of the cases these treatments have been corroborated with the scientific literature. These are very promising results within the field of rare diseases that could be used before starting a clinical trial, shortening the drug development process. As it has been demonstrated, drug repositioning would reduce costs, risks, and time, allowing to an increasing number of people suffering from these rare diseases to have an effective treatment.

For future lines of research, we would like to be able to consider a larger number of rare diseases to apply the same computational process that has been developed on them and compare results with those presented. The main limitations of the study are related to the lack of research in rare diseases, it is considered that in other types of diseases the success cases of drug repositioning would be superior, since in our case, the big problem has been not being able to validate many of the drugs obtained computationally with the scientific literature.

References

1. Delavan, B., Roberts, R., Huang, R., Bao, W., Tong, W., Liu, Z.: Computational drug repositioning for rare diseases in the era of precision medicine. Drug Discov. Today **23**(2), 382–394 (2018). https://doi.org/10.1016/j.drudis.2017.10.009

2. Stolk, P.: Rare essentials drugs for rare diseases as essential medicines. Bull. World Health Organ. **84**(9), 745–751 (2006). https://doi.org/10.2471/BLT.06.031518

3. Nguengang Wakap, S.: Estimating cumulative point prevalence of rare diseases: analysis of the Orphanet database. Eur. J. Hum. Genet. **28**(2), 165–173 (2020). https://doi.org/10.1038/s41431-019-0508-0

4. The Lancet Diabetes & Endocrinology: Spotlight on rare diseases. Lancet Diab. Endocrinol. **7**(2), 75 (2019). https://doi.org/10.1016/S2213-8587(19)30006-3

5. Sardana, D., Zhu, C., Zhang, M., Gudivada, R.C., Yang, L., Jegga, A.G.: Drug repositioning for orphan diseases. Brief. Bioinform. **12**(4), 346–356 (2011). https://doi.org/10.1093/bib/bbr021

6. Scannell, J.W., Blanckley, A., Boldon, H., Warrington, B.: Diagnosing the decline in pharmaceutical R&D efficiency. Nat. Rev. Drug Discov. **11**(3), 191–200 (2012). https://doi.org/10.1038/nrd3681

7. Roessler, H.I., Knoers, N.V.A.M., van Haelst, M.M., van Haaften, G.: Drug Repurposing for Rare Diseases. Trends Pharmacol. Sci. **42**(4), 255–267 (2021). https://doi.org/10.1016/j.tips.2021.01.003

8. Lotfi Shahreza, M., Ghadiri, N., Green, J.R.: A computational drug repositioning method applied to rare diseases: adrenocortical carcinoma. Sci. Rep. **10**(1), 8846 (2020). https://doi.org/10.1038/s41598-020-65658-x

9. Gottlieb, A., Stein, G.Y., Ruppin, E., Sharan, R.: PREDICT: a method for inferring novel drug indications with application to personalized medicine. Mol. Syst. Biol. **7**(1), 496 (2011). https://doi.org/10.1038/msb.2011.26

10. Napolitano, F., Zhao, Y., Moreira, V.M., Tagliaferri, R., Kere, J., D'Amato, M., Greco, D.: Drug repositioning: a machine-learning approach through data integration. J. Cheminformatics **5**(1), 30 (2013). https://doi.org/10.1186/1758-2946-5-30

11. Menden, M.P., Iorio, F., Garnett, M., McDermott, U., Benes, C.H., Ballester, P.J., Saez-Rodriguez, J.: Machine learning prediction of cancer cell sensitivity to drugs based on genomic and chemical properties. PLoS ONE **8**(4), e61318 (2013). https://doi.org/10.1371/journal.pone.0061318

12. Aliper, A., Plis, S., Artemov, A., Ulloa, A., Mamoshina, P., Zhavoronkov, A.: Deep learning applications for predicting pharmacological properties of drugs and drug repurposing using transcriptomic data. Mol. Pharm. **13**(7), 2524–2530 (2016). https://doi.org/10.1021/acs.molpharmaceut.6b00248

13. Prieto Santamaría, L., Ugarte Carro, E., Díaz Uzquiano, M., Menasalvas Ruiz, E., Pérez Gallardo, Y., Rodríguez-González, A.: A data-driven methodology towards evaluating the potential of drug repurposing hypotheses. Comput. Struct. Biotechnol. J. **19**, 4559–4573 (2021). https://doi.org/10.1016/j.csbj.2021.08.003

14. Prieto Santamaría, L., Díaz Uzquiano, M., Ugarte Carro, E., Ortiz-Roldán, N., Pérez Gallardo, Y., Rodríguez-González, A.: Integrating heterogeneous data to facilitate COVID-19 drug repurposing. Drug Discov. Today **27**(2), 558–566 (2022). https://doi.org/10.1016/j.drudis.2021.10.002

15. Decherchi, S., Pedrini, E., Mordenti, M., Cavalli, A., Sangiorgi, L.: Opportunities and challenges for machine learning in rare diseases. Front. Med. **8**, 747612 (2021). https://doi.org/10.3389/fmed.2021.747612

16. Cao, H., Zhang, L., Jin, B., Cheng, S., Wei, X., Che, C.: Enriching limited information on rare diseases from heterogeneous networks for drug repositioning. BMC Med. Inform. Decis. Mak. **21**(S9), 304 (2021). https://doi.org/10.1186/s12911-021-01664-x

17. Lagunes-García, G., Rodríguez-González, A., Prieto-Santamaría, L., García del Valle, E.P., Zanin, M., Menasalvas-Ruiz, E.: DISNET: a framework for extracting phenotypic disease information from public sources. PeerJ **8**, e8580 (2020). https://doi.org/10.7717/peerj.8580
18. Alto, W.A., Clarcq, L.: Cutaneous and systemic manifestations of mastocytosis. Am. Fam. Phys. **59**(11), 3047–3054 (1999)
19. Rayinda, T., Oktarina, D.A.M., Danarti, R.: Diffuse cutaneous mastocytosis masquerading as linear IgA bullous dermatosis of childhood. Dermatol. Rep. **13**(1), 9021 (2021). https://doi.org/10.4081/dr.2021.9021
20. Czarny, J., Lange, M., Ługowska-Umer, H., Nowicki, R.J.: Cutaneous mastocytosis treatment: strategies, limitations and perspectives. Adv. Dermatol. Allergol **35**(6), 541–545 (2018). https://doi.org/10.5114/ada.2018.77605

Doughnut Computing in City Planning for Achieving Human and Planetary Rights

Veronica Dahl[1] and Juan José Moreno-Navarro[2,3]

[1] Simon Fraser University, Burnaby, Canada
veronica_dahl@sfu.ca
[2] Universidad Politécnica de Madrid, Madrid, Spain
juanjose.moreno@upm.es
[3] Imdea Software Institute, Madrid, Spain
juanjose.moreno@imdea.org

Abstract. Doughnut economics provides a framework for appraising how to improve social behaviour through new relations and goals in the way humanity uses (and suffers from the lack of) resources for services. Municipalities used to have several competences and responsibilities either in the use of resources and the provision of (social) services to citizens. Usually they hold a huge amount of data and experiences that can be used to provide better planning of their responsibilities to citizens.

Cities abstract social behaviour for regeneration and distribution in two aspects: i) those related to the interaction of individuals inside big communities, basically cities, and the global beneficials obtained by social services and solidarity, and ii) the social relationship of these communities (cities and citizens) with nature, in the sense of intertwining with sustainability and reasonable use of (natural) resources.

In [9], Dahl proposed and justified *Doughnut Computing*, an AI methodology based on inferential programming that, using the Doughnut Economics model as a compass [21]), can help us achieve, both locally and globally, the goal of enabling social and ecological well-being. In this paper, we discuss how to specialize this methodology, always guided by the human and sustainability goals of Doughnut economics, to analize cities' social behaviour as communities in order to perform planning of municipal services to improve social relations, sustainability and quality of life. This paper reports our first experiences in three different cities across the world, showing a very promising interplay between computation, sustainability, and social services.

Keywords: Artificial Intelligence for Social Good · City planning of social services · Social behaviour and Doughnut Economics

J. M. Ferrández Vicente et al. (Eds.): IWINAC 2022, LNCS 13259, pp. 562–572, 2022.
https://doi.org/10.1007/978-3-031-06527-9_56

1   Motivation

Descartes' view of humans as self-contained, self-sufficient, rational, and mind-bound that pervades western thinking would have us cleanly sever biosciences from social sciences, even if more inclusive views *have* appeared throughout history, and were even already embryonically present in Plato's recognition of strong analogies between social organizations and individuals (Plato: *The Republic*, around 375 BC).

Ancient African thought tradition, for instance, escapes the dualism mind/body; self/others; humans/nature- in other words, the separation mindset that underlies the domination mentality: that of person over person, country over country, religion over religion, "man" over nature, and so on. In this view, Descartes was wrong: in fact, 'a person is a person through other persons' [4], and society is likewise inextricably intertwined with nature- so much so that in some civilizations, nature is viewed as constituted by persons (e.g. the Klamath River was granted the same rights as people according to a 2019 law passed by the Yurok tribal council, following a 2017 New Zealand court decision that granted person status to the Whanganui River [5]). Modern epigenetics points in similar directions, clarifying that neither separation, nor the "selfish gene", nor domination are our "nature": social systems create neural nets oriented towards pro-social equity & solidarity or towards domination [12].

Such is our point of view and our justification for submitting our work to a Bio-Science venue: holistic views of biology must now include the earth and the social relationships that underlie our multiple interconnected global crises if we are to have a chance to heal their causes before extinction can be stopped. In this spirit, we address in this paper a modest but important aspect of the necessary healing which we believe is crucial to success: bottom-up regeneration and distribution, city by city.

2   Main Goals

New technologies, in particular Artificial Intelligence, are revolutionizing society, services for citizens and modelling social behaviour. Unfortunately, being driven by large companies and, in some cases, by administrations, they are not always used to offer social improvements. The global preoccupation with sustainability renders opportunities for a more socially beneficial use of AI, especially for public administrations and, particularly, for those closest to the citizens, municipalities.

In this context, we define this proposal to explore, in a coordinated way between two or more municipalities of different countries, the possible manners in which Computing Science, and Artificial Intelligence in particular, can contribute to the municipal planning necessary to provide the basic necessities of all in a sustainable way, that is, respecting the ecological limits of the planet.

The use of Artificial Intelligence for Social Good (AI4SG) is gaining traction both in the social sciences and in the AI community. It has the capacity to address social problems effectively by developing AI-based applications. They include AI techniques, practices, projects, and applications collectively aiming at securing all human rights for every person on Earth [17].

We discuss the computational requisites and programming platforms needed to support an effort of that magnitude, and we argue that it should incorporate the insights offered by Doughnut Economics [21] and Bioculturalism [11].

Our initial objective is to implement computational programs that, fed with real data from the cities under consideration, permit planners to evaluate, for each topic of interest, to what degree each combination of possible actions would achieve the goals for the designated social issues in a sustainable way. For example, if the goal under consideration were to diminish the carbon footprint, the possible actions would include, for instance, optimizing the needs of daily transportation, routes and schedules; the data would include the current carbon footprint, the desired timeline, and the improvement that each feasible action would contribute annually to the total shrinking of emissions; and the programs, using this data, would propose all the possible scenarios that would achieve the goal, where by scenario, we refer to a combination of possible actions.

To date, there is only a limited understanding of what *social good* means in the framework of an AI application, and how to reproduce potential successes in terms of policies. Some discussions and experiences can be found [8,14,19,22].

2.1 Doughnut Economics

The economic theories that are encouraging for a better use of our environment and global social benefits constitute an exciting area. Notable economists are joining voices in the same general direction as here proposed, e.g. [10] proposed ecological economics to correct the flawed assumptions and excesses of the current system; Banerjee and Duflo[1] [2] focus on how to end global poverty. The UN Sustainable Development Goals is an agenda to end poverty, protect the planet, and ensure prosperity for all by 2030 [24].

Kate Raworth [21] has translated global data on human rights indicators and planetary limits into a single visualization, shaped like a Doughnut (shown in Fig. 1, left part). Red areas inside the inner circle represent lacks in human rights. Red areas outside the Doughnut represent planetary rights transgressions. Bringing us into the safe space for humanity and the natural world (the green "dough" of the Doughnut) would show as Fig. 1, right part. Various cities, like Amsterdam [15] or Portland, have explicitly adopted the Doughnut as their transformational compass.

---

[1] Esther Duflo became the second female economist to win a Nobel prize.

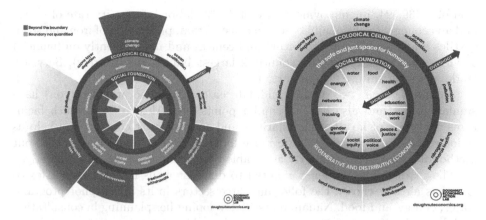

Fig. 1. Doughnut economics model & approach

3   Proof of Concept

Municipal administrations are the closest government to the citizens. They usually hold many experiences and data related to the services they offer to their residents. These data are often used for optimizing costs or procedures, and just in some few cases to improve the services from the point of view of citizenship.

Therefore, in order to achieve some of the sustainability goals pursued by the Doughnut economy framework, we have decided to further explore, following [9] how artificial intelligence, advanced planning and information technology can be used for achieving human rights and social services in the government of cities [16]. There are only a few reports on such practical experiences [25,26]. We have chosen as testbeds a city in each of Canada, Spain, and Mexico.

The Canadian city of Nanaimo has already adopted the Doughnut as its compass and is adapting it to the municipal data and objectives. Nanaimo is the second most important city, after Victoria, on Vancouver Island on the west coast of British Columbia. Nanaimo has some 100,000 inhabitants and is a major transportation hub. Traditionally, its economy has been based in forestry and today it houses a substantial cellulose plant. Services are also important for commerce and tourism.

In Spain, we are working with the city of Alcorcón, found to the south of Madrid, the capital, and around 185,000 inhabitants. Alcorcón is quite industrialized and the base of an university campus, but also serves as a commuter town for workers in the capital.

As can be seen, the profiles of these two candidate cities are similar, which facilitates a proof of concept that generalizes the results as we progress our research.

Recently, we have made a similar proposal to the municipality of Mexico City, that is also adopting the Doughnut as its compass. Mexico City has 9,209,944 inhabitants, according to the 2020 census. With an economically active population of 4,439,594, unemployment rate of 7.26%, labor informality rate of 47.1% and an economy traditionally based on construction, production of iron and steel, textiles and yarn, plastics, furniture and cement and more recently on financial services (headquarters of the country's largest banks and insurers). Services, trade, and tourism are also important.

As can be seen, two of the candidate cities (Nanaimo and Alcorcón) have similar points, and also have dissimilar points with Mexico City, which facilitates the study of how both similarities and an important contrast can help us tailor results to more cities as we move forward. Our ultimate goal is that our methodology become modularly adaptable to any municipality, quite directly.

The methodology is being adapted to different goals in each town. Mexico City has already chosen the following three sectors in its initial pilot program: water, energy, and food. Nanaimo is still developing her planning in consultation with her citizenry, related to transport services. Alcorcón wants to focus on home help, public health, and unwanted loneliness.

These local administrations are hoping to get a combination of policies and actions that can better lead to universalizing some rights and services.

We also expect to apply the advances in each town to the others, regarding different legal organization, responsibilities and structures. Other topics of interest at the start of our research would be housing, ecological footprint and gender equality in the cities of concern. But whatever the chosen theme, additional aspects of the compass will have to be taken into account, since many are interrelated.

3.1 Process

Independently of a more detailed plan, the process is described as:

1. Prioritization of the issues to address, with elements that are common to all the cities.
2. Identification of data sources.
3. Formalization of ethical aspects and data protection.
4. First prototype with results; verification with the city councils.
5. Development of visualizations of the offered solutions.
6. Final technical testing, with city councils, citizens, etc.
7. Possibility of adopting the technology to other issues.

4 Computational Methodology and Tools

To these ends, the computational tools should be reliable, explainable, transparent, and modular to be able to interact with other aspects of the compass chosen for each city (and with the global compass at the same time). Some of these features have been discussed in [18,20] from the viewpoint of freedom preservation in the automated decision-making world.

As the main programming methodology, we propose *inferential programming* over AI based statistics because the latter favours popularity over reasoned justification, and often reproduces or amplifies the social biases hidden in the data. Inferential AI can trace explanations, make inferences, accommodate change modularly, and also permits exploring hypothetical scenarios [7].

Therefore, we have chosen methods of declarative programming, in particular logic programming with restrictions, given that the inferential descriptions are what allow explanation of the reasoning carried out, and by extension transparency and reliability. Constraint Handling rules (CHR) in particular [13] permit combining information coming from various topics to take everything into account in generating results. The idea is not new and in the literature some experiences can be found [3,23].

We shall show a proof of concept programmed in Prolog plus CHR where "instructions" are rules of inference, e.g., one such rule could calculate on the basis of data such as how much extraction and waste is driven by overconsumption, what combination of actions could bring the CO_2 emissions down to zero by say, 2030. All possible scenarios (i.e., the combination of actions that together would achieve each given objective) will be output for evaluation. Scenario assessment could itself be partially automated as well, under predefined evaluating criteria.

Of course, measures may interact with each other and/or with other goals within the Doughnut rather than being independent, so the programs may involve in turn examining possible subscenarios in the same way.

This is important because, as Kate Raworth has already observed in her initial research on the Doughnut [21], the types of problems we are trying to solve involve a large number of variables, even those pertinent to another sector of the Doughnut other than the one we are considering. The interrelationship between these variables creates a complex but organized system. CHR can capture these interrelationships powerfully through its inference rules with possibly multiple premises, where each premise conjures up information that is either in the same database (or topic) that we are dealing with in the present rule, or in a database *different*, relative to some other sector of the Doughnut. This is needed, since it is necessary to take into account the possibility that some actions that are beneficial to one sector of the Doughnut represent at the same time a cost or harm to another sector - or even an extra benefit, which must also be accounted for. Although we are not considering all sectors explicitly, but focusing on a few, the methodology we propose allows us to generate consequences of our actions that can be taken into account immediately because they will be printed as part of our results, but that can also be taken up in the future and used as input to interact with the programs of other sections of the Doughnut that will be programmed later.

For example: if in the 'energy' issue we contemplate the rationing of air and land transport as a possible action to reduce CO_2 emissions, it is clear that we will have to account not only for the cost and benefits of this action on the energy issue, but also its cost and benefits on, for example, unemployment, subject that belongs to a different sector within the Doughnut. It is also clear that what constitutes a cost in one sector could well constitute a benefit to another sector, and viceversa. For instance, shutting down ecologically damaging mining operations will have an unemployment cost, yet this cost will represent a benefit in the human security sector of the Douughnut, since sexual crimes against women typically rise in areas where men camps are set up. Similarly, the cost of unemployment in the energy sector could be nullified through retraining that sector's former employees towards sectors where they are desperately needed, such as care tasks, hospital infrastructure, regenerative industries either from soil to crops, or conversion of paved areas to crops, or production of alternative energy, etc.

4.1   Planning Example

As a proof of concept for our project, and to illustrate the expressiveness of our tools, let us revisit the following grammatical logic program, developed by Dahl [9]. It consists of four rewrite rules, whose 'sentences' (the output generated) are all possible sets of actions that together, can reduce an initial amount X of CO2 emissions, in some region, to zero or less.

Rule 1) detects whether the goal G, set as 0, has been reached, and rule 2) if we have run out of actions. In both cases, the computation stops. Rule 3) adds the N-th action to those being collected, and rule 4) skips the N-th action.

```
1) actions(_, Status) --> {goal(G), Status =< G, !}, [].
2) actions(N, _) --> {number_of_actions(Max), Max=N, !, fail}, [].
3) actions(N,Status) -->
         {N1 is N+1, action(N1,A,QA), Status1 is Status-QA},
         [action(A,QA)], actions(N1,Status1).
4) action(N,Status) --> {N1 is N+1}, actions(N1,Status).
```

```
goal(0).
```

Now, we want to apply this program to choose, among the concrete actions capable of reducing emissions in a given city, a subset that together, reduces them to zero or less. Actions can be taken from the analysis of [1,6]. Using official data from the *Plan for saving energy and reducing CO2 emissions* in Alcorcón[2], we can estimate the total amount of emissions of Alcorcón at around 412 Mt CO2 eq, i.e., 412000 tons. The above-mentioned Plan has the goal to reduce emission in a 25% by 5 years, i.e. 103 Mt CO2 eq. We must therefore change the goal into 103 (see the last clause below). For each action, we can also estimate, through mining the city's databases, the number of units of tons by which each action would reduce emissions. For instance, we have estimated the gain from the action numbered 3) among those below -namely, reorganizing transport routes and fleet- as roughly 72. This figure can be found by extrapolating municipal databases of public transport use.

---

[2] Submitted to the Next Generation funds of the EU.

```
action (1, improve_climatizacion, 91).
action (2, ration_electricity_use, 76).
action (3, reorganize_transport_rutes_and_fleet, 72).
action (4, use_renovable_energy_in_public_buildings, 68).
action (5, update_electric_cars_own_vehicles,35).
action (6, regulations_and_grants, 28).
action (7, awareness_campaign, 12).
```

```
number_of_actions(7).
goal(103).
```

We could now run this grammar (or grammatical program) so that it generates all the combinations of actions capable of reducing emissions (whose initial value, if we consider Alcorcón as our region, is 412Mt CO2 eq) to a concrete goal (in our example, 103).

For explanatory purposes, meanwhile, let us show one of the solutions (out of several) that the above program finds, which is a set of two actions:

```
[action (4, use_renovable_energy_in_public_buildings, 68),
 action (5, update_electric_cars_own_vehicles, 35)]
```

We can add a cost-benefit analysis of such solutions, of any complexity we need, using CHR rules. For example, if the update of the city vehicle fleet to non-polluting vehicles generates, say, 125 unemployed people (in traditional gas stations, repair shops, etc.), we can first record this consequence simply by adding this information to the concerned "action" rule (i.e., the one numbered 5), as a call to a binary 'CHR constraint' with name "unemployment generated by action"[3], e.g.:

```
action (5, update_electric_cars_own_vehicles, 35) :-
            unemployement_generated_by_action (5, 125).
```

CHR constraints do not get evaluated as Prolog calls do; they are instead recorded in a constraint store, whose content can be consulted and updated by CHR rules. For instance, the following CHR rule (recognized as such for its use of the connector "<=>") can be added to our program to indicate that people unemployed as a result of an action N could be reinserted in the workforce in some other sector where they are needed in at least that number:

```
unemployement_generated_by_action (N, U),
new_employees_required_by (new_energies, M) <=> R is M-N, R>=0 |
        retrain_employees_sector (5, N, new_energies),
        new_employees_required_by (new_energies, M).
```

---

[3] CHR constraints are distinguished from plain Prolog calls by their being declared as such at the beginning of a program using them.

This CHR rule looks in the constraint store for elements matching its premises (i.e., those to the left of the connector), and if the calculations stated next up to the separator "|" hold, replaces those elements from the constraint store by those at the connector's right.

For instance, if the constraint store has recorded that action 5 generated 125 unemployed, as in our example, and some other sector has added to the store, the requirement of, say, 200 employees in the new energy sector, these two constraint store elements will unify with the rule's premise (with $N = 5$, $U = 125$, $M = 200$), and since 200-125>= 0 holds, will be replaced by the two new elements stating that 125 employees must be retrained from sector 5 into new energies, and that 75 new employees are then still required in the "new energies" sector. These elements, in turn, will be available for further consultation and change by other CHR rules.

Clearly, this rule is simplistic: e.g., not all of the unemployed might be able to thus relocate, but surely also the program can calculate (or ask for that data) how many of them could and would want to change professions, etc. Similarly, more details could be programmed into relocating those unemployed by the declining traditional energy sector: some could be redirected to postdisaster care, others to regeneration jobs, and so on, as needed. We hope the example has served to give an idea of how close to human reasoning the programming process is when we use inferential tools, and in particular an idea of how our programs could be useful in proposing solutions that concern or affect several sectors simultaneously. It also shows the relevance of working with adequate data, which we expect to obtain from municipality records. Once the results of the program are received, it is up to the planners whether to accept some, ask for new options from the program, etc. The idea is that all possible scenarios (i.e., combinations of actions that, together, could achieve each given goal) are calculated and printed for evaluation, as well as their consequences in terms of costs and benefits, including those that influence other sectors of the Doughnut. Notice that it is possible to find open source calculators of the CO2 footprint for cities and individual use from several sources, e.g., the Spanish Ministry of Ecologic Transition[4] or private companies[5]. However, they do not provide an adequate way to obtain the data and, more importantly, do not provide any planning or strategy to effectively reduce the emissions.

5   Conclusion

Clearly, modelling the social behaviour of cities and citizens and the transformation efforts in cities will involve much more than computational support. In degrowing what we do not need while growing universal well-being under equity, we will be giving the earth a break from the increasing dangers of unbridled "growth" and wastefulness.

---

[4] https://www.miteco.gob.es/es/cambio-climatico/temas/mitigacion-politicas-y-medidas/calculadoras.aspx.

[5] https://www.carbonfootprint.com/calculator.aspx.

With this work, we hope to help provide Doughnut-adopting cities the computational support they will need to achieve their goals.

Our next steps will be to obtain from municipalities interested in benefiting from our research, an agreement regarding what topic to focus on initially, and a list of the data and actions relevant to the selected topic, together with ways of calculating in how much each possible action would bring us closer to the goal for the chosen topic. We anticipate an initial proof of concept will reveal an extraordinary potential that will be successfully be taken advantage of by local universities, in collaboration with each municipality. Likewise, we hope that our comparisons between various distant cities can lead to an adaptation methodology that will facilitate its adoption by other cities in the world as well.

Acknowledgements. The authors want to thank UNAM researchers Eva Valencia Leñero and Michel Nader for several fruitful discussions and re. cooperation with the Mexico City project, as well as Gen Geselbracht, Karin Kronstal, Jamie Rose, Lisa Bhopalsingh, Rob Lawrence and Jeremy Holm, for likewise useful discussions re. cooperation with the municipality of Nanaimo, and Andrew Fanning, for insights on specific indicators of Doughnut Economics. Support from Veronica Dahl's NSERC grant 31611021 is gratefully acknowledged.

References

1. Balouktsi, M.: Carbon metrics for cities: production and consumption implications for policies. Build. Cities **1**(1) (2020)
2. Bancrjee, A.V., Duflo, E.: The economic lives of the poor. J. Econ. Perspect. **21**(1), 141–168 (2007)
3. Barahona, P., Ribeiro, R.: Building an expert decision support system: the integration of artificial intelligence and operations research methods. In: Schader, M., Gaul, W. (eds.) Knowledge, Data and Computer-Assisted Decisions. NATO ASI Series, vol. 61, pp. 155–168. Springer, Heidelberg (1990). https://doi.org/10.1007/978-3-642-84218-4_12
4. Birhane, A.: Indefence of uncertainty. In: Code Mesh LDN (2019)
5. Chapron, G., Epstein, Y., López-Bao, J.V.: A rights revolution for nature. Science **363**(6434), 1392–1393 (2019)
6. Chavez, A., Ramaswami, A.: Progress toward low carbon cities: approaches for transboundary GHG emissions. Carbon Manag. **2**(4), 471–482 (2011)
7. Christiansen, H., Dahl, V.: HYPROLOG. In: Logic Programming (2005)
8. Cowls, J., et al.: A definition, benchmark and database of AI for social good initiatives. Nat. Mach. Intell. **3**, 111–115 (2021). https://doi.org/10.1038/s42256-021-00296-0
9. Dahl, V.: Doughnut computing: aiming at human and ecological well-being. In: 6th International Conference on the History and Philosophy of Computing (HAPOC-6) (2021)
10. Daily, H.: Steady-State Economics. Island Press, Washington, DC (1991)
11. Eisler, R.: Human possibilities: the interaction of biology and culture. Interdiscip. J. Partnersh. Stud. **1**(1) (2015). https://doi.org/10.24926/ijps.v1i1.88
12. Eisler, R., Fry, D.P.: Nurturing Our Humanity. Oxford Scholarship Online (2019)

13. Frühwirth, T.: Theory and practice of CHR. J. Log. Program. **37**(1–3), 95–138 (1998)
14. Gorriz, J., et al.: Artificial Intelligence within the interplay between natural and artificial computation: advances in data science, trends and applications. Neurocomputing **410**, 237–270 (2020)
15. Doughnut Economics Action Lab and Biomimicry 3.8 and C40 Cities and Circle Economy: The Amsterdam City Doughnut (2020). https://www.kateraworth.com/wp/wp-content/uploads/2020/04/20200406-AMS-portrait-EN-Single-page-web-420x210mm.pdf
16. Doughnut Economics Action Lab and Biomimicry 3.8 and C40 Cities and Circle Economy: Creating City Portraits (2020). https://www.circle-economy.com/insights/creating-city-portraits
17. United Nations: United Nations Declations of Human Rights (1948). https://www.un.org/en/about-us/universal-declaration-of-human-rights
18. Alliez, P., Cosmo, R.D., et al.: Attributing and referencing (research) software: best practices and outlook from Inria. Comput. Sci. Eng. **22**(1), 39–52 (2020)
19. Pencheva, I., Esteve, M., Mikhaylov, S.J.: Big data and AI: a transformational shift for government: so, what next for research? Public Policy Adm. **33**(1), 24–44 (2020). https://doi.org/10.1177/0952076718780537
20. Di Cosmo, R.: Preserving freedom in an automated decision making world (2019). https://www.dicosmo.org/MyOpinions/index.php?post/2019/06/19/Preserving-freedom-in-an-automated-decision-making-world2. Accessed 22 Mar 2022
21. Raworth, K.: Doughnut Economics. White River Junction. Chelsea Green Publishing, Vermont (2017)
22. Mikhaylov, S.J., Esteve, M., Campion, A.: Artificial intelligence for the public sector: opportunities and challenges of cross-sector collaboration. Trans. R. Soc. A (2018). https://doi.org/10.1098/rsta.2017.0357
23. Subramanian, D.: Conceptual design and artificial intelligence. In: IJCAI, pp. 800–809 (1993)
24. UNESCO: UN Sustainable Development Goals (2015). https://www.un.org/sustainabledevelopment/. Accessed 04 Mar 2022
25. Vego, G., Kucar-Dragicevic, S., Koprivanac, N.: Application of multi-criteria decision-making on strategic municipal solid waste management in Dalmatia, Croatia. Waste Manag. **28**(11), 2192–2201 (2008). https://doi.org/10.1016/j.wasman.2007.10.002. https://www.sciencedirect.com/science/article/pii/S0956053X07003406
26. Yigitcanlar, T., Cugurullo, F.: The sustainability of artificial intelligence: an urbanistic viewpoint from the lens of smart and sustainable cities. Sustainability **12**(20) (2020). https://doi.org/10.3390/su12208548. https://www.mdpi.com/2071-1050/12/20/8548

Temperature Control and Monitoring System for Electrical Power Transformers Using Thermal Imaging

F. Segovia[1]($\boxtimes$), J. Ramírez[1], D. Salas-Gonzalez[1], I. A. Illán[1],
F. J. Martinez-Murcia[1], J. Rodriguez-Rivero[1,2], F. J. Leiva[2], C. Gaitan[2],
and J. M. Górriz[1]

[1] Department of Signal Theory, Networking and Communications,
University of Granada, Granada, Spain
fsegovia@ugr.es
[2] Endesa Distribución, Madrid, Spain

Abstract. New societal challenges due to the climate emergency will change countries' energy systems in the short and medium term. In this context, electrical energy and its production, distribution, transformation and storage will play a decisive role. The irruption of the electric car and the increased use of renewable production sources (of an intermittent character in the majority of cases), will cause greater stress on electrical systems. In order to address these challenges, the electrical infrastructure is adapting by including semi-autonomous monitoring systems that allow more efficient management of resources and potential failures.

In this work, a thermal camera-based monitoring system for electrical power transformers is demonstrated. By appropriate processing of the thermal images obtained by a camera it is possible to obtain a time series of both transformer and room temperatures. These measurements are highly correlated with operating failures, which makes it possible to predict them and thus minimize their effects. Compared to previous sensor-based monitoring systems, this approach has the advantage of being totally independent of the transformer system and has no physical contact with it. This prevents transformer failures from affecting the monitoring system. The proposed approach was applied and evaluated in 14 transformer stations of the Spanish distribution grid, obtaining accurate and reliable temperature time series, which provides some advantages over sensor-based monitoring systems.

Keywords: Thermal imaging analysis · Electrical power transformers · Connected system · mser segmentation

1 Introduction

The quality and safety of the electrical supply service has become one of the main concerns of the industry and the sector's regulators. Electrical infrastructure is

© Springer Nature Switzerland AG 2022
J. M. Ferrández Vicente et al. (Eds.): IWINAC 2022, LNCS 13259, pp. 573–582, 2022.
https://doi.org/10.1007/978-3-031-06527-9_57

fundamental to economic development, human well-being and progress. However, in recent years, changes in society are taking place that threaten the resilience of the power system. The irruption of the electric car, which demands large amounts of energy in a short time, the increased use of renewable production sources (of an intermittent character in the majority of cases) or more frequent extreme weather events are compromising the electrical systems [5].

In fact, climate change is increasing the fragility of the distribution grid, which lacks the necessary redundancy to avoid supply failures in the event of problems in any of its component. In addition, electric power systems are currently experiencing a digitization process, which involves the integration of technologies associated with computing, wireless communication, Internet of Things (IoT) devices and a multitude of applications aimed at facilitating real-time and seamless operations [10,11]. However, this digitization brings additional concerns, including cyber security concerns, that should be addressed [4].

In the case of electrical transformers, which are part of the distribution grid, their main potential failures are related to their exposure to overloads [14,20]. Transformer failures, in addition, are particularly dangerous as they can cause fires which, taking into account the urban location of transformers, can result in serious economic and personal damages [3]. In order to prevent these problems, modern electrical power transformers are equipped with a sensor system to monitor different variables such as the intensity of the input and output lines, phase unbalance or the device's temperature, allowing preventive actions to be taken if values deviate from those expected [6,16,19]. However, sensors are usually integrated in the transformer system and are not exempt from failure [2].

In this work, we demonstrate a thermal camera-based monitoring system for electrical power transformers which is intended to be a more robust alternative to sensor-based systems. Thermal cameras, installed close to but independent of the transformer, provide accurate data on temperatures in a given region of space. Subsequently, by means of appropriate image processing, it is possible to extract transformer temperature and room temperature values, which can in turn be used to predict additional electric variables and possible operation failures. This approach was implemented and evaluated in 14 transformation centers belonging to the Spanish power grid. Our experiments show that the temperature time series obtained using thermal cameras are highly correlated to that obtained by more standard systems based on sensors. In addition, the former measures appear to be more accurate and the monitoring system is not affected by transformer failures, as it is a totally independent system.

2   Materials and Methods

2.1   Thermal Camera-Based Monitoring System

The proposed monitoring system consists of several devices, namely, a thermal camera, a single board computer (SBC), a modem for mobile networks and a processing and storage server.

The thermal camera was only responsible for capturing thermal data (it did not store or process them). In our experiments, we used an Optris Xi 80, a commercial model able to provide thermal images of 80×80 pixels at a frame rate 50 Hz. It was installed at a distance of about 2 m from the transformer that, thanks to an 80° field of view, allowed us to capture both the transformer surface and the transformer protection fence.

The camera was controlled by an SBC to which it was connected via a USB interface. In our case, the SBC was based on a Raspberry Pi 4 equipped with an SD card. Since this equipment did not have a communication module that allowed connection to the Internet via mobile networks, it was necessary to use an additional device for this purpose. Specifically, we used a Teltonika RUT240, a industrial cellular router that can access to Internet using commercial mobile networks, by means of a SIM card of any carrier. The connection between the SBC and the router was carried out through the Ethernet interface.

Additionally, we used an external server, based on a general-purpose computer, to permanently store the images and process them, i.e. extract a transformer and room temperatures from each of them. A diagram showing all the devices we used and the connections between them is shown in Fig. 1. Note that to monitor more than one transformer, as many thermal cameras, SBCs and modems as transformers should be monitored are needed. However, a single server can store and process the images from all of them.

Fig. 1. Main devices required by the proposed temperature monitoring system and connections among them.

The logical control of the system was carried out by two software processes running on the SBC and an additional one running on the external server. The first process was responsible for capturing thermal images periodically (at a rate of 1 per minute) using the camera and storing them on the SD card with which the SBC is equipped and which serves as a buffer. The second process running on the SBC was in charge of sending the images stored on the SD card during the last hour to the external server. Finally, the third process was responsible for extracting the two temperatures (transformer and room temperature) from each thermal image using the segmentation procedure described below.

2.2 Image Processing

After acquisition and storage, thermal images were processed in order to extract transformer and room temperatures as numeral values. This was done in pseudo-real-time (by means of a process that was run periodically) and applying classical image processing algorithms to these data.

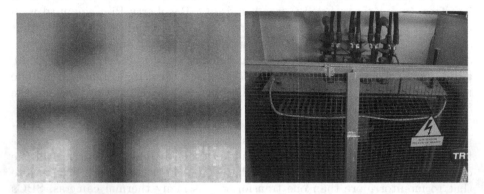

Fig. 2. Thermal image (left) and visible image (right) of an electrical power transformer currently serving a residential area in southern Spain. Note that both images were acquired with different cameras as thermal camera model used in this work provide only thermal images.

Transformer and room temperatures were computed as the average temperature of pixels in specific locations on thermal images. Transformer temperature was obtained from pixels containing the surface of the power transformer while room temperature was obtained from pixels containing the fence forming part of the metallic structure that protect the electrical power transformer. Figure 2 shows a thermal image (left) and its visible-range equivalent (right) of a power transformer currently serving a residential area in southern Spain. In this case, the T-shape blue region in the lower half correspond to the protection fence and was used to estimate the room temperature. The transformer temperature was estimated from the pixels containing the transformer surface, placed on lower left and right corners.

Thus, the calculation of the transformer and room temperature was carried out into two step. First, an *ad hoc* thermal image was segmented in order to obtain two masks, one for selecting pixels of the fence and other one for selecting pixels of the electrical power transformer surface. Then, both masks were applied to all the images in the time series to extract the pixels of the fence and the pixels of the transformer surface separately and, from them, obtain the two numeral values of temperature that form the temporal series.

The thermal image that was segmented to obtain the region masks was created from all the thermal images acquired during a day (24 h). Specifically, each pixel was calculated as the maximum of pixels at the same position in all images.

That way, we prevented the time of day (clearly related to the room temperature and indirectly related to the transformer temperature) from affecting the result.

The segmentation was performed by means of an algorithm based on Maximally Stable Extremal Regions (MSER) [13]. In particular, the procedure was as follows:

– First, the image was downsampled using the SLIC superpixel method proposed by Achanta et al. [1].
– Then, the resulted image was requantized using several thresholds computed according to [15].
– Finally, spatially separated regions of equal intensity were considered independently by applying the Maximally Stable Extremal Regions algorithm [13].

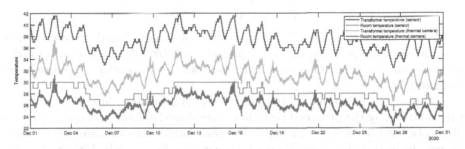

Fig. 3. Result of one of the installed monitoring systems. The comparison of transformer and room temperatures obtained by the proposed system and those obtained by sensors is shown.

3   Experiments and Results

In order to evaluate the proposed temperature monitoring system, it was implemented in several transformation centers belonging to the Spanish power grid. The electrical power transformers of these centers are equipped with a sensor-based monitoring system that has allowed us to compare the proposed system with the standard one. Figure 3 shows a comparison between the temperatures registered by the proposed system and those obtained by sensors. Note that, despite the offset, there is an almost perfect correlation between the temperatures recorded by the two systems. This correlation can be easily seen if we remove the offset, as is done in Fig. 4, where the temperature obtained from the thermal camera has been shifted so that it has the same mean as the temperature obtained from sensors.

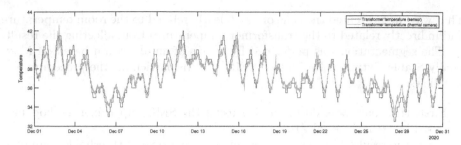

Fig. 4. Transformer temperature obtained by the proposed system based on thermal cameras (red) and by sensors (blue). The former temperature has been shifted so that both have the same mean and in order to the correlation between them can be easily appreciated. (Color figure online)

As can be seen in Figs. 3 and 4, a thermal camera-based monitoring system for electrical power transformer provides reliable information on operating temperatures and can be successfully used as an alternative to sensor-based measurements.

Finally, we carried out an analysis to study the relationship of the temperature obtained by the proposed thermal camera-based system with operation variables obtained by sensors (including the transformer temperature). Specifically, we use the method based on Wiener-Granger causality described in [18]. Figure 5 show the obtained conditional G-causality for about 8K samples acquired during the period of analysis in one of the transformers included in this study.

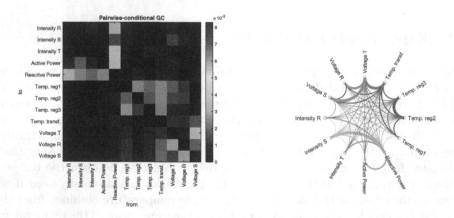

Fig. 5. Statistical inference of the conditional G-causality. We show the F matrix for relevant variables, the circular graph for strongest connections. Temp. reg 1, 2 and 3 were obtained with the proposed thermal camera-based system while the rest of measurements were obtained by sensors.

4   Discussion

The experiments carried out demonstrate that it is possible to obtain reliable information on the operating temperature of an electrical power transformer using a system based on thermal imaging [8]. Temperature is a variable of great relevance in the analysis of transformer performance. On the one hand, high temperature values can lead to complete system failure and, in the worst case, to a fire with serious economic implications. On the other hand, anomalous temperature values (higher or lower than usual) may indicate specific malfunctions of a component which, if not properly addressed, may lead to a general system failure.

In addition to the obvious relationship between ambient temperature and transformer temperature, recent studies corroborate that there is a close relationship between these two temperatures and other electrical variables involved in transformer operation. In [18], a methodology based on Granger causality is used to study the ability of some electrical variables to predict others. The results show that there is a clear relationship between the transformer temperature and other relevant variables such as current, active power, reactive power and voltage. The last experiment performed in this work has shown that this relationship is also present between the temperatures obtained by the proposed system and other electrical variables. The relationship between transformer temperature and active power has also been corroborated in [12], which shows that it is possible to predict the transformer temperature in the near future from the active power of the three transformer lines together with the ambient temperature using long short-term memory (LSTM) networks. A similar approach was also demonstrated in [17]. In this case, a non-linear autoregressive neural network with exogenous inputs (NARX) was used to predict the temperature of the transformer as a function of past values of outputs and exogenous inputs.

All in all, temperature plays a fundamental role in the performance of electrical power transformers and has a clear relationship with other electrical variables as shown in previous studies. The thermal camera-based system demonstrated in this paper could improve the temperature monitoring of electrical power transformers and, that way, reduce the probability of errors that affect the quality of the power supply and shorten the transformer lifetime.

As shown in Figs. 3 and 4, the thermal camera-based system provides more accurate temperatures (note that temperature changes are more progressive in the curves obtained with the proposed system) and has the advantage of being an external system that is not coupled to the transformer, i.e. there is no physical contact between the devices of both systems and no data transfer through the electrical network, which guarantees that errors in the transformer will not affect the monitoring system. Furthermore, the proposed approach is easily scalable to obtain a higher temperature granularity, i.e. to obtain not only the room and transformer temperatures but also those of other elements such as the connection terminals or the input and output lines. This would only require changing the image processing but no hardware changes (additional cameras, etc.) would be necessary. In addition, it would be theoretically possible to estimate other electrical variables from temperature using schemes similar to the networks proposed in [12] and [17]. In this way, the proposed system could be used to monitor not only temperature but all relevant electrical variables.

Regardless of the system used for data acquisition, data must be permanently stored in a database that allows later analyses [9]. Ideally this permanent storage is carried out externally to the transformer, i.e. in locations other than the transformer whose operation is being monitored. A communication system is therefore required between the acquisition equipment and the servers external to the transformer. Possibly, the most direct application is to use the power grid itself to transmit the monitoring data, but this makes the monitoring system vulnerable to failures in the distribution network and its implementation entails substantial costs. In order for the monitoring system to be completely autonomous from the power grid, it is necessary that the data transmission is carried out independently from the grid. However, implementing an independent data network from scratch (whether wired or wireless), involves high costs. In the proposed approach, the commercial mobile phone network is used for this purpose. This allows significantly lower implementation costs by using already deployed infrastructure, while allowing data transmission to be carried out independently of the power grid. A similar approach was previously described in [7]. Unlike the approach proposed by Jalilian et al. the communication system proposed in this paper is unidirectional. The transmission is made only from the equipment installed next to the transformer to the external database. This facilitates the system to have a certain resilience since synchronous communication is not required and in case of connection error the data are temporarily stored in a buffer memory to be sent later in a new connection attempt.

5   Conclusions

In this paper we demonstrated a thermal camera-based system to monitor the operation temperature of electrical power transformers. It uses thermal cameras located near the transformer and focused on it to capture its temperature and that of adjacent areas. Subsequently, by appropriate image processing, 2 temperatures (transformer temperature and room temperature) were obtained for each thermal image, and stored as a time series.

This approach was implemented in 14 transformation centers belonging to the Spanish electrical system and the obtained temperature time series were compared with those obtained using a sensor-based system. The results support the hypothesis that the image-based approach produces results at least as accurate as those obtained by the sensor-based system, with the added advantage of being completely independent of the electrical transformer system and having no physical contact with it.

Acknowledgement. This work was supported by the Ministerio de Ciencia e Innovación (España)/FEDER under the RTI2018-098913-B100 project, by the Consejería de Economía, Innovación, Ciencia y Empleo (Junta de Andalucía) and FEDER under CV20-45250, A-TIC-080-UGR18, B-TIC-586-UGR20 and P20-00525 projects.

References

1. Achanta, R., et al.: SLIC superpixels compared to state-of-the-art superpixel methods. IEEE Trans. Pattern Anal. Mach. Intell. **34**(11), 2274–2282 (2012). https://doi.org/10.1109/TPAMI.2012.120
2. de Melo, A.S., et al.: Applied methodology for temperature numerical evaluation on high current leads in power transformers. Int. J. Electr. Power Energy Syst. **131**, 107014 (2021). https://doi.org/10.1016/j.ijepes.2021.107014
3. Dolata, B., Coenen, S.: Online condition monitoring becomes standard configuration of transformers - practical application for optimized operation, maintenance and to avoid failures. In: E-ARWtr2016 Transformers, Advanced Research Workshop on Transformers, La Toja Island, Spain, vol. 2, October 2016
4. Elsisi, M., et al.: Effective IoT-based deep learning platform for online fault diagnosis of power transformers against cyberattacks and data uncertainties. Measurement **190** (2022). https://doi.org/10.1016/j.measurement.2021.110686
5. Foros, J., Istad, M.: Health index, risk and remaining lifetime estimation of power transformers. IEEE Trans. Power Deliv. **35**(6), 2612–2620 (2020). https://doi.org/10.1109/TPWRD.2020.2972976
6. Górriz, J.M., et al.: Artificial intelligence within the interplay between natural and artificial computation: advances in data science, trends and applications. Neurocomputing **410**, 237–270 (2020). https://doi.org/10.1016/j.neucom.2020.05.078
7. Jalilian, M., et al.: Design and implementation of the monitoring and control systems for distribution transformer by using GSM network. Int. J. Electr. Power Energy Syst. **74**, 36–41 (2016). https://doi.org/10.1016/j.ijepes.2015.07.022
8. Karakoulidis, K., Fantidis, J., Kontakos, V.: The Temperature measurement in a three-phase power transformer under different conditions. J. Eng. Sci. Technol. Rev. **8**, 19–23 (2015). https://doi.org/10.25103/jestr.085.04
9. Kunicki, M., Borucki, S., Zmarzły, D., Frymus, J.: Data acquisition system for on-line temperature monitoring in power transformers. Measurement **161** (2020). https://doi.org/10.1016/j.measurement.2020.107909
10. Li, J., Jiao, J., Tang, Y.: Analysis of the impact of policies intervention on electric vehicles adoption considering information transmission—based on consumer network model. Energy Policy **144** (2020). https://doi.org/10.1016/j.enpol.2020.111560
11. Martinez-Monseco, F.J.: An approach to a practical optimization of reliability centered maintenance. Case study: power transformer in hydro power plant. J. Appl. Res. Technol. Eng. **1**(1), 37–47 (2020). https://doi.org/10.4995/jarte.2020.13740
12. Martinez-Murcia, F.J., et al.: Prediction of transformer temperature for energy distribution smart grids using recursive neural networks. In: International Conference on Time Series and Forecasting, Granada, Spain, September 2019
13. Matas, J., Chum, O., Urban, M., Pajdla, T.: Robust wide-baseline stereo from maximally stable extremal regions. Image Vis. Comput. **22**(10), 761–767 (2004). https://doi.org/10.1016/j.imavis.2004.02.006
14. Müllerová, E., Hrůza, J., Velek, J., Ullman, I., Stříska, F.: Life cycle management of power transformers: results and discussion of case studies. IEEE Trans. Dielectr. Electr. Insul. **22**(4), 2379–2389 (2015). https://doi.org/10.1109/TDEI.2015.005025
15. Otsu, N.: A threshold selection method from gray-level histograms. IEEE Trans. Syst. Man and Cybern. **9**(1), 62–66 (1979). https://doi.org/10.1109/TSMC.1979.4310076

16. Peimankar, A., Weddell, S.J., Jalal, T., Lapthorn, A.C.: Evolutionary multi-objective fault diagnosis of power transformers. Swarm Evol. Comput. **36**, 62–75 (2017). https://doi.org/10.1016/j.swevo.2017.03.005

17. Ramírez, J., et al.: Power transformer forecasting in smart grids using NARX neural networks. In: Valenzuela, O., Rojas, F., Herrera, L.J., Pomares, H., Rojas, I. (eds.) Theory and Applications of Time Series Analysis, pp. 401–414. Contributions to Statistics, Springer International Publishing, Granada, Spain, November 2020. https://doi.org/10.1007/978-3-030-56219-9_26

18. Rodriguez-Rivero, J., et al.: Granger causality-based information fusion applied to electrical measurements from power transformers. Inf. Fusion **57**, 59–70 (2020). https://doi.org/10.1016/j.inffus.2019.12.005

19. Velasquez-Contreras, J.L., Sanz-Bobi, M.A., Galceran Arellano, S.: General asset management model in the context of an electric utility: application to power transformers. Electr. Power Syst. Res. **81**(11), 2015–2037 (2011). https://doi.org/10.1016/j.epsr.2011.06.007

20. Vitolina, S.: Development of lifetime data management algorithm for power transformers. In: 2014 5th International Conference on Intelligent Systems, Modelling and Simulation (2014). https://doi.org/10.1109/ISMS.2014.83

Visual Parking Space Estimation Using Detection Networks and Rule-Based Systems

Susana P. De Luelmo(✉) (iD), Elena Giraldo Del Viejo(✉) (iD),
Antonio S. Montemayor(✉) (iD), and Juan José Pantrigo(✉) (iD)

Universidad Rey Juan Carlos, Móstoles, Spain
{susana.deluelmo,antonio.sanz,juanjose.pantrigo}@urjc.es,
e.giraldo.2016@alumnos.urjc.es

Abstract. In this paper we propose a vision-based two-stage parking detection module. The first stage detects vehicles in images based on a deep neural network. Then, a rule-based system determines the car parking spaces in the image. Experimental results show that our proposed algorithm detects parking space but it also obtains a high false positive rate. We plan to combine visual information with other information fonts to face this drawback.

Keywords: Smart parking · Parking space detection · Detection Networks · Rule-based Systems

1 Introduction

Population growth in cities makes necessary to optimize the management of city resources. In particular, parking management is one of the main problems facing cities nowadays. Cities such as San Francisco [12], Pisa [8] or Santander [4] have started Smart Parking projects in order to reduce the environmental impact of parking search and improve urban planning.

The smart parking problem has been addressed from diverse perspectives, involving different related areas. In this work we focus on approaches that are based on visual information captured from RGB on-board cameras. Such a systems use a variety of visual information as mark parking delimiters, parking spaces, vehicles or a combination of them.

The majority of identified works in the literature try to estimate parking spaces by detecting the marks that delimit the parking spaces [5,7,10,15]. They usually work in a bottom-up stages approach that includes edge detection, filtering and parking space state (empty/occupied) estimation. Yang et al. [18] propose a parking space detection framework based on Hough transform for parking line detection. Similarly, Li et al. [9] propose a classifier based on a constant soft-cascade strategy. They also provide a public dataset called as *ps1.0*. Xu, Chen, and Xie [16] propose a neural network architecture, called as DeepPS,

© Springer Nature Switzerland AG 2022
J. M. Ferrández Vicente et al. (Eds.): IWINAC 2022, LNCS 13259, pp. 583–592, 2022.
https://doi.org/10.1007/978-3-031-06527-9_58

that focuses on visual corner detection systems. Authors release a public dataset called as *ps2.0* database.

Other works address the visual detection of the parking space itself. For this purpose, classifiers [6], and detection networks such as YOLO [17] or MobileNet [11] have been proposed. Do et al. [2] enrich the description of the scene by detecting relevant classes of objects, such as parking separating lines, cars and pillars.

Another approaches use prior knowledge of the parking capacity combined to the detection of parked cars. The system by Grassi et al. [3] detects cars with a cascade classifier. Then, these detections are combined with GPS information to determine the location of the parking space. Other systems are based on the capture of depth images [13,14]. These systems require the presence of objects in the scene that can delimit the parking spaces, such as cars, pillars, etc.

Parking space detection problem is hard and it is still open. On the one hand, it involves the detection of an empty space. An empty space visually contains objects in the background, floor, buildings facades, etc. Then it is not possible for an expert system or a machine learning method to identify discriminant features to characterize a parking space. On the other hand, parking spaces can be found in different contexts (line parking, battery parking, oblique parking, etc.), which generates a large casuistry. Additionally, it is usual to find areas in which parking is not allowed with the same visual appearance to those in which it is. Finally, when vehicle detection is used for the estimation of parking spaces, it is needed to discriminate between circulating vehicles and parked vehicles. In this work we propose a vision-based two stage parking detection module. The first stage is a visual vehicle detector that is based on a deep neural network. Given this vehicle detections, the second stage is a rule-based system that determines the car parking spaces in the image. We plan to embed this visual detection module in a parking space detection system which can be enriched with GPS information and city maps to refine the estimations provided by our visual parking space detection module.

2   Proposed Method

The proposed system is composed of two complementary stages. The first one is devoted to detect vehicles in the scene. The second one decides if there are parking space available. Next sections details these stages.

2.1   First Stage: Vehicle Detections

Starting from this premise, an important pillar in the detection of parking spaces will be the detection of vehicles. For this purpose, we use an object detector network trained using the COCO dataset. In order to chose the best network, the accuracy of different state-of-the-art networks available in the Tensorflow model garden [19] has been analyzed. The results and the tests carried out are detailed in Sect. 3.3.

2.2   Second Stage: Rule-Based Decisions

Different strategies of vehicle detections and parking space estimations are described in Fig. 1. Starting from vehicle detections (red ROIs in the figure), the spacing between them is checked (in green). For this purpose, the detections are sorted and separated according to the side of the road (left/right) in which they are located. Then, a set of rules is followed to check if there is indeed a parking gap or not.

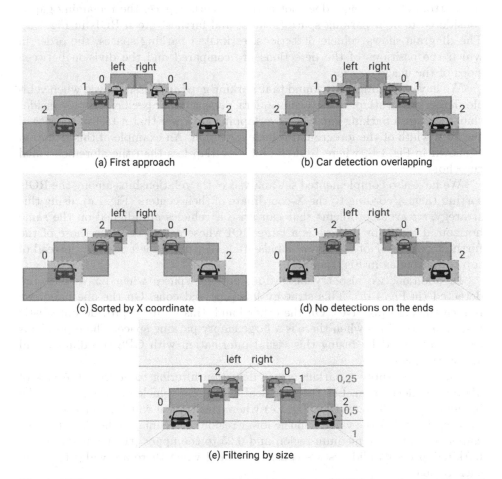

Fig. 1. Different detection strategies. Vehicle detections (ROIs) in red and estimated parking spaces in green. a) Sorting detections using the Y-coordinate, b) allowing vehicle detections overlapping, c) Sorting detections considering the X-coordinate, d) excluding final parking space estimations and e) size heuristic considerations. (Color figure online)

As discussed, the detection of parking spaces presents different problems, including labeling. We have decided to mark the space that the vehicle should occupy when parked. In the first implementation (Fig. 1.a), vehicle detections are split in left and right sides of the road, and ordered according to the Y-coordinate of their center, thus simulating the effect of depth in 2D images. On the other hand, in order to be considered as a parking space, vehicle ROIs cannot overlap. If there is no vehicle detection, the entire area is considered to be a parking space. In addition, if the last detections in each side, both at the top and at the bottom of the image, does not cover the entire space, the remaining gap is considered to be a parking space (nearest and furthest green ROIs in Fig. 1.a). The diagram shows vehicle detections, estimated parking spaces, the order in which the positions of the detections are compared and the division between sides of the image.

We have experimentally found that parking gaps are possible even when vehicle detections overlap, due to the camera perspective. Specifically, we consider that there are a parking gap when overlapping are lower that a 15% of the size of the ROI width of the foreground vehicle detection. An example of this situation is shown in Fig. 1.b, where ROIs 0 and 1 overlap less than the aforementioned threshold.

We have also complemented the analysis of the relationships among the ROIs sorting them according to the X-coordinate of their centers (Fig. 1.c). using this strategy, we avoid problems that can arise if vehicles are aligned on the same horizontal region or if there is a large ROI whose center is above those of the furthest vehicles. Note that now labels are assigned from left to right, instead of top to bottom as in Fig. 1.a and b.

In addition, we also try discarding parking spaces when no vehicles are detected (in Fig. 1.d.). This strategy has pros and cons. On the one hand, we reduce the false positives. On the other hand, this strategy provide unrealistic results in situations when there is a large empty parking space. These problems can be addressed by fusing this visual information with GPS coordinates and annotated maps.

Finally, we apply a parking space detection filtering to address the lack of 3D depth information. Let $\tilde{w}$ the typical width of a vehicle detection ROI. The image is split in 3 zones (See Fig. 1.e) where this typical width is corrected by a ratio r, that takes the value 1 in the lower region of the image (the closest to the camera), 0.5 for the medium region and 0.25 to the upper (the farthest). Then, parking spaces candidates are considered valid when there are wider to $r\tilde{w}$ in each region.

3   Experiments

3.1   Dataset

Experiments were conducted on an Intel Core i7-8700, 3.2 GHz, 32 GB RAM equipped with an NVIDIA RTX 2070 GPU. The test set is composed by a subset of the Cityscapes dataset [1] with 500 images, 152 of them presenting parking spaces. These images include a total amount of 348 parking spaces to be detected. The labels of this subset have been modified so that the detected parking spaces are marked as the space that the vehicle should occupy if it was correctly parked. Notice that we consider the use of pre-trained detection networks, making unnecessary the design and development of a training stage.

3.2   Metrics

Different approximations have been used to calculate the precision metrics. On the one hand, for the comparison between neural networks for vehicle detection, the true positives (TP), false positives (FP) and false negatives (FN) have been calculated using the intersection-over-union (IoU) metric. In this case, a minimum threshold of 0.5 has been used to consider that a detection is correct. On the other hand, in the comparison of parking space detectors, TP, FP and FN were calculated by counting the number of detections in each of the images. This approach was chosen because the exact position of the parking space is not critical.

3.3   Comparison of Object Detection Networks

We tested the accuracy of different state-of-the-art networks in detecting vehicles has been tested with the following detection networks available in Model Zoo [19]:

- CenterNet HourGlass104 (*CenterNet*) 1024 × 1024.
- EfficientDet D4 (*EfficientDet*) 1024 × 1024.
- Faster R-CNN Inception ResNet V2 (*FasterRCNN_Inception*) 1024 × 1024.
- Faster R-CNN ResNet152 V1 (*FasterRCNN*) 1024 × 1024.
- SSD MobileNet V2 FPNLite (*SSDMobilenet*) 640 × 640.
- SSD ResNet50 V1 FPN (*RetinaNet_50*) 1024 × 1024.
- SSD ResNet152 V1 FPN (*RetinaNet_152*) 1024 × 1024.

Obtained results are depicted in Table 1. As we are interested not only in quality results but also in computational performance, we report for each model the following metrics: Precision, Recall, F1 Score, Computing Time, Computing Framerate and input size.

We observe that EfficientDet obtains the best precision results while SSD-Mobilenet are the less consuming in terms of time and memory. Taking into consideration these quality and performance measures, we finally choose Faster-RCNN for vehicle detection as a reasonable compromise. This network gives us the second highest F1 Score, reducing the inference time by more than half compared to the network with the highest F1 Score.

Table 1. Performance comparison of state of the art detection networks in vehicle detection. Results obtained on the Cityscapes subset using a NVIDIA GeForce RTX 2070 GPU. FPS refers to frames per second.

Net	Precision	Recall	F1 Score	T (sec)	FPS	input size
CenterNet	0,949	0,408	0,571	0,430	2,324	1024x1024
EfficientDet	**0,966**	0,387	0,553	0,361	2,770	1024x1024
FasterRCNN_Inception	0,811	**0,560**	**0,662**	0,577	1,734	1024x1024
FasterRCNN	0,845	0,473	0,606	0,259	3,867	1024x1024
SSDMobilenet	0,945	0,288	0,441	**0,156**	**6,402**	640x640
RetinaNet_50	0,938	0,415	0,576	0,260	3,852	1024x1024
RetinaNet_152	0,951	0,415	0,578	0,2482	4,029	1024x1024

3.4 Comparison of Different Strategies

We carried out a set of test taking into account the strategies presented in Sect. 2. Table 2 resumes different combinations of the proposed methods. In this table we report the test id, if detections are allowed to overlap, the axis where we perform the sorting of detections, if we allow detections at the end of the image and if we perform parting space filtering. For each experiment we report TP, FP, FN and F1 Score results.

Table 2. Results obtained in the detection of parking spaces using the different approaches.

Test	Overlapping	Axis sort	End detections	Filtering	TP	FP	FN	F1 Score
t_0	No	Y	No	No	179	466	90	0,392
t_1	No	Y	No	Yes	148	319	121	**0,402**
t_2	No	Y	Yes	No	260	1400	9	0,270
t_3	No	Y	Yes	Yes	223	964	46	0,306
t_4	No	X	No	No	180	493	89	0,382
t_5	No	X	No	Yes	113	253	156	0,356
t_6	No	X	Yes	No	260	1439	9	0,264
t_7	No	X	Yes	Yes	203	827	66	0,312
t_8	Yes	Y	No	No	212	616	57	0,386
t_9	Yes	Y	No	Yes	148	319	121	**0,402**
t_10	Yes	Y	Yes	No	266	1577	3	0,252
t_11	Yes	Y	Yes	Yes	223	964	46	0,306
t_12	Yes	X	No	No	209	737	60	0,343
t_13	Yes	X	No	Yes	113	253	156	0,356
t_14	Yes	X	Yes	No	264	1708	5	0,235
t_15	Yes	X	Yes	Yes	203	827	66	0,312

According to the F1 Score (last column in Table 2), we can observe that allowing overlapping between vehicle detections does not provide an improvement (tests *t_8* to *t_15*). Indeed, it does not change the results in the best cases or it can penalize the performance of the parking space estimation in others. Allowing overlapping we obtained an average F1 Score of 31.9%, while not allowing it resulted in 33.2%. This may be due to a poor choice of the percentage of overlap between detections.

As with overlapping, sorting detections by X-coordinate shows no improvement over sorting detections by Y-coordinate. The average F1 Score obtained by sorting according to the X-coordinate is 31.7% versus 37.7% using the Y-coordinate for sorting. These results show that selecting the order in which to compare the detections is not trivial, and the use of depth maps may be important.

With the *End detections* column we observe that when we do not consider possible parking gaps at the ends of each side of the road, the results increase considerably. When not taking into account these possible parking gaps, the average F1 Score goes from 28.1% to 37.7%.

Filtering by size also improves the performance of the parking space estimation. In these tests, the F1 Score increases from 30.9% without filtering the parking spaces to 34.2% when filtering them.

Despite this improvement in F1 Score in the last two configurations, it should be noted that along with this improvement there is an increase in the number of false negatives. Because of this, we believe it is important to take into account the amount of false positives or false negatives that the problem can afford. In our case, a high number of false positives is not a big problem, since we intend to filter the data by GPS position later on.

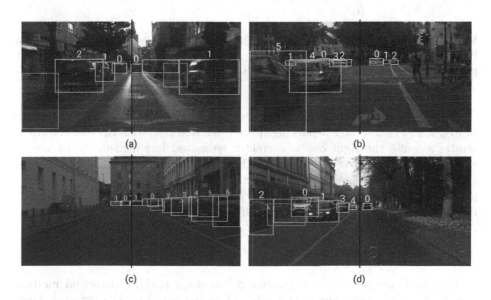

Fig. 2. Examples of error detection. Blue ROIs mark vehicle detections made by Faster-RCNN, red ROIs mark the parking space groundtruth and green ROIs mark parking space detections. (Color figure online)

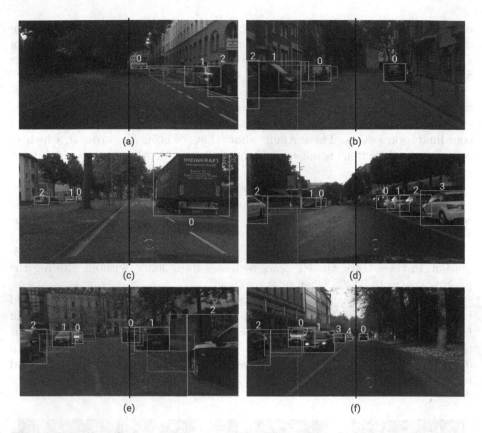

Fig. 3. Examples of correct estimations. Blue ROIs mark vehicle detections made by FasterRCNN, red ROIs mark the parking space groundtruth and green ROIs mark parking space detections. (Color figure online)

Some examples of problems in the parking space estimation can be observed in Fig. 2. In Fig. 2.a the left parking space is not detected with the *end detections* strategy, while the right one is correctly estimated but because it detected a moving vehicle as parked, and it should not. The same happens in Fig. 2.c, the green ROI detects a parking space after an incorrect vehicle labeling. Figure 2.b and 2.d show incorrect labeling and very small ROIs in green that can be easily filtered by size. Finally, Fig. 3 shows different correct scenarios.

4   Conclusions

In this work we propose a vision-based two stage parking detection module. The first one is implemented as machine learning-based vehicle detector. Once the vehicle detection is accomplished, in a second stage a rule-based system determines the car parking spaces in the image. We have found that parking space location with only visual information is a very hard problem, mainly due to the fact that it is not possible to characterize parking gap with only visual features. Experimental results show that our proposal is able to detect parking space but it suffers for a high FP rate. To address this problem, we plan to combine the visual information (images) with other information fonts as GPS signal and maps that give prior information about the location of parking areas in the city.

Acknowledgements. This research has been supported by the Spanish Government research funding RTI2018-098743-B-I00 (MICINN/FEDER) and the Comunidad de Madrid research funding grant Y2018/EMT-5062.

References

1. Cordts, M., et al.: The cityscapes dataset for semantic urban scene understanding. In: Proceedings of the IEEE Conference on Computer Vision and Pattern Recognition (CVPR) (2016)
2. Do, H.: Implementation of CNN-based parking slot type classification using around view images. In: 2020 IEEE International Conference on Consumer Electronics (ICCE) (2020)
3. Grassi, G., et al.: ParkMaster: an in-vehicle, edge-based video analytics service for detecting open parking spaces in urban environments. In: Proceedings of the Second ACM/IEEE Symposium on Edge Computing, pp. 1–14 (2017)
4. Gutiérrez, V., et al.: SmartSantander: Internet of Things research and innovation through citizen participation. In: Galis, A., Gavras, A. (eds.) FIA 2013. LNCS, vol. 7858, pp. 173–186. Springer, Heidelberg (2013). https://doi.org/10.1007/978-3-642-38082-2_15
5. Hsu, C.-M., Chen, J.-Y.: Around view monitoring-based vacant parking space detection and analysis. Appl. Sci. **9**(16), 3403 (2019)
6. Huang, J.-Q., Wang, M.-S.: Cloud adaboost feedback training machine for outside available parking spaces query service. In: IEEE International Conference on Communication, Networks and Satellite (ComNetSat), pp. 177–181 (2012)
7. Kim, S., et al.: Vacant parking slot recognition method for practical autonomous valet parking system using around view image. Symmetry **12**(10) (2020)
8. Leone, G.R., et al.: An intelligent cooperative visual sensor network for urban mobility. Sensors **17**(11), 2588 (2017)
9. Li, L.: Vision-based parking-slot detection: a benchmark and a learning-based approach. In: 20174 IEEE International Conference on Multimedia and Expo (ICME), pp. 649–654 (2017)
10. Li, W., et al.: Vacant parking slot detection in the around view image based on deep learning. Sensors **20**(7), 2138 (2020)
11. Poddar, D.: Deep learning based parking spot detection and classification in fisheye images. In: 2019 IEEE International Conference on Electronics, Computing and Communication Technologies (CONECCT), pp. 1–5 (2019)
12. Shoup, D., et al.: SFpark: Putting Theory Into Practice, August 2011
13. Suhr, J., et al.: Automatic free parking space detection by using motion stereo-based 3D reconstruction. Mach. Vis. Appl. **21**, 163–176 (2010)
14. Unger, C., Wahl, E., Ilic, S.: Parking assistance using dense motion-stereo. Mach. Vis. Appl. **25**(3), 561–581 (2014)

15. Wang, C., et al.: Automatic parking based on a bird's eye view vision system. Adv. Mech. Eng. **6**, 847406 (2014)
16. Xu, J., Chen, G., Xie, M.: Vision-guided automatic parking for smart car In: Proceedings of the IEEE Intelligent Vehicles Symposium 2000 (Cat. No.00TH8511), pp. 725–730 (2000)
17. Yamamoto, K., Watanabe, K., Nagai, I.: Proposal of an environmental recognition method for automatic parking by an Imagebased CNN. In: IEEE International Conference on Mechatronics and Automation (ICMA) **2019**, 833–838 (2019)
18. Yang, C.-F., et al.: iParking - a real-time parking space monitoring and guiding system. Veh. Commun. **9**, 301–305 (2017)
19. Yu, H., et al.: TensorFlow Model Garden (2020). https://github.com/tensorflow/models

Correction to: Real-Life Validation of Emotion Detection System with Wearables

Dominika Kunc⦿, Joanna Komoszyńska⦿, Bartosz Perz⦿,
Przemysław Kazienko⦿, and Stanisław Saganowski⦿

Correction to:
Chapter "Real-Life Validation of Emotion Detection System
with Wearables" in: J. M. Ferrández Vicente et al. (Eds.):
Bio-inspired Systems and Applications: from Robotics
to Ambient Intelligence, **LNCS 13259,**
https://doi.org/10.1007/978-3-031-06527-9_5

In an older version of this paper, there was an error in the cited reference no. 12. This has been corrected.

The updated version of this chapter can be found at
https://doi.org/10.1007/978-3-031-06527-9_5

J. M. Ferrández Vicente et al. (Eds.): IWINAC 2022, LNCS 13259, p. C1, 2022.
https://doi.org/10.1007/978-3-031-06527-9_59

Author Index